Intelligent Technologies and Techniques for Pervasive Computing

Kostas Kolomvatsos
University of Athens, Greece

Christos Anagnostopoulos
Ionian University, Greece

Stathes Hadjiefthymiades
University of Athens, Greece

A volume in the Advances in
Computational Intelligence and Robotics
(ACIR) Book Series

Managing Director:	Lindsay Johnston
Editorial Director:	Joel Gamon
Book Production Manager:	Jennifer Yoder
Publishing Systems Analyst:	Adrienne Freeland
Development Editor:	Austin DeMarco
Assistant Acquisitions Editor:	Kayla Wolfe
Typesetter:	Christina Henning
Cover Design:	Jason Mull

Published in the United States of America by
Information Science Reference (an imprint of IGI Global)
701 E. Chocolate Avenue
Hershey PA 17033
Tel: 717-533-8845
Fax: 717-533-8661
E-mail: cust@igi-global.com
Web site: http://www.igi-global.com

Library of Congress Cataloging-in-Publication Data

Intelligent technologies and techniques for pervasive computing / Kostas Kolomvatsos, Christos Anagnostopoulos and Stathes Hadjiefthymiades, editors.
    pages cm
  Summary: "This book provides an extensive discussion of such technologies, theories and practices in an attempt to shed light on current trends and issues in the adaption of pervasive system"-- Provided by publisher.
  Includes bibliographical references and index.
  ISBN 978-1-4666-4038-2 (hardcover) -- ISBN 978-1-4666-4039-9 (ebook) -- ISBN 978-1-4666-4040-5 (print & perpetual access) 1. Ubiquitous computing. 2. Multiagent systems. 3. Computational intelligence. I. Kolomvatsos, Kostas, 1973- II. Anagnostopoulos, Christos, 1978- III. Hadjiefthymiades, Stathes,
1971-
  QA76.5915.I545 2013
  006.3--dc23
                                          2013001109

This book is published in the IGI Global book series Advances in Computational Intelligence and Robotics (ACIR) Book Series (ISSN: 2327-0411; eISSN: 2327-042X)

British Cataloguing in Publication Data
A Cataloguing in Publication record for this book is available from the British Library.

Advances in Computational Intelligence and Robotics (ACIR) Book Series

ISSN: 2327-0411
EISSN: 2327-042X

MISSION

While intelligence is traditionally a term applied to humans and human cognition, technology has progressed in such a way to allow for the development of intelligent systems able to simulate many human traits. With this new era of simulated and artificial intelligence, much research is needed in order to continue to advance the field and also to evaluate the ethical and societal concerns of the existence of artificial life and machine learning.

The **Advances in Computational Intelligence and Robotics (ACIR) Book Series** encourages scholarly discourse on all topics pertaining to evolutionary computing, artificial life, computational intelligence, machine learning, and robotics. ACIR presents the latest research being conducted on diverse topics in intelligence technologies with the goal of advancing knowledge and applications in this rapidly evolving field.

COVERAGE
- Adaptive & Complex Systems
- Agent Technologies
- Artificial Intelligence
- Cognitive Informatics
- Computational Intelligence
- Natural Language Processing
- Neural Networks
- Pattern Recognition
- Robotics
- Synthetic Emotions

IGI Global is currently accepting manuscripts for publication within this series. To submit a proposal for a volume in this series, please contact our Acquisition Editors at Acquisitions@igi-global.com or visit: http://www.igi-global.com/publish/.

Titles in this Series

For a list of additional titles in this series, please visit: www.igi-global.com

Intelligent Technologies and Techniques for Pervasive Computing
Kostas Kolomvatsos (University of Athens, Greece) Christos Anagnostopoulos (Ionian University, Greece) and Stathes Hadjiefthymiades (University of Athens, Greece)
Information Science Reference • copyright 2013 • 349pp • H/C (ISBN: 9781466640382) • US $195.00 (our price)

Intelligent Planning for Mobile Robotics Algorithmic Approaches
Ritu Tiwari (ABV – Indian Institute of Information, India) Anupam Shukla (ABV – Indian Institute of Information, India) and Rahul Kala (School of Systems Engineering, University of Reading, UK)
Information Science Reference • copyright 2013 • 320pp • H/C (ISBN: 9781466620742) • US $195.00 (our price)

Simultaneous Localization and Mapping for Mobile Robots Introduction and Methods
Juan-Antonio Fernández-Madrigal (Universidad de Málaga, Spain) and José Luis Blanco Claraco (Universidad de Málaga, Spain)
Information Science Reference • copyright 2013 • 497pp • H/C (ISBN: 9781466621046) • US $195.00 (our price)

Prototyping of Robotic Systems Applications of Design and Implementation
Tarek Sobh (University of Bridgeport, USA) and Xingguo Xiong (University of Bridgeport, USA)
Information Science Reference • copyright 2012 • 321pp • H/C (ISBN: 9781466601765) • US $195.00 (our price)

Cross-Disciplinary Applications of Artificial Intelligence and Pattern Recognition Advancing Technologies
Vijay Kumar Mago (Simon Fraser University, Canada) and Nitin Bhatia (DAV College, India)
Information Science Reference • copyright 2012 • 784pp • H/C (ISBN: 9781613504291) • US $195.00 (our price)

Handbook of Research on Ambient Intelligence and Smart Environments Trends and Perspectives
Nak-Young Chong (Japan Advanced Institute of Science and Technology, Japan) and Fulvio Mastrogiovanni (University of Genova, Italy)
Information Science Reference • copyright 2011 • 770pp • H/C (ISBN: 9781616928575) • US $265.00 (our price)

Particle Swarm Optimization and Intelligence Advances and Applications
Konstantinos E. Parsopoulos (University of Ioannina, Greece) and Michael N. Vrahatis (University of Patras, Greece)
Information Science Reference • copyright 2010 • 328pp • H/C (ISBN: 9781615206667) • US $180.00 (our price)

Artificial Intelligence Applications for Improved Software Engineering Development New Prospects
Farid Meziane (University of Salford, UK) and Sunil Vadera (University of Salford, UK)
Information Science Reference • copyright 2010 • 370pp • H/C (ISBN: 9781605667584) • US $180.00 (our price)

www.igi-global.com

701 E. Chocolate Ave., Hershey, PA 17033
Order online at www.igi-global.com or call 717-533-8845 x100
To place a standing order for titles released in this series, contact: cust@igi-global.com
Mon-Fri 8:00 am - 5:00 pm (est) or fax 24 hours a day 717-533-8661

Editorial Advisory Board

Table of Contents

Section 1
Multi-Agent Systems Applications

Dimitris C. Dracopoulos, University of Westminster, UK
Dimitrios Effraimidis, University of Westminster, UK

Seyyed Abed Hosseini, Ferdowsi University of Mashhad, Iran
Mohammed-Reza Akbarzadeh-T, Ferdowsi University of Mashhad, Iran
Mohammed-Bagher Naghibi-Sistani, Ferdowsi University of Mashhad, Iran

Paolo Renna, University of Basilicata, Italy

George Karasmanoglou, Ionian University, Greece
Blerina Lika, Ionian University, Greece

Constanta-Nicoleta Bodea, Academy of Economic Studies, Romania
Radu-Ioan Mogos, Academy of Economic Studies, Romania

Section 2
Pervasive Computing Applications

Detailed Table of Contents

Section 1
Multi-Agent Systems Applications

Chapter 1

Dimitris C. Dracopoulos, University of Westminster, UK
Dimitrios Effraimidis, University of Westminster, UK

Computational intelligence techniques such as neural networks, fuzzy logic, and hybrid neuroevolutionary and neuro-fuzzy methods have been successfully applied to complex control problems in the last two decades. Genetic programming, a field under the umbrella of evolutionary computation, has not been applied to a sufficiently large number of challenging and difficult control problems, in order to check its viability as a general methodology to such problems. Helicopter hovering control is considered a challenging control problem in the literature and has been included in the set of benchmarks of recent reinforcement learning competitions for deriving new intelligent controllers. This chapter shows how genetic programming can be applied for the derivation of controllers in this nonlinear, high dimensional, complex control system. The evolved controllers are compared with a neuroevolutionary approach that won the first position in the 2008 helicopter hovering reinforcement learning competition. The two approaches perform similarly (and in some cases GP performs better than the winner of the competition), even in the case where unknown wind is added to the dynamic system and control is based on structures evolved previously, that is, the evolved controllers have good generalization capability.

Chapter 2

Seyyed Abed Hosseini, Ferdowsi University of Mashhad, Iran
Mohammed-Reza Akbarzadeh-T, Ferdowsi University of Mashhad, Iran
Mohammed-Bagher Naghibi-Sistani, Ferdowsi University of Mashhad, Iran

A novel combination of chaotic features and Adaptive Neuro-Fuzzy Inference System (ANFIS) is proposed for epileptic seizure recognition. The non-linear dynamics of the original EEGs are quantified in the form of the Hurst exponent (H), Correlation dimension (D2), Petrosian Fractal Dimension (PFD), and the Largest lyapunov exponent (λ). The process of EEG analysis consists of two phases, namely the qualitative and quantitative analysis. The classification ability of the H, D2, PFD, and λ measures is tested using ANFIS classifier. This method is evaluated with using a benchmark EEG dataset, and qualitative and quantitative results are presented. The inter-ictal EEG-based diagnostic approach achieves 98.6% accuracy with using 4-fold cross validation. Diagnosis based on ictal data is also tested in ANFIS classifier, reaching 98.1% accuracy. Therefore, the method can be successfully applied to both inter-ictal and ictal data.

Chapter 3

Paolo Renna, University of Basilicata, Italy

The automated negotiation performed by a software agent is investigated in order to improve the benefits compared to a humane face-to-face negotiation. The profitability of e-business applications can be increased by the support of automated negotiation tools. This research proposes a set of learning methodologies to support both the suppliers' and customers' negotiation activities. The learning methodologies are based on Q-learning technique, which is able to evaluate the utility of the actions without a model of the environment. The context regards one-to-many negotiation and multi-issues (volume, price, and due date). A simulation environment is developed to test the proposed methodologies and evaluate the benefits compared to a negotiation approach without learning support tool. The simulations are conducted in several market conditions, and a proper statistical analysis is performed. The simulation results show that the proposed methodologies lead to benefits both for suppliers and customers when both the opponents adopt the learning approach.

Chapter 4

George Karasmanoglou, Ionian University, Greece
Blerina Lika, Ionian University, Greece

During the last years, the emergence of Semantic Web has produced a vast amount of resources and a variety of content representation schemes. The latter has increased the complexity that the users are facing when searching for information in open environments. A representative example is Electronic Markets (EMs). In EMs users try to find and purchase products through interactions with providers. In such scenarios, shopbots can offer a number of advantages. Shopbots are agents that help users to find the products they want, saving them a lot of time and effort. However, building efficient shopbots is a challenging task. This is more imperative when shopbots interact with providers using different ontological terms for product description. In this chapter, the authors propose a generic ontology to describe products in EMs. They also introduce a matching algorithm that maps the specific provider ontology to the generic one in order to be used by a shopbot. Their algorithm, called S+, is based on a set of linguistic and semantic matching techniques. The authors present their approach and compare it with other proposed algorithms. Finally, they discuss their experimental results that reveal the performance of their methodology.

Chapter 5

Constanta-Nicoleta Bodea, Academy of Economic Studies, Romania
Radu-Ioan Mogos, Academy of Economic Studies, Romania

The chapter presents UNIRA, a multi-agent system developed by the authors for a Romanian university in order to improve the resources allocation for educational programmes and courses. Different types of resources are required to deliver programmes and courses. Considering a set of resources inquires, issued by programmes and courses, UNIRA system performs a transparent negotiation process between the managers of these resources, to find the solution for the allocation problem. During the initial stage of the multi-agent system deployment, only two types of resources are considered, professors and teaching rooms. The system is now in the validation phase. After the complete validation, the system will be integrated into the university management system. The UNIRA experience is relevant not exclusively for the academic resources management, but also for a large variety of domains, including the load distribution, production planning, computer scheduling, portfolio selection, and apportionment.

Section 2
Pervasive Computing Applications

Chapter 6

Recent interest in integrated electronic devices (sensors) that operate wirelessly creates a wide range of applications related to national security, surveillance, military, healthcare, and environmental monitoring. Many visions of the future include people immersed in an environment surrounded by sensors and intelligent devices, which use smart infrastructures to improve the quality of life. However, a fundamental feature of sensor networks is coverage: how these tiny devices can cover a certain terrain. These devices should be organized in an optimal manner, consuming the minimum energy and covering the whole area of interest. The coverage concept is subject to a wide range of interpretations due to the variety of sensors and applications. Different coverage formulations have been proposed based on the subject to be covered (area in relation to specific items and obstacles), sensor development mechanisms (random versus deterministic), and other properties of wireless sensor networks (e.g. network connectivity and minimum energy consumption). In this chapter, the authors study the coverage problem in wireless sensor networks using the most recent algorithms. The aim of this chapter is to present these algorithms and a comparison between them based on various criteria. The Node Self-Scheduling algorithm, the Centralized Voronoi Tessellation (CVT), the Particle Swarm Optimization Algorithm (PSO), the Virtual Forces Algorithm (VFA), etc. are analyzed. Through the algorithms' analysis, the interested reader can have a complete view of the proposed solutions related to the coverage problem.

Chapter 7

Wireless sensors are small-scale mobile devices that can programmatically measure physical quantities, perform simple computations, store, receive, and transmit data. The lattice built by a set of cooperating sensors is called a sensor network. Since sensor networks provide a powerful infrastructure for large-scale monitoring applications, an important issue is the network design to achieve an optimal placement of the sensors to allow (1) energy-efficient monitoring and (2) gathering meaningful data. This chapter presents a novel approach to optimize sensing node placement (e.g., for new to-be-deployed networks) and efficiently acquire data from existing sensor networks. A historical data analysis task is performed to discover spatial and temporal correlations and identify sets of correlated sensors. Then, an algorithm based on a cost function considering both distance and communication cost selects the candidate sensors, leading to the optimized network design and acquisition. Candidate sensors can then be deployed and/

or queried instead of the whole network, thus reducing the network cost and extending its lifetime in terms of energy consumption. Experiments, performed on a real wireless sensor network, demonstrate the adaptability and the effectiveness of the proposed approach in optimizing the sensor network design and the data acquisition.

    Yves Vanrompay, Ecole Centrale Paris, France
    Manuele Kirsch Pinheiro, Université Paris1 – Panthéon Sorbonne, France
    Nesrine Ben Mustapha, Ecole Centrale Paris, France
    Marie-Aude Aufaure, Ecole Centrale Paris, France

The authors propose in this chapter a context grouping mechanism for context distribution over MANETs. Context distribution is becoming a key aspect for successful context-aware applications in mobile and ubiquitous computing environments. Such applications need, for adaptation purposes, context information that is acquired by multiple context sensors distributed over the environment. Nevertheless, applications are not interested in all available context information. Context distribution mechanisms have to cope with the dynamicity that characterizes MANETs and also prevent context information from being delivered to nodes (and applications) that are not interested in it. The authors' grouping mechanism organizes the distribution of context information in groups whose definition is context based: each context group is defined based on a criteria set (e.g. the shared location and interest) and has a dissemination set, which controls the information that can be shared in the group. They propose a personalized and dynamic way of defining and joining groups by providing a lattice-based classification and recommendation mechanism that analyzes the interrelations between groups and users, and recommend new groups to users, based on the interests and preferences of the user.

    Vassileios Tsetsos, Mobics LTD, Greece
    Odysseas Sekkas, Mobics LTD, Greece
    Evagellos Zervas, TEI-A, Greece

Forest fires cause immeasurable damages to indispensable resources for human survival, destroy the balance of earth ecology, and worst of all they frequently cost human lives. In recent years, early fire detection systems have emerged to provide monitoring and prevention of the disasterous forest fires. Among them, the Meleager2 system aims to offer one of the most advanced and integrated technology solutions for fire protection worldwide by integrating several innovative features. This chapter outlines one of the major components of the Meleager system, that is the visual fire detection sybsystem. Ground-based visible range PTZ cameras monitor the area of interest, and a low level decision fusion scheme is used to combine individual decisions of numerous fire detection algorithms. Personalized alerts and induced feedback is used to adapt the detection process and improve the overall system performance.

    Leonidas Kazatzopoulos, Athens University of Economics and Business, Greece

Wireless Sensor Networks (WSNs) receive significant attention due to the wide area of applications: environment monitoring, tracking, target detection, etc. At the same time, in some cases, the captured information from the WSN might be considered as private, for example, location of an important asset. Thus, security mechanisms might be essential to ensure the confidentiality of the location of the information source. In this chapter, the authors present an approach called iHIDE (information HIding in Distributing Environments) to enable source-location privacy in WSNs. iHIDE adopts a non-geographical, overlay routing method for packet delivery. This chapter presents the architecture and assesses its performance through simulation experiments, providing comparisons with relative approaches.

Chapter 11

Sally Almanasra, Universiti Sains Malaysia, Malaysia

Khaled Suwais, Arab Open University, Saudi Arabia

Muhammad Rafie, Universiti Sains Malaysia, Malaysia

In game theory, presenting players with strategies directly affects the performance of the players. Utilizing the power of automata is one way for presenting players with strategies. In this chapter, the authors studied different types of automata and their applications in game theory. They found that finite automata, adaptive automata, and cellular automata are widely adopted in game theory. The applications of finite automata are found to be limited to present simple strategies. In contrast, adaptive automata and cellular automata are intensively applied in complex environment, where the number of interacted players (human, computer applications, etc.) is high, and therefore, complex strategies are needed.

Chapter 12

Theodoros Anagnostopoulos, National and Kapodistrian University of Athens, Greece

Mobile context-aware applications are required to sense and react to changing environment conditions. Such applications, usually, need to recognize, classify, and predict context in order to act efficiently, beforehand, for the benefit of the user. In this chapter, the authors propose a mobility prediction model, which deals with context representation and location prediction of moving users. Machine Learning (ML) techniques are used for trajectory classification. Spatial and temporal on-line clustering is adopted. They rely on Adaptive Resonance Theory (ART) for location prediction. Location prediction is treated as a context classification problem. The authors introduce a novel classifier that applies a Hausdorff-like distance over the extracted trajectories handling location prediction. Two learning methods (non-reinforcement and reinforcement learning) are presented and evaluated. They compare ART with Self-Organizing Maps (SOM), Offline kMeans, and Online kMeans algorithms. Their findings are very promising for the use of the proposed model in mobile context aware applications.

Chapter 13

Constantinos Delakouridis, Athens University of Economics and Business, Greece

Location-based services are receiving signification attention over the last few years due to the increasing use of mobile devices. At the same time, location privacy is important, since position information is considered personal information. Thus, in order to address this issue, several mechanisms have been proposed protecting the mobile user. In this chapter, the authors present an architecture to shield the location of a mobile user and preserve the anonymity on the service delivery. This architecture relies on un-trusted entities to distribute segments of anonymous location information, and authorizes other entities to combine these portions and derive the actual location of a user. The chapter describes how the architecture takes into account the location privacy requirements, and how it is used by the end users' devices, e.g., mobile phones, for the dissemination of location information to service providers. Furthermore, it notes privacy issues for further discussion and closes with proposed exercises.

    Salma Najar, Université Paris1 – Panthéon Sorbonne, France
    Manuele Kirsch Pinheiro, Université Paris1 – Panthéon Sorbonne, France
    Yves Vanrompay, Ecole Centrale Paris, France
    Luiz Angelo Steffenel, Université de Reims Champagne-Ardenne, France
    Carine Souveyet, Université Paris1 – Panthéon Sorbonne, France

The development of pervasive technologies has allowed the improvement of services availability. These services, offered by Information Systems (IS), are becoming more pervasive, i.e., accessed anytime, anywhere. However, those Pervasive Information Systems (PIS) remain too complex for the user, who just wants a service satisfying his needs. This complexity requires considerable efforts from the user in order to select the most appropriate service. Thus, an important challenge in PIS is to reduce user's understanding effort. In this chapter, the authors propose to enhance PIS transparency and productivity through a user-centred vision based on an intentional approach. They propose an intention prediction approach. This approach allows anticipating user's future requirements, offering the most suitable service in a transparent and discrete way. This intention prediction approach is guided by the user's context. It is based on the analysis of the user's previous situations in order to learn user's behaviour in a dynamic environment.

    Constantinos Delakouridis, Athens University of Economics and Business, Greece
    Leonidas Kazatzopoulos, Athens University of Economics and Business, Greece

The location privacy issue has been addressed thoroughly so far. Cryptographic techniques, k-anonymity-based approaches, spatial obfuscation methods, mix-zones, pseudonyms, and dummy location signals have been proposed to enhance location privacy. In this chapter, the authors propose an approach, called STS (Share The Secret) that segments and distributes the location information to various, non-trusted, entities from where it will be reachable by authenticated location services. This secret sharing approach prevents location information disclosure even in situation where there is a direct observation of the target. The proposed approach facilitates end-users or location-based services to classify flexible privacy levels for different contexts of operation. The authors provide the optimal thresholds to alter the privacy policy levels when there is a need for relaxing or strengthening the required privacy. Additionally, they discuss the robustness of the proposed approach against various adversary models. Finally, the authors evaluate the approach in terms of computational and energy efficiency, using real mobile applications and location update scenarios over a cloud infrastructure, which is used to support storage and computational tasks.

Preface

The aim of this book is to provide a common platform for the researchers from diverse backgrounds to present their theoretical and applied research findings in pervasive computing, multi-agent systems, and computational intelligence. This book may prove to be a building block for enhancing/developing pervasive computing and computational intelligence systems as it highlights the core concepts as well as applicability in real world problems.

Pervasive computing enables users to interact with information resources in their everyday lives. The development of computational technologies that can exist in ever-smaller devices while simultaneously increasing processing power allows such devices to blend seamlessly into tangible environments. Of special importance of this book is the usage of machine learning, swarm intelligence optimization, multi-agent systems, fuzzy logic, and neural networks providing means for contextual information representation, reasoning, and inference in pervasive computing environments. Topics that are covered by this book are: computational intelligence in pervasive computing applications, multi-agent systems, context-aware computing, event-detection systems for environmental risks, spatiotemporal optimized deployment of wireless sensor networks, and techniques for location privacy in pervasive environments. This book provides a common platform to pervasive computing and computational intelligence researchers to disseminate new ideas and techniques.

This book is organized in self-contained chapters to provide greatest reading flexibility. In response to the call for papers, the book received around 35 abstracts. Based on the suitability, the editors invited full chapters from 32 researchers of various disciplines (Computational Intelligence, Multi-Agent Systems, Soft Computing, Context-Aware Computing, and Wireless Sensor Networks) and from 7 different countries. All submitted chapters were reviewed on a double-blind review basis, by at least three reviewers. After an evaluation process by the EBM members, 15 chapters were selected. Acceptance was based on relevance, technical soundness, originality, and clarity of presentation.

This book is organized into two sections. Section 1 refers to Multi-Agent Systems Applications with five chapters, and Section 2 refers to Pervasive Computing Applications with ten chapters.

SECTION 1: MULTI-AGENT SYSTEMS APPLICATIONS

Chapter 1: Computational intelligence techniques such as neural networks, fuzzy logic, and hybrid neuroevolutionary and neuro-fuzzy methods have been successfully applied to complex control problems in the last two decades. Genetic programming, a field under the umbrella of evolutionary computation, has not been applied to a sufficiently large number of challenging and difficult control problems, in order to check its viability as a general methodology to such problems. Helicopter hovering control is considered a challenging control problem in the literature and has been included in the set of benchmarks of recent reinforcement learning competitions for deriving new intelligent controllers. This chapter shows how genetic programming can be applied for the derivation of controllers in this nonlinear, high dimensional, complex control system. The evolved controllers are compared with a neuroevolutionary approach that won the first position in the 2008 helicopter hovering reinforcement learning competition. The two approaches perform similarly (and in some cases GP performs better than the winner of the competition), even in the case where unknown wind is added to the dynamic system and control is based on structures evolved previously, that is, the evolved controllers have good generalization capability.

Chapter 2: A novel combination of chaotic features and Adaptive Neuro-Fuzzy Inference System (ANFIS) is proposed for epileptic seizure recognition. The non-linear dynamics of the original EEGs are quantified in the form of the Hurst exponent (H), Correlation dimension (D_2), Petrosian Fractal Dimension (PFD), and the Largest lyapunov exponent (λ). The process of EEG analysis consists of two phases, namely the qualitative and quantitative analysis. The classification ability of the H, D_2, PFD, and λ measures is tested using ANFIS classifier. This method is evaluated with using a benchmark EEG dataset, and qualitative and quantitative results are presented. The inter-ictal EEG-based diagnostic approach achieves 98.6% accuracy with using 4-fold cross validation. Diagnosis based on ictal data is also tested in ANFIS classifier, reaching 98.1% accuracy. Therefore, the method can be successfully applied to both inter-ictal and ictal data.

Chapter 3: The automated negotiation performed by a software agent is investigated in order to improve the benefits compared to a humane face-to-face negotiation. The profitability of e-business applications can be increased by the support of automated negotiation tools. This research proposes a set of learning methodologies to support both the suppliers' and customers' negotiation activities. The learning methodologies are based on Q-learning technique, which is able to evaluate the utility of the actions without a model of the environment. The context regards one-to-many negotiation and multi-issues (volume, price, and due date). A simulation environment is developed to test the proposed methodologies and evaluate the benefits compared to a negotiation approach without learning support tool. The simulations are conducted in several market conditions, and a proper statistical analysis is performed. The simulation results show that the proposed methodologies lead to benefits both for suppliers and customers when both the opponents adopt the learning approach.

Chapter 4: During the last years, the emergence of Semantic Web has produced a vast amount of resources and a variety of content representation schemes. The latter has increased the complexity that the users are facing when searching for information in open environments. A representative example is Electronic Markets (EMs). In EMs users try to find and purchase products through interactions with providers. In such scenarios, shopbots can offer a number of advantages. Shopbots are agents that help users to find the products they want, saving them a lot of time and effort. However, building efficient shopbots is a challenging task. This is more imperative when shopbots interact with providers using different ontological terms for product description. In this chapter, the authors propose a generic ontology to describe products in EMs. They also introduce a matching algorithm that maps the specific provider ontology to the generic one in order to be used by a shopbot. Their algorithm, called S^+, is based on a set of linguistic and semantic matching techniques. The authors present their approach and compare it with other proposed algorithms. Finally, they discuss their experimental results that reveal the performance of their methodology.

Chapter 5: The chapter presents UNIRA, a multi-agent system developed by the authors for a Romanian university in order to improve the resources allocation for educational programmes and courses. Different types of resources are required to deliver programmes and courses. Considering a set of resources inquires, issued by programmes and courses, UNIRA system performs a transparent negotiation process between the managers of these resources, to find the solution for the allocation problem. During the initial stage of the multi-agent system deployment, only two types of resources are considered, professors and teaching rooms. The system is now in the validation phase. After the complete validation, the system will be integrated into the university management system. The UNIRA experience is relevant not exclusively for the academic resources management, but also for a large variety of domains, including the load distribution, production planning, computer scheduling, portfolio selection, and apportionment.

SECTION 2: PERVASIVE COMPUTING APPLICATIONS

Chapter 6: Recent interest in integrated electronic devices (sensors) that operate wirelessly creates a wide range of applications related to national security, surveillance, military, healthcare, and environmental monitoring. Many visions of the future include people immersed in an environment surrounded by sensors and intelligent devices, which use smart infrastructures to improve the quality of life. However, a fundamental feature of sensor networks is coverage: how these tiny devices can cover a certain terrain. These devices should be organized in an optimal manner, consuming the minimum energy and covering the whole area of interest. The coverage concept is subject to a wide range of interpretations due to the variety of sensors and applications. Different coverage formulations have been proposed based on the subject to be covered (area in relation to specific items and obstacles), sensor development mechanisms (random versus deterministic), and other properties of wireless sensor networks (e.g. network connectivity and minimum energy consumption). In this chapter, the authors study the coverage problem in wireless sensor networks using the most recent algorithms. The aim of this chapter is to present these algorithms and a comparison between them based on various criteria. The Node Self-Scheduling algorithm, the Centralized Voronoi Tessellation (CVT), the Particle Swarm Optimization Algorithm (PSO), the Virtual Forces Algorithm (VFA), etc. are analyzed. Through the algorithms' analysis, the interested reader can have a complete view of the proposed solutions related to the coverage problem.

Chapter 7: Wireless sensors are small-scale mobile devices that can programmatically measure physical quantities, perform simple computations, store, receive, and transmit data. The lattice built by a set of cooperating sensors is called a sensor network. Since sensor networks provide a powerful infrastructure for large-scale monitoring applications, an important issue is the network design to achieve an optimal placement of the sensors to allow (1) energy-efficient monitoring and (2) gathering meaningful data. This chapter presents a novel approach to optimize sensing node placement (e.g., for new to-be-deployed networks) and efficiently acquire data from existing sensor networks. A historical data analysis task is performed to discover spatial and temporal correlations and identify sets of correlated sensors. Then, an algorithm based on a cost function considering both distance and communication cost selects the candidate sensors, leading to the optimized network design and acquisition. Candidate sensors can then be deployed and/or queried instead of the whole network, thus reducing the network cost and extending its lifetime in terms of energy consumption. Experiments, performed on a real wireless sensor network, demonstrate the adaptability and the effectiveness of the proposed approach in optimizing the sensor network design and the data acquisition.

Chapter 8: The authors propose in this chapter a context grouping mechanism for context distribution over MANETs. Context distribution is becoming a key aspect for successful context-aware applications in mobile and ubiquitous computing environments. Such applications need, for adaptation purposes, context information that is acquired by multiple context sensors distributed over the environment.

Nevertheless, applications are not interested in all available context information. Context distribution mechanisms have to cope with the dynamicity that characterizes MANETs and also prevent context information from being delivered to nodes (and applications) that are not interested in it. The authors' grouping mechanism organizes the distribution of context information in groups whose definition is context based: each context group is defined based on a criteria set (e.g. the shared location and interest) and has a dissemination set, which controls the information that can be shared in the group. They propose a personalized and dynamic way of defining and joining groups by providing a lattice-based classification and recommendation mechanism that analyzes the interrelations between groups and users, and recommend new groups to users, based on the interests and preferences of the user.

Chapter 9: Forest fires cause immeasurable damages to indispensable resources for human survival, destroy the balance of earth ecology, and worst of all they frequently cost human lives. In recent years, early fire detection systems have emerged to provide monitoring and prevention of the disasterous forest fires. Among them, the Meleager system aims to offer one of the most advanced and integrated technology solutions for fire protection worldwide by integrating several innovative features. This chapter outlines one of the major components of the Meleager system, that is the visual fire detection sybsystem. Ground-based visible range PTZ cameras monitor the area of interest, and a low level decision fusion scheme is used to combine individual decisions of numerous fire detection algorithms. Personalized alerts and induced feedback is used to adapt the detection process and improve the overall system performance.

Chapter 10: Wireless Sensor Networks (WSNs) receive significant attention due to the wide area of applications: environment monitoring, tracking, target detection, etc. At the same time, in some cases, the captured information from the WSN might be considered as private, for example, location of an important asset. Thus, security mechanisms might be essential to ensure the confidentiality of the location of the information source. In this chapter, the authors present an approach called iHIDE (information HIding in Distributing Environments) to enable source-location privacy in WSNs. iHIDE adopts a non-geographical, overlay routing method for packet delivery. This chapter presents the architecture and assesses its performance through simulation experiments, providing comparisons with relative approaches.

Chapter 11: In game theory, presenting players with strategies directly affects the performance of the players. Utilizing the power of automata is one way for presenting players with strategies. In this chapter, the authors studied different types of automata and their applications in game theory. They found that finite automata, adaptive automata, and cellular automata are widely adopted in game theory. The applications of finite automata are found to be limited to present simple strategies. In contrast, adaptive automata and cellular automata are intensively applied in complex environment, where the number of interacted players (human, computer applications, etc.) is high, and therefore, complex strategies are needed.

Chapter 12: Mobile context-aware applications are required to sense and react to changing environment conditions. Such applications, usually, need to recognize, classify, and predict context in order to act efficiently, beforehand, for the benefit of the user. In this chapter, the authors propose a mobility prediction model, which deals with context representation and location prediction of moving users. Machine Learning (ML) techniques are used for trajectory classification. Spatial and temporal on-line clustering is adopted. They rely on Adaptive Resonance Theory (ART) for location prediction. Location prediction is treated as a context classification problem. The authors introduce a novel classifier that applies a Hausdorff-like distance over the extracted trajectories handling location prediction. Two learning methods (non-reinforcement and reinforcement learning) are presented and evaluated. They compare ART with Self-Organizing Maps (SOM), Offline *k*Means, and Online *k*Means algorithms. Their findings are very promising for the use of the proposed model in mobile context aware applications.

Chapter 13: Location-based services are receiving signification attention over the last few years due to the increasing use of mobile devices. At the same time, location privacy is important, since position information is considered personal information. Thus, in order to address this issue, several mechanisms have been proposed protecting the mobile user. In this chapter, the authors present an architecture to shield the location of a mobile user and preserve the anonymity on the service delivery. This architecture relies on un-trusted entities to distribute segments of anonymous location information, and authorizes other entities to combine these portions and derive the actual location of a user. The chapter describes how the architecture takes into account the location privacy requirements, and how it is used by the end users' devices, e.g., mobile phones, for the dissemination of location information to service providers. Furthermore, it notes privacy issues for further discussion and closes with proposed exercises.

Chapter 14: The development of pervasive technologies has allowed the improvement of services availability. These services, offered by Information Systems (IS), are becoming more pervasive, i.e., accessed anytime, anywhere. However, those Pervasive Information Systems (PIS) remain too complex for the user, who just wants a service satisfying his needs. This complexity requires considerable efforts from the user in order to select the most appropriate service. Thus, an important challenge in PIS is to reduce user's understanding effort. In this chapter, the authors propose to enhance PIS transparency and productivity through a user-centred vision based on an intentional approach. They propose an intention prediction approach. This approach allows anticipating user's future requirements, offering the most suitable service in a transparent and discrete way. This intention prediction approach is guided by the user's context. It is based on the analysis of the user's previous situations in order to learn user's behaviour in a dynamic environment.

Chapter 15: The location privacy issue has been addressed thoroughly so far. Cryptographic techniques, k-anonymity-based approaches, spatial obfuscation methods, mix-zones, pseudonyms, and dummy location signals have been proposed to enhance location privacy. In this chapter, the authors propose an approach, called STS (Share The Secret) that segments and distributes the location information to various, non-trusted, entities from where it will be reachable by authenticated location services. This secret sharing approach prevents location information disclosure even in situation where there is a direct observation of the target. The proposed approach facilitates end-users or location-based services to classify flexible privacy levels for different contexts of operation. The authors provide the optimal thresholds to alter the privacy policy levels when there is a need for relaxing or strengthening the required privacy. Additionally, they discuss the robustness of the proposed approach against various adversary models. Finally, the authors evaluate the approach in terms of computational and energy efficiency, using real mobile applications and location update scenarios over a cloud infrastructure, which is used to support storage and computational tasks.

Kostas Kolomvatsos
National and Kapodistrian University of Athens, Greece

Christos Anagnostopoulos
Ionian University, Greece

Stathes Hadjiefthymiades
National and Kapodistrian University of Athens, Greece

Section 1
Multi-Agent Systems Applications

Chapter 1
Evolutionary Control of Helicopter Hovering Based on Genetic Programming

Dimitris C. Dracopoulos
University of Westminster, UK

Dimitrios Effraimidis
University of Westminster, UK

ABSTRACT

Computational intelligence techniques such as neural networks, fuzzy logic, and hybrid neuroevolutionary and neuro-fuzzy methods have been successfully applied to complex control problems in the last two decades. Genetic programming, a field under the umbrella of evolutionary computation, has not been applied to a sufficiently large number of challenging and difficult control problems, in order to check its viability as a general methodology to such problems. Helicopter hovering control is considered a challenging control problem in the literature and has been included in the set of benchmarks of recent reinforcement learning competitions for deriving new intelligent controllers. This chapter shows how genetic programming can be applied for the derivation of controllers in this nonlinear, high dimensional, complex control system. The evolved controllers are compared with a neuroevolutionary approach that won the first position in the 2008 helicopter hovering reinforcement learning competition. The two approaches perform similarly (and in some cases GP performs better than the winner of the competition), even in the case where unknown wind is added to the dynamic system and control is based on structures evolved previously, that is, the evolved controllers have good generalization capability.

DOI: 10.4018/978-1-4666-4038-2.ch001

INTRODUCTION

Limitations of classical control theory has led to the usage of computational intelligence techniques (neural networks, evolutionary computing, and fuzzy logic) for the control of nonlinear, noisy and other dynamic systems which involve complexities.

Genetic Programming (GP), a field which belongs to evolutionary computing techniques, aims at the automatic discovery (evolution) of computer programs for a given task given minimal or no information about the task. The computer programs are involved based on a fitness function without any other information (the details of the dynamic system, derivatives of the system, etc.) being available. Such a computer program can serve as a control law, if the underlying task for which is evolved for, is the control of a dynamical system. Following this approach, the idea of automatic generation of controllers by GP seems ideal, assuming that it can be proven successful in practice too. In the past, GP has been applied to only a small number of challenging control problems (Dracopoulos & Piccoli 2010), compared with other computational intelligence techniques (Dracopoulos, 1997; Si, Barto, Powell, & Wunch, 2004; Werbos, 2008).

One of the challenging control problems found in the literature is that of helicopter hovering. According to this, a helicopter attempts to hover as close as possible to a fixed position. The dynamics of the helicopter is nonlinear, high dimensional, complex, asymmetric and noisy (Koppejan & Whiteson 2009; Ng, Kim, Jordan, Sastry & Ballianda 2004). The problem has been included in different control competitions (e.g. Reinforcement Learning competition 2009) as a benchmark in developing new more powerful control architectures.

The control of a helicopter in hovering position must take into account the different forces of the main rotor and the tail rotor. While the main rotor rotates clockwise, the air which blows downwards generates upward thrust that keeps the helicopter in the air. Based on this, one could suggest that the balancing of the generated thrust with the force of the weight of the fuselage is sufficient to achieve hovering. However, the clockwise torque of the main rotor has as a consequence an anti-torque force, that tends to spin the main chassis. In order to balance the fuselage, the tail rotor has to blow air rightward to generate the appropriate moment to counteract the spin (Ng, Kim, Jordan, Sastry & Ballianda 2004).

This chapter describes in detail how genetic programming can be applied to the problem of generalized helicopter hovering. The results are compared with the neuroevolutionary approach which won the first position in the 2008 Reinforcement Learning (RL) competition for the same problem (Koppejan & Whiteson 2009; Reinforcement Learning Competition 2009). The problem of generalized hovering includes noise in the form of unknown wind. Wind is added to each generalized version (domain) of the problem, according to some unknown probability distribution. The controller evolved has no knowledge about the amount of the wind which is present in each domain. Any control algorithm attempting to guess the wind in a single domain, will overfit the model for that particular case and it will perform badly in the other domains which include different wind.

THE PROBLEM OF HELICOPTER HOVERING

The state of the dynamic system of a helicopter is described in Box 1: where P is the helicopter position in inertial coordinates and $\Theta = \begin{bmatrix} \varphi & \theta & \psi \end{bmatrix}^T$ are the Euler angles corresponding to the roll, pitch and yaw respectively. v^p is the velocity vector: v^p_x is the forward, v^p_y is the

Box 1.

$$q = [P \quad v^p \quad \Theta \quad w^b]^T = [x \quad y \quad z \quad v_x^p \quad v_y^p \quad v_z^p \quad \varphi \quad \theta \quad \psi \quad w_1^b \quad w_2^b \quad w_3^b]^T$$

$$u = [T_m \quad T_t \quad a_1 \quad a_2]^T$$

lateral and v_z^p is the vertical velocity. $\omega^b \in \Re^3$ is the vector which includes the angular velocities of the body.

The main rotor produces the forces $f^b \in \Re^3$ and torques $\tau^b \in \Re^3$ which are controlled by the main rotor thrust T_m and the longitudinal a_1 and lateral a_2 tilts of the tip path plane of the main rotor with respect to the shaft. The thrust T_t controls the anti-torque of the tail rotor (Gonzalez, Mahtani, Bejar & Ollero 2004).

The equations of motion of a rigid body (based on the body coordinate frame) are described by the *Newton-Euler* equations:

$$\begin{bmatrix} mI & 0 \\ 0 & I \end{bmatrix} \begin{bmatrix} \dot{v}^b \\ \dot{\omega}^b \end{bmatrix} + \begin{bmatrix} \omega^b \times mv^b \\ \omega^b \times I\omega^b \end{bmatrix} = \begin{bmatrix} f^b \\ \tau^b \end{bmatrix} \quad (1)$$

where $m \in \Re$ is the mass, $I \in \Re^{3 \times 3}$ is the identity matrix and $I \in \Re^{3 \times 3}$ is the inertial matrix (Koo, Ma & Sastry 2001).

Equations (1) can be rewritten using $v^p = R(\Theta)v^b$ and $\Theta = \Psi(\Theta)\omega^\beta$, where $R(\Theta)$ is the rotation matrix of the body axes relative to the inertial axes (superscript p):

$$\begin{bmatrix} \dot{P} \\ \dot{v}^p \\ \dot{\Theta} \\ \dot{\omega}^b \end{bmatrix} = \begin{bmatrix} v^p \\ \dfrac{1}{m} R(\Theta)f^b \\ \Psi(\Theta)\omega^b \\ I^{-1}(\tau^b - \omega^b \times I\omega^b) \end{bmatrix}$$

The previous system is coupled, non-linear, multivariable and under-actuated with fewer independent control actuators than degrees of freedom to be controlled (Gonzalez, Mahtani, Bejar & Ollero 2004).

Helicopter hovering belongs to the reinforcement learning paradigm problems (Sutton & Barto 1998; Wiering & Otterlo 2012), as it is a sequential decision making problem in which there is limited feedback during learning. Unlike supervised learning, there are no available signals which indicate the "correct" actions in sample states. The fitness of a controller is measured by the difference of the desired state and the actual one, which is then used to construct a reward or penalty (the reinforcement signal) to the controller at every point in time.

The results presented here have been obtained using an XCell Tempest helicopter simulator (Abbeel, Ganapathi & Ng 2006), which was implemented for the RL-Competition (Reinforcement learning competition 2009).

The aim in all simulations is to hover the helicopter around the origin. A single simulation lasts for 600 seconds and it consists of 6000 discrete steps (each step accounts for 0.1 seconds). A penalty (or reward) is applied to the controller at every time step. This is based on the deviation of the helicopter from the origin position. The penalty (or reward) is the reinforcement signal and it is the only information available to the controller (agent) for learning. The reward is calculated as follows:

$$R = -\sum_i \left(s_i - t_i \right)^2 \quad (2)$$

where s_i and t_i are the current value and the target value respectively, of the ith state feature.

A crash of the helicopter during a simulation results in a very large penalty, which is calculated by summing the largest penalty for every remaining step. The values of the four controls of the helicopter are normalized in the range $[-1, 1]$.

RELATED WORK

Neural Networks (NN) can approximate the input-output behavior of arbitrary dynamic systems and have the ability to learn. Supervised neural networks require training data and in the case of flying systems the source of such data can be an experienced pilot. This approach was used by Buskey (Buskey, Wyeth & Roberts 2001), where the NN was used to correlate data from Inertial Navigation System (INS) to actual responses taken from a pilot. These responses comprise the control signals. INS is a system describing the position, orientation, and velocity of an object, which as mentioned earlier are the state variables of the dynamic system of the helicopter. During the training, the INS data together with the inputs directed from the pilot are sampled and logged to the control computer. The network is then trained with the backpropagation supervised learning algorithm to generate the correct response to a given flight attitude.

The case of the yaw control, which is the angle of the helicopter diverted from the longitudinal axis, was considered from Sabatto (Zein-Sabatto, Ma & Malkani 1998). A Remote Control (RC) model helicopter was used. The main parameters that control the yaw are the speed of the main rotor and the tail blade angle. A three layer feed-forward NN was used and the perturbation algorithm was employed to adjust the weights. Although the response of the controller was not ideal, it has been proven that the whole procedure

to control the yaw angle was successful. Sabatto research on the problem investigated the control problem of the helicopter altitude (Zein-Sabatto & Yixiong Zheng 1997). A three-layer NN was trained by the back-propagation algorithm to model the non-linear behavior of the function. An intelligent controller comprised of a PID and a fuzzy controller was then used to control the collective pitch and the rotor speed. The combined intelligent controller achieved a constant rotor speed and avoided the sensitive region of the collective pitch angle.

Genetic algorithms based on floating point representation have been used by Perhinschi (Perhinschi 1997) to design the gains of a controller. He utilised a linear model around hovering and the effort was to control only the longitudinal channel. Ng (Ng & Jordan 2000) had successfully applied the PEGASUS RL algorithm, where with pre-sampling of all the required random numbers in advance and fixing them, any policy can be evaluated. Abbeel and Ng (Abbeel, Coates, Quigley, & Ng 2006) had applied RL algorithms to pilot aerobatic maneuvers, where a linear model based on flight data was constructed to predict the accelerations.

THE WINNER OF THE 2008 RL COMPETITION

The 2008 RL Competition included a helicopter hovering task. The first position in the competition for this problem was won by a neuroevolutionary reinforcement learning approach (Koppejan & Whiteson 2009) which evolved neural network controllers using the accumulated reward. The evolved neural networks corresponded to different policies mapping observations to actions. The initial population of controllers contained 50 randomly generated networks. A steady state evolutionary optimization was applied, i.e. generations of populations were not used. In every evolutionary step, the worst performing network was replaced, by modifying its weights with the application of crossover and mutation operations (Koppejan & Whiteson 2009).

Four different types of networks were used, based on their architecture and the initial configuration of their weights. Single Layer Perceptrons (SLP) and Multi-Layer Perceptrons (MLP) were the two architectures used. The MLP topology was designed by a human specialist. Additional initial knowledge was also applied to the initial population of the neural networks (in two out of the four different types of networks), by setting all the weights of one of the networks, such that it is equivalent to a base-line controller provided by the RL competition software. Although this controller avoids crashes, it is naive and cannot solve the problem satisfactorily, as it performs poorly and does not approach the hovering point. The rest of the initial population (in the case of the base controller being present) was created by mutating the weights of the base-line controller with a predefined probability. The mutation operator was defined as the random generation of a weight from a Gaussian distribution with zero mean and standard deviation of 0.8, which either replaced or added itself to the initial weight.

During the evolution process, two parent networks were selected via roulette wheel selection every time that crossover occurred. The weights of the new networks were probabilistically assigned to be, either the average of the weights of the two parents networks, or the weights of one of the parents. After the application of crossover, mutation was performed to the weights of the networks with a low probability. Mutation followed the same procedure as that described above during the generation of the initial population. If crossover was not probabilistically selected, a network was selected using the roulette wheel method and its weights were subsequently mutated. The mutation created a new neural network which replaced

the worst performing network in the population (Koppejan & Whiteson 2009).

GENETIC PROGRAMMING

Genetic Programming (GP) is an iterative evolutionary process. An initial population of individuals is randomly generated at the beginning of the process. The data structure of the individuals is a tree where the nodes are populated with functions and terminals. This tree structure allows for much more diverse and complex structures of different sizes, which are easy to map to mathematical structures or computer programs. Each individual program in the population is evaluated against a function (fitness function), to measure the performance of the individual against the problem it is addressing. In the evolutionary stage a new population of programs is created from the old population. The fitness is used as a basis to decide which programs are better than others. During the evolutionary phase the higher fit programs are more likely to contribute either in parts or entirely to individuals in the new population. The process of fitness evaluation and evolution is repeated until an optimum or near-optimum solution is generated. The flowchart of the process is shown in Figure 1.

The two main processes of the evolutionary phase are crossover and reproduction, typically to generate 90% and 10% of a new population. In crossover, two individuals and two crossover points in their tree structure are selected probabilistically. Subsequently the parts below the crossover points are interchanged resulting in two offspring, as it shown in Figure 2. Crossover imitates the sexual reproduction we find in nature. To avoid the loss of good individuals which have already been formed reproduction is used to copy some of the better individuals in successive generations. The selection mechanism in both cases is fitness proportionate. Fitness is a measure of "goodness" and typically in a control problem assesses the deviation from a desired state. During the fitness

Figure 1. Flowchart of the GP process

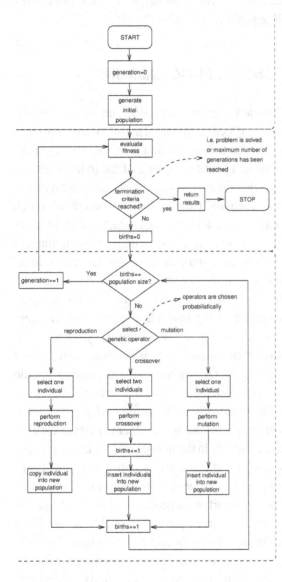

Figure 2. The crossover process

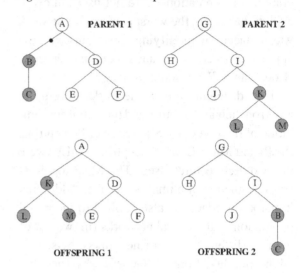

tion as a whole. A loss of diversity will result in premature convergence and sub-optimal solutions. The adoption of an elitist approach, where the top n individuals are always copied to the next generation may speed up convergence but sometimes leads to the degradation of the overall solution. For additional information and full details on the GP family of algorithms the reader can refer to the seminal book of Koza *Genetic Programming on the Programming of Computers by Means of Natural Selection* (Koza 1992).

The most obvious problem with GP is related with computer hardware. Given infinite power and memory, GP could solve any problem. As the complexity of the problems increases so the computational and memory requirements tend to increase very rapidly. The improvement of GP as a technique is still an area of very active research.

THE GENETIC PROGRAMMING APPROACH

The action space for the helicopter hovering control is continuous and includes the following four actions:

- α_1: Longitudinal cyclic pitch (aileron)

evaluation, each program (tree structure) in the population is evaluated on how well it performs in the specific problem.

The underlying principle of evolution is that of "survival of the fittest," where the good genetic material perpetuates at the expense of the bad. The method of proportional fitness or roulette wheel selection, involves calculating, for each individual, its proportion of the total population fitness, such that the sum of all individual fitnesses equals to 1.0. To allow evolution to progress, sufficient diversity must exist in the popula-

- α_2: Latitudinal cyclic pitch (elevator)
- α_3: Main rotor collective pitch (rudder)
- α_4: Tail rotor collective pitch (coll)

Unlike the traditional GP approach, the application of GP in helicopter hovering uses four independent trees allocated for each individual in the population, one for every action. Thus, the population consists of 500 quad trees.

The individuals in the initial population are generated with the 'ramped half-and-half' method (Koza 1992). The 'full' method which creates full trees of length 2 to 6 and the 'grow' method which sets the maximum length of a tree are chosen with equal probability. Creation of the same individual (duplication) was not allowed in the initial population. The initial population included an individual equivalent with the default baseline controller supplied with the RL Competition software described in the previous section. The controller can avoid helicopter crashes but it is unable to bring it close to the hovering position. It has to be emphasized, that the same baseline controller was also included in the initial population of the neuroevolutionary approach which won the RL Competition. The baseline controller is shown in Figure 3.

The GP derivation of controllers for helicopter hovering uses the normalized fitness to drive the evolution. First, the reinforcement signal of equation (2) is utilized to calculate the raw fitness. To do so, the sum of the reinforcement signal at every time step in an episode is calculated. The raw fitness is equal to this sum. The reinforcement signal is negative, therefore the standard fitness $s(i)$ of the ith individual is the negation of the raw fitness. Then the adjusted fitness is calculated by the following:

$$a(i) = \frac{1}{1 + s(i)}$$

Finally, the normalized fitness was calculated:

$$n(i) = \frac{a(i)}{\sum_{k=1}^{M} a(k)}$$

The function set chosen for the application of GP is shown in Table 1. The state of the dynamic system is described by 12 variables. However, only 9 of them are independent because the angular velocities can be calculated from the rest. Therefore, the terminal set used included only the independent variables, i.e. the coordinates x, y, z, the velocities u, v, w, the angles θ, φ, ω and the constants that were essential to construct the default baseline controller.

Figure 3. The default baseline controller in the initial GP population

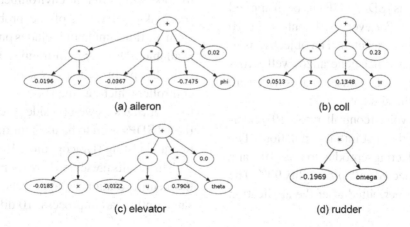

(a) aileron

(b) coll

(c) elevator

(d) rudder

Table 1. The function set used by GP for the helicopter hovering problem

Function	Symbol	Function	Symbol
Addition	ADD	Square	SQ
Subtraction	SUB	Cube	CUB
Multiplication	MUL	Greater Than	GT
Division	DIV	Sign	SIG
Absolute Value	ABS	Sin	SIN
Square Root	SQRT	Cosine	COS
Exponential	EXP		

The generalized version for the helicopter hovering problem, which includes noise in the flight dynamics, was considered by the GP process. The details of the actual noise, i.e. its magnitude and range were unknown to the controller. A derived controller should not overfit to a specific control problem (i.e. specific noise) but it should be able to hover the helicopter even when the environmental conditions (noise representing wind) change. This is what the generalized version of the problem requires (which was the case for the RL competition and its software simulator used in this work). The wind (noise) has x and y components. The wind velocities vary randomly between $-5m/sec$ and $5m/sec$ (neither the value nor the range is known to the evolving GP controllers). The helicopter hovering simulator provides 10 different wind patterns corresponding to 10 different modes of the simulation, i.e. it includes 10 different Sequential Decision Problems (SDPs). GP has been applied to all 10 of them. For every different mode, 10 different runs were executed. The objective is to derive a controller which generalizes well across different SDPs, including unseen cases which are not included in the simulator.

Each GP run evolved controllers for 119 generations (excluding the first initial population). The probability of selecting reproduction was 10% and crossover was selected with probability 90%. The maximum depth permitted after the application

of crossover operation was 17 and in the case that one of the offspring had depth which was longer than the allowed one, the selected parent tree was copied without modification. In the case that both offspring exceeded the allowed depth, both parents were copied to the new population, something which is equivalent to reproduction. The selection of an individual was proportional to fitness. Permutation and mutation were not allowed. It should be noted that the mutation operator was also tested, but it did not manage to produce successful results.

The default baseline controller was copied to the next population independently from the reproduction process, as this was proved to generate better results overall.

The output of an evolved GP controller is calculated based on the following:

$$f(x) = \frac{e^x - e^{-x}}{e^x + e^{-x}}$$

where x is the evaluation of the GP tree. The above limits the range of the control inputs to the plant in $[-1, 1]$, a requirement of the simulator.

RESULTS

To address the generalized version of the helicopter hovering problem, a controller must be able to cope with different environmental conditions (i.e. unknown wind) of the problem. The RL Competition simulator includes only 10 different available SDPs for both training and testing. In order to optimize the process of finding the best controller which can then be applied successfully to other SDPs as well (besides the 10 available), the 10 SDPs need to be used for training, validation and testing (Dracopoulos, 1997).

The results presented here for both the GP and the neuroevolutionary approaches followed the same optimization process. 10 different populations (runs) are created for every mode of the wind pattern (10 modes in total). Every run consisted of 120 generations for the GP and 120000 episodes for the neuroevolutionary method.

The optimum controller was derived by the following process:

1. The best controller of every generation were subsequently validated in the modes 0 to 4. If the controller was actually evolved on any of the modes 0 to 4, this mode was excluded from the validation. According to the performance in the validation set, the best individual for every mode was selected. Thus, the validation runs determined which individual performs better (generalizes) in unseen SDPs (i.e. SDPs not used for its evolution).

2. The 10 best controllers (one from each mode) for both approaches (GP and neuroevolution-

ary) were tested in modes 5 to 9. The comparison of the GP and the neuroevolutionary method winner of the 2008 RL competition was based on this. If a controller was evolved (trained) in one of the modes 5 to 9, this mode was excluded from the test runs. 100 episodes were run with each controller for each test mode, to obtain the test results. The best overall controller found by Genetic Programming (based on the test modes) is shown in Appendix A.

Figures 4–8 show the performance of the two approaches for the 5 test modes (SDPs). It can be seen that in most cases the performance of the GP is similar that of the SLP and MLP controllers evolved using the neuroevolutionary approach. For some modes, GP performs better. The diagrams also include the performances of the controllers of the 2 approaches in the initial population. The

Figure 4. Best agents of mode 5

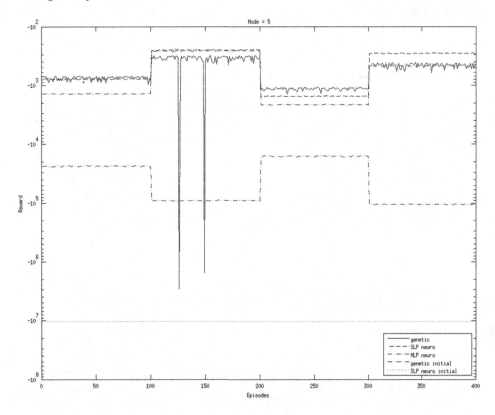

Figure 5. Best agents of mode 6

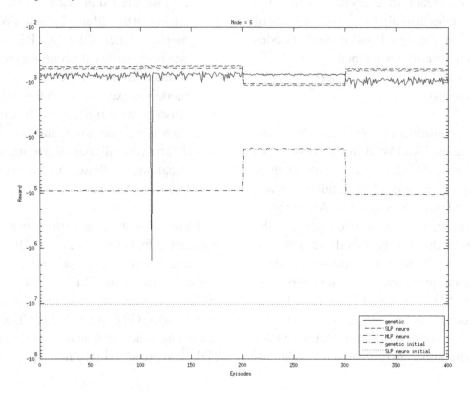

Figure 6. Best agents of mode 7

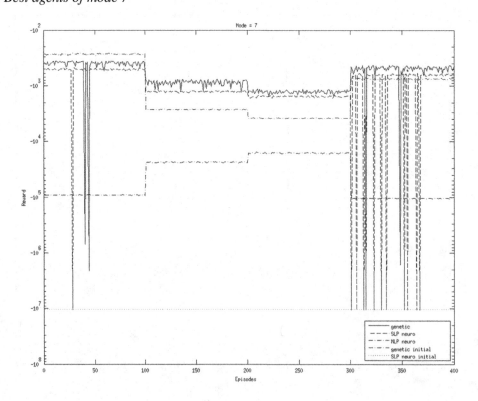

Figure 7. Best agents of mode 8

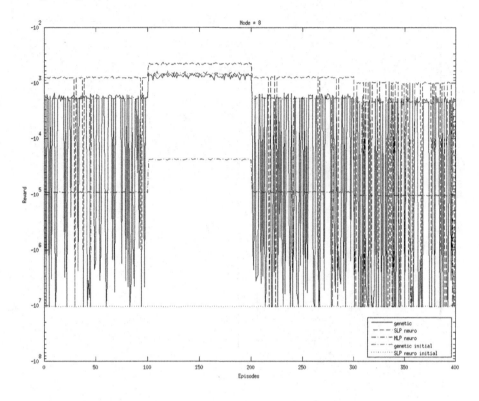

Figure 8. Best agents of mode 9

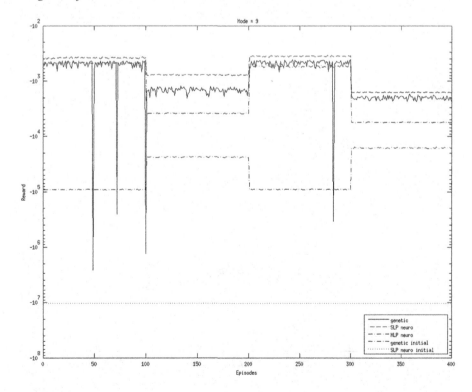

Figure 9. The performance of the best agents for the various approaches

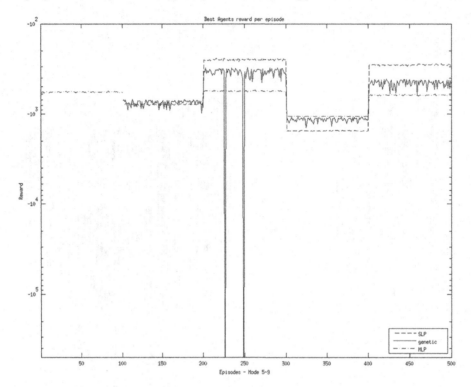

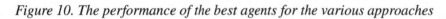

Figure 10. The performance of the best agents for the various approaches

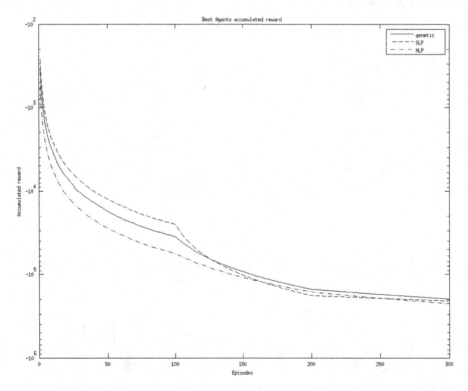

GP manages to improve the initial (baseline) controller by two orders of magnitude.

From Figure 4 it can be seen that for the different modes of testing the best performance is interchanged by the three approaches with the GP having the defect of crashing the helicopter at mode 7. In Figure 4 the GP achieves stable results slightly inferior than the neuroevolutionary approach but performs better in one case. In Figures 6 and 7 we observe that the agents trained in these modes for all approaches are crashing the helicopter numerous times. This manifests the difficulty of the control problem at hand.

Figures 9 and 10 illustrate the performance of the best controllers between all modes of training where the GP and the neuroevolutionary approaches achieve similar results. This becomes clearer if the three approaches are compared excluding the crashes. In that case the GP performs better than the other approaches in the long run.

Tables 1 and 2 detail the performance of the various controllers against key measures. These measures are the number of crashes for every mode in the test process, how many times the controller performed better than the others and the accumulated reward excluding crashes. In the comparison between the GP and SLP approaches it is apparent that the crashes occurred more often for the GP. However, when the specific episodes are compared, GP manages to outperform the SLP half of the times. In Table 2, the GP is compared with the MLP and the times of crashes for the MLP are even more infrequent in comparison with the SLP. Where GP achieved better scores against SLP, it also outperformed the MLP. This leads to the conclusion that GP optimization is robust, although it needs large number of individuals in order to achieve it (See Table 3).

CONCLUSION

The capability of GP to generate automatically controllers for challenging complex control problems has not been tested sufficiently in the literature. Here, GP is applied to the helicopter hovering problem. Helicopter hovering is a nonlinear high-dimensional control problem which have been included in the literature in the set of challenging control domains. The generalised version of helicopter hovering is considered, which includes unknown noise (in the form of wind), as an additional complexity. The problem was included in the set of benchmarks in recent RL competitions for deriving new controllers.

The details of how GP can derive controllers for this problem are described. The proposed approach is compared with a neuroevolutionary approach, which won the first position for helicopter hovering in the 2008 RL competition. The performance of the evolved controllers is tested in versions of the dynamic system that they have not encountered during evolution (training). The presented results demonstrate that GP performs similarly with the winner of the RL competition. In some cases, the GP solved controllers which lead to a crash, but this is also happening with the winner of the competition. In certain modes (SDPs), the GP performance is better than the neuroevolutionary approach.

Based on the results obtained for this problem, it can be stated that the automatic generation of computer programs by genetic programming could also provide an ideal candidate for the automatic generation of controllers for other complex control problems. This is because GP does not require any knowledge about the problem domain and evolution is driven by a fitness function. Problems which belong to the reinforcement learning paradigm, where a limited (and possibly delayed) single reward or penalty signal is only available for learning, seem suitable for the application of GP.

Table 2. Performance comparison for each mode between GP and SLP

		Mode 5			Mode 6			Mode 7			Mode 8			Mode 9		
		Crh	Bet	Acc	Crh	Bet	Acc	Crh	Bet	Acc	Crh	Bet	Acc	Crh	Bet	Acc
Agent Mode 0	GP	1	0	-87792	13	0	-83736	0	0	-83681	28	72	-88301	4	0	-123590
	SLP	0	100	-56242	0	100	-40383	0	100	-56332	0	28	-99329	0	100	-54965
Agent Mode 1	GP	3	34	-50547	0	3	-83438	4	2	-49350	0	0	-133935	2	0	-66411
	SLP	0	66	-47000	0	97	-74001	0	98	-41285	0	100	-60516	0	100	-46266
Agent Mode 2	GP	7	35	-47512	51	0	-73633	5	11	-45030	63	29	-92901	23	0	-61243
	SLP	0	65	-45238	0	100	-36679	0	89	-40606	0	71	-98758	0	100	-48464
Agent Mode 3	GP	0	100	-51732	0	100	-65718	3	97	-48658	0	1	-143389	0	100	-67374
	SLP	0	0	-96287	1	0	-109319	0	3	-90617	0	99	-130921	30	0	-154985
Agent Mode 4	GP	1	0	-87257	2	0	-176645	1	2	-82308	0	0	-226003	3	0	-134277
	SLP	0	100	-74344	0	100	-130160	0	98	-69355	0	100	-171885	0	100	-86932
Agent Mode 5	GP	-	-	-	0	79	-75581	2	0	-34468	0	100	-115604	0	0	-45969
	SLP	-	-	-	0	21	-78253	0	100	-25051	0	0	-154021	0	100	-28622
Agent Mode 6	GP	0	0	-75617	-	-	-	1	0	-73645	0	100	-72229	0	0	-93995
	SLP	0	100	-52513	-	-	-	0	100	-51048	0	0	-113669	0	100	-57072
Agent Mode 7	GP	2	97	-39566	0	98	-88398	-	-	-	0	99	-128574	2	97	-48604
	SLP	1	3	-50939	0	2	-127104	-	-	-	0	1	-155043	11	3	-63450
Agent Mode 8	GP	31	3	-178694	0	0	-75126	45	4	-174114	-	-	-	42	25	-203970
	SLP	3	97	-80322	0	100	-45421	4	96	-78954	-	-	-	27	75	-100123
Agent Mode 9	GP	3	0	-49156	0	0	-147568	1	0	-47917	0	0	-200945	-	-	-
	SLP	0	100	-38384	0	100	-77955	0	100	-35751	0	100	-159757	-	-	-

Table 3. Performance comparison for each mode between GP and MLP

		Mode 5			Mode 6			Mode 7			Mode 8			Mode 9		
		Crh	Bet	Acc	Crh	Bet	Acc	Crh	Bet	Acc	Crh	Bet	Acc	Crh	Bet	Acc
Agent Mode 0	GP	1	99	-87792	13	0	-83736	0	100	-83681	28	72	-88301	4	96	-123590
	MLP	0	1	-173088	0	100	-63677	1	0	-172145	0	28	-108277	2	4	-195310
Agent Mode 1	GP	3	0	-50547	0	100	-83438	4	0	-49350	0	100	-133935	2	0	-66411
	MLP	0	100	-33185	0	0	-259734	0	100	-33027	0	0	-397802	0	100	-46010
Agent Mode 2	GP	7	93	-47512	51	31	-73633	5	95	-45030	63	37	-92901	23	77	-61243
	MLP	0	7	-104444	0	69	-74733	0	5	-106599	0	63	-161663	0	23	-114475
Agent Mode 3	GP	0	100	-51732	0	100	-65718	3	97	-48658	0	100	-143389	0	100	-67374
	MLP	0	0	-110556	0	0	-106775	0	3	-106793	0	0	-187406	0	0	-150084
Agent Mode 4	GP	1	97	-87257	2	98	-176645	1	92	-82308	0	100	-226003	3	97	-134277
	MLP	0	3	-113862	0	2	-429170	0	8	-98078	0	0	-537801	0	3	-252467
Agent Mode 5	GP	-	-	-	0	100	-75581	2	0	-34468	0	100	-115604	0	60	-45969
	MLP	-	-	-	0	0	-139729	0	100	-25958	0	0	-214368	0	40	-46168
Agent Mode 6	GP	0	0	-75617	-	-	-	1	0	-73645	0	100	-72229	0	0	-93995
	MLP	0	100	-57107	-	-	0	0	100	-55847	0	0	-106240	0	100	-61786
Agent Mode 7	GP	2	0	-39566	0	100	-88398	-	-	-	0	100	-128574	2	98	-48604
	MLP	0	100	-26953	0	0	-266833	-	-	-	0	0	-382199	0	2	-74924
Agent Mode 8	GP	31	52	-178694	0	10	-75126	45	45	-174114	-	-	-	42	48	-203970
	MLP	1	48	-188102	0	90	-68571	2	55	-188486	-	-	-	6	52	-221276
Agent Mode 9	GP	3	54	-49156	0	100	-147568	1	82	-47917	100	100	-200945	-	-	-
	MLP	0	46	-47782	0	0	-382501	0	18	-54595	0	0	-556661	-	-	-

Future work on the application of GP to helicopter hovering should include how the avoidance of crashes could be incorporated in the evolution of GP controllers. Additional work should investigate whether the application of more than one GP controllers, depending on the operating range (state of the system), could lead to even better results.

REFERENCES

Abbeel, P., Coates, A., Quigley, M., & Ng, A. Y. (2006). An application of reinforcement learning to aerobatic helicopter flight. *Advances in Neural Information Processing Systems, 19.*

Abbeel, P., Ganapathi, V., & Ng, A. (2006). Learning vehicular dynamics, with application to modeling helicopters. *Advances in Neural Information Processing Systems, 18*(1).

Buskey, G., Wyeth, G., & Roberts, J. (2001). Autonomous helicopter hover using an artificial neural network. In *Proceedings IEEE International Conference on Robotics and Automation,* (pp. 1635–1640). IEEE.

Dracopoulos, D. C. (1997). *Evolutionary learning algorithms for neural adaptive control.* Berlin: Springer Verlag.

Dracopoulos, D. C., & Piccoli, R. (2010). Bioreactor control by genetic programming. In Schaefer, R. et al. (Eds.), *Parallel Problem Solving from Nature (PPSN) XI (LNCS) (Vol. 6239,* pp. 181–188). Springer-Verlag. doi:10.1007/978-3-642-15871-1_19.

Gonzalez, A., Mahtani, R., Bejar, M., & Ollero, A. (2004). Control and stability analysis of an autonomous helicopter. In *Proceedings of World Automation Congress,* (vol. 15, pp. 399–404). IEEE.

Koo, T. J., Ma, Y., & Sastry, S. (2001). Nonlinear control of a helicopter based unmanned aerial vehicle. *IEEE Transactions on Control Systems Technology.*

Koppejan, R., & Whiteson, S. (2009). Neuroevolutionary reinforcement learning for generalized helicopter control. In *Proceedings of the 11th Annual Conference on Genetic and Evolutionary Computation,* (pp. 145–152). ACM.

Koza, R. J. (1992). *Genetic programming on the programming of computers by means of natural selection.* Boston: MIT Press.

Ng, A. Y., & Jordan, M. (2000). PEGASUS: A policy search method for large MDPs and POMDPs. In *Proceedings of the Sixteenth Conference on Uncertainty in Artificial Intelligence.* IEEE.

Ng, A. Y., Kim, H. J., Jordan, M. I., Sastry, S., & Ballianda, S. (2004). Autonomous helicopter flight via reinforcement learning. *Advances in Neural Information Processing Systems.*

Perhinschi, G. M. (1997). A modified genetic algorithm for the design of autonomous helicopter control system. In *Proceedings of AIAA Guidance, Navigation, and Control Conference.* AIAA.

Reinforcement Learning Competition. (2009). http://www.rl-competition.org

Si, J., Barto, A. G., Powell, W. B., & Wunch, D. II, (Eds.). (2004). *Handbook of learning and approximate dynamic programming.* New York: Wiley. doi:10.1109/9780470544785.

Sutton, R. S., & Barto, A. G. (1998). *Reinforcement learning an introduction.* Boston: MIT Press.

Werbos, P. J. (2008). Foreword - ADP: The key direction for future research in intelligent control and understanding brain intelligence. *IEEE Transactions on Systems, Man, and Cybernetics. Part B, Cybernetics, 38*(4), 898–900. doi:10.1109/TSMCB.2008.924139.

Wiering, M., & van Otterlo, M. (Eds.). (2012). *Reinforcement learning: State-of-the-art*. Boston: Springer Verlag. doi:10.1007/978-3-642-27645-3.

Zein-Sabatto, S., Ma, G., & Malkani, M. J. (1998). Intelligent flight control design for helicopter yaw control. In *Proceedings of the Thirtieth Southeastern Symposium on System Theory*, (pp. 184–188). IEEE.

Zein-Sabatto, S., & Zheng, Y. (1997). Intelligent flight controllers for helicopter control. In *Proceedings of the International Conference on Neural Networks*, (pp. 617–621). IEEE.

ADDITIONAL READING

Kirk, D. E. (2004). *Optimal control theory: An introduction*. New York: Dover Publications.

Koza, R. J. (1994). *Genetic programming II*. Boston: MIT Press.

Koza, R. J., Forrest, B. H., Andre, D., & Keane, A. M. (1999). *Genetic programming III: Darwinian invention and problem solving*. San Francisco: Morgan Kaufmann. doi:10.1109/TEVC.1999.788530.

Michalewicz, Z. (1996). *Genetic algorithms + data structures = evolution programs*. Berlin: Springer Verlag. doi:10.1007/978-3-662-03315-9.

Poli, R., Langdon, W. B., & McPhee, N. F. (2008). *A field guide to genetic programming*. Retrieved from http://www.gp-field-guide.org.uk

Powell, W. B. (2011). *Approximate dynamic programming: Solving the curses of dimensionality* (2nd ed.). New York: Wiley. doi:10.1002/9781118029176.

KEY TERMS AND DEFINITIONS

Computational Intelligence: Computational Intelligence is a set of computational methodologies aim to address complex real-world problems and where the traditional approaches are ineffective or infeasible. Another major characteristic of these algorithms is that in order for Computational Intelligence to achieve its goal, it exhibits a degree of intelligence. Usually at the start there is a 'naive' structure incapable to solve the problem and through iterative steps the algorithm adapts and adjusts the initial structure. The final outcome is a highly sophisticated problem solver.

Control Theory: Control Theory is a well-established discipline of engineering and mathematics that tries to control the behaviour of dynamical systems. The dynamical system is seen as a pair of input and output and Control Theory algorithms try to devise ways to manipulate the inputs in order to obtain a desired effect on the output.

Evolutionary Computation: Evolutionary Computation applies the biological mechanisms of evolution on combinatorial optimisation problems. Evolutionary Computation employs iterative progress over a population. The population in every generation is selected through a guided random search. Evolutionary Computation is a subfield of Computational Intelligence and includes methodologies like: Genetic Algorithms, Genetic Programming, Evolutionary Strategies, Ant Colony optimisation and others.

Genetic Programming: Genetic Programming is an evolutionary methodology inspired by the biological evolution. It is a special case of Genetic Algorithms where the individuals are well-structured programs. Genetic Programming is a machine learning technique, which optimises a population of computer programs according to the program's ability to perform a given computational task.

Helicopter Control: Helicopter Control is the area which studies the methods required to control the flying behaviour of a helicopter. Usually a specific state is given and the researcher/engineer has to design controllers capable to achieve and maintain the specific state.

Neural Networks: Neural Networks is a highly adaptable mathematical model, which consists of interconnected group of neurons. The neuron constitutes the most fundamental unit of computation in the Neural Networks and it is usually described by the equation $y = w_i * x$. The high degree of structural complexity gives the Neural Networks the ability to model complex relationships and to find patterns in non-linear spaces.

Reinforcement Learning: Reinforcement Learning is a Machine Learning technique, where an agent interacts through actions with an environment and aims to maximize a specific measure, the cumulative reward. The major difference of Reinforcement Learning and the standard supervised learning is that convergence to the optimal policy is achieved without the use of correct behaviour pairs of input/output.

APPENDIX

The best individual derived through GP for which all results are presented in the paper is shown (unedited) below:

α_1 - aileron:

(-0.0196 v)(+ (* -0.0196 y)(* -0.0367 v)(+ (* -0.0196 (* phi v))(+ -0.0196 (* -0.0196 y)(* -0.0367 v)0.02)(* -0.7475 phi)0.02)0.02)0.02)(* -0.7475 phi)0.02)0.02)(+ -0.0367 (+ (* 0.02 -0.0196)(* -0.7475 v)(* (* -0.0367 v)(* -0.0196 -0.0367))0.02)(* -0.7475 phi)0.02)0.02))(* -0.0367 (* -0.0196 y))(* -0.7475 -0.0196)0.02)(+ -0.0196 (* -0.0196 v)(+ (* -0.7475 -0.0196)(+ (* (+ (* -0.0196 y)(* -0.0367 v)(* -0.7475 0.02)0.02)y)(* -0.0367 v)(* -0.7475 (* -0.0196 -0.0367))0.02)-0.0196 0.02)(+ (* -0.0196 y)(* -0.0367 v)(* -0.7475 (+ (* -0.0196 (* -0.7475 phi))(* (* -0.0367 v)v)-0.0196 0.02))0.02)) (+ (* (* -0.0367 -0.0196)(+ (* (* -0.0367 0.02)y)(* -0.0367 v)(*-0.7475 (* -0.0196 -0.0367))0.02)) (+ (* 0.02 y)(* -0.0367 v)(* -0.7475 (* phi v))0.02)(* -0.7475 phi)(* -0.0196 y))(+ 0.02 (* -0.0367 -0.0196)(+ (+ (* -0.0196 -0.0196)(* 0.02 v)(* -0.7475 -0.0367)(* -0.0196 y))(* 0.02 -0.0196)(+ (* (+ (* -0.0196 y)(* (* 0.02 -0.0196)v)(* -0.7475 -0.0196)0.02)y)(+ (* -0.7475 y)(* -0.0367 v)(* -0.7475 (* -0.0196 -0.0367))-0.0367)(* (* (+ (* -0.0196 y)(+ 0.02 (* -0.0367 v)(+ (* -0.0196 v) v (* -0.7475 phi)(* 0.02 y))0.02)(+ (* (+ (* 0.02 -0.7475)(* -0.0367 v)(+ (* -0.0196 y)(+ (* -0.0196 y)(* -0.0196 0.02)(* phi (* (* -0.0367 v)v))0.02)(* (* -0.7475 (* (* -0.0367 v)v))phi)0.02)0.02)y)(+ (* -0.0196 y)(* (* -0.0196 -0.0367)v)(* (* -0.0367 v)(* -0.0196 -0.0367))0.02)(* -0.7475 phi)0.02)0.02)(* -0.0196 -0.0367))phi)0.02)0.02)(+ (* -0.0196 v)(+ 0.02 (* -0.0367 v)(+ (* -0.0196 v)(+ 0.02 (* -0.0196 v)(+ (* -0.0196 y)(* -0.0367 v)(+ (* -0.0196 (* (* -0.0367 v)(* -0.0367 v)))(+ (* -0.0196 y)(* -0.0367 v)(* -0.0367 v)0.02)(* -0.7475 phi)0.02)0.02)0.02)(* -0.7475 phi)0.02) 0.02)(+ (* 0.02 y)(+ (* -0.0196 y)(* 0.02 v)(* (* -0.0367 (* -0.0196 y))(* -0.0196 -0.0367))0.02)(* -0.7475 phi)(* -0.0367 y))0.02)))(+ 0.02 (* -0.0367 y)(+ (* (* -0.7475 v)0.02)(+ 0.02 (* -0.0367 v) (* -0.7475 (* (* -0.0367 v)-0.0367))0.02)(* -0.7475 phi)0.02)(* -0.0196 -0.0367)))

α_2 - elevator:

(+ (* -0.0185 x)(* -0.0322 u)(+ (* -0.0185 (* -0.0185 (+ (* -0.0185 x)(* -0.0322 u)(* 0.7904 theta)0.0)))(+ (* -0.0322 x)(* -0.0185 x)(+ (* 0.7904 (* -0.0322 theta))(* -0.0322 -0.0185)(+ (* -0.0185 x)(* -0.0322 u)(+ (* -0.0185 x)(+ (+ (* -0.0185 x)(* -0.0185 x)(+ (* x x)(+ (* -0.0322 x)(* (* 0.7904 (* -0.0322 u))(* u x))(+ (* (* -0.0322 u)(* x theta))(* -0.0322 u)(+ (* -0.0185 x)(* -0.0322 u)theta (* -0.0185 -0.0185))0.0)(+ (* -0.0185 (+ (* 0.7904 x)(* (* -0.0185 u)u)(* 0.7904 theta)(+ (* -0.0185 x)-0.0185 (* -0.0322 u)-0.0322)))(* -0.0322 u)(* 0.7904 theta)(* -0.0185 u)))(+ (* -

0.0185 (+ (* u x)(* -0.0185 u)(* 0.7904 theta)0.0)(* -0.0322 u)(* x theta)(* -0.0185 x))(* -0.0185 x))(* x -0.0322))(* (* 0.7904 -0.0322)u)(* -0.0322 u)(* (* 0.7904 (+ (* -0.0185 x)(* -0.0185 x)(* (+ (* (* -0.0322 (* -0.0185 u))(* -0.0322 theta))(* u u)(+ (* -0.0185 x)(* -0.0322 u)theta (* -0.0185 x))0.0)(* (* -0.0322 u)u))(+ theta (* -0.0322 u)(* 0.7904 theta)(* (* -0.0185 x)x))))x))(+ (* (* -0.0185 x)(+ (* -0.0185 x)(* (* -0.0185 (* -0.0185 x))-0.0185)(* -0.0185 theta)0.0))(* -0.0322 u)(+ (* -0.0185 x)(* -0.0322 u)(* 0.7904 theta)(* -0.0185 x))(* -0.0185 x))(* (* 0.7904 (+ (* -0.0185 x)(* -0.0185 x)(* 0.7904 x)(+ (* -0.0185 x)(* -0.0322 u)(* 0.7904 theta)(* (* -0.0185 x)x))))x))theta)(* -0.0185 x))(+ (* -0.0185 (+ (* -0.0185 x)(* 0.0322 u)(* 0.7904 theta)(+ (* -0.0185 x)(* (* -0.0322 u)(* 0.7904 u))(* x -0.0322)-0.0322)))(* -0.0322 u)(+ (* -0.0185 x)(+ (+ (* -0.0185 x)(* -0.0185+ 0.02 (* -0.0367 v)(+ (+ (* (* -0.0196 y)(+ (* -0.0196 y)(+ (* -0.7475 -0.0196)(* -0.0367 v)(+ (* -0.0196 v)(+ 0.02 (*x)(+ (* -0.0185 x)(+ (* -0.0322 x)(* (* 0.7904 (* u u))u)(+ (* (* -0.0185 x)(* -0.0322 theta))(* -0.0322 u)

(+ (* -0.0185 x)(* -0.0322 u)theta (* -0.0185 x))0.0)(+ (* -0.0185 (+ (* -0.0185 x)(* (+ (* -0.0185 x)
(* -0.0322 u)(* 0.7904 theta)(* -0.0185 x))(* -0.0185 x))(* 0.7904 theta)(+ (* -0.0185 x)(* (* 0.7904 (*
-0.0322 x))-0.0185)(* -0.0322 u)-0.0322)))(* -0.0322 -0.0185)(* 0.7904 theta)(* (* -0.0322 u)-0.0322)))
(+ (* -0.0185 (+ (* u x)(* -0.0185 u)(* 0.7904 theta)0.0))(* -0.0185 x)(* x theta)(* -0.0185 x))(* x x))
(* (* -0.0185 -0.0185)theta))(* u u)(* x u)(+ (* -0.0185 (* u x))(* (* x theta)u)(* 0.7904 (* (* -0.0185
theta)u))(* -0.0185 u)))(+ (* -0.0185 theta)(* -0.0322 u)(* x x)(* 0.0 x))(* -0.0185 x))(* -0.0185 (*
-0.0322 u))))(+ (* (* -0.0185 x)(+ (* -0.0185 x)(* -0.0322 u)-0.0185 0.0))(* -0.0322 u)(* x theta)(*
-0.0185 x))(* -0.0185 x))(* -0.0185 x))

a$_3$ - rudder:

(* (/ (* (CUB (ABS omega))u u u)(* (ABS x)(ABS x)theta omega))(* (CUB (ABS w))(* x theta
(CUB u))(* (ABS (/ (CUB w)(ABS x)))(ABS (CUB (ABS x)))(* u u w w))theta)u)

a$_4$ - coll:

(+ z (* (+ (* 0.0513 (+ (+ (* 0.1348 w)(+ (+ 0.1348 (+ z (* z z)w)(+ (* (* z 0.1348)(* (+ (*
0.0513 z)(* 0.1348 w)0.1348)w))(* 0.1348 w))(+ (* 0.1348 z)z (+ z (* 0.1348 z)(+ (+ z (* z w)(* w
w))0.1348 (+ 0.0513 (* 0.1348 w)w))))(+ (* 0.0513 z)(* (* 0.1348 0.1348)z)(* z (+ z 0.1348 (+ z (*
0.0513 (* 0.1348 z))z)))))(+ 0.1348 0.0513 0.0513))(* z z)w))(* 0.1348 (+ (* 0.1348 z)(* 0.23 w)(* z
0.1348)))(+ 0.1348 0.1348 0.0513))w)0.23)

Chapter 2
Methodology for Epilepsy and Epileptic Seizure Recognition using Chaos Analysis of Brain Signals

Seyyed Abed Hosseini
Ferdowsi University of Mashhad, Iran

Mohammed-Reza Akbarzadeh-T
Ferdowsi University of Mashhad, Iran

Mohammed-Bagher Naghibi-Sistani
Ferdowsi University of Mashhad, Iran

ABSTRACT

A novel combination of chaotic features and Adaptive Neuro-Fuzzy Inference System (ANFIS) is proposed for epileptic seizure recognition. The non-linear dynamics of the original EEGs are quantified in the form of the Hurst exponent (H), Correlation dimension (D_2), Petrosian Fractal Dimension (PFD), and the Largest lyapunov exponent (λ). The process of EEG analysis consists of two phases, namely the qualitative and quantitative analysis. The classification ability of the H, D_2, PFD, and λ measures is tested using ANFIS classifier. This method is evaluated with using a benchmark EEG dataset, and qualitative and quantitative results are presented. The inter-ictal EEG-based diagnostic approach achieves 98.6% accuracy with using 4-fold cross validation. Diagnosis based on ictal data is also tested in ANFIS classifier, reaching 98.1% accuracy. Therefore, the method can be successfully applied to both inter-ictal and ictal data.

DOI: 10.4018/978-1-4666-4038-2.ch002

INTRODUCTION

Epilepsy is a brain disorder that is characterized by sudden and recurrent seizures. According to available reports, "approximately 1% of the world's population suffers from epilepsy" (University of Melbourne) while about 85% of them live in the developing countries (Atlas, 2005). It can cause abnormal electrical activity in the brain and may alter consciousness, perception, sensation, behavior and body movement. Patients experience varied symptoms during seizures depending on the location and extent of the affected brain tissue. Most seizures are very brief and is rarely life threatening. Depending on the extent of the involvement of brain areas during the epilepsy, it can be divided into two main types that according to the International League Against Epilepsy (ILAE), in 1981 (ILAE, 1909) includes: 1- Generalized seizures that involve almost the entire brain, 2- Partial (or focal) seizures that originate from a circumscribed area of the brain and remain restricted to that area (Guo, 2010). Generalized seizures can be divided into several main types, such as Absence, Atypical Absence, Myoclonic, Clonic, Tonic, Tonic-clonic, and Atonic seizures. Also, Partial seizures can be divided into three main types such as Simple partial, Complex partial, and Secondarily generalized seizures.

Due to a large number of patients in Intensive Care Units (ICU) and the need for continuous observation of such conditions, several methods for epileptic seizure recognition have been developed in the past. Several quantitative system approaches incorporating statistical techniques, dynamical systems and optimization for brain disorders (Chaovalitwongse, 2005). In assessment of epilepsy, brain activity plays a central role. Electroencephalography (EEG) is a technique, which contains much information about the patient's psycho-physiological state (Kumar, 2011). Therefore, EEG has become the premier diagnostic method for epilepsy recognition. EEG can be recorded in two essential ways: The first

and most common is non-invasive recording known as scalp recording. The second is invasive recording that often is known as inter-cranial EEG. Frequency bands of EEG signals are interesting to be interpreted such as delta (1-4 Hz), theta (4-8 Hz), alpha (8-13 Hz), beta (13-30 Hz) and gamma (> 30 Hz).

In principle, there are two different scenarios of how a seizure could evolve. It could be caused by a sudden and abrupt transition, in which case it would not be preceded by detectable dynamical changes in the EEG. Such a scenario would be conceivable for the initiation of seizures in primary generalized epilepsy. Alternatively, this transition could be a gradual change in dynamics, which could in theory, be detectable. This type of transition could be more likely in focal epilepsies. About dynamical states of epileptic EEG signals, there are some main classic states of inter-ictal, pre-ictal, ictal, and post-ictal; but clinical and laboratory experiments leave little doubt that a pre-seizure period exists in temporal lobe and perhaps other forms of epilepsy. Its existence, however, raises fundamental questions about what constitutes a seizure, what brain regions are involved in seizure generation, and whether discrete inter-ictal, pre-ictal, ictal, and post-ictal physiologies exist, or blend together in a continuous process (Litt, 2002).

Feature extraction process plays a very important role on the classification performance. In this book chapter, Non-linear measures like Correlation dimension, Fractal dimension, Hurst exponent and Lyapunov exponent, quantify the degree of complexity in a time series. Features are selected so that they capture the differences between the epileptic and normal EEG. Fuzzy set theory plays an important role in dealing with uncertainty when making decisions in medical applications. Fuzzy sets have attracted the growing attention and interest in modern information technology, production technique, decision making, pattern recognition, diagnostics, and data analysis. Neuro-fuzzy systems are fuzzy systems which use Artificial Neural Networks (ANNs) theory in order to determine their properties (fuzzy sets and fuzzy rules) by processing data.

In this research, an approach based on Adaptive Neuro-Fuzzy Inference System (ANFIS) was presented for the seizure recognition. The main aim of this book chapter is to produce a multi-aspect combination of chaos and ANFIS for epileptic seizure recognition using EEG signals.

The rest of this book chapter is as follows: the background, database, chaotic features and classifier are explained. Then the results and performance is illustrated. Finally, the conclusion is reported.

BACKGROUND

The behavior and dynamics of billions of interconnected neurons from the EEG signal requires knowledge of several signal-processing methods, from the linear and non-linear domains. A lot of research has been undertaken in assessment of epilepsy over the last few years. Gotman (1982) presented a computerized system for recognizing a variety of seizures, in year 1982. Murro et al. (1991) developed a seizure recognition system based on the discriminant analysis of the EEG signal recorded from the intracranial electrodes. Choosing suitable features is important for seizure recognition. Many features have been investigated based on time domain and frequency domain (Srinivasan, 2005; Nigam, 2004), wavelet transformation (Subasi, 2007; Güler, 2004), Fourier Transformation (Ktonas, 1987), energy distribution in time-frequency plane (Tzallas, 2007), and chaotic features (Lerner, 1996; Tito, 2009; Srinivasan, 2007; Kannathal, 2005; Pravin-Kumar, 2010). Subasi (2007) used a method for analysis of EEG signals using Discrete Wavelet Transform (DWT) and classification using an ANFIS. Non-linear features of EEG signals have also often explained complex structure of epilepsy (Ocak, 2009; Iasemidis, 1996). Kannathal et al.

(2005) have shown the importance of various entropies for recognition of epilepsy. Adeli et al. (2007) presented a wavelet-chaos methodology for analysis of EEGs and delta, theta, alpha, beta, and gamma sub-bands of EEGs for recognition of seizure. Ghosh-Dastidar et al. (2007) presented a wavelet-chaos-neural network methodology for classification of EEGs into healthy, ictal, and inter-ictal EEGs.

From studies reported in the literature, EEG signals can be considered chaotic. In this research, non-linear dynamics theory opens new window for understanding the behavior of EEG.

METHODS AND MATERIALS

Figure 1 shows the block diagram of the proposed system based automated epileptic recognition system.

The dataset and its partitions used are briefly discussed and the three stages (Feature extraction, Normalization, and Classification) of the method are explained in detail.

Data Selection

For studying epilepsy, the subjects that are used are either human o animal. EEG signals used for this research are obtained from Bonn University, Germany, which is available in public domain (Andrzejak, 2001). The complete datasets consists of five sets of data (denoted *A–E*), each containing 100 single-channel EEG segments. Each segment has *N*=4096 sampling points over 23.6 seconds. All EEG signals were recorded with the same 128-channel amplifier system and 12 bit A/D resolution, which the sampling rate of the data

Figure 1. Block diagram of the proposed system

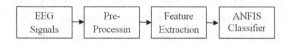

was 173.61 Hz, which it have the spectral bandwidth of the acquisition system is between 0.5 to 85 Hz. These segments were selected and cut out from continuous multi-channel EEG recordings after visual inspection for artifacts such as muscle activity, eye movements etc. Sets *A* and *B* have been recorded from external surface EEG recordings of five healthy volunteers in the wake state with eyes open and eyes closed, respectively. Sets *C*, *D* and *E* have been recorded from depth electrodes EEG recordings from five patients. Set *A* and *B* have been recorded during normal state. Set *D* were recorded from within the epileptogenic zone (Inter-ictal period), and those in set *C* from the hippocampal formation of the opposite hemisphere of the brain (Inter-ictal period). Set *E* has been recorded during seizure activity (Ictal). Figure 2 shows the sample recordings of EEG signals obtained from five sets *A-E*. For a more detailed description of the data, please refer to the (Andrzejak, 2001).

Features Extraction

Choice of the methods and measures for discriminating dynamical changes of epileptic signals highly depends on the characteristics of epileptic EEG signals, on the other hand, regarding type of seizure, specifications of individuals who data are recorded from them etc, are important parameters that have significant effect on results of recognition and classifying of epileptic EEG signals.

In this research to concentrate on the recognition of dynamic changes of EEG signals recording, a short epoch of data is selected. The time series of data are divided into 2 seconds epochs with an overlap of 1 second.

Non-linear and chaotic measures have received the most attention in comparison with the measures mentioned before such as time domain, frequency domain, time-frequency etc. There is some evidence that shows the brain signals have chaotic behavior.

Figure 2. Sample recordings of A, B, C, D, and E dataset from top to bottom

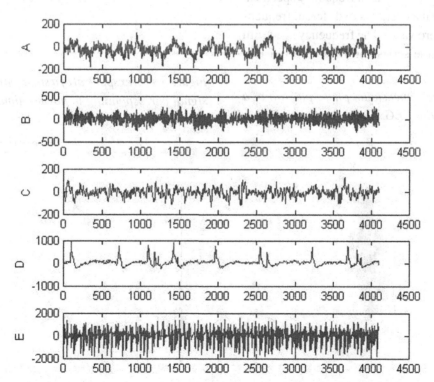

Quality Aspect: Phase Plane Portrait

The phase plane provides a method of displaying brain signal in a form that emphasizes the dynamical state in a system. A first evidence for chaotic dynamics is that EEG dynamics display a prominent sensitivity to initial conditions. The phase space portraits are shown in Figures 3 and 4 corresponding to the unfiltered normal and ictal EEG signals in three-dimensional representation, respectively. To construct phase space, we have used three dimensions, chosen as $x(t)$, $x(t+1)$, and $x(t + 2)$. As can be seen in the phase portraits in spite of chaos and noise, the system shows patterns, which are a proof of the existence of order and a structure within itself.

From Figures 3 and 4 it is clear that the value of area for epileptic signal set E, is less than non-epileptic signal set A.

Power Spectral Density

In alternating signal, energy is concentrated on certain frequencies, while in frequency spectrum of chaotic signals, energy is in different frequencies has non-zero value. The frequency spectrum of a random time series and time series of real

Figure 4. Three-dimensional phase portrait of a small part of the EEG signal corresponding to ictal time series (E)

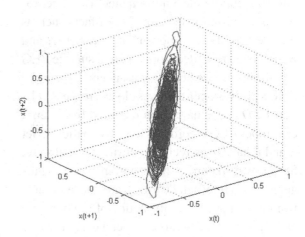

dynamical systems that are mixed with noise are also wide band, and distinguish between these cases, only through the frequency spectrum is not possible. Frequency spectrum by Burg method shown in Figures 5, 6 and 7 corresponding to the A, C and E data, respectively.

Figure 3. Three-dimensional phase portrait of a small part of the EEG signal corresponding to normal time series (A)

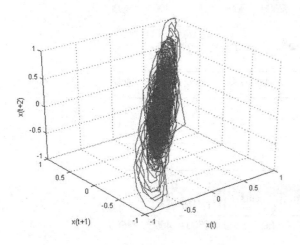

Figure 5. Power spectral of a small part of the EEG signal corresponding to normal time series (A)

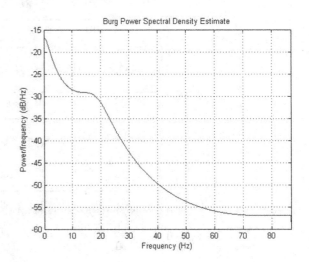

Figure 6. Power spectral of a small part of the EEG signal corresponding to inter-ictal time series (C)

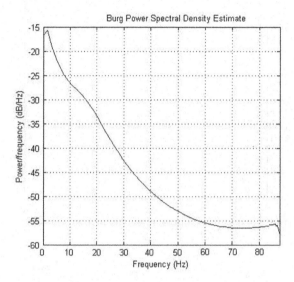

$$C(N,r) = \frac{1}{N(N-1)} \sum_{i=1}^{N} \sum_{\substack{j=1 \\ j \neq i}}^{N} \theta(r - \|V(i) - V(j)\|)$$

$$\theta(x) = \begin{cases} 0 & if\ x < 0 \\ 1 & if\ x \geq 0 \end{cases}$$

$$V_m(i) = (x(i), x(i+\tau), ..., x(i+(m-1)\tau) \qquad (1)$$

$$\|V(i) - V(j)\| = \sqrt{\sum_{k=0}^{m-1} (V(i) - V(j))^2}$$

$$D_2 = \lim_{r \to 0} \frac{Log_2 C(N,r)}{Log_2 (r)}$$

The choice of an appropriate time delay (τ) and embedding dimension (m) is important for the success of reconstructing the attractor with finite data. We calculated D_2 with d_{sat} values varying from 2 to 10 for all the subjects. As can be seen from Figure 8, D_2 saturates after the embedding dimension of 7. Therefore, we have chosen $d_{sat}=8$ for constructing the embedding space and estimation of the invariants (In this test, $m = 8$ and $\tau = 6$).

The determination is based on calculating the relative number of pairs of points in the phase-space set that is separated by a distance less than r. For a self-similar attractor, the local scaling exponent is constant, and this region is called a scaling region. This scaling exponent can be used as an estimate of the correlation dimension. If the $d_{sat}=8$ plots $C(N, r)$ vs. r on a *log-log* scale, the correlation dimension is given by the slope of the $log(C(r))$ vs. $log(r)$ curve over a selected range of r, and the slope of this curve in the scaling region is estimated by the least slope fitting (Figure 9).

Figure 7. Power spectral of a small part of the EEG signal corresponding to ictal time series (E)

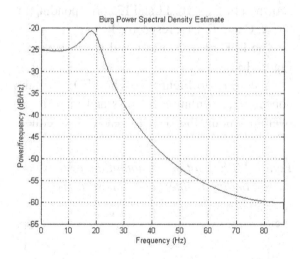

Correlation Dimension

Correlation dimension (D_2) is one of the most widely used measures of a chaotic process. In this research, for estimating D_2, we used the Grassberger and Procaccia Algorithm (GPA) (Yang, 2004), that the relations (1) are estimated.

Fractal Dimension

Fractal Dimension (FD) analysis is frequently used in biomedical signal processing, including EEG analysis (Esteller, 2001). The results of FD in time domain depend on algorithm and window length. In this research, the algorithm is used to calculate fractal dimension is Petrosian method (Petrosian,

Figure 8. A graph of the correlation dimension plotted as a function of the embedding dimension. The correlation dimension of the attractor in this case is about 8.

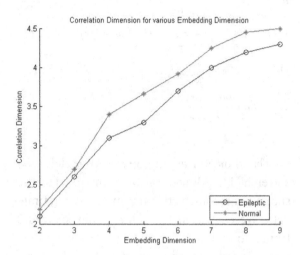

Figure 9. A plot of log (C(r)) versus log(r) for logistic map data

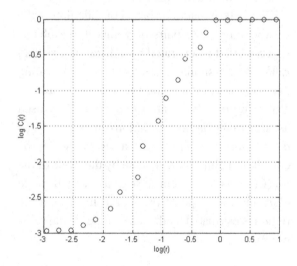

1995). Petrosian uses a quick estimate of the FD (Petrosian, 1995). Petrosian Fractal Dimension (PFD) can be defined as follows,

$$PFD = \frac{\log_{10} N}{\log_{10} N + \log_{10}(\frac{N}{N + 0.4 * N_\Delta})} \quad (2)$$

Figure 10. Fractal dimension of the EEG signal corresponding to normal time series (A)

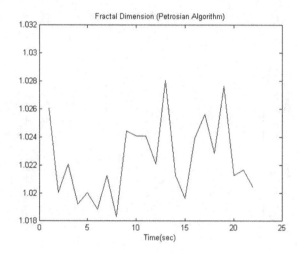

where, N is the series length of the sequence (number of points) and NΔ is the number of sign changes in the signal derivative. The PFD are shown in Figures 10, 11 and 12 corresponding to the A, C and E data, respectively.

The PFD of *A, B, C, D,* and *E* are shown in Figure 13.

According to Figure 13, The PFD is highly concentrated within each class and there is no overlap among the data for each class either.

Figure 11. Fractal dimension of the EEG signal corresponding to inter-ictal time series (C)

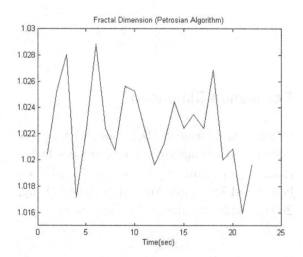

Figure 12. Fractal dimension of the EEG signal corresponding to ictal time series (E)

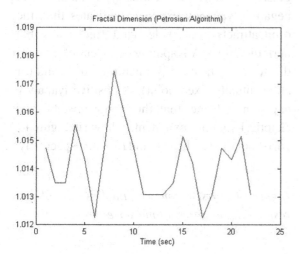

Figure 13. Average Petrosian fractal dimension of datasets

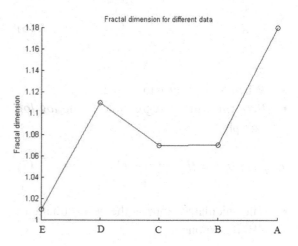

Therefore, all classes can be clearly distinguished using PFD. From the above Figure 13 it is clear that the value of Fractal dimension for epileptic signal set *E*, is less than non-epileptic signal set *A*.

Hurst Exponent

The name Hurst exponent (*H*) derives from *Harold Edwin Hurst* in 1951 (Hurst, 1951). The Hurst exponent is directly related to the Fractal dimension. The relationship between the Fractal dimension and the Hurst exponent is,

$$FD = 2 - H \qquad (3)$$

Therefore, a small Hurst exponent has a higher fractal dimension and vice versa. Brownian walks can be generated from a defined Hurst exponent. *H* has a value between 0 and 1 ($0 \leq H \leq 1$). If a value *H* in the range $0.5 < H < 1$, the random walk will be a long-term memory process (or positive correlated time series or persistent). A value *H* in the range $0 < H < 0.5$ can indicate anti-correlated time series (anti-persistent). A value of $H = 0.5$ can indicate a completely uncorrelated time series. Data sets like this are sometimes referred to as fractional Brownian motion (*fBm*). *fBm* can be

generated by several methods, such as spectral synthesis using either the Fourier transform or the wavelet transform, dispersional analysis, Hurst rescaled range analysis, autocorrelation measures.

Here the power spectral density is proportional to (4),

$$Spectral\ desity \propto \frac{1}{f^{\alpha}}, \qquad (4)$$

where a=2H+1

Dispersional analysis, also known as "Aggregated variance method" is one good candidate (Taqqu, 1995). In this method, the variance is calculated by averaging the time over bins of width *τ*. Given a fractional Gaussian noise (or *fGn*) series $\zeta_H(i)$, *i*=1,2,3,...,*N*, the algorithm can be defined as follows (Blok, 2000),

- Set the bin size to $\tau = 1$.
- Calculate the standard deviation of the *N* data points and record the point $(\tau, \tau \cdot \sigma_{\tau})$.
- Average neighboring data points and store in the original dataset as,

$$\zeta_H(i) \leftarrow \frac{1}{2}[\zeta_H(2i-1) + \zeta_H(2i)] \qquad (5)$$

- Rescale N and τ appropriately as,

$$N \leftarrow \frac{N}{2}$$
$$\tau \leftarrow 2\tau \qquad (6)$$

- When $N > 4$ return to Step 2.
- Perform a linear regression on the *log-log* graph as,

$$Log(\tau, \tau.\sigma_\tau) = H.\log(\tau) + C \qquad (7)$$

- The calculated slope is the best estimate of Hurst exponent.

Dispersional analysis can be regarded as a strong method for characterizing biological or natural time series, which generally show long-range positive correlation (Bassingthwaighte, 1995).

The Hurst exponent is estimated by a linear regression through these points. Hurst exponent are shown in Figures 14, 15 and 16 corresponding to the *A*, *C* and *E* data, respectively.

From the above Figures 14, 15, and 16, it is clear that the value of Hurst exponent for non-epileptic signal sets *A*, *B* is less than epileptic signal set *E*.

Lyapunov Exponent

The lyapunov exponents have been proven to be the useful dynamical quantity for the chaotic system analysis (Wolf, 1989). Lyapunov exponents define the average exponential rates of divergence or convergence of the nearby orbits in the phase space and can be estimated using Largest Lyapunov Exponent (λ). The λ can be defined as follows,

$$\lambda = \lim_{m \to \infty} \frac{1}{m} \sum_{k=1}^{m} Ln \left| \frac{dx_{k+1}}{dx_k} \right| \qquad (8)$$

The lyapunov exponent is useful for distinguishing among the various types of orbits. A negative lyapunov exponent indicates that, the orbit attracts to a stable fixed point (or stable periodic orbit). A lyapunov exponent of zero indicates that, the orbit is a neutral fixed point (or an eventually fixed point). A positive lyapunov exponent indicates that, the orbit is unstable and chaotic. Lyapunov exponent is shown in Figure 17 corresponding to the *A*, *C* and *E* data, respectively.

Figure 14. Hurst exponent of the EEG signal corresponding to normal time series (A)

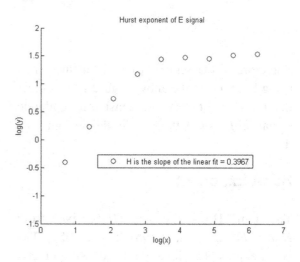

Figure 15. Hurst exponent of the EEG signal corresponding to inter-ictal time series (C)

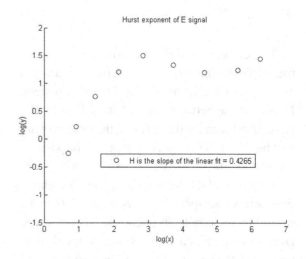

Figure 16. Hurst exponent of the EEG signal corresponding to ictal time series (E)

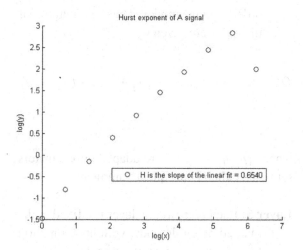

Figure 17. Plot of λ values for EEG signals between three different classes

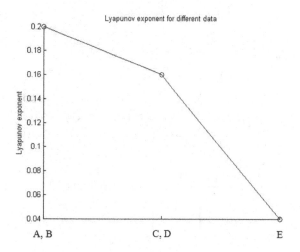

From the above Figure 17 it is clear that the value of Lyapunov exponent for epileptic signal set E, is less than non-epileptic signal sets A, B.

NORMALIZATION

In order to normalize the features in the limits of [0, 1], we used (9).

$$Y_{norm} = \frac{Y'_s + Y'_{s\min}}{Y'_{s\max} - Y'_{s\min}} \tag{9}$$

Here Ynorm is the relative amplitude.

CLASSIFICATION

Adaptive Neuro-Fuzzy Inference System Model Structure

The Adaptive Neuro-Fuzzy Inference System (ANFIS), first introduced by Jang in 1993 (Jang, 1993; Jang, 1995). The ANFIS is a fuzzy Sugeno model put in the framework of adaptive systems

to facilitate learning and adaptation (Jang, 1995). Jang showed that even if human expertise is not available it is possible to intuitively set up practical membership function and employs the neural training process to generate a set of fuzzy IF-THEN rules that Approximate a desired data set (Jang, 1995).

There are a total of 5 layers in the overall network framework, including the fuzzification layer, product layer, normalization layer, defuzzification layer and the total output layer. For each input x_i, three fuzzy sets A_i, B_i, C_i and D_i, with the corresponding membership functions $\mu_{Ai}(x_1)$, $\mu_{Bi}(x_2)$, $\mu_{Ci}(x_3)$ and $\mu_{Di}(x_4)$, respectively. Thus, the ANFIS Model has a total of $3^4 = 81$ fuzzy rules and one output (f). The node function in each layer is described below:

Layer 1: Each node in this layer is an adjustable node, marked by square node. Where x_1, x_2, x_3 and x_4 are the input of node, A_i, B_{i-3}, C_{i-6} and D_{i-9} are the linguistic variable. The membership function usually adopts Gaussian and or bell-shape with maximum and minimum equal to 1 and 0, respectively. $\mu_{Ai}(x_1), \mu_{Bi-3}(x_2),$ $\mu_{Ci-6}(x_3)$ and $\mu_{Di-9}(x_4)$ are given by:

$$\mu_{A_i}(x_1) = \cfrac{1}{1 + \left(\cfrac{x_1 - c_i}{a_i}\right)^{2b_i}} \qquad i = 1, 2, 3$$

$$\mu_{B_{i-3}}(x_2) = \cfrac{1}{1 + \left(\cfrac{x_2 - c_i}{a_i}\right)^{2b_i}} \qquad i = 4, 5, 6$$

$$\mu_{C_{i-6}}(x_3) = \cfrac{1}{1 + \left(\cfrac{x_3 - c_i}{a_i}\right)^{2b_i}} \qquad i = 7, 8, 9 \tag{10}$$

$$\mu_{D_{i-9}}(x_4) = \cfrac{1}{1 + \left(\cfrac{x_4 - c_i}{a_i}\right)^{2b_i}} \qquad i = 10, 11, 12$$

where $\{a_i, b_i, c_i\}$ are adaptable parameters. The parameters in this layer are called as premise parameters.

Layer 2: Each node in this layer is a fixed node, marked by circle node, with node function to be multiplied by input signals to serve as output signal,

$$O_i^2 = \omega_i = \mu_{A_i}(x_1)\mu_{B_i}(x_2)\mu_{C_i}(x_3)\mu_{D_i}(x_4), \\ i = 1, 2, 3, 4 \tag{11}$$

The output signal ω_i means the firing strength of a rule.

Layer 3: Each node in this layer is a fixed node, marked by circle node, with node function to normalize firing strength by calculating the ratio of this node firing strength to the sum of the firing strength. The outputs of this layer can be represented as:

$$O_i^3 = \bar{\omega}_i = \frac{\omega_i}{\omega_1 + \omega_2 + \omega_3 + \omega_4}, \\ i = 1, 2, 3, 4 \tag{12}$$

Layer 4: Each node this layer is an adjustable node, marked by square node for a first order Sugeno model. Thus, the outputs of this layer are given by:

$$O_i^4 = \bar{\omega}_i f_i = \bar{\omega}_i(p_i x_1 + q_i x_2 + s_i x_3 + t_i x_4 + r_i), \\ i = 1, 2, 3, 4 \tag{13}$$

where $\{p_i, q_i, s_i, t_i, r_i\}$ are adaptable parameters set witch called consequent parameters.

Layer 5: Each node in this layer is a fixed node, marked by circle node, with node function to compute the overall output by:

$$O_i^5 = \sum_{i=1}^{4} \bar{\omega}_i f_i, \qquad i = 1, 2, 3, 4 \\ = \bar{\omega}_1 f_1 + \bar{\omega}_2 f_2 + \bar{\omega}_3 f_3 + \bar{\omega}_4 f_4 \tag{14}$$

Hybrid learning algorithm: The task of the learning algorithm is to adjust all the adaptable parameters, namely $\{ai, bi, ci\}$ and $\{pi, qi, si, ti, ri\}$, to make the ANFIS output match the training data. When the premise parameters ai, bi and ci of the membership function are fixed, the output of the ANFIS model can be written as:

$$f = \frac{\omega_1}{\omega_1 + \omega_2 + \omega_3 + \omega_4} f_1 \\ + \frac{\omega_2}{\omega_1 + \omega_2 + \omega_3 + \omega_4} f_2 \\ + \frac{\omega_3}{\omega_1 + \omega_2 + \omega_3 + \omega_4} f_3 \\ + \frac{\omega_4}{\omega_1 + \omega_2 + \omega_3 + \omega_4} f_4 \tag{15}$$

Substituting the fuzzy IF–THEN rules into Equation (14), it becomes:

$$f = \bar{\omega}_1(p_1 x_1 + q_1 x_2 + s_1 x_3 + t_1 x_4 + r_1)$$
$$+ \bar{\omega}_2(p_2 x_1 + q_2 x_2 + s_2 x_3 + t_2 x_4 + r_2) \qquad (16)$$
$$+ \bar{\omega}_3(p_3 x_1 + q_3 x_2 + s_3 x_3 + t_3 x_4 + r_3)$$
$$+ \bar{\omega}_4(p_4 x_1 + q_4 x_2 + s_4 x_3 + t_4 x_4 + r_4)$$

which is a linear combination of the modifiable consequent parameters p_i, q_i, s_i, t_i and r_i. The least squares method can be used to identify the optimal values of these parameters easily. When the premise parameters are not fixed, the search space becomes larger and the convergence of the training becomes slower. A hybrid algorithm combining the least squares method and the gradient descent method is adopted to solve this problem. The hybrid algorithm is composed of a forward pass and a backward pass. The least squares method (forward pass) is used to optimize the consequent parameters with the premise parameters ;xed. Once the optimal consequent parameters are found, the backward pass starts immediately. The gradient descent method (backward pass) is used to adjust optimally the premise parameters corresponding to the fuzzy sets in the input domain. The output of the ANFIS is calculated by employing the consequent parameters found in the forward pass. The output error is used to adapt the premise parameters by means of a standard backpropagation algorithm. It has been proven that this hybrid algorithm is highly e?cient in training the ANFIS (Jang, 1992; Jang, 1993).

RESULTS

The process of EEG analysis consists of two states: first the qualitative analysis and second the quantitative analysis of EEG signals.

The qualitative results are presented in this section. It is clear that the value of area for epileptic signal set E, is less than non-epileptic signal set

A. In addition, the value of Fractal dimension for epileptic signal set E, is less than non-epileptic signal set A. In addition, the value of Hurst exponent for non-epileptic signal sets A, B is less than epileptic signal set E. In addition, the value of Lyapunov exponent for epileptic signal set E, is less than non-epileptic signal sets A, B. This reduce in λ, *PFD*, and D_2 and this increase in H values to mean the reduction in brain system complexity for subjects with seizure state, therefore the number of the necessary dynamic equations for the description of the brain state in the seizure state decreases.

The quantitative results and compare with other researchers presented in this section. As shown in Table 1, we designed three experiments to test the ability of our classifier to separate: 1- Normal EEG (sets A and B) vs. inter-ictal EEG (sets C and D) 2- Normal EEG (sets A and B) vs. ictal EEG (set E) 3- Inter-ictal EEG (sets C and D) vs. ictal EEG (set E)

The classifier is validated using 4-fold cross validation on 400, 300 and 300 samples, respectively, in experiments 1, 2, and 3.

In experiment 1, the accuracy using inter-ictal EEG for epileptic recognition reaches 98.6%. In experiment 2, the accuracy using ictal data reaches 98.1%. In experiment 3, 97.2% accuracy shows our system can distinguish ictal vs. inter-ictal EEG.

The sensitivity, specificity, and total classification accuracy are defined as follows:

- **Sensitivity:** Number of true positive decisions/number of actually positive cases.
- **Specificity:** Number of true negative decisions/number of actually negative cases.

Total classification accuracy: number of correct decisions/total number of cases.

The test performance of the ANFIS was evaluated by the computation of the statistical parameters such as sensitivity, specificity and total

Table 1. The classification accuracy for three experiments

Number	Experiment	Classification accuracy (%)
1	Normal vs. inter-ictal	98.6
2	Normal vs. ictal	98.1
3	Inter-ictal vs. ictal	97.2

classification accuracy, which the average results of 50 executions are given in Table 2.

There are many other methods proposed for the epileptic seizure recognition. Table 3 presents a comparison on the results between this method and other methods proposed in the literature. In this table, only methods evaluated in the same dataset are included so that a comparison between the results is feasible.

The following results are seen in Table 3. For $A - E$ classification, the accuracy obtained from methods is 100% for this dataset. For $A - E$ or A, $B - E$ classification, the result obtained from our method is better than Kannathal's and Subasi's researches with 8.1% and 4.1% difference to discriminate EEGs, respectively. The numbers of features applied in Kannathal's research are simpler and lower computation cost compared with our method. For A, B, $C - E$ classification, the accuracy obtained from Guo's research is better than Ocak's research with 1.1% difference. For $A, B, C, D - E$ classification, the accuracy obtained from Guo's research is better than Tzallas's research with 0.04% difference.

Table 2. The test performance of the ANFIS classifier

Classes	Sensitivity (%)	Specificity (%)	Classification accuracy (%)
A, B vs. C, D	98.1	99.1	98.6
A, B vs. E	97.6	98.6	98.1
C, D vs. E	97	97.4	97.2

Table 3. A comparison of the results obtained by our method and other methods for classification

Authors (Year)	Methods	Dataset	Accuracy (%)
Kannathal et al. (2005)	Entropy and ANFIS	A, E	90
Subasi (2007)	DWT and ANFIS	A, E	94
Srinivasan et al. (2007)	Entropy and Elman Neural Network	A,E	100
Tzallas et al. (2007)	Time frequency analysis and ANN	A, E	100
Tezel et al. (2009)	ANN	A, E	~100
Guo (2010)	DWT and ANN	A, E	99.6
Ocak (2009)	DWT and Entropy	(A, C, D), E	96.65
Guo (2010)	DWT and ANN	(A, C, D), E	97.75
Tzallas et al. (2007)	Time frequency analysis and ANN	(A, B, C, D), E	97.73
Guo (2010)	DWT and ANN	(A, B, C, D), E	97.77
This method (1)	H, D_2, PFD, λ and ANFIS	(A, B), (C, D)	98.6
This method (2)	H, D_2, PFD, λ and ANFIS	(A, B), E	98.1
This method (3)	H, D_2, PFD, λ and ANFIS	(C, D), E	97.2

CONCLUSION

The book chapter has presented the analysis of the EEG signals for the characterization of the epileptic behavior of the brain activity. We investigated the chaotic dynamics underlying the EEG in patients with Epilepsy's disease by non-linear analysis to understand the role of chaos in brain function. Therefore, presents a novel method for epileptic seizure recognition using chaotic features and ANFIS classifier. We calculated the Petrosian fractal dimension, Hurst exponent, Correlation dimension and the Largest lyapunov exponent for non-linear analysis of EEG signals. The process of EEG analysis consists of two states: first the qualitative analysis and second the quantitative analysis of EEG signals. The reduce in λ, *PFD*, and D_2 and this increase in *H* values to mean the reduction in brain system complexity for subjects with seizure state, therefore the number of the necessary dynamic equations for the description of the brain state in the seizure state decreases. Therefore, chaotic features could be helpful to distinguishing between epileptic EEG and normal EEG. This method is evaluated using a benchmark EEG dataset, and qualitative and quantitative results are presented. Our inter-ictal EEG based diagnostic approach achieves 98.6% accuracy in 4-fold cross validation. Diagnosis based on ictal data is also tested in ANFIS classifier, reaching 98.1% accuracy. Therefore, our method can be successfully applied to both inter-ictal and ictal data. We show that non-linear analysis can provide a promising tool for detecting relative changes in the complexity of brain dynamics, which may not be detected by conventional linear analysis. The testing performance of the model diagnostic system is found to be satisfactory and we think that this system can be used in clinical studies in the future after it is developed.

ACKNOWLEDGMENT

The authors would like to acknowledge Dr. R.G. Andrzejak of Bonn University, Germany, for providing permission to use the EEG signals available in the public domain.

REFERENCES

Adeli, H., Ghosh-Dastidar, S., & Dadmehr, N. (2007). A wavelet-chaos methodology for analysis of EEGs and EEG subbands to detect seizure and epilepsy. *IEEE Transactions on Bio-Medical Engineering, 54*(2). doi:10.1109/TBME.2006.886855 PMID:17278577.

Andrzejak, R. G., Lehnertz, K., Mormann, F., Rieke, C., David, P., & Elger, C. E. (2001). Indications of nonlinear deterministic and finite dimensional structures in time series of brain electrical activity: Dependence on recording region and brain state. *Physical Review E: Statistical, Nonlinear, and Soft Matter Physics, 64*, Retrieved from http://epileptologie-bonn.de doi:10.1103/PhysRevE.64.061907.

Bassingthwaighte, J. B., & Raymond, G. M. (1995). Evaluation of the dispersional analysis method for fractal time series. *Annals of Biomedical Engineering, 23*(4), 491–505. doi:10.1007/BF02584449 PMID:7486356.

Blok, H. J. (2000). *On the nature of the stock market: Simulations and experiments.* (PhD Dissertation). University of British Columbia. Canada.

Chaovalitwongse, W., Pardalos, P., Iasemidis, L. D., Shiau, D. S., & Sackellares, J. C. (2005). Dynamical approaches and multi-quadratic integer programming for seizure prediction. *Optimization Methods and Software, 20*(2-3), 389–400. doi:10.1080/10556780512331318173.

Esteller, R., Vachtsevanos, G., Echauz, J., & Litt, B. (2001). A comparison of waveform fractal dimension algorithms. *IEEE Transactions on Circuits and Systems: Fundamental Theory and Applications, 48*(2), 177–183. doi:10.1109/81.904882.

Ghosh-Dastidar, S., Adeli, H., & Dadmehr, N. (2007). Mixed-band wavelet-chaos-neural network methodology for epilepsy and epileptic seizure detection. *IEEE Transactions on Bio-Medical Engineering, 54*(9). doi:10.1109/TBME.2007.891945 PMID:17867346.

Gotman, J. (1982). Automatic recognition of epileptic seizures in the EEG. *Electroencephalography and Clinical Neurophysiology, 54*, 530–540. doi:10.1016/0013-4694(82)90038-4 PMID:6181976.

Gu¨ler, I˙., & U¨beyli, E. D. (2004). Application of adaptive neuro-fuzzy inference system for detection of electrocardiographic changes in patients with partial epilepsy using feature extraction. *International Journal of Expert Systems with Applications, 27*, 323–330. doi:10.1016/j.eswa.2004.05.001.

Guo, L., Rivero, D., & Dorado, J., Rabu˜nal, J. R., & Pazos, A. (2010). Automatic epileptic seizure detection in EEGs based on line length feature and artificial neural networks. *Journal of Neuroscience Methods, 191*(1), 101–109. doi:10.1016/j.jneumeth.2010.05.020 PMID:20595035.

Hurst, H. E. (1951). Long-term storage of reservoirs: an experimental study. *Transactions of the American Society of Civil Engineers, 116*, 770–799.

Iasemidis, D. L., & Sackellares, J. C. (1996). Chaos theory and epilepsy. *The Neuroscientist, 2*(2), 118–126. doi:10.1177/107385849600200213.

Jang, J.-S. R. (1992). Self-learning fuzzy controllers based on temporal backpropagation. *IEEE Transactions on Neural Networks, 3*(5), 714–723. doi:10.1109/72.159060 PMID:18276470.

Jang, J.-S. R. (1993). ANFIS: Adaptive-network-based fuzzy inference system. *IEEE Transactions on Systems, Man, and Cybernetics, 23*(3), 665–685. doi:10.1109/21.256541.

Jang, J.-S. R., & Sun, C. T. (1995). Neuro fuzzy modeling and control. *Proceedings of the IEEE, 83*(3), 378–406. doi:10.1109/5.364486.

Kannathal, N., Lim, C. M., Rajendra Acharya, U., & Sadasivan, P. K. (2005). Entropies for detection of epilepsy in EEG. *International Journal of Computer Methods and Programs in Biomedicine, 80*(3), 187–194. doi:10.1016/j.cmpb.2005.06.012 PMID:16219385.

Ktonas, P. Y. (1987). Automated spike and sharp wave (SSW) detection. In Gevins & Remond (Eds.), Methods of analysis of brain electrical and magnetic signals, (pp. 211-241). Amsterdam: Elsevier.

Kumar, Y., & Dewal, M. L. (2011). Complexity measures for normal and epileptic EEG signals using ApEn, SampEn and SEN. *International Journal of Computer & Communication Technology, 2*(7), 6–12.

Lerner, D. E. (1996). Monitoring changing dynamics with correlation integrals: Case study of an epileptic seizure. *Physica D. Nonlinear Phenomena, 97*(4), 563–576. doi:10.1016/0167-2789(96)00085-1.

Litt, B., & Lehnertz, K. (2002). Seizure prediction and the preseizure period. *Current Opinion in Neurology, 15*(2), 173–177. doi:10.1097/00019052-200204000-00008 PMID:11923631.

Murro, A. M., King, D. W., Smith, J. R., Gallagher, B. B., Flanigin, H. F., & Meador, K. (1991). Computerized seizure detection of complex partial seizures. *Electroencephalography and Clinical Neurophysiology, 79*, 330–333. doi:10.1016/0013-4694(91)90128-Q PMID:1717237.

Nigam, V.P., & Graupe, D. (2004). A neural-network-based detection of epilepsy. *Neurological Research, 26*(1), 55–60. doi:10.1179/016164104773026534 PMID:14977058.

Ocak, H. (2009). Automatic detection of epileptic seizures in EEG using discrete wavelet transform and approximate entropy. *International Journal of Expert Systems with Applications, 36*, 2027–2036. doi:10.1016/j.eswa.2007.12.065.

Petrosian, A. (1995). Kolmogorov complexity of finite sequences and recognition of different preictal EEG patterns. In *Proceedings of the 8th IEEE Symposium on Computer-Based Medical Systems*, (pp. 212–217). IEEE.

Pravin-Kumar, S., Sriraam, N., Benakop, P. G., & Jinaga, B. C. (2010). Entropies based detection of epileptic seizures with artificial neural network classifiers. *International Journal of Expert Systems with Application, 37*, 3284–3291. doi:10.1016/j.eswa.2009.09.051.

Srinivasan, V., Eswaran, C., & Sriraam, N. (2005). Artificial neural network based epileptic detection using time-domain and frequency-domain features. *Journal of Medical Systems, 29*(6), 647–660. doi:10.1007/s10916-005-6133-1 PMID:16235818.

Srinivasan, V., Eswaran, C., & Sriraam, N. (2007). Approximate entropy-based epileptic EEG detection using artificial neural networks. *IEEE Transactions on Information Technology in Biomedicine, 11*(3). doi:10.1109/TITB.2006.884369 PMID:17521078.

Subasi, A. (2007). Application of adaptive neuro-fuzzy inference system for epileptic seizure detection using wavelet feature extraction. *International Journal of Computers in Biology and Medicine, 37*, 227–244. doi:10.1016/j.compbiomed.2005.12.003 PMID:16480706.

Taqqu, M. S., Teverovsky, V., & Willinger, W. (1995). Estimators for long-range dependence: An empirical study. *Fractals, 3*(4), 785–798. doi:10.1142/S0218348X95000692.

Tezel, G., & Ozbay, Y. (2009). A new approach for epileptic seizure detection using adaptive neural network. *International Journal of Expert Systems with Application, 36*, 172–180. doi:10.1016/j.eswa.2007.09.007.

Tito, M., Cabrerizo, M., Ayala, M., Barreto, A., Miller, I., Jayakar, P., & Adjouadi, M. (2009). Classification of electroencephalographic seizure recordings into ictal and interictal files using correlationsum. *International Journal of Computers in Biology and Medicine, 39*, 604–614. doi:10.1016/j.compbiomed.2009.04.005.

Tzallas, A., Tsipouras, M., & Fotiadis, D. (2007). Automatic seizure detection based on time–frequency analysis and artificial neural networks. *Computational Intelligence and Neuroscience*, 1–13. doi:10.1155/2007/80510 PMID:18301712.

University of Melbourne. (n.d.). *Website*. Retrieved from http://www.neuroeng.unimelb.edu.au/research/epilepsy/index.html

WHO. (2005). *Atlas: Epilepsy care in the world*. Geneva: World Health Organization.

Wolf, A., Swift, J., Swinney, H., & Vastano, J. (1989). Determining lyapunov exponents from a time series. *Physica, 16D*, 285–317.

Yang, H., Wang, Y., Wang, C. J., & Tai, H. M. (2004). Correlation dimensions of EEG changes during mental tasks. In *Proceedings of the IEEE, The 26th Annual International Conference in Engineering in Medicine and Biology Society (EMBS)*, (pp. 616-619). IEEE.

ADDITIONAL READING

Firpi, H., Goodman, E. D., & Echauz, J. (2007). Epileptic seizure detection using genetically programmed artificial features. *IEEE Transactions on Bio-Medical Engineering, 54*(2). doi:10.1109/TBME.2006.886936 PMID:17278578.

Hilborn, R. C. (2000). *Chaos and nonlinear dynamics*. Oxford, UK: Oxford University Press. doi:10.1093/acprof:oso/9780198507239.001.0001.

Hosseini, S. A., & Khalilzadeh, M. A. (2010). Emotional stress recognition system for affective computing based on bio-signals. *International Journal of Biological Systems, 18*, 101–114. doi:10.1142/S0218339010003640.

Kannathal, N., Sadasivan, K. P., & Lim, C. M. (2004). Complex dynamics of epileptic EEG. In *Proceedings of the 26th Annual International Conference Engineering in Medicine and Biology Society (EMBS)*. San Francisco: EMBS.

Kurths, J., & Herzel, H. (1987). An attractor in solar time series. *Physica D. Nonlinear Phenomena, 25*, 165–172. doi:10.1016/0167-2789(87)90099-6.

Niedermeyer, E., & Lopes da Silva, F. (1987). *Electroencephalography: Basic principles, clinical application and related fields*. Munich, Germany: Urban & Schwarzenberg.

Pincus, S. M. (1991). Approximate entropy as a measure of system complexity. *Proceedings of the National Academy of Sciences of the United States of America, 88*(6), 2297–2301. doi:10.1073/pnas.88.6.2297 PMID:11607165.

KEY TERMS AND DEFINITIONS

ANFIS: The ANFIS is a fuzzy Sugeno model put in the framework of adaptive systems to facilitate learning and adaptation.

Classification: After extracting the desired good features, we still have to find the related between states. A classifier will do this process.

Electroencephalography: EEG is a technique which contains much information about the patient's psycho-physiological state. IT can be recorded in two essential ways: The first and most common is non-invasive recording known as scalp recording. The second is invasive recording that often is known as inter-cranial EEG.

Epilepsy: Epilepsy is a brain disorder that is characterized by sudden and recurrent seizures. It can cause abnormal electrical activity in the brain and may alter consciousness, perception, sensation, behavior and body movement.

Feature Extraction: Feature extraction is the process of extracting useful information from the signal.

Chapter 3
Learning Methodologies to Support E–Business in the Automated Negotiation Process

Paolo Renna
University of Basilicata, Italy

ABSTRACT

The automated negotiation performed by a software agent is investigated in order to improve the benefits compared to a humane face-to-face negotiation. The profitability of e-business applications can be increased by the support of automated negotiation tools. This research proposes a set of learning methodologies to support both the suppliers' and customers' negotiation activities. The learning methodologies are based on Q-learning technique, which is able to evaluate the utility of the actions without a model of the environment. The context regards one-to-many negotiation and multi-issues (volume, price, and due date). A simulation environment is developed to test the proposed methodologies and evaluate the benefits compared to a negotiation approach without learning support tool. The simulations are conducted in several market conditions, and a proper statistical analysis is performed. The simulation results show that the proposed methodologies lead to benefits both for suppliers and customers when both the opponents adopt the learning approach.

INTRODUCTION

The development of Information and Communication Technology (ICT) allows to develop several electronic applications in different fields. The main field is the Business to Business (B2B)

e-commerce that allows to provide real value to manufacturing industries (Aberdeen Group, 2006). Their use by firms, as a recent research of the Aberdeen Group (2006) testifies, leads to the following improvements in performance: an increase in spending under management by 36%;

DOI: 10.4018/978-1-4666-4038-2.ch003

a reduction in their requisition-to-order cycles by 75%; a reduction in their requisition-to-order costs by 48%; a reduction in their maverick spending by 36%.

The success of B2B applications depends on the real Value-Added Services (VAS) that support these applications. The VAS that can improve the profitability of the B2B application are: negotiation, coalition support tools and integration of production planning with the negotiation process (Renna and Argoneto, 2010). In particular, the negotiation process integrated with the production planning process may be considered to be a significant hindrance to the diffusion of B2B electronic commerce. The absence of appropriate tools to support the B2B platform does not allow the firms to gain significant benefits from the participation in these platforms (Calosso et al., 2004). The increasing importance of business to business electronic trading has driven interest in automated negotiation to soaring heights. The sequence of negotiation messages (proposals and counter-proposals) are modeled as the negotiation strategy of an actor (Jennings et al., 2001). In fact, it is important to distinguish between negotiation protocol and negotiation strategy. The protocol concerns the flow of messages in terms of who can say what, time of intervention, negotiation ending criteria, etc. The negotiation strategy is the sequence of the actions of the party in an effort to get the best outcome; for example, the utility function evaluation, how generate the counter-proposal and the threshold value to accept the proposals. The strategy is private information in order to gain an advantage to the negotiation opponents. The possibility of one opponent to incorporate additional knowledge of the opponents' behavior can improve its performance. The effectiveness of providing knowledge about the domain of negotiation has been demonstrated in the trade-off strategy introduced in (Faratin et al., 2003). The information about the opponents' behavior can be derived by the negotiation moves performed by that opponent during a negotiation.

Several authors proposed automated negotiation in different sectors without exploring learning possibility (Neubert et al., 2004; Hausen et al., 2006; Cheng et al., 2006; Renna, 2010). The scientific literature discussed the lack of learning opponents' strategy in automated negotiation as a field to investigate. The automated negotiation process involves several disciplinary areas as: Multi Agent Systems (Ramchurn et al., 2007), game theory (Binmore and Vulkan, 1999), optimization (Arbib and Rossi, 2000), e-business (Huang et al., 2010) and decision support systems (Kersten and Lai, 2007).

The learning process can be supported by the reinforcement learning methodology. A Reinforcement-Learning (RL) agent learns by trial-and-error interaction with its dynamic environment (Kaelbling et al., 1996). At each time step, the agent perceives the complete state of the environment and takes an action, which causes the environment to transit into a new state. The agent receives a scalar reward signal that evaluates the quality of this transition. This feedback is less informative than in supervised learning, where the agent would be given the correct actions to take (Cherkassky and Mulier, 1998) (such information is, unfortunately, not always available). The RL feedback is, however, more informative than in unsupervised learning, where the agent would be left to discover the correct actions on its own, without any explicit feedback on its performance (Sejnowski and Hinton, 1999).

The Q-learning algorithm is wide used in the multi agent fields (Pen and Williams, 1996). It is an interactive approximation structure that uses the actual experience to forecast the subsequent states. The benefit of Q-learning technique is the reduction of the complexity, because it does not use a model of the environment in which the agents operate.

The aim of this chapter is to propose a learning algorithm to forecast the opponents' strategies. The methodology proposed concerns a Q-learning algorithm. The approach proposed is general with respect to a wide variety of market mechanisms.

The approach proposed is linked to a production-planning algorithm, and a simulation environment is developed to test the proposed methodology in different market conditions.

This paper is organized as follows: in Section 2, a literature review of negotiation by Multi Agent System in Business To Business e-marketplaces is illustrated. In Section 3, the e-marketplace scenario and negotiation approaches and customers' tactics are illustrated. The simulation environment developed is described in Section 4. Section 5 presents the numerical results of the simulation. Finally, in Section 7 the conclusions and future developments are discussed.

LITERATURE REVIEW

In recent years, use of multi-attribute auctions has been consolidating as a powerful mechanism in procurement settings where multiple drivers affect the transaction outcome (David et al., 2006; Perrone et al., 2010).

Several methodologies have been proposed in scientific literature to learn the strategies of the other actors in the automated negotiation process.

Faratin et al. (2003) and Jonker et al. (2007) proposed learning techniques, but these methodologies need a higher number of moves for the negotiation protocol to obtain benefits form the learning methodologies, and individual bids do not provide much information.

The baysian learning method was proposed in multi-issue negotiation models (Zen and Sycara, 1998) to learn the reservation value, and the preferences ordering of the issues (Hindriks and Tykhonov, 2008). Kowalcyzk (2000) modeled the multi-issue negotiation process as a fuzzy constraint satisfaction problem. However, the negotiation model proposed did not consider the opponents' response in the negotiation strategies.

Luo et al. (2003) developed a fuzzy constraint based framework for bilateral multi-issue negotiations in semi-competitive trading environments.

The model uses prioritized fuzzy constraints to represent trade-offs between the different possible values of the negotiation issues and to indicate how concessions should be made when they are necessary. In addition, by incorporating the notion of a reward into their negotiation model, the agents can sometimes reach agreements that would not otherwise be possible.

Raju et al. (2006a) investigated the electronic retail markets with a single seller (without competition). The seller manages an inventory and uses the reinforcement learning to learn from the environment. The objective is the determination of the dynamic price that optimizes the seller's performance. The algorithm proposed to solve the problem is based on Q-learning algorithm. Raju et al. (2006b) considered n electronic retail market, where multiple sellers compete on price to get buyers. The Q-learning algorithm is used in case of no information sharing among the sellers.

Lin et al. (2006) assumed that affixed set of possible opponent profiles is given and known. The Bayesian algorithm is used to determine to learn what profile the opponent chooses. This approach assumes that a public information needs to be provided: the set of profiles.

Chen and Wang (2007) used fuzzy similarity to compute tradeoffs among multiple issues during bilateral negotiations. The first stage determines which behavior strategy will be taken by agents while delay event occurs, and prepares to next negotiation process; then the compensatory negotiations among agents are opened related with determination of compensations for respective decisions and strategies, to solve dynamic scheduling problem in the second stage.

The Kernel Density Estimation (KDE) was proposed for estimating issue weights of opponent's strategy (Coehoorn and Jennings, 2004) or to determining the reservation values (Osrhat et al., 2009). KDE can be an attractive method computationally; the complexity was estimated of $O(n \log n)$ (Coehoorn and Jennings, 2004).

Reinforcement learning algorithms have been successfully deployed in various decision-making processes, such as setting prices in a competitive marketplace (Tesauro & Kephart, 2002).

Renna (2009) presented a Multi Agent System architecture to sustain a catalogue-based e-marketplace by using workflow management methodologies for the design activities, the agent-based technologies and the implementation phases, and open source IT tools for the software platform development. Subsequently, the formalised e-marketplace is linked to a production planning algorithm to support the negotiation stage among the involved agents. Finally, a discrete event simulation environment is utilized to validate the proposed MAS architecture and, using an appropriate test model, to evaluate the performances of the negotiation protocol.

Yasamura et al. (2009) presented a method for acquiring a concession strategy of an agent in multi-issue negotiation by reinforcement learning method. The experimental results showed that the agents could acquire the negotiation strategy that avoids negotiation breakdown and increases profits of an agreement.

Q-learning (Watkins, 1998) was one of the first algorithms for reinforcement learning (Sutton and Barton, 1994) specifically designed to maximize reward in multistage environments.

Yoshikawa et al. (2008) presented a learning method of strategies in multi-issue negotiation under the situation where an opponent's preference is not open. They used reinforcement learning to each issue for acquiring a concession strategy. Experimental results showed that agents could acquire a negotiation strategy that avoids negotiation breakdown and increases profits of both sides.

Rahimiyan and Mashhadi (2008) and Bigdeli et al. (2010) discussed the bidding decision making problem in electricity pay-as-bid auction from a supplier's point of view. The suggested solution is generalized to consider the effect of supplier market power due to transmission congestion.

The supplier learns from past experiences using the Q-learning algorithm to find out the optimal bid price.

Huang and Lin (2008) investigated the reinforcement learning methodology in a bargaining process as a Markov decision process. The learning approach proposed was sufficiently robust and convenient, hence it is suitable for online automated bargaining in electronic commerce.

Bandyopadhyay et al. (2008) modeled reverse-auction bidding behavior by artificial agents as both two-player and n-player games in a simulation environment. The theoretical results of a mixed strategy equilibrium in capacity-constrained reverse auctions involving two dissimilar competitors are successfully replicated. They also successfully replicate the mixed-strategy equilibria in capacity-constrained reverse auctions with more than two similar sellers through the simulation results.

The RL algorithm is able to successfully converge on the pure strategy even though the agents start off initially by placing their bids according to a uniform distribution.

Wong and Ho (2010) presented a reinforcement learning approach on modelling the intelligent negotiation behavior between the track owner and train service providers. The negotiation model proposed is bilateral and the Q-learning approach is used during the negotiation process. The reinforcement learning knowledge has been stored and represented in tabular format in this study. This representation is not the most efficient as the reuse of the knowledge is not particularly flexible. Further studies on the improvement of knowledge management are necessary for more realistic behavior models.

Martin et al. (2012) proposed an agent-based system for cooperative meta-heuristic search composed of a population of autonomous meta-heuristic agents. The meta-heuristic agents run in parallel and can execute diferrent meta-heuristic and heuristic combinations with different parameter settings. The meta-heuristic agents cooperate asynchronously to exchange information on the search space using pattern matching and reinforcement learning.

The Q-learning approach was proposed to evaluate the market power in the electricity markets. In this context, the agent-based simulation developer uses Q-learning to learn how to respond to competitors' behavior and market conditions (Mashhadi and Rahimiyan, 2011).

Some authors investigated the problem using Artificial Neural Network (Carbonneau et al., 2008).

The research presented in this chapter outcomes the previous researches in the following issues:

- It is proposed a simple methodology that reduces the computational complexity, and it can be used in real-time during the negotiation process.
- The approach proposed is linked to the production-planning model in order to provide more detailed information to the negotiation process.
- The approach is tested by a simulation environment based on multi agent technology in order to provide a quantitative evaluation of the proposed approach in different environment conditions.

THE E-BUSINESS CONTEXT

The e-business context consists of a neutral linear e-marketplace owned by a third part where a set of registered buyers, and a set of registered sellers are allowed to play procurement actions. In this scenario, each customer can input an order in the e-marketplace. The generic order is characterized by the product typology, the volume required (V^*), the due date (dd^*), and the price (p^*). The suppliers of the e-marketplace reply with a counter-proposal

to maximize their utility. The negotiation process is activated to reach an agreement (for details see Argoneto and Renna, 2010).

The main characteristics of the negotiation process are the following:

- The negotiation process starts with the order submission by the customer.
- The negotiation is an interactive process with a fixed number of round. If the maximum number of round is reached without agreement, the negotiation fails.
- During each round of the negotiation process, the suppliers submit a new counter-proposal to the customer. The customer can only accepts or asks for a new counter-proposal (if the round of negotiation is lower than the maximum number of round).
- Suppliers' and customers' behavior is assumed to be rationale according to their utility functions.

The suppliers apply the production-planning algorithm (for details see Argoneto and Renna, 2010) to obtain the production planning alternatives. The production planning alternative is a vector composed by the following information: price, profit, due date and volume. Each supplier computes the matrix as shown in Table 1. For each combination of price and due date is computed the profit and the volume of the production alternative. The supplier uses the matrix obtained to evaluate the strategies during the negotiation process. At first round of negotiation, the supplier computes the proposal maximizing the profit of the matrix. When the round of negotiation increases, the supplier reduces the minimum level of the profit; the supplier computes the better proposal for the customer among the alternatives with a profit greater than the minimum level of the profit determined for the generic round of negotiation. At the last round of negotiation, the minimum level

Table 1. Production-planning alternatives

	Due date 1	**Due date 2**	**Due date *j***	**Due date *m***
Price 1	Profit [1,1]; Volume [1,1]	Profit [1,2]; volume [1,2]	Profit [1,j]; volume [1,j]	Profit [1,m]; volume [1,m]
Price 2	Profit [2,1]; volume [2,1]	Profit [2,2]; volume [2,2]	Profit [2,j]; volume [2,j]	Profit [2,m]; volume [2,m]
Price *i*	Profit [i,1]; volume [i,1]	Profit [i,2]; volume [i,2]	Profit [i,j]; volume [i,j]	Profit [i,m]; volume [i,m]
Price *n*	Profit [n,1]; volume [n,1]	Profit [n,2]; volume [n,2]	Profit [n,j]; volume [n,j]	Profit [n,m]; volume [n,m]

of the profit is the minor value that the supplier defined as lowest target. Therefore, the strategy of the supplier is the path composed by the first point (maximum level of profit of the production alternatives) connected to the last point (lowest level of profit). The learning strategies proposed in this chapter try to connect these two points in order to maximize the utility of the suppliers in a competitive situation.

Supplier Learning Algorithm

The suppliers apply a reduction profit strategy to improve the customer satisfaction and reach an agreement. In case of no learning, the reduction strategy is a neutral linear strategy; at each round of negotiation, the generic supplier reduces the minimum level of profit to compute the counter-proposal. Figure 1 shows the reduction strategy of the profit. The strategy is linear and does not

depend on the information of the past negotiations. In particular, this strategy does not evaluate the real competition among the suppliers. The competition in terms of counter-proposal formulation of the other suppliers can be evaluated only evaluating the past negotiation results (agreement/disagreement), because the information between customer, and the generic supplier is private.

The generic supplier can adopt an aggressive strategy; in this case, the supplier reduces the level of profit rapidly (See Figure 2) in order to improve the competition with the other suppliers. According to this strategy, the supplier can improve the satisfaction of the customer computing a better proposal, and it can win the competition with the other suppliers.

Otherwise, the generic supplier can adopt a waiting strategy, if it evaluates that the competition among the suppliers is lower (See Figure 3). In this case, the level of profit is reduced slowly during the rounds of the negotiation.

Figure 1. Neutral linear strategy

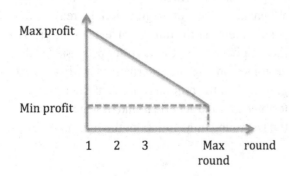

Figure 2. Aggressive strategy

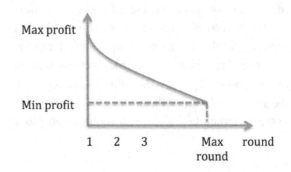

Figure 3. Waiting strategy

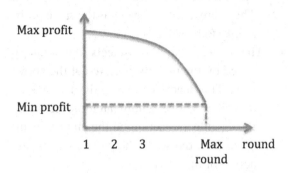

The function of the minimum level of the profit is reported in expression (1):

$$prof_{min}\left(r\right) = prof_{max}\left(1 - u\left(r\right)\right)^2$$
$$+ 2u\left(r\right)k\left(1 - u\left(r\right)\right) + prof_{last}\,u\left(r\right)^2 \qquad (1)$$

where

$$u\left(r\right) = \frac{r - 1}{r_{max} - 1}$$

k is the factor that characterizes the strategy of the supplier.

The expression (1) is a cubic spline that can be adapted to the strategy by the only factor k.

The value $prof_{max}$ is the maximum profit of the production-planning matrix computed by the supplier. The value $prof_{min}$ is the minimum profit that the supplier is available to get.

The study of the function leads to the following values for the factor k:

- **k = prof$_{max}$:** this value leads to a waiting strategy (See Figure 3).
- **k=prof$_{max}$/2:** This is a neutral strategy (See Figure 1).
- **k=1:** This is an aggressive strategy (See Figure 2).

In this chapter, a Q-learning algorithm (Watkins and Dayan, 1992) is used to select the profit strategy of the suppliers. This methodology can be easily adapted to the expression (1), because only one parameter needs to be set. The problem can be modeled as an agent, states S and a set of actions per state A. The agent selects an action a $\in A$ and it moves from one state to another state. The new state provides the agents a reward; the objective of the agent is to maximize its total reward. This objective can be performed learning what are the optimal actions.

Therefore, the algorithm has a function, which calculates the quality of a state-action combination Q. When the agent chooses an action, the agent gets a reward that depends on the state, and action selected. Figure 4 shows the interactions of the generic agent with the environment.

The learning algorithm is characterized by four main elements: a policy, a reward function, a value function and a model of the environment (optionally) (Sutton and Barto, 1998).

A policy defines the behavior of the agent. It evaluates the state and environment to take the decision. The policy can be a simple function, a complex searching process, and it can be stochastic.

A reward function defines the perceived state in terms of goodness of an action. Therefore, the agent uses the reward function to evaluate the better action to take.

Figure 4. Reinforcement learning scheme

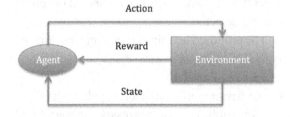

A value function is the function used to evaluate the actions that can optimize the reward of the agent. The value is estimated and re-estimated from the sequences of observation over the entire process.

The model of the environment tries to emulate the behavior of the environment composed by the other agent in order to forecast the future situations.

The algorithm is a simple value iteration update; it makes a correction of the old value based on new information (Russel and Norvig 2003).

$$Q\left(s_t, a_t\right) = Q\left(s_t, a_t\right) + a\left(s_t, a_t\right) \bullet$$
$$\left[r\left(s_{t+1}, a_{t+1}\right) + \beta \bullet \max_{a_{t+1}} Q\left(s_{t+1}, a_{t+1}\right) - Q\left(s_t, a_t\right)\right]$$
(2)

where,

$r(s_{t+1}, a_{t+1})$ is the reward obtained after performing a_t in s_t;

s_{t+1} is the new state when choosing the action a_t;

$\alpha \in [0,1]$ is the learning rate; this index determines the weight of new acquired information. The value 0 means that no learning activity is performed, while the value 1 means that it is considered only the new information.

$\beta \in [0,1]$ is the discount factor. This index evaluates the importance of future rewards. The value 0 means that the agent considers only che curren rewards, while the value 1 means that the agent considers only the future rewards.

The approach applies the learning process through interaction with the customer during the negotiation. It focuses on the positive effect (agreement with the customer) and the negative effect (no agreement reached) based on the profit strategy selected.

The proposed learning algorithm is performed by the following activities.

- At first negotiation, each supplier sets three probabilities Q1 (aggressive strategy), Q2 (neutral strategy) and Q3 (wait strategy).

All the probabilities are equal to 33%. Therefore, each strategy has the same probability to be selected.

- The generic supplier selects the strategy based on the probability fixed at the above step. This leads to choose the factor *k* as described above. The strategy selected by the agent is the action on the environment. Therefore, the set of the parameter k is the action of the agent.

- The suppliers negotiate with the customer using the strategy selected.

- At the end of the negotiation process, if one supplier reaches an agreement with the customer, it increases the probability of the strategy chosen. The negotiation process representing the environment. The reward is characterized by the agreement or no agreement of the negotiation. Then, the reward is characterized by a binary evaluation: it is positive if the negotiation ends with an agreement; otherwise, it is negative. All the suppliers that don't reach an agreement reduce the probability of the strategy chosen. In particular, the supplier that reaches an agreement uses the expression (3 and 4):

$$Q* = Q* + \Delta Q$$
(3)

$$Q = Q - \Delta Q$$
(4)

where Q* is the strategy chosen. This means that the positive reward increase the probability to select the Q* strategy in the next negotiations.

The suppliers that don't reach an agreement uses the expression (5 and 6):

$$Q* = Q* - \Delta Q$$
(5)

$$Q = Q + \Delta Q \tag{6}$$

This means that the negative reward reduces the probability to select the Q* strategy in the next negotiations.

ΔQ defines the rapidity of the strategies change. This value is the α of the Q-learning algorithm that determines the weight of the new information (in this case the agreement or not of the negotiation process).

The above process concerns only the slope of the profit strategy during the negotiation process. The learning approach can be used to choose the minimum level of profit.

In this case, the minimum level of profit depends on the strategy chosen:

- **Waiting Strategy:** Leads to a high level of the minimum level of profit.
- **Neutral Strategy:** Leads to a medium level of the minimum level of profit.
- **Aggressive Strategy:** Leads to a low level of the minimum level of profit.

The above approach allows to learn the better strategy to select based on the interaction of the negotiation process. The negotiation interaction takes into account the customer preferences and the other suppliers' counter-proposals. Therefore, the objective of the proposed approach is the possibility to learn the competitive arena in which the supplier operates.

The approach described is an algorithm characterized by a value of 0 for the discount factor, and the value ΔQ defines the learning rate.

Customer Learning Algorithm

The customer evaluates a threshold function at each round of negotiation. The first activity is the computation of the customer satisfaction for each parameter in negotiation: price, volume and due date. The satisfaction of each parameter is comprised between 0 and 1.

The volume satisfaction U_v is computed by following expression:

$$U_v = \frac{V_{sup\,plier} - V_{min}}{V_{customer} - V_{min}} \tag{7}$$

where,

- $V_{supplier}$: Is the volume proposed by the supplier.
- $V_{customer}$: Is the volume requested by the customer.
- V_{min}: Is the minimum volume accepted by the customer (in this chapter, it is fixed to 30% of the volume requested by the customer).

The price satisfaction U_p is computed as shown in expression (7) if the volume proposed by the supplier is greater than the V_{min}; otherwise the volume satisfaction is 0.

The price satisfaction is computed by the following expression:

$$U_p = 1 - \frac{P_{sup\,plier} - P_{customer}}{P_{max} - P_{customer}} \tag{8}$$

where,

- $P_{supplier}$: Is the price proposed by the supplier (for unit of product).
- $P_{customer}$: Is the price requested by the customer (for unit of product).
- P_{min}: Is the maximum price accepted by the customer (in this chapter, it is fixed to 60% of increment of the price requested by the customer).

The price satisfaction is computed as shown in expression (8) if the price proposed by the supplier is lower than the P_{max}; otherwise the price satisfaction is 0.

The price satisfaction U_p is computed as shown in expression (7) if the volume proposed by the supplier is greater than the P_{max}; otherwise the volume satisfaction is 0.

The due date satisfaction is computed by the following expressions:

$$U_d = \frac{dd_{supplier} - dd_{min}}{dd_{customer} - dd_{min}}, if \ dd_{supplier} \leq dd_{customer} \tag{9}$$

$$U_d = 1 - \frac{dd_{supplier} - dd_{customer}}{dd_{max} - dd_{customer}}, if \ dd_{supplier} > dd_{customer} \tag{10}$$

where,

- **dd$_{supplier}$:** Is the due date proposed by the supplier.
- **dd$_{customer}$:** Is the due date requested by the customer.
- **dd$_{max}$:** Is the maximum due date accepted by the customer (in this chapter, it is fixed to 5 periods of increment of the due date requested by the customer).
- **dd$_{min}$:** Is the minimum due date accepted by the customer (in this chapter, it is fixed to 5 before the due date requested by the customer).

The due date satisfaction U_d is computed as shown in the expressions (9 and 10) if the due date proposed by the supplier is lower than the dd_{max} and greater than dd_{min}; otherwise the due date satisfaction is 0.

The global satisfaction is the sum of the satisfaction of each parameter in negotiation; therefore, the global satisfaction is comprised between 0 and 3.

The customer compares the global satisfaction with a threshold value to decide if accepts or refuses the supplier proposal. The threshold function is computed by the following expression:

$$Thu(r) = Thu_{max} \bullet \left(1 - u1\left(r\right)\right)^2$$
$$+2 \bullet fat \bullet u1 \bullet \left(1 - u1\left(r\right)\right) + Thu_{min} \bullet u1\left(r\right)^2 \tag{11}$$

$$u1\left(r\right) = \frac{r-1}{r_{max} - 1} \tag{12}$$

where,

- **Thu$_{max}$:** Is the maximum value of the threshold function that is 3, because maximum value of the global satisfaction can be 3.
- **Thu$_{min}$:** Is the minimum value of the threshold decided by the customer. In this chapter is assumed a minimum value of 1.5 (the half of the maximum customer satisfaction possible).
- **r:** Is the round of the negotiation mechanism.
- **r$_{max}$:** Is the maximum round of negotiation. This value defines the deadline of the negotiation.

The expression (11) is a cubic spline; the parameter *fat* can control the slope of the function.

The investigation of the parameter *fat* allows to defines the following values:

- **fat=2.2:** This value characterizes a linear threshold function between 3 and 1.5.
- **fat= 3:** This value characterizes a threshold function similar to Figure 3.
- **fat=1:** This value characterizes a threshold function similar to Figure 2.

The learning approach proposed for the customer concerns the evaluation of the average customer satisfaction obtained by the past negotiation process.

If the average customer satisfaction of the past negotiations is greater than 2.7 value, the parameter *fat=fat+0.1*. If the value fat is greater than 3 the parameter assumes value 3. This means that the customer reduces slowly the threshold utility during the negotiation, because the average utility obtained is high. If the past negotiation leads to high customer satisfaction means that the competitive area of the suppliers is able to keep high level of satisfaction.

If the average customer satisfaction of the past negotiations is lower than 2.4 value, the parameter *fat=fat-0.1*. If the value fat is lower than 1 then the parameter assumes value 1. This means that the customer reduces quickly the threshold utility during the negotiation, because the average utility obtained is low. If the past negotiation leads to low customer satisfaction means that the competitive area of the suppliers is not able to keep high level of satisfaction.

The customer-learning model tries to evaluate the competitive arena of the suppliers in order to obtain the better value of satisfaction. The environment is characterized by the average value of the past satisfaction utility obtained, while the parameter 0.1 is the value α as learning parameter.

SIMULATION ENVIRONMENT AND TEST CASE

In order to test the proposed approach, a proper simulation environment has been developed to highlight the main benefits. The simulation environment has been developed in an open-source architecture by using Java Development Kit (JDK) package (Pidd and Cassel, 2000). The modeling formalism adopted consists in a collection of independent objects interacting via messages. This formalism is undoubtedly suitable for multi- agent systems development. In particular, each developed object represents an agent and, through a message-sending engine, the system evolves managed by a discrete event scheduler. Specifically, the following objects have been developed: customer, supplier, scheduler and statistical analysis. Each

object to represent an agent is composed by data and methods. The data is the knowledge of the agent, while the method is the intelligence of the agent. The interaction with the other agents by messages change the data and therefore the knowledge of the agent. The customer object manages the activity of the customer: input the orders and evaluate the suppliers counter-proposal. The data of the customer objects are: the orders data required (volume, due date and price); the parameters of the strategy to perform; the utility obtained by the past negotiations. The methods of the customer object are the following: the method used to evaluate the suppliers' counter-proposal; the method to select the utility function strategy during the negotiation process; the computation of the past negotiations utility satisfaction. The supplier object manages the suppliers activities: it performs the production planning, formulates the counterproposal and performs the learning algorithm. The data of the supplier object are the following: the production data (resources' costs and resources' availability); the parameters of the strategies to perform, the prodit obtained by the past negotiations. The methods of the supplier object are the following: the method used to formulate the counter-proposal; the method to select the profit reduction strategy; the production planning algorithm to plan the order. The scheduler object coordinates the activities among the customer and supplier objects: it manages the communication among the objects. The scheduler object is at the upper level and coordinates the message that the other objects exchange among them. The statistical analysis collects the simulation data and draws up the report of the simulations. In particular, the statistical object computes the confidence interval and determines the number of replications to perform. The simulation environment has been entirely developed by using open source code (Java) and architecture (Object Oriented). Therefore, it can be used to build up the real system once the design and test phase is completed. This choice allows reducing investment time and cost, thus reducing the investment risk. Figure 5 shows the UML activity diagram of the interactions between the customer and supplier agents.

The customer agent works through the following activities:

- **Order Data Input:** The first activity of the customer agent concerns the order data input in terms of technological and commercial requirement.
- **Transmits Order Requirements:** The customer transmits the order information to the customer agent.
- **Waits for Supplier Counter-Proposal:** After the data transmission, the customer waits for the supplier's counter-proposal.

- **Evaluates Counter-Proposal:** The customer evaluates the supplier counter-proposal as described in the above sections. In case of positive evaluation, the customer accepts the counter-proposal and signs the contract with the supplier. In case of negative evaluation, the customer can ask for a new counter proposal if the round of negotiation is lower than the maximum round. If the evaluation is negative and the round of negotiation is the last, the negotiation ends without agreement.

The supplier agent performs the following activities:

Figure 5. UML-activity diagram

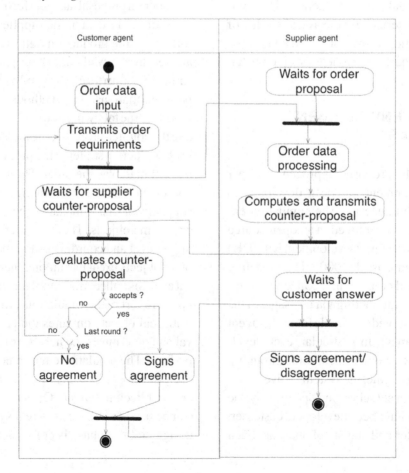

- **Waits for Order Proposal:** The supplier is in the initial state of waiting. The supplier is activated when the customer transmits the request for an order.
- **Order Data Processing:** The supplier analyzes the order data and computes the production planning alternatives.
- **Computes and Transmits Counter-Proposal:** The supplier applies its strategy to compute the counter-proposal using the information provided by the production planning alternatives. Then, the counter-proposal is transmitted to the customer.
- **Waits for Customer Answer:** The supplier waits for the answer of the customer.
- **Signs Agreement/Disagreement:** If the answer of the customer is positive, the customer and supplier sign the agreement. If the answer is negative, and the number of round negotiation is lower than the maximum number, the supplier computes a new counter-proposal. Otherwise, the negotiation ends without agreement.

The network consists of four suppliers that compete to reach an agreement with the customer. Therefore, the competitive environment concerns four players. Table 2 reports the suppliers' data. The data concerns the production planning information:

- **Fixed Cost:** It is the fixed costs needed to activate a production planning for the order requested by the customer.
- **Ordinary Cost for Unit Rime:** Unit cost per hour of regular manpower in the supplier j.
- **Overtime Cost for Unit Time:** Unit cost per hour of overtime manpower in the supplier j.
- **Outsourcing Costs for Product Unit:** It is the costs for each unit of product requested in outsourcing.

- **Ordinary Capacity:** Hours of direct and regular manpower available in the unit time period in the supplier j.
- **Overtime Capacity:** Hours of direct and overtime manpower available in the unit time period in the supplier j.
- **Outsourcing Capacity:** The maximum number of product that the supplier j can acquire in outsourcing.
- **Hours for Product Unit:** Number of manpower hours needed for a unit of product in the supplier j.

In order to investigate only the learning algorithm, it is used a simplified production planning algorithm to provide the production alternatives.

The production planning algorithm is performed through the following steps:

STEP 1: It initializes the index $i=1$ (price) and $j=1$ (due date); it sets the price and due date as the values requested by the customer. Moreover, it is defined the maximum due date possible and the maximum profit value.

STEP 2: It assigns the ordinary capacity using as soon as possible policy. If the customer volume is entirely satisfied go to STEP 5; otherwise go to STEP 3.

STEP 3: If the volume assigned at STEP 2 is not enough to satisfy the customer volume requested, then the overtime capacity is assigned using as soon as possible policy; If the customer volume is entirely satisfied go to STEP 5; otherwise go to STEP 4.

STEP 4: If the volume assigned at STEP 3 is not enough to satisfy the customer volume requested, then the outsourcing capacity is assigned using as soon as possible policy.

STEP 5: It is computed the profit and the total volume of the production alternative.

STEP 6: If the profit reached is lower than the maximum profit fixed go to STEP 7; otherwise, it increases the price of a percentage α in this chapter, it assumed $\alpha=0.1$).

Table 2. Suppliers data

	Supplier 1	Supplier 2	Supplier 3	Supplier 4
Fixed costs [unit cost]	500	300	200	100
Ordinary cost for unit time [unit cost/unit time]	20	30	35	40
Overtime cost for unit time [unit cost/unit time]	30	35	40	45
Outsourcing cots for product unit [unit cost/product]	45	40	45	50
Ordinary capacity [unit time]	8	8	16	16
Overtime capacity [unit time]	8	16	8	8
Outsourcing capacity [products]	20	32	28	40
Hours for product unit [unit time/product]	1	1	1	1

STEP 7: It increases the due date of one unit; if the due date is greater than the maximum due date possible the algorithm ends.

The customer inputs the order during a horizon of 200 unit times with eight periods as average between two consecutive orders. The orders data consists of four case studies as shown in Table 3. The four cases simulate the four combinations (high and low) for the price and volume.

The four cases are replicated in three overlap periods among the orders: 0 overlap, 4 periods of overlap and 8 periods of overlap. The overlap among the orders is a factor that affects the computation of the production alternatives.

Table 3. Orders data

	Volume	Price
Case 1: low volume and high price	UNIF[8;40]	UNIF[20;55]
Case 2: low volume and low price	UNIF[8;40]	UNIF[15;30]
Case 3: high volume and high price	UNIF[20;65]	UNIF[20;55]
Case 4: high volume and low price	UNIF[20;65]	UNIF[15;30]

Table 4 reports the approaches simulated for the environment above described.

Therefore, the total cases simulated are: 4 (orders data) X 3 (overlap periods) X 6 (approaches)-> 72 experimental classes.

For each experimental condition, the following performance indicators are reported:

- **Total Customer Utility:** It is the sum of the customer utility over all the orders submitted. If the agreement is not reached the utility is 0.
- **Suppliers Utility:** It is the total profit of the suppliers over all the orders.
- The average number of rounds to reach the agreements. It is an index of the facility of the customer and suppliers to reach the agreements.
- Unbalance of the profit distribution among the suppliers. This index is computed as follows:

$$unbalance = \sum_{i=1}^{N} \left| \frac{1}{N} - \frac{utility_{\text{sup} plier_i}}{totalutility_{\text{sup} plier}} \right| \quad (13)$$

Table 4. Simulated approaches

	Approach
1	No learning
2	Q-learning approach (slope function)
3	Q-learning approach (minimum profit level)
4	Q- learning approach (slope function and minimum level profit)
5	Q-learning approach (slope function) and customer learning
6	Q- learning approach (slope function and minimum level profit) and customer learning

If the profit is equally distributed among the suppliers, the expression (13) is equal to 0, otherwise the expression (13) is greater than 0. This index allows to highlight if some suppliers gain high profit, while other suppliers gain low profit. The capability of the e-marketplace management to distribute profit to all participants is attractive for the potential participants.

NUMERICAL RESULTS

The numerical results are analyzed considering the market environment and the overlap among the orders. The simulation results are obtained with a confidence interval of 5% and confidence level of 95%.

Table 5 shows that the negotiation process is always an added value for the customer. In each case, the customer utility improves if the negotiation process is performed. Therefore, the negotiation approach is a real value added services for the customer.

The difference of customer utility is always limited over the market case environment and over the overlap among the orders. The results show the robustness of the negotiation protocol proposed to the behavior of the suppliers. Moreover, the results highlight how the combination of price and volume (market case 3 to 4) leads to reduce significantly the customer utility. This means that the volume high has the more importance from the point of view of customer satisfaction. The overlap among the orders has the same effect but with a minor relevance. Therefore, the customer satisfaction has more sensitivity to the market conditions.

Table 6 reports the supplier utility in terms of percentage difference of the total profit compared to the profit in case of no negotiation (base of the percentage computation). In case of no negotiation, the customer accepts or refuses the proposal of the suppliers. The better utility reached for the suppliers change over the cases investigated. The main part of the better results is obtained between "Q learning 3" and "Q learning 4". These cases regard the application of the Q learning only

Table 5. Customer utility: average over the market environment case

	No learning	No nego	Q learning 1	Q learning 2	Q learning 3	Q learning 4	Q learning 5	Q learning 6
Case 1	66.51	62.61	66.11	65.54	65.86	66.09	67.59	65.26
Case 2	58.84	57.17	58.54	58.16	58.22	57.66	58.39	58.97
Case 3	51.11	45.35	50.61	49.01	49.56	48.68	50.31	50.11
Case 4	44.35	42.16	44.12	43.41	43.84	43.63	45.90	43.05
average	*55.20*	*51.82*	*54.85*	*54.03*	*54.37*	*54.01*	*55.55*	*54.35*
Over 0	58.82	55.54	58.57	57.72	58.14	57.95	59.46	57.81
Over 4	54.48	51.37	54.03	53.29	53.61	53.22	54.76	53.61
Over 8	52.32	48.56	51.94	51.09	51.37	50.88	52.43	51.62

Table 6. Supplier utility: average over the market environment case

	No learning	Q learning 1	Q learning 2	Q learning 3	Q learning 4	Q learning 5	Q learning 6
Case 1	-36.69%	-34.25%	-28.96%	-31.86%	-32.37%	-41.33%	**-26.35%**
Case 2	-52.79%	-46.75%	-36.65%	-44.15%	**-28.14%**	-45.91%	-46.70%
Case 3	-49.70%	-47.50%	-37.26%	-40.44%	**-30.15%**	-44.11%	-42.31%
Case 4	-66.06%	-60.43%	-60.73%	**-16.96%**	-32.34%	-44.84%	-77.47%
average	-52.03%	-48.05%	-41.68%	-33.17%	**-30.77%**	-44.11%	-49.33%
Over 0	-52.32%	-49.85%	-44.43%	**-35.48%**	-39.33%	-48.12%	-48.85%
Over 4	-47.42%	-42.67%	-35.46%	**-26.11%**	**-26.41%**	-38.13%	-44.24%
Over 8	-55.00%	-50.66%	-44.33%	-36.64%	**-28.80%**	-45.87%	-53.05%

to the minimum level of profit (Q learning 3) and the case with slope function and customer learning (Q learning 4). The effect of the market case has a low relevance between case 2 (low volume and high price) and 3 (low volume and low price). This mean that the volume requested by the customer is more important of the price level of the orders. This because the volume is the main effect on the production planning costs of the suppliers. The relevant result is the better result obtained when both customer and supplier apply a learning strategy.

Table 7 reports the unbalance index of the distribution of the profit among the suppliers of the network. The results are similar to the suppliers utility described above. In this case, each learning approach allows to improve this perfor-

mance index. The better learning approaches are the same of the suppliers' utility.

Table 8 reports the results if the time to reach the agreements. In case of no negotiation, the average round is one. Also for this performance the Q-learning 3 and 4 are the better solutions.

From the above numerical results, the following issues can be drawn:

- The performance of the customer utility depends by the market conditions, but the effect of the learning approaches is very low. However, if the suppliers apply a learning strategy, the customer needs to implement a learning strategy to improve the utility; otherwise, if only the suppliers apply learning strategy the customer utility decreases.

Table 7. Unbalance index: average over the market environment case

	No learning	Q learning 1	Q learning 2	Q learning 3	Q learning 4	Q learning 5	Q learning 6
Case 1	-34.03%	-39.59%	-34.97%	-34.55%	-40.43%	-35.38%	**-32.89%**
Case 2	-55.52%	-48.63%	-37.46%	-45.94%	**-29.11%**	-48.85%	-48.34%
Case 3	-57.70%	-55.71%	-43.34%	-46.90%	**-36.03%**	-52.07%	-47.20%
Case 4	-75.98%	-71.30%	-71.74%	**-32.07%**	-46.25%	-55.05%	-85.47%
average	-60.67%	-58.01%	-51.64%	**-39.54%**	**-39.33%**	-50.26%	-59.36%
Over 0	-59.19%	-56.98%	-51.13%	**-40.39%**	-44.66%	-50.18%	-56.99%
Over 4	-60.89%	-58.43%	-51.72%	**-39.00%**	-42.37%	-50.75%	-59.77%
Over 8	-61.51%	-58.35%	-51.93%	-39.41%	**-32.96%**	-49.90%	-60.67%

Table 8. Time of agreement: average over the market environment case

	No learning	Q learning 1	Q learning 2	Q learning 3	Q learning 4	Q learning 5	Q-learning 6
Case 1	**2.94**	3.10	3.19	3.11	3.52	3.36	2.83
Case 2	4.61	4.62	4.73	4.60	**4.06**	**3.93**	5.53
Case 3	5.35	5.49	5.49	5.32	**4.47**	**4.38**	6.38
Case 4	6.50	6.46	5.83	**4.62**	5.49	7.24	7.03
average	4.85	4.92	4.81	**4.41**	**4.39**	4.73	5.44
Over 0	4.99	5.06	5.05	4.56	**4.48**	5.09	5.42
Over 4	4.80	4.88	4.94	4.42	**4.07**	4.63	5.52
Over 8	4.76	4.81	4.45	**4.26**	4.60	4.47	5.38

- The suppliers improve the utility with the learning approaches. If the customer applies a learning strategy, the better strategy regards the slope of the minimum level of profit over the rounds. The combination of the slope function and the minimum level of profit does not improve significantly the suppliers performance.
- All the learning strategies allow to reduce the unbalance index. The profit among the suppliers is distributed more uniformly.
- The time to reach the agreements is reduced used the learning approaches.

Briefly, the better results are obtained when both customer and suppliers apply the learning strategy. In particular, if the suppliers apply only the slope function learning strategy.

CONCLUSION AND FUTURE DEVELOPMENT

The research presented several learning strategies for the suppliers and the customer in multi-issue negotiation. The strategies of the suppliers are based on Q-learning methodology using the information of the past negotiation. The information derived by the past negotiation is used to select the strategy to use in the negotiation process.

The learning methodology to select the strategy is developed both for customer and suppliers. A simulation environment has been developed to test the proposed approaches in several market conditions and different methodology to implement the learning technique. The numerical results are compared to the case without learning approach.

The results of this research can be summarized as follows:

- The proposed approaches allow to improve the performance of the supplier in terms of total profit and better distribution of the profit among the suppliers. The benefit for the customer is limited.
- The better combination is the case in which the suppliers apply a learning strategy on the slope of the profit function to compute the counter-proposal and customer applies a learning strategy. This means that the learning strategy needs to be applied from the two counterparts to obtain the better performance.
- The approaches proposed are simply and robust to the several market conditions. Moreover, the learning approaches proposed can be integrated in the production-planning model of the supplier with a lower computational workload. This is important for the negotiation applications.

- The approaches proposed are linked to the production-planning algorithm of the suppliers. In this context, production-planning tools allow the creation of a link between commercialization (negotiation process) and manufacturing activities, providing a better service for all the involved actors.

Further research paths can be the following:

- The influence of the network system size (number of the suppliers and customers) on the performance measure. The number of suppliers changes the competitive arena, because there is more competition among the suppliers. Further simulations need to evaluate the robustness of the proposed approaches in different network sizes.
- The development of a decision support system more complex to define the parameters of the learning approaches. It needs to investigate if complex methodologies with higher computational time can improve the global performance. For example, the game theory can be a valid decision support tool both for the negotiation and the learning methodology.

REFERENCES

Aberdeen Group. (2006). *The e-procurement benchmark report*. Aberdeen Group.

Al-Agtash, S. Y., & Al-Fahoum, A. A. (2005). An evolutionary computation approach to electricity trade negotiation. *Advances in Engineering Software*, *36*(3), 173–179. doi:10.1016/j.advengsoft.2004.07.008.

Arbib, C., & Rossi, F. (2000). Optimal resource assignment through negotiation in a multi-agent manufacturing system. *IIE Transactions*, *32*(10), 963–974. doi:10.1080/07408170008967454.

Argoneto, P., & Renna, P. (2010). Production planning, negotiation and coalition integration: A new tool for an innovative e-business model. *Robotics and Computer-integrated Manufacturing*, *26*(1), 1–12. doi:10.1016/j.rcim.2009.01.001.

Bandyopadhyay, S., Rees, J., & Barron, J. M. (2008). Reverse auctions with multiple reinforcement learning agents. *Decision Sciences*, *39*(1), 33–63. doi:10.1111/j.1540-5915.2008.00181.x.

Bigdeli, N., Afshar, K. M., & Fotuhi-Firuzabad, M. (2010). Bidding strategy in pay-as-bid markets based on supplier-market interaction analysis. *Energy Conversion and Management*, *51*(12), 2419–2430. doi:10.1016/j.enconman.2010.05.006.

Binmore, K., & Vulkan, N. (1999). Applying game theory to automated negotiation. *NETNOMICS: Economic Research and Electronic Networking*, *1*(1), 1–9. doi:10.1023/A:1011489402739.

Calosso, T., Cantamessa, M., & Gualano, M. (2004). Negotiation support for make-to-order operations in business-to-business electronic commerce. *Robotics and Computer-integrated Manufacturing*, *20*, 405–416. doi:10.1016/j.rcim.2004.03.003.

Carbonneau, R., Kersten, G. E., & Klaue, R. (2008). Predicting opponent's moves in electronic negotiations using neural networks. *Expert Systems with Applications*, *34*(2), 1266–1273. doi:10.1016/j.eswa.2006.12.027.

Chen, Y. M., & Wang, S. C. (2007). Framework of agent-based intelligence system with two stage decision-making processes for distributed dynamic scheduling. *Applied Soft Computing*, *7*, 229–245. doi:10.1016/j.asoc.2005.04.003.

Cheng, C., Chan, C. H., & Lin, K. (2006). Intelligent agents for e-marketplace: Negotiation with issue trade-offs by fuzzy inference systems. *Decision Support Systems*, *42*, 626–638. doi:10.1016/j.dss.2005.02.009.

Cherkassky, V., & Mulier, F. (1998). *Learning from data*. New York: Wiley.

Coehoorn, R. M., & Jennings, N. R. (2004). Learning an opponent's preferences to make effective multi-issue negotiation trade-offs. In *Proceedings of the 6th International Conference on Electronic Commerce*, (pp. 59-68). ACM.

David, E., Azoulay-Schwartz, R., & Kraus, S. (2006). Bidding in sealed-bid and English multi-attribute auctions. *Decision Support Systems*, *42*(2), 527–556. doi:10.1016/j.dss.2005.02.007.

Faratin, P., Sierra, C., & Jennings, N. R. (2003). Using similarity criteria to make negotiation trade-offs. *Journal of Artificial Intelligence*, *142*(2), 205–237. doi:10.1016/S0004-3702(02)00290-4.

Hausen, T., Fritz, M., & Schiefer, G. (2006). Potential of electronic trading in complex supply chains: An experimental study. *International Journal of Production Economics*, *104*(2), 580–597. doi:10.1016/j.ijpe.2005.04.010.

Hindriks, K., & Tykhonov, D. (2008). Opponent modelling in automated multi-issue negotiation using bayesian learning. In *Proceedings of the 7th International Joint Conference on Autonomous Agents and Multiagent Systems*, (Vol. 1, pp. 331-338). International Foundation for Autonomous Agents and Multiagent Systems.

Huang, C., Liang, W., Lai, Y., & Lin, Y. (2010). The agent-based negotiation process for B2C e-commerce. *Expert Systems with Applications*, *37*(1), 348–359. doi:10.1016/j.eswa.2009.05.065.

Huang, S.-L., & Lin, F.-R. (2008). Using temporal-difference learning for multi-agent bargaining. *Electronic Commerce Research and Applications*, *7*(4), 432–442. doi:10.1016/j.elerap.2007.04.001.

Jennings, N. R., Faratin, P., Lomuscio, A., Parsons, S., Wooldridge, M., & Sierra, C. (2001). Automated negotiation: Prospects, methods and challenges. *Group Decision and Negotiation*, *10*(2), 199–215. doi:10.1023/A:1008746126376.

Jonker, C., Robu, V., & Treur, J. (2007). An agent architecture for multi-attribute negotiation using incomplete preference information. *Autonomous Agents and Multi-Agent Systems*, *15*(2), 221–252. doi:10.1007/s10458-006-9009-y.

Kaelbling, L. P., Littman, M. L., & Moore, A. W. (1996). Reinforcement learning: A survey. *Journal of Artificial Intelligence Research*, *4*, 237–285.

Kersten, G., & Lai, H. (2007). Negotiation support and e-negotiation systems: An overview. *Group Decision and Negotiation*, *16*(6), 553–586. doi:10.1007/s10726-007-9095-5.

Kowalcyzk, R. (2000). On negotiation as a distributed fuzzy constraint satisfaction problem. In *Proceedings DEXA e-Negotiation Workshop*, (pp. 631– 637). DEXA.

Lin, R., Kraus, S., Wilkenfeld, J., & Barry, J. (2006). An automated agent for bilateral negotiation with bounded rational agents with incomplete information. [ECAI.]. *Proceedings of ECAI*, *2006*, 270–274.

Luo, X., Jennings, N. R., Shadbolt, N., Leung, H. F., & Lee, J. H. M. (2003). A fuzzy constraint based model for bilateral, multi-issue negotiation in semi-competitive environments. *Artificial Intelligence*, *148*(1–2), 53–102. doi:10.1016/S0004-3702(03)00041-9.

Martin, S., Ouelhadj, D., Beullens, P., & Ozcan, E. (2012). *A generic agent-based framework for cooperative search using pattern matching and reinforcement learning* (Technical Report 5861). Portsmouth, UK: University of Portsmouth.

Mashhadi, R. H., & Rahimiyan, M. (2011). Measurement of power supplier's market power using a proposed fuzzy estimator. *IEEE Transactions on Power Systems*, *26*(4), 1836–1844. doi:10.1109/TPWRS.2011.2144626.

Neubert, R., Görlitz, O., & Teich, T. (2004). Automated negotiations of supply contracts for flexible production networks. *International Journal of Production Economics*, *89*(2), 175–187. doi:10.1016/S0925-5273(03)00043-4.

Oshrat, Y., Lin, R., & Kraus, S. (2009). Facing the challenge of human-agent negotiations via e_ective general opponent modeling. In *Proceedings of The 8th International Conference on Autonomous Agents and Multiagent Systems*, (Vol. 1, pp. 377-384). International Foundation for Autonomous Agents and Multiagent Systems.

Peng, J., & Williams, R. J. (1996). Incremental multi-step Q-learning. *Machine Learning*, *22*(1–3), 283–290. doi:10.1007/BF00114731.

Perrone, G., Roma, P., & Lo Nigro, G. (2010). Designing multi-attribute auctions for engineering services procurement in new product development in the automotive context. *International Journal of Production Economics*, *124*(1), 20–31. doi:10.1016/j.ijpe.2009.10.003.

Pidd, M., & Cassel, R. A. (2000). Using java to develop discrete event simulation. *The Journal of the Operational Research Society*, *51*(4), 405–412.

Rahimiyan, M., & Mashhadi, H. R. (2008). Supplier's optimal bidding strategy in electricity pay-as-bid auction: Comparison of the q-learning and a model-based approach. *Electric Power Systems Research*, *78*(1), 165–175. doi:10.1016/j.epsr.2007.01.009.

Raju, C. V. L., Narahari, Y., & Ravikumar, K. (2006a). Learning dynamic prices in electronic markets with customer segmentation. *Annals of Operations Research*, *143*(1), 59–75. doi:10.1007/s10479-006-7372-3.

Raju, C. V. L., Narahari, Y., & Ravikumar, K. (2006b). Learning dynamic prices in multi-seller electronic retail markets with price sensitive customers, stochastic demands, and inventory replenishments. *IEEE Transactions on Systems, Man and Cybernetics. Part C, Applications and Reviews*, *36*(1), 92–106. doi:10.1109/TSMCC.2005.860578.

Ramchurn, S.D., Sierra, C., Godo, L., & Jennings, N.R. (2007). Negotiating using rewards. *Artificial Intelligence*, *171*(10-15), 805-837.

Renna, P. (2009). A multi-agent system architecture for business-to-business applications. *International Journal of Services and Operations Management*, *5*(3), 375–401. doi:10.1504/IJSOM.2009.024152.

Renna, P. (2010). Negotiation policies for e-procurement by multi agent systems. In Nag, B. (Ed.), *Intelligent Systems in Operations: Models, Methods, and Applications*. Hershey, PA: IGI Publishing. doi:10.4018/978-1-61520-605-6.ch009.

Renna, P., & Argoneto, P. (2010). Production planning and automated negotiation for SMEs: An agent based e-procurement application. *International Journal of Production Economics*, *127*(1), 73–84. doi:10.1016/j.ijpe.2010.04.035.

Russel, S., & Norvig, P. (2003). *Artificial intelligence a modern approach*. Upper Saddle River, NJ: Prentice Hall.

Sejnowski, T. J., & Hinton, G. E. (Eds.). (1999). *Unsupervised learning: Foundations of neural computation*. Cambridge, MA: MIT Press.

Sutton, R. S., & Barto, A. (1998). *Reinforcement learning: An introduction*. Boston: MIT Press.

Tesauro, G., & Kephart, J. O. (2002). Pricing in agent economies using multi-agent Q-learning. *Autonomous Agents and Multi-Agent Systems*, 5(3), 289–304. doi:10.1023/A:1015504423309.

Watkins, C. J. C. H. (1989). *Learning from delayed rewards*. (PhD Thesis). King's College. Cambridge, UK.

Watkins, C. J. C. H., & Dayan, P. (1992). Q-learning. *Machine Learning*, 8, 279–292. doi:10.1007/BF00992698.

Wong, S. K., & Ho, T. K. (2010). Intelligent negotiation behaviour model for an open railway access market. *Expert Systems with Applications*, 37(12), 8109–8118. doi:10.1016/j.eswa.2010.05.077.

Yasumura, Y., Kamiryo, T., Yoshikawa, S., & Uehara, K. (2009). Acquisition of a concession strategy in multi-issue negotiation. *Web Intelligence and Agent Systems*, 7(2), 161–171.

Yoshikawa, S. Y., Yasumura, Y., & Uehara, K. (2008). Strategy acquisition on multi-issue negotiation without estimating opponent's preference. [LNCS]. *Proceedings of Agent and Multi-Agent Systems: Technologies and Applications*, 4953, 371–380. doi:10.1007/978-3-540-78582-8_38.

Zeng, D., & Sycara, K. (1998). Bayesian learning in negotiation. *International Journal of Human-Computer Studies*, 48, 125–141. doi:10.1006/ijhc.1997.0164.

ADDITIONAL READING

Chandrashekhar, H., & Bhasker, B. (2011). Quickly locating efficient, equitable deals in automated negotiations under two-sided information uncertainty. *Decision Support Systems*, 52(1), 157–168. doi:10.1016/j.dss.2011.06.004.

Comuzzi, M., Francalanci, C., & Giacomazzi, P. (2008). Pricing the quality of differentiated services for media-oriented real-time applications: A multi-attribute negotiation approach. *Computer Networks*, 52(16), 3373–3391. doi:10.1016/j.comnet.2008.09.003.

Helander, A., & Möller, K. (2007). System supplier's customer strategy. *Industrial Marketing Management*, 36(6), 719–730. doi:10.1016/j.indmarman.2006.05.007.

Pressey, A. D., Winklhofer, H. M., & Tzokas, N. X. (2009). Purchasing practices in small- to medium-sized enterprises: An examination of strategic purchasing adoption, supplier evaluation and supplier capabilities. *Journal of Purchasing and Supply Management*, 15(4), 214–226. doi:10.1016/j.pursup.2009.03.006.

Rau, H., Chen, T. F., & Chen, C. W. (2009). Develop a negotiation framework for automating B2B processes in the RosettaNet environment using fuzzy technology. *Computers & Industrial Engineering*, 56(2), 736–753. doi:10.1016/j.cie.2008.06.016.

Wang, G., Wong, T. N., & Yu, C. (2011). Computational method for agent-based e-commerce negotiations with adaptive negotiation behaviors. *Procedia Computer Science*, 4, 1834–1843. doi:10.1016/j.procs.2011.04.199.

KEY TERMS AND DEFINITIONS

Coordination: It is the mechanism how the agent exchange information and cooperate to purse a common objective.

Discrete Event Simulation: It emulates a real system by a chronological sequence of events. Each event occurs at an instant in time and marks a change of state in the system.

E-Business: It is the application of Information and Communication Technology (ICT) to support the business activities.

Multi-Agent System: It is a system composed of multiple interacting intelligent agents.

Negotiation: It is the dialogue between two or more parties to resolve a conflict and reach an agreement.

Negotiation Tactics: It refers to the parametric functions that are used to build the offer/counter-offer in the negotiation process.

Q-Learning: It is a reinforcement learning technique that works by learning an action-value function that gives the expected utility of taking a given action in a given state and decides to follow a particular strategy.

Chapter 4
A Novel Matching Algorithm for Shopbot Agents acting in Marketplaces

George Karasmanoglou
Ionian University, Greece

Blerina Lika
Ionian University, Greece

ABSTRACT

During the last years, the emergence of Semantic Web has produced a vast amount of resources and a variety of content representation schemes. The latter has increased the complexity that the users are facing when searching for information in open environments. A representative example is Electronic Markets (EMs). In EMs users try to find and purchase products through interactions with providers. In such scenarios, shopbots can offer a number of advantages. Shopbots are agents that help users to find the products they want, saving them a lot of time and effort. However, building efficient shopbots is a challenging task. This is more imperative when shopbots interact with providers using different ontological terms for product description. In this chapter, the authors propose a generic ontology to describe products in EMs. They also introduce a matching algorithm that maps the specific provider ontology to the generic one in order to be used by a shopbot. Their algorithm, called S^+, is based on a set of linguistic and semantic matching techniques. The authors present their approach and compare it with other proposed algorithms. Finally, they discuss their experimental results that reveal the performance of their methodology.

INTRODUCTION

The rapid development of the Web and the Semantic Web leads to a huge amount of resources as well as of content representation schemes. Hence, one can find numerous information sources and among them a large number of electronic stores. However, there is a lot of information describing these products that is very difficult for customers to retrieve it. Users should search and find the appropriate products that best match to their needs. As we understand this task is out of the human

DOI: 10.4018/978-1-4666-4038-2.ch004

limitations. The number of choices for users has grown and for this they need an efficient tool that can help them in finding the appropriate products.

For this reason, autonomous entities were proposed for being responsible to find and return the appropriate products in the smallest amount of time. Such entities can be represented by intelligent agents. These entities can interact in an autonomous way in Electronic Markets (EMs). In such places, the discussed software components can negotiate and agree upon the exchange of products. Entities acting in EMs can represent buyers, sellers or can be other administrative entities helping buyers and sellers to conclude their transactions. An important category of such middle entities is shopbots. Shopbots (Shopping Robots) are agents that can operate online and help users to find and decide which products should buy. A shopbot gets the users preferences and accordingly returns information relevant to products and the characteristics that match the user needs. Shopbots enhance users shopping experiences as they collect product information from a large number of sellers. Hence, users have the opportunity to compare products characteristics. Furthermore, the product list provided by shopbots is in such form that best matches the user preferences. This way, users save time and effort. In addition, agents are able to search products lists faster than a human and choose products for user desires. The Semantic Web (SW) consists of the extension of the Web providing semantics for the information representation in order to provide a machine understandable view on the information. This way, machines are able to understand information in order to fulfill owners' requests. Ontologies, the basic component of the SW, help along this line. They facilitate the interoperability of heterogeneous information sources by providing a formalization that makes them machine accessible. Ontologies are the key for the emergence of the SW. They carry knowledge and information for reasoning.

From the above, we can understand that the combination of autonomous intelligent components with ontologies can enhance the way that the information is provided to users. Products can be described by ontological means and, thus, can be processed more efficiently by agents. However, different developers use different ways to create ontologies because they have different view on various domains. Hence, we need two main things:

- An ontology that can be used by a shopbot in order to store the products information. This ontology should be as generic as it can be in order to provide an upper level of abstraction for all the other possible ontologies. Hence, the shopbot should be able to provide to users a uniform view on all the presented products.
- A matching algorithm that will result the information retrieved by all the sub-ontologies and will be stored to the generic product ontology. However, the proposed algorithms in this domain cannot give us good results because they are not designed for the specific scenario.

In this chapter, we propose a generic product ontology and we describe the S^+ algorithm. S^+ is designed for the specific scenario. The paper is organized as follows. In prior work section, we discuss about the related work in the specific domain. In research challenge section, we present the most important research efforts for the shopbot scenario. Accordingly, in shopbot architecture section, we describe the shopbot behavior concerning its actions in an EM environment. In addition, we present our product ontology which is designed to cover the most important information about a product. This information is necessary to provide the necessary knowledge to users in order to be able to decide the appropriate product. In matching algorithm section, we present the S^+, our matching algorithm, and give the most important parts of it. In the evaluation section, we compare the S^+ with other proposed algorithms. The comparison is based on specific ontologies found in the literature. Finally, we finish our study presenting the most important conclusions.

PRIOR WORK

Shopbots are active research area for many years. In this section, we provide the most important research efforts in the discussed domain. In (Smith, 2002), authors describe the impact of shopbots on electronic markets. They present reasons that shopbots are beneficial for both consumers and retailers. Shopbots can help consumers to find the appropriate products and compare prices. Hence, consumers need smaller time to conclude a transaction. On the other side, one can allege that shopbots lead retailers to reduce their marginal cost and they do not provide them ways to differentiate their products. However, a review in the literature shows that this is not true because retailers retain numerous opportunities to differentiate their products. They leverage brand names or set strategic prices in the market.

The semantic future of shopbots is revealed in (Fasli, 2006). Semantic Web technologies will provide shopbots with the necessary tools for overcoming the limitations of the current technology. Nowadays, shopbots should rely on syntax of Web pages. Thus, they limit information provided by vendors and ignore attributes such as warranty or shipping details. Of course, the product price is a very important parameter that a buyer should rely upon. Semantic Web and the provided services can offer the necessary form of retrieved information and, thus, shopbots can process it more efficiently. This will enhance the potential of comparison based on various parameters such as the price or other attributes. Moreover, shopbots will be capable of providing the best matching between the user preferences and providers adding an additional level of efficiency in their functionality.

An economic model for shopbots is presented and analyzed in (Greenwald and Kephart, 1999). Through this model authors want to capture the role of shopbots and other economically-motivated agents with regard to consumer preferences. Shopbots decrease the cost of obtaining information in markets and can facilitate in many ways consumers. Moreover, in this research, the authors present simulations about the functionality of pricebots in electronic markets. They describe an adaptive price-setting algorithm for pricebots that being responsible to set prices for specific products. Pricebots are shown to be capable of inducing price wars leading to earn profits that are above the game-theoretic levels.

The efficient and productive shopbot design is dealt with in (Montgomery et Al, 2004). Authors develop a utility model of consumer purchasing behavior. This model takes into consideration the product price as well as other important product attributes. Moreover, it considers latency and the cognitive costs evaluating the retrieved offers. Hence, the main focus is on attributes that are important to consumers in the purchase interactions in addition to basic parameters such as waiting time, price, etc. This way, the shopbot will be more efficient when presenting results to the consumers. The main operational decisions of the shopbot are: (1) selection of stores, (2) selection of the appropriate waiting time, and, (3) selection of the appropriate products that will be presented to users. Finally, they show how the shopbot design can be optimized to lead to higher chance of selecting the shopbot than to simply visiting a favorite retailer.

As the number of the available ontologies becomes larger, there is the need for access from multiple applications. Furthermore, a common layer between multiple ontologies is necessary. Authors in (Kalfoglou and Schorlemmer, 2003) review the state of the art in the domain of ontologies mapping. The development of such mappings has been the focus of various research efforts. A classification of schema-based and ontology matching is presented in (ShvaikoEuzenat, 2005). Authors distinguish between exact and approximate techniques at element and structure level. Based on this classification they overview some of the schema or ontology matching systems describing which part of the solution space they cover.

A large number of fields (machine learning, database schemata, formal theories to heuristics, etc) are entailed in ontology mapping. We can find a number of research prototypes as well as industrial applications. Thirty five efforts have been reviewed and for some of them specific use cases were shown fully covering in detail the domain of ontology mapping. A lot of research efforts focus on the ontology mapping problem. At this point is not efficient to describe all these tools defined for ontology mapping, however, we indicated some survey papers where the interested reader can find the information related to the discussed research field.

RESEARCH CHALLENGES

In this section, we provide the research questions that our model tries to answer in the electronic commerce domain. In the literature, the importance of shopbots is fully identified and described for both the buyers and the product providers. However, in order to have shopbots that provide personalized information to every buyer the semantic representation of the product information is necessary. The reason is that using product semantic representation, shopbots will be able to overcome the limitation of relying on Web pages syntax (Fasli, 2006). Relying on ontological representations, shopbots will be capable of providing, in the minimum time and efficiently, information fully adapted in the user needs. Hence, from our point of view, a generic product ontology should be defined in order to store the necessary information for each product. This ontology should contain the appropriate information for each product, information adapted and

related to the user needs. The discussed ontology should contain only the necessary classes and be updated when the shopbot acting in the Web. The proposed ontology is presented below and its architecture is described. The usage of a generic product ontology should enable the provision of personalized product catalogues to users in the minimum time. Furthermore, the shopbot should be capable of dealing with the heterogeneity in the product information of providers. Queries posed by users can be manipulated more efficient increasing their satisfaction. Finally, according to users preferences shopbots can adapt the products catalogues giving the opportunity to users to spend less time to compare similar product information for different providers.

As mentioned, the basic technology of the Semantic Web is ontology. However, they are a lot of different ontologies defining product information for every provider. Due to the reason that there is not a common way to define product ontologies, each provider defines its own ontology increasing the heterogeneity among different provides. A shopbot acting and negotiating with such providers should be able to solve this problem. As future extension, the usage of rules combined with the product ontology will provide more efficient results increasing the performance of the shopbot.

Concerning the ontology matching/mapping algorithms, in the literature one can find many matchers available for various research domains. These matchers perform well for some cases or not so well in other cases. This makes the selection of the matcher or the combination of matchers very important for ontology matching. In our case, we need an automatic matching mechanism that will be the base for instances copy in the shopbot product ontology. However, in our case a semi-automatic methodology using manual shopbot owner intervention for ontology matching is not acceptable. The reason is that the shopbot should be able to import and use the instances retrieved by the ontology providers in an automatic way in order to save time and define an efficient mechanism for products representation. This way the shopbot is capable of returning to users in the minimum time the most appropriate results according to user needs.

Furthermore, in traditional applications automatic ontology matching algorithms usually cannot deliver high quality results (ShvaikoEuzenat, 2008). Also, the most of the techniques are generic methods for ontology matching mainly based on ontology schema. In our scenario, the shopbot needs a less complex methodology that matches the ontologies providers with the product ontology – that mainly is a shallow ontology with few levels – taking in to consideration all ontology components (classes, object and data properties, instances information, etc.).

Hence, we propose an algorithm for instances creation in the shopbot product ontology based on the information taken by ontologies providers. Our approach is fully adapted to shopbot needs for more efficient instances creation. The proposed algorithm is described in the following sections.

SHOPBOT ARCHITECTURE/ BEHAVIOR

In this section, we describe in detail the behavior of a shopbot and we show how it uses its resources and the information taken by the electronic market. In addition, we present generic product ontology in order to store the basic information that we retrieve from the sellers.

General Architecture

In this work, we consider an environment that is semantically enhanced. This means that all the participants, and more specifically sellers, use their own ontology for the description of their products. It should be noted that every seller can sell a specific type of products or it can deal with different types. For example, we can have a seller that only sells cars or we can deal with a seller that

sells vehicles in general. The shopbot knowledge base relies on a generic product ontology (see next section for the description of the ontology) which is filled with product instances. Hence, when the user decides the product that he wants to buy, he can rely on the shopbot in order to have a catalogue presenting a number of sellers dealing with the specific product. This catalogue is filled using the product ontology instances. The described scenario is depicted in Figure 1.

The internal architecture of the shopbot is depicted in Figure 2. The shopbot consists of two main components:

- **Shopbot User Interface:** It is responsible for the interaction between users and the shopbot. The shopbot through this interface can accept user preferences for products and can return a catalogue containing a number of product characteristics classified in the order that the user wants. The analytical description of the shopbot user interface is out of the scope of this paper.

- **Core Shopbot Logic:** It consists of the main logic of the shopbot where it should interact with sellers in specific time points in order to retrieve the ontological information and accordingly to update the generic product ontology. The shopbot logic could be divided into three sub-parts:
  - **Ontologies Interaction Part:** This part is responsible for the interaction with sellers and the retrieval of

Figure 1. The architecture of the shopbot scenario

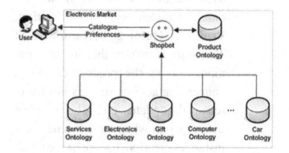

Figure 2. Shopbot internal architecture

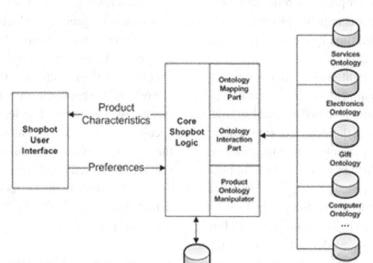

the information to the products that each sellers deals with. The shopbot retrieves the ontology schema and accordingly using the ontology mapping part can define classes and properties relations between the seller and the product ontology. Moreover, the interaction part is responsible to retrieve the seller products instances for their insertion in the generic product ontology.

○ **Ontology Mapping Part:** This part uses a set of similarity (linguistic and semantic) algorithms in order to define relations between the source (seller ontology) and the shopbot product ontology. The algorithms used are fully described in shopbot ontology matching algorithm section.

○ **Product Ontology Manipulator:** This part is responsible for the manipulation of the product ontology, concerning actions such as insertion, retrieval, update, etc. The shopbot uses this part when there is a need for instances creation, update or retrieval.

Based on the above presented architecture, the shopbot can interact with users and sellers. Through the generic product ontology, it is capable of producing efficient product catalogues according to user needs. Ontologies provide such an advantage.

Shopbot Product Ontology

In the literature, we can find two of the most widely known product categorization schemata: the United Nations Standard Products and Service Code (UNSPSC)[1] and the ecl@ss[2]. Other product classification schemes are eOTD[3] and RosettaNet Technical Dictionary[4]. For the first two coding schemes there are some efforts for their description by using OWL[5].

However, the provided ontologies are very large (size approximately to 25MB for ecl@ssOWL and 3MB for UnspscOWL) and contain a very large number of concepts. Furthermore, the names of the classes do not facilitate their automatic manipulation by an ontology mapping algorithm. For these, reasons we propose a new generic and lightweight product ontology that covers only the basic and necessary information for every product.

The upper level of the shopbot product ontology is depicted in Figure 3. It should be noted that this ontology consists of a part of the Shopbot Ontology which contains classes for the description of the shopbot knowledge base. This ontology provides means for the semantic description of the entities with which the shopbot interacts in the market. The description of this ontology is out of the scope of the current paper. We have designed this generic ontology in order to be able to store the basic information related with every product available. In Figure 3, we can see that the main class of this ontology is the '*Product*'. The class '*Product*' has the following basic properties:

- Object Properties
  - **hasCategory:** Defines the category that the product belongs.
  - **hasManufacturer:** Defines the manufacturer of the product and through the class '*Manufacturer*' its properties (address, nick name, etc).
  - **hasProvider:** Defines the seller that sells the specific product.
  - **hasShipment:** Defines the regions in which the specific product is available.
- Datatype Properties
  - *hasCurrency*
  - *hasDescription*
  - *hasDiscount*
  - *hasName*

Figure 3. The upper classes level of the shopbot product ontology

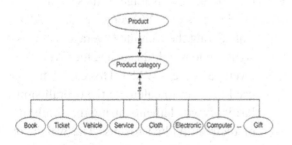

- *hasOriginCountry*
- *hasID*
- *hasPrice*
- *hasTimeValidity*

The 'hasTimeValidity' property is used to define a time interval for which the product is valid. After this time the shopbot does not take into consideration products with this field expired. The above consist of the basic information that a user may want to learn about a specific product.

At the second level, the most important concept is the 'ProductCategory'. This class has a number of sub-concepts one for every product category that we want to cover. These categories are very common in ecommerce sites. This class has a number of sub-classes each for every product category. For example, we can find a "Vehicle" class with properties that describe cars, motorcycles, etc. The depth depends on the developer's view on the specific domain. It should be noted that the properties defined for each sub-class are not the generic properties defined for the "Product" class. The main advantage of this architecture is that our proposed ontology can be extended very easily. Adding new sub categories under the "Product Category" class the ontology can store and represent new products in this new category.

SHOPBOT ONTOLOGY MATCHING ALGORITHM

In this section, we introduce the S^+, our proposed schema matching algorithm. The main functions of the S^+ are the classes and properties matching, and instances generation. In classes matching, the S^+ calculates the path (class-class) to the root of the ontology and then breaks the path to get individual tokens. The overall similarity is derived from the similarity between these tokens. The similarity value of the two classes is stored in a table called Class Similarity Matrix (CSM). Similarly, in properties matching we use a table called Property Similarity Matrix (PSM) for calculating the similarity of names, domains, and ranges of properties, respectively. After computing class and property similarity the S^+ updates the product ontology assigning instances from different ontologies providers with the help of CSM and PSM.

General Description

As said above, the matching and semantic translation processes are conducted between two ontologies. The Source Ontology (SO) is the ontology of the seller, which contains product data that we want to process. The Target Ontology or Product Ontology (PO) is the ontology of the shopbot, in which we gather data from various products and sellers for later use. It is obvious, that the PO should include as many characteristics of different products as possible, properly organized to facilitate the matching process and translation. Still, the PO should contain some stable properties to ensure the proper functionality of the algorithm. These properties are:

- **Default:** During the copying procedure of information from SO to PO, there can be some values that fit nowhere to be copied. Nevertheless, we must not lose any data when copying. So we use a property, the default property, in which we import values, which cannot be imported elsewhere in order not to lose them.
- **HasName:** Is used to store the name of the instance of the product we want to import.
- **HasSellerName:** In which the S^+ stores the name of the seller from whom the information for the product was received. The reason this information is stored is the likelihood of the same product existing from another seller. So, if a new product is to be imported in PO, the values of this property are checked. If they are same, we deduct that the product already exists in PO, from a previous match. So we renew

the values of the already existing instance with the ones exported from the new instance. If different, then the product is supplied by another seller and thus is stored as a different product.

- **HasPID:** Is used to store a number unique for each product, which characterizes it.

Please note that these properties are excluded from the process of matching, because they have specific values to be imported regardless of the property values of the SO instances. The proposed algorithm contains a combination of lexical and semantic techniques. These techniques include popular linguistic measures (Maedche and Staab, 2002; Jaro, 1989; Lin, 1989) and the strict semantic measures (Rodrigez and Egenhofer, 2003; Wu and Palmer, 1994).

Another item to mention is that the S^+ uses a tool called Similarity Matrix. The tool is used to provide fast and easy storage of the similarity values of different components (classes, properties, instances, or simple words) of ontologies, immediate recall of the similarity value between two elements and the ability to change or delete this value. Moreover, this tool also provides functions to select the most likely match, and calculate the overall similarity between two groups of elements. To calculate the overall similarity it considers every element of SO and withdraws the most likely match (i.e. with the largest value of similarity) from its matches with the elements of PO. Having, thus, a value corresponding to each element of SO, it can calculate the overall similarity of all elements in 3 ways:

- Calculating the average of these values for all elements of SO (Average Score – AS).
- Calculating the weighted average, i.e. it assigns some weight in each value (Weighted Average Score – WAS). This calculation is used in order to calculate the overall similarity of two elements, using the similarity of their individual tokens. The weight of each value is the number of symbols con-

tained in the token element of SO, divided by the number of symbols contained in all tokens of the element.

- Selects the highest similarity value, the greater value than those selected for each element of SO (Best Similarity – BS). In other words, it returns the greatest value in the array of Similarity Matrix.

Moreover, the S+ uses a technique to control weight named Weight Checking (WC). This technique, checks all the individual values of similarity before combining them, in order to deduct if they are valid. If one is not, it distributes its weight to the remaining valid, in order not to affect the combination. In other words, it excludes from the combination the values that are not valid, while ensuring that the sum of the weights of valid values is 1. A value is invalid if there is an error during its calculation (e.g. in the case of Name Matching improper use of the library WordNet). So we could say that the WC procedure is a function that processes the initial weights and the individual similarities, and returns weights to be used in the final combination of similarities.

In addition, there are some data the user provides to the algorithm for greater flexibility. One of these is an upper limit value, above which the program will accept a match, and would otherwise reject it. This limit must be of course between 0 and 1, as do the similarity values. The user also gives the name of a PO property, which will be used as the Default Property and will be excluded from the matching process.

The first step of the S+ is the initialization of weights which are to be used later. The weights are fixed and derived experimentally. Then the two ontologies, SO and PO are read, so that the S+ will be able to process their data. Once initialized the weights and opened the ontologies, the algorithm calculates the similarity of classes and properties by storing the results in CSM and PSM, respectively. Below, we present the details of these steps.

Classes Matching

In order to calculate the similarity between classes, CSM is initialized first. Then, for each pair of classes (one for each ontology) executes the following steps: It calculates the path (class-to-class) from the class in examination, to the root of the ontology. Then, it breaks the path in order to get the individual tokens that comprise it. Thus each class will include a number of words that characterize it, a bag of tokens. Finally, the resulting words are compared for every pair of classes in order to compute their similarity. The comparison is made using Class Token Similarity Matrix (CTSM). For each pair of words, one from each class, the S+ calculates the similarity by using the techniques mentioned in section above. The results/similarities of these techniques are combined together to compute an overall similarity to those bag of words, i.e. classes. The combination is calculated using the weights given by the user, after performing the WC operation. To calculate the overall similarity of two classes the function WAS is used. We use the average score because each word/token in the name of a class contains information relating that class, so it should affect the overall similarity calculation. In addition, there is a chance, two completely different classes, which should not match, to contain some common or similar words (so using a different technique such as the BS would result to a high similarity value which is wrong) but it is highly unlikely that all their words match (resulting their average- similarity value to decrease). Also, the average with weights is used, in order to decrease the influence of these similar words to the overall similarity (using a low weight). The resulting similarity value of the two classes is stored in CSM (See Listing 1).

Properties Matching

To calculate the similarity of properties, PMS is initialized first. Then, for each pair of properties (one from each ontology) the S+ executes the fol-

Listing 1. The class matching algorithm

```
Input: ProductOntologyClasses, SourceOntologyClasses, Weights
Output: ClassSimMatrix
Begin
  Initialize(ClassSimMatrix)
  Foreach ProductClass in ProductOntologyClasses
        Foreach SourceClass in SourceOntologyClasses
                GetClassPath(ProductClass)
                GetClassPath(SourceClass)
                Split(ProductClassPath)
                Split(SourceClassPath)
                Initialize(ClassTokenSimMatrix)
                ForEach HomeName in HomeTokens
                        ForEach TargetName in TargetTokens
                          CalculateSimilarity(HomeName,TargetName)
                          WeightCheck(SimilarityMetrics,Weights)
                          Calculate(WeightedSimResult)
                        EndFor
                        Update(ClassTokenSimMatrix)
                EndFor
                Calculate(ClassSimilarity)
        EndFor
        Update(ClassSimMatrix)
  EndFor
End
```

lowing steps: It Initially calculates the similarity of names of properties (NameSim). Then it calculates the similarity of their domain (DomainSim) and then the similarity of their ranges (RangeSim). Before calculating the overall similarity of the three values, it calculates an intermediate value (Median). The Median is computed using the equation:

$$Median = w_1 \cdot NameSim + w_2 \cdot DomainSim \tag{1}$$

where w1 and w2 are weights for name and domain similarity. In our experiments, we have used w1 equal to 0.4 and w2 equal to 0.6. If Median is above a given threshold (MedianThreshold), then the algorithm continues to compute the overall

similarity of the two properties in consideration, using the combination of their three similarities (NameSim, DomainSim, RangeSim). If it is below, the similarity value of two properties under consideration will be the median. In ontologies, if two properties don't have common or similar domain, there is very little chance to match. On the contrary, if they have a common domain, they may match or not, depending on the similarity of their names and ranges. If we assign a small value of weight in the domain similarity value, it is likely properties with different domain (thus not similar) to have a high similarity value due to similar names and ranges. If we assign a high value of weight in the domain similarity value, it is possible properties with similar domain to have high similarity, although their names and ranges don't match. So we use the intermediate value. If the two properties have similar domain, the median is above the MedianThreshold (because the weight 0.6 which is assigned to DomainSim is large enough to affect the value), so the S+ will continue to the combination of the three similarity values using the given weights (which for the same reasons assign a higher value of weight to the name and range similarity than the domain). If the two properties don't have similar domains, then the median is very small and below the MedianThreshold, so the similarity of these two properties would be low. Finally, the combination of the three values is computed using the weights given after the WeightCheck operation (See Listing 2).

The NameSim value is calculated in a manner similar to the similarity of classes: It first splits the names of properties in tokens just like the classes. Similarity values of these tokens will be stored in a new auxiliary array, Property Token Similarity Matrix (PTSM). In order to compute the similarity between them the same techniques are being used as in classes. Then, the weights are being checked using the WC procedure. Finally, the NameSim value is computed by using the WAS technique in the individual values of PTSM. The reason we use this technique, it is the same as in above. We must note here that the WAS technique is even more important at this point than that in classes because the names of properties are used to being written with a 'Is' or 'Has' prefix in front of them (See Listing 3).

To calculate the DomainSim of two properties, we first read all domains (direct i.e. the class which is assigned as domain by the definition of the property, and indirect i.e. all the subclasses of the direct domain) for each property. Here again a Similarity Matrix tool is being used, the Domain Similarity Matrix (DSM), which stores the similarities of their domains. These similarity values are read by the CSM. The overall similarity of domain properties is calculated using the technique BS on the DSM. That is, the DomainSim is the highest value of the array and not the average of all the values as the NameSim value. That is because, intuitively, in order for two properties to match, it is sufficient to have one common or similar domain class, even if the rest don't match. Conversely, even if we examine two similar prop-

Listing 2. The property comparison algorithm (general)

```
Input: ProductOntologyProperties, SourceOntologyProperties, Weights, Attrib-
uteWeights
Output: PropertySimMatrix
Begin
        ForEach ProductProperty in ProductOntologyProperties
            ForEach SourceProperty in SourceOntologyProperties
                CalculatePropertyNameSimilarity()
                CalculatePropertyDomainsSimilarity()
                CalculatePropertyRangesSimilarity()
                WeightCheck(SimilarityMetrics,AttributeWeights)
                Calculate(WeightedSimResult)
                Update(PropertySimMatrix,WeightedSimResult)
            EndFor
        EndFor
End
```

Listing 3. The property comparison algorithm (name)

```
Input: HomeObjectName, TargetObjectName, Weights
Output: ObjectSimilarity
Begin
        Split(HomeObjectName)
        Split(TargetObjectName)
        Initialize(TokenSimMatrix)
        ForEach HomeName in HomeTokens
                ForEach TargetName in TargetTokens
                        CalculateSimilarity(HomeName,TargetName)
                        WeightCheck (SimilarityMetrics, AttributeWeights)
                        Calculate(WeightedSimResult)
                    Update(TokenSimMatrix,WeightedSimResult)
                EndFor
        EndFor
        Return(BestSimilarityScore)
End
```

erties, it is unlikely for all their domains to match. So we use the BS technique to get the highest similarity value, which shows us the highest similarity between their domains (See Listing 4).

To calculate the RangeSim, we take into account three cases, depending on their range type:

- **The Two Properties are Both Object Properties:** In this case we get the ranges and act in a manner similar to calculating the similarity of the domain (Listing 4). That is, the ranges are being read (direct and indirect), their similarities are read from the CSM and stored in an auxiliary table, the Range_SimilarityMatrix. The RangeSim value is calculated with the BS technique for the same reasons as above.

- **One of the Properties is Object Property, While the Other is Datatype Property:** In this case we examine two other cases. If the Datatype property type is string, we assign an empirical constant value of similarity equal to 0.5. Otherwise it is equal to

0. The reason for singling out those cases is because it is likely to define the range of a property as an object (where you assign an instance as a value of the property which includes the various information about this object), but it is also likely to define the same property as a string simply because there aren't any information about this object (so there isn't any reason to define it as an object and can be represented as a name-string). Thus it is possible two properties with range objects and strings relatively can be similar. The reason we used the specific value of 0.5 is empirical. However, it is highly unlikely that there is a correspondence between an object and for e.g. an integer. That is why we used zero similarity in all the other cases.

- **Both Properties are Datatype Properties:** In this case their type is compared. If they are the same, the RangeSim is 1. If any of the types are string RangeSim is equal to 0.3 and 0 in any other case.

Listing 4. The property comparison algorithm (domain)

```
Input: ProductOntologyProperty, SourceOntologyProperty
Output: PropertySimilarity  //according to their domain
Begin
        GetDomain(ProductOntologyProperty)
        GetDomain(SourceOntologyProperty)
        Initialize(DomainSimMatrix)
        ForEach ProductDomain in ProductPropertyDomains
                ForEach SourceDomain in SourcePropertyDomains
                        GetSimilarity(ClassSimMatrix)
                        Update(DomainSimMatrix)
                EndFor
        Return(BestSimilarityScore)
End
```

Again we distinguish cases. The reason is that according to the creator of the ontology, for e.g. a value of salary could be defined as an integer or a string. The same applies to other types. In other words string type may include all other types of data. So we assign some similarity even if their types don't match, provided that at least one of them is of type string. Conversely, it is extremely unlikely that a salary value could be defined with a date format. So we give zero probability of similarity in cases where types don't match and none of them is of string format. The reason we use the value 0.3 in cases where one of them is string is still empirical (See Listing 5).

Instances Generation

The complete and as much possible, proper instance assign from SO to PO of product is a necessary function to achieve normalization of information from various sites on the Web. This assign composes a combination of other individual functions. Here, we describe these functions and how they are linked together in order to make the overall instances assignment possible.

Introduction-Initialization: At this step, the S^+ has computed the similarity values and matches between the elements and stored them in CSM and PSM. The final step of the algorithm is the assignment of instances of the SO to PO with the help of the two tables. In order to make the assignment, the algorithm initially reads the two tables to extract the most likely matches according to the similarity values of each table. This task uses the value of the upper limit mentioned above. We must be careful to maintain the completeness of the assignment, that is, we must copy all information contained in SO to PO. In order to preserve the completeness (because using the upper limit it is possible a class of SO not to match with a class of PO and therefore its instances cannot be copied to the PO), in the end, all instances of classes not matched will be copied to the Default Property. Thus, the algorithm at this step, stores all likely matches of classes and properties for later use, and rejects the rest matches.

Instances Assignment: The next step of the S^+ is to perform a search in some of the matches found during the initialization phase, and namely

Listing 5. The property comparison algorithm (range)

```
Input:ProductOntologyProperty, SourceOntologyProperty
Output: PropertySimilarity   //according to their range
Begin
        If Both Properties are Object Properties Then
                GetRange(ProductOntologyProperty)
                GetRange(SourceOntologyProperty)
                Initialize(RangeSimMatrix)
                Foreach ProductRange in ProductPropertyRanges
                        Foreach SourceRange in SourcePropertyRanges
                                Get(SimilarityValue, ClassSimMatrix)
                                Update(RangeSimMatrix)
                        EndFor
                                        EndFor
                                        Return(BestSimilarityScore)
                        Else If One is ObjectProperty and the other
is
                                        DatatypeProperty Then
                                If DatatypeProperty.RangeType is
String Then
                                                        Return(0.5)
                                Else
                                                        Return(0.0)
                                EndIf
                        Else If both are DatatypeProperties Then
                                If both RangeTypes are equal Then
                                                        Return(1.0)
                                Else If one of the RangeTypes is
String Then
                                                        Return(0.3)
                                Else
                                                        Return(0.0)
                        EndIf
        EndIf
    End
```

the elements of the PO, to find if there is any class that is subclass of the ProductCategory class. If found, then this class or classes concern the new products we want to add in PO. So we read all their instances, which will be added later as new instances of the Product class. If no such classes are found, or if they don't have any instance, the execution of the algorithm will end. Therefore the purpose of this phase is to find all individuals contained in SO, which refer directly to products, and will be later inserted in PO. Exactly how this insertion is made will be introduced introduced in Listing 6.

Listing 6. Instance assignment algorithm (general)

```
Input: ProductOntology, SourceOntology, SellerName
Output: Updated ProductOntology
Begin
        Get MatchedClasses()
        Get MatchedProperties()
        Foreach Pair in MatchedClasses
                If ProductOntologyClass.isSubclass(ProductCategory) Then
                        Get all instances from the SourceOntologyClass
                        Foreach instance in Instances
                                CreateNewProductInstance(Instance)
                        EndFor
                EndIf
        EndFor
End
```

New Product Creation: To create a new product instance in PO an instance exported from SO is needed. Which instance exactly and how it is extracted is presented in the previous section (Listing 6).

The first step of product creation is a checking process whether this particular product already exists in our ontology (Name Check) from the same source (Source Check). The reason we use these two checks, is because the same product can be available from two different sources with different information. Thus, they must be addressed as two different products. Only if they have the same name (the same product) and seller (available from the same source), we assume that the product already exists in our ontology and is not needed to create a new instance. In this case, the values of the existing instance are updated with the values of the new instance. This is because the seller may have renewed the information contained in the instance from the previous time we copied these data, e.g. the price may have been changed and we should keep only the latest values. If the two checks don't return any result, we deduct that the product does not exist in PO and a new instance of the product class must therefore be created. This instance will be used to import its property values from SO. If instead, the search found an instance, it will be used to renew its property values.

In the event that we have created a new instance, before proceeding to copying its property values from SO, we must assign some values in its stable properties. These properties are: "hasPID" where we assign the product's ID as value, "hasName" where we assign the name of the instance from SO as its value and finally "hasSellerName" where we assign the seller name/location as its value.

As a next step, we read all properties of the Product class. For each one of them, we read its matched property (matchProp) using the matches extracted in the Introduction-Initialization phase. We examine two cases depending on whether a matchProp is found or not: If a matchProp is found, then a search is performed to find its domain instance. We need this instance, in order to extract the property's value so that we can later add it to the Product's instance's property which matches with matchProp. Once the instance is found, we proceed to copying the values from matchProp to the product property using the assign functions of properties described below, depending on the type of their ranges. If a matchProp is not found, we consider two cases: If the product property is an Object or a Datatype property. If it is a Datatype property, the execution of the algorithm ends here, since there is no value to be copied to the property. So, we move on to the next property of the Product class. If it is an Object property, we try to carry out the assignment by checking the classes that constitute the range of the two properties. In particular, we read the range (direct and indirect) of the object property of the PO and find the classes that match with some of those contained in SO. If no class matches, then there is no value to be copied and therefore we again move on to the next property of the Product class. If matching classes are found, we continue by reading their instances. But since, we read all the instances of those classes, they may not all have something to do with the product we want to import and may concern other products which are already imported or will be imported later. So, we must sort out the instances to keep only those related directly or indirectly to the product whose information we are importing. To do this, we use a function which scans and finds all instances associated with an instance of the SO product that we want to import. When this function ends we will either have the instance to be assigned as value of the property of the new product, or else this cycle ends and we move to the next product property. The only thing remaining is to find the exact this new instance will be created to. This class is found by taking the domain class of the SO instance, and finding the corresponding class of PO by using the matches. We must note here that we are certain we there will be a corresponding class and do not check the case there isn't, because the instance this class has, was found by the reverse procedure.

Finally, the assignment is made using the "Assign Instance to Class" function, which essentially copies a given instance to a new instance in this class, in a manner similar to the creation of a new product we are dealing with now. Exactly how this is done will be examined in more details below

(Listing 8). The "New Product Creation" function returns the instance which was just created, or updated. So the only thing remaining is to assign this instance as value to the product property we are examining, and our goal is achieved.

Before we perform this assignment, we should check if the instance already exists as a property value (probably with older and perhaps outdated values in its own). This check is performed by taking all its values and comparing them with those of the new instance. If any value is found different during this process, it is deleted so that the new value can be assigned.

Assign Instance to Class: Here, in order to make the assignment, we consider given an instance of SO and a class of PO. The purpose of this function is to create a new instance of the PO class, which contains all the information (name, property values) the given instance has. Which are the given instances and classes and how they are chosen, appears wherever this function is called. The "Assign Instance to Class" procedure is similar to the "New Product Creation" procedure which was explained above (Listing 7). As in the new product creation, a new instance must be created or an old one updated. Then the algorithm checks all the properties which contain data of the SO instance as follows: If the property of the SO matches with a property of PO, then the values from the first are copied to the second. While copying, we must respect their value types (if they are Datatype properties, object properties, exactly what type of Datatype properties). The various cases and how the data copying is made are described later. If the property of the SO doesn't match with a property of PO, and contains data, this information is imported in the Default Property of the instance newly created/updated.

Assignment from a Datatype Property to a Datatype Property: In this assignment, as in any property assignment, we read a value from a property belonging to the SO (Copy Property), and copied to a property of the PO (Paste Property). In this case, the value extracted must be

Listing 7. Instance assignment algorithm (new product creation)

```
Input: ProductInstance
Output: Updated ProductOntology
Begin
        If ProductInstance.exists Then
                Get(ProductInstance)
        Else
                Create(ProductID)
                Create(ProductInstance)
                Fill(ProductGenericProperties)
                Get new ProductInstance
        EndIf
        ForEach Property in ProductProperties
                GetBestMatch(PropertySimMatrix)
                If  SourceMatchedProperty != null Then
                        GetSourceInstance(SourceMatchedProperty)
                        If SourceInstance != null Then
                                If  Property is ObjectProperty Then
                                        If  SourceMatchedProperty is
                                                ObjectProperty Then
                                                ObjectProp2ObjectProp()
                                        Else
                                                DatatypeProp2ObjectProp()
                                        EndIf
                                Else
                                        If  SourceMatchedProperty is
                                                ObjectProperty Then
                                                ObjectProp2DatatypeProp()
                                        Else
                                                DatatypeProp2DatatypeProp()
                                        EndIf
                                EndIf
                        EndIf
                Else If Property is ObjectProperty Then
                                GetPropertyRanges()
                                GetMatchedClasses(PropertyRanges)
                                AssignInstance2Class(ClassesInstances)
                EndIf
        EndFor
End
```

Listing 8. Instance assignment algorithm (assignment to a class)

```
Input: Instance, Class
Output: Updated ProductOntology
BeginIf  Instance.exists in ProductOntology Then
        If Instance.seller <> SourceInstance.seller Then
            Change(InstanceName)
            Create the new instance
        EndIf
     Else
        Create new Instance()
     EndIf
     Foreach Property in InstanceProperties
Get(BestSmilarityScore,PropertySimMatrix)
        If Property is ObjectProperty Then
            If SourceMatchedProperty is ObjectProperty
                Then
                ObjectProp2ObjectProp()
            Else
                ObjectProp2DatatypeProp()
            EndIf
        Else
            If SourceMatchedProperty is ObjectProperty
                Then
                DatatypeProp2ObjectProp()
            Else
                DatatypeProp2DatatypeProp()
            EndIf
        EndIf
EndFor
Update(ProductOntology,Instance)
End
```

first converted to the Datatype of the property of the PO. The data may be an integer, a float, a string, a Boolean value or have special form for dates, time etc. To make the conversion, we use an intermediate stage of the string. When reading the values in whatever form they are, we first convert them to a string. Similarly, before importing values to a property they must be converted from a string, to the format of the property range datatype. This intermediate stage is used because

for e.g. an integer format cannot be converted to a date format, but with this intermediate step the problem is eliminated. If however a problem arises with the conversions and the values cannot be converted to the proper format, they are imported in the Default Property in order not to lose the data. So initially, we read the value contained in Copy Property. If it contains a valid value, we consider two cases: if the Paste Property is also the Default Property, and the opposite case. If the

Paste Property is also the Default Property, the value to be imported is not just the value copied. It should contain more information for instance the class from which it originated and the property to which it belongs. Otherwise, we will have scattered information, with no use. In our algorithm the value to be imported will be in the form *Class_Property:Value*. Thus, it will contain enough information about the reference of this value. Before importing the new value, we will have to check if a value with the same origination already exists. The origin is checked by reading at the first two information of the value to be imported, that is: *Class_Property*. So if a value containing these information exists, that means that a value has been imported in the past from the same property (with a surpassed value). So we delete the older value, and import the newest one. In the opposite case where the Paste Property is not the Default Property, we first check if the paste property has a previous value or if it's empty. If empty, we simply add the new value. If a previous value exists, we examine two cases: If we add new values and a value already exists, then probably the old value is from another property of SO matching this property of PO and we need both old and new values. That is because many properties of SO can be matched to a property of PO. And since they contain different information we should not lose any of them, so we essentially unite them to one value. In particular, we first check if the existing value has as a substring the new value, and if it does, there is no reason to re-add it so this function ends. If it doesn't, we unite the old with the new value in the form: *OldValue_New_Value*.

Assignment from a Datatype Property to an Object Property: In order to make the assignment from a Datatype property (copy property) to an object property (paste property), a new instance should essentially be created and assigned as value of paste property with null property values and the Datatype value as its name. Its properties will necessarily remain empty since copy property

doesn't have any more data than the value which will be used as the instance's name. So as a first step we read the value of the copy property which will be converted to string format as said above.

Prior to the new instance creation we will have to check if there is any existing value (instance) in the paste property as well as whether there exists any instance having as name the value we extracted from the copy property (remember that the definition of ontology does not allow us to add items that have the same name as an existing, each element name must be unique). If an instance with the same name exists, then the execution of this function ends here. If there is an existing value in paste property, we again examine two sub-cases: If we perform the update procedure, previous values are deleted and the newest is added. Else, the previous value possibly is from a previous match of the PO property with another SO property so we combine the two values just like the Datatype to Datatype assignment before. Before combining the two values however, we should check if the newest value is a sub-string of the oldest. If it is, the execution of this function is ended. If not, then the value to be added will be in the form: *OldValue_NewValue*. As above, if there is not an already existing value, the new value is added.

Assignment from an Object Property to a Datatype Property: In this case, we must convert the information contained in an instance to a Datatype value in order to import them to the paste property. This conversion will be in the form of string just like in previous property assignments. In addition, it has to be done in a way, so that we will not lose any data contained in the instance. So the instance is read, and a string is created with its name. Then we read all its properties. For each one we get the following cases: If the property is Datatype, we add in the existing string the string with the form: *_PropertyName:PropertyValue*. If the property is object, the string to be added has the form *_PropertyName:NextString* where the term *NextString* corresponds to the result of exactly the same operation described for the instance/

value of *PropertyName* property. An example follows for better understanding of the process: Suppose we have a class '*car*' with an instance 'FiatPunto', which should be imported in an object property. This class has two properties. One of them is an object property named 'hasConstructor' with range to class 'Constructor' which has a Datatype property named 'telephone'. The other is a Datatype property named 'CC'. We assume now that the instance 'FiatPunto' is connected with an instance of 'Constructor' named 'Fiat' via the 'hasConstructor' property. The 'telephone' property of 'Fiat' is 555, and the 'CC' property of 'FiatPunto' has value: 1300. So the string conversion is created as follows: We start with the name of the instance, so the string will be 'FiatPunto'. Then we get the properties and check if they are object or datatype properties. The 'CC' property is datatype, so it will be converted to: '_CC:1300' and added to the first string which will now be: 'FiatPunto_CC:1300'. Next, the algorithm will check the next property of 'FiatPunto' which will be the 'hasConstructor' which is an object property. So it will take the specific value, and compute the corresponding string recursively as follows: It will read all the properties, ('telephone'), it will check the type of this property (Datatype) and construct the string corresponding to these properties ('_telephone:555'). Next, it will add it to its instance string so the string computed will be: 'Fiat_telephone:555'. Finally, it will add this string to the first one, and the final string computed will be: 'FiatPunto_CC:1300_hasConstructor:Fiat_telephone:555'. Using this technique all information of the instance will be read and converted to a string without any loss of data. Once we have calculated the value to be imported, the next steps for this assignment is similar to the assignment of a Datatype property to a Datatype property. In both cases, the steps are the same. The only thing changing is how we get the data. We must note here that due to the data form, the new value cannot be converted to

a Datatype form different of string. Thus, if the Datatype is of different form (e.g. integer) the value cannot be added to the paste property so it is added to the default property instead.

Assignment from an Object Property to an Object Property: In this case we need to transfer data from one instance to another. At first the instance/value of copy property is read. Next, the instance/value of paste property is read. If there are any instance in paste property, delete them in order to import the new value. The next step is to find the class in which the new instance will be created. To do this, we must read the range (which is a class) of paste property – direct range – and all its sub-classes – indirect range. We do this because if a class has a property, the property is inherited to the sub-classes of the original. However we cannot know to which of all the classes (direct and indirect range) the new instance should be created. So we compare the name of each class with the name of the instance/value of copy property, using the same techniques we used in NameSim while comparing classes or properties. Finally, we choose the class with the highest similarity value, as a candidate to import the new instance. If its value is greater than the upper limit given by the user then this is the class that the new instance will be imported. If it is lower, the instance will be created in the class of direct range. Then the function 'Assign Instance to Class' (Listing 8) is called given the instance/value of copy property and the class chosen above. This function returns the newly created instance (which is a copy of the given instance to the PO). The final step of this function is to assign the new instance as a value in paste property. Otherwise, the previous value possibly is from a previous match of the PO property with another SO property so we combine the two values just like the Datatype to Datatype assignment before. Before combining the two values however, we should check if the newest value is a sub-string of the oldest. If it is, the execution of this function is ended. If not, then the value to be added will be in the form: *OldValue_NewValue*. As stated previously, if there is not an already existing value, the new value is added.

EVALUATION

In this section, we present our experimental results depicting the performance of the S⁺ algorithm. The efficiency of our model is revealed by using a comparison of the S⁺ with several other matching algorithms proposed in the literature.

Experimental Setup

We compare the S⁺ with the following algorithms (Table 1):

- Nom (Ehrig and Sure, 2004)
- Crosi (Kalfoglou and Hu, 2005)
- Cupid (Madhavan et al., 2001)
- Anchor-Prompt(Noy, 2001)

We compare the PO, our product ontology, with one of the other two ontologies from different EMs, the book ontology from Amazon, and vehicle ontology from a vehicle EM. Each algorithm read the PO and the SO and process their data. As mentioned, each algorithm uses also several linguistic and semantic measures. This measures use weights that are derived from our experimental study. More specifically, in properties matching we use an intermediate value

Table 1. Parameters and values of the experiments

Parameters	Values
Algorithm	S⁺, Nom, Crosi, Cupid, Anchor-Prompt
Ontology	Product, Amazon Book, Vehicle
Ontological component	Class, Property
Threshold:	0.8(Classes), 0.78(Properties)

(Median). Furthermore, we set a threshold, an upper limit value, above which the program will accept a match, and would otherwise reject it. In our scenario the threshold for classes matching is equal to 0.8 and for properties matching is equal to 0.78. Finally, we calculate WAS in order to find the overall similarity between ontological components. We take similarity results for classes and properties matching.

The evaluation is based on widely known retrieval measures, precision, recall, and F-measure (Euzenat, 2007). For each algorithm's results, we calculate these metrics. More specifically, precision describes the number of correct found matches in comparison to the total number of found matches. Recall describes the number of correct found matches in comparison to the number of relevant matches. F-measure is a metric that combines both precision and recall discussed above. These metrics are defined as follows:

Precision:

$$\frac{|\{relevant\ documents\} \cap \{retrieved\ documents\}|}{|\{retrieved\ documents\}|} \quad (2)$$

Recall:

$$\frac{|\{relevant\ documents\} \cap \{retrieved\ documents\}|}{relevant\ documents} \quad (3)$$

F-measure:

$$\frac{2 \times Precision \times Recall}{(Precision + Recall)} \quad (4)$$

Results

We study two different scenarios according to the SO. In the first scenario, we examine instances defined by the Amazon book ontology and in the second scenario we take instances defined by the vehicle ontology.

Scenario 1: Amazon Book Ontology

As mentioned in this scenario we try to match ontological components defined by our product ontology with instances created by the book ontology of Amazon. We take results for classes and properties matching.

Figure 4 show that almost all algorithms have good results when matching classes. The algorithm calculates the similarity between classes, and if the similarity score is above the defined threshold it returns a matching. The matching can be correct, book – book, or wrong, book – vehicle. In this scenario the only correct and existing matching is book – book. We see that the S$^+$, Nom, Crosi, and Anchor-Prompt have large metrics' values. This happens because book classes of both ontologies have identical notation, and, thus, large linguistic and semantic similarity. However, we see that Cupid algorithm has not as good results as the rest of the algorithms. The reason is that Cupid returns one wrong matching result between classes, author – manufacturer.

Property matching differs from the classes matching results as shown in Figure 5. The algorithm calculates the similarity between properties, and if the similarity score is above or equal to 0.78 it returns a matching. We see that all algorithms used for properties matching have low recall, and, thus low F-measure. The reason is

Figure 5. Results for Amazon ontology properties

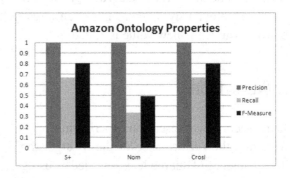

that the number of correct matches is lower than the number of existing matching. For properties the correct matches are price-hasPrice, title-hasTitle, hasAuthors-hasAuthor. All algorithms do not manage to find all these correct matches therefore recall metric is low. S$^+$ and Crosi have the same good performance.

Scenario 2: Vehicle Ontology

In this scenario, we try to match instances defined by a vehicle ontology derived from a vehicle EM with the ontological terms of the PO. For classes the correct matches are vehicle-vehicle, car-vehicle, and motorcycle-vehicle.

As shown in Figure 6, in this scenario Cupid and Anchor-Prompt have better performance. The other algorithms do not return all the correct matches, therefore, the recall metric is low. Nom

Figure 4. Results for Amazon ontology classes

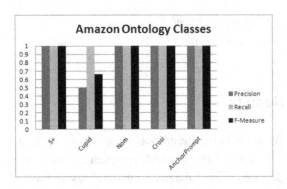

Figure 6. Results for vehicle ontology classes

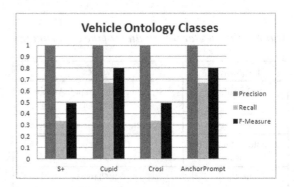

uses only one linguistic measure, therefore, does not find any matching between classes. For this reason we do not depict Nom results.

In Figure 7, we show the result for properties matching. In this case the correct matches are color-hasColor, region – hasRegion, price – hasPrice, country – hasOriginCountry, manufacturer – isManufacturer. Neither S+ nor Crosi manage to find all the correct matches. More specifically, Crosi present low metrics' values for the same reason mentioned above. Crosi presents not such good results due to the weight it uses for calculating property similarity (name, domain, and range check). As discussed in our approach, there should be a check for the property domains. If the property domains have high similarity score, the weight of this value will be low, otherwise will be high. Thus, if the domains do not match, the classes will not match. If the domains match, the algorithm will continue in order to find the range similarity. Crosi does not have this particular check, thus, has not so good performance. Furthermore, in our experiments Nom algorithm does not have satisfied results therefore we are not able to calculate any of the metrics.

In conclusion, we see that for classes and properties matching, the S^+ has good performance. More specifically, in classes matching, the S^+ uses a set of measures for calculating linguistic and semantic similarity. On the other hand, Nom is based on only one similarity measures, thus, does not return many correct matches. For the same reason, Cupid has some significant problems. Cupid uses only one linguistic similarity measure so it is mainly based on the semantic similarity. Thus, algorithms that are appropriate for schema matching on ontologies should have a set of measures for linguistic and semantic similarity.

FUTURE RESEARCH DIRECTIONS

Although we believe that we have made a progress on the schema matching problem, we do not claim that we have solved it. In this current

Figure 7. Results for vehicle ontology properties

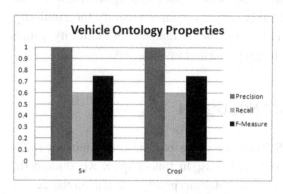

study, we cannot draw any conclusions about the performance of algorithms in general cases. However, we can draw conclusion only for the specific scenario that we mentioned. The main reason is the lack of sufficient datasets oriented in electronic marketplace environment. However, in this specific scenario the S^+ presented satisfied results. Our future goal is to extend our approach using other ontologies such as UnspscOWL and eclassOWL, mentioned above trying to provide a more generic solution. More attention needed in order to store data to the PO from different SOs. In the current study, we used a generic ontology. The design of this ontology is not subject to any conventions, thus, the provider is able to build a completely different structure. Therefore, further investigation is necessary in order to find a standard structure for the generic ontology.

Another future direction is the study of weights assignment. In this chapter, we used fixed weights in order to calculate the similarity. However, the values can be optimal for one application but for another can have an inverse result. In our study, we use weights that produce satisfied matches in all experiments. However, using methods that assign weights dynamically, related to the application, we will have better performance.

Our future goal is also the investigation of similarity values for checking the range of properties. In current study when both properties of the PO and the SO are object type the check is normal. However, if one Datatype is integer and the other is sting, respectively, the checking becomes difficult. In this case, we cannot quantify the similarity. Therefore, the assignment of similarity values should be further investigated.

CONCLUSION

Schema matching is a basic problem for many research areas. In this chapter, we studied the schema-matching problem in E-Commerce and Semantics Web domains. More specifically, we presented the behavior of shopbots when dealing with different ontologies in order to retrieve product information. In our specific scenario, shopbots interact with sellers in order to retrieve ontological information and update accordingly the generic product ontology that we propose. In addition, we presented the S+, a new matching algorithm, designed for shopbots acting in EMs. We described the main functionality of the S+, that are classes and properties matching, and instances assignment of the SO to the PO. In the experimental evaluation, we compared the performance of the S+ using several proposed schema-matching algorithms. The results were satisfied and demonstrated the strengths of our approach.

We draw the following conclusions from our experiments. Using more than one linguistic and semantic similarity techniques, we achieve better performance. In properties matching, the use of the intermediate value (Median) for calculating the overall similarity can affect the performance of the algorithm. Finally, the check of different ontological components is necessary for evaluating the performance of algorithm.

REFERENCES

Choi, N., Song, I. Y., & Han, H. (2006). A survey on ontology mapping. *SIGMOD Recommendations, 35*(3), 34–41. doi:10.1145/1168092.1168097.

Ehrig, M., & Sure, Y. (2004). Ontology mapping - An integrated approach. In *Proceedings of The Semantic Web: Research and Applications, First European Semantic Web Symposium* (pp. 76-91). Heraklion, Greece: IEEE.

Euzenat, J. (2007). Semantic precision and recall for ontology alignment evaluation. In *Proceedings of the 20th International Joint Conference on Artificial Intelligence*. Hyderabad, India: IEEE.

Fasli, M. (2006). Shopbots: A syntactic present, a semantic future. In *Proceedings of IEEE Internet Computing* (pp. 69-75). IEEE.

Greenwald, A. R., & Kephart, J. O. (1999). Shopbots and pricebots. In *Proceedings of the 16th International Joint Conference on Artificial Intelligence*. Stockholm, Sweden: IEEE.

Hirst, G., & St. Onge, D. (1998). Lexical chains as representations of context for the detection and correction of malapropisms. In Fellbaum, C. (Ed.), *WordNet: An Electronic Lexical Database* (pp. 305–332). Boston: MIT Press.

Jaccard. (1912). The distribution of the flora of the alpine zone. *New Phychologist, 11,* 37-50.

Jaro, M. A. (1989). Advances in record linking methodology as applied to the 1985 census of Tampa Florida. *Journal of the American Statistical Society, 64,* 1183–1210.

Kalfoglou, Y., & Schorlemmer, M. (2003). Ontology mapping: The state of the art. *The Knowledge Engineering Review, 18*(1), 1–31. doi:10.1017/S0269888903000651.

Kephart, J. O., & Greenwald, A. R. (1999). Shopbot economics. In *Proceedings of the 3rd Annual Conference on Autonomous Agents* (pp. 378-379). Seattle, WA: IEEE.

Leacock, C., & Chodorow, M. (1998). Combining local context and WordNet similarity for word sense identification. In Fellbaum, C. (Ed.), *WordNet: An Electronic Lexical Database* (pp. 265–283). Boston: MIT Press.

Lin, D. (1998). An information-theoretic definition of similarity. In *Proceedings of the 15th International Conf. on Machine Learning* (pp. 296–304). San Francisco: Morgan Kaufmann.

Maedche, A., & Staab, S. (2001). *Comparing ontologies: Similarity measures and a comparison study*. Paper presented at the Institute of AIFB. Karlsruhe, Germany.

Maedche, A., & Staab, S. (2002). Measuring similarity between ontologies. In *Proceedings of the 13th International Conference on Knowledge Engineering and Knowledge Management* (pp. 251-263). Singuenza, Spain: IEEE.

Monge, A. E., & Elkan, C. P. (1996). The field matching problem: Algorithms and applications. In *Proceedings of the Second International Conference on Knowledge Discovery and Data Mining*. IEEE.

Montgomery, A. L., Hosanagar, K., Krishnan, R., & Clay, K. B. (2004). Designing a better shopbot. *Management Science, 50*(2), 189–206. doi:10.1287/mnsc.1030.0151.

Needleman, S. B., & Wunch, C. D. (1970). Needleman - Wunch algorithm for sequence similarity searches. *Journal of Molecular Biology, 48*, 443–453. doi:10.1016/0022-2836(70)90057-4 PMID:5420325.

Noy, N. F. (2001). Anchor-PROMPT: Using non-local context for semantic matching. In *Proceedings of the Workshop on Ontologies and Information Sharing at the International Joint Conference on Artificial Intelligence* (pp. 63-70). IEEE.

Palmer, D. D. (1997). A trainable rule-based algorithm for word segmentation. In *Proceedings of the 35th Annual Meeting on Association for Computational Linguistics* (pp. 321-328). Madrid, Spain: ACL.

Rodriguez, M. A., & Egenhofer, M. J. (2003). Determining semantic similarity among entity classes from different ontologies. *IEEE Transactions on Knowledge and Data Engineering*. doi:10.1109/TKDE.2003.1185844.

Shvaiko, P., & Euzenat, J. (2005). A survey of schema-based matching approaches. *Journal on Data Semantics, 3730*, 146–171.

Smith, M. D. (2002). The impact of shopbots on electronic markets. *Journal of the Academy of Marketing Science, 30*(4), 446–454. doi:10.1177/009207002236916.

Smith, T. F., & Waterman, M. S. (1981). Identification of common molecular subsequences. *Journal of Molecular Biology, 147*, 195–197. doi:10.1016/0022-2836(81)90087-5 PMID:7265238.

Winkler, W. E. (1990). String comparator metrics and enhanced decision rules in the Fellegi-Sunter model of record linkage. In *Proceedings of the Section on Survey Research Methods, American Statistical Association* (pp. 354-359). ASA.

Winkler, W. E. (1999). The state of record linkage and current research problems. In *Proceedings of the Survey Methods Section,* (pp. 73-79). IEEE.

Wu, Z., & Palmer, M. (1994). Verb semantics and lexical selection. In *Proceedings of the 32nd Annual Meeting of the Association for Computational Linguistics* (pp. 133–138). Las Cruces, NM: ACL.

ADDITIONAL READING

Bernstein, P. A., Melnik, S., Petropoulos, M., & Quix, C. (2004). Industrial-strength schema matching. *SIGMOD Record, 33*, 38–43. doi:10.1145/1041410.1041417.

Clifton, C., Hausman, E., & Rosenthal, A. (1997). Experience with a combined approach to attribute-matching across heterogeneous databases. In *Proceedings of the 7th IFIP Conference on DB Semantics*. IFIP.

Evermann, J. (2009). Theories of meaning in schema matching: An exploratory study. *Journal in Information Systems, 34*.

Fensel, D., van Harmelen, F., Horrocks, I., Mc-Guiness, D. L., & Patel-Schneider, P. F. (2001). OIL: An ontology infrastructure for the semantic web. *Journal in Intelligent Systems, 16*(2), 38–45. doi:10.1109/5254.920598.

Miller, R. J. Haas, & Hernández. (2000). Schema mapping as query discovery. In *Proceedings of the 26th International Conference on Very Large Databases* (pp. 77–88). Cairo, Egypt: IEEE.

Mork, P., & Bernstein, P. A. (2004). Adapting a generic match algorithm to align ontologies of human anatomy. In *Proceedings of the 20th International Conference on Data Engineering* (pp. 787-790). Boston: IEEE.

Nandi, A., & Bernstein, P. A. (2009). HAMSTER: Using search clicklogs for schema and taxonomy matching. In *Proceedings of the VLDB Endowment* (vol. 2). VLDB.

Rahm, E., & Bernstein, P. A. (2001). A survey of approaches to automatic schema matching. *The VLDB Journal*, 334–350. doi:10.1007/s007780100057.

Smiljanic, M., van Keule, M., & Jonker, W. (2006). Effectiveness bounds for non-exhaustive schema matching systems. In *Proceedings of the 22nd International Conference on Data Engineering*. IEEE.

Unal, O., & Afsarmanesh, H. (2006). Using linguistic techniques for schema matching. In *Proceedings of 1st International Conference on Software and Data Technologies* (pp. 115–120). IEEE.

KEY TERMS AND DEFINITIONS

Class Similarity Matrix (CSM): Array used for storing similarity scores for classes of ontologies.

Electronic Marketplace (EM): A location in the Internet (open environment) where companies, sellers, disseminate information that customers, buyers, can retrieve.

Ontology: A set of representational components for describing and modeling knowledge. Ontology includes a number of concepts in a domain and relations between them. Ontologies are the key for the emergence of the Semantic Web.

Property Similarity Matrix (PSM): Array used for storing similarity scores for properties of ontologies.

S+ Algorithm: A schema matching algorithm for shopbot agents acting in marketplaces. S^+ is used in a specific scenario where shopbots interact with providers' ontologies for retrieving information.

Schema Matching: A basic problem in many domains. This problem refers to the difficulty of defining correspondences between two schemata.

Semantic Web (SW): A mesh of information that is easily understandable by machines. It is simply a way to represent information in Web. SW allows data to be shared across applications using a common framework.

Shopbot (Shopping Robot): Intelligent agent that help users, buyers or sellers, to find products according to her preferences. These agents obtain information about prices and other attributes of goods and service.

ENDNOTES

[1]   http://www.unspsc.org/
[2]   http://www.eclass-online.com/
[3]   http://www.eccma.org/whyeotd.php
[4]   http://www.rosettanet.org/TheStandards/tabid/287/Default.aspx
[5]   http://www.heppnetz.de/projects/eclassowl/

Chapter 5
A Multi–Agent System for Improving the Resource Allocation on Programmes in Higher Education

Constanta-Nicoleta Bodea
Academy of Economic Studies, Romania

Radu-Ioan Mogos
Academy of Economic Studies, Romania

ABSTRACT

The chapter presents UNIRA, a multi-agent system developed by the authors for a Romanian university in order to improve the resources allocation for educational programmes and courses. Different types of resources are required to deliver programmes and courses. Considering a set of resources inquires, issued by programmes and courses, UNIRA system performs a transparent negotiation process between the managers of these resources, to find the solution for the allocation problem. During the initial stage of the multi-agent system deployment, only two types of resources are considered, professors and teaching rooms. The system is now in the validation phase. After the complete validation, the system will be integrated into the university management system. The UNIRA experience is relevant not exclusively for the academic resources management, but also for a large variety of domains, including the load distribution, production planning, computer scheduling, portfolio selection, and apportionment.

INTRODUCTION

The Bucharest Academy of Economic Studies (AES) is the most prestigious institution of higher economic and public administration education in Romania (www.ase.ro). AES has 11 faculties, over 30.000 students and 1600 didactical and administrative personnel. In 2011-2012, the university delivers 182 education & training programmes, based on a public budget, coming from the Education and Research Ministry, and also based on its own resources.

DOI: 10.4018/978-1-4666-4038-2.ch005

Academic staff is the most important resource of the university. Without experienced and qualified professors and trainers, the educational programmes and courses cannot be successful delivered. Other important resources are proper equipped rooms, educational software, secretarial staff and financial resources. Only a small part of the activities are performs by the departments using their own resources. Most of resources are asked from other departments of the university. The resources allocation process is a negotiation process between departments of the faculty or between faculties. The university has an Enterprise Resource Planning (ERP) system in place. The information about the resources required for the delivery the education & training programmes are organized as a database, administered by the Educational Programmes Department, part of the ERP system. Even if the university is using this system, the resource allocation process is still done outside the ERP, because it is not able to perform negotiation-like processes.

RESOURCES ALLOCATION PROBLEM AND THE SOLVING APPROACHES

The resource allocation problem (RAP) is how to allocate available resources to the clients (scheduled tasks or agents, either cooperative or self-interested) in a way which maximizes the global utility (Dolgov & Durfee, 2006). RAP is relevant in many domains, such as: sociology and marketing (for ranking different objects according to consumers' economic social preferences), product design, architecture and construction, operations, network routing, transportation logistics, bandwidth allocation and commercial transactions, just to name a few. The real-world applications usually work in complex environments, with high dimensionality, dynamic, non-cooperative and uncertain, which make RAP even more complex and difficult.

RAP is expressed as a Constraint Satisfaction Problem (CSP). RAP can be easily mapped into a list-coloring problem in a special kind of graphs called interval graphs. In this case, RAP is called restricted coloring or feasible coloring problem. It is known that the usual graph-coloring problem in interval graphs is linear, but the list coloring is NP-complete (Choueiry & Faltings, 1994). As an optimization problem, RAP is a multi-objective and over-constrained problem. Even if the optimality is rarely needed in the real-world situations, the optimal solution is expected by the users. For solving RAP, a centralized or distributed approach could be undertaken. A Distributed Constraint Optimization Problem (DCOP) is more adequate in a large problem space. In this case, the problem is split into agents, each of them having a specific set of variables and constraints as well as local optimization criterion. The goal is to find a feasible solution with the highest ranking by all agents (Ridder, Brett, & Signori, 2012).

Developing academic class timetable is a real-world RAP. This problem involves the allocation of students, teachers and rooms, within certain restrictions (related to the regulations, proper utilization of resources, and satisfaction of people's preferences), for executing education activities in specific time-slots. Effective timetables for academic courses delivery are crucial for the efficient utilization of university resources and for ensuring the student satisfaction. Timetable is usually developed manually, based on valid solutions applied in the previous years. This approach does not even guarantee finding an optimal solution, even a valid one. The problem complexity is increasing when multiple criteria and types of classes are considered (Silva, Burke, & Petrovic, 2004). As hard constraints, the following could be mentioned: a student or teacher should have only one class at a time; a room should be booked only for one class at a time; a class should be assigned, at least, to one teacher; a class should be scheduled in a room having sufficient seating capacity, and which satisfies all the features required by the class; all classes must be scheduled (Blum et al., 2002; Carrasco & Pato, 2001; Carrasco & Pato, 2004; Rossi-Doria & Paechter, 2003). As main soft constraints, the following have been considered: a class should be preferred in the morning than in the afternoon the number of days per week with classes should be at minimum and the classes should be uniformly distributed over the week; preferences of teachers and students, for a time-slot or a room, should be respected (Bufe et al., 2001; Daskalaki, Birbas & Housos, 2004; Melicio, Caldeira, & Rosa, 2004).

The problem is usually addressed as a single-objective optimization problem by combining multiple criteria into one single value. The minimization of the weighted sum of the violations of hard and soft constraints is generally considered as the objective function. In recent years, several multi-objective optimization techniques have been applied to solve this problem. When studying the complexity of the problem, Even, Itai and Shamir (1976) found it as NP-complete if teachers can be unavailable at an arbitrary subset of times. Cooper and Kingston (1995) showed that the timetable problem is NP-complete in five independent cases.

RAP can be solved using the Multi-Criteria Decision Analysis (MCDA). Belton and Stewart (2002) define the Multi-Criteria Decision Analysis (MCDA) as "an umbrella term to describe a collection of formal approaches which seek to take explicit account of multiple criteria in helping individuals or groups explore decisions that matter". According to this definition, MCDA is a formal framework, requiring multiple criteria and a decision process ran by a person or a group of persons. All these characteristics are much closed to the resource allocation, which need a structured and rational approach, multiple perspectives on the resources qualities and quantities and the presence of the multiple stakeholders with specific goals and interests. MCDA shows important properties that make it very useful, such as: the possibility

to deal with multiple and conflicting criteria, the support assured in structuring the management problems, and in defining a rational and explainable decision process. MCDA approaches have been classified as multi-objective decision making and multi-attribute decision making (Korhonen et al., 1992; Hayashi, 2000; Belton and Stewart, 2002). A detailed discussion on this issue was made by Malczewski (1999) based on the works of Hwang and Yoon (1981) and Zeleny (1982). Traditional MCDM methods have limitations when dealing with complex resource allocation problems. Considering these limitations, more flexible, robust, and broad methods were proposed, such as the "soft systems methods" (Rosenhead, 1989; Checkland, 1981).

For solving the RAP problem, different classic techniques are considered, such as: integer linear programming and graph coloring theory (Chvatal, 1983; Schrijver, 1998; Wolsey, 1998; Chartrand, 1984; Jensen, 1995), as well non-classic ones, like: genetic/evolutionary algorithms, neural network, tabu search algorithm and simulated annealing (Deb, 2001; Glover & Laquna, 2004; Laarhoven & Aarts, 1987). Specific genetic representation and operators are used by Carrasco and Pato (2001) for developing an academic timetable considering the preferences of teachers and classes. Blum et al. (2002) reduces the complexity of the problem by initializing the time table solutions with a set of sequential heuristic rules. Srinivasan et al. (2002) apply an evolutionary algorithm, with heuristics and context-based reasoning for the feasible solutions initialization. A hybrid evolutionary algorithm is presented in (Bufe et al., 2001), associated with a heuristic timetable builder generating feasible solutions, and with a local search engine for a better convergence. Rossi-Doria and Paechter (2003) allow the choice of the heuristics which generate the feasible solutions. In (Lewis & Paechter, 2004) several problem specific crossover operators are defined and applied.

Computational intelligence methods, other than genetic/evolutionary algorithms are also applied to solve the academic class timetable problem. The earlier works on the class timetabling problem, using neural network, are found in (Gislen et al., 1992) and (Looi, 1992). Carrasco and Pato (2004) define two neural network architectures to solve the timetable problem, one based on continuous potts neurons and the other on discrete winner-take-all neurons. A constraint solver is defined by Rudova and Murry (2003) for developing a demand-driven academic timetable. It allows the hard constraint propagation together with the preference propagation for the soft constraints.

MULTI-AGENT SYSTEMS AND AGENT-BASED METHODOLOGIES

The multi-agent system (in short, MAS) represents an important paradigm in the field of distributed computation (Bodea, Badea and Purnus, 2011). Promoting the collaborative approach in complex problem solving, MAS is a natural implementation of the Distributed Constraint Optimization (DCOP) approach. When MAS is adopted, a collaborative planning and participatory environment in decision making can be applied, allowing the involvement and participation of multiple experts and stakeholders (Mendoza and Prabhu, 2003).

One MAS is composed by several agents that communicate and work together in an environment (application field or problem). Each of these agents is designed to have a goal. According to this goal, it will act in a specific way, at a specific moment of time. For obtaining resources, the agent's utility should be calculated. The utility is usually defined by what the agent can achieve using these resources, which is a non-trivial task, because the agent's actions might have long-term and nondeterministic effects and they are conditioned by the resources it will obtain. This leads

to cyclic dependencies, with no possibility to calculate parameterized solutions. Determining classes of utility functions (deVries & Vohra, 2003), iterative algorithms for resource allocation, preference elicitation (Sandholm & Boutilier, 2006), and concise languages for expressing agents' preferences (Boutilier, 2002) there are only some solutions for addressing this issue.

Several methods for solving the distributed Constraint Optimization version of RAP are already available through the research made in the field of resource allocation using MAS. The best known algorithms are: the Asynchronous Distributed Optimization (ADOPT) algorithm, distributed breakout (communication only among neighboring agents to reduce time in achieving synchronization), Distributed Pseudo-Tree Optimization Procedure (DPOP), No Commitment Branch and Bound (NCCB) and Autonomous Agent Constraint Optimization Distribution Algorithm (ANACONDA). In ANACONDA algorithm, each variable computed by an agent trying to locally minimize its errors subject to different constraints. The algorithm is computationally inexpensive and when combined with user friendly interface, it enables users to explore solutions along a Pareto front and find appropriate solution. In the context of cooperative agents, the concept of resources can be viewed as a compact way of representing the interactions between agents (Bererton, Gordon & Thrun, 2003). For non-cooperative agents, the goal is to allocate resources among the agents in a way that maximizes the social welfare, given that each participating agent is selfishly maximizing its own utility. For domains with self-interested agents with complex preferences that exhibit combinatorial effects between the resources, combinatorial auctions (deVries & Vohra, 2003) are often used for resource-allocation.

The YAMS model (Parunak et all, 1987) is one of the earliest system that applied multi-agents in the manufacturing domain. MACIV (Oliveira, Fonseca, & Steiger-Garcao, 1997) is a multi-agent project, enabling a decentralized management of the resources in the construction companies. The task assignment policy is based on the Contract Net Protocol, with an extension that enables negotiation among the agents. A multi-agent system, named TRACE is presented in (Fatima & Wooldridge, 2001). This system allows the resource allocation to the tasks on priority basis. CORMAS represents a multi-agent systems application for renewable resource management. An integrated usage of CORMAS, Geographic Information Systems (GIS), and participatory modeling was developed for the Senegal River Valley and reported by Aquino et al. (2002). CORMAS has also been chosen by Purnomo et al. (2005) as a platform for developing a multi-agent simulation model of a community forest.

In Bodea and Niculescu (2006), an agent-based approach to project planning and scheduling, especially in resource leveling issues is described. The ResourceLeveler system, an agent-based model for leveling project resources is presented. The objective of Resource Leveler is to find a scheduling of resources similar to the optimal theoretical solution which takes into consideration all constraints stemming from the relationships between projects, activity calendars, resource calendars, resource allotment to the activities and resource availability. ResourceLeveler was developed in C# as a plug-in for Microsoft Project. The program has the following functional modules: the interface module, the wrapper module, the leveling module, and the auction market simulation module. Comparing the ResourceLeveler with other resource leveling tools and have observed that ResourceLeveler has brought better results than the leveler implemented in Microsoft Project and found better solutions to some problems than other leveling tools. (Bodea, Badea and Mogos, 2011) discusses the MAS implementation in two scheduling problems: TCPSP (Time-Constrained Project Scheduling) and RCPSP (Resource-Constrained

Project Scheduling). An improved BDI (Beliefs, Desires, and Intentions) model is proposed and the implementation in JADE platform is presented.

Implementing MAS is a complex and laborious process and the role of the applied methodology is essential. For this reason, a lot of research is done in the agent-oriented methodologies field, revealing that methodologies are even more important in developing MAS than in any other software engineering projects (Brinkkemper, 1996; IEEE Standards Board, 1990; Sturm, Shehory, 2003).

Agent-based methodologies consider the enterprise as divided into sub-organizations where agents play one or more roles, interacting with each other. Concepts as "role", "social dependence" and "organizational rules" are used not only to model the system environment, but also to model the system itself. One of the most important aspects addressed by methodologies is the description of interactions between agents, by simulating the dependencies between agents and the roles. The methodology must assure a high abstraction degree during the agent modeling. For this reason, the object-oriented methodologies are not suitable for developing multi-agent systems. An agent-oriented methodology should be in focused on agents, the roles they have made in systems and interaction protocols.

GAIA is one of the first ABMs, using analogies from real organizations, and trying to provide both a friendly approach for a less developer and a technical one, for the skilled developers. GAIA promotes the sequential approach in software development, containing stages for requirements gathering, analysis, design and implementation. In (Zhao, Zhou & Perry, 2007) the SMART (Semantic Agreement) allowing an automatic agreement using ontology and agent technology is presented. *TROPOS* provides guidance for the most important stages of a multi-agent system development (Bresciani et. all, 2004). A framework for modeling agent objectives starting with actors, activities and system resources is included in TROPOS. This methodology is the starting point of **i*** (*i star*) modeling language (Yu, 1995) and pays special attention to the initial requirements modeling. The usage of **i*** language, especially during the analysis and design provides a high degree of flexibility especially for those who use the Agent UML notation (Huget, Odell, Bauer, 2004). In (Hadar, et al., 2010) the advantages of TROPOS are analyzed.

UNIRA: A MULTI-AGENT SYSTEM FOR RESOURCES ALLOCATION TO THE EDUCATIONAL PROGRAMMES IN UNIVERSITIES

The UNIRA multi-agent system allows the identification of the most suitable solution for resources allocation on educational programmes/courses. The resources allocation is made based on a predefined set of criteria, which have to be fulfilled in order to allocate the resources. How better the criteria must be fulfilled is interactively decided during a negotiation process. If the expectation level is too high, there is the risk for not to be able to allocate resources. Contrary, when the expectations are too low, the risk is to get low quality resources. For this reason, the negotiation process, running several negotiation rounds is a better solution than other approaches. Figure 1 presents the criteria for the two main resources: professors and teaching rooms, as they are stored in the database, named as *Broker Database*.

As it is shown in Figure 1, the criteria applied in the negotiation process for acquiring the "professor" resources are the following:

- **Teaching Experience:** In the university and in the programme/course topic.
- **Academic Evaluation:** The results of the evaluation made by the students and by the peers.

- **Scientific Activity:** Scientific papers, research projects, member of the professional associations, reviewer at scientific journals and conference.

For the teaching rooms the following criteria are considered in the negotiation:

- **The Building:** The distance from the department/chair asking a room, the distance from the main library of the university, the distance from the main facilities (dorms, restaurants, etc.), the security.
- **The Room Comfort:** Light, heat, size.
- **The Room Equipment:** Beamer, flipchart, workstation.

All these criteria are used for implementing soft constraints in the timetable engine, as preferences of programmes/courses in terms of resources (professors and teaching rooms). We assume that the resource inquirers are weakly-coupled, meaning that the programmes/courses only interact through the shared resources, and once the resources are allocated, their state transitions are independent. While this allocation assumption introduce a limitation in our approach, it also allows us to address more efficient the non-cooperative situations and to avoid the state space explosion.

The novelty of the UNIRA system is that it applies the negotiation process for incremental satisfying of the soft constraints, in a transparent way (the intermediate results are sent to all participants and their preferences might change accordingly). This approach reduces the computational complexity of the resources allocation problem. Each *resource inquirer,* representing a programme/course sets the level of expectation for each of the allocation criterion. The *resource manager* makes an offer for a specific inquiry, proposing an available resource, with specific characteristics. For each criterion, the *negotiator* matches the actual resources characteristics with

Figure 1. The UNIRA database: a) the allocation criteria for the teaching room; b) the allocation criteria for professors

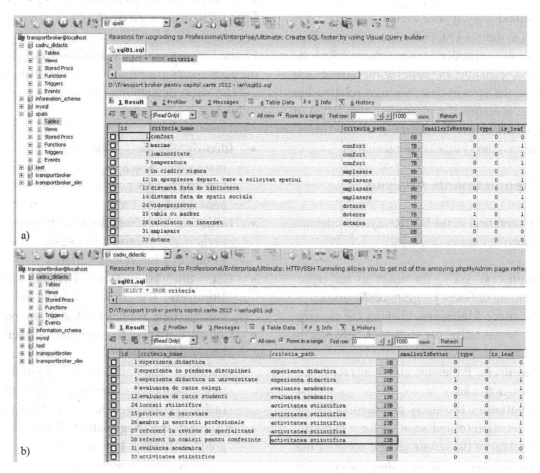

the expected ones, calculating scores, which are showing how better the different resources fulfill the criteria. For every resource participating at the negotiation process, the scores are aggregated into a single value (the overall score) and the resource having the greatest overall score is proposed for allocation. The first negotiation round is now completed. The resource managers can improve their offers, proposing another resource with more competitive characteristics. This new offer is communicated by the negotiator to all participants and another negotiation round starts. The process is repeated until the negotiation result is accepted by all participants (there is not any resource manager interested to propose another resource for the programme/course). Different resources inquires can be issued, in the same time, by different programmes/courses of the university, and different resource manager can make offers.

Another contribution of the UNIRA approach is the usage of Analytic Hierarchy Process (AHP) on the negotiation process for dealing simultaneously with multiple preference criteria. The AHP tree developed by the negotiator agent (the algorithm is presented in a separate paragraph) will be used to calculate the scores of each resource, combining different preference criteria.

THE SYSTEM DEVELOPMENT

The methodology applied for the development of UNIRA system is TROPOS. According to TROPOS, the following development phases have to be executed, sequential and iterative: the requirement analysis, the system description in relationship with the operational environment, the design of overall architecture, the design of detailed architecture, and the system implementation.

The Requirements Analysis

The environment of the UNIRA system contains the following entities (Figure 2):

- **Inquirers:** Asking for resources and representing different programmes/courses.
- **Resource Managers:** Owning the resources in the university (heads of department/char).
- **Resources:** Professors and rooms for didactical activities.
- **Negotiator:** The entity proposed by the organization to find solution for a good utilization of the resources. We consider that the negotiator is representing the organization interest for a better utilization of the resources.

The System Description in Relationship with the Operational Environment

Figure 3 presents, in hierarchical form, the goals of the participants in the resource allocation process.

The short description of these goals is the following:

- **Identify the Best Resource:** This is the main goal, which is divided into several sub-goals. This goal is solved based on a predefined set of allocation criteria.
- **Initiating the Negotiation Process:** All participants receive the message that the resources allocation is started.
- **Get the Requested Criteria from Inquirers:** The criteria stored in the database become available to the inquirers.
- **Collect Criteria:** Inquirers define their requirements regarding the resources. The inquirers can not define requirements based on the characteristics which are not included in the predefined set of criteria.
- **Running the Negotiation Process:** The goal is divided into the following sub-goals: *Receive criteria from Inquirers* (the requirements are received from the inquirers), *Receive information about Resources*

Figure 2. Environment diagram

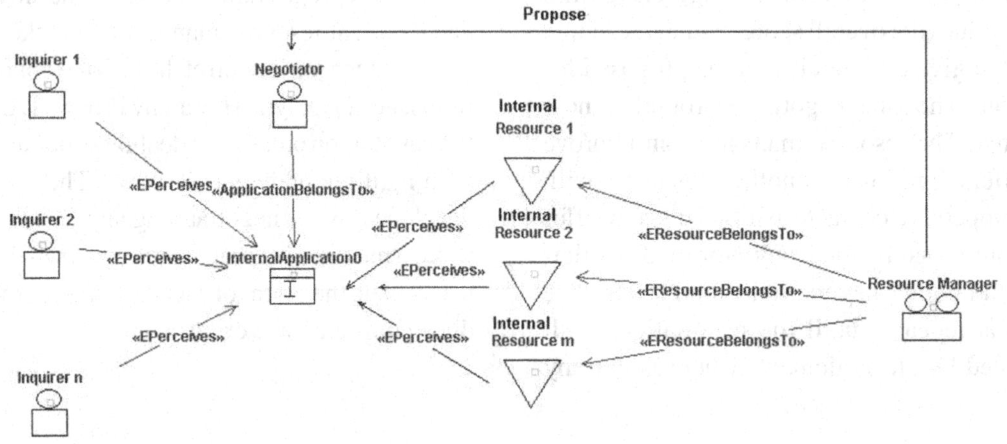

Figure 3. The UNIRA goal tree

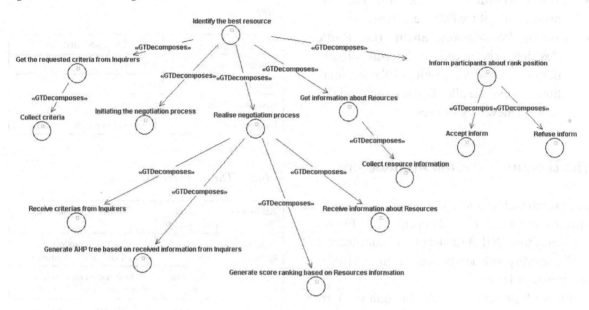

Figure 4. The roles and agents model

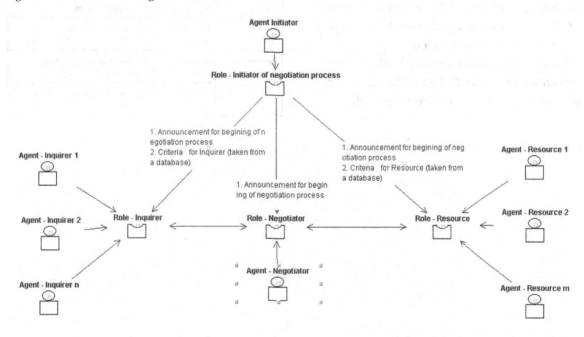

(information about the resources are received), *Generate AHP tree based on received information from Inquirers* (AHP trees are developed, based on the allocation criteria weights), *Generate score raking based on Resources information* (the resources hierarchy is developed based on the AHP tree weights multiplied by the value of the resource characteristics). The resources with the highest score will be on the first place on the resources hierarchy;

- **Collect Resource Information:** The improvements of the offers are done.
- **Inform Participants about the Rank Position**: The negotiator informs all participants about the results of the negotiation process, the allocated resource and the score achieved by this resource.

The Design of Overall Architecture

The overall architecture is defined in term of subsystems, relationships, and dependences. Figure 4 presents the UNIRA model of roles and agents.

The correspondences between agents and roles are shown in Table 1.

Figure 5 presents the roles in connection to the defined goals. Each role is associated with an agent, and each agent has to be developed for attending specific goals. This is why the connections between roles and goals have to be decided as soon as the roles are defined.

The overall architecture of the UNIRA system is presented in Figure 6. The exchange of messages between agents is presented in Table 2.

Table 1. Correspondences between agents and roles

Agent	The associated role
Inquirer Agent	Inquirer
Resource Agent	Resource
Negotiator Agent	Negotiator
Initiator Agent	Initiator of negotiation process

Table 2. The message exchange

Agent name	Send message to	Content of the message
Inquirer agent	Inquirer agent	(2) Negotiation process is started and other information
	Negotiator agent	(2) Negotiation process is started and other information
	Resource agent	(2) Negotiation process is started
Inquirer agent	Negotiator agent	(3) Allocation criteria with correspondent values
Resource agent	Negotiator agent	(4) An offer is sent (6) An improved offer is sent
Negotiator agent	Inquirer agent	(7) The winning resource agent is announced
	Resource agent	(7) The winning resource agent is announced

Figure 5. The relationships between roles and goals

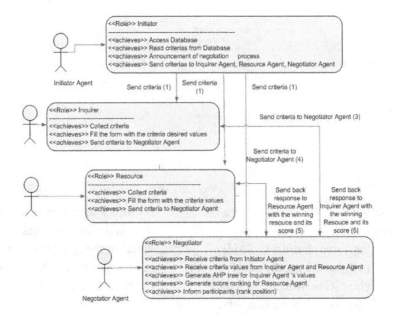

The Design of Detailed Architecture

Due to their ability to model dynamic systems, the object-oriented Petri nets are chosen to define the multi-agent system detailed architecture. The detailed architecture contains the main components (agents), the interconnections between components, and the inputs and outputs for each of them. To get clarity, the agency is represented only by inputs, outputs and a generic transaction including all places and transitions. Figure 7 presents a multi-agent architecture based on

object-oriented Petri net and Figure 8 presents the detailed architecture of the UNIRA system.

The Algorithm for Creating the Analytic Hierarchy Process (AHP) Tree

The negotiation agent, using the information sent by the Inquirer agents create an AHP tree, which is be used for the scores calculation, for each offer issued by resource agents. Figure 9 presents this algorithm in a graphical form.

Figure 6. The overall architecture of the UNIRA system

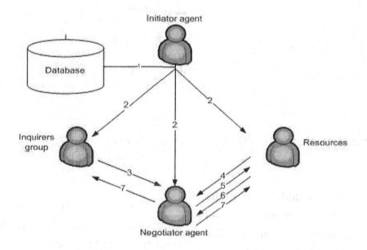

Figure 7. The architecture based on object-oriented Petri nets

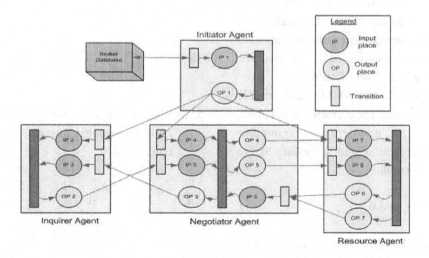

Figure 8. The UNIRA detailed architecture

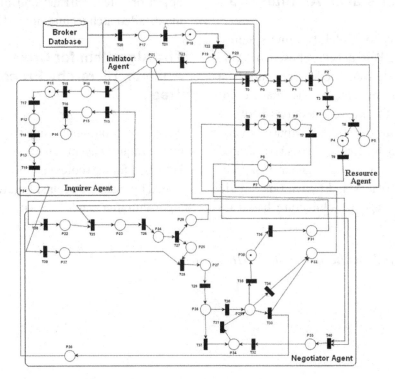

The AHP tree generation algorithm is the following:

1. A tree representation is created, based on the objective which should be achieved, a set of criteria and decision alternatives. The tree root is represented by the objective, the second level if the tree is represented by the criteria, the next levels include sub-criteria, and the leaves are represented by alternatives. The objective and the criteria form a sub-tree, allowing the evaluation of the alternatives according to a sub-set of criteria.

2. Pair-Wise Comparison (PCM) matrix and B matrix are created. The elements of B matrix, b_{ij}, with i,j-1, ..., n, where n is the number of criteria are calculated according to the following formula:

$$b_{ij} = 1/b_{ji}, \text{ for } i \neq j, \text{ and } b_{ii}=1 \qquad (1)$$

3. The principal eigenvector, M is calculated:

$$M_i = \sum_j^n b_{ij} \, (i = 1, 2, ..., n) \qquad (2)$$

M is used for setting the importance of each decision element in connection with the upper level of the APH tree.

4. The criteria weights, W_{ci} are calculated:

$$W_{ci} = M_i / \sum_i^n M_i \qquad (3)$$

5. The consistency index, CI of the B matrix and the Random Consistency Ratio (*CR*) are calculated.

$$CI = \frac{\lambda \max - n}{n-1} \text{ și } CR = \frac{CI}{RI} \qquad (4)$$

Figure 9. The AHP algorithm

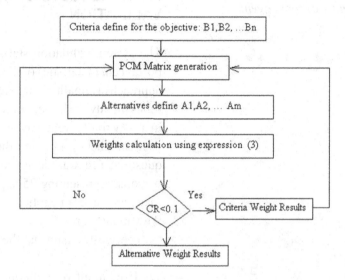

where: λ max represents the maxim eigenvalue from B and RI represents the Random Index, with a value that are depending on the number of criteria. If CR has the value less than 0.1, the consistence of the PCM based analysis is accepted, otherwise the B should be redefined.

6. The alternative weights, W_{Aij}, for alternative j ($j = 1, 2,..., m$) in connection with criteria i are calculated, then the total weight for each alternatives are set according with the formula:

$$w_{Aj} = \sum_{i=1}^{n} w_{Ai,j} * wci \qquad (5)$$

IMPLEMENTATION OF THE UNIRA SYSTEM

The multi-agent system is implemented using Jade platform, version 3.7 (http://jade.tilab.com/). The allocation scenario presented below describes a negotiation process ran when three education programmes require teaching rooms. The number of inquirer agents is 3 and the number of resources is also 3.

The allocation processes has the following steps:

1. The application agents are declared using the Jade platform. Figure 10 a) presents all the system and application agents included on the main container while the Figures 10 b) and c) show details about some of the application agents.

2. The criteria values are declared by the *Inquirer 1* agent (Figure 11 a) and sent to the negotiation agent (Figure 11b).

3. The criteria values are declared by the *Inquirer 2* and the *Inquirer 3* agents.

4. The resource agents declare the characteristics of the teaching rooms (Figure 12).

5. The negotiator agent evaluates the resources offers considering the criteria values (Figure 13 a) and calculates the overall scores (Figure 13 b).

Figure 10. The UNIRA agents: a) the main container; b) inquirer agents; c) room agents

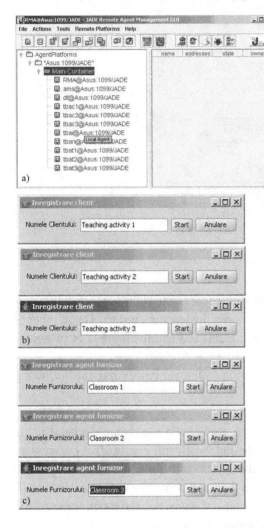

a)

b)

c)

6. The negotiation agent sent messages to the other agents, inviting the resource agents to resubmit their offers.
7. The *Resource agent 2* changes the characteristics, becoming the wining offer (Figure 14).
8. The resource agent 1 updates the resource characteristics and the offer hierarchy is updated (Figure 15).
9. The negotiation agent sent messages to all agents (Figure 16 a,b,c).

FIRST RESULTS OF THE SYSTEM VALIDATION

The system validation starts with the most important characteristics of the system, assuring the approach originality. The originality of the system relies mainly on the negotiation process, executed in a very transparent way. In order to validate the user satisfaction in using the UNIRA system, a questionnaire was designed and applied to 50 persons, representing 25 applicants, 20 resource managers, and 5 negotiators. Figure 17 presents the validation results.

The questionnaire has the following questions:

1. How intuitive is the interface of your agent (1 - very little intuitive, 5 - very intuitive).
2. Have you identified factors which you consider unnecessary for the interface? (1-No, 0-Yes) (max: 25).
3. Did you experience difficulties in the execution? (1-No, 0-Yes).
4. You needed advanced knowledge in order to work with the application? (1-No, 0-Yes).
5. Did you experience errors in the communication with the server? (1-No, 0-Yes).
6. How do you rate the quality of the allocated resources in relation to your request? (1-totally inadequate, 5 - totally appropriate) – only for the Inquirer agent.
7. How do you consider the ranking position that you have placed (1-completely unacceptable, 5 - total acceptable) – only for the resource agent.
8. How do you rate the communication with other entities? – only for the negotiator Agent.

The degree of interface understanding (the question one) is lower to the applicants (only 84%), because the grading criteria are made by comparison (the elements belonging to the same leaf node are evaluated comparing them to all

Figure 11. Defining and sending the criteria values: a) the criteria values as defined by inquirer 1; b) the values were sent to the negotiation agent

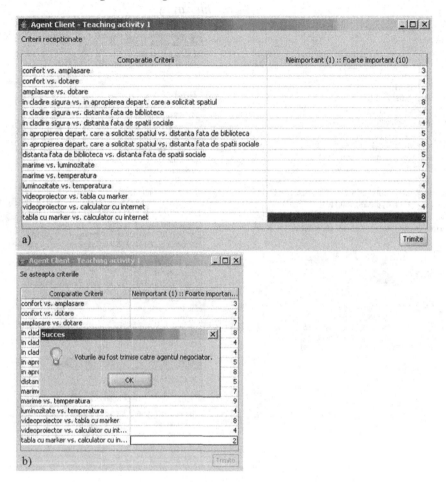

Figure 12. The characteristics of the teaching rooms: a) teaching room 1; b) teaching room 2; c) teaching room 3

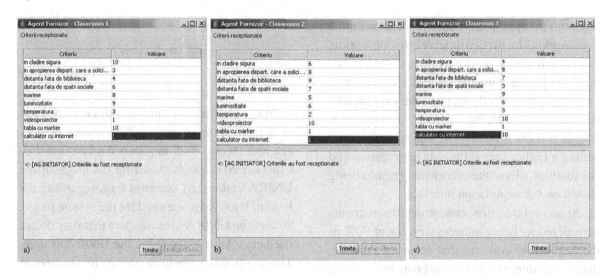

Figure 13. The negotiation scores: a) calculation results; b) the overall scores

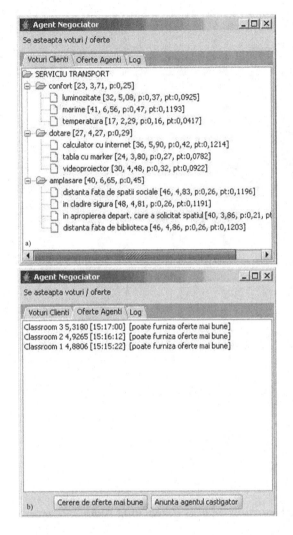

Figure 14. New negotiation iteration: a) the new offer of Resource agent 2; b) the new offers hierarchy

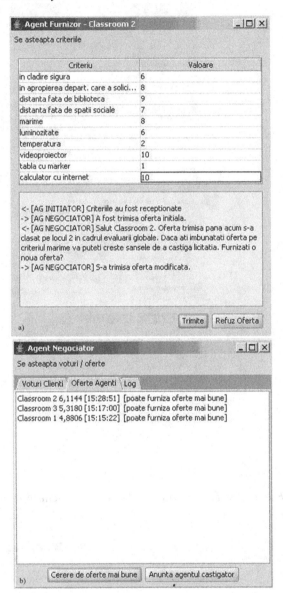

others). This approach produces confusion for the users working for the first time with the application. The resource managers get a higher score (around 90%), mainly because the values for the resource evaluation are directly input in the system. The negotiators consider that the interface as intuitive, getting a score around 92%. The reason for not getting a higher sore is the data aggregation and calculations, a lot of the intermediary results being shown on the negotiation interface.

At second question, concerning the elements considered as being unnecessary, about 70% of the negotiators consider that some information, mainly the intermediary results may be removed

from the interface. At question three, only 2 out of 5 negotiators, 9 out of 20 resource managers, and 19 out of 25 inquirers declare that they experienced difficulties during the usage of the UNIRA system. At question four, regarding the level of knowledge required for the system usage, 80% of the UNIRA users declare that they do not need prior knowledge about the UNIRA system. The question five is addressing the most common

Figure 15. Other negotiation iteration: a) the new offer of resource agent 1; b) the new offers hierarchy

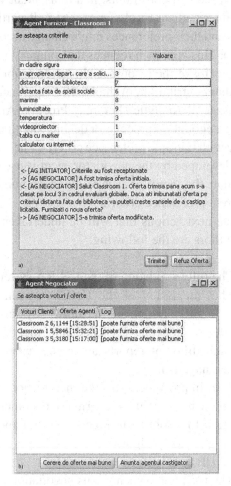

problem, the communication with the server. Only 21 out of 50 persons did not experience communication problems. Regarding the question 6.1, 60% of inquirers are satisfied with the allocation result, considering that the allocated resources meet the requirements. At question 6.2, 85% of the resource managers consider the negotiation results as acceptable. At question 7, the communication problems for the negotiators are more frequent than other entities. This is because the negotiator sends and receives the largest amount of information in the system.

The system validation will continue to assess the UNIRA system, in terms of the quality of the allocation results and the computational efficiency.

CONCLUSION AND FUTURE WORK

The chapter proposed a model based on MASs for solving the problem of allocating resources in an academic environment. The chapter includes detailed information about the system development process, using TROPOS. Several design models are presented, such as: the environment model, the roles and goals model. The detailed design of the system was done using object oriented Petri nets, considering their capacity to highlight the

Figure 16. Messages sent by the negotiation agent to other agents: a) negotiation agent to agent client (teaching activity 1); b) negotiation agent to provider agent (classroom 1); c) negotiation agent to the negotiation process winner

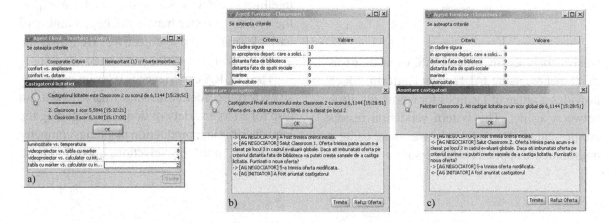

Figure 17. The validation results: a) the average values of the answers provided the applicants; b) the average values of the answers provided the resource managers; c) average values of the answers provided by the system managers

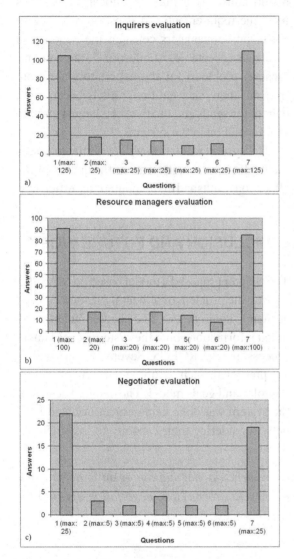

behavior of processes within MAS. The system was implemented using JADE agent platform, which provides a range of facilities for communication between agents. The system validation results are presented. The validation was done using a questionnaire applied for 50 persons.

The novelty of the UNIRA is that it applies the negotiation process for the incremental exploitation of the soft constraints, in a transparent way (the intermediate results are sent to all participants and their preferences might change accordingly). This approach reduces the computational complexity of the resources allocation problem. Another contribution of the UNIRA approach is the usage of Analytic Hierarchy Process (AHP) on the negotiation process for dealing simultaneously with multiple preference criteria. The AHP tree developed by the negotiator agent is used to calculate the scores of each resource, combining different preference criteria.

The next actions that will be undertaken by the authors are the following:

- The fully validation of the UNIRA system.
- The integration of the UNIRA system in the ERP system of the university, in order to generate the academic timetables and different reports about the resources management.
- The improvement of the negotiation approach, assuring the criteria decomposition for more than three levels and applying a fuzzy algorithm for generating the AHP tree.
- The usage of asynchronous negotiation processes, which allow a higher degree of flexibility.

These actions will increase the computational intelligence of UNIRA system and we expect the system to better handle the huge number of variables and multiple objectives. We expect the system to be faster and more robust.

The UNIRA experience is relevant not exclusively for the academic resources management, but also for a large variety of domains, including the load distribution, production planning, computer scheduling, portfolio selection, apportionment, and so on.

REFERENCES

Aquino, P., Le Page, C., Bousquet, F., & Bah, A. (2002). A novel mediating participatory modelling: the "self-design" process to accompany collective decision making. *International Journal of Agricultural Resources. Governance and Ecology, 2*(1), 59–74.

Belton, S., & Stewart, T. S. (2002). *Multiple criteria decision analysis: An integrated approach*. Boston: Kluwer Academic Publishers. doi:10.1007/978-1-4615-1495-4.

Bererton, C., Gordon, G., & Thrun, S. (2003). Auction mechanism design for multi-robot coordination. In Thrun, Saul, & Scholkopf (Eds.), *Proceedings of Conference on Neural Information Processing Systems (NIPS)*. MIT Press.

Blum, C., Correia, S., Dorigo, M., Paechter, B., Rossi-Doria, O., & Snoek, M. (2002). A GA evolving instructions for a timetable builder. In *Proceedings of the Practice and Theory of Automated Timetabling IV*. Gent, Belgium: IEEE.

Bodea, C., Badea, I. R., & Mogoş, R. (2011). A multi-agent system with application in project scheduling. *Management & Marketing. Challenges for Knowledge Society, 6*(4), 573–590.

Bodea, C., Badea, I. R., & Purnus, A. (2011). Distributed research project scheduling based on multi-agent methods. *Journal of Applied Computer Science & Mathematics, 10*(5), 20–26.

Bodea, C., & Niculescu, C. (2006). Resource leveling using agent technologies. In *Proceedings of 20th IPMA World Congress on Project Management*. China Machine Press.

Bodea, C., & Niculescu, C. (2007). Improving resource leveling in agile software development projects through agent-based approach. *Journal of Applied Quantitative Methods, 2*(2), 260–265.

Boutilier, C. (2002). Solving concisely expressed combinatorial auction problems. In *Proceedings of the Eighteenth National Conference on Artificial Intelligence (AAAI-02)*, (pp. 359–366). AAAI.

Bresciani, P., Perini, A., Giorgini, P., Giunchilia, F., & Mylopoulos, F. (2004). Tropos: An agent-oriented software development methodology. *Autonomous Agents and Multi-Agent Systems, 8*, 203–236. doi:10.1023/B:AGNT.0000018806.20944.ef.

Brinkkemper, S. (1996). Method engineering: Engineering of information systems development methods and tools. *Information and Software Technology, 38*, 275–280. doi:10.1016/0950-5849(95)01059-9.

Bufe, M., Fischer, T., Gubbels, H., Hacker, C., Hasprich, O., & Scheibel, C. Wolfangel, C. (2001). *Automated solution of a highly constrained school timetabling problem*. Paper presented at EvoWorkshop. Como, Italy.

Carrasco, M. P., & Pato, M. V. (2001). A multi-objective genetic algorithm for the class/teacher timetabling problem. In E. K. Burke & W. Erben (Eds.), *Proceedings of the Practice and Theory of Automated Timetabling, The Third International Conference* (LNCS). Springer.

Carrasco, M. P., & Pato, M. V. (2002). Solving real class/teacher timetabling problems using neural networks. In *Proceedings of the Practice and Theory of Automated Timetabling IV*. IEEE.

Carrasco, M. P., & Pato, M. V. (2004). A comparison of discrete and continuous neural network approaches to solve the class/teacher timetabling problem. *European Journal of Operational Research, 153*(1), 65–79. doi:10.1016/S0377-2217(03)00099-7.

Chartrand, G. (1984). *Introductory graph theory*. New York: Dover Publications.

Checkland, P. B. (1981). *Systems thinking, systems practice*. London: John Wiley and Sons.

Choueiry, B. Y., & Faltings, B. (1994). Interactive resource allocation by problem decomposition and temporal abstractions. In *Proceedings of the Second European Workshop on Planning*. IOS Press.

Chvatal, V. (1983). *Linear programming*. New York: W H Freeman & Co..

Cooper, T. B., & Kingston, J. H. (1995). The complexity of timetable construction problems. in E. K. Burke & P. Ross (Eds.), *Proceedings of the Practice and Theory of Automated Timetabling I* (LNCS), (Vol. 1153, pp. 283–295). Springer.

Daskalaki, S., Birbas, T., & Housos, E. (2004). An integer programming formulation for a case study in university timetabling. *European Journal of Operational Research, 153*, 117–135. doi:10.1016/S0377-2217(03)00103-6.

de Vries, S., & Vohra, R. V. (2003). Combinatorial auctions: A survey. *INFORMS Journal on Computing, 15*(3), 284–309. doi:10.1287/ijoc.15.3.284.16077.

Deb, K. (2001). *Multi-objective optimization using evolutionary algorithms*. London: John Wiley & Sons Ltd..

Dolgov, D. A., & Durfee, E. H. (2006). Resource allocation among Agents with MDP-induced preferences. *Journal of Artificial Intelligence Research, 27*, 505–549.

Even, S., Itai, A., & Shamir, A. (1976). On the complexity of timetable and multicommodity flow problems. *SIAM Journal on Computing, 5*(4), 691–703. doi:10.1137/0205048.

Fatima, S. S., & Wooldridge, M. (2001). Adaptive task and resource allocation in multi-agent systems. In *Proceedings of the Fifth International Conference on Autonomous Agents*, (pp. 537-544). Montreal, Canada: Agents.

Freed, J., & Klugman, M. (1996). *A culture for academic excellence: Implementing the quality principles in higher education*. San Francisco: Jossey-Bass Publisher.

Gislen, L., Peterson, C., & Soderberg, B. (1992). Complex scheduling with potts neural networks. *Neural Computation, 4*, 805–831. doi:10.1162/neco.1992.4.6.805.

Glover, F. W., & Laquna, M. (2004). *Tabu search*. Berlin: Springer.

Hadar, I., Reinhartz-Berger, I., Kuflik, T., Perini, A., Ricca, F., & Susi, A. (2010). An empirical study of requirements model understanding: Use case vs. tropos models. In *Proceedings 25th ACM Symposium on Applied Computing*. ACM.

Hayashi, K. (2000). Multi-criteria analysis for agricultural resource management: A critical survey and future perspectives. *European Journal of Operational Research, 122*, 486–500. doi:10.1016/S0377-2217(99)00249-0.

Huget, M., Odell, J., & Bauer, B. (2004). The AUML approach. In Bergenti, Gleizes, & Zambonelli (Eds.), Methodologies and software engineering for agent systems. Boston: Kluwer Academic Publishers.

Hwang, C. L., & Yoon, K. (1981). *Multiple-attribute decision making: Methods and applications*. Berlin: Springer-Verlag. doi:10.1007/978-3-642-48318-9.

IEEE Standards Board. (1990). *Standards coordinating committee of the computer society of the IEEE*. Washington, DC: IEEE.

Jensen, T. R. (1995). *Graph coloring problems*. New York: John Wiley & Sons.

Korhonen, P., Moskowitz, H., & Wallenius, J. (1992). Multiple criteria decision support: A review. *European Journal of Operational Research, 63*, 361–375. doi:10.1016/0377-2217(92)90155-3.

Laarhoven, P. J. M. V., & Aarts, E. H. L. (1987). *Simulated annealing: Theory and applications.* Berlin: Springer. doi:10.1007/978-94-015-7744-1.

Lewis, R., & Paechter, B. (2004). New crossover operators for timetabling with evolutionary algorithms. In A. Lofti (Ed.), *The 5th International Conference on Recent Advances in Soft Computing,* (Vol. 5, pp. 189–195). IEEE.

Looi, C. (1992). Neural network methods in combinatorial optimization. *Computers & Operations Research, 19*(3/4), 191–208. doi:10.1016/0305-0548(92)90044-6.

Malczewski, J. (1999). *GIS and multi-criteria decision analysis.* New York: John Wiley & Sons, Inc..

Melıcio, F., Caldeira, J. P., & Rosa, A. (2004). Two neighbourhood approaches to the timetabling problem. In *Proceedings of the Practice and Theory of Automated Timetabling V, Fifth International Conference.* IEEE.

Mendoza, G. A., & Prabhu, R. (2003). Qualitative multi-criteria approaches to assessing indicators of sustainable forest resource management. *Forest Ecology and Management, 174,* 329–343. doi:10.1016/S0378-1127(02)00044-0.

Mustafa, A., & Goh, M. (1996). Multi-criterion models for higher education administration, Omega. *International Journal of Management Science, 24,* 167–178.

Oliveira, E., Fonseca, J. M., & Steiger-Garcao, A. (1997). MACIV: A DAI based resource management system. In Proceedings of Applied Artificial Intelligence. AAAI.

Parunak, H. V. D., White, J. F., Lozo, P. W., Judd, R., Irish, B. W., & Kindrick, J. (1986). An architecture for heuristic factory control, DFSG 86-8. In *Proceedings of the 1986 American Control Conference.* ACC.

Politis, Y., & Siskos, Y. (2004). Multicriteria methodology for the evaluation of a Greek engineering deparment. *European Journal of Operational Research, 156,* 223–240. doi:10.1016/S0377-2217(02)00902-5.

Purnomo, H., Mendoza, G. A., Prabhu, R., & Yasmi, Y. (2005). Developing multistakeholder forest management scenarios: A multi-agent systems simulation approach applied in Indonesia. *Forest Policy and Economics, 7*(4), 475–491. doi:10.1016/j.forpol.2003.08.004.

Ridder, J. P., Brett, S. W., & Signori, D. T. (2012). *Distributed algorithms for resource allocation problems.* Paper presented at the 17th International Command and Control Research and Technology Symposium. Fairfax, VA.

Rosenhead, J. (1989). *Rational analysis of a problematic world.* New York: John Wiley and Sons.

Rossi-Doria, O., & Paechter, B. (2003). *An hyperheuristic approach to course timetabling problem using an evolutionary algorithm.* Paper presented at the First Multidisciplinary International Conference on Scheduling: Theory and Applications (MISTA 2003). New York.

Rudova, H., & Murry, K. (2003). University course timetabling with soft constraints. In Burke & Causmaecker (Eds.), *Proceedings of the Practice and Theory of Automated Timetabling IV, Fourth International Conference.* Berlin: Springer.

Sandholm, T., & Boutilier, C. (2006). Preference elicitation in combinatorial auctions. In Cramton, Shoham, & Steinberg (Eds.), Combinatorial Auctions. Boston: MIT Press.

Schrijver, A. (1998). *Theory of linear and integer programming.* New York: John Wiley & Sons.

Silva, J. D. L., Burke, E. K., & Petrovic, S. (2004). An introduction to multiobjective metaheuristics for scheduling and timetabling. *Lecture Notes in Economics and Mathematical Systems, 535,* 91–129. doi:10.1007/978-3-642-17144-4_4.

Srinivasan, D., Seow, T. H., & Xu, J. X. (2002). Automated time table generation using multiple context reasoning for university modules. In *Proceedings of IEEE International Conference on Evolutionary Computation*, (pp. 1751–1756). IEEE.

Sturm, A., & Shehory, O. (2003). A framework for evaluating agent-oriented methodologies. In Giorgini & Winikoff (Eds.), *Proceedings of the Fifth International Bi-Conference Workshop on Agent-Oriented Information Systems*. Melbourne, Australia: IEEE.

Wolsey, L. A. (1998). *Integer programming*. New York: Wiley-Interscience.

Yu, E. (1995). *Modeling strategic relationships for process reengineering*. (Doctoral Thesis). University of Toronto. Toronto, Canada.

Zeleny, M. (1982). *Multiple criteria decision making*. New York: McGraw-Hill.

Zhao, Q., Zhou, Z., & Perry, M. (2007). *Agent design of smart license management system using gaia methodology*. Ontario, Canada: University of Western Ontario. doi:10.1109/CONIELE-COMP.2007.52.

Hu, C., Mao, X., & Ning, H. (2009). Integrating model transformation in agent-oriented software engineering. In *Proceedings of the IEEE/WIC/ACM International Conference on Web Intelligence and Intelligent Agent Technology*, (Vol. 2). IEEE.

Mogoş, R. I., & Mogoş, P. L. (2009a). An agent-based intelligent platform approach based on ebXML for intelligent guidance in shopping – Stores. *Metalurgia International, 14*(9).

Mogoş, R. I., & Mogoş, P. L. (2009b). A conceptual framework based on web-services for e-business process modelling in tourism. *Revista Metalurgia International, 14*, 89–94.

Zambonelli, F., Jennings, N., & Wooldridge, M. (2003). Developing multiagent systems: The Gaia methodology. *ACM Transactions on Software Engineering and Methodology, 12*(3), 417–470. doi:10.1145/958961.958963.

Zhu, H. (2001). SLABS: A formal specification language for agent-based systems. *Journal of Software Engineering and Knowledge Engineering, 11*(5), 529–558. doi:10.1142/S0218194001000657.

ADDITIONAL READING

Hadar, I., Reinhartz-Berger, I., Kuflik, T., Perini, A., Ricca, F., & Susi, A. (2010). An empirical study of requirements model understanding: Use case vs. Tropos models. In *Proceedings of the 25th ACM Symposium on Applied Computing*. ACM.

Henderson-Sellers, B., & Giorgini, P. (2005). *Agent-oriented methodologies*. Hershey, PA: IGI. doi:10.4018/978-1-59140-581-8.

KEY TERMS AND DEFINITIONS

Agent-Based Methodologies: Methodologies that offer modeling concepts, analysis techniques, and opportunities for agent oriented systems. They vary in scope of coverage and maturity.

AHP Method: It is a multi-criteria decision method for selecting the best option from a number of alternatives, based on a set of criteria.

Multi-Agent Systems: An agent-based system that aims to model the real world. He must be able to model an interactive system through a collection of specialized agents that produce and respond to stimuli within the existing (environment).

Negotiation Process: It is an interaction that involves the existence of two or more social partners (persons, groups, organizations), with homogeneous and heterogeneous interests. Negotiation involves a mutual exchange of information governed by implicit/explicit rules aiming to adopt a mutually acceptable solution to a common problem.

Petri Networks: Mathematical objects that determine an effective theoretical description of duplication of discrete systems behavior with asynchronous interactions.

Resource Allocation Problem: To identify the configuration in which resources can be distributed in an optimal way considering some limits entities that need them for their activity. This issue falls within the resource management domain.

Software Agent: An entity that perceives the environment through sensors and acts upon the environment through effectors. There are several types of agents. The intelligent (rational) agent is that agent which acts in order to achieve success. The rationality is associated with the expected success.

Section 2
Pervasive Computing Applications

Chapter 6
Algorithms for Spatial Partitioning in Wireless Sensor Network

Kakia Panagidi
Ionian University, Greece

ABSTRACT

Recent interest in integrated electronic devices (sensors) that operate wirelessly creates a wide range of applications related to national security, surveillance, military, healthcare, and environmental monitoring. Many visions of the future include people immersed in an environment surrounded by sensors and intelligent devices, which use smart infrastructures to improve the quality of life. However, a fundamental feature of sensor networks is coverage: how these tiny devices can cover a certain terrain. These devices should be organized in an optimal manner, consuming the minimum energy and covering the whole area of interest. The coverage concept is subject to a wide range of interpretations due to the variety of sensors and applications. Different coverage formulations have been proposed based on the subject to be covered (area in relation to specific items and obstacles), sensor development mechanisms (random versus deterministic), and other properties of wireless sensor networks (e.g. network connectivity and minimum energy consumption). In this chapter, the authors study the coverage problem in wireless sensor networks using the most recent algorithms. The aim of this chapter is to present these algorithms and a comparison between them based on various criteria. The Node Self-Scheduling algorithm, the Centralized Voronoi Tessellation (CVT), the Particle Swarm Optimization Algorithm (PSO), the Virtual Forces Algorithm (VFA), etc. are analyzed. Through the algorithms' analysis, the interested reader can have a complete view of the proposed solutions related to the coverage problem.

DOI: 10.4018/978-1-4666-4038-2.ch006

INTRODUCTION

A Wireless Sensor Network (WSN) is a network of portable devices (sensors) that can monitor, compute, and store information depending on their environment. Sensor nodes, also called wireless transceivers, are tiny devices equipped with one or more sensors, one or more transceivers, processors, storage resources and, possibly, actuators, like depicted by Figure 1. Sensors have specific and, usually, small size, weight and cost. Their limited lifetime sets out restrictions on actions that they can perform (e.g. processing and communication). Due to the fact that battery replacement is not feasible in many cases; low power consumption is a critical factor, which affects the entire life of the WSN. Each of these nodes should be able to collect and send data back to a base station via a multi-hop wireless network.

A WSN is composed of a large number of nodes with sensing capabilities, in which each node can communicate with each other. After the development of the network, sensor nodes begin a process of creating groups (clusters), installing of communication channels, creating hierarchy between them etc. Sensor nodes can be organized in smaller networks and collaborate to accomplish a larger sensing task. The network is expected to operate for long periods without human intervention or supervision. It should be characterized by speediness, agility and adaptability in the environment. These features are useful in emergency situations such as natural disasters and military wars. It is important to be supported by the topology and distribution of the nodes, which should

Figure 1. The typical architecture of a sensor node

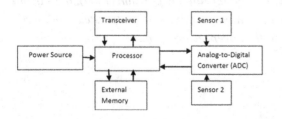

occupy the entire area of interest (ROI). The major components of a typical sensor network shown in Figure 2 are: the sensor nodes, the sensor field, the sink and the task manager or base station. The sensor field can be considered as a field in which the nodes are placed, i.e. the area where we expect a particular phenomenon to occur. The sensor nodes are the heart of the network. They are responsible for data collection and routing this information back to the sink.

The sink node is a sensor with the specific aim of taking, processing and storing data from other sensor nodes. The sink is used to reduce the total number of messages to be sent between nodes, thus resulting in low energy needs of the network. Such points are usually defined dynamically by the network. Regular nodes can also be considered as sink if they have gathered enough information. For this reason, the sink is also known as data collection point. The task manager or base station is a central control point in the network, which sends the required information back to the control network. It also provides a gateway to other networks, a powerful data processor, a data storage center and an access point for users. The base station is either a laptop or a terminal. The data is routed from sink to these terminals via the Internet, wireless channels, satellites etc. So, in some cases, hundreds of thousands of nodes extending across the ROI to create a multi-hop wireless network. The nodes can be placed very densely together as 20 nodes per m^3. The sensor nodes use the wireless media such as infrared, radio, optical devices or Bluetooth for communications. The transmission range of nodes varies depending on the communication protocol used.

Section 2 contains a reference to the study the problem related with the sensors' spatial partition, which is called coverage problem. The sensor's coverage, the sensor's energy consumption and the most usual characteristics included in the assumption of the proposed algorithms are defined. Section 3 analyzes the most recent algorithms that have been elaborated in the literature, while

Figure 2. Sensor nodes in a sensor field

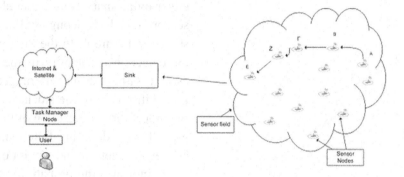

Section 4 contains a comparative evaluation of basic algorithms with their extensions. In chapter 5, there are proposals for future work and, finally, section 6 presents the conclusions.

THE COVERAGE PROBLEM

In hostile or harsh environments such as enemy territories in battlefields, fire or chemical spills, it is impossible to deploy the sensor nodes in a pre-determined regular topology. Random (possibly aerial) deployment of sensor nodes is a solution in such scenarios. After their deployment, a network should dynamically be built. Every sensor should know not only its neighbors using a sensing function, but also its position. If a sensor wants to send data back to the gateway, it should send data to the neighbors nearest to the gateway instead of aimlessly flooding the network. There are three ways for a sensor to learn its position:

- **Deterministic Placement:** The location of the sensor is manually entered. This can be done if the sensor is not randomly disposed, but deliberately placed.
- *The sensor has a GPS receiver or anything* that can be used in order to find its position, independently of the network or the rest of the sensors.

- **Multilateration:** If a sensor has three neighbors which already know their positions, it can use multilateration to deduce its position. Each neighbor can perceive the sensor at certain signal strength, and, thus, could situate it on a certain circle. By intersecting the 3 obtained circles, the sensor can thus learn its position (two circles generally yield two possible locations).

In practice, usually all three methods are used. A subset of the devices has GPS or is programmed manually and then the rest learn their position by multilateration.

These random deployments are highly susceptible to the creation of uncovered regions, referred to as coverage holes. A coverage hole, which is shown in Figure 3, is the area of not covered by sensors around a defined set of points called points of interest. There are many factors that contribute to this, including the presence of obstacles, sloping grounds like hills, strong winds or dense forestation during the deployment, etc. (Nadeem et al, 2007).

In addition, the self-organization of WSN nodes should consume the minimum amount of energy. Minimizing energy consumption to prolong the network lifetime is a major design objective for WSNs since tiny devices usually operate on limited battery power due to low cost and small size

Figure 3. Black hole example in WSN

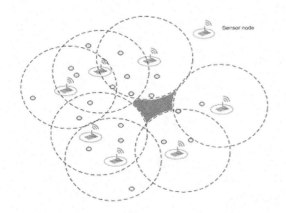

(Jianli et al, 2004). The two requirements, i.e. (1) the full coverage of the area and (2) the minimum energy consumption, are discussed in the literature and it is widely known as the sensor coverage problem. The coverage problem is trying to cover a ROI with the minimum available number of sensors. The coverage problem usually is a measure of the quality of service (QoS) (Cardei & Wu, 2005) of the sensing function and is subject to a wide range of interpretations due to a large variety of sensors and applications. The main goal is to have each location in the physical space of interest within the sensing range of at least one sensor.

SENSORS COVERAGE

General Definition of the Problem

Each sensor has a sensing range r, which is spread to all directions. It is often represented by a unit disc. Assume sensor s_i is deployed at a point (x_i, y_i). For any point $P(x, y)$, we denote the Euclidean distance between s_i and P as follows:

$$d(s_i, P) = \sqrt{(x_i - x)^2 - (y_i - y)^2} \qquad (1)$$

The coverage of each sensor can be defined either by a binary sensor model or a stochastic sensor model (Nojeong & Pramod, 2005), as shown in Figure 4. In the binary sensor model, the detection probability of the event of interest is 1 within the sensing range; otherwise, the probability is 0. In the stochastic sensor model, the probability of detection of the event of interest follows a decaying function of the distance between the sensor and a point of interest.

P_D indicates the probability detection of the event. In addition, the coverage is defined as the ratio of the union of areas (in square meters) covered by each node and the area (in square meters) of the entire ROI. The covered area of each node is defined as the circular area within its sensing radius R. Perfect detection of all interesting events in the covered area is assumed,

$$C = \frac{\bigcup\limits_{i=1}^{N} A_i}{A} \qquad (2)$$

where A_i is the area covered by the ith-node, N is the total number of nodes and A stands for the area of the ROI. The overall coverage (O_C) of a sensor network is composed of the covered regions of each sensor node. Though the coverage of a sensor is expressed by a sensor model which is binary or stochastic, the overall coverage of a sensor network depends on the locations of the sensor nodes in the sensor field. The topology including the locations and spacing of sensor nodes determines the overall coverage of the network as well as the expected lifetime of the network.

The extension of coverage problem in 3D terrain can be defined as follows:

Any sensor s_i with coordinates (x_1, y_1, z_1) can cover any point located at $P(x_2, y_2, z_2)$, if the Euclidean distance between s_i and P is less than sensing range.

Figure 4. Binary and stochastic model

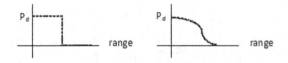

$$d(s_i,P)$$
$$= \sqrt{(x_1 - x_2)^2 + (y_1 - y_2)^2 + (z_1 - z_2)^2}$$
$$\leq \text{sensing\_range} \tag{3}$$

K-Coverage Problem

Given a set of points P= {P_1, P_2, ...,P_n } located in a ROI and a set of sensors S= {S_1, S_2, ..., S_m}, the objective is each point in ROI to be covered (or sensed) by at least k sensors. The k-coverage problem should satisfy the following requirements:

1. **On Demand Coverage:** A ROI should be covered by k sensors dynamically whenever needed; ROI may change during time.
2. **Mobility:** The sensors should be able to move to ensure the coverage of ROI.
3. **Minimum Energy:** The k-sensors should cover the ROI while they are keeping the sensing range at minimum.

Q-Coverage Problem

Let a set of sensors S= {S_1, S_2, ..., S_m} be randomly deployed and a set of points P= {P_1, P_2, ...,P_n } be the n points covered. Let Q ={ Q_1, Q_2, ..., Q_m} be a covered vector such that any given point should be covered by at least q_j ($q_j \geq 1$) active sensor nodes. A Q-cover set is a set of sensors that jointly cover all points satisfying the coverage vector specification. Formally:

$$S = \{s_i \mid \text{ for each } p_j, \text{ there are at least } q_j$$
$$number \text{ of } s_i \in S \text{ covering } p_j\} \tag{4}$$

Cluster Formation

The points and sensors will be partitioned in clusters. Let the set of clusters to be formatted as represented C ={C_1,C_2,....,C_m}. Any point p_j belongs to C_i if and only if

$$\text{distance}(p_j,s_i)$$
$$\leq \text{distance}(p_j,s_k) \begin{cases} i = k = 1,2,...,m \\ j = 1,2,...,n \end{cases} \tag{5}$$

For simple coverage, each point is associated to exactly one cluster and for k-coverage and Q-coverage, each point is associated to minimum k and q_j sensors nodes respectively (Mini et al., 2011).

Sensor Energy Consumption

The energy consumption of a sensor node is considered in literature by using the assumption that there is no sensor mobility or that the nodes have already moved to their final positions. The power consumption model for the radio hardware energy diffusion where the transmitter dissipates energy to run the radio electronics and the power amplifier, and the receiver dissipates energy to run the radio electronics. Each node is displayed inside a cluster and has short distance (dis) to the cluster head and each cluster head has a long distance (Dis) to the base station. Thus for each node to transmit an l-bit message, the required energy in a cluster is (Wu et al, 2005):

$$E_{TS}(l, dis) = l * E_{elec} + l * \varepsilon_{fs} * dis^2 \tag{6}$$

The required energy for a cluster head to transmit to the base station is (Wu et al, 2005):

$$E_{TH}(l, Dis) = l * E_{elec} + l * \varepsilon_{mp} * Dis^2 \quad (7)$$

E_{elec} is the electronic energy, and are amplifier constants.

The Coverage Algorithms

The proposed coverage algorithms are either distributed and localized or centralized. In distributed algorithms, the decision process is decentralized. By distributed and localized algorithms, we refer to a distributed decision process at each node that makes use of only neighborhood information (within a constant number of hops). Because the WSN has a dynamic topology and needs to accommodate a large number of sensors, the designed algorithms and protocols should be distributed and localized, in order to better accommodate a scalable architecture. Considering the coverage concept, different problems can be formulated, based on specific criteria:

- **Sensor Deployment Method:** Deterministic versus random. A deterministic sensor placement may be feasible in friendly and accessible environments.
- **Coverage Type:** Area versus points.
- Energy Efficiency
- Connectivity
- **Algorithm Characteristics:** Centralized versus Distributed/Localized.
- **Problem Objective:** Maximizing the life cycle of a WSN versus minimizing the nodes' coverage holes (See Figure 5), like in Equation 5:

Minimize $\sum$ coverage_hole(sensor nodes)
OR Maximizing $\sum$ life_cycle(sensor nodes)
(8)

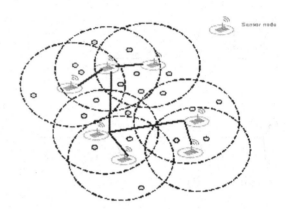

Figure 5. The objective of the problem in a ROI

Table 1 presents an overview of the nine algorithms, which are going to be covered in the following sections, according to the five criteria presented above. This table highlights the similarities and the differences between the algorithms.

PROPOSED ALGORITHMS

In this Section, we review the most important algorithms that solve the problem of the coverage problem in a specific area. Basic algorithms, such as Virtual Forces (VFA) and Particle Swarm Optimization, are studied in detail along with their characteristics. Their methodology is enhanced with pseudo-algorithms, so the reader should have an overall understanding of them. Furthermore, algorithms developed as extensions of the basic methods, like Mobility Assisted Probabilistic Protocol (MAPC) using VFA, are presented. The focus on these algorithms' extensions is the analysis of the additional characteristics.

Virtual Force Algorithm (VFA)

The Virtual Force Algorithm (VFA) is a sensor deployment strategy to enhance the coverage after an initial random placement of sensors. The VFA algorithm is inspired by disk packing theory (Locateli & Raber, 2002) and the virtual force field concept from robotics (Howard et al, 2002). For a given number of sensors, VFA attempts to maxi-

Table 1. Algorithms' overview for coverage problem

Algorithm	Coverage Type	Sensor Deployment Method	Characteristics	Problem Objectives
Node Self-Scheduling Algorithm	Area Coverage	Random	Distributed, localized	Energy- Efficiency Maximize network lifetime by reducing the number of working nodes
Centralized, Voronoi tessellation (CVT)	Area Coverage	Random	Centralized	Energy- Efficiency Maximize network lifetime by reducing the number of working nodes
Particle Swarm Optimization (PSO)	Area Coverage	Random	Distributed	Energy- Efficiency Maximize network lifetime by reducing the number of working nodes
Artificial Bee Colony (ABC)	Area Coverage	Random	Distributed	Energy- Efficiency Maximize network lifetime by reducing the number of working nodes
Mission-Oriented k-Coverage	Area Coverage	Random	Centralized & Distributed	Energy- Efficiency Maximize network lifetime by reducing the number of working nodes
Hilbert Mobile Beacon Coverage	Area Coverage	Random	Distributed using additional mobile nodes	Localization Energy- Efficiency Maximize network lifetime by reducing the number of working nodes
Virtual Force Algorithm (VFA)	Area Coverage	Random	Centralized	Energy- Efficiency Maximize network lifetime by reducing the number of working nodes
Mobility Assisted Probabilistic Protocol (MAPC)	Area Coverage	Random	Distributed, Localized & Centralizes	Energy-Efficiency Maximize network lifetime by reducing the number of working nodes
Disjoint Set Cover Heuristic ok	Point Coverage	Random	Centralized	Energy- Efficiency Maximize network lifetime by reducing the number of working nodes

mize the sensor field coverage using a combination of attractive and repulsive forces. The sensor field is represented by a two-dimensional grid. The dimensions of the grid provide a measure of the sensor field. The granularity of the grid, i.e. distance between grid points can be adjusted to trade off computation time of the VFA algorithm with the effectiveness of the coverage measure. The detection by each sensor is modeled as a circle on the grid. The center of the circle denotes the sensor while the radius denotes the detection range. The deployment of sensors can be either non-overlapped or overlapped for covering a ROI as shown in Figure 6.

An obvious drawback at the non-overlapped sensors is that a few grid points are not covered by any sensor. The alternative strategy is to allow overlap, although it needs more sensors for grid coverage. Note that in both cases, the coverage is effective only if the total area $k \cdot \pi \cdot r^2$, where r

Figure 6. Non-overlapped and overlapped sensor coverage areas

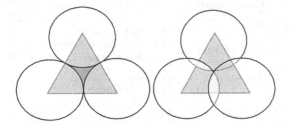

is defined as the detection range that can be covered, with the k sensors exceeds the area of the grid. Therefore, in the VFA algorithm, the first strategy is adopted.

In addition to the VFA approach, each sensor s_i is subjected to positive and negative forces F_i due to other sensors exerted by obstacles and areas of preferential coverage in the grid. Note that F_i is a vector whose orientation is determined by the vector sum of all the forces acting on s_i. This virtual force model creates a convenient method to model obstacles (negative forces) and the need for preferential coverage (positive forces). Sensor deployment must take into account the nature of the terrain, e.g., obstacles such as building and trees in the line of sight for infrared sensors, uneven surface and elevations for hilly terrain, etc. In addition, based on relative measures of security needs and tactical importance, certain areas of the grid need to be covered with greater certainty. For example consider four sensors s_1, s_2, s_3 and s_4 as shown in Figure 6. The force F_1 is given as the vector sum of the forces F_{12}, F_{13} and F_{14}, like in Equation 6.

$$F_1 = F_{12} + F_{13} + F_{14} \qquad (9)$$

The force F_{12} is the force between the sensor s_1 and sensor s_2, F_{13} is the force between s_1 and s_3 and F_{14} is the force between s_1 and s_4. The F_{ij}, in general, is expressed as the force between the

sensor s_i and s_j in polar coordinate notation. Note that $\bar{f} = (r,\theta)$ implies a magnitude of r and orientation θ for vector $\bar{f}$.

$$F_{ij} = \begin{cases} (w_A(d_{ij} - d_{th}), a_{ij}) & \text{if } d_{ij} > d_{th} \\ 0 & \text{if } d_{ij} = d_{th} \\ w_R \dfrac{1}{d_{ij}}, a_{ij} + \pi & \text{otherwise} \end{cases} \qquad (10)$$

where d_{ij} is the Euclidean distance between sensor s_i and s_j, d_{th} is the threshold on the distance s_i and s_j, a_{ij} is the orientation (angle) of a line segment from s_i to s_j and $w_A(w_R)$ is the measure of the attractive (repulsive) force. The threshold distance d_{th} controls how close sensors get to each other. In our example, if it assumed that $d_{12} > d_{th}$, $d_{13} < d_{th}$ and $d_{14} = d_{th}$, then the F_{12} is a attractive force, F_{13} is a repulsive force and F_{14} is zero, as shown in Figure 7.

In VFA algorithm, in each round the total F_i for each node s_i is computed and then the sensor moves to its next position. The next position is

Figure 7. An example of virtual forces with four sensors (adapted from Zou & Krishnendu, 2004)

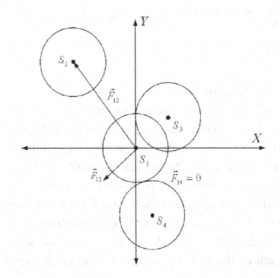

defined as the next location where the vector sum leads. The VFA algorithm is executed by the cluster head to find the appropriate sensor node locations based on the coverage requirements. The new locations are then sent to the sensor nodes, which perform a one-time movement to the designated positions. No movements are performed during the execution of the VFA algorithm. Energy constraints are also included in the sensor repositioning algorithm. The VFA pseudo-code is next described in Listing 1[REMOVED REF FIELD]. For a nxm grid with a total of k sensors deployed, the computational complexity of the VFA algorithm is $O(n \cdot m \cdot k)$ (See Box 1).

It is also proposed a novel target localization approach based on a two-step communication protocol between the cluster head and the sensors within the cluster. In the first step, sensors detecting a target report the event to the cluster head. The amount of information transmitted to the cluster head is limited; in order to save power and bandwidth, the sensor only reports the presence

of a target, and it does not transmit detailed information such as signal strength, confidence level in the detection, imagery or time series data. Based on the information received from the sensor and the knowledge of the sensor deployment within the cluster, the cluster head executes a probabilistic scoring-based localization algorithm to determine likely position of the target. The cluster head subsequently queries a subset of sensors that are in the vicinity of these likely target positions (See Figures 8 and 9).

Mobility-Assisted Probabilistic Protocol (MAPC)

In Nadeem et al (2007), the authors deal with a hybrid network consisting of a large number of static sensors deployed in a non-deterministic manner and a few mobile sensors available for plugging the coverage holes. The proposed MAPC protocol works in two distinct phases based on the idea of virtual forces. Phase I aims at estimating

Box 1. Pseudocode of the VFA algorithm (adapted from Zou & Krishnendu, 2004)

```
Algorithm: Virtual Force
Input : d(s_i, P), c_th, d_th, α, β
Output: Final proper locations of sensor nodes

loops = 0
MaxLoops = MAX_LOOPS
While (loops < MAX_LOOPS)
/*coverage evaluation */
        For P(x,y) in Grid, x ∈ [1, width], y ∈ [1, height]
                For s_i ∈ {s_1, s_2, ....., s_k}
                        Calculate c_xy(s_i, P) from the sensor model using (d(s_i, P), c_th, d_th, α, β)
                EndFor
                If coverage requirements are met
                        Break from While loop
                End if
        EndFor
/*Virtual forces among sensors*/
        For s_i ∈ {s_1, s_2, ....., s_k}
                Calculate F_ij
                Calculate F_iA
                Calculate F_iR
                F_i = ∑ F_ij + F_iR + F_iA, j ∈ [1,k], j ≠ i
        EndFor
/*move sensors virtually*/
        For s_i ∈ {s_1, s_2, ....., s_k}
                Fi(si) virtually moves si to its next position
        EndFor
        loops=loops+1
EndWhile
```

Figure 8. Initial deployment of sensors

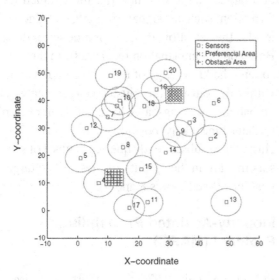

Figure 9. Sensor positions after the VFA's execution

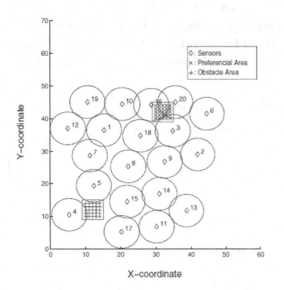

the existing coverage provided by the randomly deployed static nodes. The widely used binary detection model, assumes that the sensing coverage of a sensor node is uniform in all directions, often represented by a unit disc. However, in reality, the sensing capabilities of a sensor are often affected by environmental factors. In particular, for range-based sensor modalities such as acoustics, radio,

etc, the signal strength of the triggering signal decays as a function of distance. This implies that the detection capabilities of these sensors would exhibit similar characteristics as opposed to a uniform sensing range. In an effort to employ more realistic models in the computation of area coverage, is used the Probabilistic Coverage Algorithm (PCA) that takes into account the probabilistic sensing behavior of sensor nodes.

Phase II manages relocation of the mobile sensors. A set of coverage and energy aware variants of the Virtual Force Algorithm are proposed. These algorithms work in rounds and manage the mobile node relocation that serves a dual purpose. Firstly, this relocation increases the coverage during deployment by allowing the mobile nodes to fill in the coverage holes with minimal expenditure of energy. Secondly, the additional mobile sensors are uniformly spread at the target area for further discovery of coverage holes. The movements of the mobile nodes are controlled by novel thresholds based on real radio characteristics. This ensures that the nodes can communicate with each other, with high probability of successful transmission, during the round-by-round movements. The mobile nodes relocation in Phase II, thus, resulting in an increase in area coverage during the deployment stage. The simulation results of MAPC demonstrate that, for different type of initial deployments, this protocol consumes only 30-40% of the energy consumed by the basic Virtual Force Algorithm. MAPC is, thus, successful in enhancing area coverage to the desired degree while ensuring that minimal energy is expended by the mobile nodes.

Centralized Voronoi Tessellation (CVT)

The motivation of the algorithm presented in (Jie et al., 2005) is the effective spatial query execution in sensor networks. In the process of spatial query, the sink node needs to gather sensor data within a specific target region in order to obtain the status of the monitored target area. Sink nodes are capable machines with rich (often considered unlimited) resources, which gather data from one or more sensors for analysis and processing. An energy efficient way to respond to the query is to activate only a subset of sensor nodes to monitor the field and send back report data. The active node subset must satisfy two requirements:

- **Coverage Requirement:** Each point in the monitored region should be covered by at least one sensor in this subset.
- **Connectivity Requirement:** The communication network induced by active nodes should be connected.

For a given target region, the problem of finding a minimal subset of sensor nodes which meets the above two requirements at the same time is NP-hard. It is proposed a Centralized Voronoi Tessellation (CVT) based heuristic algorithm to compute the near optimal set of sensor nodes needed to cover the target region completely. A Voronoi diagram (Jie et al., 2005) is a special kind of decomposition of a given space, e.g., a metric space, determined by distances to a specified family of objects (subsets) in the space. These objects are usually called the sites or the generators (but other names are used, such as "seeds") and to each such object one associates a corresponding Voronoi cell, namely the set of all points in the given space whose distance to the given object is not greater than their distance to the other objects. It is called a Voronoi tessellation or a Voronoi decomposition.

In case of sensor's communication range is at least twice of its sensing range $Rc \leq 2Rs$, the constructed sensor set is connected. In other cases $Rc \leq 2Rs$ where the CVT algorithm alone cannot guarantee the network connectivity, it is designed a Steiner minimum tree (SMT) (Jie et al., 2005) based algorithm to ensure the communication connectivity. The minimal cover set can be obtained by turning off the maximal num-

ber of redundant sensors. A sensor is redundant if its sensing coverage is completely subsumed by other sensors. Turning off a redundant sensor will not leave sensing hole in the target region. The sensing hole is detected by utilizing the Voronoi tessellation of R. After all redundant sensors have been identified, they are classified in two sub-categories: independently and dependently redundant sensors. An independently redundant sensor is a redundant sensor whose Voronoi neighbors are all non redundant. A dependently redundant sensor is a redundant sensor whose Voronoi neighbors include at least one redundant sensor.

Non-redundant sensors must be kept active and independently redundant sensors are safe to be turned off. If two dependently redundant sensors, which are Voronoi neighbors each other, are turned off simultaneously, an area between them may be left uncovered, thus a sensing hole will occur. So the problem of calculating the minimal set of the active sensors is equivalent to determining the maximal set of the dependently redundant sensors that can be turned off simultaneously. A solution to this problem is to use the Redundant Dependency Graph (Jie et al., 2005) to resolve the dependency relationship. A Redundant Dependency Graph, $RDG = (Vr, Er)$, is an undirected graph, where Vr is the set of all dependently redundant sensors and $\forall v_{ri}, v_{rj} \in V_r, (v_{ri}, v_{rj}) \in V_r, (v_{ri}, v_{rj}) \in E_r$ if and only if vri and vrj are Voronoi neighbors. The problem of determining the maximal set of dependently redundant sensors that can be deactivated simultaneously is equal to the problem of calculating the Maximal Independent Set (MIS) of the RDG graph. In this paper, the greedy algorithm in Box 2 (Hochbaum, 1995) is adopted to calculate the MIS of the RDG graph.

When CVT algorithm terminates, all independently redundant sensors and all dependently redundant sensors selected into the MIS of the RDG graph form a Safe Set (SS), which includes

Box 2. Pseudo-code of CVT (adapted from Jie, et al., 2005)

```
Algorithm: CVT
Input : IS, Sensors
Output: MIS

SS=CS=0
S=IS
If R ⊄ ∪ si
      sᵢ ∈ S
      Return CS
EndIf
While S≠0
      IRS=DRS=MIS=0
      identify all redundant sensor nodes in S
      Foreach redundant sensor sᵢ ∈ S
            If sᵢ is independently redundant
                  IRS = IRS ∪ {sᵢ}
            Else
                  DRS = DRS ∪{sᵢ}
            EndIf
      EndFor
      If DRS ≠ 0
            Compute MIS of the RDG graph
            SS = SS∪IRS∪MIS
            SS=IS – SS
      Else
            SS = SS∪IRS
            Break from the While loop
      EndIf
EndWhile
CS = IS - SS
End
```

Figure 10. Graph Gc and Gc'

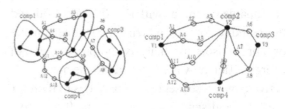

all sensors that can be deactivated safely at the same time. And all other sensors form the final cover set for the target region and must be kept active to respond a specific query. Suppose that sensors in the cover set constructed by the CVT algorithm form m separated connected components in G_c as shown in Figure 10. The connected component consists of only primary sensors (denoted by solid circular dots). A connected component in the cover set is a connected sub graph of G_c whose vertices only involve primary sensors, where G_c is the communication graph induced by

all initially deployed sensors. These components are connected through assistant sensors (denoted by hollow circular dots). Each connected component is presents as one virtual vertex and use v_i to represent $comp_i$. Then we attach to v_i all edges in G_c that connect one primary sensor in $comp_i$ and another assistant sensor. In this paper, a sensor in the cover set is called a primary sensor; otherwise it is an assistant sensor. After this conversion, an abstract communication graph (G_c') is created.

If weight is equal to 1, it is assigned to each edge in G_c, selecting the minimal number of additional sensors needed to connect the components in G_c is equivalent to solving the SMT problem in the 1-weighted graph G_c, where the virtual vertices representing components are considered as 'terminals' and the required assistant sensors are those 'Steiner points' that are necessary to construct the SMT to connect all the terminals. The SMT based connection algorithm is presented in Box 3:

In summary CVT outperforms an algorithm in terms of both the time complexity and the size of the final connected cover set (i.e., the number of sensors that must be kept active).

Particle Swarm Optimization Using Voronoi Diagrams: WSNPSO$_{con}$

In (Nor Azlina et al, 2010), the coverage problem is considered using an evolutionary algorithm. The proposed algorithm, WSNPSO$_{con}$ uses Particle Swarm Optimization (PSO or WSNPSO) to find the best locations of the sensors according to a penalty based fitness function.

Box 3. The SMT-based connection algorithm

Algorithm: SMT based Connection
Create the 1-weighted abstract communication graph G_c' as described
Calculate the Steiner Minimum Tree (SMT) to connect all virtual vertices in G_c'
Return all the assistant sensors corresponding to the Steiner points in the computed SMT
End

Particle Swarm Optimization (PSO) is a computational method developed by Kennedy and Eberhant (Kennedy & Eberhart, 1995) that optimizes a problem by iteratively trying to improve a candidate solution with regard to a given measure of quality. PSO optimizes a problem by having a population of candidate solutions, here dubbed particles, and moving these particles around in the search-space according to simple mathematical formulate over the particle's position and velocity. Let $x_i(t)$ denote the position of particle i in the search space at time step t; unless otherwise stated, t denotes discrete time steps. The position of the particle is changed by adding a velocity, vi (t), to the current position, i.e.

$$x_i(t+1) = x_i(t) + v_i(t+1) \qquad (11)$$

Each particle's movement is influenced by its local best P_i known position and is also guided toward the best known positions P_g in the search-space, which are updated as better positions are found by other particles. The pseudo-code of the PSO is shown in Box 4.

The fitness function in this approach is described by the following equation

minimize
point $\in$ interest points
$$\sum \text{coverage\_holes(point)} + {}^3 \cdot P(d_{mov}) \qquad (12)$$

where γ is a positive value penalty parameter and $P(d_{mov})$ is a penalty function. The penalty function penalizes any solution outside the feasible solu-

tion. The d_{mov} is the maximum distance moved by any sensor. The absolute penalty value, which is used in WSNPSO$_{con}$, is

$$P(d_{mov}) = \max(0,(d_{mov}\text{-}D_{max})) \qquad (13)$$

$P(d_{mov})$ is equal to zero as long as the constraint is obeyed, but when the constraint is violated, $P(d_{mov})$ is equal to some positive value. The accuracy of the approximation of the optimal solution found by the penalty method is controlled by γ. A large value of γ will result in a heavier penalty to any breach of the constraint, however, a very severe penalty will make it hard to find an optimal solution. On the contrary, a small penalty might be too lenient, thus causing infeasible solution.

The fitness function uses the Voronoi diagram to measure the quality of the coverage. A set of interest points is defined as two group of points: (1) vertices of the Voronoi polygons, obtained from the computed Voronoi diagram and (2) a number of points distributed evenly on the boundary of the polygons. The Voronoi diagram is computed based on the sensors positions encoded by the particle. The boundary points, whose number is selected experimentally, act as pulling forces that prevent the sensors from congregating around a particular point in the ROI. A fuzzy penalty system finds the penalty parameters. The Fuzzy set is used to determine the penalty parameter γ, based on the value of d_{mov} which is divided in three parts, Figure 11: are good feasible solutions while part (1) interesting infeasible solutions; infeasible but close to the feasible region (2) bad solutions that are too far from the feasible area (3).

Box 4. Pseudo-code for PSO algorithm

```
Algorithm: PSO
Input : Particles' Position (X_i) and Velocity (V_i)
Output: Final Best position of particles

Foreach particle
        Initialize X_i and V_i
EndFor
Do
        Foreach particle
                Calculate fitness value
                If the current fitness value is better than P_i
                        Update P_i
                EndIf
                Choose the particle position with the best fitness value of all the neighbors
                as the P_g
        EndFor
        Foreach particle
                Update V_i
                Update X_i
        End
While maximum iteration or ideal fitness is not attained
```

In every iteration, Figure 12, the maximum distance moved by any particle d_{mov} is passed to the fuzzy system to compute a new value of the penalty parameter γ. This value is passed to PSO to be used in the fitness function. This process will continue until either one of the stopping conditions – maximum iteration or 100% coverage with $d_{mov} - D_{max}$ is met.

WSNPSO$_{con}$ is an algorithm based on PSO for optimizing the WSN coverage problem while conserving energy. WSNPSO$_{con}$ sees the two problems as a constrained optimization problem where the coverage is maximized by moving the sensors subject to a maximum distance moved. Simulation results show that the proposed algo-

rithm succeeds in maximizing the coverage and ensures the energy is saved and kept below the threshold value.

Sensor Deployment Algorithm Based on Artificial Bee Colony

Researchers in (Mini et al., 2011) describe an algorithm for optimal deployment in 3D terrain using Artificial Bee Colony (ABC). ABC is one of the most recently defined algorithms by Dervis Karaboga (Karaboga & Akay, 2009) motivated by the intelligent behavior of honey bees. It is as simple as Particle Swarm Optimization (PSO) and uses only common control parameters such as colony size and maximum cycle number. ABC provides a population-based search procedure in which individuals called foods positions are modified by the artificial bees with time and the bee's aim is to discover the places of food sources

Figure 11. Fuzzy set for γ based on d_{mov}

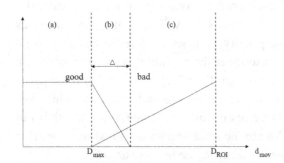

Figure 12. WSNPSOcon operation diagram

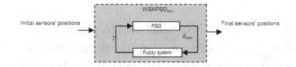

with high nectar amount and finally the one with the highest nectar. In ABC system, artificial bees fly around in a multidimensional search space and some bees (employed bees) choose food sources depending on the experience of themselves and their nest mates, and adjust their positions. Some (scouts/unemployed) fly and choose the food sources randomly without using experience. If the nectar amount of a new source is higher than that of the previous one in their memory, they memorize the new position and forget the previous one. Hence, the unemployed bee will become employed.

The foraging bee takes a load of food (nectar) from the source and returns to the hive and unloads the nectar to the food store. After unloading the food, the bee performs a special form of dance called waggle dance which contains information for:

1. Direction of food source.
2. Source's distance from the hive.
3. Source's quality rating.

Since information of about all rich sources is available to an onlooker on the dance floor, an onlooker bee probably could watch numerous dances and choose to employ itself at the most qualitative source. If a great amount of information is circulating about the qualitative sources, the greater is the possibility of onlookers choosing more qualitative sources (See Box 5).

In the proposed method, the first step is to form clusters according to their locations. Each cluster has a sensor s_i associated as cluster centroids with it. The number of clusters formed is equal to the number of sensors to be deployed. The algorithm for the clustering is described in Box 5.

The next step is to calculate the optimal sensor positions. The fitness function is calculated based on the Euclidean distances between cluster centroids and points at ROI. $F(D_i)$ refers to the nectar amount at food source located at D_i. An onlooker watches the waggle dances of foraging bees, an onlooker picks a region D_i to go with possibility (Mini et al., 2011):

$$p_i = \frac{F(D_i)}{\sum_{f=1}^{nf} F(D_f)} \qquad (14)$$

where *nf* is the total number of food sources. The next neighborhood to go in the vicinity of D_i is computed according to (Mini et al., 2011):

$$D_i(t+1) = D_i(t) + \delta_{id} \times v \qquad (15)$$

Δ_{id} is the neighborhood patch size of the dth food source, t is the current cycle and v is a random number $\in [-1, 1]$. The fitness function for the $D_i(t+1)$ and its solutions are evaluated and compared with the existing value and solutions of fitness function. If any solution is better than the existing one, the new solution replaces the old one. Otherwise scout bees search for a random feasible solution. The solution with least sensing range is finally chosen as the best solution. Algorithm is described in Box 6.

Mission-Oriented k-Coverage

The problem of k-coverage of a ROI is studied in (Habib et al., 2010), where each point is covered by at least $k \geq 3$ active sensors. The solution proposed is based on Helly's Theorem and the geometric analysis of a geometric structure, called Reuleaux triangle. The Reuleaux triangle is a constant width curve based on an equilateral triangle, as shown in Figure 13, where all points on a side are equidistant from the opposite vertex. Also, the method proposed enables sensors to move towards a ROI and ensure the k-coverage while minimizing the required energy.

Box 5. Clustering algorithm

```
For every bee
        solution=false
        while (solution==false) then
                Calculate distance between each target and all the sensor locations
                Form clusters by assigning targets to 1/k/Q sensor nodes which are
                at minimum distance
                If (all sensors form cluster) then
                        Move the sensor location to centroid of all target
                        location points that are associated with it

                        solution=true
        Else
                        Move sensors without assigned targets to random
                        target locations

        EndIf

    EndWhile
EndFor
```

Box 6. Deployment's algorithm

```
Algorithm: Deployment

cycle =1

while (cycle < maximumcycles) repeat

        Search for new solutions in the neighborhood

                if (new solution better than old solution) then

                        Memorize new solution and discard old solution

                end if

        Replace the discarded solution with a newly randomly generated
        solution through a scout bee

        Memorize the best solution

        cycle = cycle +1

EndWhile
```

Figure 13. Reuleaux triangle

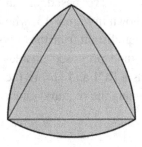

Helly's Theorum: Let K be a set of convex sets in R^n such that for $m \geq n + 1$. Any m sets of K have a non-empty intersection. Then, the intersection of all sets of K is non-empty.

Lemma 1: Let $k \geq 3$. The intersection of k sensing disks is not empty if and only if the intersection of any three of them is not empty (*Helly's Theorum in 2D space*).

In the studied type of WSN, there must be a node that is aware of the mission objectives of the network in the monitored field. We assume that the sink is aware of any region of interest in the field that needs to be k-covered and hence is responsible for computing the locations that should be occupied by the sensors in order to k-cover a region of interest. Also, it has been proved that the optimum location of the sink in terms of energy-efficient data gathering is the center of the field (Yi & Krishnendu, 2004). Based on Theorem 1, the sink randomly splits a region of interest into overlapping Reuleaux triangles of width r (or slices) such that two adjacent slices intersect in a region shaped as a lens:

Theorem 1: *Let $k \geq 3$. A region of interest is surely k-covered with a small number of sensors if for any slice in the region, there is at least one adjacent slice such that their intersection (lens) has at least k active sensors (Ammari & Guidici, 2009).*

Based on Theorem 1, Theorem 2 computes the number of sensors needed to k-cover a field of area F.

Theorem 2: *Let r be the radius of the sensors' sensing disks and $k \geq 3$. The minimum number of sensors $n(r,k)$ to k-cover a field of area F is given by:*

$$n(r,k) = \frac{6kF}{(4\pi - 3\sqrt{3})r^2}$$

The sink exploits the result of Theorem 1 so that a region of interest is k-covered by a small number of active sensors. Hence, it identifies the necessary lenses where the active sensors should be located and broadcast this information into the network. The sink for computing the lenses needs to be aware of the current locations of all the sensors. Also, the sink has to keep track of the

remaining energy of each sensor in the network. Thus, the sink is required to maintain a database for all the sensors where each entry contains a sensor's id, its current location, and remaining energy. There are two solutions proposed, i.e. a centralized and distributed method for sensors' deployment.

Centralized Approach for Mobile Sensor Selection (CAMSEL): The sink will broadcast as many queries as the number of sensors necessary to k-cover the ROI. Each query includes an id of a selected sensor or and its point location $(x,y)_{target}$ in one of the lenses of ROI. Precisely, a query has the following structure: query $= <id,(x,y)>$ point. When a sensor receives a query, it will decide whether to forward the query toward the selected sensor based on the location of the sink and the point location (x,y) in the query. Sensors move only when they are requested by the sink, because sink is aware of the current locations of all the sensors and keeps track of the remaining energy of each sensor in the network. In the centralized approach, the sink is supposed to be aware of the status of all the sensors in the network with regard to their location and energy consumption. Although centralized approach helps obtain the best schedule in terms of energy-efficient k-coverage and minimum energy consumption due to sensor movements, it would incur delay in the sensor selection phase especially for a large network that require a huge database for maintaining the current status of all the sensors in the network.

Distributed Approach for Mobile Sensor Selection (DAMSEL): The sensors will cooperate with each other to move to the region of interest to k-cover it with a small number of sensors while minimizing the energy consumption introduced by their mobility. The sink will only specify the ROI to be k-covered, which supposed to be a square that is characterized by its center (x_o,y_o) and side length a. Thus, the sink will broadcast a unique query that has the following structure: query $= <(x_o,y_o),a>$. Moreover, it is assumed that all the sensors generate the same slicing grid of the ROI. This means that all the sensors deterministically generate the same reference triangle whose center coincides with that of the ROI. This would enable all the sensors to have the same set of lenses, each of which should be occupied with at least k sensors. Also, each sensor is supposed to be moving at a constant speed until it reaches its destination in the lens it selected in the region.

The simulation results in (Habib et al., 2010) show that CAMSEL outperforms DAMSEL in terms of the number of sensors and the total moving energy required to ensure k-coverage of a ROI.

Hilbert Mobile Beacon Coverage

A different approach is studied in (Jacques et al., 2008). Researchers to reach an optimal solution try to locate the sensors at ROI (localization problem) and then to solve the coverage problem. The localization problem is a major issue which contributes to decreasing the effectiveness of WSN by decreasing geographical accuracy. To elaborate on the localization problem, the following should be considered: given a large number of sensors (also called unknown sensors) randomly deployed in a given area of known shape and a small number of mobile beacons (i.e. sensor nodes that know their global coordinates a priori using GPS, being set manually, etc.). The localization problem lies within the difficulty in finding the geographical positions of the unknown sensors while the coverage problem is related to energy optimization. This approach (Jacques et al., 2008) is based on a mobile beacon that traverses the ROI and help sensors locate themselves and find in addition a 'coverage scheduling' between them. The advantages of such approach are numerous, particularly the significant reduction of the consumed energy. Also, finding a scheduling (coverage) between sensors will dramatically simplify and reduce the initialization phase of the network, i.e. neighboring discovery and routing initialization.

To implement this method a Hilbert space filing curve is used as a trajectory for the mobile beacon. The Hilbert space filling curve is a one-dimensional curve, which visits every point exactly once without crossing itself within two- or three-dimensional space (20). The Hilbert curve avoids by constructing the co-linearity of packets, which is not the case for the scan line curve. Second, in the scan line curve, the mobile beacon travels long distances following straight lines, which of course decreases the localization precision. Moreover, the order of Hilbert curve could be changed dynamically without altering the continuity of the curve. This interesting feature could be used to get locally higher localization precision by making the trajectory of the mobile beacon closer to the unknown nodes.

Definition 1: The basic curve is said to be of order 1. To derive a curve of order i, each vertex of the basic curve is replaced by the curve of order i-1, which may be appropriately rotated and/or reflected to fit the new curve (Hilbert curve ordering) (Jacques et al., 2008).

The basic Hilbert curve for a 2x2 grid is shown in Figure 14. The procedure to derive higher orders of the Hilbert curve is to rotate and reflect the curve at vertex 0 and at vertex 3. Figure 15 also shows the Hilbert curve of order 2.

Hilbert Keys: Hilbert-keys or h-keys are defined as points order in the linear ordering going from 0 to 2^m-1.

Figure 15 shows Hilbert keys from 0 to 15 with Hilbert curve of order 2. Every Hilbert key has its correspondent coordinates in x and y-axis. For example, h=6 corresponds to the point (1, 3) in the two-dimensional space.

Definition 2: A US is a sub square section of the grid, where it encloses the basic Hilbert curve with four consecutive h-keys.

The first h-key must be divisible by 4. Figure 15 shows an example of a grid that encloses an order 2 Hilbert curve with four USs ({0, 1, 2, 3}, {4, 5, 6, 7}, {8, 9, 10, 11}, {12, 13, 14, 15}). The algorithm steps are described below (Jacques et al., 2008):

Figure 14. Hilbert curves of order 1

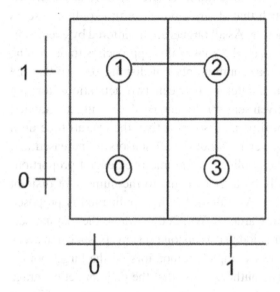

Figure 15. Hilbert curves of order 2

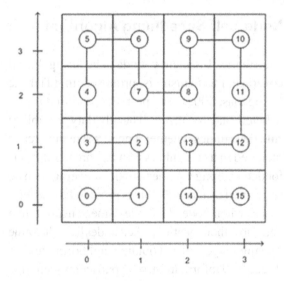

Localization

1. After sensors deployment, the Hilbert beacon (a mobile beacon that traverses the region of interest following the Hilbert space filling curve) sticks to its trajectory and sends packets. At this stage, each unknown sensor receives part of these packets, and sorts it into sets of three h-keys. The two segments joining these h-keys known as 'L' curve must have the scale s as lengths and must be parallel to the Cartesian axis.

2. The second step is to obtain the distance between sensors and the selected h-keys positions. Every sensor computes distances by using one of the ranging techniques, like Bary–Hilbert, Hilbert, Bayesian and Trilateration (Jacques et al., 2008).

3. At this step, every sensor has selected a set 'l' of 'L' curves, which contains at least one curve. The core of this step is a simple trigonometric algorithm, based on law of cosines. For every 'L' curve, the sensor begins by grouping the three h-keys into two pairs, each one containing two of different parities. One of the lines joining the components of these pairs is vertical and the second is horizontal. The vertical line is used to find the X coordinate and the horizontal one is used to find the Y coordinate. Every sensor is then running the following algorithm.

Coverage

1. From the above localization approach, every sensor within a US calculates its position.

2. The estimated position is then sent back to the mobile beacon. The condition on the order of Hilbert trajectory to be able to locate sensors and to perform coverage is

$$m \geq \left\lceil \log_2(\frac{2\sqrt{2} \max(height, width)}{R_S}) \right\rceil,$$

where m is the Hilbert curve order and R_s is the sensing range at a ROI with specific height and width. This condition ensures that every sensor located within the considered US is able to communicate with the mobile beacon.

3. Once the mobile beacon has received messages from sensors, it could determine which sensors are located within the same US ('redundant sensors'). Then, it assigns an order of activation for those sensors. The order of activation, in current implementation, is random.

4. Finally, the activation scheduling is sent back to sensors so that every sensor knows precisely when it has to be active. In this implementation, the activation of each sensor is performed until the sensor is running out of energy. Before its 'death', it activates the next sensor in the activation order.

This method exploits the interesting features of Hilbert curves to develop a low-complex localization algorithm that makes it very suitable for limited capabilities sensor sensors. In addition moving beacons are used to derive an activity scheduling between sensors in order to prolong the network lifetime.

Disjoint Set Cover Heuristic

The point coverage scenario addressed in (Cardei & Du, 2005) has military applicability. It considers a limited number of points (targets) with known location that need to be monitored. A large number of sensors are dispersed randomly in close proximity to the targets; the sensors send the monitored information to a central processing node. The requirement is that every target must be monitored at all times by at least one sensor, assuming that every sensor is able to monitor all targets within its sensing range. One method for extending the sensor network lifetime through energy resource preservation is the division of the set of sensors into disjoint sets such that every set completely covers all targets.

These disjoint sets are activated successively, such that at any moment in time only one set is active. As all targets are monitored by every sensor set, the goal of this approach is to determine a maximum number of disjoint sets, so that the time interval between two activations for any given sensor is longer. By decreasing the fraction of time a sensor is active, the overall time until power runs out for all sensors is increased and the application lifetime is extended proportionally by a factor equal to the number of disjoint sets. A solution for this application is proposed in (Cardei & Wu, 2005), where the disjoint sets are modeled as disjoint set covers, such that every cover completely monitors all the target points. The authors prove that the disjoint set coverage problem is NP-complete and propose an efficient heuristic for set covers computation using a mixed integer programming formulation.

Node Self-Scheduling Algorithm

An Energy-Efficiency node-scheduling based coverage mechanism is proposed in (Tian & Georganas, 2002). The protocol proposed is distributed and localized. The off-duty eligibility rule determines whether a node's sensing area is included in its neighbors' sensing area. Solutions for determining whether a node's coverage can be sponsored by its neighbors is provided for several cases: when nodes have the same sensing range and know their location, when nodes have the same sensing range and can obtain neighboring node's directional information, or in particular scenarios when nodes have different sensing ranges. The node scheduling scheme is divided into rounds, where each round has a self-scheduling phase followed by a sensing phase. In the self-scheduling phase, the nodes investigate the off-duty eligibility rule. Eligible nodes turn off their communication and sensing units, while all other nodes will perform sensing tasks in the sensing phase. In order to obtain neighboring information, each node broadcasts a position advertisement message at the beginning of each round, containing node ID and node location. If the off-duty eligibility rule is tested simultaneously by neighboring nodes, a node and its sponsor may decide to turn off simultaneously, triggering the occurrence of blind points. To avoid this, a back-off scheme is used, where every node starts the evaluation rule after a random time, and then broadcasts a status advertisement message to announce if it is available for turning off. Before turning off, a node waits another time to listen for neighboring nodes update.

PERFORMANCE OVERHEAD

Comparison between VFA and CEA-VFA

The simulation in the Figures 16 and 17 take into account some assumptions (Nadeem et al, 2007). In simulation the static nodes are randomly deployed in a 100m by 100m region. Values of Th_{push}, Th_{pull}, and d_{dis} are set at 25m, 33m, and 40m respectively. Initial energy of each node is 4528J and energy consumed in movement is taken as 8.274 J/m. In island distribution, mobile nodes form two disconnected clusters at opposite corners of the topology. Maximum number of rounds is set to 12. The results are averaged over two different topologies for each type of deployment.

So, Figure 16 and Figure 17 compare the total distance moved by all mobile nodes comparing the MAPC algorithm (CEA-VFA) with the basic Virtual Force Algorithm (VFA). The results show that CEA-VFA performs better than the basic VFA, for both normal and island initial deployment, for different numbers of mobile nodes. On average, CEA-VFA causes the mobile nodes to

Figure 16. Total Normal distance moved

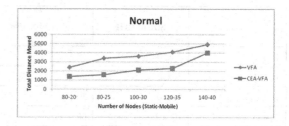

Figure 17. Total distance moved on island

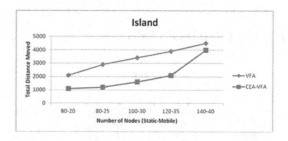

move about 63% and 57% (Nadeem et al, 2007) of the total distance moved in case of basic VFA for normal and island deployments respectively. This saving is primarily due to the coverage aware-ness that enables CEA-VFA to discover and plug the coverage holes in each round of the VFA.

Comparison between WSNPSO and WSNPSO_con

The performance overview for the two algorithms is measured from six different tests, as recorded in Table 2. The coverage, the maximum distance travelled among the sensors and the execution time averaged over 20 runs are figured in Figure 18, Figure 19 and Figure 20. The figures show that both WSNPSO and WSNPSOcon significantly improve the initial coverage of the networks. The maximum distance travelled by any sensor, when WSNPSOcon is used, is always below the threshold value of 20. The coverage of the two algorithms is similar to each other in small ROIs but the difference becomes clearer when the ROI

Table 2. Test parameters

	Size of ROI	Number of Sensors	Ideal Coverage	Description	
				ROI	Density
Test I	50x50	10	62%	Smaller	Sparse
Test II	50x50	20	100%	Smaller	Optimal
Test III	50x50	30	100%	Smaller	Dense
Test IV	100x100	60	92%	Larger	Sparse
Test V	100x100	80	100%	Larger	Optimal
Test VI	100x100	100	100%	Larger	Dense

Figure 18. Test results for coverage

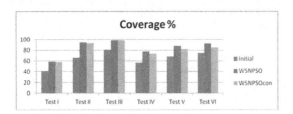

Figure 19. Test results for execution time in seconds

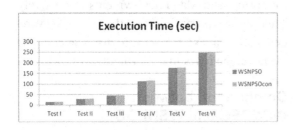

Figure 20. Test results for maximum distance travel

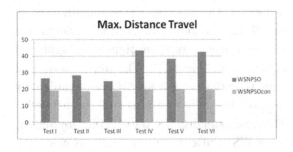

size is larger. This is expected as the constraint in large ROI is restricting the WSNPSOcon to search more severely than what it does in small ROI, hence this reduces its coverage. As for density

Figure 21. Sensing range requirement for k-coverage problem

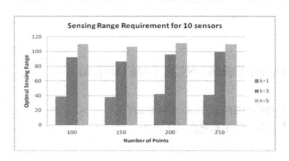

Figure 22. Sensing range requirement for Q-coverage problem

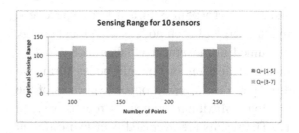

level, both algorithms show that the denser the network the better is the final coverage on the expense of longer execution time.

Comparison in ABC between k and Q-Coverage

The simulations carried out by the researchers in (Mini et al., 2011) with varying k-values and values of vector Q in order to find the minimum sensing range. We can notice that the sensing range does not increase in same proportion with increase in k and Q values. For a given number of sensors, an increase in the number of points to be covered not always need high sensing range requirement, as it is figured in Figure 21 and Figure 22.

FUTURE RESEARCH DIRECTIONS

In future work, more extensions of WSN's assumptions should be considered. Some algorithms take into consideration only one target in the sensor field, so it is necessary to extend the algorithms to facilitate the localization of multiple objects. The coordinates of the sensors are considered as predefined, but as future work the researchers should take into consideration the uncertainty in the position of the sensors due to the initial deployment. Researchers also can examine continuous coordination systems instead of discrete coordination systems and can enhance their approaches with experiments, which will help to validate the working algorithms. In addition, there should be a provision for the existing algorithms to be combined with high security levels. Wireless nodes, in the future, will not only transmit environmental observations and measurements, but also "sensitive data. As the future for WSNs is bright and the interest areas are extending, for example, sensors will be used in underwater acoustic sensor systems, in security and management of privacy or in detection of cognitive spectrum, it is necessary to upgrade the existing work with the work in other fields.

CONCLUSION

Summing up, wireless sensor networks (Wireless Sensor Network – WSN) are a recent, rapidly emerging network technology. Many argue that it is one of the most important developments of wireless and mobile communications. We observe that the scopes of WSN are numerous and are increasing over time. Specifically, WSN applications are used in environmental, military, health, ambient intelligence, etc. Scientists searching the area of WSN face many challenges relating to restrictions on power, memory, processing power, bandwidth, etc. Sensor coverage is an important element for QoS in applications in WSNs and is associated with two important properties of sensor nodes, (1) the full coverage of the area and (2) the minimum energy consumption. Large WSNs with limited resources and dynamic topology need coverage control algorithms and protocols, which will answer to their needs. The algorithms, which are presented in this chapter, meet the raising challenges. However, there are further steps in the evolution of these algorithms and their combination with other sectors such as security.

REFERENCES

Ammari, H. M., & Guidici, J. (2009). On the connected k-coverage problem in heterogeneous sensor nets: The curse of randomness and heterogeneity. In *Proceedings of IEEE ICDCS*. IEEE.

Ammari & Das. (2010). Mission-oriented k-coverage in mobile wireless sensor networks. In *Proceedings of the International Conference of Distributed Computing and Networking – ICDCN*. Berlin: Springer.

Azlina, Aziz, Mohemmed, & Zhang. (2010). Particle swarm optimization for coverage maximization and energy conservation in wireless sensor networks. *EvoApplications, 2*, 51–60.

Cardei, M., & Du, D.-Z. (2005). Improving wireless sensor network lifetime through power aware organization. *ACM Wireless Networks, 11*(3), 333–340. doi:10.1007/s11276-005-6615-6.

Cardei, M., & Wu, J. (2005). Coverage in wireless sensor networks. In Ilyas & Mahgoub (Eds.), Handbook of Sensor Networks: Compact Wireless and Wired Sensing Systems (pp. 19-1–19-12). Boca Raton, FL: CRC Press.

Hochbaum, D. S. (1995). *Approximation algorithms for np-hard problems*. PWS Publishing Company.

Howard, A., Mataric, M. J., & Sukhatme, G. S. (2002). Mobile sensor network deployment using potential field: A distributed scalable solution to the area coverage problem. In *Proceedings of the 6th International Symposium on Distributed Autonomous Robotics Systems (DARS '02)* (pp. 299–308). Fukuoka, Japan: DARS.

Jacques, M. B., Abdallah, M., & Ahmed, M. (2008). Hilbert mobile beacon for localisation and coverage in sensor networks. *International Journal of Systems Science, 39*(11), 1081–1094. doi:10.1080/00207720802085302.

Jiang, Song, Zhang, & Dou. (2005). *Voronoi-based improved algorithm for connected coverage problem in wireless sensor networks*. EUC.

Karaboga, D., & Akay, B. (2009). A survey: Algorithms simulating bee swarm intelligence. *Artificial Intelligence Review, 31*(1-4), 61–85. doi:10.1007/s10462-009-9127-4.

Kennedy, J., & Eberhart, R. (1995). Particle swarm optimization. In *Proceedings of the IEEE International Conference on Neural Networks*. IEEE.

Locateli, M., & Raber, U. (2002). Packing equal circles in a square: A deterministic global optimization approach. *Discrete Applied Mathematics, 122,* 139–166. doi:10.1016/S0166-218X(01)00359-6.

Mini, S., Udgata, S. K., & Sabat, S. L. (2011). Artificial bee colony based sensor deployment algorithm for target coverage problem in 3-D terrain. In *Proceedings of the Distributed Computing and Internet Technology - 7ᵗʰ International Conference*. Berlin, Germany: Springer.

Nadeem, A., Salil, S. K., & Sanjay, J. (2007). *Ensuring area coverage in hybrid wireless sensor network*. Berlin: Springer-Verlag.

Nojeong, H., & Pramod, K. V. (2005). Energy-efficient deployment of intelligent mobile sensor networks. *IEEE Transactions on Systems, Man, and Cybernetics. Part A, 35*(1), 78–92.

Tian, D., & Georganas, N. D. (2002). A coverage-preserving node scheduling scheme for large wireless sensor networks. In *Proceedings of the 1st ACM Workshop on Wireless Sensor Networks and Applications*. ACM.

Wu, S., & Xu, Y. Cho, & Lee. (2005). Swarm based sensor deployment optimization in ad hoc sensor networks. In *Proceedings of Embedded Software and Systems, Second International Conference, ICESS 2005* (LNCS), (Vol. 3820, pp. 533-541). Berlin: Springer.

Zhao, W. Shang, & Wang. (2004). Optimizing sensor node distribution with genetic algorithm in wireless sensor network. Berlin: Springer-Verlag.

Zou & Chakrabarty. (2004). Sensor deployment and target localization in distributed sensor networks. *ACM Transaction on Embedded Computing Systems, 3,* 61–91. doi:10.1145/972627.972631.

ADDITIONAL READING

Bang, Hock, & Di. (2009). A survey of movement strategies for improving network coverage in wireless sensor networks. *Computer Communications, 32,* 1427–1436. doi:10.1016/j.comcom.2009.05.004.

Chaudhary, M., & Pujari, A. K. (2008). Q-coverage problem in wireless sensor networks. In Garg, Wattenhofer, & Kothapalli (Eds.) ICDCN 2009 (LNCS), (Vol. 5408, pp. 325–330). Heidelberg: Springer.

Karaboga, D., & Basturk, B. (2008). On the performance of artificial bee colony (ABC) algorithm. *Applied Soft Computing, 8,* 687–697. doi:10.1016/j.asoc.2007.05.007.

Rappaport, T. S. (1996). *Wireless communications: Principles and practice.* Upper Saddle River, NJ: Prentice Hall.

Sibley, G. T., Rahimi, M. H., & Sukhatme, G. S. (2002). Robomote: A tiny mobile robot platform for large-scale ad-hoc sensor networks. In *Proceedings of IEEE International Conference on Robotics and Automation* (pp. 1143-1148). IEEE.

KEY TERMS AND DEFINITIONS

Artificial Bee Colony (ABC): An algorithm which is motivated by the intelligent behavior of honey bees. ABC provides a population-based search procedure in which individuals called foods positions are modified by the artificial bees with time and the bee's aim is to discover the places of food sources with high nectar amount and finally the one with the highest nectar.

Coverage Problem: To decide how to deploy the portable devices (sensors) in order to cover the entire area of interest (ROI).

K-Coverage Problem: To decide how to deploy at least k devices (sensors) in order to cover the entire area of interest (ROI).

Mobile Beacons: Sensor nodes that know their global coordinates a priori using GPS, being set manually, etc.

Particle Swarm Optimization (PSO): An algorithm that optimizes a problem by having a population of candidate solutions, like dubbed particles, and moving these particles around in the search-space according to simple mathematical formulate over the particle's position and velocity.

Sensor's Energy Consumption: To organize the sensors in an optimal manner-efficiently, consuming the minimum energy and covering the whole area of interest (ROI).

Virtual Force Algorithm (VFA): An algorithm that tries to maximize the sensor field coverage using a combination of attractive and repulsive forces.

Wireless Sensor Network (WSN): A network of portable devices (sensors) that can monitor, compute and store information depending on their environment.

Chapter 7
Wireless Sensor Network Design for Energy–Efficient Monitoring

Daniele Apiletti
Politecnico di Torino, Italy

Elena Baralis
Politecnico di Torino, Italy

Tania Cerquitelli
Politecnico di Torino, Italy

ABSTRACT

Wireless sensors are small-scale mobile devices that can programmatically measure physical quantities, perform simple computations, store, receive, and transmit data. The lattice built by a set of cooperating sensors is called a sensor network. Since sensor networks provide a powerful infrastructure for large-scale monitoring applications, an important issue is the network design to achieve an optimal placement of the sensors to allow (1) energy-efficient monitoring and (2) gathering meaningful data. This chapter presents a novel approach to optimize sensing node placement (e.g., for new to-be-deployed networks) and efficiently acquire data from existing sensor networks. A historical data analysis task is performed to discover spatial and temporal correlations and identify sets of correlated sensors. Then, an algorithm based on a cost function considering both distance and communication cost selects the candidate sensors, leading to the optimized network design and acquisition. Candidate sensors can then be deployed and/or queried instead of the whole network, thus reducing the network cost and extending its lifetime in terms of energy consumption. Experiments, performed on a real wireless sensor network, demonstrate the adaptability and the effectiveness of the proposed approach in optimizing the sensor network design and the data acquisition.

DOI: 10.4018/978-1-4666-4038-2.ch007

INTRODUCTION

To identify careful power management techniques in habitat-monitoring applications, we consider sensor power consumption required to collect and process data, and transmit the result to the sensor network application (through a master sensor node). While CPU overheads are very small, as no significant processing is typically performed on the nodes, the main contributors to energy consumption are communication and data acquisition from sensors (Deshpande et al., 2004). Furthermore, collected data must be relevant for the monitoring purposes. To this aim, sensor networks must be carefully designed by optimizing sensing node placement to address both meaningfulness of collected measurements and energy consumption during data collection (Baoqianga et al., 2008). Sensor positioning can be performed by application-domain experts, but unknown relationships and correlations among different sensors can affect optimal placement, which remains a hard goal to achieve (Baoqianga et al., 2008).

This chapter presents an approach to optimize sensing node placement and efficiently acquire data from deployed sensor networks. Sensor data are usually correlated both in time and space, thus a set of candidate nodes are identified to model the network state and realistic assumptions are considered (e.g., presence of outliers).

The proposed approached consists of (1) a historical data analysis phase and (2) a model building phase. If a new wireless sensor network has to be deployed, the historical data analysis task is performed during the pre-deployment phase. In the model building phase, an innovative algorithm exploiting a cost function and considering both distance and communication cost selects the candidate sensors. Candidate sensors are chosen with the aim of leading to the optimized network design and acquisition. Depending on the number of effectively deployable sensors (typically due to budget constraints), candidate sensors can then be deployed and/or queried instead of the whole network, thus reducing the network cost and extending its lifetime in terms of energy consumption.

Experiments and simulations performed on a real wireless sensor network deployed at the Politecnico di Torino headquarters (Turin, Italy) demonstrate the adaptability and the effectiveness of the proposed approach in optimizing the sensor network design and the data acquisition. The chapter is organized as follows. Section 2 presents some real-world scenarios that would benefit from the application of the proposed approach. Section 3 formalizes the problem addressed in this chapter, whereas the proposed approach is described in Section 4. Section 5 reports the experiments performed to validate the effectiveness of the proposed approach. Section 6 discusses related work, while Section 7 draws conclusions and presents future developments.

APPLICATION SCENARIOS

Some contexts which would benefit from the proposed approach are described in the following. (1) Agricultural production monitoring (Burrell at al., 2004). A sensor network can be exploited in agricultural production (1) to identify the risk of frost damage to vines, (2) to assess the risk of powdery-mildew outbreak (or to detect pests and irrigation needs), or (3) to detect the presence of birds. A trial sensor network (involved 18 nodes) has been deployed in a local Oregon vineyard to collect different measures (e.g., temperature, lighting levels, humidity, presence of birds) for several weeks during the summer of 2002 (Burrell at al., 2004). By means of this deployment it has been possible to observe some correlations among sensor data. There is a great variability across the vineyard during the day and less variation during the night, hence measurements are more correlated during the night and less during the day. Furthermore, there are different seasonal issues (e.g., risk of frost damage to vines). For example, during the winter a wireless sensor network can be exploited in an agricultural production to gather frequent temperature data and to alert the system only when a risk of frost damage is detected (i.e., temperature is lower than a given threshold). Hence, sensor data are correlated both in time and space, and a more power-efficient technique would be necessary to efficiently collect the required information, optimize sensor placement and extend the sensor network lifetime.

(2) Volcano area monitoring (Werner-Allen et al., 2005, 2006). A wireless sensor network has been deployed on Volcano Tungurahua, an active volcano in central Ecuador, to monitor volcano eruptions with low-frequency acoustic sensors (Werner-Allen et al., 2005, 2006). However, studying active volcanoes can achieve two different challenges: (1) understanding long-term trends or (2) focusing on discrete events such as eruption, earthquakes, or tremor activities. In both cases high data rates, high data fidelity, and large inter-node separations are required to perform an accurate monitoring. For the last constraint, sensors need to be able to transmit data at long distance. Since wireless sensor devices are characterized by low radio bandwidth, a good degree of redundancy is required to reduce the distance between two sensors. However, the number of deployed sensors is always greater than the required number. Since the collected measures are highly correlated, an efficient technique to identify redundant sensors and gather correlated data may be exploited. Furthermore, the network needs to run for extended period of time to study long-term trends. Hence, an ad-hoc wireless sensor network design for energy-efficient monitoring is needed.

In the above-mentioned scenarios, sensors acquire measurements (e.g., temperature, light, humidity, fire) to monitor the physical phenomena at discrete points. Each measurement is characterized by a specific time and location of acquisition. A primary issue is the network design to obtain an optimal placement of the sensors, thus allowing to gather meaningful data. Then, the acquisition of the sensor measurements is performed. Since sensors are battery-powered, collection is driven by three factors: (1) power management, (2) limited resources, and (3) real-time constraints. In this work we focus on careful power management techniques for energy saving during network design and data collection. The proposed power management strategies transmit only relevant data by reducing the network throughput and minimizing the transmission time. Furthermore, energy-saving techniques also reduce the effects of limited resource constraint by extending the sensor network lifetime.

Further real-world scenarios include agricultural applications (Zerger et al., 2010; Ulrich, 2008; Wark et al., 2007) and traffic control (Brahma et al., 2012). For example by exploiting the wireless sensing stations installed at Camalie Vineyards (Ulrich, 2008), data on both soil moisture and soil temperature could be collected and analyzed with the aim of optimizing the sensing node placement and efficiently acquire data. An efficient network deployment in agricultural applications could optimize irrigation, reduce water consumption, minimize pump energy costs, and increase vegetable quality without sacrificing yield.

PROBLEM STATEMENT

Smart wireless devices can programmatically measure physical quantities, perform simple computations, store, receive and transmit data. The lattice built by a set of cooperating smart sensors is called a sensor network. Sensed measures collected by means of a sensor network are a stream of data. Formal definitions for these concepts follow.

Definition 3.1: Measure. *A measure m is an estimation of a physical variable expressed in a unit of measurement.*

An example of measure is the temperature, which can be expressed in Celsius degree as unit of measurement.

Definition 3.2: Sensor node. *Let m be a measure and f the frequency of reading. A sensor node n senses m every t = 1/f time units. n is also characterized by its spatial coordinates expressed in a three dimensional space (e.g., n(x, y, z)) with respect to a reference point, relative (to the room or building) or absolute (geo-location coordinates on Earth).*

Definition 3.3: Sensor network. *Let $N = \{n_1, n_2, ..., n_i\}$ be a set of sensor nodes and $e(i, j) \in E$ ($\forall n_i \in N, \forall n_j \in N$) a set of edges. A sensor network SN is a network graph SN = {N, E} where $\forall (n_i, n_j) \exists e(i, j)$. e(i, j) models the communication link between two sensor nodes.*

Definition 3.4: Time band. *Let T be a sequence of time units and n a sensor node able to sense measures every $t \in T$. A time band is a continuous subset of T.*

Definition 3.5: Sample. *Let n be a sensor node able to sense measure m. A sample is the observed value of measure m at time t performed by n.*

Definition 3.6: Sensor readings. *Let n be a sensor node able to sense measures in $M = \{m_1, ..., m_k\}$. Sensor readings are an array of k samples performed by n in a time unit t.*

For example, a sensor node n can measure temperature and relative humidity in a given time unit t, thus providing an array of k = 2 sensor readings.

Definition 3.7: Aggregate operator. *Let s be a sequence of samples collected by a given sensor in T. An aggregate operator G accepts s and returns a single value. $G_{t \in T}(s_t)$ is used to compute an aggregation over values in s.*

Examples of aggregate operators are MIN, MAX, AVG, SUM, and COUNT. When these operators are used to compute aggregations over a time series, they always return a single value.

Definition 3.8: Sensor query. *Let s be a sequence of samples collected by a given sensor in T. A query Q specifies the aggregate operator G and the time band $\mu \subseteq T$ on which G has to be computed.*

Definition 3.9: Sensor data. *Let s be a sequence of samples collected by a given sensor in T, μ be a time band and G an aggregate operator defined through a query Q. Sensor data is the result of Q, i.e., it is the value obtained by $G_{t \in \mu}(s_t)$.*

Definition 3.10: Time series. *Let μ be a sequence of time units and n a sensor node able to sense measure m. A time series is a sequence of sensor data for m computed by n every $t \in \mu$. The length of the time series is $|\mu|$.*

Definition 3.11: Historical sensor data. *Let N be a set of sensor nodes, $M = \{m_1, ..., m_k\}$ a set of measures, T_{window} a time band. $\forall n \in N \forall t \in T$ sensor data are collected. Historical sensor data R are represented by a matrix whose cardinality is $|M| \times |N| \times |T_{window}|$. Each value r_{ijt} represents the sensor data of measure $m_j \in M$, performed by sensor $n_i \in N$ at time $t \in T_{window}$.*

Definition 3.12: Sensor network model. *Let R be a historical sensor data matrix with cardinality $|M| \times |N| \times |T_{window}|$, G an aggregate operator, and b the error bound (i.e., error-tolerance threshold). A sensor network model N_{model} for G computed over sensor data of measure m_j at $t \in T_{window}$ is $N_{model} \in N$ such that $|G_{\forall ni \in N}(r_{ijt}) - G_{\forall ni \in Nmodel}(r_{ijt})| = b$.*

Definition 3.13: Candidate sensors. *Let N_{model} be a sensor network model. Candidate sensors are (a subset of) sensor nodes in N_{model}.*

Definition 3.14: Model validity window. *Let R be a historical sensor data matrix with cardinality $| M | \times | N | \times | T_{window} |$, G an aggregate operator, and b the error bound (i.e., error-tolerance threshold). Let N_{model} be a sensor network model for G computed over sensor data of measure m_j at $t \in T_{window}$. The model validity window T_{model} is the largest time band in which $| G_{\forall ni} \in_N (r_{ijt}) - G_{\forall ni} \in_{Nmodel} (r_{ijt}) | = b$.*

The proposed approach identifies sensor network models and their validity windows. Models can be exploited to optimize sensing node placement and efficiently acquire data from deployed sensor networks.

SENSOR NETWORK MODELS

In this section, the main phases to build a sensor network model are described: (1) Gathering historical sensor data, i.e., learning phase (Section 4.1), (2) correlation analysis (Section 4.2), (3) selection of candidate sensors (Section 4.3), and (4) model characterization and validation (Section 4.4). Furthermore, the model evolution is discussed in Section 4.5.

Gathering Historical Sensor Data

The sensor reading collection requires a significant amount of energy (Madden et al., 2003). This communication cost mainly depends on the number of acquired samples and the number of times a query is executed through the network. While the lower bound of the sampling frequency is defined by the monitored phenomenon (Nyquist rate), the number of collected sensor data may be reduced according to the monitored phenomenon characteristics (e.g., seasonal patterns). In the proposed approach, to collect historical sensor data the gathering activity is performed for T_{window}. Since

different physical phenomena may follow a cyclic pattern (e.g., seasonal patterns, daily patterns), we exploit as T_{window} the minimum cyclic pattern of the monitored phenomena. However, the more sensor data are analyzed, the more accurate the model will be. Thus, a longer T_{window} may improve the correlation analysis and discover more interesting spatial and temporal correlations (e.g., voltage and temperature always follow the same patters (Deshpande et al., 2005a). This improvement is counterbalanced by high energy consumption. A trade-off between the communication cost and the accuracy of correlation analysis has to be found. In the proposed approach this trade-off is set according to the error-tolerance threshold t.

Correlation Analysis

Correlation analysis on sensor data may detect relationships, both in space and time, among physical phenomena and sensor data. Groups of correlated sensors are identified by means of clustering techniques. To this aim, we exploit the clustering phase of SeReNe (Apiletti et al., 2011), whose main features are described in the following. Given historical sensor data, SeReNe analyzes two types of correlations: (1) Physical correlation, which depends on the similarity of the environment where the sensors are located, and (2) time correlation, when sensor data is correlated over time. The results of the SeReNe clustering analysis are groups of correlated sensors, which are exploited as inputs of the following phase.

Selection of Candidate Sensors

To select candidate sensors from a cluster we propose an innovative algorithm, named W-Meta, which aims at achieving a trade-off between the following issues: (1) Capability of candidate sensors to represent their clusters (groups) and (2) minimization of the communication cost. For the first issue we exploit three different strategies which aim at sorting sensors in a cluster according to their adequateness to model the whole group. The proposed algorithm receives in input the number n of candidate nodes. The number of candidate nodes in each cluster is proportional to the number of cluster points (i.e., the number of sensor nodes). Reliable outliers, singled out by means of the SeReNe clustering algorithm (Apiletti et al., 2011) can be included in the candidate node set.

Accuracy of a Candidate Sensor

Three strategies to evaluate the accuracy of a sensor to model its cluster have been exploited. Given a cluster of sensors, each of which senses k measures, the objective of the proposed strategies is to sort the sensors according to their capability to model (a) correlated measures and (b) physical location of correlated sensors. Details of the proposed strategies are described in the following, while experimental results are reported in Section 5.4.

Strategy 1 (Measure Trend): Given a cluster of sensors, the objective of the measure trend strategy is to sort sensors according to their capability of approximating the measurements collected by sensors in the cluster. Hence, the proposed strategy is based on the analysis of correlated measurements. To represent both physical and temporal correlations among sensors and sensor data, we consider (a) the clustering result in a given sampling time and (b) measurements collected during the T_{Band}. Since we use the AVG operator as the main aggregate operator to describe the proposed approach, the average operation is implied in the following discussion. The measure trend strategy is characterized by the following steps:

○ Since we would like to approximate (ideally) the value obtained by averaging all measurements coming from all sensors in a given T_{Band}, we define this value as $O = (M_1, ..., M_k)$.

○ Since each sensor n_i senses k measurements, it is described by means of an array $M(n_i)=(M_{1i}, ..., M_{ki})$, in which the component M_{ji} represents the average value of the monitored variable j over T_{Band} sensed by n_i.

○ Sensors are sorted according to the distance of each node n_i from O. Distance is measured as Euclidean distance as follows $d(M(n_i), O)^2 = (M_{1i} - M_1)^2 + ... + (M_{ki} - M_k)^2$.

Strategy 2 (Cluster Shape): Given a cluster of sensors, the objective of the cluster shape strategy is to sort sensors according to the ability of their physical location to model the physical shape of the cluster. Hence, this technique is based on the physical positions of the correlated sensors in the cluster. Sensors from cluster border nodes that better detect the cluster shape appear higher in the sorted list.

The cluster shape strategy is characterized by the following steps:

- Given a cluster of m sensors, the cluster barycenter is computed as follows:

$(x, y, z) = ((x_1 +...+ x_m)/m, (y_1 +...+ y_m)/m, (z_1 +...+ z_m)/m)$ where (x_i, y_i, z_i) are the spatial coordinates of sensor n_i.

- Sensor coordinates are normalized with respect to the barycenter by computing.

$(x_i - x, y_i - y, z_i - z)$ for each sensor n_i. In other words, we consider the barycenter as the reference system center for each cluster.

- Sensors are sorted according to their distance from the barycenter. Thus, far sensors from the barycenter appear at the top of the sorted list.

Strategy 3 (Cluster shape and Core): It is an extended version of the previous strategy. In particular, this strategy extends the strategy 2 (cluster shape) by adding a cluster core node in the first position of the sorted list. In particular, the closest node with respect to the cluster barycenter is selected as core node.

Communication Cost

Sensing devices equipped with a low power wireless radio are able to communicate through distance ranges from few feet to hundreds of feet. While a multi-hop communication protocol can be exploited to gather sensor data (Madden et al., 2003), topologies based on a master node and a tree of leaves can be also exploited. Even if the communication is often broadcast, it is possible to address the data to a given node. When the message has been received by the intended neighbor node, a link-level acknowledgment is sent. To provide a certain degree of independence from network level implementations, we suppose that no end-to-end acknowledgments are provided. Hence, sensors are modeled as nodes (see Definition 3.2) and the radio link between two nodes is modeled as two oriented edges, corresponding to two independent radio links. Each edge $e(i, j)$ is characterized by a label which models the communication cost from node n_i to node n_j. We consider the function $w_c: E \rightarrow R$ to associate to each edge $e(i, j) \in E$ ($\forall n_i \in N$, $\forall n_j \in N$) a value $w(i, j) \in R$ which represents the transmission cost (in terms of power consumption) from node n_i to node n_j. Let $W(n, n)$ be the matrix related to a sensor network with n sensors. Each element $w_{ij} = w_c(i, j)$ represents the transmission cost of each successful transmission from node n_i to node n_j. We assume that each node n_i never transmits to itself $w_{ii} = \infty$, $\forall n_i \in N$.

To compute the communication cost required to send data from each couple of nodes, the average number of transmissions required to successfully complete the delivery would be needed. If this value is known, by considering p_{ij} and p_{ji} as the probabilities that a packet from n_i will reach n_j and vice versa, and by assuming that these probabilities are independent, the expected number of transmission and acknowledgment messages required to guarantee a successful transmission between n_i and n_j is $(p_{ij} \cdot p_{ji})^{-1}$. This value, set as the edge weight, can be exploited to estimate the transmission cost between n_i and n_j. Hence, p_{ij}^{-1} can be defined as the weight for each edge between nodes n_i and n_j, the network may be considered as a not-oriented graph, and the matrix W will be symmetric.

For some sensor networks, the probabilities of successful transmission p_{ij} and p_{ji} are not known. In such case, we assume that the transmission cost w_{ij} between two nodes n_i and n_j is estimated to be proportional to the Euclidean distance of their physical locations to the power 2, even if this exponent can vary depending on the specific setting (Rappaport, 2002). Specific experiments addressing the percentage of energy saving obtained by exploiting the proposed approach in different environments are reported in Section 5.6.

Candidate Node Selection Algorithm

We propose an innovative algorithm, W-Meta (See Algorithm 1), to single out candidate nodes from a set of correlated sensors. The W-Meta algorithm selects the subset of sensors (i.e., selected sensor) which best represent the network (from the measurement accuracy point of view) and minimize the communication cost to transmit sensing data to a given master collecting node.

The algorithm receives a set of input parameters:

- The set of clusters C identified by the correlation analysis.
- The set of *Outliers* (i.e., possibly noisy sensors or sensors independent from any group) identified by the clustering algorithm.

Algorithm 1. Candidate sensor selection: W-Meta

```
Input: C, Outliers, Strategy, N_rs, CF_p, c_max, Effective-Ranges,
Output: selected_sensor set of candidate sensors
 1: N_ss = 0;
 2: for all cluster in C do
 3:     N_ss-c = 0;
 4:     candidate_sensor_cost = 0;
 5:     candidate_sensor_accuracy = sorted_strategy(Strategy);
 6:     selected_sensor[0] =candidate_sensor_accuracy[0];
 7:     N_ss ++; N_ss-c ++;
 8:     repeat
 9:         for all n_i in selected_sensor do
10:             for all n_j in candidate_sensor_accuracy do
11:                 if CF_p [n_i, n_j] ≤ c_max then
12:                     candidate_sensor_cost.Add(n_j, CF_p [n_i, n_j ]); // ordered list
in ascending values of

// communication cost
13:                 end if
14:             end for
15:         end for
16:         selected_sensor[N_ss ] = candidate_sensor_cost.FirstElement;
17:         candidate_sensor_cost.Remove(FirstElement);
18:         N_ss ++; N_ss-c ++;
19:     until N_ss-c < ⌈N_rs · |cluster| / (Σ_{cluster∈C} | cluster |)) ⌉
20: end for
21: analyze_outliers(Outliers, selected_sensor, Effective-Ranges);
22: return selected_sensor
```

- The type of sorting strategy (i.e., measure trend, cluster shape, or cluster shape and core).
- The desired number of candidate sensors to be selected N_{rs}.
- The communication cost matrix W.
- The maximum communication cost c_{max} allowed for a transmission between two sensors.
- And the *Effective-Ranges* for each sensed measurement.

The last two parameters are functional inputs of our approach. While c_{max} is useful to select as candidate nodes only the nodes able to communicate by consuming less than c_{max}, *EffectiveRanges* allows the identification of reliable outliers from noisy measurements.

For each cluster in C (lines 2- 20), a subset of sensors which minimize the communication cost and maximize the accuracy is selected. For each cluster we select a number of candidate nodes proportional to the total number of the desired candidate nodes (i.e., N_{rs}) and to the percentage of the nodes in the cluster (i.e., | *cluster* |) with respect to the total number of clustered sensors (i.e., $\Sigma_{cluster \in C}$ | *cluster* |) (lines 8- 19). The list of candidate sensors which best represents the cluster from the communication cost point of view (i.e., candidate sensor cost list) and the candidate sensors number for the current cluster (i.e., N_{ss-c}) are initialized in lines 3 and 4. Sensors in the cluster are sorted according to the selected strategy (line 5) and inserted into the *candidate_sensor_accuracy* list. More accurate sensors are added at the head of the list. The sensors which best represent the cluster are selected in line 6. These are the first elements of the *candidate_sensor_accuracy* list. Then, N_{ss} and N_{ss-c} are incremented (line 7).

For each couple of sensors (n_i, n_j), n_i in *selected_sensor* list and n_j in the *candidate_sensor_accuracy*, the corresponding communication cost (i.e., $W[n_i, n_j]$) is compared to the c_{max}. If it is smaller, n_j is considered as candidate sensor (i.e., insertion on *candidate_sensor_cost* list).

The *candidate_sensor_cost* list contains one entry for each candidate sensor which best represents the cluster (from the communication cost point of view). Each entry is characterized by two attributes: Candidate sensor identifier and communication cost. The second attribute represents the minimum communication cost required to transmit a packet from the current candidate sensor to one of the sensors belonging to the *selected_sensor* list. Hence, sensor n_j is inserted to the *candidate_sensor_cost* list (line 12) if either it does not yet appear in the list or its current communication cost (i.e., $CF_p[n_i, n_j]$) is smaller than the previous cost associated to itself. The algorithm selects as candidate sensor the first element of the *candidate_sensor_cost* list (line 16), providing good accuracy and low communication cost towards one of the previously selected sensors. The selected sensor is removed from the *candidate_sensor_cost* list (line 17) and the number of selected sensors is increased (line 18). Then, outlier sensors are analyzed one by one (line 21) to identify sensors whose measures are not noise but only independent from others. An outlier is selected as candidate if its measurements belong to the effective ranges (i.e., *Effective-Ranges*) of the sensed measurements. Finally, the *selected_sensor* list, which contains the best candidate sensors for all clusters including outlier sensors, is returned (line 22).

Model Validation and Characterization

After selecting the candidate sensors representing the network state in different time instants, the model validity window in which this model holds (i.e., the error bound of the result is less or equal to the desired *b*) has to be determined.

Given the largest time band, an accuracy threshold and a subset of candidate sensors, the largest subset of contiguous sampling times in which the model provides a good approximation of the monitored environment is identified. This time band, denoted as T_{model}, is the model validity window. At first, we estimate the approximate value Mr_j of a measurement *j* as the average on values collected by all candidate sensors. The best approximation M_j is the average on the values gathered by querying all sensors. For each subset of contiguous sampling times the percentage of contiguous samples in which | $Mr_j - M_j$ |$\le b$ is considered.

Selected candidate nodes shared among different time bands are included in the larger T_{model}. To this subset, given by the intersection of the selected candidate nodes in different time bands, non-shared selected candidate nodes are added until the desired number of nodes is reached (the target is usually budget-driven). These additional nodes are sorted according to their capability of approximating the network state, by minimizing the measurement error.

Furthermore, two model parameters are identified for each query: The minimum and the maximum value of *Q*, computed over T_{model} by querying only the selected candidate sensors. This range, extended by the error-tolerance threshold b, is Ω. When a sensor which does not belong to the selected candidate sensors computes a value of Q outside the range Ω, it sends its local measure.

Evolving the Model

Since only the selected candidate sensors are queried to monitor a given environment, two issues are to be considered.

(1) Nodes that do not belong to the selected candidate sensors do not send their collected measurements, unless their Q value is outside Ω. Hence, the ability of learning the current state of the network is lost and the network model cannot be reliably adapted to changing patterns. In this case, smart sensors can be deployed (Deshpande et al., 2005a). They can exploit a selective transmission strategy to send their measurements only when they are queried or when their own measurements are not correctly represented by the sensor network model. Hence, to always learn the current state of the network, the desired query is broadcast to all sensors. The selected candidate sensors always reply to the query, whereas other sensors only reply if they are currently not represented by the model.

(2) The network topology may change over time. In this case, the model needs to be adapted to the new configuration. Two issues should be addressed: (a) Change detection and (b) model maintenance. The goal of change detection is to quantify the difference, in terms of sensor reading distribution, between the data related to the old network configuration and the new one (e.g., new nodes are added to the network). The goal of model maintenance, instead, is to maintain a sensor network model when new or relocated nodes are incrementally added to the network or sensors are turned off. Three event types may change the network state: (1) A new sensor is added to the network, (2) a sensor is turned off, and (3) new measurements, gathered from a sensor, are very different from the modeled ones. While, case (1) is automatically detected because a sensor always sends its measurements when it is turned on for the

first time, case (3) is addressed by means of the selective transmission strategy. A small number of such events can be managed by incrementally evolving the cluster model, whereas a large number of network modification events requires a new clustering session, followed by the candidate selection process.

Finally, case (2) is interesting only when the sensor is a selected candidate sensor. In this case, at the first occurrence of a missed reply, a new sensor node is temporary selected among the candidates to get the desired result. After a user-defined threshold (time period or number of occurrences) of continuous missed replies from the currently selected candidate sensor, it is replaced with the first available sensor in the sorted list of candidates.

EXPERIMENTAL RESULTS

We validated the proposed approach by performing different experimental sessions focused on analyzing (1) the effectiveness in detecting sensor correlations (see Section 5.3), (2) the accuracy of the candidate sensors in modeling the sensor network (see Section 5.4), (3) number of selected sensors (see Section 5.5), and (4) the effectiveness of the proposed approach in reducing power consumption (see Section 5.6).

Experimental results on data from a real sensor network described in Section 5.1, highlight the effectiveness of the proposed approach in identifying the subset of sensors that better model the network. In particular, candidate sensors are selected to optimize sensing node placement in new networks and efficiently acquire data from deployed sensor networks.

Sensor Network Settings

To perform the experiments we exploited historical sensor data collected by means of the sensor network deployed at the Politecnico di Torino labs (Turin, Italy). The network consists of 23 nodes, of which 15 have been actually included in the analyses. Excluded nodes have been affected by hardware failures and low-level problems which are beyond the scope of this chapter. During the tests, a few more problems have been encountered, ranging from node thefts to temporary issues (e.g., unexpected battery shortage). Hence, not all the 15 nodes have always been available for analysis.

Each node consists of a Tmote Sky module (i.e., a low power wireless module for sensor networks). It features an IEEE 802.15.4 wireless transceiver with antenna, a USB connection, and integrates humidity, light, and temperature sensors.

All the nodes have been configured to transmit their daily measures in bulk at a certain time of the day. In particular, antennas were switched on for half hour at 5:30 pm each day. The half-hour period allowed us to avoid transmission losses due to drift in the mote clocks. The bulk transmission have been chosen instead of the real-time monitoring because it greatly improved the mote lifetime, which was up to a month on average. The switching of the antenna, however, affected the measurements: the temperature always showed a suddenly increasing trend during the half-hour period of antenna power up. Collected sensor measurements are publicly available upon request to the authors.

We considered historical sensor data collected from April 1st to April 30th, 2009. The Tmote Sky modules collected temperature, humidity, and light values once every 15 minutes by means of the TinyOS platform. The x and y coordinates of sensors expressed in meters with respect to the laboratory map are also known. The location of the experiments consists of 7 consecutive lab rooms connected by a long corridor. We exploited the concept of epochs to introduce absolute time references. Epoch 0 is defined as the beginning of the measurement session, i.e., April 1st 2009, at 0:00, then 1 epoch has been set as equivalent to 60 seconds.

Experimental Setting

To build a sensor network model, as discussed in Section 4, the following activities need to be performed: (1) Gathering historical sensor data, (2) performing correlation analysis, (3) selection of candidate sensors, and (4) model characterization and validation. Since data collected by means of the sensor network deployed at the Politecnico di Torino labs are characterized by different trends during the weekdays and during the holidays, we analyzed two different sensor network models, one for the holidays and one for the weekdays. Both models are exploited to optimize sensing node placement and efficiently acquire data from deployed sensor networks.

For task (1) we considered historical sensor data collected during Thursday, April 2nd, 2009 in 12 hours of monitoring, from 8:00 am to 8:00 pm, as the training set to study the weekday model, whereas sensor data collected during Sunday, April 5th, 2009 from 8:00 am to 8:00 pm, have been used as the training set to study the holiday model. For the weekday sensor network model, candidate sensors are selected from physically correlated sensor clusters related to epoch 2400, while for the holiday model candidate sensors are singled out from physically correlated sensor clusters related to the epoch 6600. Analyses have been performed by considering both temperature and humidity measures. Before each run of the experiments, a preprocessing phase has been performed consisting in a normalization step by means of a standard filter (measurement values are normalized in the (0,1) interval).

To perform task (2), we exploited the SeReNe framework (Apiletti et al., 2011) to discover both physical and temporal sensor correlations among sensors and sensor data. After the correlation analysis, the model validity window T_{model} for the weekday model ranges from epoch 1920 to epoch 2640 (i.e., 12 hours, from 8:00 am to 8:00 pm), while for the holiday model T_{model} ranges from epoch 6240 to epoch 6960.

The algorithms for task (3) and (4) have been developed by means of the Python programming language. Experiments have been performed on a 3.2 GHz Pentium IV PC with 2.5 GB of main memory running Linux kernel 2.6.32.

Sensor Correlations

To study sensor correlations, we exploited the SeReNe framework (Apiletti et al., 2011). Different clustering sessions have been performed to analyze all measurements collected from all sensors at a given epoch. We have run experiments on both the weekday and the weekend time bands. In particular, our analyses considered the DBSCAN (Ester et al., 1996) algorithm as a representative clustering algorithm among the algorithms available in SeReNe. The default values of DBSCAN parameters: epsilon (i.e., radius of the neighborhood) and min points (i.e., minimum number of points within radius epsilon) have been set to 0.05 and 2 respectively. Distance between two sensor measurements has been computed by exploiting the Euclidean distance (Tan et al., 2006).

By studying sensor correlations we identified the following reference trend during weekdays. Since air-conditioning is switch on during working days, sensor data are grouped together into two main clusters: Sensors in labs and sensors in the corridor. Thus, laboratories behave like one big group, whereas the corridor has a completely different behavior. The 2160 epoch corresponding to Thursday, April 2nd, 2009 is discussed as a representative epoch of the weekday results. Figure 1

graphically shows the clusters of temperature and humidity measures, collected on epoch 2160. In the map sensors are indicated by a round mark, whose color depends on the cluster they belong to. The corridor covers all the lower (southern) part of the map, laboratories are the rooms located along the upper (northern) part.

During holidays, sensor correlations are represented by a different trend because air-conditioning is inactive. Thus, sensors are grouped into different clusters according to the sensor physical positions. Figure 2 graphically shows the clusters of temperature and humidity measures, collected on Sunday, April 5th, 2009 (epoch 6420). Since each room tends to drift away in its own way, different clusters emerge for each laboratory besides the corridor.

Accuracy of the Candidate Sensors

To evaluate the accuracy of the candidate sensors we exploited the Root Mean Square Deviation (RMSD) (Tan et al., 2006), also called Root Mean Square Error (RMSE). RMSD is a common measure of precision to evaluate the differences between values predicted by a model and the values actually observed from the phenomenon being modeled. We exploited the RMSD to evaluate the precision of both holiday and weekday models with respect to the whole network.

The root mean square deviation is computed in T_{model} according to the following formula.

Figure 1. Physical correlation result, epoch 2160

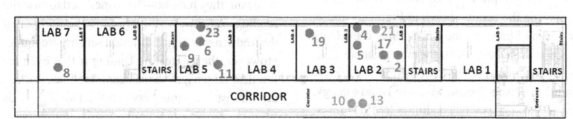

Figure 2. Physical correlation result, epoch 6420

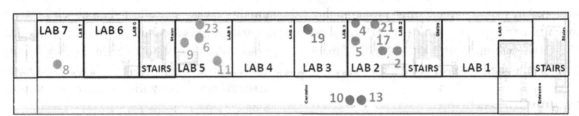

$$\sqrt{\frac{1}{epoch\#}\sum_{t \in T\text{model}}\left(M_{rt} - M_t\right)^2}$$

M_{rt} is the average measure value computed by querying the candidate sensors in a given epoch t and M_t is the value obtained by querying all deployed sensor network nodes in the same epoch t. Figure 3 and Figure 4 graphically show the Root Mean Square Deviation for the candidate sensors selected by the W-Meta algorithm by exploiting the three selection strategies (i.e., Measure Trend, Cluster Shape, or Cluster Shape and Core) in T_{model} and for different percentages of selected candidate sensors. The RMSD in Figure 3 has been computed by considering the temperature measure while the RMSD in Figure 4 is related to the humidity measure.

Each plot in both Figures 3 and 4 reports two lines, one for each considered T_{model}. Recall that T_{model} in the 1920-2640 epoch range is related to the weekday model, while T_{model} in the 6240-6960 epoch range is related to the holiday model.

Since our aim is to optimize sensing node placement and efficiently acquire data from deployed sensor nodes, we need to identify the set of candidate sensors able to maximize the accuracy of the collected measurements in any epoch (power consumption will be addressed later). By comparing the results shown in Figures 3 and 4, the Cluster Shape and the Cluster Shape and Core selection strategies provide the most accurate models, by leading to lower RMSD values with few candidate sensors than the Measure Trend strategy, The two strategies yielded similar RMSD trends,

with the Cluster Shape slightly outperforming the other with very low percentages of selected sensors (e.g., 20%-30%). Instead, the Measure Trend strategy achieved the highest values of RMSD, in particular with few selected sensors. Thus, from the accuracy point of view, the W-Meta algorithm is able to identify more accurate candidate sensors when it exploits either the Cluster Shape or the Cluster Shape and Core strategies.

Number of Selected Sensors

To single out the set of selected candidate sensors optimizing the sensor network design for energy-efficient monitoring, we analyzed the candidate sensors selected in the two T_{model}, (i.e., weekday and weekend), to maximize the accuracy of the model in any epoch and minimize the power consumption. Figure 5 shows for different sensor ratios the number of (1) desired sensors (i.e., an input of the algorithm, equivalent to the sensor ratio multiplied by the total number of sensors), (2) common, and (3) different sensors between the two sets of selected candidate sensors in the considered T_{model} (weekday and weekend). The analysis has been performed for all the selection strategies exploited by W-Meta algorithm.

The sum of common and different sensors is constant, they have both been included to ease the reading. As expected, increasing the number of desired sensors, more common sensors are found. However, the interesting finding is that even for few desired sensors, the selected candidate sensors are almost the same between the two T_{model}, as

Figure 3. (a) Measure trend – RMSD on the temperature measure; (b) cluster shape – RMSD on the temperature measure; (c) cluster shape and core – RMSD on the temperature measure

Figure 4. (a) Measure trend – RMSD on the humidity measure; (b) cluster shape – RMSD on the humidity measure; (c) cluster shape and core – RMSD on the humidity measure

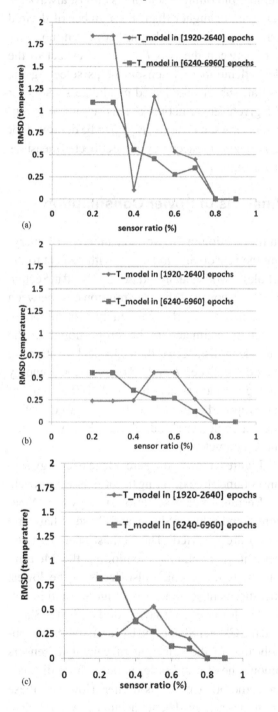

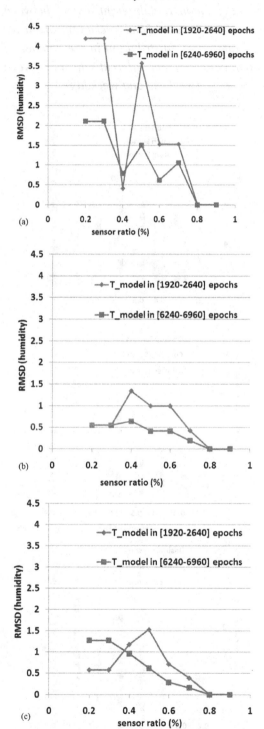

Figure 5. (a) Measure trend – distribution in the number of desired, common, and different sensors between the two T_{model} (weekend and weekday); (b) cluster shape – distribution in the number of desired, common, and different sensors between the two T_{model} (weekend and weekday); (c) cluster shape and core – distribution in the number of desired, common, and different sensors between the two T_{model} (weekend and weekday)

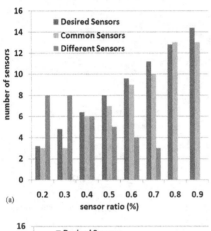

(a)

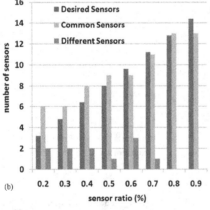

(b)

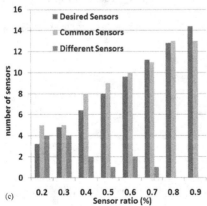

(c)

proved by common sensor values close to desired ones. In particular, considering the Cluster Shape and the Cluster Shape and Core strategies, the number of common sensors is almost always the same as (or higher than) the number of desired sensors. Having a high number of common sensors between the two T_{model} with respect to the desired number of sensors helps selecting the overall subset of selected candidate sensors for the given sensor network. This set of nodes represents the sensors (i.e., N_{model}) to be deployed for maximizing the accuracy of the collected measures in any epoch.

Analysis of Power Consumption

In this section the power consumption of querying the sensors in $Model_{sensors}$ with respect to the whole network is analyzed. As discussed in Section 4.3.2, we consider the transmission cost between two sensors to be the main energy consumption, which is estimated to be proportional to the Euclidean distance of their physical locations to the power 2 (i.e., $k = 2$). To analyze the energy saving we addressed two issues: (1) the saving of the proposed approach with respect to querying the whole network and (2) the trend by varying the k parameter.

Figure 6 reports the percentage of energy saving obtained by exploiting the proposed approach.

Results for each selection strategy (i.e., Measure Trend, Cluster Shape, and Cluster Shape and Core) are reported. The highest energy saving percentage is obtained exploiting the Measure Trend strategy, which also leads to the lowest measurement accuracy (See Figure 3 and Figure 4). The lower energy saving of the Cluster Shape and the Cluster Shape and Core strategies is probably due to the selection of candidate sensors among the cluster border nodes, whose distance from the other nodes is higher. However, these strategies achieved better accuracy. According to the context-specific requirements, the sensor

Figure 6. Energy saving percentage with respect to deploying the whole network

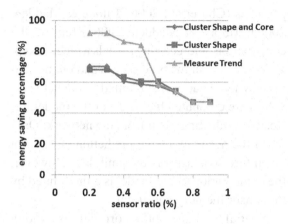

Figure 7. (a) Measure trend – saving percentage on power consumption by varying k parameter; (b) cluster shape – saving percentage on power consumption by varying k parameter; (c) cluster shape and core – saving percentage on power consumption by varying k parameter

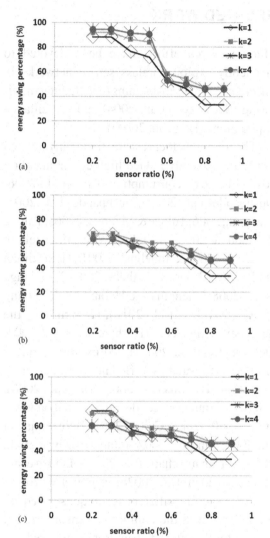

network designer should select the strategy that better fits the application needs, finding the optimal trade off.

The proposed approach yields to a relatively high saving percentage (50%) even selecting most of the available sensors. This behavior is probably due to the selection of the master node, with respect to which the transmission cost is computed from all the other sensors. To take into account possible transmission optimizations, for each subset of selected candidate sensors, the master node is chosen as the node minimizing the overall transmission costs. For a fair comparison, the same approach has been applied when using the whole network. Hence, removing few nodes from the original network makes the optimal master node nearer to the remaining selected sensors, further lowering the total transmission cost.

Figure 7 shows the energy saving when the sensor network is deployed into different environments (e.g., indoor, outdoor, etc.). As described in (Rappaport, 2002), different environments may affect the propagation of wireless data. This behavior can be approximated by varying the k value. Experiments for k values in the range $(1, 4)$ lead to different trends depending on the selection strategy. The Measure Trend strategy consistently yielded an increasing energy saving percentage

for higher values of k independently of the sensor ratio. Instead, the Cluster Shape and the Cluster Shape and Core strategies showed higher energy saving with higher k for low values of sensor ratio (up to 0.6), and vice-versa for high sensor ratios (0.8 and 0.9). However, all the trends reflected the main trend already seen for k = 2 with no significant differences. Thus, we consider the approach to be applicable for sensor networks in different environments.

RELATED WORK

Many research efforts have been devoted to efficiently exploit wireless sensor networks in different application domains (e.g., habitat monitoring (Szewczyk et al., 2004) and surveillance applications (He et al., 2004)).

The research focuses are frequently related to (1) significantly reduce high communication cost and energy consumption (Chu et al., 2006; Deshpande et al., 2005b; Deshpande et al., 2004; Chu et al., 2006; Tulone & Madden, 2006a; Tulone & Madden, 2006b; Kotidis, 2005; Silberstein et al., 2006; Goel & Imielinski 2001; Heinzelman et al., 2000; Yoon & Shahabi, 2007; Baoqianga et al., 2008; Zhengmao & Habib, 2009; Zhuang et al., 2010; Du et al., 2010), (2) minimize the query execution cost (Deshpande et al., 2004; Deshpande et al., 2005a), (3) exploiting query similarity to support efficient multiple query execution (Trigoni et al., 2005; Xia et al., 2006), and (4) routing protocol design (Intanagonwiwat et al., 2000; Hui & Culler, 2004; Heinzelman et al., 2002; Lindsey, 2002; Intanagonwiwat et al., 2000; Krishnamachari et al., 2002; Madden et al., 2002a; Madden et al., 2002b; Meliou et al., 2006).

For issue (1) different techniques based on the reduction in the number of sensors needed to monitor the interested environment have been proposed. For example, the approaches presented in (Deshpande et al., 2004; Chu et al., 2006; Deshpande et al., 2005b) are based on integrating statistical models of real-world processes into the query processing architecture of the sensor network. These statistical models are then used to answer queries when the estimated accuracy is above a given threshold. Otherwise the query is redirected to the whole network. Other approaches (Chu et al., 2006; Tulone & Madden, 2006a; Tulone & Madden, 2006b) rely on the construction of forecasting models which are kept synchronized on the base station and on the sensors. When a query is submitted to the network, values are computed by means of the model, instead of collecting them from the network. Only when the accuracy of the prediction is below a given threshold sensors transmit data. However, the computation of the model is quite limited by the sensor memory constraint.

Spatial and temporal correlations among measures have been also exploited to reduce the number of queried sensors (Kotidis, 2005; Silberstein et al., 2006; Apiletti et al., 2011). In (Kotidis, 2005) nodes exchange a set of messages with their neighbors to elect some of them as representatives of the surrounding environment. Values are transmitted by a subset of sensors chosen as representatives of their neighborhood if the value is changed since the last transmission (Silberstein et al., 2006). In (Apiletti et al., 2011) a step further toward more energy-aware query processing has been done by exploiting the correlations among sensor measurements of faraway nodes. The approach in (Apiletti et al., 2011) does not require message exchanges among sensors to elect representative nodes, and it is not restricted to sensor neighborhood when analyzing correlations. The proposed approach enhances (Apiletti et al., 2011) by being more general and extends the application scope. The new approach aims at: (1) optimizing sensing node placement (e.g., for new to-be-deployed networks) and (2) efficiently acquiring data from existing sensor networks. Furthermore, this chapter also presents a new algorithm based on a cost function considering both distance and communication cost to identify the candidate sensors, leading to the optimized network design and acquisition.

In the last few years, an increasing effort has been devoted by the researcher community to exploiting clustering techniques to efficiently query sensor networks (Goel & Imielinski 2001; Heinzelman et al., 2000; Yoon & Shahabi, 2007). Any of the above approaches is efficient. However (Goel & Imielinski 2001) requires the a-priori knowledge of the cluster topology, (Heinzelman et al., 2000) is not able to detect correlations among faraway sensors, and (Yoon & Shahabi, 2007) transmits only one measure for each cluster. The correlation analysis exploited in this chapter overcomes the previous limitations since the cluster topology is not required for the analysis process, correlations among faraway sensors are easily detected, and different candidate sensors are selected from each cluster.

To minimize the execution cost in terms of energy consumption, approaches in (Deshpande et al., 2004; Deshpande et al., 2005a; Trigoni et al., 2005); Xia et al., 2006) proposed to select the best execution plan to collect data from the network. In (Deshpande et al., 2004, 2005a) correlation among attributes is exploited to identify the appropriate plan. If two attributes are correlated, the execution plan always considers the attribute whose acquisition cost is lower. However, this approach queries the entire network. In (Trigoni et al., 2005; Xia et al., 2006) query similarity is exploited to efficiently support multiple query execution. Query similarity allows merging similar queries in a single query, which will be disseminated through the network. These approaches reduce both the number of data requests submitted by the base station, and the total execution cost, which is lower bounded by the cost of a single query. When the query is disseminated through the network, this approach queries all sensors. Hence, efficient query execution strategies are still needed.

Finally, many studies in wireless sensor network research have been devoted to the design of efficient routing protocols. The aim of a routing protocol is to define the rules exploited to efficiently deliver data from the base station to the sensor nodes and from the sensor nodes to the base station. Two classes of routing protocols have been identified: Data collection protocols (Intanagonwiwat et al., 2000) and dissemination protocols (Hui & Culler, 2004). In the former, cluster based (Heinzelman et al., 2002; Lindsey, 2002) and tree based (Intanagonwiwat et al., 2000; Krishnamachari et al., 2002; Madden et al., 2002a; Madden et al., 2002b) routing algorithms have been exploited, whereas in the latter, simple flooding techniques are typically used. While data collection protocols are used when all sensors are queried, dissemination protocols are used to broadcast the query to all the network nodes. Another class of routing protocols is able to gather data from a selected set of nodes in the network (Meliou et al., 2006). These protocols are exploited when a subset of sensors is queried. Thus, they could be exploited to collect data by querying only the candidate sensors selected by the approach proposed in this chapter.

CONCLUSION AND FUTURE WORK

The proposed approach aims at optimizing sensing node placement and efficiently acquiring data from deployed sensor networks. Sensor data are usually correlated both in time and space, thus a set of candidate nodes are identified to model the network state.

An innovative algorithm exploiting a cost function and considering both distance and communication cost selects the best nodes to be deployed in a new network or to be queried in an existing network, thus reducing the network cost and extending its lifetime in terms of energy consumption.

Experiments and simulations performed on a real wireless sensor network deployed at the Politecnico di Torino headquarters (Turin, Italy) demonstrate the adaptability and the effectiveness of the proposed approach in optimizing the sensor network design and the data acquisition.

The wireless sensor network design for energy-efficient monitoring presented in this chapter could be easily exploited in different real sensor applications, such as agricultural applications (Zerger et al., 2010; Ulrich, 2008; Wark et al., 2007) and traffic control (Brahma et al., 2012). For example by exploiting the wireless sensing stations installed at Camalie Vineyards (Ulrich, 2008), data on both soil moisture and soil temperature could be collected and analyzed with the aim of optimizing the sensing node placement and efficiently acquire data. An efficient network deployment in agricultural applications could optimize irrigation, reduce water consumption, minimize pump energy costs, and increase vegetable quality without sacrificing yield.

The proposed approach could be extended to deal with different data types collected by means of novel sensing technologies. For example, the wireless sensor network presented in (Garcia-Sanchez et al., 2010) integrated photographic monitoring with tracking devices to study animal behaviors in reactions to wildlife passage structures. Furthermore, the sensor network model proposed in this chapter could be extended to support the analysis of heterogeneous data, collected by means of different sensing devices, to optimize the placement of different sensing nodes.

REFERENCES

Abadi, D. J., Madden, S., & Lindner, W. (2005). REED: Robust, efficient filtering and event detection in sensor networks. In *Proceedings of 31st International Conference on Very Large DataBases* (pp. 769–780). IEEE.

Apiletti, D., Baralis, E., & Cerquitelli, T. (2011). Energy-saving models for wireless sensor networks. *Knowledge and Information*, *28*(3), 615–644. doi:10.1007/s10115-010-0328-6.

Baoqianga, K., Lia, C., Hongsongb, Z., & Yongjunb, X. (2008). Accurate energy model for WSN node and its optimal design. *Journal of Systems Engineering and Electronics*, *19*(3), 427–433. doi:10.1016/S1004-4132(08)60102-4.

Brahma, S., Chatterjee, M., Kwiat, K., & Varshney, P. K. (2012). Traffic management in wireless sensor networks: Decoupling congestion control and fairness. *Computer Communications*, *35*(6). doi:10.1016/j.comcom.2011.09.014 PMID:22267882.

Burrell, J., Brooke, T., & Beckwith, R. (2004). Vineyard computing: Sensor networks in agricultural production. *IEEE Pervasive Computing/IEEE Computer Society [and] IEEE Communications Society*, *3*(1), 38–45. doi:10.1109/MPRV.2004.1269130.

Chu, D., Deshpande, A., Hellerstein, J. M., & Hong, W. (2006). Approximate data collection in sensor networks using probabilistic models. In *Proceedings of The 22nd International Conference on Data Engineering* (pp. 48). IEEE.

Deshpande, A., Guestrin, C., Hong, W., & Madden, S. (2005). Exploiting correlated attributes in acquisitional query processing. In *Proceedings of The 21st International Conference on Data Engineering* (pp. 143–154). IEEE.

Deshpande, A., Guestrin, C., & Madden, S. (2005). Using probabilistic models for data management in acquisitional environments. In *Proceedings of The Conference on Innovative Data Systems Research* (pp. 317–328). IEEE.

Deshpande, A., Guestrin, C., Madden, S. R., Hellerstein, J. M., & Hong, W. (2004). Model-driven data acquisition in sensor networks. In *Proceedings of The 30th international conference on Very Large Data Bases* (pp. 588–599). IEEE.

Du, W., Mieyeville, F., & Navarro, D. (2010). Modeling energy consumption of wireless sensor networks by SystemC. In *Proceedings of The 5th International Conference on Systems and Networks Communications* (pp. 94–98). IEEE.

Ester, M., Kriegel, H.-P., Sander, J., & Xu, X. (1996). A density-based algorithm for discovering clusters in large spatial databases with noise. In *Proceedings of The 2nd International Conference on Knowledge Discovery and Data Mining* (pp. 226–231). IEEE.

Garcia-Sanchez, A.-J., Garcia-Sanchez, F., Losilla, F., Kulakowski, P., Garcia-Haro, J., & Rodríguez, A. et al. (2010). Wireless sensor network deployment for monitoring wildlife passages. *Sensors (Basel, Switzerland)*, *10*(8), 7236–7262. doi:10.3390/s100807236 PMID:22163601.

Goel, S., & Imielinski, T. (2001). Prediction-based monitoring in sensor networks: Taking lessons from mpeg. *SIGCOMM Computer and Communications Review*, *31*(5), 82–98. doi:10.1145/1037107.1037117.

He, T., Krishnamurthy, S., Stankovic, J. A., Abdelzaher, T., Luo, L., & Stoleru, R. Krogh, B. (2004). Energy-efficient surveillance system using wireless sensor networks. In *Proceedings of The 2nd International Conference on Mobile Systems, Applications, and Services* (pp. 270–283). IEEE.

Heinzelman, W. B., Chandrakasan, A. P., & Balakrishnan, H. (2002). An application-specific protocol architecture for wireless microsensor networks. *IEEE Transactions on Wireless Communications*, *1*(4), 660–670. doi:10.1109/TWC.2002.804190.

Heinzelman, W. R., Chandrakasan, A., & Balakrishnan, H. (2000). Energy-efficient communication protocol for wireless microsensor networks. In *Proceedings of The 33rd Hawaii International Conference on System Sciences*. IEEE.

Hui, J. W., & Culler, D. (2004). The dynamic behavior of a data dissemination protocol for network programming at scale. In *Proceedings of The 2nd International conference on Embedded Networked Sensor Systems* (pp. 81–94). IEEE.

Intanagonwiwat, C., Govindan, R., & Estrin, D. (2000). Directed diffusion: A scalable and robust communication paradigm for sensor networks. In *Proceedings of The 6th Annual International Conference on Mobile Computing and Networking* (pp. 56–67). IEEE.

Kotidis, Y. (2005). Snapshot queries: Towards data-centric sensor networks. In *Proceedings of The 21st International Conference on Data Engineering* (pp. 131–142). IEEE.

Krishnamachari, B., Estrin, D., & Wicker, S. (2002). The impact of data aggregation in wireless sensor networks. In *Proceedings of The 22nd International Conference on Distributed Computing Systems* (pp. 575-578). IEEE.

Lindsey, S. R. C. (2002). Pegasis: Power-efficient gathering in sensor information systems. In *Proceedings of Aerospace Conference*. Academic Press.

Madden, S., Franklin, M. J., Hellerstein, J. M., & Hong, W. (2002). TAG: A tiny aggregation service for ad-hoc sensor networks. In *Proceedings of the ACM Symposium on Operating System Design and Implementation*. ACM.

Madden, S., Franklin, M. J., Hellerstein, J. M., & Hong, W. (2003). The design of an acquisitional query processor for sensor networks. In *Proceedings of The 2003 ACM SIGMOD International Conference on Management of Data* (pp. 491–502). ACM.

Madden, S., Szewczyk, R., Franklin, M. J., & Culler, D. E. (2002). Supporting aggregate queries over ad-hoc wireless sensor networks. In *Proceedings of The 4th IEEE Workshop on Mobile Computing Systems and Applications* (pp. 49–58). IEEE.

Meliou, A., Chu, D., Hellerstein, J., Guestrin, C., & Hong, W. (2006). Data gathering tours in sensor networks. In *Proceedings of The 5th International Conference on Information Processing in Sensor Networks* (pp. 43–50). IEEE.

Rappaport, T. (Ed.). (2002). *Wireless communications: Principles and practice*. Englewood Cliffs, NJ: Prentice Hall.

Silberstein, A., Braynard, R., & Yang, J. (2006). Constraint chaining: on energy-efficient continuous monitoring in sensor networks. In *Proceedings of The 2006 ACM SIGMOD International Conference on Management of Data* (pp. 157–168). ACM.

Szewczyk, R., Osterweil, E., Polastre, J., Hamilton, M., Mainwaring, A., & Estrin, D. (2004). Habitat monitoring with sensor networks. *Communications of the ACM, 47*(6), 34–40. doi:10.1145/990680.990704.

Tan, P.-N., Steinbach, M., & Kumar, V. (Eds.). (2006). *Introduction to data mining*. Reading, MA: Addison-Wesley.

Trigoni, Yao, Demers, Gehrke, & Rajaraman. (1989). *Multi-query optimization for sensor networks* (TR2005-1989). Ithaca, NY: Cornell University.

Tulone, D., & Madden, S. (2006). An energy-efficient querying framework in sensor networks for detecting node similarities. In *Proceedings of The 9th ACM International Symposium on Modeling Analysis and Simulation of Wireless and Mobile Systems*. ACM.

Tulone, D., & Madden, S. (2006). PAQ: Time series forecasting for approximate query answering in sensor networks. In *Proceedings of The 3rd European Workshop on Wireless Sensor Networks*. IEEE.

Ulrich, T. (2008). *Wireless network monitors H2O*. Wines & Vines.

Wark, T., Corke, P., Sikka, P., Klingbeil, L., Guo, Y., & Crossman, C. et al. (2007). Transforming agriculture through pervasive wireless sensor networks. *IEEE Pervasive Computing/IEEE Computer Society [and] IEEE Communications Society, 6*(2), 50–57. doi:10.1109/MPRV.2007.47.

Werner-Allen, G., Johnson, J., Ruiz, M., Lees, J., & Welsh, M. (2005). Monitoring volcanic eruptions with a wireless sensor network. In *Proceedings of The 2nd European Workshop on Wireless Sensor Networks*. IEEE.

Werner-Allen, G., Lorincz, K., Welsh, M., Marcillo, O., Johnson, J., Ruiz, M., & Lees, J. (2006). Deploying a wireless sensor network on an active volcano. *IEEE Internet Computing, 10*(2), 18–25. doi:10.1109/MIC.2006.26.

Xia, P., Chrysanthis, P., & Labrinidis, A. (2006). Similarity-aware query processing in sensor networks. In *Proceedings of The 20th International Parallel and Distributed Processing Symposium* (pp. 178). IEEE.

Yoon, S., & Shahabi, C. (2007). The clustered aggregation (CAG) technique leveraging spatial and temporal correlations in wireless sensor networks. *ACM Transactions on Sensor Networks, 3*(1), 1–38. doi:10.1145/1210669.1210672.

Zerger, A., Viscarra Rossel, R. A., Swain, D., Wark, T., Handcock, R. N., & Doerr, V. A. J. et al. (2010). Environmental sensor networks for vegetation, animal and soil sciences. *International Journal of Applied Earth Observation and Geoinformation, 12*(5), 303–316. doi:10.1016/j.jag.2010.05.001.

Zhengmao, Y., & Habib, M. (2009). WSN topology control design via integration of Kalman filtering and adaptive estimation. In *Proceedings of The 6th International Conference on Electrical Engineering, Computing Science and Automatic Control* (pp. 1–5). IEEE.

Zhuang, Y., Pan, J., & Cai, L. (2010). Minimizing energy consumption with probabilistic distance models in wireless sensor networks. In *Proceedings of The IEEE INFOCOM* (pp. 1–9). IEEE.

ADDITIONAL READING

Berry, J., Hart, W. E., Phillips, C. E., Uber, J. G., & Watson, J. P. (2006). Sensor placement in municipal water networks with temporal integer programming models. *Journal of Water Resources Planning and Management, 132*(4), 18–224. doi:10.1061/(ASCE)0733-9496(2006)132:4(218).

Berry, J. W., Fleischer, L., Hart, W. E., Phillips, C. A., & Watson, J. P. (2005). Sensor placement in municipal water networks. *Journal of Water Resources Planning and Management, 131*(3), 237–243. doi:10.1061/(ASCE)0733-9496(2005)131:3(237).

Di Francesco, M., Das, S. K., & Anastasi, G. (2011). Data collection in wireless sensor networks with mobile elements: A survey. *ACM Transactions on Sensor Networks, 8*(1), 1–31. doi:10.1145/1993042.1993049.

Garetto, M., Gribaudo, M., Chiasserini, C.-F., & Leonardi, E. (2007). A distributed sensor relocation scheme for environmental control. In *Proceedings of the IEEE International Conference on Mobile Adhoc and Sensor Systems* (pp. 1-10). IEEE.

Gehrke, J., & Madden, S. (2004). Query processing in sensor networks. *IEEE Pervasive Computing/ IEEE Computer Society [and] IEEE Communications Society, 3*(1), 46–55. doi:10.1109/MPRV.2004.1269131.

Gupta, H., Zhou, Z., Das, S. R., & Gu, Q. (2006). Connected sensor cover: Self-organization of sensor networks for efficient query execution. *IEEE/ ACM Transactions on Networking, 14*(1), 55–67. doi:10.1109/TNET.2005.863478.

Han, J., & Kamber, M. (Eds.). (2006). *Data mining: Concepts and techniques*. San Francisco: Morgan Kaufmann Publishers.

Jiang, N. (2007). A data imputation model in sensor databases. *Lecture Notes in Computer Science, 4782*, 86–96. doi:10.1007/978-3-540-75444-2_14.

Lai, T. T.-T., Chen, W.-J., Li, K.-H., Huang, P., & Chu, H.-H. (2012). TriopusNet: Automating wireless sensor network deployment and replacement in pipeline monitoring. In *Proceedings of The 11th International Conference on Information Processing in Sensor Networks* (pp. 61-72). IEEE.

Römer, K., & Mattern, F. (2004). The design space of wireless sensor networks. *IEEE Wireless Communications, 11*(6), 54–61. doi:10.1109/MWC.2004.1368897.

Tilak, S., Abu-Ghazaleh, N. B., & Heinzelman, W. (2002). A taxonomy of wireless micro-sensor network models. *MC2R, 6*(2), 28–36.

Tu, Z., Wang, Q., Qi, H., & Shen, Y. (2012). Flocking based distributed self-deployment algorithms in mobile sensor networks. *Journal of Parallel and Distributed Computing, 72*(3), 437–449. doi:10.1016/j.jpdc.2011.11.013.

Zhu, Y., Vedantham, R., Park, S. J., & Sivakumar, R. (2008). A scalable correlation aware aggregation strategy for wireless sensor networks. *Information Fusion, 9*, 354–369. doi:10.1016/j.inffus.2006.09.002.

Zou, Y., & Chakrabarty, K. (2004). Sensor deployment and target localization in distributed sensor networks. *ACM Transactions on Embedded Computer Systems, 3*(1), 61–91. doi:10.1145/972627.972631.

KEY TERMS AND DEFINITIONS

Clustering Algorithm: It is a well-known unsupervised data mining techniques that allows to discover groups of correlated objects without a-priori knowledge on the data.

RMSD or RMSE: The root mean square deviation, also called root mean square error is a common measure of precision. It is the square root of the variance. Formally, it quantifies the square root of the amount by which an estimator differs from the true value of the quantity being estimated.

Routing: It is the process to select the transmission schedule to send data from network nodes to the base station. In a sensor network environment, routing is usually static, i.e. the base station com-

municates to each sensor node the path along which send data. Thus, the base station is responsible for the transmission fault tolerance, energy consumption, and latency. These goals can be achieved by optimizing the selection of routing paths for each query submitted through the network.

Sensor Node: A smart wireless device characterized by computational, communication and sensing capabilities (i.e., able to monitor a set of physical variables, e.g., temperature, humidity, light).

TinyOS: It is an open-source operating system designed for wireless sensor networks. It features a component-based architecture which allows fast implementation while minimizing code size as required by the memory constraints inherent in sensor networks.

Chapter 8
Context–Based Grouping and Recommendation in MANETs

Yves Vanrompay
Ecole Centrale Paris, France

Nesrine Ben Mustapha
Ecole Centrale Paris, France

Manuele Kirsch Pinheiro
Université Paris1 – Panthéon Sorbonne, France

Marie-Aude Aufaure
Ecole Centrale Paris, France

ABSTRACT

The authors propose in this chapter a context grouping mechanism for context distribution over MANETs. Context distribution is becoming a key aspect for successful context-aware applications in mobile and ubiquitous computing environments. Such applications need, for adaptation purposes, context information that is acquired by multiple context sensors distributed over the environment. Nevertheless, applications are not interested in all available context information. Context distribution mechanisms have to cope with the dynamicity that characterizes MANETs and also prevent context information from being delivered to nodes (and applications) that are not interested in it. The authors' grouping mechanism organizes the distribution of context information in groups whose definition is context based: each context group is defined based on a criteria set (e.g. the shared location and interest) and has a dissemination set, which controls the information that can be shared in the group. They propose a personalized and dynamic way of defining and joining groups by providing a lattice-based classification and recommendation mechanism that analyzes the interrelations between groups and users, and recommend new groups to users, based on the interests and preferences of the user.

INTRODUCTION

Context distribution is a key aspect for successful applications in mobile and ubiquitous computing environments. Such applications typically need context information that is acquired by multiple context sensors distributed over the environment. Context-aware applications collect and react to this information, exploiting it through predefined adaptation mechanisms. Such mechanisms may vary from content adaptation to resource-driven adaptation and application deployment (Preuve-

DOI: 10.4018/978-1-4666-4038-2.ch008

neers et al. 2009). Context information on which these adaptation mechanisms rely is also extremely varied, being potentially any information that can be used to characterize the situation of an entity (a person, place, or object) considered as relevant to the interaction between a user and an application (Dey et al. 2001). Context-aware applications adapt their operations to such context information in order to increase usability and effectiveness by taking environmental context into account (Baldauf et al. 2007).

The success of such adaption mechanisms depends then on the availability of context information, which is disseminated in Mobile Ad Hoc Networks (MANETs). However, in practice, only a fraction of all the observable context information is of interest for the user or application. For instance, in a metro station, a wide variety of information can be available: temperature and humidity, available computing infrastructure, network status, etc. Each context-aware application running in such an environment will use a subset of all available information. A travel guide application requires available computing infrastructure, network status and user profile information, but does not need temperature and humidity information, which is context information exploited by maintenance and control applications. Context distribution, which is defined as the capability to gather and deliver context information to interested entities (Bellavista et al., 2013), has to cope with this reality and adapt the distribution process to application needs.

In previous work (Kirsch Pinheiro et al., 2008), we designed a context-based grouping mechanism in which groups of peers were defined based on a criteria set (e.g. the shared location and interest) and a dissemination set (i.e. which information can be shared in the group). This approach relied on a rather static perception of groups, being defined explicitly by the developer at design time. Inference or recommendation of new groups taking into account the interests and preferences of the user was not considered. We supposed that the

initiative to search for a specific group and the decision to join it was the responsibility of the user. In this chapter, we propose a more personalized and dynamic way of joining groups by providing a mechanism that makes it possible for the system to analyze the interrelations between groups and users, and recommend new groups to users, based on the situation and profile of the user, and representing concepts and groups by Galois lattices. Galois lattices are well defined and exhaustive representations of concepts embedded in data sets (Ventos & Soldano, 2005), which can be used to represent conceptual hierarchies that are inherent in data (Stummer et al 2001).

In this chapter, we present a context-based grouping mechanism, which allows the definition of groups based on contextual characteristics shared among members of the group. Each group is defined by these characteristics and specifies which context information can be distributed among group members. New groups can be inferred from existing ones by the incorporation of conceptual clustering with Galois lattices. This allows us to discover and analyze relations between different groups and the nodes contained in them. Based on a user profiles' similarity with the elements specifying the group and the current situation of the user, the system can decide to give a recommendation to the user to join a group. This leads to a dynamic, proactive, and personalized user experience.

This chapter is organized as follows: Section 2 presents an overview of related work; Section 3 introduces a motivating scenario that illustrates the application of the proposed context grouping mechanism; Section 4 introduces the basic context grouping definition, after which the use of Galois lattices to automatically infer these groups is explained in section 5; Section 6 presents the context grouping mechanism's applicability to MANETs, including a lattice-based approach for joining suitable groups. Finally we discuss future work directions and conclusions.

Related Work

Context information is a central element of context-aware applications. Such information, often acquired by multiple context sensors distributed over the environment, is used by context-aware applications for multiple adaptation purposes (Preuveneers et al. 2009). Thus, the success of such mechanisms depends on the availability of context information, which is disseminated in Mobile Ad Hoc Networks (MANETs).

Information dissemination is a common topic in many distributed system approaches, including Peer-to-Peer ones. Architectures such as (Harjula et al., 2006; Khambatti et al. 2003) propose different ways to manage and distribute information over a set of peers. Harjula et al. (2006) proposes a topic-based publish-subscribe system with SIP/SIMPLE. This proposal uses P2P SIP for the structure and maintenance of a P2P overlay. Khambatti et al. (2003) propose a grouping mechanism based on the notion of community. Communities are groups formed based on users (or peers) common interests, declared as peer attributes. Thus, communities are automatically defined over common claimed attributes, which correspond to published attributes from the set of all observable/available attributes: a community C is a non-empty set N of peers sharing a common signature, a signature S is the intersection set of claimed attributes claim(k) for all k in N. Nevertheless, these proposals usually handle stable information sets. For instance, communities proposed by Khambatti et al. (2003) are based on claimed attributes that are not supposed to evolve quickly. This is not the case for context-aware applications. Context information on ubiquitous environments can be characterized by its dynamicity, evolving with environment changes and user's movements. In other words, context-aware applications need proper context distribution mechanisms that are able to cope with context data and with mobile and ubiquitous environments.

Context distribution can be defined as the function in charge of distributing relevant context data to interested entities (Bellavista et al. 2013). Context distribution is typically handled by middleware systems on top of which these applications are built. Different approaches have been proposed in the literature, starting from centralized solutions in which a central server concentrates and manages context information collected from the environment (Baladauf et al., 2007). Examples of such centralized architecture for context distribution include Henricksen et al. (2005) and Paganelli et al. (2006), which propose centralized entities (context repositories for the former and a domain server for the latter), managing the context information and handling the client requests for it. These centralized approaches are prone to scalability and single point of failures.

A different approach is then required in which the generation and the management of context information is distributed over the network. Such a distributed approach has to match requirements such as heterogeneity, scalability and robustness (Baladauf et al. 2007). In addition to these, an effective context distribution mechanism has to fulfill some extra requirements, among them (Bellavista et al., 2013):

1. **Decoupling Among Context Producers and Consumers:** Context producers and consumers do not need to know each other, context distribution has to transparently route produced context data from producers to all interested consumers.

2. **Adaptation to Mobile and Heterogeneous Environments:** Context distribution has to promptly adapt to mobile nodes moving in and out, sometimes randomly.

3. **Appropriate Enforcement to Context Visibility Scope:** Context data has typically a limited visibility scope that depends on the physical or logical neighborhood Context distribution must enforce such scope to avoid useless management overload.

Despite the importance of these requirements for context distribution over mobile and ubiquitous environments, many of the proposed solutions in the literature do not reach all these requirements. For instance, Romero et al. (2010) propose a distribution mechanism that handles context data as a RESTFul resource. Even if this approach successfully handles context data interoperability, it fails in decoupling context producers and consumers. Indeed, context producers and consumers declare themselves using a component-based definition language. Communication among these elements is guaranteed by REST principles, which obliges consumers to know the multiple producers. Similarly, Devlic and Klintskog (2007) have proposed a context engine providing mechanisms to retrieve, synthesize and distribute context information in distributed mobile environments. This engine uses a query principle in which a node can query context information from another node. Again, context consumers and producers have to know each other in order to allow context distribution.

In order to cope with the previously mentioned requirements, some context distribution mechanisms propose a P2P approach. For instance, Ye et al. (2007) proposes a context sharing mechanism in which context information remains locally stored on the peers and only an access reference is registered on remote peers. The discovery of new peers is performed by broadcasting messages and context queries to remote peers are sent through unicast messages. Even if this mechanism matches the first two requirements, it fails on fulfilling the third one, since broadcasting registration messages is performed regardless of peer interests on context data. Peers have to manage such context discovery process by themselves. Besides, such a flat structure may raise scalability issues in ubiquitous environments, since every peer potentially registers references to available context data on every discovered peer.

A grouping mechanism can be used in order to prevent such flat structure. For instance, Paridel et al. (2011) propose a context-based grouping mechanism particularly designed for vehicular networks. Such mechanism intends to reduce network traffic by controlling context propagation between groups. However, such groups are defined based on a strict criterion defined by vehicle location and direction. No logical neighborhood (other than location) can be defined, which may comprise the visibility scope of some context data.

Context grouping mechanisms, such as Paridel et al. (2011), can be considered as an *informed context data distribution*, since it exchanges context data according to a dynamic adapted distribution process, in opposition to an *uninformed context data distribution*, which blindly routes context data without inspecting their content (Bellavista et al., 2013). In a previous work (Kirsch-Pinheiro et al., 2008), we have proposed an informed context distribution mechanism, which is inspired by P2P dynamic group definition proposals. However, different from traditional P2P mechanisms, context groups can be seen as communities defined using common context information. We have designed a context-based grouping mechanism in which groups of peers were defined based on a criteria set (e.g. the shared location and interest) and a dissemination set (i.e. which information can be shared in the group). This approach relied on a rather static perception of groups, which had to be defined explicitly by the developer at design time. Inference or recommendation of new groups taking into account the interests and preferences of the user was not taken into account. We supposed that the initiative to search for a specific group and the decision to join it was the responsibility of the user. This lack of dynamicity on group definition can be considered as a limitation, since groups should be previously defined and cannot adapt themselves to interests of nodes that are currently available in the network.

We propose a more personalized and dynamic way of joining groups by providing a mechanism that makes it possible for the system to analyze the interrelations between groups and users, and recommend new groups to users. Recommendation systems have moved from being used by Websites like Amazon.com to key elements for realizing personalization and user-centric computing. Recent research combines context-aware computing with recommendation systems and user profiles in order to flexibly and dynamically meet user needs on mobile devices in changing environments (Nauer & Toussaint, 2007). A promising way to achieve even further personalization is the representation of the available information by concept lattices (Mao et al., 2010; Li et al., 2007; Kwon & Kim, 2009). Our goal is to dynamically recommend context-based groups to the user in a personalized way leveraging concept clustering by these lattices. Inspired by these works, we propose in this chapter a new context grouping mechanism, capable of adapting the grouping definition by recommending new groups to users, based on the analysis of Galois lattices representing concepts and groups.

Motivating Scenario

In order to demonstrate the importance of the context grouping mechanism, we describe a motivating scenario in a metro station. Let us consider Jim, a tourist visiting Paris. Jim is looking for a restaurant and he is using a travel assistant application in order to better organize (and enjoy) his stay on Paris. The travel assistant application is a context-aware application that observes and distributes context information in the network. Indeed, this application will gather information about location, network status, available infrastructure (e.g. available devices and display screens), personal details, visited locations, supplier booking references (for restaurants, hotels, or travel agencies), and user preferences around Jim in order to adapt its content and behavior to the available resources (using, for instance, a big screen available in the metro station to show Jim how to reach the restaurant). Some of these data will be locally gathered on Jim's device (e.g. Jim's location), but others will be made available by other devices (nodes) in the neighborhood.

As stated earlier in this chapter, in a metro station, several context-aware applications coexist. Among the different nodes executing these applications, different context information is gathered and can be exchanged among these nodes. Groups of nodes can then be logically formed based on the nodes interests in context information.

Nevertheless, the travel assistant application is not the only context-aware application running in the metro station. We have also a traffic information application and metro maintenance applications. Each of these applications will gather and distribute different context information, according to their needs. A traffic information application will be interested on context information such as location, network status and direction, while a maintenance application will be more interested in user role, humidity, temperature and available infrastructure. If every node connected to this network starts distributing all collected context information, devices connected to it will quickly overload, and Jim's phone will probably waste too much time filtering context data it receives.

In order to prevent disagreements that can be caused by such unnecessary processing, applications may constitute groups of nodes sharing common interests on context information. Such groups can be defined based considering node neighborhood, not only network or physical neighborhood, but also logical neighborhood, defined using common context information. Group templates can be manually defined, based on a static perception of user interests on lodging, attraction sites, travel location, transport issues. Since each interest category contains a lot of dimensions, this leads to a combinatorial explosion of the number of templates.

For instance, Jim is using his mobile device and asks for the restaurant the most visited in Paris providing Italian food. The travel assistant should search in group templates repositories to find an exact matching with *Jim's interest*.

Two possible scenarios can happen. The first one concerns the fact that no exact matching is found so that the system will rely only on shared information about restaurant suppliers and will provide the user with a long list of restaurant. In a second case, the system finds many general templates that are not relevant for Jim's request.

In both cases, the travel assistant cannot find dynamically the appropriate group template according to the user interest and Jim will abandon the use of his travel assistant since he can by himself search over the Web for the most visited Italian restaurants. This is due mainly to two facts:

- Manually defined group templates do not reflect the actually shared information about user interests.
- A static context grouping mechanism cannot carry out deep personalization as it is based on static matching with predefined criteria in templates.

With the aim of these two problems, the main motivation resides on providing a spontaneous way to build group templates by formally analyzing the large amount of data about user interests. Group templates have to be built based on the most common criteria associated with a high number of similar user interests.

For instance, the travel assistant application can enter in a group defined based on user preferences and location information, including travelers located in the same metro station that have similar interests, while a maintenance application can get in a group defined based on the user role. In each group, nodes can share different context information: network status, available infrastructure for the former, humidity and temperature for the latter. By separating nodes in groups, based on shared context information, we can isolate Jim's phone from context information coming from nodes interested only in the maintenance application. However, let us consider that there is no other traveler in the metro station that shares Jim's preferences. Based on the group definition used by travel assistant application, Jim will not receive any context in-

formation, since no other node shares with him context values used as criteria for defining the group. Even if the context information needed by Jim's travel assistant is available on other nodes, Jim's node will be outside groups sharing such information. For instance, let us consider that the traffic information application defines a group based only on location information and shares context information related to network status, available infrastructure and direction. In this case, Jim's phone may detect that there is another group in the network and decide to enter this group in order to receive the context information it needs.

In this chapter, we handle context distribution by proposing a context grouping mechanism that allows the definition of groups based on common shared context information.

Additionally, we propose using Galois lattices in order to improve such grouping mechanism. Lattices are used for recommendation purposes, adapting the groups to the current situation of the node neighborhood. Indeed, lattices provide a natural and formal setting to discover and represent groups of interests hierarchies. "Formal concept analysis" is mainly used for data analysis, i.e. for investigating and processing explicitly given information (Szathmary & al., 2008; Gao and Lai, 2010). Lattice-based analysis can bring out context-based groups that were not predefined by the applications or the middleware.

CONTEXT-BASED GROUPING WITH GROUP TEMPLATES

Context dissemination is organized in groups, which are defined using context information. The main principle consists in forming groups with nodes that share common observable context items (for example, the same location, the same network connection, etc.). Within these groups, it is specified which type of context information will be disseminated. The disseminated information typically corresponds to interests shared amongst the members of the group like traffic alerts or weather information. Grouping can be seen as corresponding to the node neighborhood. The notion of neighborhood is semantically extended to include not only the notion of network neighborhood (nodes in the same network), but also geographical neighborhood (nodes in the same location) or other application-defined criteria (nodes executing over similar devices, nodes acting on behalf of users playing a given role in an organization, etc.). Thus, applications can determine the criteria for the group formation. These criteria for forming context groups depend on the context characteristics, which can be described by the context model used. All context elements defined in the context model can be used and combined by the application or the middleware to form groups (for example, groups based on the location, on the network connection, etc.). Once the criteria are defined, the groups are formed and used as context addresses for distribution purposes. Figure 1 gives an illustration of the grouping definition. This figure shows a set of nodes forming two groups: (1) a first group is formed based on the node location (group formation criterion) and disseminates information about device available memory, screen size and battery; (2) a second group is defined based on the user role and the group disseminates location information. The criteria defining the groups are at runtime translated to real values of observable context information (e.g. location = room x, user role = expert),

Figure 1. Two context group definition composed by group criteria ("location," "userrole") and corresponding dissemination set ("memory, screensize, battery," "location")

UserRole group
< [UserRole], [Location] >

Location group
< [Location], [Memory, ScreenSize, Battery] >

which are used to disseminate the allowed context information, i.e. device resource information for the first group, user location for the second one. In this sense, this context grouping mechanism can be seen as a decentralized publish-subscribe mechanism since applications can decide to join only groups disseminating context information, which the application is interested in.

Only information related to the group is disseminated to group members. We consider two types of context requests: pull requests in which nodes query context information from other nodes in the neighborhood, and push requests in which nodes proactively send context information to other nodes in the neighborhood. The group definition becomes then central for context distribution over the network. A context group G_D is defined as follows:

$$G_D = < C_D, I_D >,$$

where C_D is the criteria set, i.e. set of context elements that determine the context group. I_D is the dissemination set, also called the working set. It is the context information that can be disseminated in this group, i.e. the context elements that are allowed to be disseminated (by push requests) or requested (by pull requests) in this group.

Initially the group definition is established at design time. Each application defines its groups based on its context information needs. Thus, for group management, the application has to determine the criteria for forming a group and the context information, which is allowed to be distributed in this group. An application defines a *group template* in which it stipulates, using queries in a Context Query Language (CQL) (Reichle et al. 2008), the criteria and dissemination sets that define the group. The CQL (Reichle et al. 2008) allows the expression of fine-grained groups through complex queries, exploiting logical constraints and semantic references to entities represented in the context model. As an example, Figure 2 shows two CQL queries defining, respectively, the criteria set (Figure 2a) and the dissemination set (Figure 2 b), which act as a template for a context group. This template defines a context group based on the user's location information (Figure 2 a). It expresses that the shared context item by which the group is defined is equal to the room the user is in. The group allows the dissemination of context information related to the user's device memory status (Figure 2 b). For readability purposes, we express this group template using a literal representation as illustrated by Figure 2 c.

For the application, the group definition remains stable over time, since its template remains the same. However, since this definition relies on context information, it is naturally dynamic. The values corresponding to the group criteria and the dissemination set are updated by the reasoning layer according to the runtime context changes. The context group template is used to instantiate an actual context group: the query representing the group criteria is processed and the current values of the corresponding context elements are used to form the concrete context group. For example, given a group G1 defined by <[position],

[memory]>, as was illustrated in Figure 2, its definition criterion is translated to [position = room x], corresponding to the current value of this context element. Once the value of the context elements used as criteria change (e.g. the user goes into another room), the group definition is updated to the new value ([position = room y]), and accordingly to this new situation, nodes may leave and join (or create) the corresponding group at the network level.

Based on the group definitions, the context group mechanism organizes the context dissemination and requests, by handling accordingly the context query messages and dissemination messages coming from other nodes over the network, as well as context request messages coming from the application. The context group mechanism hides from the application dynamic changes related to the context groups. Nevertheless, the grouping mechanism depends on the query that determines the grouping criteria. If this query is not well-formed or is ambiguous, the context grouping mechanism is unable to interpret it and to form or join the context groups. For instance, given a location-based context group, an applica-

Figure 2. Context definition in XML

```
<contextQL>                                                              (a)
    <ctxQuery>
        <action type="SELECT"/>
        <entity ontConcept="prefix:music:username">#user</entity>
        <scope ontConcept="prefix:music:Location"
               ontRep="prefix:music:DefaultLocationRep">#location</scope>
        <conds>
            <cond type="ONVALUE">
                <constraint param="#location.#room" op="EQ"/>
            </cond>
        </conds>
    </ctxQuery>
</contextQL>

<contextQL>                                                              (b)
    <ctxQuery>
        <action type="SELECT"/>
        <entity ontConcept="prefix:music:devicename">#any</entity>
        <scope ontConcept="prefix:music:Resource"
               ontRep="prefix:music:DefaultMemoryRep">#memory</scope>
    </ctxQuery>
</contextQL>
```

$$G_d = < [\ position\ ], [\ memory\ ] > \qquad (c)$$

tion can consider that two users are in the same location if they are in the same room (such as in the query in Figure 2 a), or in the same city, or in the same coordinate interval. Even if the CQL allows a query just indicating the context concept location, this is not enough to indicate without ambiguity what the application treats as being in the same location. Applications using the proposed context grouping mechanism should avoid queries with any ambiguity when defining context grouping criteria.

Such context grouping definition performed at design time has an important drawback: group criteria remain stable and it does not adapt to networks variations and opportunities. For instance, a node can find itself alone in a group whose criteria are not shared by any other node. We supposed that the initiative to search for a specific group and the decision to join it was the responsibility of the user. In this chapter, we propose a more personalized and dynamic way of joining groups by providing a mechanism that makes it possible for the system to analyze the interrelations between groups and users, and recommend new groups to users, based on the situation and profile of the user, and representing concepts and groups by Galois lattices. In next section, we present how lattices can contribute to the group formation and management, realizing an important inference method for group templates.

LATTICE-BASED GROUP FORMATION AND MANAGEMENT

Although group profiles can be defined explicitly by the application developer, this is not optimal because it restricts the kind of groups that can be formed. In general, it is not possible to know at design time what groups will be relevant in a given context. In order to provide a personalized experience to the user, in which groups can be dynamically recommended in function of the situation and interests of the user, we propose the use of concept lattices. Contextual elements that (potentially can) specify groups are represented as concepts in a Galois lattice, which allows conceptual clustering and the discovery of novel groups that match user's needs. Lattice-based formal concept analysis takes as input a matrix specifying the set of nodes in the MANET (the *objects*) and the corresponding context elements (the *properties* or *attributes*) specifying the groups each node belongs to. This representation allows us to:

- **Find "Natural" Node Clusters:** The set of all nodes that share a common subset of context elements.
- **Find "Natural" Context Element Clusters:** The set of all context elements shared by one of the natural node clusters.

Natural context element clusters correspond with natural node clusters, and a concept is a pair containing both a natural property cluster and its corresponding natural object cluster.

By analyzing and visualizing this emerging and evolving concept lattice, we gain the following three features. (1) group membership and dependencies between groups can be inferred to dynamically *form new groups* based on group templates suitable to the overall user interests. (2) we can efficiently *recommend possibly interesting groups* to users. The detection of potentially suitable groups uses similarity metrics between the elements specifying a group and the users' interests, which are represented as scores associated with concepts and attributes in an ontology. Alternatively, similarity between different users can be calculated in order to recommend groups based on collaborative filtering. (3) By showing in real time (using existing visualization tools) the evolution of the (relative) size of and relations between groups, *"hot topics"* can be detected and used for commercial purposes.

In the next section we explain how group templates can be inferred using Galois lattices. Then, we present how this approach can help in recommending interesting groups to users.

Inference of Group Templates

We propose techniques based on formal concept analysis (FCA) to identify (1) sets of users that share common interests and (2) relations and dependencies between interests. Analyzing this information allows us to automatically derive appropriate group templates.

In FCA, a concept is identified both by an extent, i.e. a set of objects that share the concept's attributes, and an intent, the set of attributes common to the concept. The starting point of FCA is a formal context, which is defined as a triple (G, M, I), where G is a set of objects, M a set of attributes and I a binary relation over $G \times M$. A formal context corresponds to a binary matrix with the rows being the objects and the columns the attributes. Given $O \subseteq G$, O' is defined as the set of attributes of M which are shared by all elements of O. Given $A \subseteq M$, A' is defined as the set of objects that share all attributes in A. A formal concept of a context is a pair (O, A), O being the objects that share all attributes of A. O is the extent and A the intent, i.e. $O = A'$ and $A = O'$. The set of all concepts derived from the formal context can be represented as a lattice, based on the subconcept relation $\leq$ for partial ordering: $(O_1, A_1) \leq (O_2, A_2)$ if $O_1 \subseteq O_2$ or equivalently that $A_2 \subseteq A_1$. The maximum element in this ordering is the concept with an empty extent, and the minimum is the concept with an empty intent.

Contrary to the design time and rather static definition of groups by application developers, our goal is to infer suitable candidates for group templates by analyzing a set of users with their interests, and the relations between these interests. The user's interests and preferences are expressed in ontology modules as entities and attributes that

are annotated with scores $-1 \leq w_i \leq 1$ indicating a user's (dis-)interest in a particular item. Each ontology module is domain-specific, representing for example interests in houses for sale or restaurants. Figure 3 shows a hierarchical modular ontology for the tourism domain. Each leaf node corresponds to a specific ontology sub-module representing an entity with attributes according to the specified schema. For example, the restaurant sub-module contains attributes like location, food type and dress code. Scores associated with these attributes indicate whether the user prefers e.g. Indian or Italian restaurants, or whether the dress code should be formal or casual.

Each scored ontology module serves as input for the construction of the formal context (G, M, I). The set G holds all users, while M contains relevant attributes (interests). I is defined as follows:

$$I(g_i, m_j): G \times M \rightarrow \{0, 1\} = 1 \text{ if } w_j(u_i) \geq T, \text{ otherwise } 0$$

$w_j(u_i)$ is the score assigned for user i to attribute j, and T is a threshold between 0 and 1. An example formal context, the crosses indicating a value of 1 for I, is shown in Figure 4.

Based on this formal context, we build a concept lattice (illustrated in Figure 4) allowing us to identify the sets of attributes which are best suited to be taken into account for the definition

Figure 3. Hierarchical modular ontology for tourism

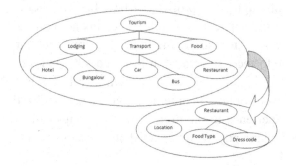

Figure 4. Example formal context and corresponding Galois lattice for restaurant module

	LOC:PARIS14	FT:ITALIAN	FT:INDIAN	...	DC:CASUAL	DC:FORMAL
U₁	X		X			X
U₂	X	X	X		X	
U₃		X	X	X	X	
...				X	X	
Uᵢ	X	X			X	
...		X	X		X	
Uₙ	X			X		

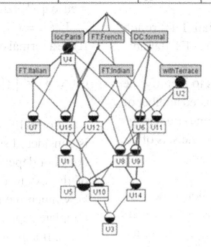

of group templates. The lattice assigns users to (sets of) interests, which are the building blocks for the group template definition. A user U_i is interested in all attributes that are connected to and hierarchically higher in the lattice than the node the user is assigned to.

From the Galois lattice we can automatically infer association rules like the ones shown in the box below. For example, rule 1 states that 7 users are interested in restaurants with formal dress code, and 6 users out of these 7 prefer french food. From the association rules, we infer suitable group templates, which balance generality and specificity. Group templates should not be too general because contextual information must be disseminated as much as possible only to users that are interested in that information. Users do not have to be flooded with all kinds of information. On the other hand, templates should not be too specific, because this leads to a large number of sparsely populated groups. Intuitively, this

corresponds to concepts in the lattice on a not too high and not too low level, i.e. somewhere in the middle.

1. < 7 > DC:formal =[86%]=> < 6 > FT:French;
2. < 7 > FT:Indian =[86%]=> < 6 > loc:Paris;
3. < 5 > loc:Paris DC:formal =[100%]=> < 5 > FT:French;
4. < 6 > FT:French DC:formal =[83%]=> < 5 > loc:Paris;
5. < 6 > loc:Paris FT:French =[83%]=> < 5 > DC:formal;
6. < 6 > FT:Italian =[83%]=> < 5 > FT:French;
7. < 6 > FT:Italian =[83%]=> < 5 > loc:Paris;
8. < 4 > loc:Paris FT:Italian FT:French =[100%]=> < 4 > DC:formal;
9. < 4 > FT:Italian DC:formal =[100%]=> < 4 > loc:Paris FT:French;
10. < 4 > FT:Indian FT:French =[100%]=> < 4 > loc:Paris;

11. < 4 > FT:French withTerrace =[100%]=> < 4 > DC:formal;
12. < 4 > DC:formal withTerrace =[100%]=> < 4 > FT:French;
13. <5> conn:wifi =[80%]=> <4> FT:Indian;
14. < 5 > loc:Paris FT:French DC:formal =[80%]=> < 4 > FT:Italian;
15. < 5 > FT:Italian FT:French =[80%]=> < 4 > loc:Paris DC:formal;
16. < 3 > loc:Paris FT:Indian FT:French DC:formal =[100%]=> < 3 > FT:Italian;

The association rules allow us to identify the group templates that realize a balanced number of groups with users who share common interests. Two basic metrics are used to find the sets of attributes defining the group templates:

- **Support S:** This metric denotes the proportion of users that expressed their interest in a set of attributes. For example, association rule 4 indicates that 6 users (out of the total of 15) have an interest in restaurants serving French food with formal dress code, meaning support = 0.4.
- **Confidence C:** This metric expresses the proportion of users having an interest in the rules' consequent, given they have an interest in the rules' antecedent. In rule 4 for example, 5 out of 6 users that are interested in French restaurants with formal dress code are interested in Parisian restaurants. So confidence in this case is 0.83.

The group templates' dissemination set is defined as the attributes of those association rules which have a minimal support s_{min} and minimal confidence c_{min}. These minimal values can be tuned according to the application needs and priorities. For example, if it is important that not much information is disseminated in groups that is irrelevant for some users, c_{min} should be put rather high. For our purposes, we set s_{min} to 0.4 and c_{min} to 0.8. Minimal support ensures that only

concepts with extents having at least $100.s_{min}$ % of all users are considered candidates for the group templates. Algorithms for computing frequent item sets are used to build such a so called Iceberg lattice (Stumme et al. 2002).

As soon as the appropriate candidate attribute sets for the group templates are identified, a second filtering step takes place using the stability index metric φ (Kuznetsov et al., 2007).

Let K = (G, M, I) be a formal context and (A, B) be a formal concept of K. Then φ is as follows:

$$\varphi (A, B) = \left| \{C \subseteq A \mid C' = B\} \right| / 2^{|A|}$$

Informally, a concept (i.e. group in our case) is considered stable if its intent (set of interests) does not depend much on each particular object of the extent (set of users). Stability expresses how much the set of attributes forming a group template depends on the interests of its individual users. If a group is persistent, it does not depend on a few users: some users leaving the group should not change the set of interests the group represents. It should be noted that we already minimize this risk by incorporating the minimal confidence metric in step 1. A stable group also does not merge with a different group or split into several independent subgroups when some users leave the group.

Apart from the "intensional" stability, we also use the extensional stability, which measures how the users of a particular group depend on the particular attributes. If we remove some attributes from the group template definition, does the set of users remains more or less the same. Extensional stability indicates how much the group of users depends on a particular interest.

Group Recommendation Using Local Views

The previous section explained how group templates can be derived given the interests of a set of users by building a global lattice. This lattice gives a global view of the group templates and serves as a bootstrap to start users joining and leaving groups according to their needs. When a user found a group that matches his interests and joins it, the members of the group can recommend other possibly interesting groups to the newly joined that they themselves are member of. This collaborative filtering process allows to exploit the local knowledge of each user about groups he is a member of to efficiently recommend other groups. Indeed, a group can be seen as a community, and groups that are popular in that community can be of interest for the newly joint user.

The local information is represented by local lattices, where the objects are the users and the attributes are groups that the users are member of. The formal context defines a membership function of users to groups for one specific group A, as is exemplified for a group with 4 users in Table 1.

When a user U5 joins group A, it will publish its group membership information and the local lattice is updated. First, the local lattice, shown in Figure 5, is used to check which groups are popular in group A, and groups are accordingly recommended to U5. In our example, the support for group B is 0.75 and this group is recommended to U5. In case U5 is already a member of one or more of the groups in the local lattice, a recommendation will be made containing the direct children of these groups.

Lattice-Based GroupING in MANETs

The context grouping definition, as presented in the previous section, can be applied in many different settings. Indeed, it is independent from the architecture adopted by the hosting system. Nevertheless, a context grouping mechanism like this one is particularly interesting for highly dynamic environments, in which entities may appear and disappear at any moment, such as MANETs. When considering MANETs, one should consider its dynamic nature. As a consequence of this dynamic nature, assuming any centralized approach

Table 1. Group with four users

A	B	C	D	F
U1	X	X		
U2	X		X	
U3				X
U4	X	X		

in such environment is impractical. We cannot suppose neither any previous knowledge about the nodes availability on the network. In such conditions, a peer-to-peer (P2P) approach imposes itself as an interesting solution for handling such dynamic environments. In this section, we present a P2P-based architecture for nodes adopting our context grouping mechanism and we discuss its applicability to MANETs.

Architecture

Several works (Hu et al., 2008; Ye et al., 2007; Paridel et al., 2011) have proposed P2P-based approaches for context distribution, some of them dividing peers according to their roles or capabilities. Hu et al. (2008) considers three kind of peers, mainly according to device capabilities and

Figure 5. Local lattice for group A

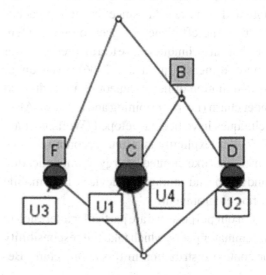

associated roles for context distribution purposes: (1) sensor peers, which correspond to devices providing only raw context data (typically, context sensors); (2) consumer peers, resource-constrained devices that need polished (and synthesized) context information; (3) disseminator peers, which represent peers providing both provider and consumer functionalities, they provide context distribution services and perform the context reasoning. We agree with this distinction, since, for us, the heterogeneous nature of nodes involved in the context distribution process cannot be ignored and should be considered. Such distinction on three kinds of nodes allows a better applicability of the grouping mechanism to different kinds of mobile devices. Nodes with limited device capabilities can be used as sensor or consumer peers, while more powerful devices, typically last generation smartphones, will be used as disseminator peers. Indeed, current smartphones are more and more powerful compared to older mobile phones. Dual-core processors are now equipping several models, and quad-core devices are expected for the next generation of smartphones and tablets (Olivarez-Giles, 2012; Petric, 2012). This kind of devices, which is becoming extremely popular nowadays, can be used as disseminator peers, since they have enough computational power to support both context providing and reasoning. Moreover, information distribution becomes more and more feasible since recent approaches optimize the efficiency of peer-to-peer content distribution techniques close to a theoretical lower bound (Kangasharju et al., 2006), even under the assumption of heterogeneous bandwidth and under churn (i.e. peers joining and leaving). Also, techniques have been developed (Wolfson et al., 2007) that explicitly take into account resource constraints like limited energy, communication bandwidth and storage of devices in a mobile ad-hoc environment.

For our purpose, we are particular interested in disseminator peers, which take full responsibility for context distribution in this architecture. Be-

sides, we consider that some of these disseminator nodes play also a relay role, connecting different groups in the network. These relay nodes, acting as super-peers, can keep a partial knowledge of the network state that can be applied for lattice construction (cf. previous section).

Each disseminator peer has a multilayer architecture represented in Figure 6: a "reasoning" layer, which manages the context grouping (together with other context reasoning functionalities, which is out of the scope of this chapter), and a "distribution" layer, which handles the context dissemination according to the grouping definitions. In this way, the grouping mechanism can be defined independently of the actually used distribution technologies. Each layer is represented by a service that is in charge of layer responsibilities. Thus, each disseminator peer offers, as illustrated by Figure 6, a "Context Service", which provides context clients with a way to query context or to subscribe to context updates, and a "Distribution Service", which disseminates context information in a certain scope.

In the reasoning layer, the *context service* is in charge of interpreting group criteria for forming groups depending on the context characteristics. Context data is represented using a particular context model, which defines and describes context information. The context model delimits what context elements can be potentially used as grouping criteria: all context elements defined in the context model can be used and combined to form groups (for example, groups based on the location, on the network connection, etc.). In our case, we adopt the MUSIC Context Model (Reichle et al. 2008). This model enables the representation of context information in terms of *context elements*, which provide context information about *context entities* (the concrete subjects the context data refers to: a user, a device, etc.) belonging to specific *context scopes*. The Context Query Language (Reichle et al. 2008), used for describing the group profile, adopts the same model. It allows applications to submit to the context service queries about

Figure 6. Disseminator peer architecture

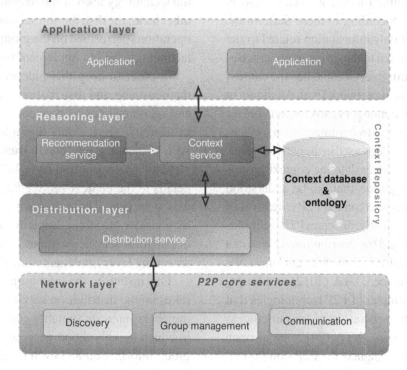

an entity and referred to a context scope, specifying a set of constraints that represent the filters of the query.

The context service interprets group criteria, represented using a CQL query, and uses this information to manage the group membership according to context changes. It provides the group management mechanisms to create, update, and leave context groups. In addition to managing peer groups, the context service also handles the application requests for context information, in the form of pull or push requests. Based on the group definitions, the context service organizes the context dissemination and requests, by handling accordingly the context query messages and dissemination messages coming from other peers over the network, as well as context request messages coming from the application.

Besides, the reasoning layer offers a recommendation service, which is responsible for analyzing network information and eventually recommend new groups to the context service.

Periodically, this recommendation service gathers context information from the different peers belonging to the same groups the peer belongs to. Disseminator peers acting as relay peers are particularly well-placed for gathering context information from groups and build a more complete lattice representing peers interests, sharing this information on each "context gather" request performed by neighborhood peers. Based on this information, the recommendation service builds a lattice and may then recommend new groups, as explained previously in this chapter. It may recommend these new groups to the applications, on the application layer, requiring then an explicit user validation, or directly to the context service (corresponding to an implicit validation), according to user's preferences.

Concerning the *distribution layer*, it acts as a mediator between the reasoning layer and the mechanisms offered by the P2P core service at the network layer. The *distribution service* interprets the groups defined by the context service and controls the distribution of the context information over the network according to these definitions. It guarantees that only information related to the group is disseminated to the group members. Besides, the distribution service handles the context group formation at the network level. As shown in Figure 6, the distribution service is responsible for isolating the context and recommendation services from real P2P technology used in the network level. This means it has to translate the context groups to traditional P2P groups that can be understood by the technologies used on the P2P core level of the architecture. Actually, different P2P technologies are available and the distribution service can be potentially confronted to different ones. We may cite, for instance, JXTA (2012) and Pastry (2012) as two examples of P2P technologies that can be used in the network level for our context grouping mechanism. JXTA (2012) is an open network platform designed for P2P computing, which provides a common set of open protocols for peer-to-peer communication. Basically, it standardizes the manner in which peers perform common operations such as discovering each other, self-organizing into peer groups, communicating, etc. Developers can leverage open source implementations of JXTA protocols for creating point-to-point applications. Pastry (2012) is a generic, scalable and efficient substrate for P2P applications. Pastry nodes form a decentralized, self-organizing and fault-tolerant overlay network within the Internet. It provides efficient request routing, deterministic object location, and load balancing in an application-independent manner. Furthermore, Pastry provides mechanisms that support and facilitate application-specific object replication, caching, and fault recovery. FreePastry is an open-source implementation of Pastry intended for deployment in the Internet. Such multiplicity of available P2P technologies is the main reason behind the separation between reasoning and distribution layers in the proposed architecture. On the one hand, the context grouping mechanism can be defined independently of the technology used at the network level. On the other hand, the distribution service decouples the operations performed on the groups from the P2P technology used to implement these operations.

In order to keep this independence between the reasoning and distribution layer, the context and recommendation services interact with the distribution service only through a well defined API. This interface defines the functionalities supplied by the distribution layer, hiding technology details to the context service and to recommendation service. Through this API, it is possible to consider different implementations for the distribution service, without compromising the reasoning layer implementation.

For instance, the recommendation service relies on the distribution service API for gathering peers interests (notably context information in which neighborhood peers are interested on), group information and even neighborhood local lattices.

Applicability to MANETS

This section describes how we can efficiently search across the P2P network exploiting local and global view lattices. A query for a specific group is not flooded over the network, but routed over a super-peer structure. A hybrid P2P network includes a set of peers P and super-peers SP. Links exist exclusively as pairs $\{SP_i, SP_j\}$ and $\{SP_i, P_j\}$. Compared to pure P2P systems, an architecture with super-peers has several advantages. The search is much faster since it is broken into a search for information from a smaller set of super-peers, each having their own indexed information from their set of peers. The problem of network flooding associated with pure P2P systems is hereby resolved. Also, each super-peer cluster corresponds to an autonomous unit not depending on a central server for information exchange. Lastly, super-peers introduce load balancing by only allowing nodes with sufficient computing power to act as super-peer.

Figure 7. Physical super-peer clusters with peers expressing their concept interest

SuperPeer SP1	Concept interest		
	C1 (hotel)	C2(restaurant)	C3(transport)
P11	0	0	1
P12	0	0	1
P13	0	1	1
P14	0	1	0
P15	1	0	0
P16	1	0	0
P17	1	1	0

SuperPeer SP2	Concept interest		SuperPeer SP3	Concept interest	
	C3(transport)	C4 (museum)		C1(hotel)	C2(restaurant)
			P31	1	0
P21	1	0	P32	1	0
P22	1	1	P33	1	0
P23	0	1	P34	0	1
P24	1	1	P35	0	1
P25	1	1	P36	1	0
P26	0	1	P37	1	0
P27	1	1			

In the following, we explain the lattice-based group finding approach by a running example. The tables in Figure 7 show three super-peer clusters with their associated peers. For each peer it is indicated whether there is an interest in high-level concepts like hotels, restaurants, museums, or transport. The super-peers with their clusters are depicted in Figure 8. The global view lattice for each super-peer cluster, derived from the tables in Figure 7, is also shown. The virtual groups formed by the common interests of the peers are represented by the ovals. For example, P15, P16, and P17 are interested in hotel information and form a virtual group within cluster SP1.

Suppose a user P18 is searching for museum information (C4) having a set of attribute values (AT1_V2, AT2_V2 and AT3_V1) and is connected physically to SP1. The super-peer SP1 searches in its lattice for groups that are associated to museum interests (i.e. concept C4). As can be seen in Figure 8, there are no groups in cluster SP1 that can satisfy the user request. So SP1 will transfer the request to the super-peers in its neighborhood, being SP2.

In cluster SP2, the same search process is performed and it found a possibly relevant group associated to C4, consisting of 6 peers. Next, a deep search is carried out inside these groups to find the suitable subgroup that matches with the set of attribute values (ATi_Vi), which is the specific part of the user request.

For this, we use the local view lattice of concept C4 in cluster SP2, shown in Figure 9. The local view lattice for each concept shows the detailed interests of the peers belonging to the virtual group of the concept museum. Since P18 is specifically interested in attributes AT1_V2, AT2_V2, and AT3_V1, we assign it to the context group shown in the box in Figure 9, and which already contains P24 and P25.

Finally, Figure 10 shows P18 in cluster SP1 having joined the appropriate museum group, after which the global lattice of cluster SP1 is updated to reflect this change.

FUTURE RESEARCH DIRECTIONS

The proposed context grouping mechanism represents a first step for the combination of context distribution and recommendation systems. Context-based recommendation systems are already an important tendency (Adomavicius et al. 2005; Abbar et al. 2009). Nonetheless, this work considers a different point of view: the use of recommendation techniques for context distribution. We

Figure 8. Super-peer networks with global view lattices

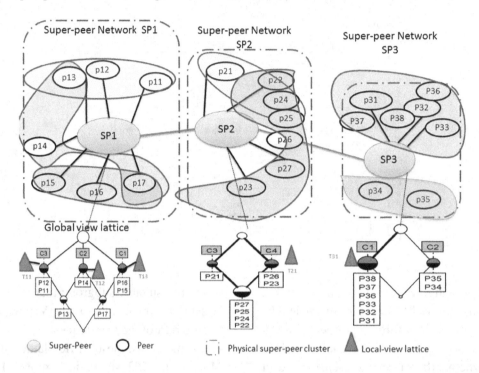

Figure 9. Local view lattice for museum concept in SP2

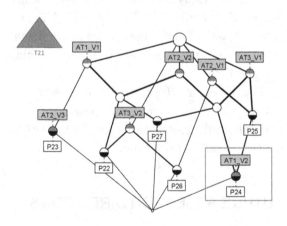

are strongly convinced that context information is more than a simple parameter for adaptation purposes, it is the key for providing a personalized experience to the user. More than a new context distribution mechanism, what we propose here is a fully context-based distribution mechanism that can be used to distribute not only necessary context information, but also to distribute any information corresponding to current user's needs in real-time. By considering concept lattices for analysing emerging groups of interests, we can efficiently recommend possibly interesting groups to users, which represents a new opportunistic adaptation mechanism for context-aware computing. We can also detect and visualize "hot topics", which may represent an important source of information for application designers in the future.

Distribution mechanisms like this one that explore both context information and recommendation techniques, represent new opportunities to be explored by context-aware application, notably the applicability to social computing. Such applications, which represent an important application domain for pervasive computing, can heavily benefit from initiatives like this one. Nevertheless, a more formal analysis of the complexity presented by lattice building is still missing. Even if such analysis is particular important considering lattice-based recommendation techniques,

Figure 10. P18 joined the appropriate museum group, after which SP1's global lattice is updated

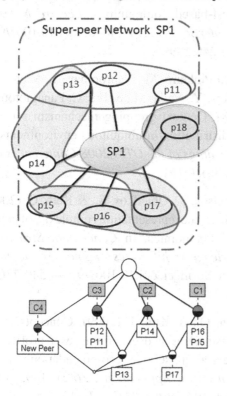

we have to consider that, contrarily to traditional recommendation systems, in this particular case of context-based grouping, not the number of users, nor the attribute set will be very large in real life cases. A practical evaluation of the proposed mechanism will be realized in order to validate this hypothesis and to supply necessary data to complete this analysis.

CONCLUSION

In this chapter, we have proposed a context grouping mechanism for context distribution over MANETs. This grouping mechanism allows the management of groups of peers based on shared context information. However, a static definition of group profiles at design time, is not enough since it is quite difficult to predefine groups that will be relevant for users in a given context. In

order to tackle this problem, we have considered that groups could be dynamically recommended by the grouping mechanism. Thus, we proposed an improved context grouping mechanism that is capable of recommending to users new groups based on current available context elements and on user's interests (including interests on context information itself). The improved grouping mechanism uses Galois lattices in order to recommend groups that best match the interests. By using Galois lattices, we can automatically infer suitable candidates for group templates by analyzing a set of users with their interests and the relations between these interests.

The next step in this work includes its evaluation in a more practical scenario. A Java implementation is under development for this purpose. A practical evaluation of the proposed lattice-based context grouping mechanism will allow us to analyze performance of the proposed mechanism, and notably the lattice-based recommendation, and to demonstrate the feasibility of this approach, mainly through a formal analysis of the complexity of lattice building.

REFERENCES

Abbar, S., Bouzeghoub, M., & Lopez, S. (2009). Context-aware recommendation systems: A service-oriented approach. In *Proceedings of the 35th International Conference on Very Large Data Bases (VLDB)*. VLDB.

Adomavicius, G., & Tuzhilin, A. (2005). Toward the next generation of recommender systems: A survey of the state-of-the-art and possible extensions. *IEEE Transactions on Knowledge and Data Engineering*, *17*(6), 734–749. doi:10.1109/TKDE.2005.99.

Baldauf, M., Dustdar, S., & Rosenberg, F. (2007). A survey on context-aware systems. *International Journal of Ad Hoc Ubiquitous Computing*, *2*, 263–277. doi:10.1504/IJAHUC.2007.014070.

Bellavista, P., Corradi, A., Fanelli, M., & Foschini, L. (2013). A survey of context data distribution for mobile ubiquitous systems. *ACM Computing Surveys, 45*(1), 1–49.

Devlic, A., & Klintskog, E. (2007). Context retrieval and distribution in a mobile distributed environment. In *Proceedings of the Third Workshop on Context Awareness for Proactive Systems (CAPS 2007)*. Guildford, UK: CAPS.

Gao, J., & Lai, W. (2010). Formal concept analysis based clustering for blog network visualization. *ADMA, 1*, 394–404.

Harjula, E., Ala-Kurikka, J., Howie, D., & Yli-anttila, M. (2006). Analysis of peer-to-peer SIP in a distributed mobile middleware system. In *Proceedings of IEEE Global Telecommunications Conference (GlobeCom06)* (pp. 1–6). IEEE.

Henricksen, K., Indulska, J., McFadden, T., & Balasubramaniam, S. (2005). Middleware for distributed context-aware systems. *Lecture Notes in Computer Science, 3760*, 846–863. doi:10.1007/11575771_53.

Hu, X., Ding, Y., Paspallis, N., Bratskas, P., Papadopoulos, G., & Vanrompay, Y. Berbers, Y. (2008). A hybrid peer-to-peer solution for context distribution in mobile and ubiquitous environments. In *Proceedings of the 17th International Conference on Information Systems Development (ISD2008)* (pp. 501-510). ISD.

JXTA. (n.d.). *The language and platform independent protocol for P2P networking*. Retrieved from http://jxta.kenai.com/

Kangasharju, J., & Kangasharju, J. (2006). An optimal basis for efficient peer-to-peer content distribution algorithms. In *Proceedings of the 15th International Conference on Computer Communications and Networks* (pp. 481-486). IEEE.

Khambatti, M., Dong Ryu, K., & Dasgupta, P. (2003). Structuring peer-to-peer networks using interest-based communities. *Lecture Notes in Computer Science, 2944*, 48–63. doi:10.1007/978-3-540-24629-9_5.

Kirsch Pinheiro, M., Vanrompay, Y., Victor, K., Berbers, Y., Valla, M., & Frà, C. Panagiotou, G. (2008). Context grouping mechanism for context distribution in ubiquitous environments. In *Proceedings of the OTM 2008 Conferences* (pp. 571-588). OTM.

Kuznetsov, S., Obiedkov, S., & Roth, C. (2007). Reducing the representation complexity of lattice-based taxonomies. In *Conceptual Structures: Knowledge Architectures for Smart Applications*. Berlin: Springer. doi:10.1007/978-3-540-73681-3_18.

Kwon, O., & Kim, J. (2009). Concept lattices for visualizing and generating user profiles for context-aware service recommendations. *Expert Systems with Applications, 36*(2), 1893–1902. doi:10.1016/j.eswa.2007.12.064.

Li, K., Du, Y., & Xiang, D. (2007). Collaborative recommending based on core-concept lattice. *Advances in Soft Computing, 42*, 583–592. doi:10.1007/978-3-540-72434-6_59.

Mao, Q., Feng, B., Pan, S., Zheng, Q., & Liu, J. (2010). New collaborative recommendation approach based on concept lattice. [FSKD]. *Proceedings of Fuzzy Systems and Knowledge Discovery, 4*, 1803–1807.

Nauer, E., & Toussaint, Y. (2007). Dynamical modification of context for an iterative and interactive information retrieval process on the web. In *Proceedings of CLA 2007*. CLA.

Olivarez-Giles, N. (2012). *Does Samsung's Galaxy S III smartphone even need quad-core power? Gadget lab*. Retrieved from http://www.wired.com/gadgetlab/2012/05/quad-core-vs-dual-core-phones-tablets-nvidia-samsung-galaxy/

Paganelli, F., Bianchi, G., & Giuli, D. (2007). A context model for context-aware system design towards the ambient intelligence vision: experiences in the etourism domain. In *Proceedings of the 9th Conference on User Interfaces for All*, (pp. 173–191). Berlin: Springer-Verlag.

Paridel, K., Yasar, A., Vanrompay, Y., Preuveneers, D., & Berbers, Y. (2011). Teamwork on the road: Efficient collaboration in VANETs with context-based grouping. In *Proceedings of The International Conference on Ambient Systems, Networks and Technologies (ANT-2011)*, (vol. 5, pp. 48-57). Elsevier.

Pastry. (n.d.). *A substrate for peer-to-peer applications*. Retrieved from www.freepastry.org

Petric, D. (2012). *Quad-core smartphones dominated mobile world congress 2012*. Retrieved from http://www.brighthand.com/default.asp?newsID=18664&news=Mobile+World+Congress+MWC2012

Preuveneers, D., Victor, K., Vanrompay, Y., Rigole, P., Kirsch Pinheiro, M., & Berbers, Y. (2009). Context-aware adaptation in an ecology of applications. In Stojanovic, D. (Ed.), *Context-Aware Mobile and Ubiquitous Computing for Enhanced Usability: Adaptive Technologies and Applications*. Hershey, PA: IGI Global. doi:10.4018/978-1-60566-290-9.ch001.

Reichle, R., Wagner, M., Khan, M. U., Geihs, K., Lorenzo, L., & Valla, M. Papadopoulos, G.A. (2008). A comprehensive context modeling framework for pervasive computing systems. In Meier & Terzis (Eds.) DAIS 2008 (LNCS), (vol. 5053). Berlin: Springer.

Reichle, R., Wagner, M., Khan, M. U., Geihs, K., Valla, M., & Fra, C. Papadopoulos, G.A. (2008). A context query language for pervasive computing environments. In *Proceedings of the 5th IEEE Workshop on Context Modeling and Reasoning (CoMoRea)*, (pp. 434–440). IEEE.

Romero, D., Rouvoy, R., Seinturier, L., & Loiret, F. (2010). Integration of heterogeneous context resources in ubiquitous environments. In *Proceedings of the 36th EUROMICRO International Conference on Software Engineering and Advanced Applications* (pp. 123-126). ACM Press,

Stumme, G., Taouil, R., Bastide, Y., Pasquier, N., & Lakhal, L. (2002). Computing iceberg concept lattices with TITANIC. *Data & Knowledge Engineering*, *42*, 189–222. doi:10.1016/S0169-023X(02)00057-5.

Szathmary, L., Valtchev, P., Napoli, A., & Godin, R. (2008). Constructing iceberg lattices from frequent closures using generators. In *Proceedings of the 11th International Conference on Discovery Science (DS '08)*, (pp. 136-147). Budapest, Hungary: DS.

Ventos, V., & Soldano, H. (2005). Alpha galois lattices: An overview. [ICFCA.]. *Proceedings of the ICFCA*, *2005*, 299–314.

Wolfson, O., Xu, B., & Tanner, R. M. (2007). Mobile peer-to-peer data dissemination with resource constraints. In *Proceedings of the 2007 International Conference on Mobile Data Management* (pp. 16-23). MDM.

Ye, J., Li, J., Zhu, Z., Gu, X., & Shi, H. (2007). PCSM: A context sharing model in peer-to-peer ubiquitous computing environment. In *Proceedings of the International Conference on Convergence Information Technology* (pp. 1868–1873). IEEE.

ADDITIONAL READING

Bartlang, U. (2010). Architecture and methods for flexible content management in peer-to-peer systems. Wiesbaden, Germany: Vieweg+Teubner.

(2006). InBen Yahia, S., Mephu Nguifo, E., & Belohlavek, R. (Eds.). Lecture Notes in Computer Science: *Vol. 4923. Concept lattices and their applications.*

Bolchini, C., Curino, C., Quintarelli, E., Schreiber, F., & Tanca, L. (2007). A data-oriented survey of context models. *SIGMOD Record, 36*(4), 19–26. doi:10.1145/1361348.1361353.

Buchholz, T., Hamann, T., & Hubsch, G. (2004). Comprehensive structured context profiles: Design and experiences. In *Proceedings of the Second IEEE Annual Conference on Pervasive Computing and Communications Workshops* (pp. 43). IEEE.

Lukasiewics, T. (1995). Uncertain reasoning in concept lattices. In *Proceedings of the 3rd European Conference on Symbolic and Quantitative Approaches* (LNCS), (vol. 496, pp. 293-300). Berlin: Springer.

Paspallis, N., Rouvoy, R., Barone, P., Papadopoulos, G., Eliassen, F., & Mamelli, A. (2008). A pluggable and reconfigurable architecture for a context-aware enabling middleware system. *Lecture Notes in Computer Science, 5331*, 553–570. doi:10.1007/978-3-540-88871-0_40.

Schilit, B., Adams, N., & Want, R. (1994). Context-aware computing applications. In *Proceedings of the Workshop on Mobile Computing Systems and Applications* (pp. 85-90). IEEE.

Szathmary, L., & Napoli, A. (2004). Knowledge organization and information retrieval using galois lattices. *Lecture Notes in Computer Science, 3257*, 511–512. doi:10.1007/978-3-540-30202-5_50.

KEY TERMS AND DEFINITIONS

Adaptive System: A system that is aware of its context, and is able to react on changing context in order to express optimal behavior with respect to a goal.

Concept Lattice: A formal representation of concepts in a domain consisting of objects having attributes.

Context: Any information that is considered to be relevant for the user and the application in a given situation.

Context Distribution: The dissemination of context information in a network of nodes amongst context-aware applications.

Disseminator Peer: Resource-rich device in a P2P network, responsible for managing, reasoning with, and distributing context information.

MANET: Mobile Ad-hoc Network. A network of mobile nodes that organizes and manages itself.

Ontology: A formal explicit specification of a shared conceptualization.

Personalization: The customization of a system taking into account the characteristics, preferences and interests of a particular user.

Recommendation: The ability to recommend things of potential interest to users, mainly based on the interests of the user himself and on the interest of similar users.

Chapter 9
A Forest Fire Detection System:
The Meleager Approach

Vassileios Tsetsos
Mobics LTD, Greece

Odysseas Sekkas
Mobics LTD, Greece

Evagellos Zervas
TEI-A, Greece

ABSTRACT

Forest fires cause immeasurable damages to indispensable resources for human survival, destroy the balance of earth ecology, and worst of all they frequently cost human lives. In recent years, early fire detection systems have emerged to provide monitoring and prevention of the disasterous forest fires. Among them, the Meleager[1] system aims to offer one of the most advanced and integrated technology solutions for fire protection worldwide by integrating several innovative features. This chapter outlines one of the major components of the Meleager system, that is the visual fire detection sybsystem. Groundbased visible range PTZ cameras monitor the area of interest, and a low level decision fusion scheme is used to combine individual decisions of numerous fire detection algorithms. Personalized alerts and induced feedback is used to adapt the detection process and improve the overall system performance.

INTRODUCTION

Reliable fire detection systems with minimum detection latency are of great importance for fast reaction to prevent fire expansion and minimize damages. Traditional forest watch towers tend to be replaced by automatic detection systems that range from IR sensors (Arrue et al., 2000), LIDAR (Light Detection and Ranging systems) (Utkin et al., 2002), satellite platforms (Akasuma et al., 2002), to computer vision based systems (Martinez de Dios et al., 2008; Li et al., 2005)

DOI: 10.4018/978-1-4666-4038-2.ch009

and WSN (wireless sensor network) systems) (Lloret et al., 2009). Aligned with the latter, the Meleager system aims to offer one of the most advanced and integrated technology solutions for fire protection worldwide by integrating the following important innovative features: • A visual fire detection subsystem, which consists of high resolution cameras with embedded digital signal processing and machine vision algorithms.

- The simulation subsystem which has the unique feature of the parallel execution of multiple simulations for different scenarios of environmental parameters. The fire simulator handles the high variability of forest fires, by examining a set of environmental parameters (e.g., wind direction and speed) and creating dynamic hazard maps for the ongoing crisis. The fire simulator uses an innovative design that allows it to perform multiple snapshots of the perturbations from the average recorded values of environmental parameters.
- The data fusion subsystem that incorporates a two-tier data fusion scheme for better assessment of the field observations and for developing safer conclusions about the crisis and risk. The two-tier organization of the fusion scheme allows the scaling of the mechanism and the effective implementation of various versions of the Meleager system (large scale/prefectures, local authorities, private installations).
- **Open Protocols and Interfaces:** Meleager is based entirely on open standards for information exchange to ensure interoperability with existing systems, e.g., crisis management systems, GIS data, cartographic systems and systems for registration of land use.
- **Crisis Management with Advanced Algorithms:** The part of crisis management incorporates applications based on

spatial data (e.g., firefighting resource management). The dynamic positioning of various resources allows more efficient treatment of environmental risk and minimizes the impact on the lives and property of citizens and firefighting forces. This subsystem can optimize the firefighting equipment deployment and the citizen evacuation process of the affected region.

- **Open GIS and Interfaces:** An innovative feature is the ability to record real-time information on the fire evolution, and reproduce at a later time and time scales selected by the system user (e.g., real-time reproduction, fast, slow, transition to a specific point in time).
- Implementation of personalized alerts/alarms and automatic activation of fire protection/sprinkler systems. The implementation of advanced technology and the major innovations incorporated in the system enhance the system functionality, usability, efficiency and interoperability while at the same time they can reduce costs.

This paper aims to describe the visual fire detection subsystem that was adopted by the Meleager project. Video-based fire detection has many advantages over traditional methods, such as low latency response and theoreticaly no space limits. Numerous techniques have been proposed that make use of the visual features of fire and smoke including color, motion, geometry, flickering and texture. Some of these techniques are summarized in Section Related Work, where related work on computer vision based wildfire detection methods is presented. Section System Architecture outlines the Meleager system architecture for the fire detection subsytem, whereas Section Experimenatl Results presents some preliminary results. Finally, conclusions are drawn in Conslusions Section.

RELATED WORK

There is a lot of research for fire and smoke detection based on image processing. In general, fire detection algorithms are mainly based on the analysis of motion and color information in video sequences to detect the flames (Toreyin et al., 2006). In (Toreyin et al., 2005)) authors use hidden markov models to detect flames in video. Color based detection methods are introduced in (Ebert & Shipley, 2009; Zhang et al., 2009). The fire detection method proposed in (Chen et al., 2004) adopts the RGB color chromatic model and uses disorder measurement. In (Celik et al., 2007) authors introduced the statistic color model for generic fire model and studied the fire detection method using foreground object information. Authors in (Gunay et al., 2009) propose a system for fire detection at night, while in (Zhang et al., 2008) a method is presented for forest fire detection using FFT and wavelets.

Smoke detection is also vital for fire alarm systems. In an uncontrolled fire, smoke can be detected by a camera more easily than flames. This results in early detection of the fire. Various research activities for video smoke detection are available in the literature. In (Yu et al., 2009) the motion and color characteristics of the smoke are used for detection. A system that uses a fast accumulative motion orientation model is proposed in (Yuan 2008). The method that is presented in (Xiong et al., 2007) exploits techniques such as backround substraction, flickering extraction and contour classification. A similar contour based solution using wavelets is proposed in (Toreyin et al., 2006).

Most of the above mentioned methods for flames and smoke detection were tested in a limited experimental environment and are prone to increased false alarm rate according to the environmental conditions. Moreover, the majority of the systems detect either flames or smoke. Furthermore, heuristic fixed thresholds are used for the detection process. In this paper, a hybrid day/night system for flame and smoke detection is proposed. Hierarchical design approach and novel scene tile segmentation ensure early detection and reduced false alarm rate. Finally, user feedback and historical data are incorporated in the detection process thus making the system capable for automatic threshold calculation without empirical fixed threshold values.

SYSTEM ARCHITECTURE

System Set-Up

The flowchart of the Meleager fire detection subsystem is presented in Figure 1. The scene is segmented in tiles as it is shown in Figure 2 and the detection process is repeated for each tile in a round robin fashion.

This segmentation is critical for several reasons.

- First of all there are image segments where the presence of fire is impossible. This is for example the case of tiles I and V in Figure 2 that contain regions of the sky. These tiles are prone to false alarms since clouds are often mistaken for smoke by a machine vision automatic detection system. By excluding these regions from further processing we not only speed up the detection process but we reduce considerably the false alarm rate. However, these segments are not totally worthless. There is always the possibility to search for smoke in these segments, since smoke tends to move upwards, and then fuse this information with the decision taken in the spatially lower tiles.
- By segmenting an image in small tiles we obtain a finer characterization of the scene. For example, in Figure 2 tile II can be characterized as far, tile III as mid- distanced, whereas tile IV can be character-

Figure 1. Fire detection subsystem flowchart

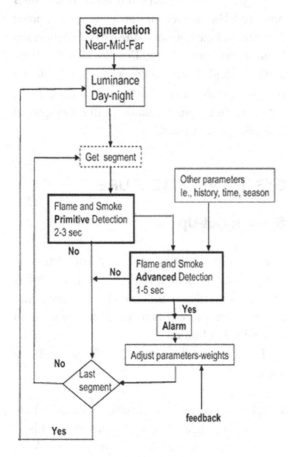

Figure 2. Scene tile segmentation

analaysis) and are applied to whole images. Therefore, small size images reduce memory and processing requirements.

Primitive Detection Algorithms

Following the flowchart of Figure 1, luminance conditions are taken into account before fire detection takes place. Smoke is not detectable at nights and flames are not always visible during the day especially in the first stages of the fire event. Thus, the type of algorithms and the various thresholds used depend heavily on the luminance conditions.

The primitive detection algorithms explore two basic features of flames and smoke, that is motion and color. Three techniques are employed for motion detection.

- Temporal difference of two successive frames.
- **Background Subtraction:** Needs background modeling.
- Optical Flow.

Temporal difference schemes exhibit large noise disturbance and a dilation-erosion technique followed by deletion of small blobs is used to reduce noise. Alternatively, to reduce disturbance of noise we sum up pixels in a block (i.e 4×4) and then calculate difference of sums block by

ized as near. Although motion of flames and smoke is a key feature for fire detection, for distant objects motion is hard to be detected promptly. In this case, either the sensitivity of the detection algorithms should be increased or their weight in the final decision should be decreased.

- Segmentation results in tiles with almost uniform texture. Therefore, fire detection techniques are more suitable than others for specific backgrounds. For example, in areas with swaying trees, a Mixture of Gaussian background model seems more appropriate to detect motion due to flames or smoke.
- Computational complexity reduction also justifies scene tesselation. Some methods, such as the eigenbackgrounds approach, are based on PCA (principal component

block as in (Yuan 2008). Several background subtraction methods have been adopted for the Meleager sytem. The technique in (Toreyin et al., 2006) estimates the background using a first order IIR filter for each pixel in a sequence of frames. In (Gunay et al., 2009) the same approach is used but two background images are created (day and night) depending on updating rates. A *running Gaussian average* (Collins 1999) is another technique where each pixel is modeled as a Gaussian random variable. This method is suitable for unimodal backgrounds. An extension of this method that works with RGB and treats colors independenty (Celik et al., 2007) is also included in the pool of algorithms. To deal with multimodal backgrounds the Mixture of Gaussians model (Stauffer & Grimson, 1999), has been also incorporated.

An approximation of the background pdf can be obtained by the histogram of the most recent pixels classified as background values. To avoid poor modeling due to the missing distribution tails, each sample is smoothed with a Gaussian kernel. This technique, which is referred as KDE (Kernel Density Estimation) (Elgammal et al., 2000), is also suitable for multimodal backgrounds. A method faster than KDE, with low memory requirements, is the Sequential Kernel Density Approximation (SKDA) (Han et al., 2004). The method uses the mean shift algorithm to detect the modes of the pdf, which are later propagated by adapting them with new samples. A different method of background modeling is the Cooccurence of image variations (Seki et al., 2003). The method is based on the fact that neighboring blocks of pixels belonging to the background experience similar variations over time. Finally, a method termed Eigenbackground approach (Oliver et al., 2000) has been also adopted by the Meleager system. The method is based on the Principal Component Analysis as applied to sequences of frames.

Regarding the optical flow motion detection schemes, we have incorporated the most representative one, that is the Lucas Kanade method,

and its variant the pyramidal Lucas Kanade. The latter uses smaller resolution of images and it is appropriate to detect motion of nearby objects.

At the output of the motion detection process we should find connected regions (blobs) that represent the moving objects. These blobs will be tested for flame or smoke using color information. Three flame color detection schemes are used. The first was proposed in (Celik et al., 2007) and works in the RGB color space. Three conditions should be met simultaneously in order to classify a pixel as a fire pixel. The R component should be greater than R_{mean}, the double inequality $R > G > B$ should be satisfied, and the ratio of the G, B to the R compnent should be within certain limits. The second method (Gubay et al., 2009), works in the LUV color space and uses brightness to detect fires during night. The third method (Toreyin et al., 2006) models fire color as a mixture of Gaussians in RGB space. The proposed number of Gaussians is 10. If a pixel color lies within $2 \cdot \sigma$ of the center (mean) of a Gaussian is classified as fire pixel.

Similarly to the flame color detection, three models are use for smoke. The first one, proposed in (Chen et al., 2004), classify a pixel as smoke if the following condition is met:

$$\max\{R, G, B\} - \min\{R, G, B\}$$
$$< \alpha \quad AND \quad k_1 \leq L \leq K_2$$

where L is the luminance and $\alpha = 15 - 20$. For dark gray smoke $K_1 = 80, K_2 = 150$ whereas for light gray smoke $K_1 = 150, K_2 = 220$. The second method (Yuan, 2008) is similar to the previous one with an additional criterion in case of bluish color smoke:

$$B = \max\{R, G, B\} \; AND$$

$$\max\{R, G, B\} - \min\{R, G, B\} < \beta$$

where β is a suitably chosen thresold. Finally, the third method [26] uses the criteria

$$|R - G| < T, \quad |G - B| < T, \quad |R - B| < T$$

with suggested threshold value $T \in [15, 25]$. Additionally, for early detection, smoke low temperature induces a white-bluish to white color which means small saturation. Therefore an additional criterion is (working in HSV color space).

$$S \leq 0.1$$

Advanced Detection Algorithms

If some blobs pass the motion and color screen tests, then they are processed further in an effort to reduce the false alarm rate. The algorithms that the Meleager system uses, for this advanced detection, explore other features of flames and smoke such as the geometry and the spatial and temporal variability. Regarding geometry the pool of algorithms consists of four techniques. In the first technique we take advantage of the turbulant shape of flames and smoke as in (Xiong et al., 2007). If P is the perimeter of the cadidate fire blob and A its area, then we form the metric

$$T = P2\pi^{1/2}A^{1/2}$$

The value of T for circular schemes, such as the bright areas of car headlights, is equal to 1. Deviations from this value is a strong indication for flames or smoke. The second algorithm (Toreyin et al., 2006) is also based on the roughness of the boundary of fire or smoke blobs. A 1-D signal is created using the distances from the center of mass of a cadidate fire or smoke blob to the points of its perimeter. In case of a rough boundary, this signal exhibits large variations which can be detected using a simple one stage

wavelet filter. The third technique was originally proposed in (Zhang et al., 2008). We assume that the boundary of a cadidate region consists of N pixels, which in complex notation are written as $\{z_i = x_i + jy_i\}$. Using these points we find the DFT of the 1-D boundary signal. The first 2-3 dozens of the DFT coefficients are sufficient to describe the shape of the underlying blob. If flickering is present, due to fire or smoke, it can be detected by analyzing the variability of the DFT coefficients from frame to frame. This analysis can be achieved using simple wavelet filters. Finally, the fourth geometry detection algorithm has been proposed in (Borges et al., 2008) and it is based on the change of shape of fire or smoke regions from frame to frame. We may define the normalized area change, ΔA_i, from the $i-1$-frame to the i-frame as

$$\Delta A_i = |A_i - A_{i-1}| A_i$$

and compare it with a suitably chosen threshold in order to decide for fire or smoke. Similarly, we can use the change of the perimeter ΔC_i of the cadidate blob instead of ΔA_i.

Many algorithms have been proposed for fire detection that are based on the spatial and temporal variance of fire regions. The Meleager system has adopted at least 10 methods but their assessment has not be done thoroughly yet. Next, we outline some of these methods. The chrominance components of fire blobs exhibit large spatial variance due to the random nature of fires. Experimental results (Borges et al., 2008) show that a standard deviation greater than 50 is a good indicator for the presence of fire. According to (Ebert & Shipley, 2009), the G component, in RGB images, exhibits large variations for fire blobs and therefore we can base decisions on the difference $\max G - \min G$ of adjacent pixels over small blocks.

Saturation of the G and R channel of fire pixels move the histogram of the corresponding values to the upper side. This phenomenon can be detected using a third order statistic, called skewness. The authors in (Borges et al., 2008) state that skewness obtains values less than -1 for fire blobs.

The significant spatial variance in fire areas can be explored using a 2-D wavelet filter. The authors in (Toreyin et al., 2006) base decisions on the sum of low-high, high-low and high-high wavelet images of fire-colored moving regions. Wavelet filters can also be used for temporal analysis. If a pixel at position $(k.l)$ belongs to a fire region, then its value (either the Y component in the YUV color space or the R component in the RDB color space) in successive frames will exhibit large variations. A two stage wavelet filter bank fed by the 1-D signal $x_n(k,l)$ (n is the frame index) can be used to detect such variations. The zero-crossings of the high frequency subband signals in a time window of 2-3 sec is a good indicator for the presence or not of fire. Flickering is also detected using the cumulative time derivative signal, estimated as

$$a_n(k.l) = wa_{n-1}(k,l) + (1-w)d_n(k,l)$$

where $d_n(k,l) = |Y_n(k,l) - Y_{n-1}(k,l)|$ is the time derivative of the luminance component (in the YUV space) at the (k,l) position. The authors in (Ebert & Shipley, 2009) proposed an improvement in the estimation, that further decreases false alarm rate. In their approach $d_n(k.l)$ is weighted by the factor $Y_n(k,l)I_{Y_n(k,l)>\delta}$, where I_A is an indicator function.

Decision Fusion and User Feedback

The final decision about a fire event will be based on both primitive and advanced algorithms. For each tile N frames are used for background modeling as it is shown in Figure 3. N is a variable that depends on the motion algorithm used and ranges from 1, in case of the temporal difference algorithm, to 60-80, for more complex algorithms like the Mixture of Gaussian or the SKDA algorithm. There is no need to re-estimate the background model each time the process returns to the same tile. The parameters of the previously estimated model can be stored and then updated, in a selective or blind fashion, using more recent frames.

After background estimation, a motion detection algorithm leaves G frames to pass, to increase detection probability for slowly moving objects, and then checks the following L frames for possible moving objects. Having detected the moving objects, color detection algorithms are applied. A moving object is characterized as fire blob if

$$\sum_i w_i c_i > T_c$$

where c_i are binary decisions for the existence of fire, w_i are normalized weights (initialized to the same value) and T_c is a suitably chosen threshold. Detected fire blobs in successive frames correspond to the same fire source if their convex hulls exhibit considerable overlapping. After the association of fire blobs in the L frames, a final decision is taken using the m out of L majority rule. That is, if at least m fire blobs (corresponding to the same fire source) exist in a sequence of L frames then we decide for fire event. Note that

Figure 3. Motion and color based decision

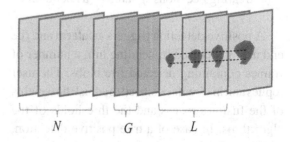

this decision, call it d_j, is binary and depends on the motion detection algorithm used. To increase system's reliability we can test more than one motion detection algorithms and combine the results. In this case, we allow d_j to take $L+1$ values, representing the number of fire blobs detected in the sequence of L frames, and we combine them in a linear fashion as

$$\sum_j p_j d_j > T_m$$

where p_j are weights summing to one and T_m is a predetermined threshold.

If the previous condition is satisfied then the control is passed to more sophisticated techniques as it is shown in Figure 1. These algorithms operate on the fire blobs detected by the motion algorithm that maximizes d_j, that is

$$\hat{j} = arg\max d_j$$

Geometry based decisions, g_j, and spatial/temporal variance decisions, v_j, are fused in a higher level to reach a final decision. In the framework of the Meleager project three fusion schemes are under investigation, that is

- A majority voting rule, using binary decisions g_j and v_j.
- Thresholding of linear weighted sums, using soft decisions g_j and v_j.
- Dempster-Shafer rule of combination, treating decisions g_j and v_j as beliefs.

A positive detection triggers an alarm and the end user is notified by sending him a number of frames containing detected fire blobs. The user replies and his feedback is used to adjust the weights of the fusion process and the thresholds of the algorithms. In case of a true positive detection,

all algorithms that favor the fire decision increase their weights. The rest of the algorithms lower their thesholds to become more sensitive. On the contrary, in case of a false positive (false alarm), all the algorithms favoring the fire decision increase their thresholds whereas the rest increase their weights. Two more situations may exist, that is true negative and false negative. These situations are detected by other means, ie. temperature sensors in the field, or periodic feedback regardless the presence of a fire event. For false negative, the detection algorithms that miss the event decrease their thresholds thus becoming more sensitive, while the rest increase their weights. On the other hand for true negative, detecting algoritms increase thresholds and non detecting algorithms increase weights. The process is summarized in Table 1.

EXPERIMENTAL RESULTS

In this section we present some initial experimental results. Algorithms for primitive detection of fire and smoke have been ported and mapped on a System on Chip, OMAP3530. The chip includes one general purpose processor, ARM Cortex A8, one special purpose processor, Texas Instrument TMS320C64x+ and one graphic accelerator. For the algorithm implementation both the generic purpose and the special purpose processor have been used. For primitive fire detection we implemented the algorithm proposed in (Yuan, 2008)

Table 1: Adjustment of weights and thresholds

	Detecting Algorithms	Non Detecting Algorithms
True Positive	Weights ↑	Thresholds ↓
False Positive	Thresholds ↑	Weights ↑
True Negative	Thresholds ↑	Weights ↑
False Negative	Weights ↑	Thresholds ↓

to detect motion. We have used blocks of 4x4 pixels. The output of this process, that represents connected regions (blobs) is fed to the next phase where the fire color detection technique proposed in (Celik et al., 2007) is applied. The results are depicted in the Figure 4. As we can see at the end of primitive phase the flames are detected successfully. However, some blocks that constitute false alarms are also present.

For smoke we use the same motion detection technique as before. For the subsequent color analysis the rule proposed in (Borges et al., 2008) is applied with the use of empirical thresholds.

Again, the smoke region is detected successfully and the existence of blocks outside this region represents false alarms as depicted in Figure 5. The false alarm rate (false alarm blocks/total image blocks) at the end of primitive detection is less than 4% for the fire video and 5% for the smoke video. Such rates are extremely encouraging taking into account that we have implement one motion detection algorithm and one color detection algorithm. The primitive detection phase will incorporate more than one of similar techniques as described in the previous section.

Figure 4. Flame detection in video. Initial video snapshot (top) and flames (green blocks) detected in primitive phase.

Figure 5. Smoke detection in video. Initial video snapshot (top) and smoke (green blocks) detected in primitive phase.

CONCLUSION

In this chapter we presented the functionality of the visual component, as a part of the overall Meleager architecture, regarding the early detection of potential fires. The images are obtained from PTZ cameras that supervise an area of interest. To cope with various environmental conditions and deliver alarms with increased accuracy and confidence a layered hierarchical scheme has been adopted. Furthermore a scene segmentation technique is applied in order to facilitate and speed-up the detection process. On the primitive stage, motion and color detection algorithms are implemented. On the second stage, advanced algorithms are used in an effort to reduce the false alarm rate. The decision about flame or smoke presence is taken through various fusion schemes. Moreover, personalized alerts and induced feedback is used to adapt the detection process and improve the overall system performance. Algorithms for primitive detection of fire and smoke have been implemented on a DSP thus making the solution distributable. The first experimental results are encouraging in terms of detection rate.

REFERENCES

Arrue, B. C., Ollero, A., & Martinez de Dios, J. R. (2000). An intelligent system for false alarm reduction in infrared forest-fire detection. *IEEE Intelligent Systems*, *15*(3), 64–73. doi:10.1109/5254.846287.

Asakuma, K., Kuze, H., Takeuchi, N., & Yahagi, T. (2002). Detection of biomass burning smoke in satellite images using texture analysis. *Atmospheric Environment*, *36*, 1531–1542. doi:10.1016/S1352-2310(01)00547-7.

Borges, P., Mayer, J., & Izquierdo, E. (2008). Efficient visual fire detection applied for video retrieval. In *Proceedings of European Signal Processing Conference (EUSIPCO)*. EUSIPCO.

Celik, T., Demirel, H., Ozkaramanli, H., & Uyguroglu, M. (2007). Fire detection using statistical color model in video sequences. *Journal of Visual Communication and Image Representation*, *18*, 176–185. doi:10.1016/j.jvcir.2006.12.003.

Chen, T. H., Wu, P. H., & Chiou, Y. C. (2004). An early fire-detection method based on image processing. In *Proceedings of the IEEE International Conference on Image Processing (ICIP)*, (pp. 1707- 1710). IEEE.

Collins. (1999). A system for video surveillance and monitoring. In *Proceedings of American Nuclear Society (ANS)*. ANS.

de Dios, M. et al. (2008). Computer vision techniques for forest fire perception. *Image and Vision Computing*, *26*(4).

Ebert, J., & Shipley, J. (2009). Computer vision based method for fire detection in color videos. *International Journal of Imaging*.

Elgammal., et al. (2000). Nonparametric model for background subtraction. In *Proceedings of ECCV 2000*, (pp. 751-767). ECCV.

Gunay, O., Tasdemir, K., Toreyin, B. U., & Cetin, A. E. (2009). Video based wildfire detection at night. *Fire Safety Journal*, *44*, 860–868. doi:10.1016/j.firesaf.2009.04.003.

Han., et al. (2004). Sequential kernel density approximation through mode propagation: Applications to background modeling. In *Proceedings Asian Conference on Computer Vision*. IEEE.

Li, J., Qi, Q., Zou, X., Peng, H., Jiang, L., & Liang, Y. (2005). Technique for automatic forest fire surveillance using visible light image. In *Proceedings of International Geoscience and Remote Sensing Symposium*, (vol. 5, pp. 31–35). IEEE.

Lloret, J., Garcia, M., Bri, D., & Sendra, S. (2009). A wireless sensor network deployment for rural and forest fire detection and verification. *Sensors (Basel, Switzerland)*, *9*, 8722–8747. doi:10.3390/s91108722 PMID:22291533.

Oliver, et al. (2000). A Bayesian computer vision system for modeling human interaction. *IEEE Transactions on Pattern Analysis and Machine Intelligence*, *22*(8). doi:10.1109/34.868684.

Seki., et al. (2003). Background subtraction based on cooccurence of image variations. In *Proceedings CVPR 2003*, (Vol. 2, pp. 65-72). CVPR.

Stauffer & Grimson. (1999). Adaptive background mixture models for real-time tracking. In *Proceedings IEEE CVRP 1999*. IEEE.

Toreyin, B. U., Dedeoglu, Y., & Cetin, A. E. (2005). Flame detection in video using hidden markov models. In *Proceedings of ICIP '05*, (pp. 1230-1233). ICIP.

Toreyin, B. U., Dedeoglu, Y., Gudukbay, U., & Cetin, A. E. (2006). Computer vision based system for real-time fire and flame detection. *Pattern Recognition Letters*, *27*, 49–58. doi:10.1016/j.patrec.2005.06.015.

Toreyin, Dedeoglu, & Cetin. (2006). Contour based smoke detection in video using wavelets. In *Proceedings of the 14th European Signal Processing Conference (EUSIPCO)*. Florence, Italy: EUSIPCO.

Utkin, A. B., Lavrov, A. V., Costa, L., Simoes, F., & Vilar, R. (2002). Detection of small forest fires by lidar. *Applied Physics. B, Lasers and Optics*, *74*(1), 77–83. doi:10.1007/s003400100772.

Xiong, Z., Caballero, R., Wang, H., Finn, A. M., Lelic, M. A., & Peng, P.-Y. (2007). *Video-based smoke detection: Possibilities, techniques, and challenges.* Paper presented at SUPDET, 2007. New York.

Yu, C., Fang, J., Wang, J., & Zhang, Y. (2009). Video fire smoke detection using motion and color features. *Fire Technology*, *46*(3), 651–663.

Yuan, F. N. (2008). A fast accumulative motion orientation model based on integral image for video smoke detection. *Pattern Recognition Letters*, *29*, 925–932. doi:10.1016/j.patrec.2008.01.013.

Zhang, Z., Zhao, J., Yuan, Z., Zhang, D., Han, S., & Qu, C. (2009). Color based segmentation and shape based matching of forest fires from monocular images. In *Proceedings of the International Conference on Multimedia Information Networking and Security*. IEEE.

Zhang, Z., Zhao, J., Zhang, D., Qu, C., Ke, Y., & Cai, B. (2008). Contour based forest fire detection using FFT and Wavelet. In *Proceedings of the International Conference on Computer Science and Software Engineering*. IEEE.

ADDITIONAL READING

Celil, T., Ozkaramanli, H., & Demirel, H. (2007). Fire and smoke detection without sensors: Image processing based approach. [EUSIPCO.]. *Proceedings of Eusipco*, *2007*, 1794–1798.

Toreyin, B., Dedeoglu, Y., & Cetin, A. (2005). Flame detection in video using hidden Markov models. In *Proceedings of Image Processing, International Conference of Image Processing* (pp. 1230-1233). IEEE.

Wren, et al. (1997). Pfinder: Real time tracking of the human body. *IEEE Transactions on Pattern Analysis & Machine Intelligence, 19*(7).

Zervas, E., Mpimpoudis, A., Anagnostopoulos, C., Sekkas, O., & Hadjiefthymiades, S. (2011). Multisensor data fusion for fire detection. *Information Fusion Journal, 12*(3), 150–159. doi:10.1016/j.inffus.2009.12.006.

KEY TERMS AND DEFINITIONS

Data Fusion: The process of integration of multiple data and knowledge representing the same real-world object into a consistent, accurate, and useful representation.

Fire Alarm System: A system designed to detect the presence of fire by monitoring environmental changes associated with combustion.

Fire Detection Algorithm: The process of information related to environmental paramaters and optimal signals in order to detect and infer flames in a specific geographical area.

Information Integration: The merging of information from disparate sources with differing conceptual and contextual representations.

Sensor: A converter that measures a physical quantity and converts it into a signal which can be read by an observer or by an instrument.

ENDNOTES

[1] This work performed in the context of the Meleager project co-funded by the EU and GSRT (Contract No. 14KAIN2009A).

[2] This work performed in the context of the Meleager project co-funded by the EU and GSRT (Contract No. 14KAIN2009A).

Chapter 10
Enhancing Location Privacy in WSN:
The iHide Case

Leonidas Kazatzopoulos
Athens University of Economics and Business, Greece

ABSTRACT

Wireless Sensor Networks (WSNs) receive significant attention due to the wide area of applications: environment monitoring, tracking, target detection, etc. At the same time, in some cases, the captured information from the WSN might be considered as private, for example, location of an important asset. Thus, security mechanisms might be essential to ensure the confidentiality of the location of the information source. In this chapter, the authors present an approach called iHIDE (information HIding in Distributing Environments) to enable source-location privacy in WSNs. iHIDE adopts a non-geographical, overlay routing method for packet delivery. This chapter presents the architecture and assesses its performance through simulation experiments, providing comparisons with relative approaches.

INTRODUCTION

The WSNs technology aims to provide useful tools on monitoring and location-based applications. Contrary to stand-alone sensors, WSNs consist of cooperative nodes that forward, process, aggregate, route and disseminate information to other nodes, and finally to a central sensor, so called the sink, for further processing. From the sink, the information is passed to the users and service platforms. The WSN architecture that utilizes one or more sinks is considered as the most prevailing (Akyildiz et al., 2002; Heinzelman et al., 1999; Tilak et al., 2002), whilst other configurations have been designed, as well (Akyildiz et al., 2002). WSNs by default are not robust against

DOI: 10.4018/978-1-4666-4038-2.ch010

adversaries. An unauthorized opponent can gain access to classified data either by accessing aggregated information that is stored in sensors or by sensing and pilfering wireless transmissions. Thus, the deployment of WSNs arise privacy concerns. Privacy might not a primary issue for several types of WSNs, such as environmental monitoring installations. On the other hand, it is crucial when WSNs are used by military applications, and especially for locating valuable assets or people. Lopez identifies two types of privacy in WSNs (Tilak et al., 2002)[REMOVED REF FIELD]: social and network privacy. Social privacy incorporates the concerns for collecting and manipulating our personal data. Network privacy is associated with the content that is stored, aggregated, and communicated between the WSN's nodes. It also concerns the identity privacy, since the IDs of the nodes are subject to spoofing. Finally, it deals with the location privacy and the inferring of the physical position of a node, or of the asset that is monitored. This issue is addressed here, and the iHIDE architecture, which was originally introduced in (Kazatzopoulos et al., 2006), shields the position of the information source, i.e., the sensor that captures and reports the existence of an asset (i.e., target). iHIDE is applicable for WSNs deployed in a predefined geographical area to track a specific object with e.g., an embedded RF tag, or objects of a particular category, such as children, elderly, artifacts or even pandas (Lopez Munoz, 2005). In this type of WSNs the location information is eavesdropped either by monitoring the packet routing algorithm, or by intercepting the contents of the data packets. iHIDE uses a lightweight, end-to-end, cryptographic technique to protect the information content, and a hop-by-hop routing scheme to prevail the physical location of the source sensor.

The structure of this chapter is as follows. Firstly, next section introduces the iHIDE architecture and the mechanisms that enforce location privacy. The threats and security issues related to the iHIDE scheme are discussed in Section 'Identifying Privacy Issues'. Subsequently, Section 'Simulation Experiments' provides the experimental setup and the evaluation of the scheme. Section 'Exercises' notes issues for further discussion and the chapter closes with some proposed exercises.

iHIDE ARCHITECTURE AND ROUTING PLAN

Before describing in details the iHIDE scheme, it is essential to define what we consider as Location Information (*LocInfo*). As *LocInfo* we use a variation of the definition introduced in (Kamat et al., 2005), i.e., we use the triple of the following form: *{SensorID, RTargetID, Time}*. Thus, *LocInfo* is defined as a combination of sensor that identifies the target, the identification of the target, and the time instance of the target existence.

iHIDE consists of the following functional elements and structures: *Sensing Nodes (SEN)*, *Bus Nodes (BUN)*, one *Sink Node (SIN)*, one *Bus* and several *Rings*. We could visualize this through a configuration that consists of one rope with Rings attached to it (Figure 1). *SENs* organize the *Ring* structures, whilst *BUNs* construct the *Bus* struc-

Figure 1. An example of the iHIDERP

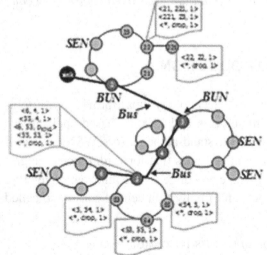

ture (i.e. the rope). As previously mentioned, we assume static sensors and mobile targets. In this static structure, every iHIDE node, *SEN* or *BUN*, forwards packets according to a specific plan, called *Routing Plan (RP)*. This plan concerns all the sensors, and it is constructed and distributed periodically by a central authority, e.g., the sink, which maintains prior knowledge of the field and the network structure.

Functional Entities and Structures

Sensing Nodes: SEN are typical sensors spread around the field. Each *SEN's* main duty is to identify the presence of an asset in its coverage area. For iHIDE, they are part of a *Ring* structure and their main concern is to place packets in the *Ring* or forward incoming packets only to *SENs* and the *BUN* of their *Ring*, according to the *RP*. A *SEN* might participate in more than one *Rings*. If a *SEN* cannot physically communicate with two or more *SENs*, then it cannot participate in a *Ring* directly. In such a case, it participates indirectly, and it is placed as a leaf of one *SEN* that relies in the *Ring*.

Bus Nodes: BUNs are *SENs*, exploiting similar functionality. They are also assigned with an extra duty to forward packets to the *SIN*. Each *Ring* has exactly one *BUN*. *BUNs* are networked with each other based on the *RP*, to form the *Bus*. The upper end of the *Bus* is the *SIN*. As the packets are routed through the *Bus* towards the sink node, the *BUNs* re-route these packets in the *Rings*, according to a predefined probability.

Sink Node: The *SIN* is a sensor node with enhanced processing, storage and energy capabilities. This central node is responsible for the collection of the packets originated from *SENs*, to process and fusion the *LocInfo*, or to pass this information to end-users and applications. The *RP* contains exactly one *SIN*.

Ring: A *Ring* is a virtual, not geographically oriented, circle structure that consists of one *BUN* and a static number of *SENs*. Each *Ring* has

exactly one *BUN*. *Rings* differ on the number of *SENs* that they consist of. In each *Ring* a packet is circulated hop-by-hop, among the nodes that form the *Ring*. This circulation maybe repeated, as it will be discussed later. The *BUN* node of the *Ring* is responsible to place the packet in the *Bus*.

Bus: The *Bus* is a virtual "rope" that connects each *Ring* with the *SIN*. Once a *BUN* receives a *LocInfo* packet for the first time, it forwards this packet on the uplink *BUN* towards the *SIN*. The upper end of the *Bus* is the *SIN*.

Routing Plan Dissemination

In the iHIDE *RP*, each sensor node maintains a *Routing Table (RT)* that consists of entries of the form <*IncomingSensorID, OutgoingSensorID, p_f*>, where p_f is the forwarding probability. Whenever a node receives a packet originated from a specific *IncomingSensorID* it consults its *RT* and determines the next node (*OutgoingSensorID*) to forward the *LocInfo* packet with a probability, p_f. Note that for the *SENs* the *RT* contains exactly one forwarding entry per *Ring* that it participates, unless it is connected to a leaf node. On the other hand, the *BUNs* contain additional records to cover the routing in both the *Ring* and the *Bus*. The probability p_f is set to one ($p_f=1$) for the entry in a *SEN*, even if this SEN is connected with a leaf *SEN*, or it is a leaf *SEN* itself. For the entries of *BUNs* p_f is also set to one ($p_f=1$) for uplink forwarding, and to a value that is less than one ($p_f<1$) for re-routing packets in the *Ring*. For instance, as depicted in Figure 1, the *BUN* with ID 5 (*BUN* 5) will forward packets arrived from the *BUN* 6 to the *BUN* 4 with probability one ($p_f=1$). Using the same probability it will also forward a packet arrived from the *SEN* 55 to the *BUN* 4. Additionally, when the *BUN* 5 receives a packet from the *BUN* 6, it will place the packet in its *Ring* with probability $p_f=p_{RING}$. For simplicity reasons, Figure 1 does not depict the case where one *SEN* is a member of multiple *Rings*. The extra re-routes enhance the privacy level. As a packet travels though the *Bus* each *BUN* forwards the packet to the next *BUN* and place a replica to its *Ring* structure with probability $p_f = p_{ring}$. As it will be discussed later, modifying the value of p_f we alter the balance between privacy and performance.

To generate and disseminate the *RP*, that is to configure the *RTs* in the nodes, parameters such as sensor's coverage area, nodes that can communicate directly with each other, and system parameters, such as minimum *Ring* and *Bus* size, have been considered. The *RP* should satisfy the iHIDE preconditions, such as:

- Each *Bus* should have one *SIN*.
- Each *Ring* should have one *BUN*.
- One *SEN* can participate in multiple *Rings*.
- One BUN cannot participate in multiple Rings as BUN, but it can exist in multiples Rings as SEN.

Upon *RP* generation, iHIDE distributes the new *RP* to the sensor nodes, through the use of a common data delivery protocol, such as the one that is used in Directed Diffusion (Kamat et al., 2005), SPIN (Intanagonwiwat et al., 2000), GBR (Kulik et al., 2002), or through other, structure-based, routing protocols for flat networks, described in (Schurgers et al., 2001). Assume that a source sensor, say with ID *K*, realizes the presence of a panda, and wishes to send the *LocInfo* packet to the *SIN*. First, it sends this packet to the next *Ring* node, i.e. a *SEN* in its *Ring*. If sensor *K* is a member of multiple *Rings*, it randomly selects one to initially forward the packet. One after another, the *SENs* circulate the packet among the *SENs* of the *Ring*. When the *BUN* receives the *LocInfo* packet, apart from forwarding the packet to the next *SEN* with probability $p_f = 1$, it stores the *LocInfo* to its local cache, and places it into the *Bus* after a randomly selected future time instance. To avoid the eternal circulation of one copy of the *LocInfo* packet in the *Ring* of *K*, we use a *Time-To-Live* (*TTL*) flag. Sensor *K* might set the *TTL* field equal to its hop distance from the *BUN*. However such an option

helps the eavesdropper to retrieve the packet and easily identify the originator *K*. To overcome this weakness, we consider a different approach on the functionality of the *TTL*. *K* sets the *TTL* equal to a random number *A*. Each node that receives this packet will subtract a random value *B=X*, where *X* follows a uniform distribution. The precondition is that the *A* and *B* values should be set in such a way that the packet can perform at least a full circle in the *Ring*. If *M* is the number of nodes in the *Ring* and *S* is a security parameter that indicates an approximation to the number of circles the packet will perform, then the following formulas are used for calculating *A* and *B*.

$$A = S*E[X]*M, \text{ where } S > 1$$

$$F(X) = 1/M, \text{ and}$$

$$B = X$$

Figure 2 depicts the iHIDE approach when the *SEN* A is the originator of the packet. The *BUN* node D receives the packet illustrating *TTL=12*. It forwards the packet to the next *SEN* (ID=E) since the circulation was no completed, and places the packet in the *Bus* to reach the *SIN*. Node C, discards the packet since it founds the TTL equal to zero.

Figure 2. TTL applied for circulating

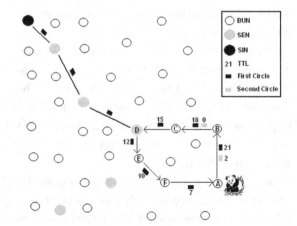

The structure of the *LocInfo* packet is depicted in Figure 3. The *LocInfo* is encrypted (E_{SIN_PU}) by the originator *SEN* using the *SIN's* public key (PU), and signed (S_{ORI_PR}) through the originator's private key (PR). These actions are performed once, i.e., at the originator of the *LocInfo*. On the other hand, the *TTL* parameter is altered in each hop, as previously mentioned. Finally, *NextNode$_{ID}$*is the next *SEN* or *BUN* that should capture the packet, according to the *RP*. Sensors that overhear the *LocInfo* packet they should drop it, if is not directed to them. Since a *LocInfo* packet might be circulated many times inside different *Rings*, its replicas might arrive multiple times to the *SIN*. In such a case, the *SIN* drops the duplicate packets using the decrypted *LocInfo*.

IDENTIFYING PRIVACY ISSUES

Let us assume the intrusion of a hunter in the pandas monitoring field. Hunter's goal is to locate and capture the panda, i.e., identify the sensor that detected and reported its existence. We assume that the hunter is equipped with efficient data traffic analyzers to eavesdrop the wireless data streams and he has knowledge of the exact position of each sensor in the field. A hunter's strategy is to remain next to a sensor node and wait until his equipment captures a packet that is forwarded to the sink. When that happens, he examines packet's contents. If the payload of the packet directly reveals the *LocInfo*, i.e., identifies the sensor node that tracked the panda, then the hunter moves towards the physical location of the named sensor, which is the originator of the *LocInfo*. For this reason, we assume that the payload, that is the content

Figure 3. The LocInfo data packet

SenderID	$E_{SIN}S_{ORI}$[LocInfo]	TTL	NextNodeID

of the data packet, is encrypted. For that reason a lightweight approach might be used, such as the Elliptic Curve Cryptography, which is considered less resource demanding than other algorithms (Al-Karaki et al., 2004; Tilak et al., 2002; Khalili et al., 2003; Mahimkar & Rappaport, 2004; Malan et al., 2004; Perrig et al., 2004). In iHIDE we assume that sensors use their unique private key that authenticates the origin of *LocInfo*, and the public key of the sink to encrypt the *LocInfo*. For the key pre-distribution and management several schemes can be found in the literature, such as (Al-Karaki et al., 2004; Song et al., 2003; Chan et al., 2003; Eschenauer et al., 2002; Liu & Ning, 2003; Mahimkar & Rappaport, 2004).

In iHIDE, only the source sensor encrypts and authenticates the *LocInfo*. Intermediate sensors that rely in the path to the sink do not decrypt, and perform only forwarding and routing. This option protects the *LocInfo* payload from the malicious hunter, which might compromise an intermediate's sensor data manipulation or aggregation unit. Additionally, it saves energy, extends the time life of the field sensors, but, on the other hand, reveals a footprint of the routing path. Without encrypting the routing fields of the networking layer packets, the hunter will always be able to track the preceding node in the routing path. Thus, assuming a periodic *LocInfo* packet stream, the hunter will eventually reveal panda's location. In contrary, using a hop-by-hop secure routing scheme, the routing information is decrypted and authenticated in each one of the wireless packets, but the battery of each sensor is sharply consumed, since each sensor decrypts and encrypts each received and forwarded packet, respectively. Additionally, in the hop-by-hop secure routing if one sensor is compromised then the location info might be revealed. Somehow, hop-by-hop secure routing requires the implementation of a IPSec-like functionally in sensors, e.g., using the Encapsulating Security Payload (ESP) for both encryption and authentication (Kent & Atkinson, 1996). Additionally, the Non-Disclosure Method (Fasbender et al., 1996) considers the existence of independent security agents that are distributed on the network. Each security agent holds a pair of keys and forwards the packets in an encrypted format. The sender routes a packet to a receiver through a path that consists of security agents. Finally, the Mist System (Al-Muhtadi et al., 2002) handles the problem of routing a packet though a network while keeping the target's location private from intermediate routers (i.e. sensors), the receiver (i.e., the sink) and eavesdroppers (i.e., hunters). The system consists of a number of routers, called Mist routers, ordered in a hierarchical structure. According to Mist, special routers, called "Portals", are aware of the target's location, without knowing the corresponding identity, whilst "Lighthouse" routers are aware of the target's identity without knowing the exact location of the target. The aforementioned approaches require additional resources to be depleted for encryption and decryption per hop and transmitted packet, and, thus, they are considered unfeasible for WSNs. To the best of our knowledge the work in (Kamat et al., 2005) is focused on location privacy in sensor networks without hop-by-hop encryption. The authors propose a *Phantom Routing (PhR)* which uses a two-phase procedure, a pure random or directed walk, and a subsequent flooding/single-path phase, for delivering the packet to the sink. Somehow, this approach borrows ideas from the Mobile IP protocol, since it mirages the actual location of the originator to another, far-way, node. Finally, in (Gruteser et al., 2003) the issue of location privacy through a distributed anonymity algorithm that is applied in a sensor network is addressed.

Attacker's Strategy: Initially, the eavesdropper does not have any prior knowledge about the WSN configuration. Instead, he might realize the precise position of sensors, but, on the other hand, their identification and classification (i.e., *BUN* or *SEN* node) are initially unknown. Only after systematic observations of the *LocInfo* packets the hunter will realize the actual identities of the nodes. For instance, consider a hunter waiting

to overhear near a sensor node, say *SEN* 54 of Figure 1. Doing so, his equipment will report that packets with alternated $NextNode_{ID}$, i.e., 54 and 55, are detected. The former ID corresponds to the packet that was forwarded from *SEN* 53 to *SEN* 54, and the latter from *SEN* 54 to *SEN* 55. Then the hunter will realize that the identity of this *SEN* is either 54 or 55, and marks this sensor ID as pending. Assume that the hunter is moving in the field, and the closest sensor it reaches is *SEN* 53, without knowing its real identity. It follows the same strategy, and waits until to spy the *LocInfo* packets. As previously, his equipment captures packets with alternated $NextNode_{ID}$, i.e., 53 and 54. Finally, it reaches the other nearby sensor, i.e. 55, and captures packets with destination addresses 55 and 5. Through these observations, the node's IDs are exposed. If the hunter repeats this strategy he will finally reveal the ID of each sensor, and, thus, he will potentially expose the *RP*. In fact, this procedure has unconquerable difficulties, because:

- The actual packet structure is initially unknown.
- *Rings* might be geographically overlapping.
- Eavesdropping on node e.g., 53 does not analyze only the transmissions initiated from *SENs* 5 and 53. It captures *SEN's* 54 transmissions, as well. Hence, conclusions about the location of node 54 are not straightforward. This is deteriorated for the hunter, due to the proximity of other nodes, which reside in different *Rings* or the *Bus*. The situation will get worse when the hunter is spying near a *Bus* node, since his equipment will overhear transmissions from the antecedent and subsequent nodes in the *Bus*, as well as from the first and the last nodes in its *Ring*, as well as from other nearby nodes that do not belong in the *Bus* or its *Ring*.

Even if the revelation of the nodes' IDs and *RP* is practically improbable, we introduce a replacement policy on the values of the fields *SenderNode*$_{ID}$ and *NextNode*$_{ID}$ to enhance the identity privacy. According to this policy each node is not assigned with a specific ID, but with a set of IDs, called *SID*. This set is unique for each node, and as *SIDi* we denote the set of IDs of node *i*. In alignment to its *RT,* each node *i* is aware of the *SIDj* of every adjacent node *j* in the *RT*. Thus, taking into account Figure 1, the *BUN* 5 is aware of the SID$_4$, and the SID$_{53}$, among others. Whenever *BUN* 5 wants to transmit a packet to *SEN* 53, it randomly selects an ID from the SID$_{53}$ set and puts it at the *NextNode*$_{ID}$ of the packet. Additionally, because *SEN* 53 and *BUN* 4 are aware of the SID$_5$, the BUN 5 uses values of its SID$_5$ for the *SenderNode*$_{ID}$ field. This approach requires large number generators due to the population explosion of WSNs. For this issue we propose the usage of a trigonometric function, depicted in Eq. 1. According to the function *f(x)*, as *Node*$_{ID}$ (*Sender* or *Next*) we consider a unique among all nodes value which is randomly selected from the domain space of the *f(x)*. Thus, if the *Node*$_{ID}$ of the node *i* is *S* (where *S* belongs to the domain space of f(x)), then the *SID*$_i$ is comprised of all the x_j such that $f(x_j)=S$.

$$f(x) = \sum_{i=1}^{n} a_i * \sin(b_i * x), a_i, \ b_i > 0 \ \text{and} \ n \in \aleph \tag{1}$$

The parameters *n, a*$_i$ and *b*$_i$ are associated with the robustness of the function *f(x)*. Here the robustness is defined as the total number of different x_p and x_q for which $f(x_p)=f(x_q)$, that is cardinality of the *SID*. The cardinality of the *SID* depends on the amplitude parameter a_i and the frequency parameter b_i. More specifically, for a$_i$ and b$_i$ it holds that if $a_i<a_{i+1}$ then $b_i<b_{i+1}$. Figure 4a depicts the *f(x)* when *n=3,* (b1, b2, b3) = (1/10, 1, 10) and (a1, a2, a3) = (10, 20, 40). Furthermore, Figure

4b depicts the *f(x)* for the same n, b1, b2, and b3, but for (a1, a2, a3) = (40, 20, 10). It is obvious that the total number of different x_p and x_q is dramatically increased when compared with the results illustrated in Figure 4a. This is proved theoretically as well, by considering the function *g(x)=S*, where *S* is a constant and represents the *Node*$_{ID}$ of a node, and by solving the equation *S=f(x)*. Furthermore, the number of the different x_p and x_q for which $f(x_p)=f(x_q)$, depends on the period of the trigonometric function *f(x)*. The period of the Eq. 1 is equal to the *Least Common Multiple (LCM)* of the periods of each sin term of Eq. 1.

Since *LCM* is increased when the volume of the b$_i$ is increased, by increasing the value of *n* we can enchase the robustness of the function, and, thus, the size of the *SIDs*. According to this *Node*$_{ID}$ replacement scheme the eavesdropper of the *LocInfo* packet will never reveal the actual identity of the sender or next node in the *RP*, since the sender uses values from the domain space of

Figure 4. a) graph of function f(x)= 10sin(0.1x)+ 20sin(x)+40sin(10x); b) graph of function f(x)= 40sin(0.1x)+20sin(x)+10sin(10x)

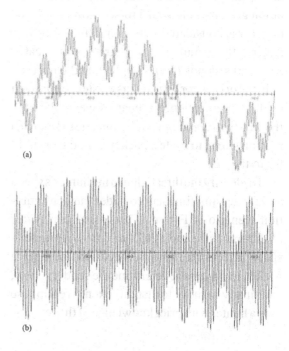

(a)

(b)

the *f(x)* in the *SenderNode*$_{ID}$ and *NextNode*$_{ID}$ fields of the packet. *SIDs* are distributed to the nodes during the bootstrapping period.

SIMULATION EXPERIMENTS

The iHIDE system was evaluated using the J-Sim simulator (http://www.j-sim.org), and the SensorSim (Sobeih et al., 2005), a subpart of the J-Sim that provides libraries to simulate WSNs. We have used three topologies:

- 5 *BUNs* with 10 *SENs* each (5B-10S scenario)
- 10 *BUNs* with 5 *SENs* each (10B-5S scenario)
- 10 *BUNs* with 10 *SENs* each (10B-10S scenario)

The distance between the circle nodes was set to 50m and between the *BUNs* was set to 100m. Thus, we covered a 200000 m^2 field area. Each simulation lasted 10000 seconds. We conducted two types of simulations. We first considered a target that performed a random walk in the simulation grid, moving with 5 m/sec. Afterwards the target was considered static, on a fixed location. During the simulation the target was located every 20 seconds (500 Samples), and each time only the originator detected its existence. On each of the aforementioned scenarios we applied the iHIDE, the *Flooding* and the *Shortest Path (SP)* routing plans, to route a packet from the originator to the *SIN*.

To identify the threats due to the hunter's speed and processing time lets consider the configuration scenario of Figure 4. It consists of 7 *Rings* of different size and a *BUS* of 7 *BUNs*. Hunter's speed affects the time he needs to overhear a packet, to process it, determine the sender sensor, and finally to move to that direction. We suppose here a hunter with prior knowledge of the sensors'

locations. We further assume that the hunter follows a variant of the cautious adversary model, described in (Lopez Munoz, 2005). Our variation is the usage of the trigonometric function in Eq. 1. This function forces a hunter that waits on a sensor, say *Si*, and senses a *LocInfo* packet, to randomly select and move to one of the neighbor sensors (say *Ni* neighbors), using a uniform distribution. The hunter waits to overhear a packet in the new sensor, say *Si ^{j}*, *j≤Ni*, for a predefined interval. In the case where no packet is sensed, the hunter moves to another *Si ^{jk}*, *k≤Ni-1*. If no packet is sensed when the cautious hunter has moved and waited in all the *Ni* neighbors of *Si*, the hunter returns to the last sensor that he sensed a packet.

Figure 5 illustrates hunter's effort (i.e., steps) to locate a static panda that resides in twelve (12) different locations, when the cautious hunter starts eavesdropping from *SIN*. These twelve locations correspond to *SENs* that reside in three discrete *Rings*, i.e., *Ring* 7 (*SENs* 76, 48, 84, and 27), *Ring* 6 (26, 66, 46, and 18), and *Ring* 2 (83, 73, 42, and 61).

Figure 6 illustrates the hunter's effort to locate the moving panda, when he starts sensing the *SIN*. As in the case of the static panda, in *Flooding* the steps required by the hunter are maximized, but this introduces energy depletion. iHIDE provides a considerable location determination delay than the *PhR* (Lopez Munoz, 2005). In most of the moving panda scenarios the tolerance delay is increased by a factor of 40%-50%. This delay, actually, can be considered as the privacy factor that each routing scheme provides. When the delay is high, the privacy is increased. In the following we compare the three routing algorithms in terms of costs and privacy. We use the function *Score* (Eq. 2), where *w* is the weight of *cost* or *privacy*. *Cost* is considered as the number of *LocInfo* packets that all the nodes of the WSN receive, manipulate, drop, or transmit. *Privacy* is considered as the hunter's effort to locate the target.

Figure 5. The 5B-10S WSN configuration

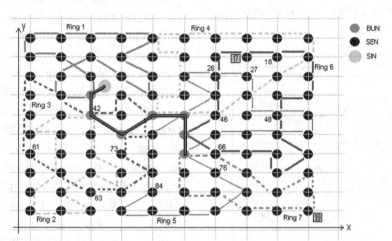

$$Score = A * privacy + (100 - A) * Cost \quad (2)$$

We consider the three discrete cases of privacy in iHIDE: a) the best, b) the worst, and c) the average case of *privacy*. We take into account these cases to compare the *Score* in Figure 7a-c.

In the best case (Figure 7a) scenarios, iHIDE gives higher score than the *PhR* for all the values of *w*. Additionally, it is better than the *Flooding* when *w<75*. Thus, when iHIDE provides the best privacy (i.e., the hunter's effort to locate the panda is maximized), it requires the exchange of less *LocInfo* packets than *PhR*. Hence, at the same time it saves energy. This is also observed when iHIDE is compared with *Flooding* when *w<75*.

Figure 6. Hunter's effort to locate a static target for different LocInfo originators

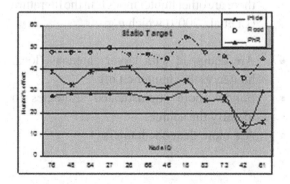

In the worst-case scenarios (Figure 7b), iHIDE scores higher than *PhR* and *Flooding* when *w<50*. Thus, in the half of the cases where the *privacy* that is provided by the iHIDE is minimized, the *score* remains higher than *PhR* and *Flooding*. Finally, in the cases where iHIDE returns average privacy (Figure 7 c), the *score* is better than *PhR* for all the values of *w*. The same conclusion applies in comparison with the *Flooding* algorithm for *w<55*.

As it is depicted in Figure 6, for each sensor *i* in the field, the hunter requires a discrete effort *Ei* to locate the panda, if it is starts is adversary journey from *SIN*. Let as now consider that the originator sensor *i* reports the location of a panda every T_i time units (position update period is *Ti*). Let assume that the cautious hunter covers the distance between two adjacent sensors in t_m time units. According to his adversary strategy he waits next to a sensor to capture a *LocInfo* packet for t_w time units. The hunter keeps trying to find the panda for t_e time units, i.e., until his resources will be elapsed. The update period *Ti* is defined as

$$T_i = (2 * t_e / E_i) + 2t_m$$

Figure 7. Scores of the three routing algorithms: (a) best iHIDE privacy, (b) worst iHIDE privacy, (c) mean iHIDE privacy

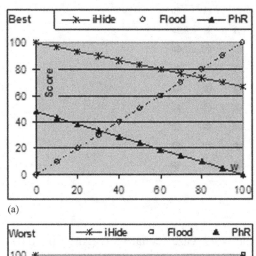

(a)

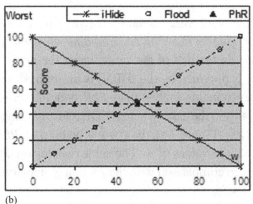

(b)

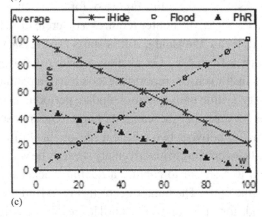

(c)

DISCUSSION

According to (Heinzelman et al., 1999), a WSN forms a path between the monitored phenomenon, i.e., the target, and the observer, i.e., the sink. WSNs are classified in two main categories: static and mobile. In static WSNs there is no motion among communicating sensors, the observer and the phenomenon. For instance environmental monitoring deployments fall in this category. Mobile WSNs are further distinguished in mobile observer, mobile sensors and mobile target (Heinzelman et al., 1999). In the mobile observer case the sink is moving with respect to the sensors and the target. In the mobile sensors scenario, the sensors are moving with respect to each other, the sink and the target. Finally, in the mobile target scenario, only the monitored subject is moving. Typical examples are WSNs deployed for children or animal detection. We concentrate on the mobile target scenario, and assume that an Animal Protecting Organization (APO) has deployed a WSN in a forest to track and monitor endangered species, say pandas. APO has attached on each panda a tag for unique identification. When a panda enters the field, it is detected and its location is reported. Only the sensor in its vicinity is activated to forward this information to the sink. This event-driven approach avoids sensors to be active all the time. In-node aggregation of location data in some powerful sensors is not essential in this case.

EXERCISES

Exercise 1: As described in the previous section, we consider a cautious hunter which is equipped with simple antenna. However, there are other hunter models in the literature (Li et al., 2009) which e.g.

- Are equipped with larger antennas (local hunter, global hunter e.t.c.)
- Follow more sophisticated strategies to identify the source
- Are more than one hunters

Elaborate on the available hunter models and identify differences.

Exercise 2: In order to create the *Routing Plan (RP)*, we used the dijkstra algorithm. Review the following pseydocode and try to consider alternative methods to create the RP.

1. Select a sensor that is able to communicate directly to the SIN
2. Set sensor of step 2 as BUN_0
3. Find the neighborhood NH_0 (i.e. sensors located within its transmission range) of BUN_0
4. Randomly select a sensor from NH_0 and set it as BUN_1
5. Until creating the desired length of *BUS:*
   a. Find the neighborhood NH_{i-1} of BUN_{i-1}
   b. Randomly selected a sensor from NH_{i-1} and set it as BUN_i
   c. Increase i by 1, where $i>=2$
6. Create a graph by creating a node for each sensor of the network
7. For each pair of nodes that are able to directly communicate (i.e. are located within their transmission range) assign an arc
8. Use a random number generator and assign to each arc a weight. Since the length of the shortest path of the step 9a is based on variation of these weights, do not over limit the random number generator (i.e. >100 and <1000 would be sufficient)
9. For each node BUN_i in *BUS:*
   a. Run dijkstra to find the shortest path from BUN_i to all other nodes
   b. Assume that the average Ring length is *RL*, select a random node N_{tmp} that its distance in hops from BUN_i is *RL/2*
   c. Store the path of step 9b as it will be the half of an *iHide Ring*
   d. Shuffle the weights of the graph
   e. Run dijkstra to find the shortest path from N_{tmp} to all other nodes
   f. Append to the path of step 9c the path from N_{tmp} to BUN_i
   g. Assign the path from BUN_i to N_{tmp} and back to BUN_i as the ring that corresponds to BUN_i
10. If there are more than one *SIN* repeat steps 1 to 9

REFERENCES

Akyildiz, F. et al. (2002). *Wireless sensor networks: A survey.* London: Elsevier.

Al-Karaki, J. N., & Kamal, A. E. (2004). Routing techniques in wireless sensor networks: A survey. *IEEE Wireless Communications Magazine, 11.*

Al-Muhtadi, J., et al. (2002). Routing through the mist: privacy preserving communication in ubiquitous computing environments. In *Proceedings of the International Conference of Distributed Computing Systems.* IEEE.

Chan, H., et al. (2003). Random key predistribution schemes for sensor networks. In *Proceedings of IEEE Symposium on Security and Privacy.* IEEE.

Eschenauer, L., et al. (2002). A key-management scheme for distributed sensor networks. In *Proceedings of ACM Conference on Computer and Communication Security.* ACM.

Fasbender, A., et al. (1996). Analysis of security and privacy in mobile IP. In *Proceedings of the 4th International Conference on Telecommunications Systems, Modeling and Analysis.* IEEE.

Friday, A., et al. (2002). A lightweight approach to managing privacy in location-based services. In *Proceedings of the Equator Annual Conference.* IEEE.

Gruteser, M., et al. (2003). Privacy-aware location sensor networks. In *Proceedings of the 8th USENIX Workshop on Hot Topics in Operating Systems*. USENIX.

Heinzelman, W. R., Kulik, J., & Balakrishnan, H. (1999). Adaptive protocols for information dissemination in wireless sensor networks. In *Proceedings of the 5th ACM/IEEE International Conference on Mobile Computing and Networking*. ACM.

Intanagonwiwat, C., et al. (2000). Directed diffusion: A scalable and robust communication paradigm for sensor networks. In *Proceedings of the 6th International Conference on Mobile Computing and Networking*. IEEE.

Kamat, P., et al. (2005). Enchasing source-location privacy in sensor network routing. In *Proceedings of the 25th International Conference on Distributed Computing Systems*. IEEE.

Kazatzopoulos, L., Delakouridis, C., Marias, G. F., & Georgiadis, P. (2006). iHIDE: Hiding sources of information in WSNs. In *Proceedings of the 2nd International Workshop on Security, Privacy and Trust in Pervasive and Ubiquitous Computing (IEEE SecPerU2006)*. Lyon, France: IEEE.

Kent, S., & Atkinson, R. (1998). Encapsulating security payload. *IETF Network Working Group RFC 2406*. Retrieved from http://www.ietf.org

Khalili, A., et al. (2003). Toward secure key distribution in truly ad-hoc networks. In *Proceedings of the Symposium Applications and the Internet Workshops*. IEEE.

Kulik, J., et al. (2002). Negotiation-based protocols for disseminating information in wireless sensor networks. *Wireless Networks Magazine, 8*.

Li, N., Zhang, N., Das, S. K., & Thuraisingham, B. M. (2009). Privacy preservation in wireless sensor networks: A state-of-the-art survey. *Ad Hoc Networks, 7*(8), 1501–1514. doi:10.1016/j.adhoc.2009.04.009.

Liu, D., & Ning, P. (2003). Establishing pairwise keys in distributed sensor networks. In *Proceedings of the 10th ACM Conference on Computer and Communication Security*. ACM.

Lopez-Munoz, J. (2005). *Wireless sensor networks: The new security challenge?* Paper presented In 1st International Workshop on Privacy and Trust in Pervasive and Ubiquitous Computing. New York.

Mahimkar, A., & Rappaport, T. S. (2004). SecureDAV: A secure data aggregation and verification protocol for sensor networks. In *Proceedings of the IEEE Globecom*. IEEE.

Malan, D. J., et al. (2004). A public-key infrastructure for key distribution in TinyOS based on elliptic curve cryptography. In *Proceedings of the 1st IEEE Communications Society Conference on Sensor and Ad Hoc Communications & Networks*. IEEE.

Perrig, A., Stankovic, J., & Wagner, D. (2004). Security in wireless sensor networks. *Communications of the ACM, 47*(6). doi:10.1145/990680.990707.

Schurgers, C., et al. (2001). Energy efficient routing in wireless sensor networks. In *Proceedings of the MILCOM Communications for Network-Centric Operations*. MILCOM.

Sobeih, A. et al. (2005). *J-sim: A simulation and emulation environment for wireless sensor networks*. IEEE Wireless Communication Magazine.

Song J.-H., et al. (2003). Secure routing with tamper resistant module for mobile ad hoc networks. *ACM Mobile Computing and Communication Review, 7*(3).

Tilak, S., et al. (2002). A taxonomy of wireless micro-sensor network models. *ACM Mobile Computing and Communications Review, 6*(2).

Zhu, S., et al. (2003). LEAP: Efficient security mechanisms for large-scale distributed sensor networks. In *Proceedings of the 10th ACM Conference on Computer and Communication Security*. ACM.

ADDITIONAL READING

Cachin, C., Kursawe, K., Lysyanskaya, A., & Strobl, R. (2002). Asynchronous verifiable secret sharing and proactive cryptosystems. In *Proceedings of the 9th ACM Conference Computer and Communications Security*. ACM.

Cachin, C., Kursawe, K., & Shoup, V. (2005). Random oracles in Constantinople: Practical asynchronous Byzantine agreement using cryptography. *Journal of Cryptology, 18*(3), 219–246. doi:10.1007/s00145-005-0318-0.

Chang, T. Y., Hwang, M. S., & Yang, W. P. (2005). An improvement on the Lin–Wu (t,n) threshold verifiable multi-secret sharing scheme. *Applied Mathematics and Computation, 163*(1), 169–178. doi:10.1016/j.amc.2004.01.029.

Chor, B., Goldwasser, S., Micali, S., & Awerbuch, B. (1985). Verifiable secret sharing and achieving simultaneity in the presence of faults. In *Proceedings of the 26th IEEE Symposium on Foundations of Computer Science*. IEEE.

Dehkordi, M. H., & Mashhadi, S. (2008). New efficient and practical verifiable multi-secret sharing schemes. *Information Sciences, 178*, 2262–2274. doi:10.1016/j.ins.2007.11.031.

Feldman, P. (1987). A practical scheme for non-interactive verifiable secret sharing. In *Proceedings of the 28th IEEE Symposium on Foundations of Computer Science*. IEEE.

Fitzi, M., Garay, J., Gollakota, S., Rangan, C. P., & Srinathan, K. (2006). Round-optimal and efficient verifiable secret sharing. In *Proceedings of the Third Theory of Cryptography Conference – TCC'06*. TCC.

Goldreich, O. (2012). *Secure multiparty computation*. Retrieved from http://www.wisdom. weizman.ac.il/oded/pp.html

Katz, J., Koo, C., & Kumaresan, R. (2008). Improved the round complexity of VSS in point-to-point networks. In *Proceedings of the ICALP 2008*. Berlin: Springer.

Maurer, U. (2006). Secure multi-party computation made simple. *Discrete Applied Mathematics, 154*(2), 370–381. doi:10.1016/j.dam.2005.03.020.

Patra, A., Choudhary, A., Rabin, T., & Rangan, C. P. (2009). The round complexity of verifiable secret sharing revisited. In *Proceedings of the Crypto '09*. Crypto.

Schultz, D., Liskov, B., & Liskov, M. (2008). Brief announcement: Mobile proactive secret sharing. In *Proceedings of the PODC '08*. PODC.

Shao, J., & Cao, Z. (2005). A new efficient (t,n) verifiable multi-secret sharing (VMSS) based on YCH scheme. *Applied Mathematics and Computation, 168*(1), 135–140. doi:10.1016/j. amc.2004.08.023.

Zhou, L. (2005). APSS: Proactive secret sharing in asynchronous systems. *ACM Transactions on Information and System Security, 8*(3), 259–286. doi:10.1145/1085126.1085127.

KEY TERMS AND DEFINITIONS

Cryptographic Technique: Technique used for secure communication or information exchange.

Intelligent Location Service: The capability of handling complex phenomena using location and time information.

Location-Based Service: General class of computer program level service used to include specific controls for location and time data.

Location Privacy: Controlling the access in location information.

Secret Sharing Scheme: Technique for distributing a secret among a group of participants each of them is allocated a share of the secret.

Chapter 11
The Applications of Automata in Game Theory

Sally Almanasra
Universiti Sains Malaysia, Malaysia

Khaled Suwais
Arab Open University, Saudi Arabia

Muhammad Rafie
Universiti Sains Malaysia, Malaysia

ABSTRACT

In game theory, presenting players with strategies directly affects the performance of the players. Utilizing the power of automata is one way for presenting players with strategies. In this chapter, the authors studied different types of automata and their applications in game theory. They found that finite automata, adaptive automata, and cellular automata are widely adopted in game theory. The applications of finite automata are found to be limited to present simple strategies. In contrast, adaptive automata and cellular automata are intensively applied in complex environment, where the number of interacted players (human, computer applications, etc.) is high, and therefore, complex strategies are needed.

INTRODUCTION

Any problem with interacted participants and actions can be treated as a game. When car drivers put a plan to drive in heavy traffic, they are actually playing a driving game. When users bid on bidding-based Websites, they are actually playing an auctioning game. In election, choosing the platform is a political game. The owner of a factory

deciding the price of his product is an economic game. Obviously, game theory can be presented in wide range of applications.

Game theory is a mathematical tool that can analyze the interactions between individuals strategically. The interactions between agents, who may be individuals, groups, firms are interdependent. These interdependent interactions are controlled by the available strategies and their corresponding

DOI: 10.4018/978-1-4666-4038-2.ch011

payoffs to participants. However, game theory studies the rational behavior in situations involving interdependency (McMillan, 1992). Therefore, game theory will only work when people play games rationally and it will not work on games with cooperational behavior.

Generally, the game consists of the following entities:

- **Players:** Where one side of the game tries to maximize the gain (*payoff*), while the other side tries to minimize the opponent's score. However, these players can be humans, computer applications or any other entities.
- **Environment:** This includes board position and the possible moves for the players.
- **Successor Function:** The successor function includes actions and returns a list of (move, state) pairs, where each pair indicates a legal move and the resulting state.
- **Terminal Test:** The terminal test specifies when the game is over and the terminal state is reached.
- **Utility Function:** The utility function is the numeric value for the terminal states.

The scientists of inter-disciplinary community believe that the time has come to extend game theory beyond the boundaries of full rationality, common-knowledge of rationality, consistently aligned beliefs, static equilibrium, and long-term convergence (Izquierdo, 2007). These concerns have led various researchers to develop formal models of social interactions within the framework of game theory.

The first formal study of games was done by Antoine Cournot in 1838. A mathematician, Emile Borel suggested a formal theory of games in 1921, which was extended by another mathematician John von Neumann in 1928. Game theory was established as a field in its own right after the 1944 publication of the monumental volume Theory of Games and Economic Behavior by von Neumann

and other economists. In 1950, John Nash proved that finite games have always have an equilibrium point, at which all players choose actions which are best for them given their opponents' choices. This concept has been a basic point of analysis since then. In the 1950s and 1960s, game theory was extended and developed theoretically and applied to problems of war and politics. Since the 1970s, it has created a revolution in economic theory. Moreover, it has found applications in sociology and psychology, and found links with evolution and biology. Game theory received special attention in 1994 with the awarding of the Nobel Prize in economics to Nash (Almanasra, 2007).

The attractive point in studying games is that models used in games are applicable to be used in real-life situations. Because of this, game theory has been broadly used in economics, biology, politics, low, and also in computer sciences. Examples on the use of game theory in computer science include interface design, network routing, load sharing and allocate resources in distributed systems and information and service transactions on Internet (Platkowski & Siwak, 2008).

One of the crucial factors which affect the performance of players in a given game is the behavior (strategy) representation. We found that different techniques are used to represent players' behavior in different games. One of the successful techniques is the use of automata-based model to represent and control participated agents. In the next sections, we will discuss different types of automata and their affect on games.

AUTOMATA TYPES

An automaton (plural: automata or automatons) is a self-operating machine. The output to one automaton is a combination between the consequences of the current input and the history of the machine's previous input. An automaton is designed to automatically follow a predetermined sequence of operations or respond to encoded instructions. There are many types of well known automata, such as finite automata, turing machines, push–down automata, adaptive automata as well as other variations such as, random access machines, parallel random access machines and arrays automata. Experimental simulations of automata methods carried out in different researchers have recommended the automaton approach in the solution of many interesting examples in parameter optimization, hypothesis testing, and in game theory (Almanasra & Rafie, 2010).

Learning Automata Theory

Learning is strongly associated with past experiences, where these experiences are meant to permanently change the entity behavior. Learning system is characterized by its ability to improve its behavior with time in some sense tending towards an ultimate goal (Narendra & Wright, 1977). Numerous approaches have been proposed for developing learning systems. One of the approaches which gained considerable attention is based on automata. This approach tends to present a given problem as one of finding the optimal state among a set of possible states. This approach is referred to by learning automaton. Figure 1 illustrates the concept of automaton, where the possible states are presented by S1, S2, S3, S4, and S5.

A learning automaton operates in a random environment. The actions are chosen based on the inputs received from the environment to find the optimal. The learning schemes come in two structures: fixed structure and variable structure. Fixed

Figure 1. The concept of automaton

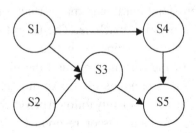

structure schemes in stationary random environments are described by homogeneous Markov chains. On the other hand, variable structure schemes are described by Markov processes. Much of the effort in these areas has been directed towards achieving expedient, optimal behavior (Narendra & Wright, 1977). However, learning automaton has a finite number of output actions, one of which is selected at each instant. Every selected action will be either rewarded or punished by the environment, which leads to update the probability distribution defined over the actions. Choosing the proper updating algorithms, leads to desirable asymptotic behavior of the learning automaton (Thathachar, 1985).

Finite-State Automata

Finite automaton is one of the well-studied computation models in theoretical computer science. Finite automata are composed of fixed finite memory, which takes its decisions using that finite memory, a finite non-empty alphabet, a transition function, an initial state and a set of final states. Transitions map ordered pairs specifying the current state and the current input symbol into a new state (Maenner, 2008). Finite Automata are classified into Deterministic Finite Automaton (DFA) and Non-Deterministic Finite Automaton (NFA). DFA is only permitted to be in one state in any time. On the contrast, NFA can be in two or more states at any given time. Technically, adding restrictions to DFA is sufficient to transform it to NFA. However, there are two types of transitions from state A to state B: *Input transitions* (**A**, *r*) → **B**, with an input symbol *r*, and *Empty transitions* (**A**, *α*) → **B**, which do not modify the input (Figure 2).

DFA can be viewed in two schemes: Graph-based (*transition diagram*) and Table-based transition-listing schemes. Graph-based scheme is considered efficient for visually represent player's behavior, while Table-based transition-listing scheme is efficient for computer simulation (Sipser, 1997). However, the classifications pre-

Figure 2. Input and empty transitions from A to B

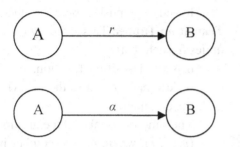

sented in (Ghneamat, 2005) showed that automata can be weighted, and therefore these types of automata are referred to by weighted automata (*Transducers*). Transducers are automata which generate new output based on a given input and/ or a state using action. Transducers come in two types as follows:

- **Moore Machines:** The output depends only on a state (e.g. entry state, random state, etc.). Moore machine is efficient in simplifying a given behavior.
- **Meally Machines:** The output depends on specific input and a state. Meally machine is efficient in reducing the number of states.

Mathematically (Guerberoff, Queiroz, & Sichman, 2010), finite automata are 4-tuple structures described by R as follows:

$$\mathbf{R}=(S, I, F, S_0) \qquad (1)$$

where:

- S is a set of states
- I is an input symbol
- $F: S \times I \mapsto S$ is a transition function
- $S_0 \in S$ is an initial state

This definition induces the concept of current state for a given input sequence. That is, given a sequence of inputs $i^* = (i_1, i_2, \ldots, i_t) \in I^t$, the current state S_t is defined recursively for $t > 0$ as:
$S_t = t(S_{t-1}, i_t)$ together with the initial state S_0.

Finite automata are widely used in game theory. For instance, in the iterated *n*-player prisoners' dilemma (INPPD), finite automata can be used to represent players' strategies. The automata states represent the players' action and the input is the strategy profile observed from the other players (e.g. the number of cooperated agents). Therefore, if *n* represent the number of players in the game, then the set I is defined as $I = \{0, 1, \ldots, n-1\}$. The set of states S can be divided two states C and D, such that the player cooperate or defect if $s_t \in C$ or $s_t \in D$, respectively. Figure 3 shows an example of a strategy for the NPPD with 3 participants.

The automaton presented in Figure 3 has four states: C1, C2, D1 and D2. The arcs between the states represent the transitions. The four states can only be triggered by the numbers associated with the arcs, resulting in a transition between the states. In this example, $F(C1, 0) = D1$ and $F(D2, 2) = C2$, and so on. The initial state is the one with an empty arrow in its direction ($S_0 = C1$). The following sequence of plays illustrates the role which finite automata can play in representing strategies:

- First, the player selects "C" as its initial state.
- If in this round none of the other two players played "C", the total number of cooperator will be 0 (excluding the player itself).

Figure 3. Example on representing INPPD strategy

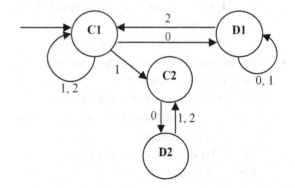

- The transition "0" will change the current state from C1 to D1.
- In the following round, the agent will play "D", since the current state is D1.
- Assume that one player is cooperated; therefore the total number of cooperator will be 1.
- The transition "1" change the state from D1 to D1 itself.
- In the next round, the player will play "D" again.

However, using finite automata as a modeling language has its limitations. Finite automata are only capable to recognize regular languages (Guerberoff, Queiroz, & Sichman, 2010). In other words, it is possible to guarantee arrival at a specific state only for a determined class of input sequences.

Pushdown Automata

The pushdown automata are finite automata equipped with stack. Several operations can be applied on the stack including read, push and pop operations. Mathematically, pushdown automata can be defined as a septuple **R** as follows:

$$R= (S; \alpha; \Gamma; \delta; I_0; Z_0; F) \qquad (2)$$

- **State Tuples:** This category includes tuples S, I_0 and F, such that:
  - ○ **S** is a finite set of states.
  - ○ I_0 is the initial state of the pushdown automata.
  - ○ **F** is the final (acceptance) state.
- **Input Tuples:** This category includes tuples α and Z_0, such that:
  - ○ α is a finite set of input symbols.
  - ○ Z_0 is the initial input symbol to pushdown automata.
- **Stack Tuples:** This category includes tuple Γ, such that:

- ○ Γ is finite stack alphabets that are allowed to be pushed onto the stack.
- **Transition Tuples:** This category includes tuples δ, such that:
  - ○ δ is the transition function, where δ is designed to control the behavior of the automaton.
  - ○ The function δ takes three arguments (m, n, r), where m is a member in **S**, n is a member in α and r is a member in Γ.

The output of this function is a finite set of pairs (p, q), where p is the new generated state and q is the string of the stack that replaces r from the top of the stack.

Turing Machine

A Turing machine is an abstract computing device which consists of a finite control, unbounded memory (represented by tapes), and a finite program. The program is a list of instructions that guide the machine to take actions based on the current state of its finite control and the bits in its current 'window' on the information on the tapes. A step normally involves both a change of state in the finite control, a rewrite of the bits in the window, and a move of the window to the left or to the right by one position (van Leeuwen & Wiedermann, 2001).

Turing Machines were first proposed by Alan Turing (Sipser M., 1997). The idea was to model what humans do in order to solve a problem when following instructions through symbolic means. Alan tried to extract the basic entities of the process together with the basic operations that allow a computer to carry out the process of following a set of instructions. Turing machine assumes that at the entire input data is available on the input tape at the beginning of the computation. The rest of the input tape is blank. If the machine approaches the accepting state, the input is said to be accepted. The result of the computation is given by the contents of the tapes at this time. Once a new set of input data is started, all previous information will be erased. The framework of Turing machines is suitable for studying the power and efficiency of algorithms, considering the achievements of computability and complexity theory(van Leeuwen & Wiedermann, 2001).

Technically, Turing machines are extended versions of pushdown automata. Similar to the transition function (δ) in pushdown automata, Turing machine has a central component which can be in one of a finite number of states and an infinite tape used for storage. However, several characteristics are responsible for distinguishing Turing machines from pushdown automata, including (Sipser M., 1997):

- The tape used by a Turing machine is infinite in both directions.
- Turing machine receive its input written on the tape which they use for storage.
- Turing machine control the head position to where reading and writing on the tape is performed.

Mathematically (Thakkar, 2004), pushdown automata can be defined as a septuple **R** as follows:

$$\mathbf{R} = (S; \alpha; \Gamma; \delta; I_0; B; F) \tag{3}$$

where the tuples of R are classified into the following categories:

- **State Tuples:** This category includes tuples S, I_0 and F, such that:
  - ◦ **S** is a finite set of states.
  - ◦ I_0 is the initial state of the Turing machine.
  - ◦ **F** is the final (acceptance) state.
- **Input Tuples:** This category includes tuples α and B, such that:
  - ◦ α is a finite set of input symbols.

  - ◦ **B** is the blank symbol. **B** is a member in Γ but not in α. The blank appears initially in all but the finite number of initial cells that hold input symbols.
- **Tape Tuples:** This category includes tuple Γ, such that:
  - ◦ Γ is a complete set of tap symbols.
- **Transition Tuples:** This category includes tuples δ, such that:
  - ◦ δ is the transition function, where δ is the central processing part of Turing machine.
  - ◦ The function δ takes three arguments (t, u, d), where t is the next state, u is a symbol in Γ that is written in the cell being scanned, replacing whatever symbol was there, and d is the direction (L: left and R:right), indicating the direction of the head tape.

The output of this function is a finite set of pairs (p, q), where p is the new generated state and q is the string of the stack that replaces r from the top of the stack.

Adaptive Automata

Many studies have been conducted on the field of adaptive and learning systems. The attention on such studies comes from the suitability of those systems in modeling many real world complex systems. In typical Learning Automata (LA) systems, a self-operating machine (Automaton) responds to a sequence of actions to achieve a specific goal. The Automaton, in turn, may responds based on pre-determined rules, or it may adapt to its environmental dynamics. In other words, adaptive actions are attached to the state-transition rules of the adaptive automata and they are activated whenever the transition is applied by removing or inserting new elements to the automaton's transition set.

In Psychology, the term learning refers to the act of acquiring knowledge and modifying one's behavior based on the experience gained. Therefore, in LA, the adaptive automaton aims to learn the best possible actions from a set of possible actions that are offered to it by the environment in which it operates. The Automaton, thus, acts as a decision maker to arrive at the best action

Adaptive automata are internally based on the structured pushdown automata. Structured pushdown automata are equivalent to classical pushdown automata (Neto & Bravo, 2003). A structured pushdown automaton consists of a set of states, a finite non-empty alphabet, initial state, set of final states, pushdown alphabet and a transition function. The transition function is composed of two transitions levels: internal and external. The internal transitions are similar to those in finite-state automata. On the other hand, the external transitions are responsible for the calling and returning scheme. In each transition of an adaptive automaton, the current state and the current input symbol of the automaton determine a set of possible transitions to be applied.

Mathematically (Pistori, Martins, & Jr, 2005), adaptive automata can be defined as a 10-tuple **R** as follows:

$$\mathbf{R} = (S; \alpha; I_0; F; \delta; U; \Gamma; H; Q; \Delta) \qquad (4)$$

where the tuples of R are classified into the following categories:

- **State Tuples:** This category includes tuples S, I_0 and F, such that:
  - ◦ S is a set of states.
  - ◦ I_0 is the initial state of the automaton.
  - ◦ F is the final (acceptance) state.
- **Input Tuples:** This category includes tuples α and Γ, such that:
  - ◦ α is a set of input symbols.
  - ◦ Γ is a set of parameters and variables.
- **Transition Tuples:** This category includes tuples δ, U, H, Q and Δ, such that:

- ◦ δ is the transition relation, where this relation takes two elements: an element from U and a set of mapped parameters from Q.
- ◦ U is a set of adaptive function labels.
- ◦ H is a set of generators.
- ◦ Q is used for mapping parameters, variables and generators to **U**.
- ◦ Δ is a set of adaptive actions {+,-,?}.

Each adaptive action consists of the *type* and the *transition* of the adaptive action. The action type can be either a query, remove or insert actions, represented by (?), (-) and (+) respectively. Adaptive actions are formulated as calls to adaptive functions with a set of parameters. These actions describe the modifications which should be applied to the adaptive automaton whenever they are called. Technically, simple finite automaton can be turned into an adaptive automaton by allowing its rules to change dynamically (adaptive mechanism). Figure 4 illustrates the concept of adaptive automata, where the discrete arrow between D1 and C2 is created when the transaction between C1 and C2 is accomplished.

Cellular Automata

The structure of Cellular Automata (CA) is based on lattice of cells where each cell may be in a predetermined number of discrete states. Updating the states of CA in each time step requires a pre-determination process of the neighborhood relation, indicating the communication structure between the cells. Updating the state of each

Figure 4. Adaptive automata

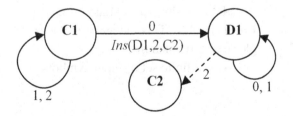

cell is carried out using a transition rule. Each transition rule takes the states of all the cells in its neighborhood as input to the automaton, and updates all cells in CA synchronously.

For simplicity, the following are the basic properties and characteristics of a given CA (Hegselmann & Flache, 1998):

- The cells are regularly arranged in n-dimensional grid.
- Each cell has an initial state selected from a finite set of states.
- Update is carried out in a discrete time step.
- Changing the state of the cells depends on the set of local rules.
- The selected transition rule is applied to all cells.
- The update process is carried out simultaneously for all cells.

Mathematically (Kari, 2011), a cellular automaton is defined as a 4-tuple **R** as follows:

$$R= (n; S; P; F) \qquad (5)$$

where

- n is the dimension of the lattice space.
- S is a finite set of states.
- P is a finite set of neighborhoods.
- F is the local rule of CA.

However, cellular automata are considered easy to implement and emulate on a computer. In addition, CA exhibits a wide range of possible nonlinear behavior and thus it is capable of producing output at the highest complexity level of formal language theory (Albin S., 1998).

Stochastic Automata

Stochastic learning automaton can be defined as an element which interacts with a random environment to improve a specified performance (Narendra, 1974). This is possible by changing the automaton action probabilities based on the responses received from the corresponding environment. The stochastic automaton works as follows:

- The automaton starts with no information about the optimal action.
- The probabilities are equally attached to all actions.
- One action is selected at random.
- Based on the response of the environment, the action probabilities are changed.
- New action is selected according to the updated action probabilities, and the procedure is repeated.

Mathematically (Chandrasekaran & Shen, 1972), a cellular automaton is defined as a 6-tuple **R** as follows:

$$R= (S; F; \Phi; G; \pi; \Gamma) \qquad (6)$$

where

- S is a set of inputs to the automaton.
- F is a set of outputs from the automaton.
- Φ is a finite set of states.
- G is the output function which maps the state to a specific output (one-to-one).
- π is the state probability.
- Γ is the reinforcement operator that specify the manner in which π is to change according to the environment.

Another form of stochastic automata is the Multiplicity automata (Oncina, 2008). Multiplicity automata are stochastic automata with only one initial state and no restrictions to force the normalization (distribute probabilities). In fact, automata with output are called automata with multiplicities (Ghneamat, 2005).

We can conclude that automata theory provides us with a simple presentation for a given problem. Automata theory is found to depend on simple rules instead of random behavior. However, automata theory shows that the simplicity of the structure of automata can obviously allow them to handle complex problems. Therefore, automata theory has been widely applied to different games in the field of game theory.

THE APPLICATIONS OF AUTOMATA IN GAME THEORY

Automata theory has presented various types of automata with different characteristics. In this section we will go through the applications which have successfully utilized the concept of automata in game theory.

Applications of Finite Automata

Back to 1985 (Neyman, 1985), Neyman tries to model the fact that players can do only bounded computation, by modeling the iterated prisoner's dilemma players as finite automata. One year later, Rubinstein (Rubinstein, 1986) tries to show that costly computation may affects an agent's utility. Rubinstein assumed that players choose a finite automaton to play the game instead of choosing a strategy directly. It was clearly stated that a player's utility depends on the automaton's moves and the complexity of the automaton structure (number of states of the automaton). In other words, automata that use more states are capable to represent more complicated procedures (Halpern, 2008). In 2000, Dodis et al. (Dodis, 2000) were the first who formalized the idea of finite automata in prisoner's dilemma instead of modeling players as polynomially bounded Turing machine.

Recently, Finite automata have been widely used to represent player strategies in game theory. For instance, the researchers of the work mentioned in (Bó & Sichman, 2004) have conducted several experiments and the results showed that finite automata have significantly improved the performance of n-player Prisoner's Dilemma. The study presented in (Maenner, 2008) showed

that infinitely repeated games, such as prisoner's dilemma and Matching Pennies, have problems in learning and presenting the strategies. Therefore, the study introduced dynamic systems where agents start the game with randomly chosen strategies which are represented by finite state automata. The agents are also allowed to change their strategies during the game.

In (Lindgren & Nordahl, 1994) the authors have presented a model which utilizes genetic algorithms and finite automata for presenting the strategies of Prisoner's Dilemma with changeable memory size. The work presented in (Bouhmala & Granmo, 2010) showed the benefits of finite learning automata which help agents to find the action that minimizes the expected number of penalties received, or maximizes the expected number of payoffs received.

On the other hand, there is a difference between the environments for representation the players in lattices, trees, or graphs using EAs techniques, based on many factors that in turn affect back the outcome of the evolution of strategies. Some of these factors include the number of players, technique of evolutionary computation, type of automata and neighborhood structures. In (Dworman, Kimbrough, & Laing, 1995) the authors have reported that they build their 3-players model using a genetic programming technique to discover high-quality negotiation policies, where the behavior of the players was presented by finite automata.

However, finite automata are found efficient in representing simple strategies in game theory. Nevertheless, game theory is interested in representing simple strategies since many real life applications do not require complex strategies to achieve their goals.

Applications of Adaptive Automata

Adaptive automata-based devices have been presented as powerful tools for defining complex languages. Adaptive automata have the following important features (Neto & Iwai, 1998):

- The accepting procedure performed by an adaptive automaton is done efficiently, due to their structure which is based on finite-state or structured pushdown automata.
- Adaptive automata can handle context dependencies in a strict syntactical way, without the aid of auxiliary semantic procedures.
- The structure of adaptive automata can extended to implement transducers, allowing the generation of parse trees as a side effect of parsing sentences.
- Generally, adaptive automata have cheaper implementations compared to other mechanisms.
- Adaptive automata can be considered as alternative to existing solutions of natural language processing.

In order for adaptive automata to do self-modification, adaptive acts adhered to their state-transition rules are activated whenever the transition is used. Adaptive mechanism can be defined as Adaptive actions which change the behavior of adaptive automata by modifying the set of rules defining it. The simple notation for representing adaptive automata should have some features such as, being, at least, compact, simple, expressive, unambiguous, readable, and easy to learn, understand and maintain (Neto & Iwai, 1998).

The work presented in (Ghnemat, Oqeili, & Bertelle, 2006) has paid more attention to the iterated prisoner dilemma. An original evaluative probabilistic automaton was created for strategy modeling. It has been shown that genetic automata are well-adapted to model adaptive strategies. As a result, we noticed that modeling the player behavior needs some adaptive attributes. However, the computable models related to genetic automata are good tools to model such adaptive strategy. In (Ghneamat, 2005) the authors used genetic algorithms to generate adaptive behaviors to be

applied for modeling an adaptive strategy for the prisoner dilemma. They used adaptive automata-based model for the modeling agent behavior.

The work presented in (Zhang J., 2009) has formed the collection of automata in a tree-like structure, and the modification of action possibility continued at different levels according to the reward signs provided for all hierarchical levels. Another work presented in (Bertelle, Flouret, Jay, Olivier, Ponty, & du Havre, 2002) has focused on the models which can be used for simulating Prisoner's Dilemma. The work showed how existing models and algorithms, in game theory, can be used with automata for representing the behaviors of players. The dynamical and adaptive properties can be described in term of specific operators based on genetic algorithms. In addition, the work showed that genetic operators on probabilistic automata enable the adaptive behavior to be modeled for prisoner dilemma strategies.

Adaptive automata have computational power equivalent to a Turing Machine (Guerberoff, Queiroz, & Sichman, 2010). Thus, strategies presented by adaptive automata may show more complex behaviors than the ones described by finite automata. For instance, learning mechanisms can be constructed using adaptive automata to represent adaptive learning mechanism based on specific input parameters.

However, finite automata are a particular case of adaptive automata. If the automata have no rules associating adaptive functions to transitions, the model can be reduced to finite automata. This characteristic is considered important to use adaptive automata naturally where finite automata are required.

Applications of Cellular Automata

Cellular automata can be complex systems by themselves, or they can offer good ways of studying the behavior of complex systems (Schut, 2010). In this section we overview the existing models and algorithms which have successfully utilized cellular automata for analyzing or achieving desired dynamics of a complex system.

The presented work in (Szilagyi, 2008) has modeled the participated agents, in a given game, as stochastic learning cellular automata. Stochastic learning means that behavior is not determined it is shaped by its consequences. In the same context, other works have modeled the agents differently, such as modeling agents as a combination of cellular automata (Wolfram, 1994; Hegselmann, Flache, & Möller, 1998) and as stochastic learning automata (Narendra & Thathachar, 1989; Flache & Macy, 1996).

Back to 1975, Albin was the first person who models the checkerboard models as cellular automata (Albin, 1975). In his book The Analysis of Complex Socioeconomic Systems, Albin has showed the cellular automata can provide enormous potentials for understanding social dynamics. In 1990 (Nowak & Latané, 1990), Nowak et al. have developed a two-dimensional cellular automata-based model of evolution for social attitudes. In the field of economics, a one-dimensional cellular automata model has been proposed to model and analyze pricing in a spatial setting (Keenan & O'Brien, 1993).

Recently, cellular automata have been used to simulate agents with different strategies (Chiong & Kirley, 2009). In that work, the researchers showed the ability of co-evolutionary learning used to evolve cooperative strategies in structured populations using the N-Player Iterated Prisoner's Dilemma (NIPD). In addition, they examined the effects of both fixed and random neighborhood structures on the evolution of cooperative behavior in a lattice-based NIPD model. Ghnemat et al. have presented a model to simulate and solve complex systems (Ghnemat, Bertelle, & Duchamp, 2009). The model is based on cellular automata with some approaches for agents programming, such as artificial intelligence, automata modeling, distributed computing, swarm intelligence, and genetic algorithms.

Simulating the n-player iterated prisoner's dilemma as a bidding game using cellular automata is one way of incorporating cellular automata in game theory (Ishibuchi, Namikawa, & Ohara, 2006). In that work, the authors intended to show why cooperation only emerges in the triangular neighborhood structure but not in the rectangular and the random pairing neighborhood structures. The authors in (Zhang, Zhang, Li, Gao, & Li, 2009) and (Szilagyi, 2003) have investigated how the evolution of cooperation is influenced in Prisoner's Dilemma model using cellular automata. In (Su, Hui, Zhang, & Li, 2009) the researchers examined how the spatial structure of environment loss affects the eco-epidemic. They simulated the heterogeneous lattice landscape by defining two environment states, i.e. suitable and unsuitable.

We can conclude that representing the behavior of n-players prisoner's dilemma models using cellular automata has a great benefit, since most of the researchers can utilize it to distinguish the effects of neighborhood structure on the evolution of cooperative behavior.

CONCLUSION

Presenting players strategies in game theory is one of the factors which affect the players' performance significantly. In this work we have analyzed the characteristics and the underlying structure of existed types of automata. Consequently, we have explored the applications of automata in game theory.

However, this study revealed that only few types of automata have been utilized in game theory. We found that finite automata have been widely used to represent simple agents' behavior. On the other hand, adaptive automata and cellular automata are mainly used to represent complex agents' behavior. The complexity level of both adaptive automata and cellular automata is determined by the number of states in the automata. The more states we have, the higher is the capability for those automata to handle complex strategies.

ACKNOWLEDGMENT

The authors would like to express their thanks to Universiti Sains Malaysia for supporting this study under the USM Fellowship.

REFERENCES

Albin, P. (1975). *The analysis of complex socio-economic systems*. London: Lexington Books.

Albin, S. (1998). *Barriers and bounds to rationality: Essays on economic complexity and dynamics in interactive systems*. Princeton, NJ: Princeton University Press.

Almanasra, S. (2007). Learning opponent behavior in game theory using genetic algorithms. Jordan: Al-Balqa' Applied University.

Almanasra, S., & Rafie, M. (2010). Comprehensive survey on automata-based game theory. In *Proceedings of the 1st International Symposium on Computing in Science & Engineering* (pp. 643-647). IEEE.

Bertelle, C., Flouret, M., Jay, V., Olivier, D., Ponty, J., & du Havre, L. (2002). *Adaptive behaviour for prisoner dilemma strategies based on automata with multiplicities*. Dresden, Germany: Academic Press.

Bó, I. G., & Sichman, J. S. (2004). *Strategy representation complexity in an evolutionary n-players prisoner's dilemma model*. Retrieved March 20, 2012, from www.econ.fea.usp.br/complex/Artigos/24_04_08_Ináciol.pdf

Bouhmala, N., & Granmo, O. (2010). Combining finite learning automata with GSAT for the satisfiability problem. *Engineering Applications of Artificial Intelligence, 23*, 715–726. doi:10.1016/j.engappai.2010.01.009.

Chandrasekaran, B., & Shen, D. (1972). Stochastic automata games. *IEEE Transactions on Systems, Man, and Cybernetics*, 145–149.

Chiong, R., & Kirley, M. (2009). Co-evolutionary learning in the n-player iterated prisoner's dilemma with a structured environment. In *Proceedings of the 4th Australian Conference on Artificial Life: Borrowing from Biology* (pp. 32-42). IEEE.

Dodis, Y. S. (2000). A cryptographic solution to a game theoretic problem. In *Proceedings of CRYPTO 2000: 20th International Cryptology Conference* (pp. 112-130). Springer-Verlag.

Dworman, G., Kimbrough, S., & Laing, J. (1995). On automated discovery of models using genetic programming: Bargaining in a three-agent coalitions game. *Journal of Management Information Systems, 12*(125).

Flache, A., & Macy, M. (1996). Weakness of strong ties: Collective action failure in a highly cohesive group. *Mathematical Sociology, 21*, 3–28. doi:10.1080/0022250X.1996.9990172.

Ghneamat, R. (2005). *Genetic algorithms and application to adaptive automata for game theory*. Al-Balqa University.

Ghnemat, R., Bertelle, C., & Duchamp, G. (2009). A methodology for urban and land-use management simulation using spatial self-organization processes. *Dynamics of Continuous, Discrete and Impulsive Systems-series B, 16*, 501–513.

Ghnemat, R., Oqeili, S., & Bertelle, C. (2006). Automata-based adaptive behavior for economic modelling using game theory. In *Emergent Properties in Natural and Artificial Dynamical Systems* (pp. 171–183). Academic Press. doi:10.1007/3-540-34824-7_9.

Guerberoff, I., Queiroz, D., & Sichman, J. S. (2010). On the effect of the expressiveness of strategy representation languages in multiagent based simulations: an experiment with an evolutionary model of the iterated n-players prisoner's dilemma. *1re Soumission à RIA Special Issue on Agent Based Social Simulation*.

Halpern, J. Y. (2008). *Algorithmic rationality: Game theory with costly computation*. Academic Press.

Hegselmann, R., & Flache, A. (1998). Understanding complex social dynamics: A plea for cellular automata based modelling. *Journal of Artificial Societies and Social Simulation, 1*(3).

Hegselmann, R., Flache, A., & Möller, V. (1998). Solidarity and social impact in cellular worlds - Results and sensitivity analyses. In *Proceedings of Social Science Microsimulation: Tools for Modeling, Parameter Optimization and Sensitivity Analysis*. Berlin: Springer.

Ishibuchi, H., Namikawa, N., & Ohara, K. (2006). Effects of spatial structures on evolution of iterated prisoner's dilemma game strategies in single-dimensional and two-dimensional grids. In *Proceedings of CEC 2006 IEEE Congress on Evolutionary Computation* (pp. 976 - 983). IEEE.

Izquierdo, L. R. (2007). *Advancing learning and evolutionary game theory with an application to social dilemmas*. Academic Press.

Kari, J. (2011). *Cellular automata*. Lecture Note.

Keenan, D. C., & O'Brien, M. J. (1993). Competition, collusion, and chaos. *Journal of Economic Dynamics & Control, 17*, 327–353. doi:10.1016/0165-1889(93)90001-9.

Lindgren, K., & Nordahl, M. (1994). Evolutionary dynamics of spatial games. *Physica D. Nonlinear Phenomena, 75*, 292–309. doi:10.1016/0167-2789(94)90289-5.

Maenner, E. (2008). Adaptation and complexity in repeated games. *Games and Economic Behavior, 63*(1), 166–187. doi:10.1016/j.geb.2007.07.008.

McMillan, J. (1992). *Games, strategies, and managers: How managers can use game theory to make better business decisions*. New York: Oxford University Press.

Narendra, K. (1974). Learning automata - A survey. *IEEE Transactions on Systems, Man, and Cypernetics, 4*.

Narendra, K., & Thathachar, M. (1989). *Learning automata (an introduction)*. Englewood Cliffs, NJ: Prentice–Hall.

Narendra, K. S., & Wright, A. (1977). Application of learning automata to telephone traffic routing and control. *IEEE Transactions on Systems, Man, and Cybernetics, 7*(11), 785–792. doi:10.1109/TSMC.1977.4309623.

Neto, J., & Iwai, K. (1998). Adaptive automata for syntax learning. In Proceedings of Anais da XXIV Conferencia Latinoamericana de Informática - CLEI 98 (pp. 135–149). Quito, Equador: CLEI.

Neto, J. J., & Bravo, C. (2003). *Adaptive automata - A reduced complexity proposal*. Lecture Notes in Computer Science Berlin: Springer.

Neyman, A. (1985). Bounded complexity justifies cooperation in finitely repeated prisoner's dilemma. *Economics Letters, 19*, 227–229. doi:10.1016/0165-1765(85)90026-6.

Nowak, A. S., & Latané, B. (1990). From private attitude to public opinion - Dynamic theory of social impact. *Psychological Review*, 362–376. doi:10.1037/0033-295X.97.3.362.

Oncina, J. (2008). Using multiplicity automata to identify transducer relations from membership and equivalence queries. In *Proceedings of 9th International Colloquium on Grammatical Inference,* (vol. 5278, pp. 154–162). Berlin: Springer.

Pistori, H., & Martins, P. S. (2005). Adaptive finite state automata and genetic algorithms: Merging individual adaptation and population evolution. In *Proceedings of the International Conference on Adaptive and Natural Computing Algorithms – ICANNGA*. Coimbra: ICANNGA.

Platkowski, T., & Siwak, M. (2008). Mean-field approximation for two-and three-person prisoner's dilemmas. *Physica A: Statistical Mechanics and its Applications, 387*.

Rubinstein, A. (1986). Finite automata play the repeated prisoner's dilemma. *Journal of Economic Theory, 39*, 83–96. doi:10.1016/0022-0531(86)90021-9.

Schut, M. (2010). On model design for simulation of collective intelligence. *Information Sciences, 180*, 132–155. doi:10.1016/j.ins.2009.08.006.

Sipser, M. (1997). *Introduction to the theory of computation*. Boston: Academic Press.

Su, M., Hui, C., Zhang, Y., & Li, Z. (2009). How does the spatial structure of habitat loss affect the ecoepidemic dynamics? *Ecological Modelling, 220*, 51–59. doi:10.1016/j.ecolmodel.2008.09.009.

Szilagyi, M. (2003). An investigation of n-person prisoners' dilemmas. *Complex Systems, 14*(2).

Szilagyi, M. N. (2008). Agent-based simulation of n-person games with crossing payoff functions. *Complex Systems, 17*(4), 427.

Thakkar, D. (2004). *Game theoretic models of computation*. New York: Academic Press.

Thathachar, M. A. (1985). Learning systems: Stochastic automata models. *Defence Science Journal, 35*(3), 361–366.

van Leeuwen, J., & Wiedermann, J. (2001). *The turing machine paradigm in contemporary computing*. Mathematics Unlimited. doi:10.1007/978-3-642-56478-9_30.

Wolfram, S. (1994). *Cellular automata and complexity* (*Vol. 10*). Reading, MA: Addison–Wesley.

Zhang, H., Zhang, F., Li, Z., Gao, M., & Li, W. (2009). Evolutionary diversity and spatiotemporal dynamics of a spatial game. *Ecological Modelling, 220*, 2353–2364. doi:10.1016/j.ecolmodel.2009.06.005.

Zhang, J. (2009). Adaptive learning via selectionism and Bayesianism: Part I: Connection between the two. *Neural Networks, 22*(3), 220–228. doi:10.1016/j.neunet.2009.03.018 PMID:19386469.

Chapter 12

Reinforcement and Non–Reinforcement Machine Learning Classifiers for User Movement Prediction

Theodoros Anagnostopoulos
National and Kapodistrian University of Athens, Greece

ABSTRACT

Mobile context-aware applications are required to sense and react to changing environment conditions. Such applications, usually, need to recognize, classify, and predict context in order to act efficiently, beforehand, for the benefit of the user. In this chapter, the authors propose a mobility prediction model, which deals with context representation and location prediction of moving users. Machine Learning (ML) techniques are used for trajectory classification. Spatial and temporal on-line clustering is adopted. They rely on Adaptive Resonance Theory (ART) for location prediction. Location prediction is treated as a context classification problem. The authors introduce a novel classifier that applies a Hausdorff-like distance over the extracted trajectories handling location prediction. Two learning methods (non-reinforcement and reinforcement learning) are presented and evaluated. They compare ART with Self-Organizing Maps (SOM), Offline kMeans, and Online kMeans algorithms. Their findings are very promising for the use of the proposed model in mobile context aware applications.

INTRODUCTION

In order to render mobile context-aware applications intelligent enough to support users everywhere/anytime and materialize the so-called ambient intelligence, information on the present

context of the user has to be captured and processed accordingly. A well-known definition of context is the following: "context is any information that can be used to characterize the situation of an entity. An entity is a person, place or object that is considered relevant to the integration between

DOI: 10.4018/978-1-4666-4038-2.ch012

a user and an application, including the user and the application themselves" (Dey, 2001). Context refers to the current values of specific ingredients that represent the activity of an entity/situation and environmental state (e.g., attendance of a meeting, location, temperature).

One of the more intuitive capabilities of the mobile context-aware applications is their *pro-activity*. Predicting user actions and contextual ingredients enables a new class of applications to be developed along with the improvement of existing ones. One very important ingredient is location. Estimating and predicting the future location of a mobile user enables the development of innovative, location-based services/applications (Hightower & Borielo, 2001; Priggouris et al., 2006). For instance, location prediction can be used to improve resource reservation in wireless networks and facilitate the provision of location-based services by preparing and feeding them with the appropriate information well in advance. The accurate determination of the context of users and devices is the basis for context-aware applications. In order to adapt to changing demands, such applications need to reason based on basic context ingredients (e.g., time, location) to determine knowledge of higher-level situation.

Prediction of context is quite similar to information classification/prediction (*offline* and *online*). In this paper, we adopt ML techniques for predicting location through an adaptive model. ML is *the study of algorithms that improve automatically through experience*. ML provides algorithms for learning a system to cluster pre-existing knowledge, classify observations, predict unknown situations based on a history of patterns and adapt to situation changes. Therefore, ML can provide solutions that are suitable for the location prediction problem. Context-aware applications have a set of pivotal requirements (e.g., flexibility and adaptation), which would strongly benefit if the learning and prediction process could be performed in real time. We argue that the most

appropriate solutions for location prediction are offline and online clustering and classification. Offline clustering is performed through the Offline kMeans algorithm while online clustering is accomplished through the Self-Organizing Maps (SOM), Online kMeans and Adaptive Resonance Theory (ART). Offline learners typically perform complete model building, which can be very costly, if the amount of samples rises. Online learning algorithms are able to detect changes and adapt/update only parts of the model thus providing for fast adaptation of the model. Both forms of algorithms extract a subset of patterns/clusters (i.e., a knowledge base) from an initial dataset (i.e., a database of user itineraries). Moreover, online learning is more suited for the task of classification/prediction of the user mobility behavior as in the real life user movement data often needs to be processed in an online manner, each time after a new portion of the data arrives. This is caused by the fact that such data is organized in the form of a data stream (e.g., a sequence of time-stamped visited locations) rather than a static data repository, reflecting the natural flow of data. Classification involves the matching of an unseen pattern with existing clusters in the knowledge base. We rely on a Hausdorff-like distance (Belogay et al., 1997) for matching unseen itineraries to clusters (such metric applies to convex patterns and is considered ideal for user itineraries). Finally, location prediction boils down to location classification w.r.t. Hausdorff-like distance.

We assess two training methods for training an algorithm: (1) the "nearly" *zero-knowledge* method in which an algorithm is incrementally trained starting with a little knowledge on the user mobility behavior and the (2) *supervised* method in which sets of known itineraries are fed to the classifier. Moreover, we assess two learning methods for the online algorithms regarding the success of location prediction: (1) the *non-Reinforcement Learning* (nRL), in which a misclassified instance is no further used in the model-training phase, thus, the classifier is no longer aware of unsuccessful predictions, and (2) the *Reinforcement Learning* (RL), in which a misclassified instance is introduced into the knowledge base updating appropriately the model.

We evaluate the performance of our models against the movement of mobile users. Our objective is to predict the users' future location (their next move) through an on-line adaptive classifier. We establish some important metrics for the performance assessment process taking into account low system-requirements (storage capacity) and effort for model building (processing power). Specifically, besides the prediction accuracy, i.e., the precision of location predictions, we are also interested in the size of the derived knowledge base; that is the produced clusters out of the volume of the training patterns, and the capability of the classifier to adapt the derived model to unseen patterns. Surely, we need to keep storage capacity as low as possible while maintaining good prediction accuracy. Lastly, our objective is to assess the *adaptivity* of the proposed schemes, i.e., the capability of the predictor to detect and update appropriately the specific part of the trained model. The classifier (through the location prediction process) should rapidly detect changes in the behavior of the mobile user and adapt accordingly through model updates, however, often at the expense of classification accuracy (note that an ambient environment implies high dynamicity). We show that increased adaptivity leads to high accuracy and dependability.

The rest of the paper is structured as follows. In Section Machine Learning Models we present the considered ML models by introducing the Offline *k*Means, Online *k*Means, ART and SOM algorithms. In Section Context Representation we elaborate on the proposed model with context representation. Section Mobility Prediction Model presents the proposed mobility prediction model based on the ART algorithm. The performance assessment of the considered model is presented

in Section Prediction Evaluation, where different versions of that model are evaluated. Moreover, in Section Comparison with Other Models, we compare the ART models with the Offline/Online *k*Means and SOM algorithms as long as we report the computational complexity of all the algorithms discussed. Related work is discussed in Section Prior Work and we conclude the paper in Section Conclusions.

MACHINE LEARNING MODELS

In this section we briefly discuss the clustering algorithms used throughout the paper. Specifically, we distinguish between offline and online clustering and elaborate on the Offline/Online *k*Means and ART.

Offline kMeans

In Offline *k*Means (Alpaydin, 2004) we assume that there are $k > 1$ initial clusters (groups) of data. The objective of this algorithm is to minimize the reconstruction error, which is the total Euclidean distance between the instances (patterns), u_t, and their representation, i.e., the cluster centers (clusters), c_i. We define the reconstruction error as follows:

$$E\left(\left\{\mathbf{c}_i\right\}_{i=1}^k \mid U\right) = \frac{1}{2}\sum_t\sum_i b_{i,t} \parallel \mathbf{u}_t - \mathbf{c}_i \parallel^2 \tag{1}$$

$$b_{i,t} = \begin{cases} 1, & if \parallel \mathbf{u}_t - \mathbf{c}_i \parallel = \min_l \parallel \mathbf{u}_t - \mathbf{c}_l \parallel \\ 0, & otherwise \end{cases}$$

$U = \{\mathbf{u}_t\}$ is the total set of patterns and $C = \{\mathbf{c}_i\}$, $i = 1,\dots, k$ is the set of clusters. $b_{i,t}$ is 1 if $\mathbf{c}_i$ is the closest center to $\mathbf{u}_t$ in Euclidean distance. For each incoming $\mathbf{u}_t$ each $\mathbf{c}_i$ is updated as follows:

$$\mathbf{c}_i = \frac{\sum_t b_{i,t} \mathbf{u}_t}{\sum_t b_{i,t}} \qquad (2)$$

Since the algorithm operates in offline mode, the initial clusters can be set during the training phase and cannot be changed (increased or relocated) during the testing phase.

Online kMeans

In Online kMeans (Alpaydin, 2004) we assume that there are $k > 1$ initial clusters that split the data. Such algorithm processes unseen patterns one by one and performs *small* updates in the position of the appropriate cluster (c_i) at each step. The algorithm does not require a training phase. The update for each new (unseen) pattern u_t is the following:

$$\mathbf{c}_i = \mathbf{c}_i + \eta \cdot b_{i,t} \cdot \left(\mathbf{u}_t - \mathbf{c}_i \right)$$

This update moves the *closest* cluster (for which $b_{i,t} = 1$) toward the input pattern u_t by a factor of η. The other clusters (found at bigger distances from the considered pattern) are not updated. The semantics of $b_{i,t}$, η and $(u_t - c_i)$ are:

- $b_{i,t} \in \{0, 1\}$ denotes which cluster is being modified.
- $\eta \in [0, 1]$ denotes how much is the cluster shifted toward the new pattern.
- $(u_t - c_i)$ denotes the distance to be learned.

Since the algorithm is online, the initial clusters should be known beforehand[1] and can only be relocated during the testing phase. The number of clusters remains constant. Therefore, the algorithm exhibits limited flexibility.

Adaptive Resonance Theory

The ART approach (Duada et al., 2001) is an online learning scheme in which the set of patterns U is not available during training. Instead, patterns are received one by one and the model is updated progressively. The model has three crucial properties:

1. A normalization of the total network activity. Biological systems are usually very adaptive to large changes in their environment.
2. Contrast enhancement of input patterns. The awareness of subtle differences in input patterns can mean a lot in terms of survival. Distinguishing a hiding panther from a resting one makes all the difference in the world.
3. Short-term memory storage of the contrast-enhanced pattern. Before the input pattern can be decoded, it must be stored in the short-term memory. The long-term memory implements an arousal mechanism (i.e., the classification), whereas the STM is used to cause gradual changes in the LTM.

The system consists of two layers which are connected to each other via the long term memory. The input pattern is received at the first layer and classification takes place in the second layer. The term *competitive learning* is used for ART denoting that the (local) clusters *compete* among themselves to assume the "responsibility" for representing an unseen pattern. The model is also called *winner-takes-all* because one cluster "wins the competition" and gets updated, and the others are not updated at all.

The ART approach is *incremental*, meaning that one starts with one cluster and adds a new one, if needed. Given an input u_t, the distance b_t is calculated for all clusters c_i, $i = 1, .., k$, and the closest (e.g., minimum Euclidean distance) to u_t is updated. The closest cluster is called "winner". Specifically, if the minimum distance b_t is smaller than a certain threshold value, named the *vigilance*, ρ, the update is performed as in Online kMeans (see Eq.(3)). Otherwise, a new center c_{k+1} representing the corresponding input u_t is added in the model (see Eq.(3)). It is worth noting that the vigilance threshold refers to the criterion of considering two patterns equivalent or not during the learning phase of a classifier. As it will be shown, the value of vigilance is considered essential in obtaining high values of corrected classified patterns. The following equations are adopted in each update step of ART:

$$b_t = \| c_i - u_t \| = \min_{l=1}^{k} \| c_l - u_t \|$$
$$\begin{cases} c_{k+1} \leftarrow u_t & \text{if } b_t > \rho \\ c_i = c_i + \eta(u_t - c_i) & \text{otherwise} \end{cases} \tag{3}$$

Self-Organizing Maps

By adopting the ART algorithm, all clusters apart from the winner cluster are not updated once an input u_t is given. In the *Self-Organizing Maps* (SOM) algorithm the winner cluster and some of the other clusters are updated w.r.t. an input u_t to a certain extent. Specifically, SOM defines the *neighborhood* of a c_i cluster as the set $V_i(n)$ of those n clusters c_l closest to c_i, i.e., $V_i(n) = \{c_l: c_l = argmin_k \| c_k - c_i \|, k = 1,..., n\}$. When c_i is the winner cluster then, in addition to c_i, its neighbor clusters are also updated. For instance, if the neighborhood is of size $n = 2$, then the two closest clusters to c_i are also updated but with less weight as the neighborhood increases. The clusters $c_l \in V_i(n)$ are updated as:

$$c_l = c_l + \eta e(l, i)(u_t - c_l) \tag{3a}$$

$$e(l, i) = \frac{1}{\sqrt{2\pi}\sigma} e^{-\frac{(l-i)^2}{2\sigma^2}} \tag{3b}$$

CONTEXT REPRESENTATION

Several approaches have been proposed in order to represent the movement history (or history) of a mobile user (Cheng et al., 2003). We adopt a spatiotemporal history model in which the movement history is represented as the sequence of 3-D points (3DPs) visited by the moving user, i.e., time-stamped trajectory points in a 2D surface. The spatial attributes in that model denote latitude and longitude.

Let $e = (x, y, t)$ be a 3DP. The *user trajectory* u consists of several time-ordered 3DPs, $u = [e_i] = [e_1, ..., e_N]$, $i = 1, ..., N$ and is stored in the system's database. It holds that $t(e_1) < t(e_2) < ... < t(e_N)$, i.e., time-stamped coordinates. The x and y dimensions denote the latitude and the longitude while t denotes the time dimension (and $t(\cdot)$ returns the time coordinate of e). Time assumes values between 00:00 and 23:59. To avoid state information explosion, trajectories contain time-stamped points sampled at specific time instances. Specifically, we sample the movement of each user at $1.66 \cdot 10^{-3}$ Hertz (i.e., once every 10 minutes). Sampling at very high rates (e.g., in the order of a Hertz) is meaningless, as the derived points will be highly correlated. In our model, u is a finite sequence of N 3DPs, i.e., u is a $3 \cdot N$ dimension vector. We have adopted a value of $N = 6$ for our experiments meaning that we estimate the future position of a mobile terminal from a movement history of 50 minutes (i.e., 5 samples). Specifically, we aim to query the system with a $N-1$ 3DP sequence so that our classifier/predictor returns a 3DP, which is the predicted location of the mobile terminal.

A *cluster trajectory* c consists of a finite number of 3DPs, $c = [e_i]$, $i = 1, ..., N$ stored in the knowledge base. Note that a cluster trajectory c and a user trajectory u are vectors of the same length N. This is because c, which is created from ART based on unseen user trajectories, is a representative itinerary of the user movements. In addition, the *query trajectory* q consists of a number of 3DPs, $q = [e_j]$, $j = 1, ..., N-1$. It is worth noting that q is a sequence of $N-1$ 3DPs. Given a q with a $N-1$ history of 3DPs we predict the e_N of the closest c as the next user movement.

MOBILITY PREDICTION MODEL

From the ML perspective the discussed location prediction problem refers to an $m+l$ model (Curewitz et al., 1993). In $m+l$ models we have m steps of user movement history and we want to predict the future user movement after l steps (the steps have time-stamped coordinates). In our case, $m = N$-1, i.e., the query trajectory q, while $l = 1$, i.e., the predicted e_N. We develop a new spatiotemporal classifier (C) which given q can predict e_N. Specifically, q and c are trajectories of different length thus we use a Hausdorff-like measure for calculating the $\|q - c\|$ distance. Given query q, the proposed classifier C attempts to find the nearest cluster c in the knowledge base and, then, take e_N as the *predicted* 3DP. For evaluating C, we compute the Euclidean distance between the predicted 3DP and the *actual* 3DP (i.e., the real user movement). If such distance is greater than a preset error threshold θ then prediction is not successful. After predicting the future location of a mobile terminal, the C classifier may receive feedback from the environment considering whether the prediction was successful or not, and reorganize the knowledge base accordingly (Narendra & Thathachar, 1989). In our case, the feedback is the actual 3DP observed in the terminal's movement. We can have two basic versions of the C classifier:

1. The C-RL classifier, which reacts with the environment and learns new patterns through reinforcement learning once an unsuccessful prediction takes place,
2. The C-nRL classifier, which is unaware of unsuccessful predictions.

Specifically,

*   In case of an unsuccessful prediction, the C-RL appends the actual 3DP to q and reinforces such extended sequence in the model considering as new knowledge, i.e., an unseen user movement behavior.

*   In the case of a successful prediction, we do not reinforce C to learn. A successful prediction refers to a well-established prediction model for handling unseen user trajectories.

The heart of the proposed C classifier is the ART algorithm. ART clusters unseen user trajectories to existing cluster trajectories or creating new cluster trajectories depending on the vigilance value. ART is taking the u_1 pattern from the incoming set U of patterns and stores it as the c_1 cluster in the knowledge base. For the t-th unseen user trajectory the following procedure is followed (see Table 1): The algorithm computes the Euclidean distance b_t between u_t and the closest c_i. If b_t is smaller than the vigilance ρ then c_i is updated from u_t by the η factor. Otherwise, a new cluster $c_j \equiv u_t$ is inserted into the knowledge base. The ART algorithm is presented in Table 1.

Let T, P be subsets of U for which it holds that $T \subseteq P \subseteq U$. The T set of patterns is used for training the C classifier, that is, C develops a knowledge base corresponding to the supervised training method. The P set is used for performing on-line predictions. We introduce the C-RLT and the C-nRLT classifier versions, which are the C-RL and C-nRL classifiers trained with the T set, respectively. In addition, once the T set is null then the

Table 1. The ART algorithm for the C classifier

1.	$j \leftarrow 1$
2.	$c_j \leftarrow u_j$
3.	For ($u_t \in U$) Do
4.	$b_t = \|c_j - u_t\| = \min_{i=1,...,j}\|c_i - u_t\|$
5.	If ($b_t > \rho$) Then/*expand knowledge*/
6.	$j \leftarrow j + 1$ $c_j \leftarrow u_t$
7.	Else
8.	$c_j \leftarrow c_j + \eta(u_t - c_j)$/*update model locally*/
9.	End If
10.	End for

C classifier is not trained beforehand corresponding to the zero-knowledge training method and performs on-line prediction with the set P. In this case, we get the C-RLnT and the C-nRLnT classifiers corresponding to the C-RL and C-nRL classifiers, respectively, when the training phase is foreseen.

Moreover, in order for the C classifier to achieve prediction, an approximate Hausdorff-like metric (Belogay et al., 1997) is adopted to estimate the distance between q and c. Specifically, the adopted formula calculates the point-to-vector distance between $e_j \in q$ and c, $\delta'(e_j, c)$, as follows:

$$\delta'\left(\mathbf{e}_j, \mathbf{c}\right) = \| \mathbf{f}_i - \mathbf{e}_j \|_{\min_{f_i} |t(f_i) - t(e_j)|}$$

where $\| \cdot \|$ is the Euclidean norm for $f_i \in c$ and e_j. The $\delta'(e_j, c)$ value indicates the minimum distance between e_j and f_i w.r.t. the time stamped information of the user itinerary, that is the Euclidean distance of the closest 3DPs in time. Hence, the overall distance between the N-1 in length q and the N in length c is calculated as

$$\delta_{N-1}(\mathbf{q}, \mathbf{c}) = \frac{1}{N-1} \sum_{e_j \in q} \delta'(\mathbf{e}_j, \mathbf{c}) \qquad (4)$$

Figure 1 depicts the process of predicting the next user movement considering the diverse versions of the proposed C classifier. Specifically, once a query trajectory q arrives, then C attempts to classify q into a known c_i in the knowledge base w.r.t. Hausdorff metric. The C classifier returns the predicted $e_N \in c_i$ of the closest c_i to q. Once such result refers to an unsuccessful prediction w.r.t. a preset error threshold θ then the C-RLT (or the C-RLnT) extend the q vector with the actual 3DP and insert q into the knowledge base for further learning according to the algorithm in Table 1 (feedback). By adopting the non-reinforcement learning method, the C classifier (the C-nRLT/-nRLnT versions) does not give feedback to the knowledge base.

Figure 1. The proposed adaptive classifier for location prediction

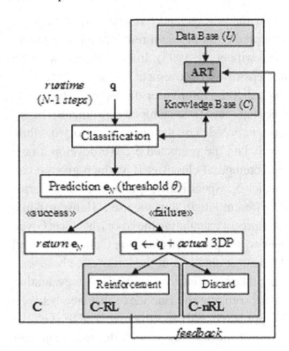

PREDICTION EVALUATION

We evaluated our adaptive model in order to assess its performance. In our experiments, the overall user movement space has a surface of 540 Km². Such space derives from real GPS trace captured in Denmark (OpenStreetMap). The GPS trace was fed into our model and the performance of the C system w.r.t. predefined metrics was monitored. Table 2 indicates the parameters used in our experiments.

The GPS traces including 1200 patterns were preprocessed and we produced two training files and two test files as depicted in Figure 2. The first training file, *TrainA*, is produced from the first half of the GPS trace records. The second training file, *TrainB*, consists of a single trace record. The first test file, *TestA*, is produced from the entire set of trace records, including—in ascending order—the first half of the GPS traces and the other half of unseen traces. Finally the second test file, *TestB*, is produced from the entire set of the GPS trace records, including—in ascending or-

Table 2. Experimental parameters

Parameter	Value	Comment
Learning rate (r)	0.5	In case of a new pattern u_t, the closest cluster c_i is moved toward u_t by half of the spatial and temporal distance.
Spatial coefficient of vigilance (ρ_s)	100m	Two 2D points are considered different over one hundred meters.
Temporal coefficient of vigilance (ρ_t)	10min	Two time-stamps are different over ten minutes.
Precision threshold/location accuracy (θ)	10m	The predicted location is within a valuable area of ten meters.

Figure 2. The generated GPS trace files for experimentation

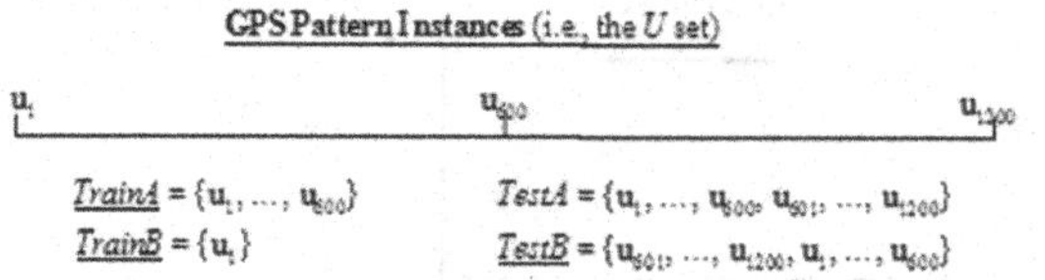

der—the second half of unseen traces and the first half of the GPS traces. During the generation of the training/test files, white noise was artificially induced into the trace records.

We have to quantitatively and qualitatively evaluate the proposed model. For that reason, we introduce the following quantitative and qualitative parameters: (a) the precision achieved by the prediction scheme—the higher the precision the more accurate the decisions on the future user location—(b) the size of the underlying knowledge base—we should adopt solutions with the lowest possible knowledge base size (such solutions are far more efficient and feasible in terms of implementation), and (c) the capability of the model to rapidly react to changes in the movement pattern of the user/mobile terminal and re-adapt. We define *precision*, p, as the fraction of the correctly predicted locations, p_+, against the total number of predictions made by the C system, p_{total}, that is,

$$p = \frac{p_+}{p_{total}}$$

In the following sub-sections, we evaluate the diverse versions of the C classifier w.r.t. training and learning methods by examining the classifier convergence (speed of learning and adaptation) and the derived precision on prediction future locations.

Convergence of C-RLT and C-RLnT

The C classifier converges once the knowledge base does not expand with unseen patterns, i.e., the set U does not evolve. In Figure 3, we plot the number of the clusters, $|U|$, that are generated from the C-RLT/-RLnT models with reinforcement learning during the testing phase. The horizontal axis denotes the incoming (time-ordered) GPS patterns. The point (.) marked line depicts the behavior of the C-RLT-1 model trained with *TrainA* and tested with *TestA*. In the training phase, the first 600 patterns of *TrainA* have gradually generated 70 clusters in U. In the testing phase, the first 600 patterns are known to the classifier so there is no new cluster creation. On the other hand, in the rest 600 unseen patterns, the number of clusters scales up to 110 indicating that the ART algorithm is "reinforced" to learn such new patterns.

The circle (o) marked line depicts the C-RLT-2 model, which is trained with *TrainA* and tested with *TestB*. Since the train file is the same as in the C-RLT-1 model, the first generated clusters are the same in number ($|U| = 70$). In the testing phase, we observe a significant difference. ART does not know the second 600 unseen patterns,

Figure 3. Convergence of C-RLT/-RLnT based on the reinforcement learning method

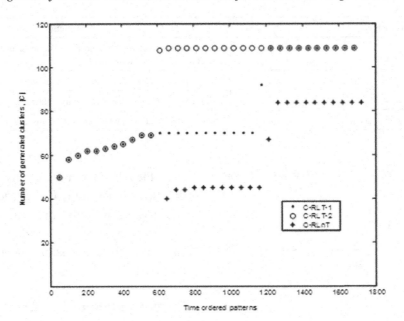

thus, it is gradually "reinforced" to learn new patterns up to 110 clusters. In the next 600 known patters, C-RLT-2 does not need to learn additional clusters thus it settles at 110 clusters.

We now examine the behavior of the C-RLnT model corresponding to the zero-knowledge training method. The asterisk (*) marked line depicts the training phase (with *TrainB*) followed by the testing phase (with *TestA*) of C-RLnT. In this case, we have an incremental ART that does not need to be trained. For technical consistency reasons, it only requires a single pattern, which is the unique cluster in the knowledge base at the beginning. In the testing phase, for the first 600 unseen patterns of *TestA* we observe a progressive cluster creation (up to 45 clusters). For the next 600 unseen patterns, we also observe a gradual cluster creation (up to 85 clusters) followed by convergence. Comparing the C-RLT-1/-2 and C-RLnT models, the latter one achieves the minimum number of clusters (22.72% less storage cost). This is due to the fact that C-RLnT starts learning only from unsuccessful predictions in an incremental way by adapting pre-existing knowledge base to new instances. Nevertheless, we also have to take

into account the prediction accuracy in order to reach safe conclusions about the efficiency and effectiveness of the proposed models.

Precision of C-RLT and C-RLnT

In Figure 4 we examine the precision achieved by the algorithms adopting reinforcement learning. The vertical axis depicts the precision value p achieved during the testing phase. The point (.) marked line depicts the precision of the C-RLT-1 model trained with *TrainA* and tested with *TestA*. During the test phase, for the first 600 known patterns C-RLT-1 achieves precision value ranging from 97% to 100%. In the next 600 unseen patterns, we observe that for the first instances the precision drops smoothly to 95% and as C-RLT-1 is reinforced to learn, i.e., learn new clusters and optimize the old ones, the precision converges to 96%.

The circle (o) marked line depicts the precision behavior for the C-RLT-2 model tested with *TestB* and trained with *TrainA*. With the first 600 totally unseen patterns during the test phase, C-RLT-2 achieves precision from 26% to 96%. This

Figure 4. Precision of C-RLT/-RLnT based on the reinforcement learning method

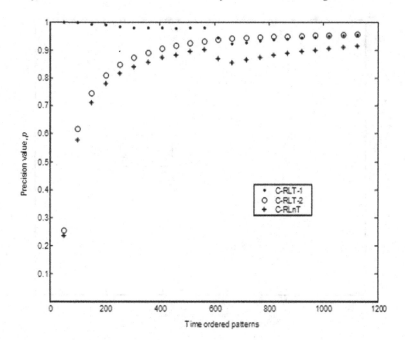

indicates that the model is still learning during the test phase adopting the reinforcement learning method increasing the precision value. In the next 600 known patterns, the model has nothing to learn and the precision value converges to 96%.

The asterisk (*) marked line depicts the precision behavior of the C-RLnT model tested with *TestA* and trained with *TrainB*. In this case, C-RLnT is trained with only one pattern instance, i.e., the algorithm is fully incremental, thus, all the instances are treated as unseen. In the test phase, for the first 600 patterns, the model achieves precision, which ranges from 25% to 91% (due to the reinforcement mechanism). In the next 600 patterns, we can notice that for the first instances the precision drops smoothly to 88% and as the model is "reinforced" to learn, precision gradually converges to 93%.

Evidently, the adoption of the training method, i.e., the C-RLT-1/-2 models, yields better precision. However, if we correlate our findings with the results shown in Figure 3, we infer that a small improvement in precision has an obvious storage

cost. Specifically, we need to store 110 clusters, in the case of C-RLT, compared to 85 clusters in the case of C-RLnT (22.72% less storage cost). Furthermore, the user movement patterns can be changed repeatedly over time. Hence, by adopting the training method, one has to regularly train and rebuild the model. Nevertheless, we have to examine the behavior of the C-nRLT and C-nRLnT models in order to decide on the appropriate model for the discussed domain.

Convergence of C-nRLT and C-nRLnT

In Figure 5, we see the number of clusters that are generated by C-nRLT/-nRLnT assuming the non-reinforcement learning method. The vertical axis indicates the generated clusters during the training and the testing phase. The point (.) marked line depicts the training phase with *TrainA* and the testing phase with *TestA* for the C-nRLT-1 model. As we can see in the training phase, the first 600 patterns (*TrainA*) have gener-

Figure 5. Convergence of C-nRLT/-nRLnT based on the non-reinforcement learning method

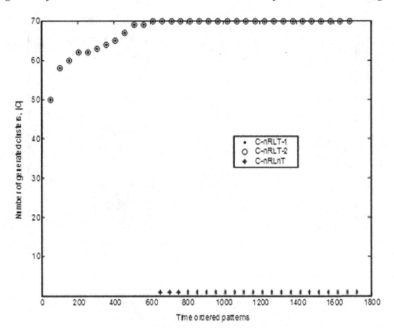

ated 70 clusters. In the testing phase, the model knows the first 600 patterns thus there is no new cluster creation. Contrast to the C-RLT-1 model (Section Prediction Evaluation), the remaining 600 unseen patterns cannot be further learned by the C-nRLT-1, thus, the total of clusters remains constant at 70 clusters.

The circle (o) marked line depicts the training phase with *TrainA* and the testing phase with *TestB* for the C-nRLT-2 model. Since the train file is the same, (i.e., *TrainA*), the count of the generated clusters is the same (70 clusters) as before. In contrast to C-RLT-2, in the testing phase we do not observe a change in the number of clusters. The model does not know the second 600 unseen patterns and is not reinforced to learn new ones, thus, the total cluster count remains constant at 70. In the next 600 known patterns, the model retains the same cluster count (70 clusters).

Finally, the asterisk (*) marked line depicts generated number of clusters for the C-nRLnT model tested with *TestA*. In this case, we have an incremental, non-reinforcement model that is not trained. In the testing phase, for the first 600

unseen patterns we observe that there is no extra cluster generation except the unique cluster (of the *TrainB* file). In addition, for the next 600 unseen patterns, no additional cluster generation is observed. We only notice that the C-nRLT/-nRLnT models achieve a lower amount of clusters than the C-RLT/-RLnT models.

Precision of C-nRLT and C-nRLnT

In Figure 6, we see the precision of the models adopting the non-reinforcement learning. The vertical axis shows the precision value achieved during the testing phase. The point (.) marked line refers to the C-nRLT-1 model (trained with *TrainA*, tested with *TestA*). In the testing phase, the first 600 known patterns achieve precision levels ranging from 97% to 100%. In the next 600 unseen patterns, we notice that the precision value drops gradually to 59%. This is attributed to the fact that there are no new clusters to optimize the old ones due to the lack of the reinforcement learning mechanism. This indicates that C-nRLT-1 model does not adapt to new knowledge.

Figure 6. Precision of C (-nRLT/-nRLnT) based on the non-reinforcement learning method

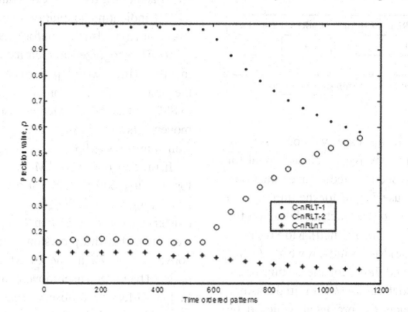

The circle (o) marked line refers to the C-nRLT-2 model (trained with *TrainA*, tested with *TestB*). In the testing phase, the first 600 unseen patterns achieve precision levels ranging from 16% to 19% because the reinforcement mechanism is not used and, thus, new clusters cannot derive. In the next 600 known patterns, we notice that the precision value converges to 59%.

Finally, the asterisk (*) marked line depicts the behavior of the precision of the C-nRLnT model (loaded with *TrainB*, tested with *TestA*). In this scenario, the classifier is fully incremental and all instances are treated as unseen. As we can see in the testing phase the first 600 patterns achieve precision levels ranging from 10% to 14% and, in the next 600 pattern instances, we notice that the precision value drops smoothly to 7%. Evidently, the C-nRLT/-nRLnT models achieve much lower precision than their counterparts C-RLT/-RLnT since the former models do not support adaptation.

Therefore, the adoption of the reinforcement learning method for location prediction produces better results than a non-reinforcement classifier. Each approach has certain advantages and limitations. If the major concern is to keep the storage

cost as lightweight as possible, the C-RLnT and C-nRLnT models should be chosen. If the mobile context-aware application aims at maximizing the supported quality of service w.r.t. precision, while keeping the storage cost stable, the C-RLnT model should be adopted. Table 3 summarizes our conclusions with respect to the comparison of the four alternative models discussed throughout the paper. Comparing the four versions of the C classifier, we can clearly distinguish the C-RLnT model as the most efficient classifier for location prediction.

COMPARISON WITH THE OTHER MODELS

We compare the C-RLnT model with other known models that can be used for location prediction. Such models implement the Offline *k*Means and Online *k*Means algorithms. Such models require a predefined number of $k > 1$ initial clusters for constructing the corresponding knowledge base. We should stress here that, the greater the k the greater the precision value achieved by Offline/

Table 3. Models comparison

Metric/Model	C-RLT	C-RLnT	C-nRLT	C-nRLnT
Precision	++	+	-	--
Storage	--	+	--	++
++: *Excellent performance*, --: *Very poor performance*				

Online *k*Means. In our case, we could set $k = 110$, which is the convergence cluster-count for the C-RL models (Section Prediction Evaluation). For C-RLnT, we use *TrainB* for the training and *TestA* for the testing phase (such model adopts the zero-knowledge training method). Moreover, for the Offline/Online *k*Means models we use *TrainA* for the training and *TestA* for the testing phase because both models require $k > 1$ initial clusters.

Figure 7 depicts the precision achieved by the C-RLnT (the point (.) marked line), Offline *k*Means (the asterisk (*) marked line) and Online *k*Means (the circle (o) marked line) models. The horizontal axis represents the ordered instances and the vertical axis represents the achieved precision. We can observe in the first 600 patterns C-

RLnT achieves precision levels ranging from 25% to 91% indicating adaptation to new knowledge. This is attributed to the reinforcement mechanism (C-RLnT recognizes and learns new user movements). In the next 600 patterns we notice that for the first instances, the precision drops smoothly to 88% and as the knowledge base adapts to new movements and optimizes the existing ones, precision converges to 93%.

In the case of Offline *k*Means, we observe that for the first 600 patterns, it achieves precision levels ranging from 96% to 98% once the initial clusters are set to $k = 110$. In the next 600 patterns we notice that the precision drops sharply and converges to 57% as the knowledge base is not updated by unseen user movements. By adopting Online *k*Means we observe that for the testing phase (the first 600 patterns) it achieves precision levels ranging from 94% to 97% given the train file *TrainA*. In the next 600 patterns we notice that for the first instances the precision drops rather smoothly to 86% and, as the knowledge base is incrementally adapting to new patterns, the precision value converges to 65%. Evidently,

Figure 7. Comparison of C-RLnT with the offline/online kmeans models

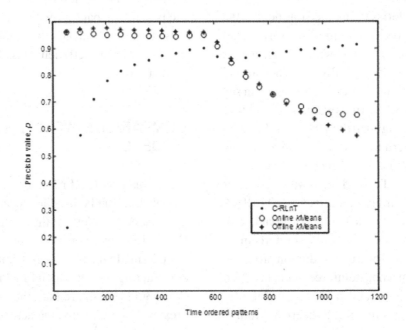

by comparing such three models, the most suitable model for location prediction is the C-RLnT since (i) it achieves greater precision through model adaptation and (ii) requires a smaller size of the underlying knowledge base (i.e., less clusters) than the Offline/Online kMeans models.

Moreover, we compare the C-RLnT model with the SOM model. We have experimented with $n = 5$ and $n = 10$ neighboring clusters of the winner cluster. In Figure 8 we can observe that the precision value for the SOM model (the asterisk (*) and point (.) marked line) increases as the number of neighboring clusters decreases. In case of $n = 0$, that is, no neighboring clusters are updated, i.e., the C-RLnT model (the circle (o) marked line), we can achieve the best precision.

Up to this point we have concluded that the C-RLnT model achieves good precision with limited memory requirements, which are very important parameters for mobile context-aware systems. However, we need to perform some tests with C-RLnT in order to determine the best value for the spatiotemporal parameter vigilance ρ. In other words, we aim to determine the best values

for both spatial ρ_s and temporal ρ_t vigilance coefficients in order to obtain the highest precision with low memory requirements. We introduce the weighted sum γ as follows:

$$\gamma = w \cdot p + (1 - w) \cdot (1 - a)$$

where a is the proportion of the generated clusters by the classifier (i.e., the size of the knowledge base in clusters) out of the total movement patterns (i.e., the size of the database in patterns), that is: $a = |C|/|U|$; $|C|$ is the cardinality of the set C. The weight value $w \in [0, 1]$ indicates the importance of precision and memory requirements; a value of $w = 0.5$ assigns equal importance to a and p. In our assessment, we set $w = 0.7$. We require that a assumes low values minimizing the storage cost of the classifier. A low value of a indicates that the applied classifier appropriately adopts and learns the user movements without retaining redundant information. The value of γ indicates which values of ρ_s and ρ_t maximize the precision while, on the same time, minimize the memory requirements. Hence, our aim is to achieve a high

Figure 8. Comparison of the C-RLnT with the SOM model for n = 5 and n = 10 neighboring clusters

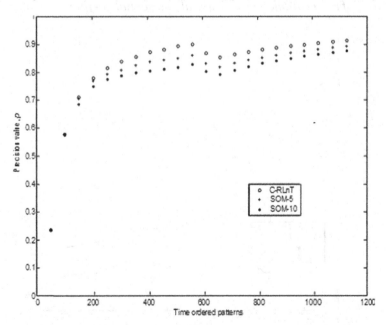

value of γ indicating an adaptive classifier with high value of precision along with low storage cost. As illustrated in Figure 9, we obtain a global maximum value for γ once $\rho_s = 100m$ and $\rho_t = 10min$ (which are the setting values during the experiments – See Table 3).

In addition, we examine the adaptivity capability of a model M that does not have prior knowledge, i.e., $M \in \{\text{C-RLnT, SOM-5, SOM-10}\}$. The term adaptivity capability for a model M refers to the time need M to reach a convergent precision value $p_{max}(M)$ given a change in the user mobility pattern. Specifically, adaptivity denotes how fast the precision value $p(M)$ for a model M reaches at $p_{max}(M)$. Consider a user that changes K times its mobility pattern, that is, the user alters its itineraries. This reflects to K changes to some set of clusters in the knowledge base. Let also the jth change in the mobility pattern of a user. The jth change is characterized by the convergent value $p^j_{max}(M)$ since a model M converges each time a change occurs. We introduce the metric $\delta_j(M)$ for a model M (w.r.t. a given user) that denotes the rate at which the precision value $p_{ij}(M)$ reaches $p^j_{max}(M)$ during the jth change, that is,

$$\delta_j\left(\mathbf{M}\right) = \sum_{i=1}^{|U_j|} |\; p^j_{max}\left(\mathbf{M}\right) - p_{ij}\left(\mathbf{M}\right)\;|$$

where U_j is the set time ordered patterns that refer to the jth change. The $\delta_j(M)$ value sums the differences of the precision value $p_{ij}(M)$ (achieved by model M at the ith pattern in U) from the convergent value $p^j_{max}(M)$. We require that $\delta_j(M)$ assume low values, which denotes that the model M quickly converges after a jth change. Hence, the metric

$$\delta\left(\mathbf{M}\right) = \sum_{j=1}^{K} \delta_j\left(\mathbf{M}\right) \qquad (5)$$

Assumes low values, w.r.t. all time ordered patterns in U, denoting that the model M adapts quickly to each jth change, $j = 1, ..., K$. The adaptivity curve $\delta(M)$ should be sharp until the first convergence (in the 1st change the knowledge base attempts to adapt to each input pattern in U_1). For the changes $j = 2, ..., K$ the difference between $\delta_j(M)$ and $\delta_{j+1}(M)$ should be as low as possible thus leading to quick adaptation.

Figure 9. The behavior of the γ parameter vs. temporal and spatial coefficients of the vigilance threshold

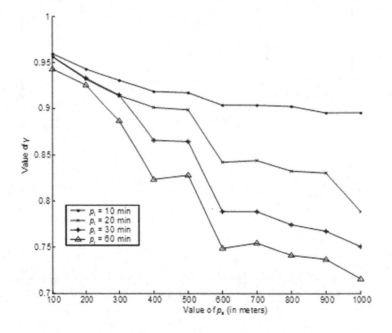

Figure 10 depicts the behavior of δ(M) for K = 2 changes. We can observe that δ(SOM-5) and δ(SOM-10) assume higher sums and less sharpness from the first convergence until the second one than δ(C-RLnT). This is attributed to the fact that in SOM-5 the five neighboring clusters to the winner one are moved towards the new input pattern. This implies that, the SOM-5 has to achieve convergence for all (possibly different) five neighbors given an input pattern. Hence, SOM-5 reaches at p^j_{max} (SOM-5) later than C-RLnT, for all j. The same holds for SOM-10. According to this metric, the C-RLnT model is deemed appropriate in our domain.

In the following, we report the time and space complexity of the models in order to predict future location. Given the set of patterns U and the set of clusters C, the time and space complexities are given in Table 4.

The Offline kMeans has time complexity O($|U||C|$), where C is fixed in advance. This means that Offline kMeans has linear time complexity w.r.t. the size of U. Its corresponding space complexity is O($|U|+|C|$), as it requires additional space to store the initial set of patterns. The Online

Table 4. Time and space complexity

Model	Time Complexity	Space Complexity
Offline kMeans	O($|U||C|$)	O($|U|+|C|$)
Online kMeans	O($|U||C|$)	O($|C|$)
ART	O($|U||C|$)	O($|C|$)
SOM	O($|U||C|$)	O($|C|$)

kMeans, ART and SOM models have space complexity depending on the number of possible generated clusters only (i.e., O($|C|$)). The corresponding time complexity is linearly to the set of patterns (i.e., O($|U||C|$)) (Lensu & Koikkalainen, 2002).

PRIOR WORK

Previous work in the area of mobility prediction includes the model in (Choi & Shin, 1998), which uses Naïve Bayes classification over the user movement history. Such model does not deal with fully/semi- random mobility patterns

Figure 10. Adaptivity capability for C-RLnT, SOM-5, SOM-10 incremental models

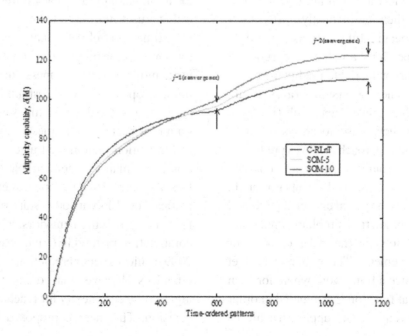

and assumes a normal density distribution of the underlying data. However, such assumptions are not considered in our model as long as mobility patterns refer to real human traces with unknown distribution. Moreover, the learning automaton in (Hadjiefthymiades & Merakos, 2003) follows a linear reward-penalty reinforcement learning method for location prediction. However, such model does not assume satisfactory correct predictions, as reported in (Hadjiefthymiades & Merakos, 2003). The authors in (Karmouch & Samaan, 2005) apply evidential reasoning in mobility prediction when knowledge on the mobility patterns is not available (i.e., like our case). Yet, such model assumes large computational complexity (derived from the adopted Dempster-Schafer algorithm) once the amount of possible locations (the user moves to) increases and requires detailed user information (e.g., daily profile, preferences, favorite meeting places). Other methods for predicting trajectory have also been proposed in the literature (Viayan & Holtman, 1993) but these have generally been limited in scope since they consider rectilinear movement patterns only (e.g., highways) and not unknown patterns, as dealt with in our model. A closely related work has been carried out in (Ashrook & Starner, 2002), where a GPS system is used to collect location information. The proposed system then automatically clusters GPS data taken into meaningful locations at multiple scales. These locations are then incorporated into a similar Markov model to predict the user's future location. The authors in (Yavas et al., 2005) adopt a data mining approach (i.e., rule extraction) for predicting user locations in mobile environments. This approach achieves prediction accuracy lower than ours (i.e., in the order of 80% for deterministic movement). In (Katsaros et al., 2003), the authors adopt a clustering method for the location prediction problem. Prediction accuracy is still low (in the order of 66% for deterministic movement). The authors in (Tao et al., 2004) introduce a framework where for each user an individual function is computed in order to capture its movement. This approach achieves

prediction accuracy lower than ours (i.e., in the order of 70% for deterministic movement). In (Nhan & Ryu, 2006), the authors apply movement rules in mobility prediction given the user's past movement patterns. Prediction accuracy is still low (i.e., in the order of 65% for deterministic movement). The authors in (Xiao et al., 2007) introduce a prediction model that uses grey theory (i.e., a theory used to study uncertainty). This approach achieves prediction accuracy lower than ours (i.e., in the order of 82% for deterministic movement). The authors in (Samaan & Karmouch, 2005) apply evidential reasoning for location prediction when knowledge on the mobility patterns is not available. This model suffers from increased computational complexity attributed to the Dempster-Shafer algorithm. It also requires detailed user information (e.g., daily movement profile, favorite meeting places).

The authors in (Jeung et al., 2008) apply a hybrid model for location prediction. The key component of the model in (Jeung et al., 2008) is a database of association rules. Such model uses association rule mining for specific user patterns. If no rules can be exploited (i.e., an unknown user pattern) the query engine uses a Recursive Motion Function (RMF) to predict the next user location. A major drawback of the hybrid model is that it uses more detailed mobility information (i.e., time and velocity) than our LPs. The performance of the proposed scheme is not assessed w.r.t. movement randomness. In the prediction model proposed in (Anagnostopoulos et al., 2007) a single, quantized timestamp is attached to each training trajectory. This timestamp refers to the last cell transition seen in the trajectory. The prediction performance is comparable to some of our LPs. Also, in (Anagnostopoulos et al., 2009), we compare our LPs with other state-of-art predictors for varying moving behaviors. The multi-expert combination method in (Anagnostopoulos et al., 2009) achieves better prediction accuracy than the other LPs. However, that comes at the expense of higher time complexity for reaching a prediction decision. The method proposed in (Akoush &

Sameh, 2007) uses Bayesian learning to train a Neural Network and Markov chain Monte Carlo methods (MCMC) to obtain a prediction. In addition, the authors in (Burbey, 2008) exhibit a Prediction-by-Partial-Match model. The key component of the proposed model is a variable order Markov Model which uses various lengths of previous patterns to build a predictive model. Both prediction models in (Akoush & Sameh, 2007) and (Burbey, 2008) assume high computational complexity due to the adopted Markov model.

CONCLUSION

We presented how ML techniques can be applied to the engineering of mobile context-aware applications for location prediction. Specifically, we use ART (a special Neural Network Local Model) and introduce two learning methods: one with non-reinforcement learning and one with reinforcement learning. Furthermore, we deal with two training methods for each learning method: in the supervised method, the model uses training data in order to make classification and in the zero-knowledge method, the model incrementally learns from unsuccessful predictions. We evaluated our models with different spatial and temporal parameters. We examine the knowledge bases storage cost (i.e., emerged clusters) and the precision measures (prediction accuracy). Our findings indicate that the C-RLnT model suits better to context-aware systems. The advantage of C-RLnT model is that (1) it does not require pre-existing knowledge in the user movement behavior in order to predict future movements, (2) it adapts its on-line knowledge base to unseen patterns, and (3) it does not consumes much memory to store the emerged clusters. For this reason, C-RLnT is quite useful in context-aware applications where no prior knowledge about the user context is available. Furthermore, through experiments, we decide on which vigilance value achieves the appropriate precision w.r.t. memory limitations and prediction error.

REFERENCES

Alpaydin, E. (2004). *Introduction to machine learning*. Boston: The MIT Press.

Ashbrook, D., & Starner, T. (2002). Learning significant locations and predicting user movement with GPS. In *Proceedings of the Sixth International Symposium on Wearable Computers (ISWC 2002)*, (pp. 101-108). ISWC.

Belogay, E., Cabrelli, C., Molter, U., & Shonkwiler, R. (1997). Calculating the Hausdorff distance between curves. *Information Processing Letters*, *64*(1), 17–22. doi:10.1016/S0020-0190(97)00140-3.

Cheng, R., Jain, E., & van den Berg. (2003). Location prediction algorithms for mobile wireless systems. In *Wireless Internet handbook: Technologies, standards, and application*, (pp. 245-263). Boca Raton, FL: CRC Press.

Choi, S., & Shin, K. G. (1998). Predictive and adaptive bandwidth reservation for hand-offs in QoS-sensitive cellular networks. In *Proceedings of ACM SIGCOMM*. ACM.

Curewitz, K. M., Krishnan, P., & Vitter, J. S. (1993). Practical Prefetching via Data Compression. *Proceedings of ACM SIGMOD*, pp. 257-266.

Dey, A. (2001). Understanding and using context. *Personal and Ubiquitous Computing*, *5*(1), 4–7. doi:10.1007/s007790170019.

Duda, R., Hart, P., & Stork, D. (2001). *Pattern Classification*. Wiley-Interscience.

Hadjiefthymiades, S., & Merakos, L. (2003). *Proxies+Path Prediction: Improving Web Service Provision in Wireless-Mobile Communications* (*Vol. 8*, p. 4). ACM/Kluwer Mobile Networks and Applications, Special Issue on Mobile and Wireless Data Management.

Hightower, J., & Borriello, G. (2001). *Location Systems for Ubiquitous Computing* (*Vol. 34*, p. 8). IEEE Computer.

Karmouch, A., & Samaan, N. (2005). A Mobility Prediction Architecture Based on Contextual Knowledge and Spatial Conceptual Maps. *IEEE Transactions on Mobile Computing, 4*(6).

Katsaros, D., Nanopoulos, A., Karakaya, M., Yavas, G., Ulusoy, O., & Manolopoulos, Y. (2003). Clustering Mobile Trajectories for Resource Allocation in Mobile Environments. *In Proceedings IDA*, pp. 319-329.

Lensu, A., & Koikkalainen, P. (2002). *Artificial Neural Networks*. ICANN.

Narendra, K., & Thathachar, M. A. L. (1989). *Learning Automata – An Introduction*. Prentice Hall.

Nhan, V. T. H., & Ryu, K. H. (2006). Future Location Prediction of Moving Objects Based on Movement Rules. *Springer ICIC 2006. LNCIS, 344*, 875–881.

OpenStreetMap. Webite: http://www.openstreetmap.org/traces/tag/Denmark

Priggouris, I., Zervas, E., & Hadjiefthymiades, S. (2006). Location Based Network Resource Management. In Ibrahim, I. K. (Ed.), *Handbook of Research on Mobile Multimedia*. Idea Group Inc. doi:10.4018/978-1-59140-866-6.ch011.

Tao, Y., Faloutsos, C., Papadias, D., & Liu, B. (2004). *Prediction and Indexing of Moving Objects with Unknown Motion Patterns*. ACM SIGMOD. doi:10.1145/1007568.1007637.

Viayan, R., & Holtman, J. (1993). *A model for analyzing handoff algorithms* (*Vol. 42*, p. 3). IEEE Trans. on Veh. Technol.

Xiao, Y., Zhang, H., & Wang, H. (2007). Location Prediction for Tracking Moving Objects Based on Grey Theory. *IEEE FSKD 2007.*

Yavas, G., Katsaros, D., Ulusoy, O., & Manolopoulos, Y. (2005). A data mining approach for location prediction in mobile environments. *Data & Knowledge Engineering, 54*(2). doi:10.1016/j.datak.2004.09.004.

ADDITIONAL READING

Akyildiz, I. F. et al. (1999). Mobility management for next generation wireless systems. *Proceedings of the IEEE, 87*(8), 1347–1385. doi:10.1109/5.775420.

Anagnostopoulos, T., Anagnostopoulos, C., & Hadjiefthymiades, S. (2009). An online adaptive model for location prediction. In *Proceedings of ICST Autonomics 2009*. Limassol, Cyprus: ICST.

Anagnostopoulos, T., Anagnostopoulos, C., & Hadjiefthymiades, S. (2011). An adaptive machine learning algorithm for location prediction. *International Journal of Wireless Information Networks, 18*, 88–99. doi:10.1007/s10776-011-0142-4.

Bharghavan, V., & Jayanth, M. (1997). Profile-based next-cell prediction in indoor wireless LAN. In *Proceedings of IEEE SICON*. Singapore: IEEE.

Biesterfeld, J., Ennigrou, E., & Jobmann, K. (1997). Location prediction in mobile networks with neural networks. In *Proceedings of the International Workshop on Applied Neural Networks to Telecommunications*, (pp. 207-214). IEEE.

Chan, J., Zhou, S., & Seneviratne, A. (1998). A QoS adaptive mobility prediction scheme for wireless networks. In *Proceedings of IEEE Globecom*. Sydney, Australia: IEEE.

Das, S. K., & Sen, S. K. (1999). Adaptive location prediction strategies based on a hierarchical network model in a cellular mobile environment. *The Computer Journal, 42*(6), 473–486. doi:10.1093/comjnl/42.6.473.

Erbas, F., et al. (2001). A regular path recognition method and prediction of user movements in wireless networks. In *Proceedings of the IEEE Vehicular Technology Conference (VTC)*. IEEE.

Jain, R., Lin, Y.-B., & Mohan, S. (1999). Location strategies for personal communications services. In Gibson, J. (Ed.), *Mobile Communications Handbook* (2nd ed.). Boca Raton, FL: CRC.

Jiang, S., He, D., & Rao, J. (2001). A prediction-based link availability estimation algorithm for mobile ad hoc networks. In *Proceedings of IEEE InfoCom*. IEEE.

Krishna, P., Vaidya, N., & Pradhan, D. (1996). Static and adaptive location management in mobile wireless networks. *Computer Communications, 19*(4), 321–334. doi:10.1016/0140-3664(96)01070-5.

Liu, T., Bahl, P., & Chlamtac, I. (1998). Mobility modeling, location tracking, and trajectory prediction in wireless ATM networks. *IEEE Journal on Selected Areas in Communications, 16*(6), 922–936. doi:10.1109/49.709453.

Madi, M., Graham, P., & Barker, K. (1996). *Mobile computing: predictive connection management with user input (Technical Report)*. Manitoba, Canada: University of Manitoba.

Zhang, T. et al. (2001). Local predictive reservation for handoff in multimedia wireless IP networks. *IEEE Journal on Selected Areas in Communications, 19*, 1931–1941. doi:10.1109/49.957308.

KEY TERMS AND DEFINITIONS

Adaptive Resonance Theory: Theory that involves a number of neural network models in order to address problems such as pattern recognition or prediction.

Classification: The identification of the correct category where a new observation belongs.

Context Awareness: Sensing the environment of some devices and adapting the behavior of a system.

Location Prediction: Predicting the location of a mobile user or device.

Machine Learning: Branch of artificial intelligence that is concerned by the development of algorithms that take as input empirical data and yield patterns or prediction of the underlying mechanism.

Online Clustering: Clustering technique that processes data points in serial, one at a time as they enter into the system, with the aim of saving computational time when used in real time applications.

ENDNOTES

[1] One possible approach to determine the initial k clusters is to select the first k distinct instances of the input sample U.

Chapter 13
Enhancing Location Privacy in Location–Based Services:
The STS Case

Constantinos Delakouridis
Athens University of Economics and Business, Greece

ABSTRACT

Location-based services are receiving signification attention over the last few years due to the increasing use of mobile devices. At the same time, location privacy is important, since position information is considered personal information. Thus, in order to address this issue, several mechanisms have been proposed protecting the mobile user. In this chapter, the authors present an architecture to shield the location of a mobile user and preserve the anonymity on the service delivery. This architecture relies on un-trusted entities to distribute segments of anonymous location information, and authorizes other entities to combine these portions and derive the actual location of a user. The chapter describes how the architecture takes into account the location privacy requirements, and how it is used by the end users' devices, e.g., mobile phones, for the dissemination of location information to service providers. Furthermore, it notes privacy issues for further discussion and closes with proposed exercises.

INTRODUCTION

As the cost of mobile devices and mobile broadband drops across the globe, the popularity of location based services, shoots up. The convergence of these two trends is influencing the vastly changing world. A number of applications, by using the capabilities of the smartphones (GPS receivers), provide services that affect the way we live, work and interact with each other. Through the aforementioned services, we are able to navigate to destination by avoiding traffic jams, to locate the closest points of interests, to discover the nearby friends, to share location tagged pictures etc. However, this new trend comes at a certain price. The networking technologies (e.g., GSM/

DOI: 10.4018/978-1-4666-4038-2.ch013

GPRS) offer the infrastructure for advertisement of the location information, and, thus, potential eavesdropping and unauthorized use (or misuse) of it. An adversary can potentially derive location information at different layers of the network stack, from the physical to the network layer (Gruteser & Grunwald, 2003a). Furthermore, data collection and mining techniques might produce historical location data and movement patterns (Gruteser & Grunwald, 2003), which they are subject to unauthorized use, as well. Minch presents and discusses several risks that are associated with the unauthorized disclosure, collection, retention, and usage, of location information (Minch, 2004). Additionally, the Location Privacy Protection Act, announced on 2001 in the United States, addresses the necessity and identifies several risks related to the privacy of the location information (U.S. Privacy location act, 2001). Location privacy is considered of high importance, since individuals should be able and free to explicitly identify what location information will be disclosed, when this can happen, how this information will be communicated and to whom this information will be revealed. Even through anonymization, as defined in (Pfitzmann & Koehntopp, 2000), personal data collection is bind with privacy, the disclosure of the personal identity might be useful for the delivery of personalized, pervasive or location-aware, services, especially when accounting and charging is a requirement.

In this chapter we discuss about an innovative architecture, called STS, originally introduced in (Marias et al., 2006), to address several aspects of the location privacy issue. Firstly, it elaborates on the control of privacy that an individual should have over his/her location. It enables individuals to define different levels or rules of privacy (i.e. secrecy) over different portion of location data, depending on the operation environment (e.g., hostile) and the service that indents or asks to use location data. This is achieved through data and secret sharing techniques, which are discussed in a later section. Additionally, it gives users, or location targets, the capability to explicitly identify

services or pervasive applications that might collect, store, and use location information. Finally, it provides anonymity on the distribution of the location information. STS architecture is designed to operate within an un-trusted environment. Portions of a target's location data are distributed to public available nodes, which act as intermediate and temporal location servers. Targets authorize, on-demand, the pervasive or LBS services to access and combine the distributed location information. This is accomplished implicitly, through the disclosure of the mapping between a pseudonym and user's or target's location data. In the last few years, several methods have been proposed which deal with the location privacy issue on the lower layers of the communication stack (e.g., the IP layer). STS address location privacy in the application layer, enabling end-user to disclosure location information to authenticated pervasive applications and location-based services. The STS architecture is applicable to environments that consist of user devices with several idiosyncrasies, such as luck of energy autonomy, memory and processing power. To provide secrecy it avoids complex computational tasks, such as producing key pairs, hashing and message authenticated codes. Instead, it deals with the division of location data into pieces and the distribution of these pieces to serving entities. Thus, it is applicable to smart spaces featuring ubiquitous services through the involvement of small gadgets, RF-tags, sensors and actuators that activated to infer the location of a user or target.

The remainder of this chapter is structured as follows. In Section 2 we provide the assumptions that STS considers for its operation. In Section 4 we present the STS architecture and the entities that it consists of. It introduces the secret share mechanism that enables the anonymity and privacy of location information. Subsequently, in Section 5, we discuss the procedures followed by the entities of the architecture. In Section 6, we note some issues for further discussion and finally in Section 7, we close with some proposed exercises.

DEFINITIONS AND ASSUMPTIONS

Location Information

Before describing in details the STS architecture it is essential to define what we consider as location data and which are the possible technologies, currently available, for position retrieval. As Location Information *(LocInfo)* we use a variation of the definition introduced in (Friday et al., 2002), i.e., we use the triple of the following form: *{Position, Time, ID}*. Thus, *LocInfo* is defined as a combination of the *"Position"* that the entity with identifier *"ID"* maintained at time *"Time"*, within a given coordinate system. This triple is adopted in order to emphasize that, within the STS architecture, time is considered as a critical parameter in terms of location identification, as well. Friday et al. in (Friday et al., 2002), provide further details on the semantics of this definition.

The STS scheme incorporates multiple user profiles to provide different precision of *LocInfo* i.e. a drive-navigation service needs high precision location data to provide exact instructions, whilst a Point Of Interest service requires data of lower precision. A user could use different pseudonyms per service and choose a discrete profile to denote the required level of the precision on the *LocInfo*. We assume that each STS server keeps a table called "Location Information Table" *(LIT)*. Each record of the *LIT* table keeps a pair of values *(ID, σ(LocInfo))*, where *σ(LocInfo)* is a random segment of the *LocInfo* of the corresponding user, produced from the SSA algorithm, as will be discussed later.

Positioning Technologies

As previously mentioned, position technologies differ in terms of scale, accuracy, time-to-first-fix, installation and operation costs. Additionally, the *Position* of an object can be either physical (e.g., at 38014´49"N by 23031´94"W) or symbolic (e.g. in the office, in Athens). Another classification uses the absolute or relative *Position* definitions.

Absolute position is depicted on a common co-ordinates system, and the *Position* for an object is the same and unique for all the observers. Unlike, the relative position represents the *Position* of a located object in reference to the observer. *LocInfo* is defined to incorporate any of the four aforementioned *Position* semantics.

In terms of scale, GPS is a technology that focuses on outdoor, wide range, location identification, providing high accurate results (less than 30 feet) using a trilateration positioning method in the three-dimensional space (Bajaj et al., 2002). Location determination can also be achieved through terrestrial, infrastructure-based, positioning methods. These positioning methods rely on cellular networks equipment to infer an estimation of a mobile users' position. In (Marias et al., 2004) a general brokerage architecture that gathers the location information independently of the positioning technology, such as Time Of Arrival, Enhanced Observed Time Difference, and Global Cell ID, is proposed. Location retrieval can rely on the infrastructure of the wireless LAN communication network, such as the IEEE 802.11, to provide higher accuracy, especially in indoor environments. Positioning systems like RADAR (Bahl & Padmanabhan, 2000) and Nibble (Castro et al., 2001) operate using the IEEE 802.11 data network to gather the location of a user or object. For context-aware services that require higher accuracy, specialized positioning infrastructure needs to be established (e.g., sensors or RF-tags). Among the positioning systems that have been proposed to provide finer granularity to the pervasive applications is the *Active Badge,* a proximity system that uses infrared emissions emitted by small infrared badges, carried by objects of interest (Want et al., 1992). *Active Bat* resembles the Active Badge using an ultrasound time-of-flight lateration technique for higher accuracy (Harter et al., 1999). *Cricket* relies on beacons, which transmit RF signals and ultrasound waves, and on receivers attached to the objects (Priyantha et al., 2000). *SpotON* measures the signal strength emitted by RF tags on the objects of interest and perceived by RF base stations (Hightower et al., 2000). *Pseudolites* are devices that are installed inside buildings and emulate the operation of the GPS satellites constellation, (Kee et al., 2000). *MotionStar* incorporates electromagnetic sensing techniques to provide position-tracking. Additionally, according to (Hightower & Borriello, 2001), there are several other types of tags and sensors that provide user's location with high accuracy, depending the requirements of the ubiquitous service. *Easy Living* uses computer vision to recognize and locate the objects in a 3D environment. *Smart Floor* utilizes pressure sensors to capture footfalls in order to track the position of pedestrians. *Pin Point 3D-iD* uses the time-of-flight lateration technique for RF signals emitted and received by proprietary hardware. Positioning technologies are further divided into two main categories: centralized and distributed. Technologies of the former category rely on a centralized, dedicated, server, responsible for calculating the position of the registered users. Methods of the latter category are based on specialized software of hardware, installed on the subject's device, which performs advanced calculations to estimate user's current position. The STS framework takes advantage of the distributed approach; the entity *ID* determines the *Position*, either autonomously or using contributed measurements, based on calculations performed at a given *Time*.

STS ARCHITECTURE AND ALGORITHMS

The STS architecture enables location privacy without relying on the existence of trusted parties (e.g., TTPs, LS). The main idea is to divide the location information into pieces and distribute it to multiple servers, called STS Servers. These are no-trustworthy, intermediate, entities, assigned to store, erase and provide segments of location information that anonymous users register or update. Third party services, such as LBS

or pervasive applications, access multiple STS servers to determine user's location data through the combination of the distributed pieces. This is achieved after a well-defined authentication process motivated by the corresponding user. Furthermore, due to the decentralized STS architecture, a possible collusion between STS servers, each of one maintaining only partial knowledge of the user location, is fruitless. The secret i.e. (location of a user) is not distributed to specific STS Servers, and, furthermore, each user dynamically chooses different servers to distribute the location information segments, according to the requested service (e.g., location-based friend-find service) and to policy rules. Additionally, even if multiple STS Servers collude successfully, the actual location information is not revealed, since the segments are stored through pseudonyms. The main characteristics of the STS are:

- Location privacy is offered as a service to users who desire to hide their location information.
- Different privacy levels can be defined based on users' profiles, policies or end-applications that the users are registered to (e.g., segmentation of location information into different number of pieces).
- The user maintains full control over the location data. The position is calculated on the user's device, the user defines which STS servers will have partial knowledge of it, and which third-party services are authorized to access and combine it.
- The location privacy is achieved within rational or distrusted environments; it does not employ trustworthy or reliable entities for data storage.

Architecture

The STS architecture does not rely on the existence of a single and trusted third party. Multiple STS servers are geographically distributed. A subset of them is assigned to store portions of the location information of a target. The segments of the location information are constructed through the "Secret Share Algorithm" (SSA), a novel threshold scheme that is proposed here to cope with location privacy.

Figure 1 illustrates the entities of the proposed STS architecture. STS servers might offered by a Wireless Internet Service Provider (WISP), an Internet feed provider, a VAS and content provider, or offered by a mobile operator. In the ad-hoc networking scenario, in the presence of STS servers the targets might use these as location information storage areas. If the STS servers are unreachable, ad-hoc nodes, RF tags and sensors might use the local nodes caches to store the *LocInfo* segments, based on mutual intensives for privacy and reciprocity principles.

The Value Added Service (VAS) provider offers location based and pervasive services to subscribers (registered users) or to ephemeral users (pay per view model). VAS might offer a wide range of services, such as indoor/outdoor navigation, proximity services (e.g., find-friend), positioning and point-of-interest, tracking person's location (e.g., children, elderly), localized advertisement and content delivery (e.g., city sightseeing), and emergency (e.g., E911). Hereafter we use the term *Service* to denote value added or pervasive applications that require the location information of a user, asset or device to operate and provide a location service. Each *Service* requires the location information, maintained in intermediate STS servers, to provide the required level of service to an individual.

Secret Share Algorithm

Several variations of the SSA have been proposed (Hoffman et al., 2004). The basic algorithm is the "Trivial Secret Sharing". According to this basic form, the secret is divided into n pieces and all the pieces are required to restore it. An improved SSA, called "Perfect Scheme", assumes that the secret is shared among the n out of m available entities ($n<m$) and any set of at most $n-1$ entities cannot rebuild the secret. The SSA we have adopted for the STS architecture is the perfect sharing scheme of Shamir, referenced to as *threshold scheme* (Shamir, 1979). Shamir's algorithm is based on the fact that to compute the equation of a polynomial of degree n, one must know at least $n+1$ points that it lies on. For example, in order to determine the equation of a line (i.e., $n=1$) it is essential to know at least two points that it lies on. Let assume that the secret is some data L, which is (or can be easily made) a number. According to Shamir's (n,m) threshold scheme, to divide L into pieces L_i one can pick a random, $n-1$ degree, polynomial

Figure 1. Entities of the STS architecture

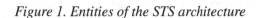

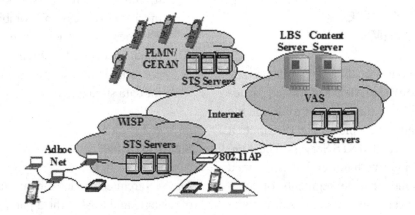

$$f(x) = S_0 + S_1 x^1 + S_2 x^2 + ... + S_{n-1} x^{n-1}$$

STS PROCEDURES

Using real life identifiers, such as user names, in each *LIT* entry enables STS servers to collude and, eventually, reconstitute the location information of a user, based on his/her username. To prevent collusions and the disclosure of *LocInfo*, we replace the username of the *LIT* entries with a pseudonym. Although, this approach does not prevent malicious users from obtaining the location of an entity, combining entries with identical pseudonyms, it discourages them from obtaining the location of a specific user. Only the entities that have a prior knowledge about the mapping between a pseudonym and a real identity can combine segments to produce useful conclusions.

To increase the security level, the pseudonym is divided into parts, as well. Each segment of the *LocInfo* is sent to the STS server along with a discrete part of the related pseudonym. As a result, a potential eavesdropper should map multiple pseudonym's segment (say p_i) in order to obtain the correct record $(p_i, \sigma_i(LocInfo))$ from all the STS servers for the monitored user. If a perfect SSA is used, the pseudonym is divided into *m* parts where *m* corresponds to the "*n* out of *m*" perfect scheme. Regulating the value of *m*, one can increase the complexity, and the privacy level. Note that for each *ID* only one *LIT* record is stored on a STS server.

We assume that a software random integer generator is running on user's device and performs the generation of the pseudonym. If there are *m* STS servers and at least *n* (*m>n*) can rebuild the *LocInfo*, the random integer generator generates a random *m*k*-bits number (i.e., the pseudonym). This number is then divided into *m* segments (*1...k* bits represent the first segment, *k+1...2k* represents the second segment etc.) where each segment acts as user's pseudonym.

The robustness of the aforementioned scheme could be enhanced if the secret is not shared to *m* STS servers but to *x*, randomly selected, servers, where *x≤m*. In this approach the secret can be recovered from *y* segments, *y<x* (i.e., a "*y* out of *x*" perfect scheme). This variation increases the complexity required by an eavesdropper to identify which STS servers keep the location of a specific user. To provide a paradigm let assume that a farm of 15 STS servers are available and the secret is being shared among *x*, randomly selected, servers, where *8≤x≤12*. An attacker should first determine the value of *x* and then calculate all the possible, C_1, combinations of the STS servers in order to combine the pseudonym

$$C_1 = \sum_{i=m-A}^{m} \binom{15}{i}$$

Assume *m* STS servers, where *x* of them have the secret, and *y (y<x)* is the minimum number of servers required to obtain the *LocInfo*. Furthermore, let each pseudonym constitutes of *k*x* bits. The random pseudonym generator splits the pseudonym into *x* segments (p_x), each of *k*-bit length. The variable *x* takes values from *(m-A, m)* where *A* *(A≥0)* is an integer that affects the desired security level of the STS architecture. More specifically, if *A* is small, an attacker has to gain access to a greater number of STS servers. However, small *A* reduces the number of different combinations of STS servers keeping the secret's segments, and, thus, the security level of the system is diminished. On the other hand, for a large *A*, the number of different combinations of STS servers sharing the secret is increased. However, large *A* reduces the number of servers that an attacker has to gain access to reveal the secret. Regarding the maximum value of variable *y*, this is set to *x-t*, where *t* *(t>0)* is an integer that depends on the desired robustness of the STS architecture. If *t* is set close to zero and *B* out of *x* STS servers go down at the same time, where *B>t*, the system eventually runs

Table 1. Steps and target

step 1. Find a random x, such that $m-A<x<m$ step 2. Generate a random $x*k-$ bit length number step 3. Split that number into x segments of $k-$ bit length each step 4. Register to the x STS servers	Pseudonym and STS registration procedure
step 5. Apply the SSA at the *LocInfo* to derive the σi pieces step 6. Produce the pairs $(p_x, \sigma_x(LocInfo))$ step 7. Find a random set of x out of the m STS servers step 8. Send to each one of the x STS servers the *LIT* pair $(p_x, \sigma_x(LocInfo))$	LocInfo segmentation and update procedure
step 9. If *LocInfo* is changed go to step 4	

out of service. The variables A and t may vary per *Service*, based on e.g., charging policy or the user profile. Furthermore the value of t is a function of x, $(t=f(x))$, where as x increases t increases, as well. The steps followed by the target during the creation of its pseudonym, the calculation of the updated *LIT entries* and the dissemination of these to the STS servers (location update procedure) are shown in Table 1.

Steps 1–4 are followed once, per user and per *Service* that requires the *LocInfo*. Each time the location information is altered, the target performs the steps 5 – 8 to inform STS servers and update the *LIT* entries.

Registration to the STS: The random generators that reside in different user's device might produce identical pseudonyms. In such a case, one STS server might receive two location segments (i.e., σ_x) that belong to the *LocInfo* of two discrete users, but associated with the same pseudonym. As a result, the STS server might forward an inaccurate segment to the *Service* that requested the user's *LocInfo*. To avoid such a conflict, the STS scheme requires from each user to perform a registration procedure (step 4), and to enter his/her pseudonym's segments to the x STS servers

Location Retrieval Procedure: When the *Service* requires user's location, it sends a request to

each one of the x STS servers. When the x segments are received, the *Service* rebuilds user's location.

LIT Update Procedures: On the other hand, when an STS server receives an update request (step 8) it searches the existing *LIT* records to determine whether the p_x already exists. If so, it updates the corresponding *LIT* entry, importing the $(p_x, \sigma_x(LocInfo))$ record.

Registration to a Service: Beyond the registration procedure to the STS servers, user has to provide to the *Service* provider the details of how to obtain his/her location information. Therefore, the user provides the following information during the registration procedure to the *Service*:

- The x STS servers that store his/her location information (e.g., IP address or URL).
- His/her pseudonym's segments, created by the user for the specific *Service*.
- The mapping between pseudonym's segments and STS servers (i.e., to which STS server each segment corresponds).

LIT Entries Remove Policy: Normally, the end-user authorizes a *Service* to access his/her location information for a given period of time, (e.g. a month), through a selection of a predefined policy. Consequently, *LIT* records of each STS server should be deleted after that period. This can be performed explicitly or implicitly. In the former case the user sends a specialized message requiring the deletion of the *LIT* entry from a specific STS server. In the latter case, an extra field on the $(p_i, \sigma_i(LocInfo))$ record is added to enable end-user to define the time-to-live (*TTL*) value for the record.

Location Information Validity Period: In ubiquitous environments users are characterized by high mobility. Thus, the location information that is stored on the STS servers must be associated with a Validity Period (*VP*). VP is an additional field on the $(p_i, \sigma_i(LocInfo), TTL_i)$ record. The *VP* period depends on several parameters, such as:

- **The Nature of the Service Provided:** A navigation *Service* might require higher location-update rates to provide exact instructions, whilst a tourist guide *Service* needs periodical updates.
- **User's Velocity:** For a driver the location is continuously altered, while for a walker the location changes at a slower rate. The former requires lower *VP*, whilst a higher *VP* is sufficient for the latter.

DISCUSSION

Other Approaches: Several approaches that enable location privacy focus on the secrecy of Medium Access Control (MAC) identifiers or IP-layer address. On the MAC layer, the problem of interface identifiers is discussed in (Gruteser & Grunwald, 2003b) that uniquely identify each client, allowing tracking of her location over time. The authors in (Gruteser & Grunwald, 2003b) introduce a location privacy scheme through the frequent disposal of a client's interface identifier. In the IP layer, Mobile IP (Fasbender et al., 1996a) implicitly addresses location privacy by associating two different IPs to the same subject (e.g., mobile user); (i) the static one, corresponding to the home network of the user, and (ii) the dynamic one, corresponding to the current access network of the user. The Non-Disclosure Method (Fasbender et al., 1996b) considers the existence of independent, security (software) agents that are distributed on the IP network. Each security agent holds a pair of keys and forwards messages in an encrypted format. The sender routes a message to a receiver through the path determined by the security agents. Moreover, the Mist System (Al-Muhtadi et al., 2002) handles the problem of routing a message though a mobile network by keeping the sender's location private from intermediate routers, the receiver and possible eavesdroppers. The Mist System consists of several routers ordered in a hierarchical structure. Specifically, portal routers are aware of the

location of the mobile user without knowing the identity of the user, while the lighthouse routers are aware of the user's identity without knowing her/his exact location.

The aforementioned approaches enforce location privacy in the MAC or IP-layer. Beyond these solutions that apply to the lower layers of the OSI stack, the *anonymity-based* approach has been proposed to address the location privacy issue on the application layer -Through anonymity the location information is unlinked from the subject prior to the information collection process. This means that subjects are reporting their location, but the use nicknames or pseudonyms such that anybody that gain access to the location information will not be able to determine the owner of this information. The idea of using pseudonyms instead of the identities of the users is used by the authors in (Leonhardt et al., 1998). They propose the replacement of the identity with a sequence of chained idempotent filters governed by a specific policy language. The authors in (Kesdogan et al., 1998) adopt temporary pseudonymous identities to protect the identity of users in GSM. Also work in (Beresford & Stajano, 2004) uses dynamic pseudonyms, and work in (Bettini et al., 2005) relies on quasi identifiers$k$-anonymity approaches are also applicable for location privacy, such as adaptive cloaking (Mokbel et al., 2006), CliqueCloak approach (Gedik & Liu, 2005), strong k-anonymity (Zhang & Huang, 2009), adaptive nearest neighborhood cloaking (Talukder & Ahamed, 2010) and historical k-anonymity. Further extensions of k-anonymity which consider multiple attributes and personal context of a mobile user include p-sensitivity (Solanas et al., 2008), t-closeness (Li et al., 2007), and l-diversity (Machanavajjhala et al., 2007). Furthermore, the IETF Geopriv Workgroup[1] addresses the location privacy issue by introducing the use of a Location Server (LS). The LS registers the position of the subject and discloses position information using specific rules. Such rules are generated by a rule maker (e.g., by the subject) and managed by a specific service (a rule holder). Each subject can explicitly specify the desired level of privacy. Beresford et al. (Beresford & Stajano, 2004) proposed the idea of mixed-zones where the user´s positions are protected within these zones. In (Beresford & Stajano, 2004) this is realized within a zone by not sending any location updates. A mixed-zone based approach, called MobiMix is proposed in (Palanisamy & Liu, 2011). In (Ouyang et al., 2008) mix-zones are adapted depending on user´s location. Additionally, in spatial obfuscation approaches privacy in enhanced by intentionally reducing the precision of the location information. In the approach of Ardagna et al. (Ardagna et al., 2007), the user uses circular areas as location info instead of his exact positions. In SpaceTwist method presented in (Yiu et al., 2008) private queries are supported by pretending that the user issued the query from a fake location. Gruteser et al. also considered spatio-temporal obfuscation to protect movement trajectories of users (Gruteser & Grunwald, 2003c).

Threats Against STS: Another important issue are the potential threats that exist against the STS architecture. In (Marias et al., 2006) we further elaborate on the several threat models and evaluate the performance and robustness of the STS.

EXERCISES

As stated in section 3, we adapted Shamir's perfect scheme (Shamir, 1979) as STS secret sharing mechanism for location. Several secret sharing approaches have been proposed in the literature like (Jun-Chou et al., 2010; Hillery et al., 1999; DNSSEC Root key split among seven people, 2010; Zhao et al., 2007; Feldman, 1987; Feigenbaum, 1991; Coppersmith, 1995). Review the alternate approaches.

REFERENCES

Al-Muhtadi, J., Campbell, R., Kapadia, A., Mickunas, D., & Yi, S. (2002). Routing through the mist: Privacy preserving communication in ubiquitous computing environments. In *Proceedings of the International Conference of Distributed Computing Systems*. IEEE.

Ardagna, C., Cremonini, M., Damiani, E., De Capitani di Vimercati, S., & Samarati, P. (2007). Location privacy protection through obfuscation-based techniques. In *Proceedings of the 21st Annual IFIP Conference on Data and Applications Security*. IFIP.

Bahl, P., & Padmanabhan, V. N. (2000). RADAR: An in-building RF-based user location and tracking system. In Proceedings of of IEEE INFOCOM2000, (Vol. 2, pp. 775-784). IEEE.

Bajaj, R., Ranaweera, S. L., & Agrawal, D. P. (2002). GPS: Location- tracking technology. In *Proceedings of IEEE Computer*, (pp. 92-94). IEEE.

Beresford, A. R., & Stajano, F. (2004). Mix zones: User privacy in location-aware services. In *Proceedings of PerCom Workshops* (pp. 127–131). PerCom. doi:10.1109/PERCOMW.2004.1276918.

Bettini, C., Wang, X., & Jajodia, S. (2005). Protecting privacy against location-based personal identification. In Jonker & Petkovic (Eds.), Secure Data Management (LNCS), (Vol. 3674, pp. 185-199). Berlin: Springer.

Castro, P., Chiu, P., Ted, K., & Muntz, R. (2001). A probabilistic room location service for wireless networked environments. In *Proceedings of Ubicom 2001*. Atlanta, GA: Ubicom. doi:10.1007/3-540-45427-6_3.

Coppersmith, D. (1995). Proactive secret sharing or: How to cope with perpetual leakage. In Proceedings of Advances in Cryptology — CRYPT0' 95, (Vol. 963, pp. 339-352). CRYPTO.

Fasbender, A., Kesdogan, D., & Kubitz, O. (1996a). Variable and scalable security: Protecting of location information in mobile IP. In *Proceedings of the 46th IEEE VTC*. IEEE.

Fasbender, A., Kesdogan, D., & Kubitz, O. (1996b). Analysis of security and privacy in mobile IP. In *Proceedings of the 4th International Conference on Telecommunication Systems, Modeling and Analysis*. IEEE.

Feigenbaum, J. (1991). Non-interactive and information-theoretic secure verifiable secret sharing. In Proceedings of Advances in Cryptology - CRYPT0' 91, (Vol. 576, pp. 129-140). CRYPTO.

Feldman, P. (1987). A practical scheme for non-interactive verifiable secret sharing. In *Proceedings of the 28th Annual Symposium on Foundations of Computer Science*, (pp. 427-438). IEEE.

Friday, A., Muller, H., Rodden, T., & Dix, A. (2002). A lightweight approach to managing privacy in location-based services. In *Proceedings of the Equator Annual Conference*. Brockenhurst, UK: Equator.

Gedik, B., & Liu, L. (2005). Location privacy in mobile systems: A personalized anonymization model. [ICDCS.]. *Proceedings of, ICDCS2005*, 620–629.

Gruteser, M., & Grunwald, D. (2003a). Anonymous usage of location-based services through spatial and temporal cloaking. [MobiSys.]. *Proceedings of MobiSys*, *03*, 31–42.

Gruteser, M., & Grunwald, D. (2003b). Enhancing location privacy in wireless LAN through disposable interface identifiers: A quantitative analysis. In *Proceedings of WMASH'03*. WMASH.

Gruteser, M., & Grunwald, D. (2003c). A methodological assessment of location privacy risks in wireless hotspot networks. In *Proceedings of Security in Pervasive Computing*. Boppard, Germany: IEEE.

Harter, A., Hopper, A., Steggles, P., Ward, A., & Webster, P. (1999). The anatomy of a context-aware application. In *Proceedings of the 5th ACM/IEEE International Conference on Mobile Computing and Networking, Mobicom 99*, (pp. 59-68). Seattle, WA: ACM/IEEE.

Hightower, J., & Borriello, G. (2001). *Location systems for ubiquitous computing*. Seattle, WA: University of Washington.

Hightower, J., Borriello, G., & Want, R. (2000). *SpotON: An indoor 3D location sensing technology based on RF signal strength*. Seattle, WA: University of Washington.

Hillery, M., Buzek, V., & Berthiaume, A. (1999). Quantum secret sharing. *Physical Review A.*, 59.

Hoffman, B. C., et al. (2004). Secret sharing schemes, project specification. *In Proceedings of COSC*. COSC.

Jun-Chou, et al. (2010). A novel secret sharing technique using QR code. *International Journal of Image*, *4*(5), 468–475.

Kee, C., et al. (2000). Development of indoor navigation system using asynchronous pseudolites. In *Proceedings of ION GPS -2000*. Salt Lake City, UT: ION GPS.

Kesdogan, D., Reichl, P., & Junghärtchen, K. (1998). Distributed temporary pseudonyms: A new approach for protecting location information in mobile communication networks. In *Proceedings of the 5th European Symposium on Research in Computer Security*. IEEE.

Leonhardt, U., & Magee, J. (1998). Security considerations for a distributed location service. *Journal of Network and Systems Management, 6*(1). doi:10.1023/A:1018777802208.

Li, N., Li, T., & Venkatasubramanian, S. (2007). t-closeness: Privacy beyond k-anonymity and l-diversity. In *Proceedings of the IEEE 23rd International Conference on Data Engineering (ICDE 2007)*, (pp. 106-115). IEEE.

Machanavajjhala, A., Kifer, D., Gehrke, J., & Venkitasubramaniam, M. (2007). L-diversity: Privacy beyond k-anonymity. *ACM Transactions on Knowledge Discovery from Data, 1*(1).

Marias, G. F., Delakouridis, C., Kazatzopoulos, L., & Georgiadis, P. (2006). Applying privacy on the dissemination of location information. *Elsevier Telematics and Informatics Journal, 23*(3), 211–219. doi:10.1016/j.tele.2005.07.006.

Marias, G. F., Prigouris, N., Papazafeiropoulos, G., Hadjiefthymiades, S., & Merakos, L. (2004). Brokering positioning data from heterogeneous infrastructures. *Wireless Personal Communications, 30*(2-4), 233–245. doi:10.1023/B:WIRE.0000049402.33897.15.

Minch, R. P. (2004). Privacy issues in location-aware mobile devices. In *Proceedings of the 37th Hawaii International Conference on System Sciences*. IEEE.

Mokbel, M. F., Chow, C. Y., & Aref, W. G. (2006). The new casper: Query processing for location services without compromising privacy. In *Proceedings of (VLDB '06)*, (pp. 763-774). VLDB.

Ouyang, Y., Xu, Y., Le, Z., Chen, G., & Makedon, F. (2008). Providing location privacy in assisted living environments. [PETRA.]. *Proceedings of PETRA, 08*, 1–8. doi:10.1145/1389586.1389633.

Palanisamy, B., & Liu, L. (2011). Mobimix: Protecting LOCATION PRIVACY with mix-zones over road networks. [ICDE.]. *Proceedings of ICDE, 11*, 494–505.

Pfitzmann, A., & Koehntopp, M. (2000). Anonymity, unobservability, and pseudonymity – A proposal for terminology. In *Proceedings of the Workshop on Design Issues in Anonymity and Unobservability*. IEEE.

Priyantha, N. B., Chakraborty, A., & Balakrishnan, H. (2000). The cricket location-support system. In *Proceedings of the 6th ACM MOBICOM*, (pp. 32-43). ACM.

Schneier on Security. (n.d.). *DNSSEC root key split among seven people*. Retrieved July 28, 2010 from http://www.schneier.com/blog/archives/2010/07/dnssec_root_key.html

Shamir. (1979). How to share a secret. *Communications of the ACM, 22*, 612-613.

Solanas, A., Seb, E. F., & Domingo-Ferrer, J. (2008). Micro-aggregation-based heuristics for p-sensitive k-anonymity: One step beyond. In *Proceedings of the 2008 International Workshop on Privacy and Anonymity in Information Society (PAIS '08)*, (pp. 61-69). PAIS.

Talukder, N., & Ahamed, S. I. (2010). Preventing multi-query attack in location-based services. In *Proceedings of the Third ACM conference on Wireless Network Security*, (pp. 25-36). ACM.

US Government. (2001). *U.S. location privacy protection act of 2001, bill number s.1164, introduced July 11, 2001*. Retrieved from http://www.techlawjournal.com/cong107/privacy/location/s1164is.asp

Want, R., Hopper, A., Falcao, V., & Gibbons, J. (1992). The active badge location system. *ACM Transactions on Information Systems, 10*(1), 91–102. doi:10.1145/128756.128759.

Yiu, M. L., Jensen, C. S., Huang, X., & Lu, H. (2008). Spacetwist: Managing the trade-offs among location privacy, query performance, and query accuracy in mobile services. [ICDE.]. *Proceedings of, ICDE2008*, 366–375.

Zhang, C., & Huang, Y. (2009). Cloaking locations for anonymous location based services: A hybrid approach. *Journal Geoinformatica, 13*, 159–182. doi:10.1007/s10707-008-0047-2.

Zhao, J., Zhang, J., & Zhao, R. (2007). A practical verifiable multi-secret sharing scheme. *Computer Standards & Interfaces, 29*, 138–141. doi:10.1016/j.csi.2006.02.004.

ADDITIONAL READING

Cachin, C., Kursawe, K., Lysyanskaya, A., & Strobl, R. (2002). Asynchronous verifiable secret sharing and proactive cryptosystems. In *Proceedings of the 9th ACM Conference Computer and Communications Security*, (pp. 88–97). ACM.

Cachin, C., Kursawe, K., & Shoup, V. (2005). Random oracles in Constantinople: Practical asynchronous Byzantine agreement using cryptography. *Journal of Cryptology, 18*(3), 219–246. doi:10.1007/s00145-005-0318-0.

Chang, T. Y., Hwang, M. S., & Yang, W. P. (2005). An improvement on the Lin–Wu (t,n) threshold verifiable multi-secret sharing scheme. *Applied Mathematics and Computation, 163*(1), 169–178. doi:10.1016/j.amc.2004.01.029.

Chor, B., Goldwasser, S., Micali, S., & Awerbuch, B. (1985). Verifiable secret sharing and achieving simultaneity in the presence of faults. In *Proceedings of the 26th IEEE Symposium on Foundations of Computer Science*, (pp. 383-395). Portland, OR: IEEE Computer Society.

Dehkordi, M. H., & Mashhadi, S. (2008). New efficient and practical verifiable multi-secret sharing schemes. *Information Sciences, 178*, 2262–2274. doi:10.1016/j.ins.2007.11.031.

Fitzi, M., Garay, J., Gollakota, S., Rangan, C. P., & Srinathan, K. (2006). Round-optimal and efficient verifiable secret sharing. In *Proceedings of the Third Theory of Cryptography Conference – TCC'06*, (pp. 329-342). New York, NY: ACM.

Goldreich, O. (2012). *Secure multiparty computation*. Retrieved from http://www.wisdom.weizman.ac.il/oded/pp.html

Katz, J., Koo, C., & Kumaresan, R. (2008). Improved the round complexity of VSS in point-to-point networks. In *Proceedings of the ICALP 2008* (LNCS), (vol. 5126, pp. 499-510). Reykjavik, Iceland: Springer.

Maurer, U. (2006). Secure multi-party computation made simple. *Discrete Applied Mathematics, 154*(2), 370–381. doi:10.1016/j.dam.2005.03.020.

Patra, A., Choudhary, A., Rabin, T., & Rangan, C. P. (2009). The round complexity of verifiable secret sharing revisited. In *Proceedings of Advances in Cryptology, the Crypto '09* (pp. 487–504). Santa Barbara, CA: Crypto. doi:10.1007/978-3-642-03356-8_29.

Schultz, D., Liskov, B., & Liskov, M. (2008). Brief announcement: Mobile proactive secret sharing. In *Proceedings of the PODC '08*. Toronto, Canada: PODC.

Shao, J., & Cao, Z. (2005). A new efficient (t,n) verifiable multi-secret sharing (VMSS) based on YCH scheme. *Applied Mathematics and Computation, 168*(1), 135–140. doi:10.1016/j.amc.2004.08.023.

Zhou, L. (2005). APSS: Proactive secret sharing in asynchronous systems. *ACM Transactions on Information and System Security, 8*(3), 259–286. doi:10.1145/1085126.1085127.

KEY TERMS AND DEFINITIONS

Cryptographic Technique: Technique used for secure communication or information exchange.

Intelligent Location Service: The capability of handling complex phenomena using location and time information.

Location-Based Service: General class of computer program level service used to include specific controls for location and time data.

Location Privacy: Controlling the access in location information.

Secret Sharing Scheme: Technique for distributing a secret among a group of participants each of them is allocated a share of the secret.

ENDNOTES

[1] http://datatracker.ietf.org/wg/geopriv/charter/.

Chapter 14
Intention Prediction Mechanism in an Intentional Pervasive Information System

Salma Najar
Université Paris1 – Panthéon Sorbonne, France

Manuele Kirsch Pinheiro
Université Paris1 – Panthéon Sorbonne, France

Yves Vanrompay
Ecole Centrale Paris, France

Luiz Angelo Steffenel
Université de Reims Champagne-Ardenne, France

Carine Souveyet
Université Paris1 – Panthéon Sorbonne, France

ABSTRACT

The development of pervasive technologies has allowed the improvement of services availability. These services, offered by Information Systems (IS), are becoming more pervasive, i.e., accessed anytime, anywhere. However, those Pervasive Information Systems (PIS) remain too complex for the user, who just wants a service satisfying his needs. This complexity requires considerable efforts from the user in order to select the most appropriate service. Thus, an important challenge in PIS is to reduce user's understanding effort. In this chapter, the authors propose to enhance PIS transparency and productivity through a user-centred vision based on an intentional approach. They propose an intention prediction approach. This approach allows anticipating user's future requirements, offering the most suitable service in a transparent and discrete way. This intention prediction approach is guided by the user's context. It is based on the analysis of the user's previous situations in order to learn user's behaviour in a dynamic environment.

DOI: 10.4018/978-1-4666-4038-2.ch014

INTRODUCTION

Nowadays, the development of mobile and pervasive technologies has allowed a significant increase of services offered to users by Information System (IS). Instead of having Information Technology (IT) in the foreground, triggered and manipulated by users, IT is gradually residing in the background, monitoring user's activities, processing this information and intervening when required (Kouruthanassis & Giaglis, 2006). In other terms, we are observing the emergence of a Pervasive Information System (PIS) that intends to increase user's productivity by making IS available anytime and anywhere. Indeed, PIS arise from the ambition to provide pervasive access to IS, while adapting itself to user's context. The notion of context is employed in order to make these systems more intelligent and adaptive. It corresponds to any entity considered as relevant to the interaction between the user and the application (Dey, 2001).

Contrarily to traditional IS, whose interaction paradigm is the desktop, PIS deals with a multitude of heterogeneous devices, providing the interaction between the user and the physical environment (Kouruthanassis & Giaglis, 2006). As pointed out by Kouruthanassis & Giaglis (2006), the main characteristics of PIS are not only the heterogeneity of devices, but also the property of context-awareness. Therefore, the evolution of IS into PIS leads us to consider PIS as more than a simple set of logical services.

Weiser (1991) suggests that a pervasive environment will be characterized by its transparency and homogeneity. Twenty years later, we can notice that this pervasive environment, which was meant to be an invisible or unobtrusive one, represents a technology-saturated environment. This environment combines several devices highly present and visible. PIS has to deal with such an environment, in which a rapidly evolving and increasing number of services is available, with multiple implementations. In spite of this rapid evolution, PIS remains too complex for the user,

who just wants a service that satisfies his needs. This complexity requires considerable effort from the user in order to understand what is happening around him and in order to select the service that best fulfils his needs.

Nowadays, pervasive environments represent reactive systems based only on current user's context. The proactive and anticipatory behaviour of PIS, notably by predicting the user's future situation, is hardly developed. Thus, most research on this topic remains on a technical level, discovering next context information or suitable service implementations. They do not consider the intentional requirements behind the user's experience. As a consequence, the user is often provided with several possibilities, even if he is not always able to understand what is proposed to him. We believe that, in order to achieve transparency advocated by Weiser (1991), PIS must reduce the user's understanding effort. PIS must hide the complexity of such multiple implementations and context situations. This will only be possible through a user-centred vision. This vision is based on the prediction of user's future requirements in a given context. It ensures a transparent access to a "space of services". This space of services hides technical details concerning how to perform these services.

In this chapter, we propose a new vision of PIS based on a space of services and on an intentional prediction approach. Our purpose is to predict the user's future intention based on his context, in order to offer the most suitable service that can interest him in a transparent and discrete way. This approach considers PIS through the notion of intention. The notion of intention can be seen as the goal that a user wants to achieve without saying how to perform it (Kaabi & Souveyet, 2007). It is described also as a goal to be achieved by performing a process presented as a sequence of goals and strategies to the target goal (Bonino et al., 2009). In other words, an intention is a requirement that a user wants to be satisfied without really caring about how to perform it or what service allows him to do so. This intentional vision allows us to focus on the *why* of the service instead of the *how*. By adopting this vision, we propose to improve the transparency by considering, on the one hand, the intention a service allows a user to satisfy, and on the other hand, the context on which this intention emerges. Based on this information, we propose an intention prediction approach that tries to anticipate user's future intention on a given context. The main purpose of such approach is to provide to the user a service that can fulfil his needs in a fairly understandable and non-intrusive way, reducing user's understanding effort.

To better illustrate this approach, we present in this chapter our middleware, called IPSOM (Intentional Pervasive Service Oriented Middleware). The purpose of IPSOM is to satisfy the user's intention by discovering, predicting and selecting for him the most suitable service in a given context. IPSOM integrates an intentional prediction mechanism guided by the context. This prediction mechanism is based on the assumption that, even in a dynamic and frequently changing pervasive information system, *common situations can be found*. Based on this assumption, this prediction mechanism considers a set of time series representing observed user's situations. A situation represents a user's *intention* in a given *context* satisfied by a specific *service*. Thus, we are able to track and store these situations in a database, after each successful discovery process (history). By analysing the user's history, represented by these triplets *<Intention, Context, Service>*, a prediction mechanism can learn user's behaviour in a dynamic environment, and therefore deduce his immediate future intention.

This chapter is organized as follow: The next section presents an overview of related work. Then, we introduce our IPSOM, after which we detail after our proposed intention prediction mechanism. Next we present a discussion and future work. Finally, we conclude this chapter in the last section.

RELATED WORK

Nowadays, pervasive environments are merely reactive. Decisions are taken solely based on the current context. Indeed, research in the anticipatory and proactive behaviour of PIS, notably by predicting the user's future situation, is hardly done. By avoiding focusing on the prediction of future user's situation, current systems lack an important element in the search for transparency and homogeneity.

In order to help end users obtain their desired services, some research on Ubiquitous Computing (Abbar et al., 2009; Adomavicius et al., 2005; Boytsov & Zaslavsky, 2011; Sigg et al., 2010; Vanrompay, 2011) proposes mechanisms to automatically predict or recommend services using user's context. These researches focus especially on context prediction and on context based recommendation systems.

Concerning the first aspect, we have major contributions towards generic context prediction, such as Mayrhofer, Harald et al.(2003), Sigg et al. (2010) and Petzold et al. (2005). According to Vanrompay (2011), Mayrhofer et al. (2003, 2004) propose an architecture and a framework for high-level context prediction. It is based on an unsupervised classification, which tries to find previously unknown classes from input data. This architecture is based on five steps: sensor data acquisition, feature extraction, classification, labelling and prediction.

Similar to Mayrhofer et al. (2003,2004), Sigg et al. (2008, 2010) provide a formal definition of the context prediction task. They propose a context prediction architecture based on an alignment method, from which missing low-level context information is deduced. This alignment method is based on typical pattern and on alignment technique. It allows predicting the continuation of the typical sub-sequence the most similar to the suffix of the observed sequence.

Petzold et al. (2003, 2005) present an approach restricted to the prediction of primary context information (time, location, activity), which is less generic. In 2005, Petzold et al. propose to predict the user's next location in a 'smart office' based on previously visited locations.

Moreover, particular applications of context prediction have been developed by Hong et al. (2009), Lee & Cho (2010) and Meiners et al. (2010). First, Hong et al. (2009) propose a framework to automatically personalize services. They extract the relationships between user profiles and services under the same contextual situation. For this they analyse the user's context history. Meiners et al. (2010) present a generic and structured approach to context prediction based on two key principles. Firstly, developers can incorporate the knowledge of the application domain at design time. Secondly, multiple exchangeable prediction techniques, which are appropriate for the domain, can be selected and combined by the application developers. However, this work does not allow for the selection of appropriate prediction algorithms at runtime.

More recently, in 2011, challenges related to context prediction and applications of the prediction of context information have been identified by Boytsov & Zaslavsky. These authors propose an architecture based on reinforcement learning. They mention that an automated decision-making is a major challenge concerning context prediction. This should be based on the quality of the predicted context (Boytsov & Zaslavsky, 2011). In 2010, Boytsov and Zaslavsky extend the context spaces theory to enable context prediction and proactive adaptation (Boytsov et al., 2009). In context spaces theory, any kind of data that is used to reason about context is called a context attribute. A context attribute corresponds to a domain of values of interest. Context state refers to the set of all relevant context attributes at a certain time. A set of all possible context states constitutes application space. Therefore, application space can be viewed as a multi-dimensional space where the number of dimensions is equal to the number of context attributes in the context state. The state of the system is represented by a point in the application space and the behaviour of the system is represented by a trajectory moving through the application space over time. Situation space represents a real life situation and it is defined as a subspace of the application space. Prediction of context information in this work occurs only on a high-level, i.e., situation space, using various machine-learning algorithms like Markov chains and Bayesian networks. A number of well-known machine learning approaches are evaluated on their appropriateness for context spaces. To decide on the execution of a specific adaptation given a prediction, authors propose a reinforcement learning approach.

We must also cite the contribution of authors on recommendation systems, which aim to propose services based on the user's context. For example, Adomavicius et al. (2005) propose the integration of contextual information into recommendation processes in order to improve recommender capabilities. In 2005, Adomavicius and Tuzhilin propose a multidimensional approach. This approach is based on ratings that are sensitive to contextual information such as time, place, and accompanying people.

In 2008, Yang et al. design an event-driven rule based system. This system recommends services according to user's context changes. Abbar et al. (2009) provide a similar approach, in which services are recommended based on user's log files and current context. Nevertheless, in order to select and recommend services, those approaches require historical data, which are not always available.

Without relying on log files, Xiao et al. (2010) propose an approach to dynamically derive a context model from ontologies and recommend services using context. They automatically extend the semantics of the context value using public available ontologies. Then, they use this semantics to recommend services.

All these works try to anticipate user's needs in order to offer him more transparency. Context prediction approaches (Boytsov & Zaslavsky, 2011; Meiners et al. 2010; Sigg, 2010; Vanrompay, 2011) try to predict user's next context based on the user's current context and history. However, none of these works consider the services a user invokes on a given context. Hence, most recommendation systems (Abbar et al., 2009; Adomavicius et al., 2005) propose a next service to users based solely on their context information, without considering the user's requirements behind a service, i.e., its goals. They propose an implementation to the user, ignoring why this service is needed.

Today, an important challenge in the field of PIS is to position itself at the user level. Current research remains on the technical level, discovering next context information or suitable service implementations, without considering the intentional requirements behind the user's experience. As a consequence, several possibilities are offered to the user, who is not always able to understand what is proposed to him.

INTENTIONAL PERVASIVE SERVICE ORIENTED MIDDLEWARE: IPSOM

Overview

In this chapter, we present a new vision of Pervasive Information System (PIS). It is based on a 'space of services', representing a user-centred approach. This approach emerges from our ambition to achieve more transparency for PIS, while addressing the limitations of existing approaches. Indeed, those existing approaches focus primarily on context adaptation, including the location and devices, neglecting therefore the intentional needs of the user.

Today, it is clear that the evolution of IS into PIS brings much more than a simple set of logical services into the IS. With the development of pervasive technologies, IT becomes embedded in the physical environment. It offers innovative services to the users evolving in this environment. However, contrarily to traditional IS, PIS may offer both logical and physical services. For this reason we introduce the notion of *space of services*. This notion is represented as a way to develop such user-centred view through a space not only including logical services, representing traditional information systems themselves, but also physical services embedded on the physical world. We consider that, in a PIS, a user evolves in a space of services. This space offers him a set of heterogeneous services whose focus is to accommodate user's needs. It allows representing knowledge about users and their environment, in order to discover and predict the most appropriate service that satisfies a user's intention in a given context.

This new approach aims to deal with the user's overload. This overload comes from the many possible implementations for each service, on one side, and from the effort required to understand them, on the other side. This new approach is able to hide the complexity of the pervasive environment through an intentional approach guided by the user's context of use. We advocate that understanding user's intention can lead to a better understanding of the real use of a service. Consequently, it leads to the selection of the most appropriate service that satisfies user's needs. To meet these requirements, contextual information plays a central role since it influences the selection of the best strategies of the intention satisfaction.

The key elements of our approach are highlighted in Figure 1. The different modules constitute our *Intentional* and *Pervasive Service Oriented Middleware* (IPSOM). IPSOM is a platform for service discovery and prediction based on the intention and context of the user.

The first element of IPSOM is the *Context Manager* (CM). The purpose of CM is to hide the context management complexity by providing a uniform way to access context information. First, the CM receives raw context data from different

Figure 1. Intentional pervasive information system approach

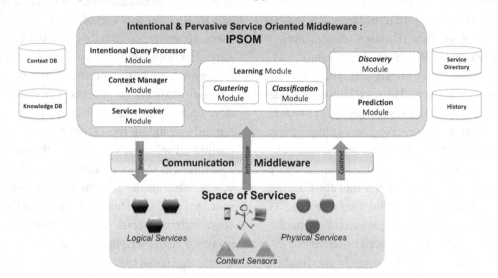

physical and logical sensors (GPS, RFID...). Then, it interprets such data in order to derive context knowledge represented on a higher level. Finally, this knowledge is stored in a knowledge database using a context model.

Next, the *Intentional Query Processor* (IQP) is in charge of processing user's request. Such request represents user's intention, expressed by a verb, a target and a set of optional parameters. This intention is represented according to a specific template (Kaabi & Souveyet, 2007; Rolland et al., 2010). The IQP enriches this request with context obtained from CM. This enriched request, represented in XML format, is then transferred to the discovery module.

Then, the service Discovery Module (DM) allows the satisfaction of the immediate user's intention. It is in charge of discovering and selecting the most appropriate service that fulfils his immediate intention in a given context. The DM mechanism is based on a semantic service description and a matching algorithm, which is detailed in next sections.

Next, the *Learning Module* (LM) is responsible for dynamically determining the user's behaviour model (classification). This module is based on the recognized clusters representing similar user's

situations (clustering). The user's behaviour model, learned and maintained by the LM, will then be used by the prediction module.

Finally, the *Prediction Module* (PM), guided by the user's intention and context, is based on the results from the discovery process previously stored in a history database. From this data, the PM is able to anticipate the user's future needs. Then, it is able to propose him, in a proactive manner, a service that may be of interest. Thus, when the DM selects a service, the triplet <*intention, context, service*> is sent to the prediction module. From the user's behaviour model proposed by the LM, the PM will determine the future user's intention and select the service that can meet its future needs. Thus, the PM is responsible for selecting, from the user's behaviour model, the situation that best represents the current user's situation. As a result, a service selected by the DM or by the PM will be presented in the form of an URI and sent to the *service invoker module*, which is in charge of invoking and executing it.

In next sections, we present our proposed extension of OWL-S service description in details. This extension takes into account the notion of intention and context. We also present an overview of our service discovery process associated to IPSOM.

Semantic Service Description

When a user requests a service, he chooses the intention that the service is supposed to satisfy. To be more exact, this intention emerges in a given context, which can also be used to characterize the service. Thus, from this assumption, we propose to enrich the OWL-S service description in order to include information about the context and the intention that characterizes a service (Najar et al., 2011). The information related to the intention is described through the addition of a sub-ontology. This sub-ontology represents the intention that a service is supposed to satisfy. Expert communities sharing a common vision of their respective fields establish the ontologies defining the intention, like community-supported ontologies proposed by Mirbel and Crescenzo (2010). This vision fits perfectly with the PIS, since the services offered in these systems are tailored to a specific user community. Moreover, information related to context is described by a URL referring to an external resource. It allows the service provider to easily update the context information related to the service description. With this extension of OWL-S, we can describe the intention that a service is deemed to satisfy and the context conditions under which this service is valid and can be executed. This semantic service description is briefly described in next section. More detailed explanation of this extension can be found in Najar et al. (2011).

Intentional Description

According to an intentional perspective, a user requires a service because he has an intention that the service (Sv) is supposed to satisfy. Hence, the importance of considering user's intentions emerges on service orientation. This new dimension is central to the definition of a service.

The term *intention* has several different meanings. According to Jackson (1995), an intention is an "optative" *statement expressing a state that is expected to be reached or maintained*. The no-tion of intention can be seen as *the goal that we want to achieve without saying how to perform it* (Kaabi & Souveyet, 2007). Bonino et al. (2009) define an intention as the *goal to be achieved by performing a process presented as a sequence of intentions and strategies to the target intention*. Moreover, Ramadour and Fakhri (2011) characterize an intention as the *formulation of needs as a service* in order to satisfy a *composition*.

Even if they differ, all these definitions let us consider an *intention* as a *user's requirement representing the goal that a user wants to be satisfied by a service without saying how to perform it*. It represents a requirement formulated by the user, who knows exactly what he expects from the service, but who has no ability to indicate how to perform it.

The intention can be formulated according to a specific template. This template is based on a linguistic approach (Prat, 1997), representing user and service's requirements. This approach is inspired by the Fillmore's case grammar (Fillmore, 1968) and its extensions by dick (Dick, 1989). According to this, an intention is formalized as follows:

Intention: [verb] [target] ([parameter])*

In this template, an intention (**I**) is composed by two mandatory elements: verb (V) and target (T). The *verb* exposes the action allowing the realization of the intention. Possible verbs can be organized in a verb ontology that recognizes significant verbs for a given community. Then, the *target* represents either the *object* existing before the satisfaction of the intention or the *result* created by the action allowing the realization of the verb. Finally, a parameter represents additional information needed by the verb.

We propose to enrich OWL-S service description with the intention associated to it. This is done, as illustrated in Figure 2, by adding a new sub-ontology that describes the intentional information of the service.

Figure 2. Service intention in OWL-S (based on Martin et al., 2004)

Figure 2. Service intention in OWL-S (based on Martin et al., 2004)

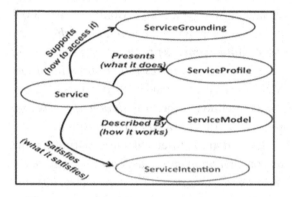

This sub-ontology first adds a property to the Service that we called *'satisfies'*. The range of this property is the added class 'Service Intention'. Thus, each instance of *Service* will satisfy a *Service Intention* description. The *Service Intention* provides the information needed to discover the appropriate service that satisfies a specific intention. Besides, the service intention presents "what the service satisfies," in a way that is suitable to determine whether the service fulfils the user's intention.

This part of the service description, as illustrated in Figure 3, presents the main intention of the service. This intention is formulated, as we described above, according to a specific template (Rolland et al., 2010), in which an intention is represented by a verb, a target and a set of parameters, as described above.

Contextual Description

The notion of context (**C**) represents a key characteristic of any pervasive information system. It corresponds to a very wide notion. Most of the definitions agree that context has something to do with interactions between the user and the information system. The widely acknowledged definition describes the context as any information that can be used to characterize the situation of an entity (a person, place, or object considered as

relevant to the interaction between a user and an application) (Dey, 2001). Also, Truong & Dustdar (2009) consider context elements as any additional information used in order to improve the service's behaviour in a specific situation. This contextual information allows service to operate better or more appropriately (Truong & Dustdar, 2010).

Furthermore, the notion of context is central to context-aware services that use it for adaptation purposes. Context information can stand for a plethora of information, from user's location, device resources (Reichle et al., 2008), up to user's agenda and other high level information (Kirsch-Pinheiro et al., 2004). Nevertheless, in order to perform such adaptation processes, context should be modelled appropriately. The way context information is used depends on what it is observed and how it is represented. Besides, the context adaptation capabilities depend on the context model (Najar et al., 2009).

Different kinds of formalism for context representation have been proposed. Nevertheless, an important tendency can be observed in most recent works: the use of ontologies for context modelling (Najar et al., 2009). According to Najar et al. (2009), different reasons motivate the use of ontologies, such as their capability of enabling knowledge sharing in a non-ambiguous manner and their reasoning possibilities.

A formal context representation was proposed by Reichle et al. (2008). They represent context information based on three main concepts: (1) the *entity* specifying the element to which the context information refers; (2) the *scope* identifying the exact attribute of the selected entity that it characterizes; and (3) the *representation* used to specify the internal representation used to encode context information in data-structures. According to this context model, we directly associate the scope that we observe with the entity that the context element refers to. This let us consider that, in order to have the value for a given scope, we have to observe its corresponding entity. However, this raises an ambiguity since some scopes are not

Figure 3. Example of enriched service description in OWL-S

```
1   ...
2   <service:Service rdf:ID="PREPARE_PROPOSAL_SERVICE">.. </service:Service>
3   <profile:Profile rdf:ID="PREPARE_PROPOSAL_PROFILE">
4   ...
5       <eprofile:context rdf:resource="http://193.55.98.54/iSOA/
6       ExtensionOWL-S/ContextDescription.xml#condition1"/>
7       <iprofile:hasintention rdf:ID="INTENTION_PREPARE_PROPOSAL_INTENTION"/>
8   ...
9   </profile:profile>
10  <intention:Intention rdf:ID="INTENTION_PREPARE_PROPOSAL_INTENTION">
11      <intention:Verb rdf:resource="http:// www.crinfo.univ-paris1.fr/iSOA/
    ExtensionOWL-S/Intention.owl#concept.intention.verb">
12          prepare
13      </intention:Verb>
14      <intention:Target rdf:resource="http://
    www.crinfo.univ-paris1.fr/iSOA/ExtensionOWL-S/Intention.owl#concept.intention.target">
15          <intention:Object rdf:resource="http://
    www.crinfo.univ-paris1.fr/iSOA/ExtensionOWL-
    S/Intention.owl#concept.intention.target.object">
16              proposal
17          </intention:Object>
18      </intention:Target>
19  </intention:Intention>
```

directly related to a precise entity. Therefore, in order to make this context model more meaningful, we believe that we must clearly separate the notion of entity that we want to represent from the property that we want to observe.

Based on Reichle et al. (2008), we define our context model illustrated in Figure 4. In this context model, context information is identified by two important concepts, the *entity* and the *attribute*. The distinction between these two concepts is adopted in order not to mix up the entity to which the context information refers to (e.g. user, device, etc.) with the attribute that characterize the property

that we want to observe. The attribute represents a piece of context information about the environment (location, time...), a user (profile, role...) or a computational entity (resource, network...).

Our context model is based on a multi-level ontology, illustrated in Figure 5, representing knowledge and describing context information. It consists of an upper level, defining general context information (e.g. profile, activity, location, network, etc.), and a lower level, with more specific context information (temperature, latency, etc.). Besides, it provides flexible extensibility to add specific concepts in different domains. All

Figure 4. Context model

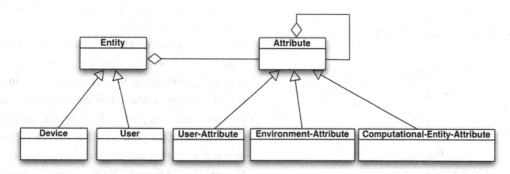

Figure 5. *Multi-level context ontology*

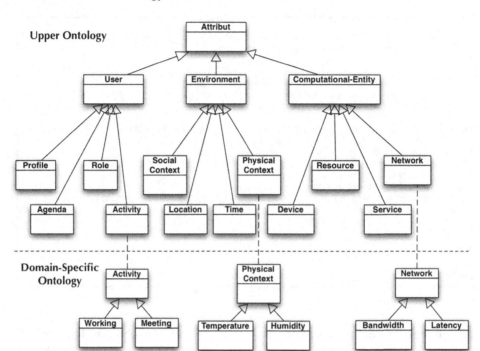

these domains share common concepts that can be represented using a general context model, but they differ in some specific details.

The importance of context information can differ from a user to another according to their preferences. Consequently, we propose a *profile context model*, as illustrated in Figure 6. According to this model, we assign to each context *entity* a *profile*. The *profile* allocates a *weight* to each context *attribute*. The weight reflects the importance of the context attribute. It is represented using the scale indicated bellow:

Figure 6. *Profile context model*

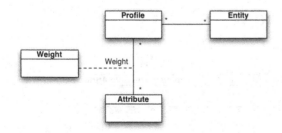

- **Nil:** {0.0}
- **Poor:** {0.1, 0.2, 0.3}
- **Medium:** {0.4, 0.5, 0.6}
- **Good:** {0.7, 0.8, 0.9}
- **Excellent:** {1.0}

Accordingly, the importance of the context attribute is proportional to its weight. When the weight decreases, the importance of the attribute decreases. When the weight increases, the importance of the attribute grows.

Then, we assume that a service is valid in a given context and needs to satisfy a set of context conditions in order to be executed. According to this, we propose to extend the service profile. This extension allows the service provider to define context information that characterizes an intentional service. Contextual information can then be considered as part of the service description, since it indicates context conditions to which the service is better suited. However, according to Kirsch-Pinheiro et al. (2008), context information can not be statically stored in the service profile due to its dynamic nature. Context properties related to service execution can evolve (e.g., server load may affect properties of services running on it), whereas a service profile is supposed to be a static description of the service.

Thus, in order to handle dynamic context information on a static service description, we enrich the OWL-S service profile with a context attribute (Kirsch-Pinheiro et al., 2008). This context attribute represents a URL pointing to a context description file (See Figure 3). Since context information is dynamic and can not be statically stored on the service profile description, we opt to describe context elements in an external file to allow the service provider to easily update such context information related to the service description itself. The context description of a service describes, on the one side, the situation status of the requested service (environment in which the service is executed), and on the other side, the contextual conditions (requirements) to execute the service. Both information elements can be the used for service discovery purpose that is described in the next section.

Service Discovery

The Intentional Pervasive Service Oriented Middleware (IPSOM), which has been presented above, integrates a Service Discovery module. This module is based on a service discovery mechanism guided by user's intention and context. This intentional and contextual mechanism is proposed in order to hide implementation complexity, and consequently to achieve the transparency promised by pervasive environments. The intention concept is used to expose services and to implement a user-centred vision of PIS in a given context. Besides, contextual information plays a central role since it influences the selection of the best strategies of the intention satisfaction.

The service discovery, based on these two concepts (context and intention), will help users by discovering the most appropriate service for them, i.e., the service that satisfies the immediate user's intention in a given context. This service discovery is based on a semantic service description, as presented above, and on a semantic service discovery algorithm. This algorithm performs a semantic matching process in order to select the most appropriate service to the user. The goal of this matching algorithm is to rank the available services based on their contextual and intentional information. Then, it selects the most suitable one for the user. This algorithm semantically compares the user's intention with the intention that the service satisfies and user's current context with the service's context conditions. Then the service having the highest matching score is selected. It represents the most appropriate service that satisfies user's immediate intention in his current context.

More specifically, the semantic matching algorithm, as illustrated in Figure 7, is a two-step process (Najar et al. 2012): *intention matching* and *context matching*. In the first step, the intention matching is based on the use of ontologies, semantic matching and degree of similarity. Concerning the intention formulation, the intention matching is especially based on a verb and target matching. For the verb matching, we use an ontology of verbs. This ontology of verbs contains a domain-specific set of verbs, their different meanings and relations. The degree of similarity is then based on a semantic matching performed using this ontology. It reflects the existence of a semantic link between two verbs in the verb ontology, i.e., the relation between them. We define 5 levels of similarity:

- **Exact:** To which we attribute the score 1.
- **Synonym:** To which we attribute the score 0,9.

Figure 7. Service discovery process

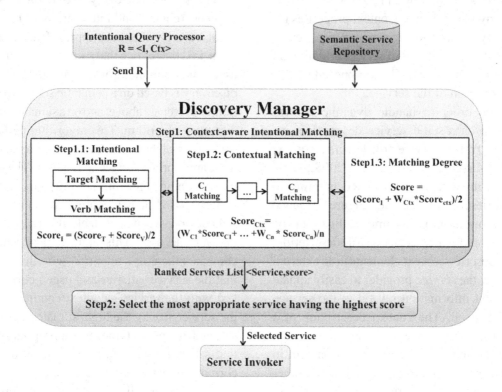

- **Hyponym:** i.e., The required verb is more specific than the provided verb, to which we attribute the score 0,7.
- **Hypernym:** i.e., The required verb is more general than the provided verb, to which we attribute the score 0,5.
- **Fail:** To which we attribute the score 0.

Similarly, for the target matching, we use a domain-specific ontology. This ontology represents the possible targets in a specific domain, from required targets T_U and provided target T_S. The degree of similarity is based on a semantic similarity calculated using the target ontology. This similarity represents a distance calculated based on the semantic link between two targets in the ontology. This semantic similarity is based on the algorithm proposed by Paoluci et al. (2002), using the following 4 levels:

- **Exact:** the required target is equivalent to the provided target.

- **Plug-In:** the provided target subsumes the required target.
- **Subsume:** the required target subsumes the provided target.
- **Fail:** there is no subsumption between the two targets.

Thus, the intention matching between user's intention $I_U = <V_U, T_U>$ and service's intention $I_S = <V_S, T_S>$ is calculated based on the *target matching* and on the *verb matching* (Najar et al., 2012).

The second step, i.e. the context matching, is based on a context ontology, semantic similarity and a set of similarity measures. It matches individually the different context elements constituting the user (C_U) and service context descriptions (C_S). The context description for a user (C_U) or a service (C_S) represents a set of observable context elements, in which $C_U = \{c_j\}_{j>0}$ and $C_S = \{c_i\}_{i>0}$. Each context element is described by an entity (to which the context element refers), an attribute (that characterizes the property that we observe) and a set of observed values. Thus, the context matching is based on *entity matching, attribute matching* and *value matching*. In order to optimize our matching algorithm, we set a threshold below which the context matching process is stopped. This threshold can be customised according to the IS. It is based on the existence of a semantic link between the concepts in the ontology. By default, to proceed with the matching process, it is required that the distance between the concepts c_i and c_j in the ontology does not exceed two links. Accordingly, the threshold is calculated as a matching score: $1/(L+1) = 1/(2+1) = 0,33$), where L represents the number of links between two concepts in the ontology.

Thus, the context element match proceeds as follows: for each c_i and c_j, we (1) match semantically the entity of c_i with the entity of c_j; if the matching score between them is higher than 0,33 then we (2) match the attribute of c_i with the attribute of c_j; if the matching score between them is higher than 0,33 then we (3) match the different values one by one. The matching of the context attribute takes into account the weight assigned to it as explained in the section contextual description. The final score of the attribute matching is equal to the weight assigned to it multiplied by the score of matching between them. More details about the service discovery mechanism are presented in Najar et al. (2012).

INTENTION PREDICTION MECHANISM

In this chapter, we detail an approach predicting the future user's intention (I). This approach provides proactively a service (Sv) that can fulfil the user's future needs. Indeed, this approach is based on the assumption that common situations (S) can be detected, even in a dynamic and frequently chang-

ing Pervasive Information System. Based on this assumption, this prediction mechanism considers a set of time series representing the user's observed situation. We define the notion of situation (S) as the user's intention (I), in a given context (C), satisfied by a specific service. These observations are time stamped and stored in a database after each service discovery process (history). Thus, by analysing the history (H) represented by the triplet <intention, context, service>, the prediction mechanism can learn the user's behaviour model (M) in a dynamic environment, and thus deduce its future immediately intention.

Two main processes compose this intention prediction mechanism: the *learning process* and the *prediction process*, as illustrated in Figure 8. In the learning process, similar situations (**S**) are grouped into clusters, during the *clustering step*. It is a way to reduce the size of the history log by looking for recurring situations. In the next step, these clusters are interpreted as states of a state machine. The transition probabilities from one state to another are then calculated based on the history. This step, called *classification* step, aims to represent, from the recognized clusters, the user's behaviour model (M) based on his situations (S). By interpreting situation changes as a trajectory of states, we can anticipate his future needs. In our approach, this process consists of estimating the probabilities of moving from one situation to other possible future situations.

The intention prediction process is based on the user's behaviour model (M), on the current user's intention (I) and the current user's context (C). Based on this information, the prediction process allows predicting the user's future needs. Thus, it provides him a service that can meet his needs in a fairly understandable way.

Before detailing these processes, we should describe the structure of the history used by these processes. This represents the trace management, described in the following section.

Figure 8. Service prediction mechanism

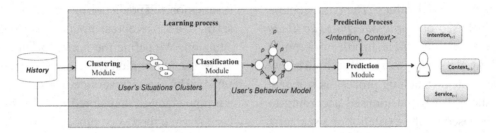

Trace Management

The service discovery process is based on the current user's intention (I) and context (C) in order to find the most appropriate service. The service, which best meets the immediate user's intention in his current context, is selected. We define the notion of situation (S) as follows:

Situation = <intention, context, service>

Indeed, the intention prediction mechanism is based not only on the current situation of the user, but also on its previously observed situations. As a consequence, these observations may be saved for future needs, such as the intention prediction. Therefore, we refer to time series of observed situations as the user's history (H). Each time series represents a time stamped observed situation, as illustrate the Table 1.

Whenever a service is selected, the situation of the user is registered at the end of the history

Table 1. The structure of the user's history

Time/Date	Intention	Context	Service
t_1	intention$_1$	context$_1$	service$_1$
t_2	intention$_2$	context$_2$	service$_2$
t_3	intention$_3$	context$_3$	service$_3$
...	..	..	..
t_i	intention$_i$	context$_i$	service$_i$
...	..	..	..
t_n	intention$_n$	context$_n$	service$_n$

base in order to keep a trace of the user's past situations. The *intention* is represented as an XML schema containing two mandatory elements, namely the *verb* and the *target*. Then, the *context* is also represented as an XML schema containing the context description. Finally, the *service* represents the name of the service selected to satisfy this intention in this context.

Let the user's history H be defined as a set of all the observed situations ξi ordered according to their time of occurrence.

$$H = \{\xi i\} \ i \in [1,n]$$

with n the history size

Each observation ξi represents a user's situation Si, observed at the time ti:

$$\xi i = \{ <Si, ti > \ | \ \forall i \in [1, n], Si \in H \land \ \text{TimeStamp}(Si) = ti \}$$

The user's observed situation Si is composed of the user's intention Ii, his context Ci and the selected service Svi at the time ti.

$$Si = \{< Ii, Ci, Svi > \ | \ \forall i \in [1, n], Ii, Ci, Svi \in H \land \text{TimeStamp}(Ii, Ci, Svi) = ti \}$$

Thus, maintaining the log of the user's observed situations helps the learning process in order to deduce the user's behaviour. This learning process will be explained in the following section.

Learning Process

To realize anticipatory and proactive behaviour of PIS, we first need first to dynamically learn about the user and his behaviour in a frequently changing environment. This represents an important step for the prediction mechanism.

The learning process is based on the analysis of this history in order to reduce the size of existing data. We proceed by grouping the different observed situations into clusters of similar situations and learn the user's behaviour model. It is triggered independently of the prediction step, and may be characterized as a background task that runs periodically. As a result, this process is responsible for dynamically determining the user's behaviour model (*classification*) from the recognized clusters representing similar situations (*clustering*).

Clustering

The first step of our intentional prediction mechanism is the clustering of user's logs. As the history log contains several user's observed situations, it is likely that some of them are similar. Since the size of this history in a dynamic environment can be quite large, clustering similar situations for a user represents an appropriate solution to reduce the data size. Also, the analysis of the clusters allows a better definition on user's habits, which can improve the accuracy of our prediction mechanism. The input of this step represents vectors representing user's situation stored in the history (Table 1).

The main task of the clustering is to detect recurrent situations (S) from all the situations observed before. In fact, the clustering is responsible for determining the situation that is the closest to a set of situations corresponding to highly similar intentions in quite similar context. This provides us with a powerful mechanism to evaluate the user's intention. A user can express the same intention in a slightly different way by using verbs and targets that are semantically similar enough.

Based on verb and target ontologies, we perform a semantic matching between two intentions in order to determine their degree of similarity

On the other hand, the user's context represents highly heterogeneous data: numerical, nominal, qualitative, etc. In addition, the same context element class may have different representations (e.g., the location can be expressed as GPS coordinates, postal address, predefined location, etc.). Thus, to compare two context descriptions, we also use a semantic matching between the context elements. This is based on using similarity measures between the values of context element. Therefore, the clustering will help to find these situations and represent them by one common situation that is closest to all the members of the same cluster.

However, to better adapt to the PIS, the clustering algorithm must meet certain requirements. These are shown in Table 2, based on Mayrhofer et al. (2003, 2004). It represents some essential criteria for pervasive information systems:

- **Unsupervised:** Clusters must be trained in an automatic manner without prior knowledge and without the help of the user.
- **Adaptable:** The clustering process needs to update the clusters already recognized as the user's behaviour can change.
- **Offline:** Clusters must be updated regularly without hindrance to the normal functioning of the system, suggesting a strategy 'offline'. This can be based on a clustering parameter that defines after how long time this process will be triggered. This parameter can be defined according to the dynamics of systems that employ them.
- **Privacy:** We must take into account that the user prefers that some context information will not be used in the clustering process.
- **Limited Resources:** We must consider the capacity constraints of the application in which the algorithm may be deployed.

Table 2. Clustering algorithms comparison (based on Mayrhofer et al., 2003, 2004)

	KM	FKM	SOM	NG	GNG
Online	✓	✓	✓	✓	✓
Adaptability	✓		Variants		✓
Soft Classification		✓	✓		✓
Limited Resource	✓	✓	✓	✓	Depends on growing
Privacy	✓	✓	✓	✓	✓
Real-Time Execution	---	---	--	-	-
Unbounded Clusters					✓
Variable Topology					✓

Algorithms consuming fewer resources are recommended.

Given the dynamic of PIS and in order to cope with changes in the dimensionality of the inputs, the clustering algorithm must be *unsupervised* with a *variable topology*. Since the main objective is to minimize user intervention, clustering must be *unsupervised*. It should not ask for a priori knowledge about the clusters to be recognized and should be able to adapt itself dynamically when a change occurs. Moreover, in order to reduce costs, while keeping up-to-date the clusters, the clustering algorithm should be *offline* using a clustering parameter. This parameter defines after which time we can handle the clustering process. It must be set according to the dynamics of the system in question.

Table 2 illustrates a comparison between different clustering algorithms. Through this table, we can observe that the algorithms K-Means (KM) (Daszykowski et al., 2002) and Fuzzy K-Means (FKM) (Nelles, 2001) cannot be applied in our case. Indeed, they require a priori knowledge about the clusters to learn and have a relatively high real-time execution. In addition, Fuzzy K-Means algorithm does not adapt itself dynamically to change. The NG (Martinetz et al., 1993), which also presents an extension of K-means taking into account the property of neighbor's classification, requires a priori specification of the number of cluster to use. This constraint has led to the elimination of NG since it is difficult to determine the number of clusters a priori in a dynamic pervasive environment. Moreover, SOM (Self-Organizing Map) (Kohonen, 1995) can also be eliminated for the same reasons that K-Means. Furthermore, according to Mayrhfer et al. (2003), SOM tend to forget quickly the clusters previously recognized due to its learning strategy and not the variability of the topology.

Therefore the algorithm GNG (Growing Neural Gas) (Daszykowski et al., 2002) seems to be the most appropriate candidate, since it is closest to our criteria. It adapts itself to the dynamics of the environment, does not require knowledge a priori and has a reasonable real-time execution. The GNG (Daszykowski et al., 2002), compared to other algorithms, offers more flexibility, allowing it to cope with frequent changes in PIS.

The Growing Neural Gas (GNG) shares the same structure with many neural networks. The role of GNG is to recognize and update a set of clusters according to the input vector. It connects the input to a set of outputs nodes that we called 'clusters'. The GNG apply the neighbour property by connecting some neighbour nodes together. Applied to our clustering step, the input represents user's situation composed by an intention, a context, and a service. The output represents the recognised clusters representing similar situations.

Once the clustering process is completed, recognized clusters are then interpreted as states of the user's behaviour model. This is the classification process, presented in the next section.

Classification

In a pervasive environment, users follow a set of behaviour schemas that change over time and depend on the user's situations (S). The user cannot be described accurately in advance. Therefore, a dynamic user's behaviour model is necessary. It must be able to adapt to user's change and take into account the probabilistic nature of his behaviour.

From the recognized clusters and the user's history, the classification module determines and maintains a user's behaviour model. This model represents the user's behaviour as a set of states with a transition probability. This probability determines the probability of moving from one state to another.

Similar to the clustering algorithms, classification algorithms pose some requirements. These algorithms must follow the change and the dynamic of pervasive environments, and therefore adapts themselves accordingly. Moreover, in such environment, it is difficult to establish a priori knowledge about the user's behaviour. Thus, among the requirement necessary for a better classification in a pervasive environment, we can list:

- **Unsupervised:** the model must be estimated in an automatic manner without a prior knowledge and without the help of the user.
- **Online:** the model must continuously adapt itself to user's change.
- **Incremental:** When a new cluster is recognized, the model must increase its internal structure incrementally, without requiring a full learning.
- **Heterogeneous and Multidimensional Data:** the user's situations are represented by heterogeneous data that can be of nomi-

nal, ordinary, numeric, etc. These different types of data must be taken into account.

- **Memory and Load Processes:** in a PIS, a classification algorithm may be deployed on different mobile devices with limited memory capacity often.

Several classification techniques exist. Among these techniques, we note the Bayesian network (BN) (Friedman et al., 1997), Markov Chain (Feller, 1968), Hidden Markov Model (HMM) (Rabiner, 1989), ARMA (Hsu et al., 1998), Support Vector Machines (SVM) (Burges, 1998), Active Lempel Ziv (ALZ) (Gopalratnam & Cook, 2003). Firstly, the BN (Friedman, et al., 1997) works with discrete variables. It requires a priori knowledge and must specify, from the beginning, the different states and hidden variables, which does not meet the above prerequisites. Then, the SVM (Burges, 1998) is a classification method treating only numerical data. In addition, it requests a fixed size of the space of input data. ARMA (Hsu et al., 1998), meanwhile, represents one of the most efficient and most appropriate classification techniques in our field. Nevertheless, the major drawback is its limitation in numeric data processing, making difficult its application to intention and some contextual data having a symbolic nature. The HMM (Rabiner, 1989) represents one of the well-known classification technique. However, this technique can not be applied in a pervasive environment, which requires a dynamic and automatic adaptation to changes, mainly due to the its supervised method.

Thus, Markov chains (Feller, 1968) are more suitable than the HMM for its unsupervised and online characteristic. Moreover, Markov chains are able to classify multidimensional and heterogeneous data in a pervasive environment. Therefore, Markov chains are the most suitable candidates for Pervasive Information Systems, which best meet the criteria outlined above.

The Markov chain (Feller, 1968) is a well-known method for representing a stochastic process in discrete time with discrete state space. We represent the Markov chains model (M) as the doublet $M = (S, p)$, with S representing the different states and $p \in [0,1]$ the probability of transition from one state to another.

In our case, at a given time t, the user is in a situation (state) $s \in S$ representing its intention in a given context. In a pervasive information system, the intention of the user and his context may change. Therefore, the user moves from the situation s to the situation $s' \in S$. The situation s' is the successor state of s with a certain probability p. This transition probability represents the ratio of the transition from s to s' divided by the number of all the possible transitions from s. This probability is represented as follows:

$$p\left(s, s'\right) = P\left(Xt + 1 = s' \mid Xt = s\right) = \frac{Nss'}{\sum_{s'' \in s} Nss''}$$

The prediction process, described in the next section, is mainly based on the results of the classification to predict the next user's intention.

Prediction Process

A more proactive behaviour can be obtained with the prediction of future user's needs. The purpose of this prediction process is to predict the future user's intention in order to propose him the next service that can meet his future intention. This process is triggered when the user sends his intention to the IPSOM middleware. Based on the user's intention (I) and his current context (C), IPSOM is able not only to select the service that best fulfils his immediate needs (service discovery), but also to propose him the next step (service prediction). Based on the user's behaviour model (M), his current intention and context, the prediction module is responsible for finding the state that is the most similar to the current situation of the user.

The Figure 9 illustrates our proposed algorithm for predicting the future user's intention and consequently the most appropriate next service. The line 9 of Figure 9 shows the first step of the prediction process. It illustrates the semantic matching between the intention and context of each state of the model with the user's immediate intention and context. First, this step is based on a semantic matching between the user's intentions and the intention of the state. As mentioned above, an intention consists of a verb and a target. The semantic matching of intentions is therefore based on ontologies describing these elements in order to calculate the matching score between them. Then, the algorithm performs a semantic matching between the user's context description and the context descriptions of the different states of the model. This matching is based on a domain-specific ontology and on similarity measures between the values of context (see Najar et al., 2011, for more details on the different ontologies).

The final matching score represents the sum of the intention matching score and the context matching score. This information is stored with the state identifier. Going through all the states

Figure 9. Service prediction algorithm

Algorithm 1 Service Prediction
1:   **Procedure** SERVICEPREDICTION $(\mathcal{I}_t, \mathcal{C}_t, \mathcal{M})$
2:   Result $= \varnothing$
3:   State$_{ranked} = \varnothing$
4:   State$_{Observed} = \varnothing$
5:   State$_{Successor} = \varnothing$
6:   Score $= 0$
7:   ID $=$ GetStatesID$(\mathcal{M})$
8:   **for each** id $\in$ ID **do**
9:       Score $=$ Match $(\mathcal{I}_t, \mathcal{C}_t,$ id$)$
10:      State$_{ranked}$.add(id, score)
11:   **end for**
12:   **if** State$_{ranked}$ is not empty **then**
13:      State$_{Observed} =$ MaxScore(S$_{ranked}$)
14:      State$_{Successor} =$ FindNextState(State$_{Observed}$, $\mathcal{M}$)
15:      $Su =$ GetService (State$_{Successor}$)
16:      $\mathcal{I} =$ GetIntention (State$_{Successor}$)
17:      $\mathcal{C} =$ GetContext (State$_{Successor}$)
18:      Result.add($\mathcal{I}, \mathcal{C}, Su$)
19:   **end if**
20:   **return** Result
21:   **end procedure**

of the model, we can determine the state the most similar to the current user's situation (line 13).

Subsequently, if a state is identified, IPSOM is responsible for selecting the next state based on the transition probabilities (line 14). This transition probability must exceed a certain threshold. If several successor states are retrieved, then the one having the highest transition probability is chosen. By this choice, we derive the successor state, which represents the future user's intention in a given context. We anticipate the user's future needs by offering him the most appropriate service that can interest him.

When a new service is added to the semantic service directory, IPSOM checks whether this new service can best respond to the situations represented as a state in the user's behaviour model. In this case, the state is updated with the new service. Therefore, the service to be offered to the user during the prediction process remains the most appropriate service according to the user's intention in its context of use.

DISCUSSION AND FUTURE RESEARCH DIRECTIONS

According to Weiser (Weiser, 1991), *pervasive systems* are characterised by their *transparency*. In 1991, Mark Weiser described "the most profound technologies as those that disappear. They weave themselves into the fabric of everyday life until they are indistinguishable from it". Twenty years later, it is clear that we have not reached the homogeneity and invisibility described by Weiser. However, this does not mean that pervasive computing is not already a reality. According to Bell and Dourish (2007), pervasive computing has simply taken a different form than expected by Weiser, in which mobile devices represents the central element of our everyday life. In fact, we interact with a variety of devices and services offered by Information Systems (IS) surround-

ing us. While great efforts have been focused on context adaptation, especially on location and on used devices, today we can observe the limitations of these approaches.

More specifically, in 2007, Kourouthanassis and Giaglis define pervasive information systems as: "interconnected technological artefacts diffused in their surrounding environment, which work together to sense, process, store, and communicate information to ubiquitously and unobtrusively support their user's objectives and tasks in a context-aware manner." However, due to the complexity, heterogeneity, and lack of transparency of our environment, the transition from a *controlled information system* to an *information system available anytime and anywhere*, is still in progress. Moreover, current PIS propose to user different implementations for the same service. Thus, the user, requesting services offered by IS, focuses no longer on his real requirement and on the tasks that really interest him. He finds himself spending time to understand the offered choices in order to select the best implementation, which affect the transparency of such pervasive information system.

An important challenge in Pervasive Computing and especially for Pervasive Information System is to achieve more transparency and invisibility. This is indeed order to make these systems more productive and efficient in a dynamic environment. The real challenge is to hide the complexity of existing systems in order to reduce the intervention and the effort of users by making PIS non-intrusive. By satisfying the user's needs in an invisible manner, PIS can let the user focus on more important tasks that really interest him, instead of spending his time to understand what is happening around him in order to choose the best service implementation.

Thus, the user-centred vision of PIS that we propose represents an interesting step towards the expected transparency. We are strongly convicted that this new vision of PIS represents a more intelligent and personalized systems that concentrate especially on user's requirements in order to satisfy his needs with the most effective way. In fact, what we present here is a proactive PIS based on an intentional prediction approach representing user's requirement as an intention. This intention is emerged, and is more significant, in a specific context. Thus, by considering the *intention* a user wants to satisfy and the *context* on which this intention emerges, we contribute to the improvement of the transparency of PIS, by hiding its complexity and letting the user concentrate on his real tasks.

The user-centred PIS proposed in this chapter presents new opportunities to be explored in different area. Then, and in order to make these systems more personalized and intelligent, a robust mechanism is needed in order to discover user's requirements, and design new services accordingly. This comes from the analysis of user's needs based on requirement elicitation methods. Besides, we consider that a service composition process has to be explored in such systems in order to cope with more complex user's requirements and services. Thus, the specification of a service composition process becomes essential for the improvement of this user-centred PIS.

Finally, an evaluation of our proposed intentional prediction mechanism with a real case study will be conducted in order to demonstrate its validity, efficiency, and precision.

CONCLUSION

Nowadays, our environment is characterized by the evolution of pervasive technologies and the growth of services offered to the user. However, pervasive information systems that derived from using current IS on pervasive environments are quite complex requiring an important user's understanding effort. Indeed, user still has to understand by his own the different service implementations offered by the system and choose the one that is most appropriate to his needs.

Therefore, we propose in this chapter a user-centred vision of PIS based on an intentional prediction approach in a space of services, in order to hide PIS complexity. This approach allows us to anticipate the future user's needs, in order to propose a service that can interest him in a fairly understandable and less intrusive way. By this approach, we believe contributing to the improvement of PIS transparency and productivity through a user-centred view. This view perceives the PIS by the intentions it allows the user to satisfy in a given context.

Thus, we propose an intentional prediction mechanism guided by the context, being integrated in our proposed IPSOM middleware. This prediction mechanism allows: (1) clustering similar user's situations in a set of clusters, (2) learning the user's behaviour model according to recognized clusters, and user's history (3) deducing the user's future intention based on his behaviour's model and on his current context and intention.

This intention prediction mechanism highlights the anticipatory and proactive behaviour of our proposed vision of PIS. We strongly believe that an intentional prediction approach can answer to transparency and homogeneity requirements, necessary for fully acceptation of Pervasive Information System.

Currently, we are finishing the first implementation of the prediction and learning module and its integration in our proposed Intentional & Pervasive Service Oriented Middleware (IPSOM). Based on this implementation, we plan to evaluate our intentional prediction mechanism under a real usage scenario in order to: (1) verify the behaviour of our system with different services under different context configurations; and (2) demonstrate its validity, efficiency and precision. Besides, we are currently working on a methodology for setting the clustering parameter. This parameter should be customized according to the system and its use.

REFERENCES

Abbar, S., Bouzeghoub, M., & Lopez, S. (2009). Context-aware recommendation systems: A service-oriented approach. In *Proceedings of the 35th International Conference on Very Large Data Bases (VLDB)*. Paris, France: VLDB.

Adomavicius, G., Sankaranarayanan, R., Sen, S., & Tuzhilin, A. (2005). Incorporating contextual information in recommender systems using a multidimensional approach. *ACM Transactions on Information Systems*, *23*(1), 103–145. doi:10.1145/1055709.1055714.

Adomavicius, G., & Tuzhilin, A. (2005). Toward the next generation of recommender systems: A survey of the state-of-the-art and possible extensions. *IEEE Transactions on Knowledge and Data Engineering*, *17*(6), 734–749. doi:10.1109/TKDE.2005.99.

Bell, G., & Dourish, P. (2007). Yesterday's tomorrows: Notes on ubiquitous computing's dominant vision. *Personal and Ubiquitous Computing*, *11*(2), 133–143. doi:10.1007/s00779-006-0071-x.

Bonino da Silva Santos, L. O., Guizzardi, G., Pires, L. F., & Van Sinderen, M. (2009). From user goals to service discovery and composition. In *Proceedings of ER Workshops*, (pp. 265-274). ER.

Boytsov, A., & Zaslavsky, A. (2010). Extending context spaces theory by proactive adaptation. In *Proceedings of the Third Conference on Smart Spaces and Next Generation Wired, and 10th International Conference on Wireless Networking*. Berlin: Springer-Verlag.

Boytsov, A., & Zaslavsky, A. (2011). Context prediction in pervasive computing systems: Achievements and challenges. In Burstein, F., Brezillon, P., & Zaslavsky, A. (Eds.), *Supporting Real Time Decision-Making* (pp. 35–63). Springer. doi:10.1007/978-1-4419-7406-8_3.

Boytsov, A., Zaslavsky, A., & Synnes, K. (2009). Extending context spaces theory by predicting run-time context. In *Proceedings of the 9th International Conference on Smart Spaces and Next Generation Wired/Wireless Networking and Second Conference on Smart Spaces*. Berlin: Springer-Verlag.

Burges, C. J. C. (1998). A tutorial on support vector machines for pattern recognition. *Data Mining and Knowledge Discovery*, *2*(2), 121–167. doi:10.1023/A:1009715923555.

Chen, I. Y. L., Yang, S. J. H., & Jiang, J. (2006). Ubiquitous provision of context aware web services. In *Proceedings of the IEEE International Conference on Services Computing*, (pp. 60-68). IEEE.

Daszykowski, M., Walczak, B., & Massart, D. L. (2002). On the optimal partitioning of data with k-means, growing k-means, neural gas, and growing neural gas. *Journal of Chemical Information and Computer Sciences*, *42*(1), 1378–1389. doi:10.1021/ci020270w PMID:12444735.

Dey, A. (2001). Understanding and using context. *Personal and Ubiquitous Computing*, *5*(1), 4–7. doi:10.1007/s007790170019.

Dik, S. C. (1989). *The theory of functional grammar*. Dodrecht, The Netherlands: Foris Publications.

Feller, W. (1968). *An introduction to probability theory and its applications*. Englewood Cliffs, NJ: Wiley.

Fillemore, C. J. (Ed.). (1968). *The case for case, in universals in linguistic theory*. New York: Holt, Rinehat and Winston.

Friedman, N., Geiger, D., & Goldszmidt, M. (1997). Bayesian network classifiers. *Machine Learning*, *29*(2-3), 131–163. doi:10.1023/A:1007465528199.

Gopalratnam, K., & Cook, D. J. (2003). Active lezi: An incremental parsing algorithm for sequential prediction. In *Proceedings of the Florida Artificial Intelligence Research Symposium (FLAIRS)*, (pp. 38-42). FLAIRS.

Hong, H., Suh, E. H., Kim, J., & Kim, S. (2009). Context-aware system for proactive personalized service based on context history. *Expert Systems with Applications, 36*(4), 7448–7457. doi:10.1016/j.eswa.2008.09.002.

Hsu, W. H., Gettings, N. D., Lease, V. E., Pan, Y., & Wilkins, D. C. (1998). Heterogeneous time series learning for crisis monitoring. In *Proceedings of Predicting the Future: AI Approaches to Time-Series Problems, Workshop held in Conjunction with the Fifteenth National Conference on Artificial Intelligence*, (pp. 34–41). IEEE.

Jackson, M. (1995). *Software requirements and specifications: A lexicon of practice, principles and prejudices*. Reading, MA: Addison Wesley Press.

Jiménez Molina, A., Koo, H. M., & Ko, I. Y. (2007). A template-based mechanism for dynamic service composition based on context prediction in ubicomp applications. In *Proceedings of the International Workshop on Intelligent Based Tools IWBT*. IEEE.

Kaabi, R. S., & Souveyet, C. (2007). Capturing intentional services with business process maps. In *Proceedings of the 1ˢᵗ IEEE International Conference on Research Challenges in Information Science (RCIS)*, (pp. 309-318). IEEE.

Kirsch-Pinheiro, M., Gensel, J., & Martin, H. (2004). Representing context for an adaptive awareness mechanism. In G.J. de Vreede, L.A. Guerrero, & G.M.Raventos (Ed), *X Workshop on Groupware (CRIWG)*, (pp. 339-348). Springer.

Kirsch-Pinheiro, M., Vanrompay, Y., & Berbers, Y. (2008). Context-aware service selection using graph matching. In *Proceedings of the 2nd Non Functional Properties and Service Level Agreements in Service Oriented Computing Workshop (NFPSLA-SOC'08), ECOWS*. CEUR.

Kohonen, T. (1995). *Self-organising maps*. Berlin: Springer. doi:10.1007/978-3-642-97610-0.

Kouruthanassis, P. E., & Giaglis, G. M. (2006). A design theory for pervasive information systems. In *Proceedings of the 3rd International Workshop on Ubiquitous Computing (IWUC)*, (pp. 62-70). IWUC.

Lee, K. C., & Cho, H. (2010). A general bayesian network-assisted ensemble system for context prediction: An emphasis on location prediction. In Kim, Lee, Kang, & Slezak (Ed.), FGIT (LNCS), (vol. 6485, pp. 294–303). Springer.

Martin, D., Paolucci, M., Mcilraith, S., Burstein, M., Mcdermott, D., & Mcguinness, D. Sycara, K. (2004). Bringing semantics to web services: The OWL-S approach. In J. Cardoso & A. Sheth (Eds.), SWSWPC 2004 (LNCS), (vol. 3387, pp. 26-42). Springer.

Martinetz, T. M., Berkovich, S. G., & Schulten, K. J. (1993). Neural-gas network for vector quantization and its application to time-series prediction. *IEEE Transactions on Neural Networks, 4*(4), 558–569. doi:10.1109/72.238311 PMID:18267757.

Mayrhofer, R. (2004). *An architecture for context prediction*. (PhD Thesis). Johannes Kepler University of Linz. Linz, Germany.

Mayrhofer, R., Harald, R., & Alois, F. (2003). Recognizing and predicting context by learning from user behaviour. In. W. Schreiner, G. Kotsis, A. Ferscha, & K. Ibrahim (Ed.), *International Conference on Advances in Mobile Multimedia (MoMM2003)*, (pp. 25–35). MoMM.

Meiners, M., Zaplata, S., & Lamersdorf, W. (2010). Structured context prediction: A generic approach. In R. Kapitza & F. Eliassen (Eds.), *Proceedings of the 10th IFIP International Conference on Distributed Applications and Interoperable Systems (DAIS 2010),* (pp. 84–97). Springer.

Mirbel, I., & Crescenzo, P. (2010). From end-user's requirements to web services retrieval: A semantic and intention-driven approach. In J.-H. Morin, J. Ralyte, & M. Snene (Eds.), *Exploring service science: First international conference on exploring services sciences (IESS),* (pp. 30-44). Springer.

Najar, S., Kirsch-Pinheiro, M., & Souveyet, C. (2011). The influence of context on intentional service. In *Proceedings of the 5th International IEEE Workshop on Requirements Engineerings for Services (REFS)- IEEE Conference on Computers, Software and Applications (COMPSAC),* (pp. 470-475). IEEE.

Najar, S., Kirsch-Pinheiro, M., & Souveyet, C. (2011). Towards semantic modeling of intentional pervasive information systems. In *Proceedings of the 6th International Workshop on Enhanced Web Service Technologies WEWST,* (pp. 30-34). WEWST.

Najar, S., Kirsch-Pinheiro, M., Souveyet, C., & Steffenel, L. A. (2012). Service discovery mechanism for an intentional pervasive information system. In *Proceeding of 19th IEEE International Conference on Web Services (ICWS),* (pp. 520-527). Honolulu, HI: IEEE.

Najar, S., Saidani, O., Kirsch-Pinheiro, M., Souveyet, C., & Nurcan, S. (2009). Semantic representation of context models: A framework for analyzing and understanding. In J. M. Gomez-Perez, P. Haase, M. Tilly, & P. Warren (Ed.), *1st Workshop on Context, Information and Ontologies CIAO, European Semantic Web Conference ESWC'2009,* (pp. 1-10). ACM.

Nelles, O. (2001). *Nonlinear system identification.* Berlin, Germany: Springer. doi:10.1007/978-3-662-04323-3.

Nurmi, P., Martin, M., & Flanagan, J. A. (2005). Enabling proactiviness through context prediction. In *Proceedings of the Workshop on Context Awareness for Proactive Systems,* (pp. 159-168). IEEE.

Paolucci, M., Kawmura, T., Payne, T., & Sycara, K. (2002). Semantic matching of web services capabilities. In *Proceedings of the First International Semantic Web Conference* (LNCS), (vol. 2342). Sardinia, Italy: Springer.

Petzold, J. (2005). *State predictors for context prediction in ubiquitous systems.* (PhD Thesis). University of Augsburg. Augsburg, Germany.

Petzold, J., Bagci, F., Trumler, W., & Ungerer, T. (2005). Next location prediction within a smart office building. In *Proceedings of the 1st International Workshop on Exploiting Context Histories in Smart Environments (ECHISE05), 3rd International Conference on Pervasive Computing.* ECHISE.

Prat, N. (1997). Goal formalisation and classification for requirements engineering. In *Proceedings of the 3rd International Workshop on Requirements Engineering: Foundations of Software Quality (REFSQ'97).* Presses Universitaires de Namur.

Rabiner, L. R. (1989). A tutorial on hidden Markov models and selected applications in speech recognition. *Proceedings of the IEEE, 77,* 257–286. doi:10.1109/5.18626.

Ramadour, P., & Fakhri, M. (2011). Modèle et langage de composition de services. In *Proceedings of INFORSID,* (pp. 59-76). INFORSID.

Reichle, R., Wagner, M., Khan, M., Geihs, K., Lorenzo, L., & Valla, M. Papadopoulos, G.A. (2008). A comprehensive context modeling framework for pervasive computing systems. In *Proceedings of the 8th IFIP Conference on Distributed Applications and Interoperable Systems (DAIS)*. Springer.

Rolland, C., Kirsch-Pinheiro, M., & Souveyet, C. (2010). An intentional approach to service engineering. *IEEE Transactions on Service Computing, 3*(4), 292–305. doi:10.1109/TSC.2010.26.

Sigg, S. (2008). *Development of a novel context prediction algorithm and analysis of context prediction schemes*. (PhD thesis). Kassel University. Kassel, Germany.

Sigg, S., Haseloff, S., & David, K. (2010). An alignment approach for context prediction tasks in ubicomp environments. *IEEE Pervasive Computing/IEEE Computer Society [and] IEEE Communications Society, 9*(4), 90–97. doi:10.1109/MPRV.2010.23.

Truong, H. L., & Dustdar, S. (2009). A survey on context-aware web service systems. *International Journal of Web Information Systems, 5*(1), 5–31. doi:10.1108/17440080910947295.

Truong, H. L., & Dustdar, S. (2010). Context coupling techniques for context-aware web service systems: an overview. In *Enabling Context-Aware Web Services: Methods, Architectures, and Technologies* (pp. 337–364). Boca Raton, FL: Chapman and Hall/CRC. doi:10.1201/EBK1439809853-c12.

Vanrompay, Y. (2011). *Efficient prediction of future context for proactive smart systems*. (PhD Dissertation). Katholieke Universiteit. Leuven, Germany

Weiser, M. (1991). The computer of the 21st century. *Scientific American, 265*(3), 94–104. doi:10.1038/scientificamerican0991-94.

Xiao, H., Zou, Y., Ng, J., & Nigul, L. (2010). An approach for context-aware service discovery and recommendation. In *Proceedings of the 17th IEEE International Conference on Web Services (ICWS)*, (pp. 163-170). IEEE.

Yang, S. J. H., Zhang, J., & Chen, I. Y. L. (2008). A JESS-enabled context elicitation system for providing context-aware web services. *Expert Systems with Applications, 34*(4), 2254–2266. doi:10.1016/j.eswa.2007.03.008.

ADDITIONAL READING

Aljoumaa, K., Assar, S., & Souveyet, C. (2011). Reformulating user's queries for intentional services discovery using an ontology-based approach. In *Proceedings of the 4th IFIP International Conference on New Technologies, Mobility and Security (NTMS)*. Paris, France: IFIP.

Baldauf, M., Dustdar, S., & Rosenberg, F. (2007). A survey on context-aware systems. *International Journal of Ad Hoc and Ubiquitous Computing, 2*, 263–277. doi:10.1504/IJAHUC.2007.014070.

Baresi, L., & Pasquale, L. (2010). Adaptive goals for self-adaptive service compositions. In *Proceedings of IEEE International Conference on Web Services*, (pp. 353- 360). IEEE.

Olsson, T., Chong, M. Y., Bjurling, B., & Ohlman, B. (2011). Goal refinement for automated service discovery. In *Proceedings of the 3rd International Conference on Advanced Service Computing, Service Computation'11*, (pp. 46-51). Rome, Italy: Computation.

Welke, R., Hirschheim, R., & Schwarz, A. (2011). Service-oriented architecture maturity. *IEEE Computer, 44*(2), 61–67. doi:10.1109/MC.2011.56.

KEY TERMS AND DEFINITIONS

Classification: Is the process that determines, based on predefined set of cluster, which cluster a new object belongs to.

Clustering: Is the process that tries to group a set of object into clusters whose members are similar in some way.

Context: Can be defined as any information that can be used to characterize the situation of an entity (a person, place, or object considered as relevant to the interaction between a user and an application).

Intention: Can be defined as a user's requirement that represents a goal that a user wants to be satisfied by a service without saying how to perform it.

Pervasive Information System (PIS): Is a new vision of Information Systems available anytime and anywhere, while adapting itself to user's context.

Service Discovery: Is the process allowing to find and to select a service, among the available ones, that answers to an immediate user's request.

Service Prediction: Is the process allowing the anticipation of the user's needs and the selection for him the service that can interest him and that can answer to his future needs.

Chapter 15

On the Use of Optimal Stopping Theory for Secret Sharing Scheme Update

Constantinos Delakouridis
Athens University of Economics and Business, Greece

Leonidas Kazatzopoulos
Athens University of Economics and Business, Greece

ABSTRACT

The location privacy issue has been addressed thoroughly so far. Cryptographic techniques, k-anonymity-based approaches, spatial obfuscation methods, mix-zones, pseudonyms, and dummy location signals have been proposed to enhance location privacy. In this chapter, the authors propose an approach, called STS (Share The Secret) that segments and distributes the location information to various, non-trusted, entities from where it will be reachable by authenticated location services. This secret sharing approach prevents location information disclosure even in situation where there is a direct observation of the target. The proposed approach facilitates end-users or location-based services to classify flexible privacy levels for different contexts of operation. The authors provide the optimal thresholds to alter the privacy policy levels when there is a need for relaxing or strengthening the required privacy. Additionally, they discuss the robustness of the proposed approach against various adversary models. Finally, the authors evaluate the approach in terms of computational and energy efficiency, using real mobile applications and location update scenarios over a cloud infrastructure, which is used to support storage and computational tasks.

INTRODUCTION

Location-based services are becoming more popular than ever, mainly motivated by the convenience and leisure that they provide to everyday leaving, as well as by the availability of smart mobile phones that are equipped with ambient location appliances. The Mobile users' location is estimated based on GPS sensors, triangulation, or proximity techniques. Then, they are assisted with navigation instructions, whilst sometimes much more intelligence is provided to avoid traffic jams, receive

DOI: 10.4018/978-1-4666-4038-2.ch015

proximity discounts from retails shops, restaurants, or pubs, pay insurance services proportionally to their driving ranges, enjoy different toll prices depending the distance covered on high ways, or locate the nearest point of interest. Teenagers, on the other hand, post location-tagged pictures or videos on social networks, upload geo-coded comments, receive in real-time distance calculations when running, discover nearby friends and socialized using proximity criteria.

But all these euphoria for mobile phones' smart applications, intelligent location services and modern gadgets comes with a penalty. Legitimate service provides use location information for profit but without the previous consent of end-users, or they reveal location information to unauthorized third parties. Additionally, the location information is subject of inference or target by malicious attackers, traders, or marketers. The location privacy scheme, called Share The Secret (STS), originally proposed in (Marias et al., 2005), supports privacy using non-trusted servers. In this paper, we (1) enhance the basic STS algorithm in (Marias et al., 2005) to optimize the use of the location information distribution scheme, (2) apply consistency on combining location segments, (3) evaluate the STS scheme using real mobile devices and an "Infrastructure as a Service" (IaaS) cloud, and (4) discuss the robustness of the STS scheme against various adversary models.

In comparison to related location privacy approaches, the STS scheme enhances privacy even if adversaries have direct observation of the position of the end-user. Additionally, STS achieves privacy in cases where the multiple servers that store location information are compromised or collude to reveal the position of the end-user. Thus, non-trustworthy entities can be used to store and provide the location information. In the first prototype implementation, a cloud service was used for location information storage. Furthermore, a time-optimized location updating policy have been designed, so the location segmentation and updating procedure is limited, and, thus, informa-

tion leakage to opponents is minimised. Finally, different privacy levels can be defined through various users' profiles, policies or mobile applications that the users are registered.

The structure of the paper is as follows: Section 1 reports related work on location privacy. In Section 2 and Section 3 we introduce the STS scheme and discuss the basic modules and mechanisms. Section 4 reports robustness issues for the proposed scheme while Section 5 we evaluate the scheme using an IaaS cloud. In Section 6 we conclude the paper and discuss on going work.

PRIOR WORK

Several approaches that enable location privacy focus on the secrecy of Medium Access Control (MAC) identifiers or IP-layer address. On the MAC layer, the problem of interface identifiers is discussed in (Gruteser & Grunwald, 2003) that uniquely identify each client, allowing tracking of her location over time. The authors in (Gruteser & Grunwald, 2003) introduce a location privacy scheme through the frequent disposal of a client's interface identifier. In the IP layer, Mobile IP (Fasbender et al., 1996b) implicitly addresses location privacy by associating two different IPs to the same subject (e.g., mobile user); (1) the static one, corresponding to the home network of the user, and (2) the dynamic one, corresponding to the current access network of the user. The Non-Disclosure Method (Fasbender et al., 1996a) considers the existence of independent, security (software) agents that are distributed on the IP network. Each security agent holds a pair of keys and forwards messages in an encrypted format. The sender routes a message to a receiver through the path determined by the security agents. Moreover, the Mist System (Al-Muhtadi et al., 2002) handles the problem of routing a message though a mobile network by keeping the sender's location private from intermediate routers, the receiver and possible eavesdroppers. The Mist System consists of several routers ordered in a hierarchical structure. Specifically, portal routers are aware of the location of the mobile user without knowing the identity of the user, while the lighthouse routers are aware of the user's identity without knowing her/his exact location.

The aforementioned approaches enforce location privacy in the MAC or IP-layer. Beyond these solutions that apply to the lower layers of the OSI stack, the *anonymity-based* approach has been proposed to address the location privacy issue on the application layer -Through anonymity the location information is unlinked from the subject prior to the information collection process. This means that subjects are reporting their location, but the use nicknames or pseudonyms such that anybody that gain access to the location information will not be able to determine the owner of this information. The idea of using pseudonyms instead of the identities of the users is used by the authors in (Leonhardt & Magee, 1998). They propose the replacement of the identity with a sequence of chained idempotent filters governed by a specific policy language. The authors in (Kesdogan et al., 1985) adopt temporary pseudonymous identities to protect the identity of users in GSM. In addition, work in (Beresford & Stajano, 2004) uses dynamic pseudonyms, and work in (Bettini et al., 2005) relies on quasi identifiers k-anonymity approaches are also applicable for location privacy, such as adaptive cloaking (Mokbel et al., 2006), CliqueCloak approach (Gedik & Liu, 2005), strong k-anonymity (Zhang & Huang, 2009), adaptive nearest neighborhood cloaking (Talukder & Ahamed, 2010), and historical k-anonymity. Further extensions of k-anonymity which consider multiple attributes and personal context of a mobile user include p-sensitivity (Solanas et al., 2008), t-closeness (Li & Li, 2007), and l-diversity (Machanavajjhala et al., 2007).

Furthermore, the IETF Geopriv Workgroup[1] addresses the location privacy issue by introducing the use of a Location Server (LS). The LS registers the position of the subject and discloses position information using specific rules. Such rules are generated by a rule maker (e.g., by the subject) and managed by a specific service (a rule holder). Each subject can explicitly specify the desired level of privacy.

Beresford et al. (Beresford & Stajano, 2004) proposed the idea of mixed-zones where the user's positions are protected within these zones. In (Beresford & Stajano, 2004) this is realized within a zone by not sending any location updates. A mixed-zone based approach, called MobiMix is proposed in (Palanisamy & Liu, 2011). In (Ouyang et al., 2008) mix-zones are adapted depending on user's location.

Additionally, in spatial obfuscation approaches privacy in enhanced by intentionally reducing the precision of the location information. In the approach of Ardagna et al. (Ardagna et al., 2007), the user uses circular areas as location info instead of his exact positions. In SpaceTwist method presented in (Yiu et al., 2008) private queries are supported by pretending that the user issued the query from a fake location. Gruteser et al. also considered spatio-temporal obfuscation to protect movement trajectories of users (Gruteser & Grunwald, 2003).

The proposed STS architecture enables location privacy without relying on the existence of trusted parties (TTPs). The main idea is to divide the location information into shares and distribute it to multiple servers, called STS Servers. These are no-trustworthy entities, assigned to store, erase and provide segments of location data that anonymous users register. Third party services, such as LBS, personal assisting or pervasive applications, access multiple STS servers to determine the location of the user through the combination of the distributed pieces.

SHARE THE SECRET SCHEME

A fundamental approach adopted for secure multiparty computations is the Secret Sharing Scheme (SSS) (Blakley, 1979; Shamir, 1979). In such scheme, a *secret* is divided into various shares for distribution among participants (i.e., private data), and, thus, a subset of participants has to cooperate in order to reveal the secret. A SSS involves a dealer, who owns a secret, a set of m parties, and a subset A of these parties. A SSS for A is a method by which the dealer distributes shares to the parties such that: (1) any subset of parties from A reconstructs the secret from the corresponding shares, and (2) any subset of parties, which does not belong to A is not able to reveal any piece of information concerning the secret. Originally motivated by the problem of secure information storage (Garay et al., 2000), the SSS found numerous applications in cryptography and distributed computing, e.g., Byzantine agreement (Rabin, 1983), secure multiparty computations (Ben-Or et al., 1988; Chaum et al., 1988; Cramer et al., 2000), threshold cryptography (Desmedt & Frankel, 1992), access control (Naor & Wool, 1998), attribute-based encryption (Goyal et al., 2006; Waters, 2008), and generalized oblivious transfer (Shankar et al., 2008; Tassa, 2011).

The proposed Share the Secret (STS) scheme addresses several aspects of location privacy issue.

- STS elaborates on the control of privacy that entities should have over their location. That is, entities are able to define different levels of privacy over different portion of location information, depending on (1) the operation environment (e.g., friendly or hostile) and (2) the location-based service that asks to use the location information.
- STS provides end-users with the ability to explicitly identify applications that collect, process, store, and use location information.
- STS provides anonymity on the distribution and storage of location information.

The proposed STS architecture is designed to make use of un-trusted infrastructures (e.g., grids clouds). Shares of the location information are distributed to public available nodes on a cloud, called STS servers, which act as intermediate and temporal location information storage elements. In that sense, the end-users can authorize location based services to access and combine such distributed location information. This is implicitly achieved through the disclosure of the mapping between a user's pseudonym and her/his location information. STS does not rely on the existence of third trusted parties and avoids complex computational tasks like using public key pairs. Thus, STS architecture is applicable even to tiny devices with several limited resources, such as energy autonomy, memory and processing power (e.g., handheld devices, cellular phones, smartphones).

The STS servers are assigned to store, delete, or provide on request segments (i.e., shares) of the location information that the users register or update anonymously. Third party services, such as LBS, can access the STS servers to determine the location information of a user through the combination of the corresponding distributed shares. This is achieved after a specific authentication process motivated by the corresponding end-user. Furthermore, due to the decentralized nature of the STS scheme, a possible collusion among STS servers, each one maintaining only partial knowledge on the user location information, is ineffective. The secret, i.e. the location information of a user, is never distributed to a specific STS server, and each user dynamically selects different STS servers to distribute the shares, according to the requested service (e.g., location-based friend-find service) and to her policy rules. In the case where multiple STS servers collude successfully, the actual location information of a user is not revealed. The user keeps control over the location information. The position information is estimated locally on the user's device, the user defines which STS servers will obtain partial knowledge of such location information and authorizes third party LBS services to access and reconstruct the location information.

The STS servers can be offered by a Wireless Internet Service Provider (WISP), an Internet feed provider, a VAS or content provider, specialised industry sector, a mobile operator or even a cloud provider. In our reference implementation (described in section 5.1), we used a cloud infrastructure to establish the STS architecture. Hereafter we use the term LBS to denote the value added or pervasive applications that require the location information of a user, asset or device. Each LBS requires the location information, maintained in intermediate STS servers, to provide the required level of service to a subscriber or third party (e.g., tolls operator, parking administration, safety agents, etc.) (See Figure 1).

Location Information Representation

As location information $p(t)$ of a moving object at time t we use a variation of the definition introduced in (Friday et al., 2002), i.e., we define $p(t)$ as the 3-tuple

$$p(t) = \langle (x, y), t, \text{ID} \rangle$$

(*username*, $\sigma(p(t))$)

The Secret Share Algorithm

A secret, that is the $p(t)$ 3-tuple, is shared among m available entities, i.e., the STS servers, in such a way that a minimum set of entities is required to reconstruct the secret. Specifically, we can divide the $p(t)$ into m pieces, $p_1, p_2, ..., p_m$ in such a way that (1) knowledge of any n or more p_i pieces makes $p(t)$ easily computable and reproducible, and (2) knowledge of any n-1 or fewer p_i pieces leaves $p(t)$ completely undetermined. This scheme is called (n, m) threshold scheme (Shamir, 1979); if $n = m$ then all pieces of $p(t)$, p_i, are required to reconstruct the secret $p(t)$. We adopt the Shamir's perfect Sharing threshold Algorithm (SSA) in (Shamir, 1979). Consider that the secret $p(t)$ is a number (or can be easily mapped to a number). We need n points to define a polynomial of degree n-1. We choose at random n-1 real coefficients $a_1, a_2, ..., a_{n-1}$ and set $a_0 = L$. The reference polynomial is then

$$f(x) = a_0 + a_1 x + a_2 x^2 + ... + a_{n-1} x^{n-1}$$

Figure 1. Entities of the STS architecture

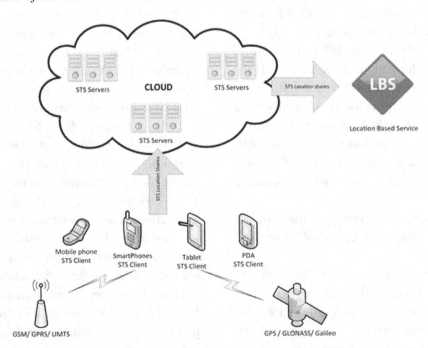

We construct any m points out of $f(x)$, i.e., the set $\{(i, f(i))\}$, $i = 1, \ldots, m$ and let $p_i = f(i)$. Given any subset of n of these p_i, we can find the coefficients of the polynomial $f(x)$ using interpolation (e.g., Lagrange polynomial interpolation) and the secret $p(t)$ is the constant term a_0. It is worth noting that the knowledge of at most n-1 of the p_i values is not sufficient to determine $p(t)$. We refer to $\sigma_i(p(t)) = p_i$ as the i-th share ($i = 1, \ldots, m$) produced by the SSA algorithm. To enhance the privacy level, the selected pseudonym is hashed based on a Lamport S/Key scheme (Lamport, 1981). The pseudonym q of the user that will be used for the j-th transaction equals to $h_j(q)$, where h is a secure hash function that the user and the LBS service have agreed.

To increase further the privacy level, the pseudonym $h_j(q)$, is divided into parts, as well. Each segment of the $p(t)$ is sent to the STS server along with a discrete part of the related pseudonym. As a result, a potential eavesdropper should map multiple pseudonym's segment (say q_i) in order to obtain the correct record $(q_i, \sigma_i(p(t))$ from all the STS servers. If a perfect SSA is used, the pseudonym is divided into m parts where m corresponds to the (n, m) perfect scheme. Regulating the value of m, one can increase the complexity, and the privacy level.

The robustness of the aforementioned pseudonym segmentation approach is enhanced, because the secret is not shared to m STS servers but to l, randomly selected, servers, where $l \leq m$. In this approach the secret can be recovered from s segments, $s < l$ (i.e., a (s, l) perfect scheme). This variation increases the complexity required by an eavesdropper to identify which STS servers keep the location of a specific user.

STS and Service Registration

To produce pseudonyms we employ random generators that reside in user's device. In such a case, an STS server might receive two location shares that belong to two discrete users, but are associated with identical pseudonym q_i. As a result, the STS server might forward an inaccurate segment to the LBS that requested the user's location information. To avoid such a conflict, the STS scheme requires from each user to perform a registration procedure and enter his/her pseudonym's segments to the l STS servers. This procedure requires a handshake between the user and each STS server, which is further discussed in (Marias et al., 2005).

Beyond the registration procedure to the STS servers, user has to provide to the LBS provider the details of how to obtain user's location information. Therefore, the user provides the following information during the registration procedure to the Service:

- The l STS servers that store user's location information (e.g., IP address or URL).
- The user's pseudonyms segments, created by the user for the specific Service.
- The mapping between pseudonym's segments and STS servers (i.e., to which STS server each segment corresponds).

The aforementioned information is communicated to the Service, through a public key scheme, ensuring authentication, confidentiality and integrity.

THE STS UPDATE MECHANISM

The LIT Entry Update Policy

The user authorizes a LBS to access his/her location information for a given period of time, (e.g., a month for toll service billing), through a selection of a predefined policy. Consequently, LIT records of each STS server should be deleted after that period. This can be performed explicitly or implicitly. In the former case the user sends a specialized message requiring the deletion of the LIT record from a specific STS server. This message can be sent when the user desires to prohibit a previously authorized LB from accessing user's location information. A multicast message can inform the entire set of the m STS servers to perform a deletion, as it is described in (Marias et al., 2005). In the latter case, an extra field is added to the tuple, i.e., $(q_i, \sigma_i(p(t), TTL_i)$, which enables user to define a Time-To-Live (TTL_i) value for the record. The STS server checks this field, and in the case it expires, the record is deleted. When the LBS requires user's location, it sends a request to each one of the m STS servers. When the m segments are received, the LBS reconstructs user's location. During the location retrieval some LIT records might not be synchronized among the STS servers. To avoid this, each LIT record is tagged with a sequential number (SEQ).

Location Information Validity Period

In ubiquitous environments mobile users are nomadic; they characterized by high mobility. Thus, the location information, which is stored on the STS servers, must be associated with a Validity Period (VP). VP is an additional field on the $(q_i, \sigma_i(p(t), TTL_i)$ tuple, thus, $(q_i, \sigma_i(p(t), TTL_i, VP)$. The VP period depends on the following parameters:

- **The Type of the LBS Provided:** For instance, a navigation Service might require frequent location updates to provide exact instructions, whilst a tourist guide Service needs periodical updates.
- **The User's Velocity:** For a driver the location information is continuously altered, while for a walker the location information changes at a slower rate. The former requires lower VP value, whilst a higher VP value is sufficient for the latter mobility pattern.

The STS Servers Update Mechanism

When a secret sharing technique is used for shares distribution, users distribute the shares among either trustworthy or/and un-trusted entities. In the former case, an adversary will try to compromise these entities in order to get access to shares, and eventually infer the original location information. In the latter case, there is always a potential threat to employ entities that might collude in order to reveal to secret. The time period required for an attack to reveal the original information is subject to several factors that are difficult to measure.

In this section we focus on possible threats, and analyse when users should update their STS scheme in order to defend against potential attacks. The update of the STS scheme is actually the procedure in which the STS servers that a user employs to store location shares are changed to a completely different set. In such a case, upon selection of a new STS servers' set, the user informs the LBS for that update, and sends the location shares to the new STS servers that have been selected. Apart from selecting new STS servers to store location shares, the end-user might alter the SSS algorithm parameters (i.e., m and n), as well. Since the probability of a successful attack depends on system vulnerabilities, the attackers' knowledge, skills and the methods he used, it is difficult to estimate a probability function for a successful attack. On the other hand, it is preferable to know in advance when the risk of an attack is high enough in order to update in priori the STS scheme. In other words, instead of estimating the absolute time for the STS update, we could force an update when the risk of an attack is relatively high. For the rest of the analysis, we assume that an attack is successful when the attacker compromises the STS servers, thus, grant access to location information shares, and reconstructs the location information.

Consider an established STS scheme and several LBSs which are used by various mobile users. When users store their location information to the STS servers, they should be ensured that their location information is accessible only by the authorized LBSs, for a particular period of time. Additionally, opponents are attempting to compromise STS servers and to reveal the location of the users during the same period of time. If we take a snapshot of the system during runtime, we will notice that the number of location shares that each STS server stores for a particular user increases with time. Intuitively, the probability of reconstructing location information from shares increases as the number of the location updates for a specific user to specific LBS increases. Hence, once the number of the LIT records for specific pseudonym increases, the risk of the location information to be revealed by an eavesdropper increases. In order to avoid this we propose an STS scheme update mechanism.

The Share Update Problem Definition

The STS scheme update procedure introduces additional cost, i.e., transmission of information to LBSs, communication overhead, or even a small interruption of the offered LBS service. Such a communication overload is getting more significant as the STS scheme update procedure is performed frequently.

Ideally we would like to perform just one STS scheme update, the initial one, and no any other. One objective in order to minimize the overhead is to intentionally delay the interval between successive STS scheme updates. Specifically, we would like to decrease the frequency of distributing shares per user among the STS servers, thus, minimize the rate of initiating STS scheme updates. We run the risk of shares revelation once we continue the process of using the same STS servers for long periods since, at each stage of the process plethora of location information shares is circulated among servers. This is risky since an eavesdropper inferences information and analyzes all disseminated information in order to extract knowledge on how to reveal the secret. We are about to stop the process once our belief that the eavesdropper is capable to extract knowledge from the disseminated information is high. Such degree of belief certainty comes along with the decision on when to stop the process, initiate a STS scheme update, at the expense of computational cost and network overhead. The open issue, though, is to find when to decide on an STS scheme update in order to balance the risk of shares revelation and the system overhead.

A possible solution is to regularly (periodically) signal the STS scheme update procedure. However, this is arbitrarily decided and there is no information on how to estimate a possibly effective period of the update. A more sophisticated decision is to observe (1) the volume of the disseminated pieces of information, i.e., a set of shares $\{\sigma_j(p(k))\}$, $j = 1, ...,$ among servers at time k, say X_k, (2) the cumulative information up to time k, i.e., $X_1 + X_2 + ... + X_k$, and (3) the amount of time period from the antecedent STS scheme update procedure, and use all the aforementioned parameters in order to decide when to stop the share dissemination process. The volume of the disseminated pieces of information X_k cannot be predicted at time k since it depends on the mobility pattern of the mobile user, the number of the current registered LBSs at time k, and the requirement of any LBS for using recent and fresh location information. Moreover, a reasonable hypothesis is that the probability that an entity reveals the location information from the disseminated shares can increase with (1) the time passed from the previous initiation of the STS scheme update procedure and (2) with the volume of the information assembled up to time k. Hence, we attempt to delay the share dissemination process as much as possible in order to disseminate a significant amount of information among the STS servers however in fear of location revelation by a possible eavesdropper.

The problem is to find a stopping time in order to stop the process of disseminating shares among STS servers and initiate the STS scheme update procedure. This problem can be treated as an Optimal Stopping Time problem with infinite horizon. In the remainder we propose two optimal stopping policies which calculate the condition (a.k.a. optimal stopping rule) that determines if a STS scheme update should take place.

Optimal Stopping Policies for Share Update

We briefly report the Optimal Stopping Theory (OST) and then introduce the two optimal stopping policies. The Optimal Stopping Theory (OST) (Peskir & Shiryaev, 2006) is related to the problem of choosing the best time instance to take the decision of performing a certain action. This decision is based on sequentially observed random variables in order to maximize the expected payoff or minimize the expected risk/cost (Ferguson, 2012). OST problems are characterized by the availability, at each stage of the process, of a controlling entity—Decision Maker (DM)—that stops the evolution of the process. At each stage the DM observes the current state of the system and decides whether to continue (perhaps at a certain cost) or stop the process and incur a certain loss or discount. The best time, at which the DM stops the process, is the *optimal stopping time*. There are many problems with optimal solutions derived through OST (Shiryaev, 1978). In a OST problem, the DM observes a sequence $X_1, X_2, ...,$ of independent and identically distributed (i.i.d.) random variables, each with cumulative distribution function $P(x) = Prob(X < x)$ and $E\{X\} < +\infty$. At each stage $t = 1, 2, ...,$ after observing $x_1, x_2, ..., x_k$ values, the DM may continue and observe x_{k+1}. The optimal stopping rule is to stop at some stage k^* in order to maximize the expected payoff (Bertsekas, 2005). An OST problem has a finite horizon if there is a known upper bound on the number of stages at which the entity stops. Such

problems can be solved by the method of 'backward induction'. An OST problem with unknown upper bound of stages refers to as infinite-horizon OST problem.

Consider at discrete time $k = 1, 2, ...$ that the STS server receives X_k pieces of information (shares). We assume that X_k are i.i.d. non-negative random variables, $X_1, X_2, ...$ having finite mean, μ. Let $Z_1, Z_2, ... Z_k$ be the random variables that indicate whether the eavesdropper reveals all pieces of information up to k with $Z_k = 0$ denoting that at time k the eavesdropper reveals the location shares and $Z_k = 1$ indicating that the eavesdropper is not able to reveal the k up to k having all pieces of information. We assume that the Z_k are i.i.d. We propose two policies: in the Static optimal Stopping Policy (SSP) we consider that the probability that the eavesdropper reveals the location shares remains constant for all k with $P(Z_k = 1) = \beta$ and $P(Z_k = 0) = 1 - \beta$ where $0 < \beta < 1$. In the Dynamic optimal Stopping Policy (DSP) we consider that the probability that the eavesdropper reveals the location shares increases with time. This is reasonable since the more information the eavesdropper compiles, i.e., observing the $X_1, X_2, ..., X_k$ process, the more capable is the eavesdropper in order to reveal the location shares. In this case we assume $P(Z_k = 1) = \beta^{k-1}$ and $P(Z_k = 0) = 1 - \beta^{k-1}$ with $P(Z_1 = 1) = 1$; we assume that at $k = 1$ the eavesdropper observing only X_1 has a little knowledge for revealing the location shares and the system is considered almost surely robust. We provide the two corresponding optimal stopping rules for both policies.

The aim of the system is to delay the process in order to transfer as much pieces of information as possible in fear of an eavesdropper capable of revealing the location shares. That is, the system (DM in the OST context) by adopting either SSP or DSP should stop the process at the stopping time k^* in order to maximize the sum $X_1 + X_2 + ... + X_{k^*}$ w.r.t. the probability of revealing the location shares. We define payoff for both policies the quantity

$$Y_k = \left(\prod_{t=1}^{k} Z_t\right) \sum_{t=1}^{k} X_t \qquad (1)$$

for $k = 1, 2, \ldots$ and we obtain $Y_\infty = 0$. The stopping time k^* through which Y_k is maximized in Eq(1) is referred to as *optimal stopping time*. We propose an optimal stopping rule in order to find k^* for each policy. Let F_k denote the σ-algebra generated by both $X_1, X_2, \ldots, X_k$ and $Z_1, Z_2, \ldots, Z_k$. Based on the principle of optimality (Peskir & Shiryaev, 2006), the DM should stop the process at k once $Y_k \geq E\{Y_{k+1}| F_k\}$ w.r.t. the one-stage look-ahead optimal stopping rule. The reader could refer to (Bertsekas, 2005) for this class of rules. We are interested in finding the k^* provided that at time k the eavesdropper has not revealed the location shares, that is, we compute $E\{Y_{k+1}| F_k\}$ on $\prod_{t=1}^{k} Z_t = 1$. Hence, we obtain that

$$E\{Y_{k+1} \mid F_k\} = E\left\{ Z_{k+1} \sum_{t=1}^{k+1} X_t | F_k \right\} \qquad (2)$$

Let $S_k = \prod_{t=1}^{k} X_t$, thus, $Y_k = S_k$. In the case of SSP, we obtain from Eq(2) that:

$$E\left\{ Z_{k+1} \sum_{t=1}^{k+1} X_t | F_k \right\}$$

$$= \left(P\left(Z_{k+1} = 0\right) \cdot 0 + P\left(Z_{k+1} = 1\right) \cdot 1 \right) \cdot \left(\sum_{t=1}^{k} X_t + \mu \right)$$

$$= \beta \left(S_k + \mu \right)$$

with $\mu = E\{X_{k+1}\}$.

Hence the optimal stopping rule for the SSP is

$$k^* = \min\{k \geq 1 \mid S_k \geq {}^2 \left(S_k + \tfrac{1}{4} \right)\}$$
$$= \min\left\{ k \geq 1 | S_k \geq \frac{2\,\tfrac{1}{4}}{1 - {}^2} \right\} \qquad (3)$$

The optimal stopping rule for SSP refers to stopping the process at the first k at which the accumulated pieces of information $X_1 + X_2 + \ldots + X_k$ is at least $\beta\mu/(1-\beta)$. That is, the DM stops the process once the criterion in Eq(3) holds true and then the STS scheme update phase takes place. After the STS scheme update the process starts-off and the DM starts with new observations on the X_k process. In a similar way we obtain the optimal stopping rule for DSP in Eq(4):

$$k^* = \min\left\{ k \geq 1 | S_k \geq \frac{2^k \tfrac{1}{4}}{1 - 2^k} \right\} \qquad (4)$$

It is worth noting that the stopping threshold in Eq(3) for the SSP, i.e.,, remains constant for all k. such policy refers to as the optimal policy for the *burglar problem* or the *discounted sum problem* in the context of OST. In the DSP, the stopping threshold in Eq(4) decreases with k thus enforcing the DM not to delay the process since the probability of revealing the location shares increases. Moreover, the β value denotes the sensitivity/self-confidence of the system in light of taking a risk to delay the process. A high β value indicates that the system renders secure enough. This results to longer periods between keys replacement. A low β value denotes a less risky system in delaying the process, thus, resulting in high frequency of STS scheme update.

PERFORMANCE EVALUATION

From a performance point of view, the STS client side induces processing overhead to generate multiple shares for each $p(t)$ update. Secret sharing and distribution are executed on the user's mobile handset, with limited energy and processing power. In addition, possible delays on performing STS tasks due to the aforementioned limitations may affect the overall LBS quality of service and experience. On the other hand, the STS server side is assumed to be a resilient infrastructure, with adequate processing power, bandwidth and storage. Hence, we concentrate on mobile devices performance when STS tasks are used.

Simulation Setup

Configuring a reliable STS-servers architecture is not complicated. We need to assure that STS servers are deployed on various network locations with adequate storage, bandwidth, and processing capabilities, and globally accessible. Hence, we considered an "Infrastructure as a Service" (IaaS) cloud network model as the most appropriate choice. In the IaaS service model, a service is provided with processing, storage and networking resources in order to apply and run arbitrary software tasks, which can include operating systems, public services, or applications. The user does not manage or control the underlying cloud. From the public available, open source IaaS service model we have used Nimbus[2]. Nimbus supports open source development practices via modular and extensible code, which has been reported as ideal for the academic community (Sempolinski & Thain, 2010).

We established our network-layer structure on the Nimbus cloud provided by the Future Grid[3], an ongoing academic project for developing collaboratively a high-performance grid testbed. For the underlying network establishment on Nimbus, we deployed multiple Virtual Machines (VMs), each one emulating a physical computing environment. Requests for CPU, memory, storage or networking are managed by the virtualization layer. For our network establishment, each VM is running a Linux Debian version 5[4]. Each VM has each own virtual network interface, and therefore is directly accessible via the Internet.

Once our VM network is established we have deployed the STS architecture. The STS servers and the Look up service modules were developed in Java[5], following a Web service concept and integrated on Apache Tomcat[6] HTTP server. Each STS server module was deployed on a different VM. From the client side, we developed the STS client for two of the most popular mobile operating systems namely iOS and Google Android. In the former case, the mobile handset application was developed under the 4.1 Apple iPhone SDK[7] in objective C. For the latter, the STS application was developed under Android version 2.2 (Froyo)[8]. We have installed the mobile applications in corresponding real mobile devices. Both applications have configured to gain hardware access (e.g., GPS) in order to collect GPS location information, apply STS and forward the shares to the corresponding STS servers on the cloud.

To evaluate the performance of the mobile devices we used the following modules.

- iOS: For CPU usage we have used the Apple's Instruments application[9]. Using Instruments we can trace different aspects for specific process behaviour. For memory consumption we have used the mach build-in library[10].

- Android: For energy consumption we have used PowerTutor, a power management and activity state component that uses the model generated by PowerBooter for online power estimation (Zhang et al., 2010). Furthermore, for CPU usage and memory consumption we have used the TOP command provide from the Android operating system (See Figure 2).

Finally, for the evaluation of the overall architecture, we implemented a Location Based Service module which required user's location information to provide a corresponding service. The required $p(t)$ refresh rate varies per LBS, based on the type of the service provided. The aforementioned module was developed in Java and deployed on the cloud network.

Figure 2. Android (left) and iOS (right) applications' screen shots

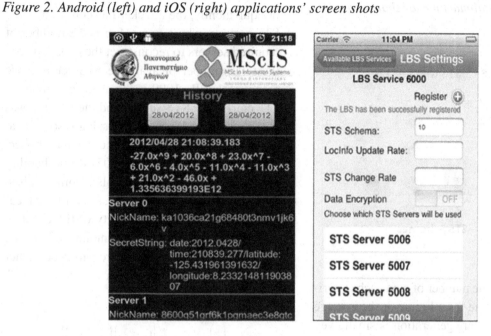

Experimental Results

Processing Overhead

In the scenario where the generation rate of shares remains static, and thus $p(t)$ updates are periodic, the evaluation is concentrated on the overheard introduced by different STS schemes. Thus, we have applied different Shamir sharing schemes and estimated the average required time for share generation. We have deployed a static number of 30 available STS servers on the cloud.

According to Shamir's algorithm (Shamir, 1979), the complexity for producing shares is related to values n and m (i.e. the degree of Shamir's polynomial and the total number of shares correspondingly). By increasing those values, the total shares computational time increases as well. Thus, we have used two different configurations for evaluation. In the first configuration, we have considered that the STS client application distributes the location shares among a certain number of STS servers whilst the number of servers required to reconstruct the secret varies. Sequentially, in the second configuration, for the same number of n STS servers, we altered the total number of STS servers where the secret was distributed.

Figure 3 and Figure 4 depict the results of our experiments when the iOS application was used. The results presented in (Marias et al., 2005) shown that following a *(7,10)* scheme provides a high level of privacy. Hence, we evaluated the STS architecture, following the aforementioned configuration. For the first configuration, we set

Figure 3. Computational time for shares creation when n varies

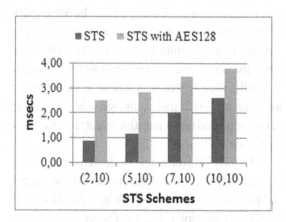

Figure 4. Computational time for shares creation when m varies

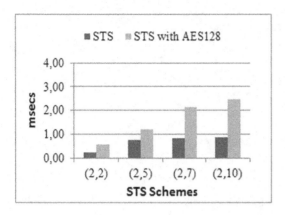

$m=10$ and adjust the number of n on each experiment. As we can see from Figure 3, the average time for location share generation is small even for complex STS schemes i.e., *2.6 msecs* for a *(10,10)* scheme. Furthermore, as *n* increases the corresponding time to compute the shares is not significantly increased. Thus, although the complexity (i.e. the degree of Shamir's polynomial and the total number of shares) of the adopted STS scheme is increased, the computational time for shares creation remains tolerable (~0.58 msecs on average). Hence, since the location privacy level offered by the STS architecture depends on the complexity of the used scheme, we can enhance privacy and at the same time keep the computational overhead on acceptable levels.

In the second configuration, we have measured the time to compute the STS shares in case where *n* is fixed and *m* varies (Figure 4). In our experiments, we set *n=2*, and alter m i.e. the number of servers that maintain the shares. The observed time for share generation on average is small. Actually, the computational time is increased on average by ~0.2 msecs as we add one more server required for storing the secret (i.e., increase m by one).

The STS Scheme is also evaluated on scenarios where STS servers collude to reveal the secret, or are compromised. The authors in (Marias et al., 2005) assumed that z STS servers collude,

or equivalently, the attacker has compromised z STS servers, where $n \leq z < M$, n is the number of required servers to reconstruct the *p(t)*, and *M* is the total number of available STS servers. We assumed that R=1000 is the average number of LIT entries per STS server, and the attacker was outfitted with adequate processing resources to check 10^{12} pseudonym segment combinations/sec. According to (Marias et al., 2005), the probability that an attacker, which controls z compromised STS servers in order to reconstruct a user location, is equal to the probability of the event E, defined as E = "The minimum number of the STS servers that a user selects to reconstruct his/her location is y, or y+1, or ...,or z, where y<=z". P(E) is defined as,

$$P\left(E\right) = \frac{\begin{pmatrix} z \\ z \end{pmatrix} + \sum_{i=1}^{z-y} \left[\begin{pmatrix} z \\ z-i \end{pmatrix} \begin{pmatrix} M-z \\ i \end{pmatrix} \right]}{\begin{pmatrix} M \\ z \end{pmatrix}}$$

The attacker must try on average of *(R^z+1)*0,5* possible combinations in order to find out if the location segments obtained from the z servers are sufficient to reconstruct the location information of any user, and this requires some time T (second location privacy parameter). Table 1 shows the location privacy parameter levels for different STS schemes, measured using the values for M, z and y that were used in simulations.

Figure 5 and Figure 6 show an extended view of the privacy level in terms of the probability P(E). In details, in Figure 5 we plot P(E) when z=10 and y varies from 1 to 10, for different

Table 1. Privacy level

M	z	y	P(E)	T (years)
30	10	7	0,0048	
30	10	5	0,1687	
30	10	2	0,7229	

Figure 5. Privacy level in terms of P(E)

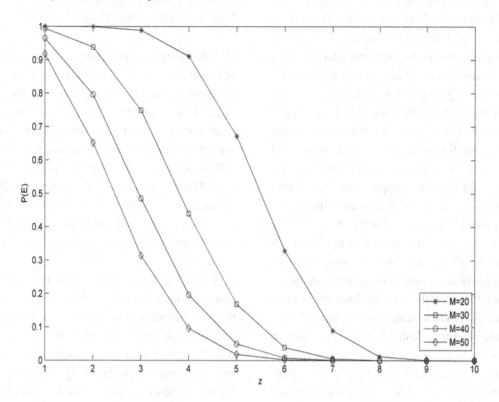

Figure 6. Privacy level in terms of P(E)

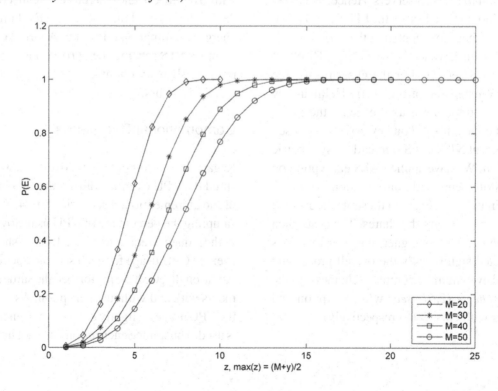

values of M. On the other hand, in Figure 6 we plot P(E) when y=2 and m varies from 2 to (M+y)/2, for different values of M.

Taking the two configurations into account, we have noticed that the increase in the computational time is greater for n, when equivalently modify n and m. Actually, the results from Figure 3 and 4 are following Shamir's theory. Since the Shamir's algorithm is based on polynomials and *n* is related to the degree of the polynomial, the computational time to compute the shares will increased as *n* increases (i.e. a more complex *n* x *n* system should be solved). On the other hand by altering *m*, we keep the degree of the Shamir's polynomial definite and thus the computational time is slightly increased as m increase. A useful conclusion though is the actual difference between the two rates. When n increases the required time is growing ~3 times faster rather than when m increases.

To enhance further the privacy mechanism, upon generating the LIT shares we have applied symmetric encryption over each share before its distribution to the STS servers. Hence, an eavesdropper should first decrypt the LIT shares before combining them to reconstruct the *p(t)*. The key was agreed in advance between the STS client and the LBS service. For the experiments, the OAKLEY extension of the Diffie-Hellman key agreement protocol was used once for the establishment of an AES 128 bit key. AES was chosen as the current NIST FIPS standard for symmetric encryption. We have applied AES encryption on all the aforementioned configurations and scenarios. Figure 3 and Figure 4 illustrate the average to create and encrypt the shares. The cost when encryption is used is higher, however this does not affected significantly the overall processing overhead even in more complex schemes e.g. the *(10,10) scheme* (*2,61msecs* w/o encryption and *3,8msecs* with encryption respectively).

Energy Consumption and Computation Overhead

For the energy consumption, we conducted experiments in which we aimed to estimate the STS client overload. In order to achieve this, the STS client was set to generate shares on high refresh rates, based on a complex SSA. Figure 7, depicts the aggregated energy consumption when an *(10,10)* scheme was used, every 1 sec, 5 sec, 10 sec, 30 sec. (scenarios 1 to 4 respectively). The application was deployed on an HTC Desire Bravo smartphone, running Android 2.3. We have run each scenario 15 times, each run was lasted 10 minutes.

From Figure 7, we can see that the energy consumption increases for higher refresh rates as the experiment progresses. The increase rate follows a linear curve. Furthermore, for the highest refresh rate (1 sec) the aggregated energy consumption was approximately 250 joules. The mobile handset we used, which is considered as an average capability device, has a 3,7 Volt battery with 1800mAh, and therefore it can consume 23976 Joules without charging. Excluding the energy consumption due to the Android OS, this complex STS scheme (i.e., *(10,10)*) is capable to produce shares without encryption for approximately 15 hours.

Computational Overheads

Regarding the computational overhead, we measured the CPU overload during the running time of the aforementioned scenarios 1 to 4. We were sampling the percentage of CPU usage over time with frequency equal to 1 sec. Table 2 shows the average CPU usage for each scenario per device. Additionally, we have performed the same experiments with and without encryption. As expected the CPU usage is slightly greater when encryption is used. Thus, since encryption does not introduce

Figure 7. Energy consumption

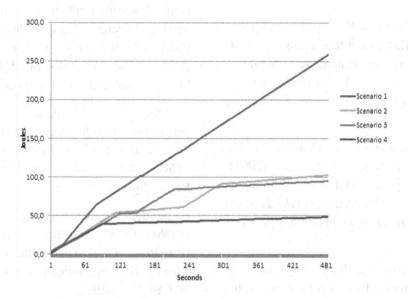

significant overhead, the encryption could be easily adopted. However the average CPU usage for both devices is not crucial when the location update frequency is lower than 1 update per second. To the best of our knowledge, there is no any LBS application that requires such dense location updates. Thus, since encryption will not introduce significant computational cost, the location share encryption policy could be easily adopted.

CONCLUSION

In this chapter, we propose the STS scheme that segments and distributes the location information to various, non-trusted, entities from where it will be reachable for reconstruction by authorized LBS. The STS scheme does not require any TTP. It is combined with pseudonyms to prevent location information disclosure even when there is a direct observation attack or target isolation. In addition, we introduce a mechanism for updating the STS servers based on the Optimal Stopping Theory. Furthermore, we analyze the proposed approach against various adversary models. We have found that STS approach is resilient to common attacks. Additionally, we discuss the consistency of the proposed STS scheme and evaluate it in terms of computational and energy efficiency. The results of the evaluation show that STS does not overload the mobile operations.

Table 2. Average percentage of CPU usage

Scenario	Plain Location Share		Encrypted Location Share	
	Android	iPhone	Android	iPhone
1	29,6	25,52	31,96	27,02
2	8,04	7,13	8,8	9,87
3	5,22	5,94	6,45	7,08
4	3,3	3,29	3,98	4,37

REFERENCES

Al-Muhtadi, J., Campbell, R., Kapadia, A., Mickunas, D., & Yi, S. (2002). Routing through the mist: Privacy preserving communication in ubiquitous computing environments. In *Proceedings International Conference of Distributed Computing Systems*. IEEE.

Ardagna, C., Cremonini, M., Damiani, E., De Capitani di Vimercati, S., & Samarati, P. (2007). Location privacy protection through obfuscation-based techniques. In *Proceedings of the 21st Annual IFIP Conference on Data and Applications Security*. IFIP.

Ben-Or, M., Goldwasser, S., & Wigderson, A. (1988). Completeness theorems for non-cryptographic fault-tolerant distributed computations. In *Proceedings of the 20th ACM Symposium on the Theory of Computing*, (pp. 1-10). ACM.

Beresford, A. R., & Stajano, F. (2004). Mix zones: User privacy in location-aware services. In *Proceedings of PerCom Workshops* (pp. 127–131). PerCom. doi:10.1109/PERCOMW.2004.1276918.

Bertsekas, D. P. (2005). *Dynamic programming and optimal control* (3rd ed.).

Bettini, C., Wang, X., & Jajodia, S. (2005). Protecting privacy against location-based personal identification. In Jonker & Petkovic (Eds.), Secure Data Management (LNCS), (Vol. 3674, pp. 185-199). Berlin: Springer.

Blakley, G. R. (1979). Safeguarding cryptographic keys. In *Proceedings of the National Computer Conference*, (vol. 48, pp. 313-317). AFIPS.

Chaum, D., Crepeau, C., & Damgard, I. (1988). Multiparty unconditionally secure proto-cols. In *Proceedings of the 20th ACM Symposium on the Theory of Computing*, (pp. 11-19). ACM.

Cramer, R., Damgard, I., & Maurer, U. (2000). General secure multi-party computation from any linear secret-sharing scheme. In Preneel, B. (Ed.), *Advances in Cryptology, EUROCRYPT 2000 (LNCS)* (Vol. 1807, pp. 316–334). Berlin: Springer-Verlag. doi:10.1007/3-540-45539-6_22.

Desmedt, Y., & Frankel, Y. (1992). Shared generation of authenticators and signatures. In Feigenbaum, J. (Ed.), *Advances in Cryptology - CRYPTO '91 (LNCS)* (Vol. 576, pp. 457–469). Berlin: Springer-Verlag.

Fasbender, A., Kesdogan, D., & Kubitz, O. (1996a). Analysis of security and privacy in mobile IP. In *Proceedings of the 4th International Conference on Telecommunication Systems, Modeling and Analysis*. IEEE.

Fasbender, A., Kesdogan, D., & Kubitz, O. (1996b). Variable and scalable security: Protecting of location information in mobile IP. In *Proceedings of the 46th IEEE VTC*. IEEE.

Ferguson, T. S. (2012). *Optimal stopping and applications*. Retrieved from http://www.math.ucla.edu/tom/Stopping/Contents.html

Friday, A., Muller, H., Rodden, T., & Dix, A. (2002). A lightweight approach to managing privacy in location-based services. In *Proceedings of the Equator Annual Conference*. Equator.

Garay, Gennaro, Jutla, & Rabin. (2000). Secure distributed storage and retrieval. *Theoretical Computer Science*, *243*(1-2), 363–389. doi:10.1016/S0304-3975(98)00263-1.

Gedik, B., & Liu, L. (2005). Location privacy in mobile systems: A personalized anonymization model. [ICDCS.]. *Proceedings of, ICDCS2005*, 620–629.

Goyal, V., Pandey, O., Sahai, A., & Waters, B. (2006). Attribute-based encryption for ne-grained access control of encrypted data. In *Proceedings of the 13th ACM conference on Computer and Communications Security*, (pp. 89-98). ACM.

Gruteser, M., & Grunwald, D. (2003). Anonymous usage of location-based services through spatial and temporal cloaking. [MobiSys.]. *Proceedings of MobiSys, 03*, 31–42.

Gruteser, M., & Grunwald, D. (2003). Enhancing location privacy in wireless LAN through disposable interface identifiers: A quantitative analysis. In *Proceedings of the WMASH '03*. WMASH.

Kesdogan, D., Reichl, P., & Junghärtchen, K. (1998). Distributed temporary pseudonyms: A new approach for protecting location information in mobile communication networks. In *Proceedings of the 5th European Symposium on Research in Computer Security*. IEEE.

Lamport, L. (1981). Password authentication with insecure communication. *Communications of the ACM, 24*(11), 770–772. doi:10.1145/358790.358797.

Leonhardt, U., & Magee, J. (1998). Security considerations for a distributed location service. *Journal of Network and Systems Management, 6*(1). doi:10.1023/A:1018777802208.

Li, N., Li, T., & Venkatasubramanian, S. (2007). t-Closeness: Privacy beyond k-anonymity and l-diversity. In *Proceedings of the IEEE 23rd International Conference on Data Engineering (ICDE 2007)*, (pp. 106-115). IEEE.

Machanavajjhala, A., Kifer, D., Gehrke, J., & Venkitasubramaniam, M. (2007). L-diversity: Privacy beyond k-anonymity. *ACM Transactions on Knowledge Discovery from Data, 1*(1).

Marias, G. F., Delakouridis, C., Kazatzopoulos, L., & Georgiadis, P. (2005). Location privacy through secret sharing techniques. In *Proceedings of the 1st IEEE International Workshop on Trust, Security and Privacy for Ubiquitous Computing*, (pp. 614-620). IEEE.

Mokbel, M. F., Chow, C. Y., & Aref, W. G. (2006). The new casper: Query processing for location services without compromising privacy. In *Proceedings of (VLDB '06)*, (pp. 763-774). VLDB.

Naor, M., & Wool, A. (1998). Access control and signatures via quorum secret sharing. *IEEE Transactions on Parallel and Distributed Systems, 9*(1), 909–922. doi:10.1109/71.722223.

Ouyang, Y., Xu, Y., Le, Z., Chen, G., & Makedon, F. (2008). Providing location privacy in assisted living environments. [PETRA.]. *Proceedings of PETRA, 2008*, 1–8. doi:10.1145/1389586.1389633.

Palanisamy, B., & Liu, L. (2011). Mobimix: Protecting location privacy with mix-zones over road networks. [ICDE.]. *Proceedings of ICDE, 2011*, 494–505.

Peskir, G., & Shiryaev, A. (2006). *Optimal stopping and free boundary problems*. Zuerich, Switzerland: Birkhauser.

Rabin, M. O. (1983). Randomized byzantine generals. In *Proceedings of the 24th IEEE Symposium on Foundations of Computer Science*, (pp. 403-409). IEEE.

Sempolinski, P., & Thain, D. (2010). A comparison and critique of eucalyptus, open nebula and nimbus. In *Proceedings of IEEE International Conference on Cloud Computing Technology and Science*, (pp. 417-426). IEEE.

Shamir, A. (1979). How to share a secret. *Communications of the ACM, 22*(11), 612–613. doi:10.1145/359168.359176.

Shankar, B., Srinathan, K., & PanduRangan, C. (2008). Alternative protocols for generalized oblivious transfer. In S. Rao, M. Chatterjee, P. Jayanti, C. S. Murthy, & S. K. Saha (Eds.), *Proceedings of ICDCN 2008* (LNCS), (vol. 4904, pp. 304-309). Berlin: Springer-Verlag.

Shiryaev, A. (1978). *Optimal stopping rules*. New York: Springer-Verlag.

Solanas, A. Seb_e, F., & Domingo-Ferrer, J. (2008). Micro-aggregation-based heuristics for p-sensitive k-anonymity: One step beyond. In *Proceedings of the 2008 International Workshop on Privacy and Anonymity in Information Society (PAIS '08)*, (pp. 61-69). PAIS.

Talukder, N., & Ahamed, S. I. (2010). Preventing multi-query attack in location-based services. In *Proceedings of the 3rd ACM Conference on Wireless Network Security (WiSec '10)*, (pp. 25-36). ACM.

Tassa, T. (2011). Generalized oblivious transfer by secret sharing. *Designs, Codes and Cryptography*, 58.

Waters, B. (2008). *Ciphertext-policy attribute-based encryption: An expressive, efficient, and provably secure realization*. Retrieved from http://eprint.iacr.org/

Yiu, M. L., Jensen, C. S., Huang, X., & Lu, H. (2008). Spacetwist: Managing the trade-offs among location privacy, query performance, and query accuracy in mobile services. [ICDE.]. *Proceedings of, ICDE2008*, 366–375.

Zhang, C., & Huang, Y. (2009). Cloaking locations for anonymous location based services: A hybrid approach. *Journal Geoinformatica*, *13*, 159–182. doi:10.1007/s10707-008-0047-2.

Zhang, L., Tiwana, B., Qian, Z., Wang, Z., Dick, R. P., Mao, Z. M., & Yang, L. (2010). Accurate online power estimation and automatic battery behavior based power model generation for smartphones. In *Proceedings International Conference Hardware/Software Codesign and System Synthesis*, (pp. 105–114). IEEE.

ADDITIONAL READING

Cachin, C., Kursawe, K., Lysyanskaya, A., & Strobl, R. (2002). Asynchronous verifiable secret sharing and proactive cryptosystems. In *Proceedings of the 9th ACM Conference Computer and Communications Security*, (pp. 88–97). ACM.

Cachin, C., Kursawe, K., & Shoup, V. (2005). Random oracles in Constantinople: Practical asynchronous Byzantine agreement using cryptography. *Journal of Cryptology*, *18*(3), 219–246. doi:10.1007/s00145-005-0318-0.

Chang, T. Y., Hwang, M. S., & Yang, W. P. (2005). An improvement on the Lin–Wu (t,n) threshold verifiable multi-secret sharing scheme. *Applied Mathematics and Computation*, *163*(1), 169–178. doi:10.1016/j.amc.2004.01.029.

Chor, B., Goldwasser, S., Micali, S., & Awerbuch, B. (1985). Verifiable secret sharing and achieving simultaneity in the presence of faults. In *Proceedings of the 26th IEEE Symposium on Foundations of Computer Science*. IEEE Computer Society.

Dehkordi, M. H., & Mashhadi, S. (2008). New efficient and practical verifiable multi-secret sharing schemes. *Information Sciences*, *178*, 2262–2274. doi:10.1016/j.ins.2007.11.031.

Feldman, P. (1987). A practical scheme for non-interactive verifiable secret sharing. In *Proceedings of the 28th IEEE Symposium on Foundations of Computer Science*. IEEE Computer Society.

Fitzi, M., Garay, J., Gollakota, S., Rangan, C. P., & Srinathan, K. (2006). Round-optimal and efficient verifiable secret sharing. In *Proceedings of the Third Theory of Cryptography Conference*. New York, NY: ACM.

Goldreich, O. (2012). *Secure multiparty computation*. Retrieved from http://www.wisdom.weizman.ac.il/oded/pp.html

Katz, J., Koo, C., & Kumaresan, R. (2008). Improved the round complexity of VSS in point-to-point networks. In *Proceedings of the ICALP 2008* (LNCS), (vol. 5126, pp. 499-510). Berlin: Springer-Verlag.

Maurer, U. (2006). Secure multi-party computation made simple. *Discrete Applied Mathematics*, *154*(2), 370–381. doi:10.1016/j.dam.2005.03.020.

Patra, A., Choudhary, A., Rabin, T., & Rangan, C. P. (2009). The round complexity of verifiable secret sharing revisited. In *Proceedings of Advances in Cryptology, Crypto '09* (pp. 487–504). Santa Barbara, CA: Crypto. doi:10.1007/978-3-642-03356-8_29.

Schultz, D., Liskov, B., & Liskov, M. (2008). Brief announcement: mobile proactive secret sharing. In *Proceedings of the PODC '08*. PODC.

Shao, J., & Cao, Z. (2005). A new efficient (t,n) verifiable multi-secret sharing (VMSS) based on YCH scheme. *Applied Mathematics and Computation*, *168*(1), 135–140. doi:10.1016/j.amc.2004.08.023.

Zhou, L. (2005). APSS: Proactive secret sharing in asynchronous systems. *ACM Transactions on Information and System Security*, *8*(3), 259–286. doi:10.1145/1085126.1085127.

KEY TERMS AND DEFINITIONS

Cloud Infrastructure: The infrastructure (machines or resources) provided by Cloud Computing.

Cryptographic Technique: Technique used for secure communication or information exchange.

Intelligent Location Service: The capability of handling complex phenomena using location and time information.

Location-Based Service: General class of computer program level service used to include specific controls for location and time data.

Location Privacy: Controlling the access in location information.

Optimal Stopping Theory: Theory studying the right time for taking a specific action under specific conditions.

Secret Sharing Scheme: Technique for distributing a secret among a group of participants each of them is allocated a share of the secret.

ENDNOTES

[1] http://datatracker.ietf.org/wg/geopriv/charter/
[2] http://www.nimbusproject.org,
[3] https://portal.futuregrid.org
[4] http://www.debian.org/index.en.html
[5] http://www.java.com/en
[6] http://tomcat.apache.org
[7] https://developer.apple.com/iphone
[8] http://developer.android.com/sdk/android-2.2.html
[9] https://developer.apple.com/library/ios/#documentation/developertools/conceptual/InstrumentsUserGuide/Introduction/Introduction.html
[10] http://www.opensource.apple.com/source/xnu/xnu-792.13.8/osfmk/mach/mach.h

Compilation of References

Abadi, D. J., Madden, S., & Lindner, W. (2005). REED: Robust, efficient filtering and event detection in sensor networks. In *Proceedings of 31st International Conference on Very Large DataBases* (pp. 769–780). IEEE.

Abbar, S., Bouzeghoub, M., & Lopez, S. (2009). Context-aware recommendation systems: A service-oriented approach. In *Proceedings of the 35th International Conference on Very Large Data Bases (VLDB)*. Paris, France: VLDB.

Abbeel, P., Coates, A., Quigley, M., & Ng, A. Y. (2006). An application of mreinforcement learning to aerobatic helicopter flight. *Advances in Neural Information Processing Systems, 19*.

Abbeel, P., Ganapathi, V., & Ng, A. (2006). Learning vehicular dynamics, with application to modeling helicopters. *Advances in Neural Information Processing Systems, 18*(1).

Aberdeen Group. (2006). *The e-procurement benchmark report*. Aberdeen Group.

Adeli, H., Ghosh-Dastidar, S., & Dadmehr, N. (2007). A wavelet-chaos methodology for analysis of EEGs and EEG subbands to detect seizure and epilepsy. *IEEE Transactions on Bio-Medical Engineering, 54*(2). doi:10.1109/TBME.2006.886855 PMID:17278577.

Adomavicius, G., Sankaranarayanan, R., Sen, S., & Tuzhilin, A. (2005). Incorporating contextual information in recommender systems using a multidimensional approach. *ACM Transactions on Information Systems, 23*(1), 103–145. doi:10.1145/1055709.1055714.

Adomavicius, G., & Tuzhilin, A. (2005). Toward the next generation of recommender systems: A survey of the state-of-the-art and possible extensions. *IEEE Transactions on Knowledge and Data Engineering, 17*(6), 734–749. doi:10.1109/TKDE.2005.99.

Akyildiz, F. et al. (2002). *Wireless sensor networks: A survey*. London: Elsevier.

Al-Agtash, S. Y., & Al-Fahoum, A. A. (2005). An evolutionary computation approach to electricity trade negotiation. *Advances in Engineering Software, 36*(3), 173–179. doi:10.1016/j.advengsoft.2004.07.008.

Albin, P. (1975). *The analysis of complex socioeconomic systems*. London: Lexington Books.

Albin, S. (1998). *Barriers and bounds to rationality: Essays on economic complexity and dynamics in interactive systems*. Princeton, NJ: Princeton University Press.

Al-Karaki, J. N., & Kamal, A. E. (2004). Routing techniques in wireless sensor networks: A survey. *IEEE Wireless Communications Magazine, 11*.

Almanasra, S. (2007). Learning opponent behavior in game theory using genetic algorithms. Jordan: Al-Balqa' Applied University.

Almanasra, S., & Rafie, M. (2010). Comprehensive survey on automata-based game theory. In *Proceedings of the 1st International Symposium on Computing in Science & Engineering* (pp. 643-647). IEEE.

Al-Muhtadi, J., Campbell, R., Kapadia, A., Mickunas, D., & Yi, S. (2002). Routing through the mist: Privacy preserving communication in ubiquitous computing environments. In *Proceedings International Conference of Distributed Computing Systems*. IEEE.

Al-Muhtadi, J., et al. (2002). Routing through the mist: privacy preserving communication in ubiquitous computing environments. In *Proceedings of the International Conference of Distributed Computing Systems*. IEEE.

Alpaydin, E. (2004). *Introduction to machine learning.* Boston: The MIT Press.

Ammari & Das. (2010). Mission-oriented k-coverage in mobile wireless sensor networks. In *Proceedings of the International Conference of Distributed Computing and Networking – ICDCN*. Berlin: Springer.

Ammari, H. M., & Guidici, J. (2009). On the connected k-coverage problem in heterogeneous sensor nets: The curse of randomness and heterogeneity. In *Proceedings of IEEE ICDCS*. IEEE.

Andrzejak, R. G., Lehnertz, K., Mormann, F., Rieke, C., David, P., & Elger, C. E. (2001). Indications of nonlinear deterministic and finite dimensional structures in time series of brain electrical activity: Dependence on recording region and brain state. *Physical Review E: Statistical, Nonlinear, and Soft Matter Physics, 64*, Retrieved from http://epileptologie-bonn.de doi:10.1103/PhysRevE.64.061907.

Apiletti, D., Baralis, E., & Cerquitelli, T. (2011). Energy-saving models for wireless sensor networks. *Knowledge and Information, 28*(3), 615–644. doi:10.1007/s10115-010-0328-6.

Aquino, P., Le Page, C., Bousquet, F., & Bah, A. (2002). A novel mediating participatory modelling: the "self-design" process to accompany collective decision making. *International Journal of Agricultural Resources. Governance and Ecology, 2*(1), 59–74.

Arbib, C., & Rossi, F. (2000). Optimal resource assignment through negotiation in a multi-agent manufacturing system. *IIE Transactions, 32*(10), 963–974. doi:10.1080/07408170008967454.

Ardagna, C., Cremonini, M., Damiani, E., De Capitani di Vimercati, S., & Samarati, P. (2007). Location privacy protection through obfuscation-based techniques. In *Proceedings of the 21st Annual IFIP Conference on Data and Applications Security*. IFIP.

Argoneto, P., & Renna, P. (2010). Production planning, negotiation and coalition integration: A new tool for an innovative e-business model. *Robotics and Computer-integrated Manufacturing, 26*(1), 1–12. doi:10.1016/j.rcim.2009.01.001.

Arrue, B. C., Ollero, A., & Martinez de Dios, J. R. (2000). An intelligent system for false alarm reduction in infrared forest-fire detection. *IEEE Intelligent Systems, 15*(3), 64–73. doi:10.1109/5254.846287.

Asakuma, K., Kuze, H., Takeuchi, N., & Yahagi, T. (2002). Detection of biomass burning smoke in satellite images using texture analysis. *Atmospheric Environment, 36*, 1531–1542. doi:10.1016/S1352-2310(01)00547-7.

Ashbrook, D., & Starner, T. (2002). Learning significant locations and predicting user movement with GPS. In *Proceedings of the Sixth International Symposium on Wearable Computers (ISWC 2002)*, (pp. 101-108). ISWC.

Azlina, Aziz, Mohemmed, & Zhang. (2010). Particle swarm optimization for coverage maximization and energy conservation in wireless sensor networks. *EvoApplications, 2*, 51–60.

Bahl, P., & Padmanabhan, V. N. (2000). RADAR: An in-building RF-based user location and tracking system. In Proceedings of of IEEE INFOCOM2000, (Vol. 2, pp. 775-784). IEEE.

Bajaj, R., Ranaweera, S. L., & Agrawal, D. P. (2002). GPS: Location- tracking technology. In *Proceedings of IEEE Computer*, (pp. 92-94). IEEE.

Baldauf, M., Dustdar, S., & Rosenberg, F. (2007). A survey on context-aware systems. *International Journal of Ad Hoc Ubiquitous Computing, 2*, 263–277. doi:10.1504/IJAHUC.2007.014070.

Bandyopadhyay, S., Rees, J., & Barron, J. M. (2008). Reverse auctions with multiple reinforcement learning agents. *Decision Sciences, 39*(1), 33–63. doi:10.1111/j.1540-5915.2008.00181.x.

Baoqianga, K., Lia, C., Hongsongb, Z., & Yongjunb, X. (2008). Accurate energy model for WSN node and its optimal design. *Journal of Systems Engineering and Electronics*, *19*(3), 427–433. doi:10.1016/S1004-4132(08)60102-4.

Bassingthwaighte, J. B., & Raymond, G. M. (1995). Evaluation of the dispersional analysis method for fractal time series. *Annals of Biomedical Engineering*, *23*(4), 491–505. doi:10.1007/BF02584449 PMID:7486356.

Bellavista, P., Corradi, A., Fanelli, M., & Foschini, L. (2013). A survey of context data distribution for mobile ubiquitous systems. *ACM Computing Surveys*, *45*(1), 1–49.

Bell, G., & Dourish, P. (2007). Yesterday's tomorrows: Notes on ubiquitous computing's dominant vision. *Personal and Ubiquitous Computing*, *11*(2), 133–143. doi:10.1007/s00779-006-0071-x.

Belogay, E., Cabrelli, C., Molter, U., & Shonkwiler, R. (1997). Calculating the Hausdorff distance between curves. *Information Processing Letters*, *64*(1), 17–22. doi:10.1016/S0020-0190(97)00140-3.

Belton, S., & Stewart, T. S. (2002). *Multiple criteria decision analysis: An integrated approach*. Boston: Kluwer Academic Publishers. doi:10.1007/978-1-4615-1495-4.

Ben-Or, M., Goldwasser, S., & Wigderson, A. (1988). Completeness theorems for non-cryptographic fault-tolerant distributed computations. In *Proceedings of the 20th ACM Symposium on the Theory of Computing*, (pp. 1-10). ACM.

Bererton, C., Gordon, G., & Thrun, S. (2003). Auction mechanism design for multi-robot coordination. In Thrun, Saul, & Scholkopf (Eds.), *Proceedings of Conference on Neural Information Processing Systems (NIPS)*. MIT Press.

Beresford, A. R., & Stajano, F. (2004). Mix zones: User privacy in location-aware services. In *Proceedings of PerCom Workshops* (pp. 127–131). PerCom. doi:10.1109/PERCOMW.2004.1276918.

Bertelle, C., Flouret, M., Jay, V., Olivier, D., Ponty, J., & du Havre, L. (2002). *Adaptive behaviour for prisoner dilemma strategies based on automata with multiplicities*. Dresden, Germany: Academic Press.

Bertsekas, D. P. (2005). *Dynamic programming and optimal control* (3rd ed.).

Bettini, C., Wang, X., & Jajodia, S. (2005). Protecting privacy against location-based personal identification. In Jonker & Petkovic (Eds.), Secure Data Management (LNCS), (Vol. 3674, pp. 185-199). Berlin: Springer.

Bigdeli, N., Afshar, K. M., & Fotuhi-Firuzabad, M. (2010). Bidding strategy in pay-as-bid markets based on supplier-market interaction analysis. *Energy Conversion and Management*, *51*(12), 2419–2430. doi:10.1016/j.enconman.2010.05.006.

Binmore, K., & Vulkan, N. (1999). Applying game theory to automated negotiation. *NETNOMICS: Economic Research and Electronic Networking*, *1*(1), 1–9. doi:10.1023/A:1011489402739.

Blakley, G. R. (1979). Safeguarding cryptographic keys. In *Proceedings of the National Computer Conference*, (vol. 48, pp. 313-317). AFIPS.

Blok, H. J. (2000). *On the nature of the stock market: Simulations and experiments*. (PhD Dissertation). University of British Columbia. Canada.

Blum, C., Correia, S., Dorigo, M., Paechter, B., Rossi-Doria, O., & Snoek, M. (2002). A GA evolving instructions for a timetable builder. In *Proceedings of the Practice and Theory of Automated Timetabling IV*. Gent, Belgium: IEEE.

Bó, I. G., & Sichman, J. S. (2004). *Strategy representation complexity in an evolutionary n-players prisoner's dilemma model*. Retrieved March 20, 2012, from www.econ.fea.usp.br/complex/Artigos/24_04_08_Ináciol.pdf

Bodea, C., & Niculescu, C. (2006). Resource leveling using agent technologies. In *Proceedings of 20th IPMA World Congress on Project Management*. China Machine Press.

Bodea, C., Badea, I. R., & Mogoş, R. (2011). A multi-agent system with application in project scheduling. *Management & Marketing. Challenges for Knowledge Society*, *6*(4), 573–590.

Bodea, C., Badea, I. R., & Purnus, A. (2011). Distributed research project scheduling based on multi-agent methods. *Journal of Applied Computer Science & Mathematics*, *10*(5), 20–26.

Bodea, C., & Niculescu, C. (2007). Improving resource leveling in agile software development projects through agent-based approach. *Journal of Applied Quantitative Methods*, 2(2), 260–265.

Bonino da Silva Santos, L. O., Guizzardi, G., Pires, L. F., & Van Sinderen, M. (2009). From user goals to service discovery and composition. In *Proceedings of ER Workshops*, (pp. 265-274). ER.

Borges, P., Mayer, J., & Izquierdo, E. (2008). Efficient visual fire detection applied for video retrieval. In *Proceedings of European Signal Processing Conference (EUSIPCO)*. EUSIPCO.

Bouhmala, N., & Granmo, O. (2010). Combining finite learning automata with GSAT for the satisfiability problem. *Engineering Applications of Artificial Intelligence*, 23, 715–726. doi:10.1016/j.engappai.2010.01.009.

Boutilier, C. (2002). Solving concisely expressed combinatorial auction problems. In *Proceedings of the Eighteenth National Conference on Artificial Intelligence (AAAI-02)*, (pp. 359–366). AAAI.

Boytsov, A., & Zaslavsky, A. (2010). Extending context spaces theory by proactive adaptation. In *Proceedings of the Third Conference on Smart Spaces and Next Generation Wired, and 10th International Conference on Wireless Networking*. Berlin: Springer-Verlag.

Boytsov, A., Zaslavsky, A., & Synnes, K. (2009). Extending context spaces theory by predicting run-time context. In *Proceedings of the 9th International Conference on Smart Spaces and Next Generation Wired/Wireless Networking and Second Conference on Smart Spaces*. Berlin: Springer-Verlag.

Boytsov, A., & Zaslavsky, A. (2011). Context prediction in pervasive computing systems: Achievements and challenges. In Burstein, F., Brezillon, P., & Zaslavsky, A. (Eds.), *Supporting Real Time Decision-Making* (pp. 35–63). Springer. doi:10.1007/978-1-4419-7406-8_3.

Brahma, S., Chatterjee, M., Kwiat, K., & Varshney, P. K. (2012). Traffic management in wireless sensor networks: Decoupling congestion control and fairness. *Computer Communications*, 35(6). doi:10.1016/j.comcom.2011.09.014 PMID:22267882.

Bresciani, P., Perini, A., Giorgini, P., Giunchilia, F., & Mylopoulos, F. (2004). Tropos: An agent-oriented software development methodology. *Autonomous Agents and Multi-Agent Systems*, 8, 203–236. doi:10.1023/B:AGNT.0000018806.20944.ef.

Brinkkemper, S. (1996). Method engineering: Engineering of information systems development methods and tools. *Information and Software Technology*, 38, 275–280. doi:10.1016/0950-5849(95)01059-9.

Bufe, M., Fischer, T., Gubbels, H., Hacker, C., Hasprich, O., & Scheibel, C. Wolfangel, C. (2001). *Automated solution of a highly constrained school timetabling problem*. Paper presented at EvoWorkshop. Como, Italy.

Burges, C. J. C. (1998). A tutorial on support vector machines for pattern recognition. *Data Mining and Knowledge Discovery*, 2(2), 121–167. doi:10.1023/A:1009715923555.

Burrell, J., Brooke, T., & Beckwith, R. (2004). Vineyard computing: Sensor networks in agricultural production. *IEEE Pervasive Computing/IEEE Computer Society [and] IEEE Communications Society*, 3(1), 38–45. doi:10.1109/MPRV.2004.1269130.

Buskey, G., Wyeth, G., & Roberts, J. (2001). Autonomous helicopter hover using an artificial neural network. In *Proceedings IEEE International Conference on Robotics and Automation*, (pp. 1635–1640). IEEE.

Calosso, T., Cantamessa, M., & Gualano, M. (2004). Negotiation support for make-to-order operations in business-to-business electronic commerce. *Robotics and Computer-integrated Manufacturing*, 20, 405–416. doi:10.1016/j.rcim.2004.03.003.

Carbonneau, R., Kersten, G. E., & Klaue, R. (2008). Predicting opponent's moves in electronic negotiations using neural networks. *Expert Systems with Applications*, 34(2), 1266–1273. doi:10.1016/j.eswa.2006.12.027.

Cardei, M., & Wu, J. (2005). Coverage in wireless sensor networks. In Ilyas & Mahgoub (Eds.), Handbook of Sensor Networks: Compact Wireless and Wired Sensing Systems (pp. 19-1–19-12). Boca Raton, FL: CRC Press.

Cardei, M., & Du, D.-Z. (2005). Improving wireless sensor network lifetime through power aware organization. *ACM Wireless Networks*, *11*(3), 333–340. doi:10.1007/s11276-005-6615-6.

Carrasco, M. P., & Pato, M. V. (2001). A multiobjective genetic algorithm for the class/teacher timetabling problem. In E. K. Burke & W. Erben (Eds.), *Proceedings of the Practice and Theory of Automated Timetabling, The Third International Conference* (LNCS). Springer.

Carrasco, M. P., & Pato, M. V. (2002). Solving real class/teacher timetabling problems using neural networks. In *Proceedings of the Practice and Theory of Automated Timetabling IV*. IEEE.

Carrasco, M. P., & Pato, M. V. (2004). A comparison of discrete and continuous neural network approaches to solve the class/teacher timetabling problem. *European Journal of Operational Research*, *153*(1), 65–79. doi:10.1016/S0377-2217(03)00099-7.

Castro, P., Chiu, P., Ted, K., & Muntz, R. (2001). A probabilistic room location service for wireless networked environments. In *Proceedings of Ubicom 2001*. Atlanta, GA: Ubicom. doi:10.1007/3-540-45427-6_3.

Celik, T., Demirel, H., Ozkaramanli, H., & Uyguroglu, M. (2007). Fire detection using statistical color model in video sequences. *Journal of Visual Communication and Image Representation*, *18*, 176–185. doi:10.1016/j.jvcir.2006.12.003.

Chan, H., et al. (2003). Random key predistribution schemes for sensor networks. In *Proceedings of IEEE Symposium on Security and Privacy*. IEEE.

Chandrasekaran, B., & Shen, D. (1972). Stochastic automata games. *IEEE Transactions on Systems, Man, and Cybernetics*, 145–149.

Chaovalitwongse, W., Pardalos, P., Iasemidis, L. D., Shiau, D. S., & Sackellares, J. C. (2005). Dynamical approaches and multi-quadratic integer programming for seizure prediction. *Optimization Methods and Software*, *20*(2-3), 389–400. doi:10.1080/10556780512331318173.

Chartrand, G. (1984). *Introductory graph theory*. New York: Dover Publications.

Chaum, D., Crepeau, C., & Damgard, I. (1988). Multiparty unconditionally secure proto-cols. In *Proceedings of the 20th ACM Symposium on the Theory of Computing*, (pp. 11-19). ACM.

Checkland, P. B. (1981). *Systems thinking, systems practice*. London: John Wiley and Sons.

Chen, I. Y. L., Yang, S. J. H., & Jiang, J. (2006). Ubiquitous provision of context aware web services. In *Proceedings of the IEEE International Conference on Services Computing*, (pp. 60-68). IEEE.

Chen, T. H., Wu, P. H., & Chiou, Y. C. (2004). An early fire-detection method based on image processing. In *Proceedings of the IEEE International Conference on Image Processing (ICIP)*, (pp. 1707- 1710). IEEE.

Cheng, R., Jain, E., & van den Berg. (2003). Location prediction algorithms for mobile wireless systems. In *Wireless Internet handbook: Technologies, standards, and application*, (pp. 245-263). Boca Raton, FL: CRC Press.

Cheng, C., Chan, C. H., & Lin, K. (2006). Intelligent agents for e-marketplace: Negotiation with issue trade-offs by fuzzy inference systems. *Decision Support Systems*, *42*, 626–638. doi:10.1016/j.dss.2005.02.009.

Chen, Y. M., & Wang, S. C. (2007). Framework of agent-based intelligence system with two stage decision-making processes for distributed dynamic scheduling. *Applied Soft Computing*, *7*, 229–245. doi:10.1016/j.asoc.2005.04.003.

Cherkassky, V., & Mulier, F. (1998). *Learning from data*. New York: Wiley.

Chiong, R., & Kirley, M. (2009). Co-evolutionary learning in the n-player iterated prisoner's dilemma with a structured environment. In *Proceedings of the 4th Australian Conference on Artificial Life: Borrowing from Biology* (pp. 32-42). IEEE.

Choi, S., & Shin, K. G. (1998). Predictive and adaptive bandwidth reservation for hand-offs in QoS-sensitive cellular networks. In *Proceedings of ACM SIGCOMM*. ACM.

Choi, N., Song, I. Y., & Han, H. (2006). A survey on ontology mapping. *SIGMOD Recommendations*, *35*(3), 34–41. doi:10.1145/1168092.1168097.

Choueiry, B. Y., & Faltings, B. (1994). Interactive resource allocation by problem decomposition and temporal abstractions. In *Proceedings of the Second European Workshop on Planning*. IOS Press.

Chu, D., Deshpande, A., Hellerstein, J. M., & Hong, W. (2006). Approximate data collection in sensor networks using probabilistic models. In *Proceedings of The 22nd International Conference on Data Engineering* (pp. 48). IEEE.

Chvatal, V. (1983). *Linear programming*. New York: W H Freeman & Co..

Coehoorn, R. M., & Jennings, N. R. (2004). Learning an opponent's preferences to make effective multi-issue negotiation trade-offs. In *Proceedings of the 6th International Conference on Electronic Commerce*, (pp. 59-68). ACM.

Collins. (1999). A system for video surveillance and monitoring. In *Proceedings of American Nuclear Society (ANS)*. ANS.

Cooper, T. B., & Kingston, J. H. (1995). The complexity of timetable construction problems. in E. K. Burke & P. Ross (Eds.), *Proceedings of the Practice and Theory of Automated Timetabling I* (LNCS), (Vol. 1153, pp. 283–295). Springer.

Coppersmith, D. (1995). Proactive secret sharing or: How to cope with perpetual leakage. In Proceedings of Advances in Cryptology — CRYPT0' 95, (Vol. 963, pp. 339-352). CRYPTO.

Cramer, R., Damgard, I., & Maurer, U. (2000). General secure multi-party computation from any linear secret-sharing scheme. In Preneel, B. (Ed.), *Advances in Cryptology, EUROCRYPT 2000 (LNCS)* (Vol. 1807, pp. 316–334). Berlin: Springer-Verlag. doi:10.1007/3-540-45539-6_22.

Curewitz, K. M., Krishnan, P., & Vitter, J. S. (1993). Practical Prefetching via Data Compression. *Proceedings of ACM SIGMOD*, pp. 257-266.

Daskalaki, S., Birbas, T., & Housos, E. (2004). An integer programming formulation for a case study in university timetabling. *European Journal of Operational Research*, *153*, 117–135. doi:10.1016/S0377-2217(03)00103-6.

Daszykowski, M., Walczak, B., & Massart, D. L. (2002). On the optimal partitioning of data with k-means, growing k-means, neural gas, and growing neural gas. *Journal of Chemical Information and Computer Sciences*, *42*(1), 1378–1389. doi:10.1021/ci020270w PMID:12444735.

David, E., Azoulay-Schwartz, R., & Kraus, S. (2006). Bidding in sealed-bid and English multi-attribute auctions. *Decision Support Systems*, *42*(2), 527–556. doi:10.1016/j.dss.2005.02.007.

de Dios, M. et al. (2008). Computer vision techniques for forest fire perception. *Image and Vision Computing*, *26*(4).

de Vries, S., & Vohra, R. V. (2003). Combinatorial auctions: A survey. *INFORMS Journal on Computing*, *15*(3), 284–309. doi:10.1287/ijoc.15.3.284.16077.

Deb, K. (2001). *Multi-objective optimization using evolutionary algorithms*. London: John Wiley & Sons Ltd..

Deshpande, A., Guestrin, C., & Madden, S. (2005). Using probabilistic models for data management in acquisitional environments. In *Proceedings of The Conference on Innovative Data Systems Research* (pp. 317–328). IEEE.

Deshpande, A., Guestrin, C., Hong, W., & Madden, S. (2005). Exploiting correlated attributes in acquisitional query processing. In *Proceedings of The 21st International Conference on Data Engineering* (pp. 143–154). IEEE.

Deshpande, A., Guestrin, C., Madden, S. R., Hellerstein, J. M., & Hong, W. (2004). Model-driven data acquisition in sensor networks. In *Proceedings of The 30th international conference on Very Large Data Bases* (pp. 588–599). IEEE.

Desmedt, Y., & Frankel, Y. (1992). Shared generation of authenticators and signatures. In Feigenbaum, J. (Ed.), *Advances in Cryptology - CRYPTO '91 (LNCS)* (Vol. 576, pp. 457–469). Berlin: Springer-Verlag.

Devlic, A., & Klintskog, E. (2007). Context retrieval and distribution in a mobile distributed environment. In *Proceedings of the Third Workshop on Context Awareness for Proactive Systems (CAPS 2007)*. Guildford, UK: CAPS.

Dey, A. (2001). Understanding and using context. *Personal and Ubiquitous Computing*, *5*(1), 4–7. doi:10.1007/s007790170019.

Dik, S. C. (1989). *The theory of functional grammar*. Dodrecht, The Netherlands: Foris Publications.

Dodis, Y. S. (2000). A cryptographic solution to a game theoretic problem. In *Proceedings of CRYPTO 2000: 20th International Cryptology Conference* (pp. 112-130). Springer-Verlag.

Dolgov, D. A., & Durfee, E. H. (2006). Resource allocation among Agents with MDP-induced preferences. *Journal of Artificial Intelligence Research*, *27*, 505–549.

Dracopoulos, D. C. (1997). *Evolutionary learning algorithms for neural adaptive control*. Berlin: Springer Verlag.

Dracopoulos, D. C., & Piccoli, R. (2010). Bioreactor control by genetic programming. In Schaefer, R. et al. (Eds.), *Parallel Problem Solving from Nature (PPSN) XI (LNCS)* (*Vol. 6239*, pp. 181–188). Springer-Verlag. doi:10.1007/978-3-642-15871-1_19.

Du, W., Mieyeville, F., & Navarro, D. (2010). Modeling energy consumption of wireless sensor networks by SystemC. In *Proceedings of The 5th International Conference on Systems and Networks Communications* (pp. 94–98). IEEE.

Duda, R., Hart, P., & Stork, D. (2001). *Pattern Classification*. Wiley-Interscience.

Dworman, G., Kimbrough, S., & Laing, J. (1995). On automated discovery of models using genetic programming: Bargaining in a three-agent coalitions game. *Journal of Management Information Systems*, *12*(125).

Ebert, J., & Shipley, J. (2009). Computer vision based method for fire detection in color videos. *International Journal of Imaging*.

Ehrig, M., & Sure, Y. (2004). Ontology mapping - An integrated approach. In *Proceedings of The Semantic Web: Research and Applications, First European Semantic Web Symposium* (pp. 76-91). Heraklion, Greece: IEEE.

Elgammal., et al. (2000). Nonparametric model for background subtraction. In *Proceedings of ECCV 2000*, (pp. 751-767). ECCV.

Eschenauer, L., et al. (2002). A key-management scheme for distributed sensor networks. In *Proceedings of ACM Conference on Computer and Communication Security*. ACM.

Esteller, R., Vachtsevanos, G., Echauz, J., & Litt, B. (2001). A comparison of waveform fractal dimension algorithms. *IEEE Transactions on Circuits and Systems: Fundamental Theory and Applications*, *48*(2), 177–183. doi:10.1109/81.904882.

Ester, M., Kriegel, H.-P., Sander, J., & Xu, X. (1996). A density-based algorithm for discovering clusters in large spatial databases with noise. In *Proceedings of The 2nd International Conference on Knowledge Discovery and Data Mining* (pp. 226–231). IEEE.

Euzenat, J. (2007). Semantic precision and recall for ontology alignment evaluation. In *Proceedings of the 20th International Joint Conference on Artificial Intelligence*. Hyderabad, India: IEEE.

Even, S., Itai, A., & Shamir, A. (1976). On the complexity of timetable and multicommodity flow problems. *SIAM Journal on Computing*, *5*(4), 691–703. doi:10.1137/0205048.

Faratin, P., Sierra, C., & Jennings, N. R. (2003). Using similarity criteria to make negotiation trade-offs. *Journal of Artificial Intelligence*, *142*(2), 205–237. doi:10.1016/S0004-3702(02)00290-4.

Fasbender, A., et al. (1996). Analysis of security and privacy in mobile IP. In *Proceedings of the 4th International Conference on Telecommunications Systems, Modeling and Analysis*. IEEE.

Fasbender, A., Kesdogan, D., & Kubitz, O. (1996). Analysis of security and privacy in mobile IP. In *Proceedings of the 4th International Conference on Telecommunication Systems, Modeling and Analysis*. IEEE.

Fasbender, A., Kesdogan, D., & Kubitz, O. (1996). Variable and scalable security: Protecting of location information in mobile IP. In *Proceedings of the 46th IEEE VTC*. IEEE.

Fasli, M. (2006). Shopbots: A syntactic present, a semantic future. In *Proceedings of IEEE Internet Computing* (pp. 69-75). IEEE.

Fatima, S. S., & Wooldridge, M. (2001). Adaptive task and resource allocation in multi-agent systems. In *Proceedings of the Fifth International Conference on Autonomous Agents*, (pp. 537-544). Montreal, Canada: Agents.

Feigenbaum, J. (1991). Non-interactive and information-theoretic secure verifiable secret sharing. In Proceedings of Advances in Cryptology - CRYPT0' 91, (Vol. 576, pp. 129-140). CRYPTO.

Feldman, P. (1987). A practical scheme for non-interactive verifiable secret sharing. In *Proceedings of the 28th Annual Symposium on Foundations of Computer Science,* (pp. 427-438). IEEE.

Feller, W. (1968). *An introduction to probability theory and its applications.* Englewood Cliffs, NJ: Wiley.

Ferguson, T. S. (2012). *Optimal stopping and applications.* Retrieved from http://www.math.ucla.edu/tom/Stopping/Contents.html

Fillemore, C. J. (Ed.). (1968). *The case for case, in universals in linguistic theory.* New York: Holt, Rinehat and Winston.

Flache, A., & Macy, M. (1996). Weakness of strong ties: Collective action failure in a highly cohesive group. *Mathematical Sociology, 21,* 3–28. doi:10.1080/0022250X.1996.9990172.

Freed, J., & Klugman, M. (1996). *A culture for academic excellence: Implementing the quality principles in higher education.* San Francisco: Jossey-Bass Publisher.

Friday, A., et al. (2002). A lightweight approach to managing privacy in location-based services. In *Proceedings of the Equator Annual Conference.* IEEE.

Friday, A., Muller, H., Rodden, T., & Dix, A. (2002). A lightweight approach to managing privacy in location-based services. In *Proceedings of the Equator Annual Conference.* Brockenhurst, UK: Equator.

Friedman, N., Geiger, D., & Goldszmidt, M. (1997). Bayesian network classifiers. *Machine Learning, 29*(2-3), 131–163. doi:10.1023/A:1007465528199.

Gao, J., & Lai, W. (2010). Formal concept analysis based clustering for blog network visualization. *ADMA, 1,* 394–404.

Garay, Gennaro, Jutla, & Rabin. (2000). Secure distributed storage and retrieval. *Theoretical Computer Science, 243*(1-2), 363–389. doi:10.1016/S0304-3975(98)00263-1.

Garcia-Sanchez, A.-J., Garcia-Sanchez, F., Losilla, F., Kulakowski, P., Garcia-Haro, J., & Rodríguez, A. et al. (2010). Wireless sensor network deployment for monitoring wildlife passages. *Sensors (Basel, Switzerland), 10*(8), 7236–7262. doi:10.3390/s100807236 PMID:22163601.

Gedik, B., & Liu, L. (2005). Location privacy in mobile systems: A personalized anonymization model.[ICDCS.]. *Proceedings of, ICDCS2005,* 620–629.

Ghneamat, R. (2005). *Genetic algorithms and application to adaptive automata for game theory.* Al-Balqa University.

Ghnemat, R., Bertelle, C., & Duchamp, G. (2009). A methodology for urban and land-use management simulation using spatial self-organization processes. *Dynamics of Continuous, Discrete and Impulsive Systems-series B, 16,* 501–513.

Ghnemat, R., Oqeili, S., & Bertelle, C. (2006). Automata-based adaptive behavior for economic modelling using game theory. In *Emergent Properties in Natural and Artificial Dynamical Systems* (pp. 171–183). Academic Press. doi:10.1007/3-540-34824-7_9.

Ghosh-Dastidar, S., Adeli, H., & Dadmehr, N. (2007). Mixed-band wavelet-chaos-neural network methodology for epilepsy and epileptic seizure detection. *IEEE Transactions on Bio-Medical Engineering, 54*(9). doi:10.1109/TBME.2007.891945 PMID:17867346.

Gislen, L., Peterson, C., & Soderberg, B. (1992). Complex scheduling with potts neural networks. *Neural Computation, 4,* 805–831. doi:10.1162/neco.1992.4.6.805.

Glover, F. W., & Laquna, M. (2004). *Tabu search.* Berlin: Springer.

Goel, S., & Imielinski, T. (2001). Prediction-based monitoring in sensor networks: Taking lessons from mpeg. *SIGCOMM Computer and Communications Review, 31*(5), 82–98. doi:10.1145/1037107.1037117.

Gonzalez, A., Mahtani, R., Bejar, M., & Ollero, A. (2004). Control and stability analysis of an autonomous helicopter. In *Proceedings of World Automation Congress,* (vol. 15, pp. 399–404). IEEE.

Gopalratnam, K., & Cook, D. J. (2003). Active lezi: An incremental parsing algorithm for sequential prediction. In *Proceedings of the Florida Artificial Intelligence Research Symposium (FLAIRS)*, (pp. 38-42). FLAIRS.

Gotman, J. (1982). Automatic recognition of epileptic seizures in the EEG. *Electroencephalography and Clinical Neurophysiology*, *54*, 530–540. doi:10.1016/0013-4694(82)90038-4 PMID:6181976.

Goyal, V., Pandey, O., Sahai, A., & Waters, B. (2006). Attribute-based encryption for ne-grained access control of encrypted data. In *Proceedings of the 13th ACM conference on Computer and Communications Security*, (pp. 89-98). ACM.

Greenwald, A. R., & Kephart, J. O. (1999). Shopbots and pricebots. In *Proceedings of the 16th International Joint Conference on Artificial Intelligence*. Stockholm, Sweden: IEEE.

Gruteser, M., & Grunwald, D. (2003). Enhancing location privacy in wireless LAN through disposable interface identifiers: A quantitative analysis. In *Proceedings of the WMASH '03*. WMASH.

Gruteser, M., & Grunwald, D. (2003). Enhancing location privacy in wireless LAN through disposable interface identifiers: A quantitative analysis. In *Proceedings of WMASH'03*. WMASH.

Gruteser, M., et al. (2003). Privacy-aware location sensor networks. In *Proceedings of the 8th USENIX Workshop on Hot Topics in Operating Systems*. USENIX.

Gruteser, M., & Grunwald, D. (2003). Anonymous usage of location-based services through spatial and temporal cloaking.[MobiSys.]. *Proceedings of MobiSys*, *03*, 31–42.

Gruteser, M., & Grunwald, D. (2003). A methodological assessment of location privacy risks in wireless hotspot networks. In *Proceedings of Security in Pervasive Computing*. Boppard, Germany: IEEE.

Gu¨ler, I˙., & U¨ beyli, E. D. (2004). Application of adaptive neuro-fuzzy inference system for detection of electrocardiographic changes in patients with partial epilepsy using feature extraction. *International Journal of Expert Systems with Applications*, *27*, 323–330. doi:10.1016/j.eswa.2004.05.001.

Guerberoff, I., Queiroz, D., & Sichman, J. S. (2010). On the effect of the expressiveness of strategy representation languages in multiagent based simulations: an experiment with an evolutionary model of the iterated n-players prisoner's dilemma. *1re Soumission à RIA Special Issue on Agent Based Social Simulation*.

Gunay, O., Tasdemir, K., Toreyin, B. U., & Cetin, A. E. (2009). Video based wildfire detection at night. *Fire Safety Journal*, *44*, 860–868. doi:10.1016/j.firesaf.2009.04.003.

Guo, L., Rivero, D., & Dorado, J., Rabu˜nal, J. R., & Pazos, A. (2010). Automatic epileptic seizure detection in EEGs based on line length feature and artificial neural networks. *Journal of Neuroscience Methods*, *191*(1), 101–109. doi:10.1016/j.jneumeth.2010.05.020 PMID:20595035.

Hadar, I., Reinhartz-Berger, I., Kuflik, T., Perini, A., Ricca, F., & Susi, A. (2010). An empirical study of requirements model understanding: Use case vs. tropos models. In *Proceedings 25th ACM Symposium on Applied Computing*. ACM.

Hadjiefthymiades, S., & Merakos, L. (2003). *Proxies+Path Prediction: Improving Web Service Provision in Wireless-Mobile Communications* (*Vol. 8*, p. 4). ACM/Kluwer Mobile Networks and Applications, Special Issue on Mobile and Wireless Data Management.

Halpern, J. Y. (2008). *Algorithmic rationality: Game theory with costly computation*. Academic Press.

Han., et al. (2004). Sequential kernel density approximation through mode propagation: Applications to background modeling. In *Proceedings Asian Conference on Computer Vision*. IEEE.

Harjula, E., Ala-Kurikka, J., Howie, D., & Ylianttila, M. (2006). Analysis of peer-to-peer SIP in a distributed mobile middleware system. In *Proceedings of IEEE Global Telecommunications Conference (GlobeCom06)* (pp. 1–6). IEEE.

Harter, A., Hopper, A., Steggles, P., Ward, A., & Webster, P. (1999). The anatomy of a context-aware application. In *Proceedings of the 5th ACM/IEEE International Conference on Mobile Computing and Networking, Mobicom 99*, (pp. 59-68). Seattle, WA: ACM/IEEE.

Hausen, T., Fritz, M., & Schiefer, G. (2006). Potential of electronic trading in complex supply chains: An experimental study. *International Journal of Production Economics*, *104*(2), 580–597. doi:10.1016/j.ijpe.2005.04.010.

Hayashi, K. (2000). Multi-criteria analysis for agricultural resource management: A critical survey and future perspectives. *European Journal of Operational Research*, *122*, 486–500. doi:10.1016/S0377-2217(99)00249-0.

He, T., Krishnamurthy, S., Stankovic, J. A., Abdelzaher, T., Luo, L., & Stoleru, R. Krogh, B. (2004). Energy-efficient surveillance system using wireless sensor networks. In *Proceedings of The 2nd International Conference on Mobile Systems, Applications, and Services* (pp. 270–283). IEEE.

Hegselmann, R., & Flache, A. (1998). Understanding complex social dynamics: A plea for cellular automata based modelling. *Journal of Artificial Societies and Social Simulation*, *1*(3).

Hegselmann, R., Flache, A., & Möller, V. (1998). Solidarity and social impact in cellular worlds - Results and sensitivity analyses. In *Proceedings of Social Science Microsimulation: Tools for Modeling, Parameter Optimization and Sensitivity Analysis*. Berlin: Springer.

Heinzelman, W. R., Chandrakasan, A., & Balakrishnan, H. (2000). Energy-efficient communication protocol for wireless microsensor networks. In *Proceedings of The 33rd Hawaii International Conference on System Sciences*. IEEE.

Heinzelman, W. R., Kulik, J., & Balakrishnan, H. (1999). Adaptive protocols for information dissemination in wireless sensor networks. In *Proceedings of the 5th ACM/IEEE International Conference on Mobile Computing and Networking*. ACM.

Heinzelman, W. B., Chandrakasan, A. P., & Balakrishnan, H. (2002). An application-specific protocol architecture for wireless microsensor networks. *IEEE Transactions on Wireless Communications*, *1*(4), 660–670. doi:10.1109/TWC.2002.804190.

Henricksen, K., Indulska, J., McFadden, T., & Balasubramaniam, S. (2005). Middleware for distributed context-aware systems. *Lecture Notes in Computer Science*, *3760*, 846–863. doi:10.1007/11575771_53.

Hightower, J., & Borriello, G. (2001). *Location systems for ubiquitous computing*. Seattle, WA: University of Washington.

Hightower, J., Borriello, G., & Want, R. (2000). *SpotON: An indoor 3D location sensing technology based on RF signal strength*. Seattle, WA: University of Washington.

Hillery, M., Buzek, V., & Berthiaume, A. (1999). Quantum secret sharing. *Physical Review A.*, *59*.

Hindriks, K., & Tykhonov, D. (2008). Opponent modelling in automated multi-issue negotiation using bayesian learning. In *Proceedings of the 7th International Joint Conference on Autonomous Agents and Multiagent Systems*, (Vol. 1, pp. 331-338). International Foundation for Autonomous Agents and Multiagent Systems.

Hirst, G., & St. Onge, D. (1998). Lexical chains as representations of context for the detection and correction of malapropisms. In Fellbaum, C. (Ed.), *WordNet: An Electronic Lexical Database* (pp. 305–332). Boston: MIT Press.

Hochbaum, D. S. (1995). *Approximation algorithms for np-hard problems*. PWS Publishing Company.

Hoffman, B. C., et al. (2004). Secret sharing schemes, project specification. *In Proceedings of COSC*. COSC.

Hong, H., Suh, E. H., Kim, J., & Kim, S. (2009). Context-aware system for proactive personalized service based on context history. *Expert Systems with Applications*, *36*(4), 7448–7457. doi:10.1016/j.eswa.2008.09.002.

Howard, A., Mataric, M. J., & Sukhatme, G. S. (2002). Mobile sensor network deployment using potential field: A distributed scalable solution to the area coverage problem. In *Proceedings of the 6th International Symposium on Distributed Autonomous Robotics Systems (DARS '02)* (pp. 299–308). Fukuoka, Japan: DARS.

Hsu, W. H., Gettings, N. D., Lease, V. E., Pan, Y., & Wilkins, D. C. (1998). Heterogeneous time series learning for crisis monitoring. In *Proceedings of Predicting the Future: AI Approaches to Time-Series Problems, Workshop held in Conjunction with the Fifteenth National Conference on Artificial Intelligence*, (pp. 34–41). IEEE.

Hu, X., Ding, Y., Paspallis, N., Bratskas, P., Papadopoulos, G., & Vanrompay, Y. Berbers, Y. (2008). A hybrid peer-to-peer solution for context distribution in mobile and ubiquitous environments. In *Proceedings of the 17th International Conference on Information Systems Development (ISD2008)* (pp. 501-510). ISD.

Huang, C., Liang, W., Lai, Y., & Lin, Y. (2010). The agent-based negotiation process for B2C e-commerce. *Expert Systems with Applications, 37*(1), 348–359. doi:10.1016/j.eswa.2009.05.065.

Huang, S.-L., & Lin, F.-R. (2008). Using temporal-difference learning for multi-agent bargaining. *Electronic Commerce Research and Applications, 7*(4), 432–442. doi:10.1016/j.elerap.2007.04.001.

Huget, M., Odell, J., & Bauer, B. (2004). The AUML approach. In Bergenti, Gleizes, & Zambonelli (Eds.), Methodologies and software engineering for agent systems. Boston: Kluwer Academic Publishers.

Hui, J. W., & Culler, D. (2004). The dynamic behavior of a data dissemination protocol for network programming at scale. In *Proceedings of The 2nd International conference on Embedded Networked Sensor Systems* (pp. 81–94). IEEE.

Hurst, H. E. (1951). Long-term storage of reservoirs: an experimental study. *Transactions of the American Society of Civil Engineers, 116*, 770–799.

Hwang, C. L., & Yoon, K. (1981). *Multiple-attribute decision making: Methods and applications.* Berlin: Springer-Verlag. doi:10.1007/978-3-642-48318-9.

Iasemidis, D. L., & Sackellares, J. C. (1996). Chaos theory and epilepsy. *The Neuroscientist, 2*(2), 118–126. doi:10.1177/107385849600200213.

IEEE Standards Board. (1990). *Standards coordinating committee of the computer society of the IEEE.* Washington, DC: IEEE.

Intanagonwiwat, C., et al. (2000). Directed diffusion: A scalable and robust communication paradigm for sensor networks. In *Proceedings of the 6th International Conference on Mobile Computing and Networking.* IEEE.

Intanagonwiwat, C., Govindan, R., & Estrin, D. (2000). Directed diffusion: A scalable and robust communication paradigm for sensor networks. In *Proceedings of The 6th Annual International Conference on Mobile Computing and Networking* (pp. 56–67). IEEE.

Ishibuchi, H., Namikawa, N., & Ohara, K. (2006). Effects of spatial structures on evolution of iterated prisoner's dilemma game strategies in single-dimensional and two-dimensional grids. In *Proceedings of CEC 2006 IEEE Congress on Evolutionary Computation* (pp. 976 - 983). IEEE.

Izquierdo, L. R. (2007). *Advancing learning and evolutionary game theory with an application to social dilemmas.* Academic Press.

Jaccard. (1912). The distribution of the flora of the alpine zone. *New Phychologist, 11,* 37-50.

Jackson, M. (1995). *Software requirements and specifications: A lexicon of practice, principles and prejudices.* Reading, MA: Addison Wesley Press.

Jacques, M. B., Abdallah, M., & Ahmed, M. (2008). Hilbert mobile beacon for localisation and coverage in sensor networks. *International Journal of Systems Science, 39*(11), 1081–1094. doi:10.1080/00207720802085302.

Jang, J.-S. R. (1992). Self-learning fuzzy controllers based on temporal backpropagation. *IEEE Transactions on Neural Networks, 3*(5), 714–723. doi:10.1109/72.159060 PMID:18276470.

Jang, J.-S. R. (1993). ANFIS: Adaptive-network-based fuzzy inference system. *IEEE Transactions on Systems, Man, and Cybernetics, 23*(3), 665–685. doi:10.1109/21.256541.

Jang, J.-S. R., & Sun, C. T. (1995). Neuro fuzzy modeling and control. *Proceedings of the IEEE, 83*(3), 378–406. doi:10.1109/5.364486.

Jaro, M. A. (1989). Advances in record linking methodology as applied to the 1985 census of Tampa Florida. *Journal of the American Statistical Society, 64,* 1183–1210.

Jennings, N. R., Faratin, P., Lomuscio, A., Parsons, S., Wooldridge, M., & Sierra, C. (2001). Automated negotiation: Prospects, methods and challenges. *Group Decision and Negotiation, 10*(2), 199–215. doi:10.1023/A:1008746126376.

Jensen, T. R. (1995). *Graph coloring problems.* New York: John Wiley & Sons.

Jiang, Song, Zhang, & Dou. (2005). *Voronoi-based improved algorithm for connected coverage problem in wireless sensor networks.* EUC.

Jiménez Molina, A., Koo, H. M., & Ko, I. Y. (2007). A template-based mechanism for dynamic service composition based on context prediction in ubicomp applications. In *Proceedings of the International Workshop on Intelligent Based Tools IWBT.* IEEE.

Jonker, C., Robu, V., & Treur, J. (2007). An agent architecture for multi-attribute negotiation using incomplete preference information. *Autonomous Agents and Multi-Agent Systems, 15*(2), 221–252. doi:10.1007/s10458-006-9009-y.

Jun-Chou, et al. (2010). A novel secret sharing technique using QR code. *International Journal of Image, 4*(5), 468–475.

JXTA. (n.d.). *The language and platform independent protocol for P2P networking.* Retrieved from http://jxta.kenai.com/

Kaabi, R. S., & Souveyet, C. (2007). Capturing intentional services with business process maps. In *Proceedings of the 1ˢᵗ IEEE International Conference on Research Challenges in Information Science (RCIS),* (pp. 309-318). IEEE.

Kaelbling, L. P., Littman, M. L., & Moore, A. W. (1996). Reinforcement learning: A survey. *Journal of Artificial Intelligence Research, 4,* 237–285.

Kalfoglou, Y., & Schorlemmer, M. (2003). Ontology mapping: The state of the art. *The Knowledge Engineering Review, 18*(1), 1–31. doi:10.1017/S0269888903000651.

Kamat, P., et al. (2005). Enchasing source-location privacy in sensor network routing. In *Proceedings of the 25ᵗʰ International Conference on Distributed Computing Systems.* IEEE.

Kangasharju, J., & Kangasharju, J. (2006). An optimal basis for efficient peer-to-peer content distribution algorithms. In *Proceedings of the 15ᵗʰ International Conference on Computer Communications and Networks* (pp. 481-486). IEEE.

Kannathal, N., Lim, C. M., Rajendra Acharya, U., & Sadasivan, P. K. (2005). Entropies for detection of epilepsy in EEG. *International Journal of Computer Methods and Programs in Biomedicine, 80*(3), 187–194. doi:10.1016/j.cmpb.2005.06.012 PMID:16219385.

Karaboga, D., & Akay, B. (2009). A survey: Algorithms simulating bee swarm intelligence. *Artificial Intelligence Review, 31*(1-4), 61–85. doi:10.1007/s10462-009-9127-4.

Kari, J. (2011). *Cellular automata.* Lecture Note.

Karmouch, A., & Samaan, N. (2005). A Mobility Prediction Architecture Based on Contextual Knowledge and Spatial Conceptual Maps. *IEEE Transactions on Mobile Computing, 4*(6).

Katsaros, D., Nanopoulos, A., Karakaya, M., Yavas, G., Ulusoy, O., & Manolopoulos, Y. (2003). Clustering Mobile Trajectories for Resource Allocation in Mobile Environments. *In Proceedings IDA,* pp. 319-329.

Kazatzopoulos, L., Delakouridis, C., Marias, G. F., & Georgiadis, P. (2006). iHIDE: Hiding sources of information in WSNs. In *Proceedings of the 2ⁿᵈ International Workshop on Security, Privacy and Trust in Pervasive and Ubiquitous Computing (IEEE SecPerU2006).* Lyon, France: IEEE.

Kee, C., et al. (2000). Development of indoor navigation system using asynchronous pseudolites. In *Proceedings of ION GPS -2000.* Salt Lake City, UT: ION GPS.

Keenan, D. C., & O'Brien, M. J. (1993). Competition, collusion, and chaos. *Journal of Economic Dynamics & Control, 17,* 327–353. doi:10.1016/0165-1889(93)90001-9.

Kennedy, J., & Eberhart, R. (1995). Particle swarm optimization. In *Proceedings of the IEEE International Conference on Neural Networks.* IEEE.

Kent, S., & Atkinson, R. (1998). Encapsulating security payload. *IETF Network Working Group RFC 2406.* Retrieved from http://www.ietf.org

Kephart, J. O., & Greenwald, A. R. (1999). Shopbot economics. In *Proceedings of the 3rd Annual Conference on Autonomous Agents* (pp. 378-379). Seattle, WA: IEEE.

Kersten, G., & Lai, H. (2007). Negotiation support and e-negotiation systems: An overview. *Group Decision and Negotiation, 16*(6), 553–586. doi:10.1007/s10726-007-9095-5.

Kesdogan, D., Reichl, P., & Junghärtchen, K. (1998). Distributed temporary pseudonyms: A new approach for protecting location information in mobile communication networks. In *Proceedings of the 5th European Symposium on Research in Computer Security*. IEEE.

Khalili, A., et al. (2003). Toward secure key distribution in truly ad-hoc networks. In *Proceedings of the Symposium Applications and the Internet Workshops*. IEEE.

Khambatti, M., Dong Ryu, K., & Dasgupta, P. (2003). Structuring peer-to-peer networks using interest-based communities. *Lecture Notes in Computer Science, 2944,* 48–63. doi:10.1007/978-3-540-24629-9_5.

Kirsch Pinheiro, M., Vanrompay, Y., Victor, K., Berbers, Y., Valla, M., & Frà, C. Panagiotou, G. (2008). Context grouping mechanism for context distribution in ubiquitous environments. In *Proceedings of the OTM 2008 Conferences* (pp. 571-588). OTM.

Kirsch-Pinheiro, M., Gensel, J., & Martin, H. (2004). Representing context for an adaptive awareness mechanism. In G.J. de Vreede, L.A. Guerrero, & G.M.Raventos (Ed), *X Workshop on Groupware (CRIWG)*, (pp. 339-348). Springer.

Kirsch-Pinheiro, M., Vanrompay, Y., & Berbers, Y. (2008). Context-aware service selection using graph matching. In *Proceedings of the 2nd Non Functional Properties and Service Level Agreements in Service Oriented Computing Workshop (NFPSLA-SOC'08),ECOWS*. CEUR.

Kohonen, T. (1995). *Self-organising maps*. Berlin: Springer. doi:10.1007/978-3-642-97610-0.

Koo, T. J., Ma, Y., & Sastry, S. (2001). Nonlinear control of a helicopter based unmanned aerial vehicle. *IEEE Transactions on Control Systems Technology*.

Koppejan, R., & Whiteson, S. (2009). Neuroevolutionary reinforcement learning for generalized helicopter control. In *Proceedings of the 11th Annual Conference on Genetic and Evolutionary Computation*, (pp. 145–152). ACM.

Korhonen, P., Moskowitz, H., & Wallenius, J. (1992). Multiple criteria decision support: A review. *European Journal of Operational Research, 63,* 361–375. doi:10.1016/0377-2217(92)90155-3.

Kotidis, Y. (2005). Snapshot queries: Towards data-centric sensor networks. In *Proceedings of The 21st International Conference on Data Engineering* (pp. 131–142). IEEE.

Kouruthanassis, P. E., & Giaglis, G. M. (2006). A design theory for pervasive information systems. In *Proceedings of the 3rd International Workshop on Ubiquitous Computing (IWUC)*, (pp. 62-70). IWUC.

Kowalcyzk, R. (2000). On negotiation as a distributed fuzzy constraint satisfaction problem. In *Proceedings DEXA e-Negotiation Workshop*, (pp. 631– 637). DEXA.

Koza, R. J. (1992). *Genetic programming on the programming of computers by means of natural selection*. Boston: MIT Press.

Krishnamachari, B., Estrin, D., & Wicker, S. (2002). The impact of data aggregation in wireless sensor networks. In *Proceedings of The 22nd International Conference on Distributed Computing Systems* (pp. 575-578). IEEE.

Ktonas, P. Y. (1987). Automated spike and sharp wave (SSW) detection. In Gevins & Remond (Eds.), Methods of analysis of brain electrical and magnetic signals, (pp. 211-241). Amsterdam: Elsevier.

Kulik, J., et al. (2002). Negotiation-based protocols for disseminating information in wireless sensor networks. *Wireless Networks Magazine, 8*.

Kumar, Y., & Dewal, M. L. (2011). Complexity measures for normal and epileptic EEG signals using ApEn, SampEn and SEN. *International Journal of Computer & Communication Technology, 2*(7), 6–12.

Kuznetsov, S., Obiedkov, S., & Roth, C. (2007). Reducing the representation complexity of lattice-based taxonomies. In *Conceptual Structures: Knowledge Architectures for Smart Applications*. Berlin: Springer. doi:10.1007/978-3-540-73681-3_18.

Kwon, O., & Kim, J. (2009). Concept lattices for visualizing and generating user profiles for context-aware service recommendations. *Expert Systems with Applications, 36*(2), 1893–1902. doi:10.1016/j.eswa.2007.12.064.

Laarhoven, P. J. M. V., & Aarts, E. H. L. (1987). *Simulated annealing: Theory and applications.* Berlin: Springer. doi:10.1007/978-94-015-7744-1.

Lamport, L. (1981). Password authentication with insecure communication. *Communications of the ACM, 24*(11), 770–772. doi:10.1145/358790.358797.

Leacock, C., & Chodorow, M. (1998). Combining local context and WordNet similarity for word sense identification. In Fellbaum, C. (Ed.), *WordNet: An Electronic Lexical Database* (pp. 265–283). Boston: MIT Press.

Lee, K. C., & Cho, H. (2010). A general bayesian network-assisted ensemble system for context prediction: An emphasis on location prediction. In Kim, Lee, Kang, & Slezak (Ed.), FGIT (LNCS), (vol. 6485, pp. 294–303). Springer.

Lensu, A., & Koikkalainen, P. (2002). *Artificial Neural Networks.* ICANN.

Leonhardt, U., & Magee, J. (1998). Security considerations for a distributed location service. *Journal of Network and Systems Management, 6*(1). doi:10.1023/A:1018777802208.

Lerner, D. E. (1996). Monitoring changing dynamics with correlation integrals: Case study of an epileptic seizure. *Physica D. Nonlinear Phenomena, 97*(4), 563–576. doi:10.1016/0167-2789(96)00085-1.

Lewis, R., & Paechter, B. (2004). New crossover operators for timetabling with evolutionary algorithms. In A. Lofti (Ed.), *The 5th International Conference on Recent Advances in Soft Computing,* (Vol. 5, pp. 189–195). IEEE.

Li, J., Qi, Q., Zou, X., Peng, H., Jiang, L., & Liang, Y. (2005). Technique for automatic forest fire surveillance using visible light image. In *Proceedings of International Geoscience and Remote Sensing Symposium,* (vol. 5, pp. 31–35). IEEE.

Li, N., Li, T., & Venkatasubramanian, S. (2007). t-closeness: Privacy beyond k-anonymity and l-diversity. In *Proceedings of the IEEE 23rd International Conference on Data Engineering (ICDE 2007),* (pp. 106-115). IEEE.

Li, K., Du, Y., & Xiang, D. (2007). Collaborative recommending based on core-concept lattice. *Advances in Soft Computing, 42,* 583–592. doi:10.1007/978-3-540-72434-6_59.

Lin, D. (1998). An information-theoretic definition of similarity. In *Proceedings of the 15th International Conf. on Machine Learning* (pp. 296–304). San Francisco: Morgan Kaufmann.

Li, N., Zhang, N., Das, S. K., & Thuraisingham, B. M. (2009). Privacy preservation in wireless sensor networks: A state-of-the-art survey. *Ad Hoc Networks, 7*(8), 1501–1514. doi:10.1016/j.adhoc.2009.04.009.

Lindgren, K., & Nordahl, M. (1994). Evolutionary dynamics of spatial games. *Physica D. Nonlinear Phenomena, 75,* 292–309. doi:10.1016/0167-2789(94)90289-5.

Lindsey, S. R. C. (2002). Pegasis: Power-efficient gathering in sensor information systems. In *Proceedings of Aerospace Conference.* Academic Press.

Lin, R., Kraus, S., Wilkenfeld, J., & Barry, J. (2006). An automated agent for bilateral negotiation with bounded rational agents with incomplete information.[ECAI.]. *Proceedings of ECAI, 2006,* 270–274.

Litt, B., & Lehnertz, K. (2002). Seizure prediction and the preseizure period. *Current Opinion in Neurology, 15*(2), 173–177. doi:10.1097/00019052-200204000-00008 PMID:11923631.

Liu, D., & Ning, P. (2003). Establishing pairwise keys in distributed sensor networks. In *Proceedings of the 10th ACM Conference on Computer and Communication Security.* ACM.

Lloret, J., Garcia, M., Bri, D., & Sendra, S. (2009). A wireless sensor network deployment for rural and forest fire detection and verification. *Sensors (Basel, Switzerland), 9,* 8722–8747. doi:10.3390/s91108722 PMID:22291533.

Locateli, M., & Raber, U. (2002). Packing equal circles in a square: A deterministic global optimization approach. *Discrete Applied Mathematics, 122,* 139–166. doi:10.1016/S0166-218X(01)00359-6.

Looi, C. (1992). Neural network methods in combinatorial optimization. *Computers & Operations Research, 19*(3/4), 191–208. doi:10.1016/0305-0548(92)90044-6.

Lopez-Munoz, J. (2005). *Wireless sensor networks: The new security challenge?* Paper presented In 1st International Workshop on Privacy and Trust in Pervasive and Ubiquitous Computing. New York.

Luo, X., Jennings, N. R., Shadbolt, N., Leung, H. F., & Lee, J. H. M. (2003). A fuzzy constraint based model for bilateral, multi-issue negotiation in semi-competitive environments. *Artificial Intelligence, 148*(1–2), 53–102. doi:10.1016/S0004-3702(03)00041-9.

Machanavajjhala, A., Kifer, D., Gehrke, J., & Venkita-subramaniam, M. (2007). L-diversity: Privacy beyond k-anonymity. *ACM Transactions on Knowledge Discovery from Data, 1*(1).

Madden, S., Franklin, M. J., Hellerstein, J. M., & Hong, W. (2002). TAG: A tiny aggregation service for ad-hoc sensor networks. In *Proceedings of the ACM Symposium on Operating System Design and Implementation.* ACM.

Madden, S., Franklin, M. J., Hellerstein, J. M., & Hong, W. (2003). The design of an acquisitional query processor for sensor networks. In *Proceedings of The 2003 ACM SIGMOD International Conference on Management of Data* (pp. 491–502). ACM.

Madden, S., Szewczyk, R., Franklin, M. J., & Culler, D. E. (2002). Supporting aggregate queries over ad-hoc wireless sensor networks. In *Proceedings of The 4th IEEE Workshop on Mobile Computing Systems and Applications* (pp. 49–58). IEEE.

Maedche, A., & Staab, S. (2001). *Comparing ontologies: Similarity measures and a comparison study.* Paper presented at the Institute of AIFB. Karlsruhe, Germany.

Maedche, A., & Staab, S. (2002). Measuring similarity between ontologies. In *Proceedings of the 13th International Conference on Knowledge Engineering and Knowledge Management* (pp. 251-263). Singuenza, Spain: IEEE.

Maenner, E. (2008). Adaptation and complexity in repeated games. *Games and Economic Behavior, 63*(1), 166–187. doi:10.1016/j.geb.2007.07.008.

Mahimkar, A., & Rappaport, T. S. (2004). SecureDAV: A secure data aggregation and verification protocol for sensor networks. In *Proceedings of the IEEE Globecom.* IEEE.

Malan, D. J., et al. (2004). A public-key infrastructure for key distribution in TinyOS based on elliptic curve cryptography. In *Proceedings of the 1st IEEE Communications Society Conference on Sensor and Ad Hoc Communications & Networks.* IEEE.

Malczewski, J. (1999). *GIS and multi-criteria decision analysis.* New York: JohnWiley & Sons, Inc..

Mao, Q., Feng, B., Pan, S., Zheng, Q., & Liu, J. (2010). New collaborative recommendation approach based on concept lattice.[FSKD]. *Proceedings of Fuzzy Systems and Knowledge Discovery, 4*, 1803–1807.

Marias, G. F., Delakouridis, C., Kazatzopoulos, L., & Georgiadis, P. (2005). Location privacy through secret sharing techniques. In *Proceedings of the 1st IEEE International Workshop on Trust, Security and Privacy for Ubiquitous Computing,* (pp. 614-620). IEEE.

Marias, G. F., Delakouridis, C., Kazatzopoulos, L., & Georgiadis, P. (2006). Applying privacy on the dissemination of location information. *Elsevier Telematics and Informatics Journal, 23*(3), 211–219. doi:10.1016/j.tele.2005.07.006.

Marias, G. F., Prigouris, N., Papazafeiropoulos, G., Hadjiefthymiades, S., & Merakos, L. (2004). Brokering positioning data from heterogeneous infrastructures. *Wireless Personal Communications, 30*(2-4), 233–245. doi:10.1023/B:WIRE.0000049402.33897.15.

Martin, D., Paolucci, M., Mcilraith, S., Burstein, M., Mcdermott, D., & Mcguinness, D. Sycara, K. (2004). Bringing semantics to web services: The OWL-S approach. In J. Cardoso & A. Sheth (Eds.), SWSWPC 2004 (LNCS), (vol. 3387, pp. 26-42). Springer.

Martin, S., Ouelhadj, D., Beullens, P., & Ozcan, E. (2012). *A generic agent-based framework for cooperative search using pattern matching and reinforcement learning* (Technical Report 5861). Portsmouth, UK: University of Portsmouth.

Martinetz, T. M., Berkovich, S. G., & Schulten, K. J. (1993). Neural-gas network for vector quantization and its application to time-series prediction. *IEEE Transactions on Neural Networks, 4*(4), 558–569. doi:10.1109/72.238311 PMID:18267757.

Mashhadi, R. H., & Rahimiyan, M. (2011). Measurement of power supplier's market power using a proposed fuzzy estimator. *IEEE Transactions on Power Systems, 26*(4), 1836–1844. doi:10.1109/TPWRS.2011.2144626.

Mayrhofer, R. (2004). *An architecture for context prediction*. (PhD Thesis). Johannes Kepler University of Linz. Linz, Germany.

Mayrhofer, R., Harald, R., & Alois, F. (2003). Recognizing and predicting context by learning from user behaviour. In. W. Schreiner, G. Kotsis, A. Ferscha, & K. Ibrahim (Ed.), *International Conference on Advances in Mobile Multimedia (MoMM2003)*, (pp. 25–35). MoMM.

McMillan, J. (1992). *Games, strategies, and managers: How managers can use game theory to make better business decisions*. New York: Oxford University Press.

Meiners, M., Zaplata, S., & Lamersdorf, W. (2010). Structured context prediction: A generic approach. In R. Kapitza & F. Eliassen (Eds.), *Proceedings of the 10th IFIP International Conference on Distributed Applications and Interoperable Systems (DAIS 2010)*, (pp. 84–97). Springer.

Melicio, F., Caldeira, J. P., & Rosa, A. (2004). Two neighbourhood approaches to the timetabling problem. In *Proceedings of the Practice and Theory of Automated Timetabling V, Fifth International Conference*. IEEE.

Meliou, A., Chu, D., Hellerstein, J., Guestrin, C., & Hong, W. (2006). Data gathering tours in sensor networks. In *Proceedings of The 5th International Conference on Information Processing in Sensor Networks* (pp. 43–50). IEEE.

Mendoza, G. A., & Prabhu, R. (2003). Qualitative multi-criteria approaches to assessing indicators of sustainable forest resource management. *Forest Ecology and Management, 174*, 329–343. doi:10.1016/S0378-1127(02)00044-0.

Minch, R. P. (2004). Privacy issues in location-aware mobile devices. In *Proceedings of the 37th Hawaii International Conference on System Sciences*. IEEE.

Mini, S., Udgata, S. K., & Sabat, S. L. (2011). Artificial bee colony based sensor deployment algorithm for target coverage problem in 3-D terrain. In *Proceedings of the Distributed Computing and Internet Technology - 7th International Conference*. Berlin, Germany: Springer.

Mirbel, I., & Crescenzo, P. (2010). From end-user's requirements to web services retrieval: A semantic and intention-driven approach. In J.-H. Morin, J. Ralyte, & M. Snene (Eds.), *Exploring service science: First international conference on exploring services sciences (IESS)*, (pp. 30-44). Springer.

Mokbel, M. F., Chow, C. Y., & Aref, W. G. (2006). The new casper: Query processing for location services without compromising privacy. In *Proceedings of (VLDB '06)*, (pp. 763-774). VLDB.

Monge, A. E., & Elkan, C. P. (1996). The field matching problem: Algorithms and applications. In *Proceedings of the Second International Conference on Knowledge Discovery and Data Mining*. IEEE.

Montgomery, A. L., Hosanagar, K., Krishnan, R., & Clay, K. B. (2004). Designing a better shopbot. *Management Science, 50*(2), 189–206. doi:10.1287/mnsc.1030.0151.

Murro, A. M., King, D. W., Smith, J. R., Gallagher, B. B., Flanigin, H. F., & Meador, K. (1991). Computerized seizure detection of complex partial seizures. *Electroencephalography and Clinical Neurophysiology, 79*, 330–333. doi:10.1016/0013-4694(91)90128-Q PMID:1717237.

Mustafa, A., & Goh, M. (1996). Multi-criterion models for higher education administration, Omega. *International Journal of Management Science, 24*, 167–178.

Nadeem, A., Salil, S. K., & Sanjay, J. (2007). *Ensuring area coverage in hybrid wireless sensor network*. Berlin: Springer-Verlag.

Najar, S., Kirsch-Pinheiro, M., & Souveyet, C. (2011). The influence of context on intentional service. In *Proceedings of the 5th International IEEE Workshop on Requirements Engineerings for Services (REFS)- IEEE Conference on Computers, Software and Applications (COMPSAC)*, (pp. 470-475). IEEE.

Najar, S., Kirsch-Pinheiro, M., & Souveyet, C. (2011). Towards semantic modeling of intentional pervasive information systems. In *Proceedings of the 6th International Workshop on Enhanced Web Service Technologies WEWST*, (pp. 30-34). WEWST.

Najar, S., Kirsch-Pinheiro, M., Souveyet, C., & Steffenel, L. A. (2012). Service discovery mechanism for an intentional pervasive information system. In *Proceeding of 19th IEEE International Conference on Web Services (ICWS)*, (pp. 520-527). Honolulu, HI: IEEE.

Najar, S., Saidani, O., Kirsch-Pinheiro, M., Souveyet, C., & Nurcan, S. (2009). Semantic representation of context models: A framework for analyzing and understanding. In J. M. Gomez-Perez, P. Haase, M. Tilly, & P. Warren (Ed.), *1st Workshop on Context, Information and Ontologies CIAO, European Semantic Web Conference ESWC'2009*, (pp. 1-10). ACM.

Naor, M., & Wool, A. (1998). Access control and signatures via quorum secret sharing. *IEEE Transactions on Parallel and Distributed Systems*, 9(1), 909–922. doi:10.1109/71.722223.

Narendra, K. (1974). Learning automata - A survey. *IEEE Transactions on Systems, Man, and Cypernetics, 4*.

Narendra, K. S., & Wright, A. (1977). Application of learning automata to telephone traffic routing and control. *IEEE Transactions on Systems, Man, and Cybernetics*, 7(11), 785–792. doi:10.1109/TSMC.1977.4309623.

Narendra, K., & Thathachar, M. (1989). *Learning automata (an introduction)*. Englewood Cliffs, NJ: Prentice–Hall.

Nauer, E., & Toussaint, Y. (2007). Dynamical modification of context for an iterative and interactive information retrieval process on the web. In *Proceedings of CLA 2007*. CLA.

Needleman, S. B., & Wunch, C. D. (1970). Needleman - Wunch algorithm for sequence similarity searches. *Journal of Molecular Biology*, 48, 443–453. doi:10.1016/0022-2836(70)90057-4 PMID:5420325.

Nelles, O. (2001). *Nonlinear system identification*. Berlin, Germany: Springer. doi:10.1007/978-3-662-04323-3.

Neto, J., & Iwai, K. (1998). Adaptive automata for syntax learning. In Proceedings of Anais da XXIV Conferencia Latinoamericana de Informática - CLEI 98 (pp. 135–149). Quito, Equador: CLEI.

Neto, J. J., & Bravo, C. (2003). *Adaptive automata - A reduced complexity proposal*. Lecture Notes in Computer Science Berlin: Springer.

Neubert, R., Görlitz, O., & Teich, T. (2004). Automated negotiations of supply contracts for flexible production networks. *International Journal of Production Economics*, 89(2), 175–187. doi:10.1016/S0925-5273(03)00043-4.

Neyman, A. (1985). Bounded complexity justifies cooperation in finitely repeated prisoner's dilemma. *Economics Letters*, 19, 227–229. doi:10.1016/0165-1765(85)90026-6.

Ng, A. Y., & Jordan, M. (2000). PEGASUS: A policy search method for large MDPs and POMDPs. In *Proceedings of the Sixteenth Conference on Uncertainty in Artificial Intelligence*. IEEE.

Ng, A. Y., Kim, H. J., Jordan, M. I., Sastry, S., & Ballianda, S. (2004). Autonomous helicopter flight via reinforcement learning. *Advances in Neural Information Processing Systems*.

Nhan, V. T. H., & Ryu, K. H. (2006). Future Location Prediction of Moving Objects Based on Movement Rules. *Springer ICIC 2006. LNCIS*, 344, 875–881.

Nigam, V. P., & Graupe, D. (2004). A neural-network-based detection of epilepsy. *Neurological Research*, 26(1), 55–60. doi:10.1179/016164104773026534 PMID:14977058.

Nojeong, H., & Pramod, K. V. (2005). Energy-efficient deployment of intelligent mobile sensor networks. *IEEE Transactions on Systems, Man, and Cybernetics. Part A*, 35(1), 78–92.

Nowak, A. S., & Latané, B. (1990). From private attitude to public opinion - Dynamic theory of social impact. *Psychological Review*, 362–376. doi:10.1037/0033-295X.97.3.362.

Noy, N. F. (2001). Anchor-PROMPT: Using non-local context for semantic matching. In *Proceedings of the Workshop on Ontologies and Information Sharing at the International Joint Conference on Artificial Intelligence* (pp. 63-70). IEEE.

Nurmi, P., Martin, M., & Flanagan, J. A. (2005). Enabling proactiviness through context prediction. In *Proceedings of the Workshop on Context Awareness for Proactive Systems*, (pp. 159-168). IEEE.

Ocak, H. (2009). Automatic detection of epileptic seizures in EEG using discrete wavelet transform and approximate entropy. *International Journal of Expert Systems with Applications, 36*, 2027–2036. doi:10.1016/j.eswa.2007.12.065.

Olivarez-Giles, N. (2012). *Does Samsung's Galaxy S III smartphone even need quad-core power? Gadget lab.* Retrieved from http://www.wired.com/gadgetlab/2012/05/quad-core-vs-dual-core-phones-tablets-nvidia-samsung-galaxy/

Oliveira, E., Fonseca, J. M., & Steiger-Garcao, A. (1997). MACIV: A DAI based resource management system. In Proceedings of Applied Artificial Intelligence. AAAI.

Oliver, et al. (2000). A Bayesian computer vision system for modeling human interaction. *IEEE Transactions on Pattern Analysis and Machine Intelligence, 22*(8). doi:10.1109/34.868684.

Oncina, J. (2008). Using multiplicity automata to identify transducer relations from membership and equivalence queries. In *Proceedings of 9th International Colloquium on Grammatical Inference,* (vol. 5278, pp. 154–162). Berlin: Springer.

OpenStreetMap. Webite: http://www.openstreetmap.org/traces/tag/Denmark

Oshrat, Y., Lin, R., & Kraus, S. (2009). Facing the challenge of human-agent negotiations via e_ective general opponent modeling. In *Proceedings of The 8th International Conference on Autonomous Agents and Multiagent Systems,* (Vol. 1, pp. 377-384). International Foundation for Autonomous Agents and Multiagent Systems.

Ouyang, Y., Xu, Y., Le, Z., Chen, G., & Makedon, F. (2008). Providing location privacy in assisted living environments.[PETRA.]. *Proceedings of PETRA, 2008,* 1–8. doi:10.1145/1389586.1389633.

Paganelli, F., Bianchi, G., & Giuli, D. (2007). A context model for context-aware system design towards the ambient intelligence vision: experiences in the etourism domain. In *Proceedings of the 9th Conference on User Interfaces for All,* (pp. 173–191). Berlin: Springer-Verlag.

Palanisamy, B., & Liu, L. (2011). Mobimix: Protecting location privacy with mix-zones over road networks. [ICDE.]. *Proceedings of ICDE, 2011,* 494–505.

Palmer, D. D. (1997). A trainable rule-based algorithm for word segmentation. In *Proceedings of the 35th Annual Meeting on Association for Computational Linguistics* (pp. 321-328). Madrid, Spain: ACL.

Paolucci, M., Kawmura, T., Payne, T., & Sycara, K. (2002). Semantic matching of web services capabilities. In *Proceedings of the First International Semantic Web Conference* (LNCS), (vol. 2342). Sardinia, Italy: Springer.

Paridel, K., Yasar, A., Vanrompay, Y., Preuveneers, D., & Berbers, Y. (2011). Teamwork on the road: Efficient collaboration in VANETs with context-based grouping. In *Proceedings of The International Conference on Ambient Systems, Networks and Technologies (ANT-2011),* (vol. 5, pp. 48-57). Elsevier.

Parunak, H. V. D., White, J. F., Lozo, P. W., Judd, R., Irish, B. W., & Kindrick, J. (1986). An architecture for heuristic factory control, DFSG 86-8. In *Proceedings of the 1986 American Control Conference.* ACC.

Pastry. (n.d.). *A substrate for peer-to-peer applications.* Retrieved from www.freepastry.org

Peng, J., & Williams, R. J. (1996). Incremental multistep Q-learning. *Machine Learning, 22*(1–3), 283–290. doi:10.1007/BF00114731.

Perhinschi, G. M. (1997). A modified genetic algorithm for the design of autonomous helicopter control system. In *Proceedings of AIAA Guidance, Navigation, and Control Conference.* AIAA.

Perrig, A., Stankovic, J., & Wagner, D. (2004). Security in wireless sensor networks. *Communications of the ACM, 47*(6). doi:10.1145/990680.990707.

Perrone, G., Roma, P., & Lo Nigro, G. (2010). Designing multi-attribute auctions for engineering services procurement in new product development in the automotive context. *International Journal of Production Economics, 124*(1), 20–31. doi:10.1016/j.ijpe.2009.10.003.

Peskir, G., & Shiryaev, A. (2006). *Optimal stopping and free boundary problems.* Zuerich, Switzerland: Birkhauser.

Petric, D. (2012). *Quad-core smartphones dominated mobile world congress 2012.* Retrieved from http://www.brighthand.com/default.asp? newsID=18664&news=Mobile+World+Congress+MWC2012

Petrosian, A. (1995). Kolmogorov complexity of finite sequences and recognition of different preictal EEG patterns. In *Proceedings of the 8ᵗʰ IEEE Symposium on Computer-Based Medical Systems*, (pp. 212–217). IEEE.

Petzold, J. (2005). *State predictors for context prediction in ubiquitous systems*. (PhD Thesis). University of Augsburg. Augsburg, Germany.

Petzold, J., Bagci, F., Trumler, W., & Ungerer, T. (2005). Next location prediction within a smart office building. In *Proceedings of the 1st International Workshop on Exploiting Context Histories in Smart Environments (ECHISE05), 3rd International Conference on Pervasive Computing*. ECHISE.

Pfitzmann, A., & Koehntopp, M. (2000). Anonymity, unobservability, and pseudonymity – A proposal for terminology. In *Proceedings of the Workshop on Design Issues in Anonymity and Unobservability*. IEEE.

Pidd, M., & Cassel, R. A. (2000). Using java to develop discrete event simulation. *The Journal of the Operational Research Society, 51*(4), 405–412.

Pistori, H., & Martins, P. S. (2005). Adaptive finite state automata and genetic algorithms: Merging individual adaptation and population evolution. In *Proceedings of the International Conference on Adaptive and Natural Computing Algorithms – ICANNGA*. Coimbra: ICANNGA.

Platkowski, T., & Siwak, M. (2008). Mean-field approximation for two-and three-person prisoner's dilemmas. *Physica A: Statistical Mechanics and its Applications, 387*.

Politis, Y., & Siskos, Y. (2004). Multicriteria methodology for the evaluation of a Greek engineering deparment. *European Journal of Operational Research, 156*, 223–240. doi:10.1016/S0377-2217(02)00902-5.

Prat, N. (1997). Goal formalisation and classification for requirements engineering. In *Proceedings of the 3rd International Workshop on Requirements Engineering: Foundations of Software Quality (REFSQ'97)*. Presses Universitaires de Namur.

Pravin-Kumar, S., Sriraam, N., Benakop, P. G., & Jinaga, B. C. (2010). Entropies based detection of epileptic seizures with artificial neural network classifiers. *International Journal of Expert Systems with Application, 37*, 3284–3291. doi:10.1016/j.eswa.2009.09.051.

Preuveneers, D., Victor, K., Vanrompay, Y., Rigole, P., Kirsch Pinheiro, M., & Berbers, Y. (2009). Context-aware adaptation in an ecology of applications. In Stojanovic, D. (Ed.), *Context-Aware Mobile and Ubiquitous Computing for Enhanced Usability: Adaptive Technologies and Applications*. Hershey, PA: IGI Global. doi:10.4018/978-1-60566-290-9.ch001.

Priggouris, I., Zervas, E., & Hadjiefthymiades, S. (2006). Location Based Network Resource Management. In Ibrahim, I. K. (Ed.), *Handbook of Research on Mobile Multimedia*. Idea Group Inc. doi:10.4018/978-1-59140-866-6.ch011.

Priyantha, N. B., Chakraborty, A., & Balakrishnan, H. (2000). The cricket location-support system. In *Proceedings of the 6th ACM MOBICOM*, (pp. 32-43). ACM.

Purnomo, H., Mendoza, G. A., Prabhu, R., & Yasmi, Y. (2005). Developing multistakeholder forest management scenarios: A multi-agent systems simulation approach applied in Indonesia. *Forest Policy and Economics, 7*(4), 475–491. doi:10.1016/j.forpol.2003.08.004.

Rabin, M. O. (1983). Randomized byzantine generals. In *Proceedings of the 24th IEEE Symposium on Foundations of Computer Science*, (pp. 403-409). IEEE.

Rabiner, L. R. (1989). A tutorial on hidden Markov models and selected applications in speech recognition. *Proceedings of the IEEE, 77*, 257–286. doi:10.1109/5.18626.

Rahimiyan, M., & Mashhadi, H. R. (2008). Supplier's optimal bidding strategy in electricity pay-as-bid auction: Comparison of the q-learning and a model-based approach. *Electric Power Systems Research, 78*(1), 165–175. doi:10.1016/j.epsr.2007.01.009.

Raju, C. V. L., Narahari, Y., & Ravikumar, K. (2006). Learning dynamic prices in electronic markets with customer segmentation. *Annals of Operations Research, 143*(1), 59–75. doi:10.1007/s10479-006-7372-3.

Ramadour, P., & Fakhri, M. (2011). Modèle et langage de composition de services. In *Proceedings of INFORSID*, (pp. 59-76). INFORSID.

Ramchurn, S. D., Sierra, C., Godo, L., & Jennings, N. R. (2007). Negotiating using rewards. *Artificial Intelligence, 171*(10-15), 805-837.

Rappaport, T. (Ed.). (2002). *Wireless communications: Principles and practice.* Englewood Cliffs, NJ: Prentice Hall.

Reichle, R., Wagner, M., Khan, M. U., Geihs, K., Lorenzo, L., & Valla, M. Papadopoulos, G.A. (2008). A comprehensive context modeling framework for pervasive computing systems. In Meier & Terzis (Eds.) DAIS 2008 (LNCS), (vol. 5053). Berlin: Springer.

Reichle, R., Wagner, M., Khan, M. U., Geihs, K., Valla, M., & Fra, C. Papadopoulos, G.A. (2008). A context query language for pervasive computing environments. In *Proceedings of the 5th IEEE Workshop on Context Modeling and Reasoning (CoMoRea)*, (pp. 434–440). IEEE.

Reinforcement Learning Competition. (2009). http://www.rl-competition.org

Renna, P. (2009). A multi-agent system architecture for business-to-business applications. *International Journal of Services and Operations Management, 5*(3), 375–401. doi:10.1504/IJSOM.2009.024152.

Renna, P. (2010). Negotiation policies for e-procurement by multi agent systems. In Nag, B. (Ed.), *Intelligent Systems in Operations: Models, Methods, and Applications.* Hershey, PA: IGI Publishing. doi:10.4018/978-1-61520-605-6.ch009.

Renna, P., & Argoneto, P. (2010). Production planning and automated negotiation for SMEs: An agent based e-procurement application. *International Journal of Production Economics, 127*(1), 73–84. doi:10.1016/j.ijpe.2010.04.035.

Ridder, J. P., Brett, S. W., & Signori, D. T. (2012). *Distributed algorithms for resource allocation problems.* Paper presented at the 17th International Command and Control Research and Technology Symposium. Fairfax, VA.

Rodriguez, M. A., & Egenhofer, M. J. (2003). Determining semantic similarity among entity classes from different ontologies. *IEEE Transactions on Knowledge and Data Engineering.* doi:10.1109/TKDE.2003.1185844.

Rolland, C., Kirsch-Pinheiro, M., & Souveyet, C. (2010). An intentional approach to service engineering. *IEEE Transactions on Service Computing, 3*(4), 292–305. doi:10.1109/TSC.2010.26.

Romero, D., Rouvoy, R., Seinturier, L., & Loiret, F. (2010). Integration of heterogeneous context resources in ubiquitous environments. In *Proceedings of the 36th EUROMICRO International Conference on Software Engineering and Advanced Applications* (pp. 123-126). ACM Press

Rosenhead, J. (1989). *Rational analysis of a problematic world.* New York: John Wiley and Sons.

Rossi-Doria, O., & Paechter, B. (2003). *An hyperheuristic approach to course timetabling problem using an evolutionary algorithm.* Paper presented at the First Multidisciplinary International Conference on Scheduling: Theory and Applications (MISTA 2003). New York.

Rubinstein, A. (1986). Finite automata play the repeated prisoner's dilemma. *Journal of Economic Theory, 39,* 83–96. doi:10.1016/0022-0531(86)90021-9.

Rudova, H., & Murry, K. (2003). University course timetabling with soft constraints. In Burke & Causmaecker (Eds.), *Proceedings of the Practice and Theory of Automated Timetabling IV, Fourth International Conference.* Berlin: Springer.

Russel, S., & Norvig, P. (2003). *Artificial intelligence a modern approach.* Upper Saddle River, NJ: Prentice Hall.

Sandholm, T., & Boutilier, C. (2006). Preference elicitation in combinatorial auctions. In Cramton, Shoham, & Steinberg (Eds.), Combinatorial Auctions. Boston: MIT Press.

Schneier on Security. (n.d.). *DNSSEC root key split among seven people.* Retrieved July 28, 2010 from http://www.schneier.com/blog/archives/2010/07/dnssec_root_key.html

Schrijver, A. (1998). *Theory of linear and integer programming.* New York: John Wiley & Sons.

Schurgers, C., et al. (2001). Energy efficient routing in wireless sensor networks. In *Proceedings of the MILCOM Communications for Network-Centric Operations.* MILCOM.

Schut, M. (2010). On model design for simulation of collective intelligence. *Information Sciences, 180,* 132–155. doi:10.1016/j.ins.2009.08.006.

Sejnowski, T. J., & Hinton, G. E. (Eds.). (1999). *Unsupervised learning: Foundations of neural computation.* Cambridge, MA: MIT Press.

Seki., et al. (2003). Background subtraction based on cooccurence of image variations. In *Proceedings CVPR 2003,* (Vol. 2, pp. 65-72). CVPR.

Sempolinski, P., & Thain, D. (2010). A comparison and critique of eucalyptus, open nebula and nimbus. In *Proceedings of IEEE International Conference on Cloud Computing Technology and Science,* (pp. 417-426). IEEE.

Shamir, A. (1979). How to share a secret. *Communications of the ACM, 22*(11), 612–613. doi:10.1145/359168.359176.

Shankar, B., Srinathan, K., & PanduRangan, C. (2008). Alternative protocols for generalized oblivious transfer. In S. Rao, M. Chatterjee, P. Jayanti, C. S. Murthy, & S. K. Saha (Eds.), *Proceedings of ICDCN 2008* (LNCS), (vol. 4904, pp. 304-309). Berlin: Springer-Verlag.

Shiryaev, A. (1978). *Optimal stopping rules.* New York: Springer-Verlag.

Shvaiko, P., & Euzenat, J. (2005). A survey of schema-based matching approaches. *Journal on Data Semantics, 3730,* 146–171.

Sigg, S. (2008). *Development of a novel context prediction algorithm and analysis of context prediction schemes.* (PhD thesis). Kassel University. Kassel, Germany.

Sigg, S., Haseloff, S., & David, K. (2010). An alignment approach for context prediction tasks in ubicomp environments. *IEEE Pervasive Computing/IEEE Computer Society [and] IEEE Communications Society, 9*(4), 90–97. doi:10.1109/MPRV.2010.23.

Si, J., Barto, A. G., Powell, W. B., & Wunch, D. II, (Eds.). (2004). *Handbook of learning and approximate dynamic programming.* New York: Wiley. doi:10.1109/9780470544785.

Silberstein, A., Braynard, R., & Yang, J. (2006). Constraint chaining: on energy-efficient continuous monitoring in sensor networks. In *Proceedings of The 2006 ACM SIGMOD International Conference on Management of Data* (pp. 157–168). ACM.

Silva, J. D. L., Burke, E. K., & Petrovic, S. (2004). An introduction to multiobjective metaheuristics for scheduling and timetabling. *Lecture Notes in Economics and Mathematical Systems, 535,* 91–129. doi:10.1007/978-3-642-17144-4_4.

Sipser, M. (1997). *Introduction to the theory of computation.* Boston: Academic Press.

Smith, M. D. (2002). The impact of shopbots on electronic markets. *Journal of the Academy of Marketing Science, 30*(4), 446–454. doi:10.1177/009207002236916.

Smith, T. F., & Waterman, M. S. (1981). Identification of common molecular subsequences. *Journal of Molecular Biology, 147,* 195–197. doi:10.1016/0022-2836(81)90087-5 PMID:7265238.

Sobeih, A. et al. (2005). *J-sim: A simulation and emulation environment for wireless sensor networks.* IEEE Wireless Communication Magazine.

Solanas, A., Seb, E. F., & Domingo-Ferrer, J. (2008). Micro-aggregation-based heuristics for p-sensitive k-anonymity: One step beyond. In *Proceedings of the 2008 International Workshop on Privacy and Anonymity in Information Society (PAIS '08),* (pp. 61-69). PAIS.

Song J.-H., et al. (2003). Secure routing with tamper resistant module for mobile ad hoc networks. *ACM Mobile Computing and Communication Review, 7*(3).

Srinivasan, D., Seow, T. H., & Xu, J. X. (2002). Automated time table generation using multiple context reasoning for university modules. In *Proceedings of IEEE International Conference on Evolutionary Computation,* (pp. 1751–1756). IEEE.

Srinivasan, V., Eswaran, C., & Sriraam, N. (2005). Artificial neural network based epileptic detection using time-domain and frequency-domain features. *Journal of Medical Systems, 29*(6), 647–660. doi:10.1007/s10916-005-6133-1 PMID:16235818.

Srinivasan, V., Eswaran, C., & Sriraam, N. (2007). Approximate entropy-based epileptic EEG detection using artificial neural networks. *IEEE Transactions on Information Technology in Biomedicine, 11*(3). doi:10.1109/TITB.2006.884369 PMID:17521078.

Stauffer & Grimson. (1999). Adaptive background mixture models for real-time tracking. In *Proceedings IEEE CVRP 1999*. IEEE.

Stumme, G., Taouil, R., Bastide, Y., Pasquier, N., & Lakhal, L. (2002). Computing iceberg concept lattices with TITANIC. *Data & Knowledge Engineering, 42*, 189–222. doi:10.1016/S0169-023X(02)00057-5.

Sturm, A., & Shehory, O. (2003). A framework for evaluating agent-oriented methodologies. In Giorgini & Winikoff (Eds.), *Proceedings of the Fifth International Bi-Conference Workshop on Agent-Oriented Information Systems*. Melbourne, Australia: IEEE.

Subasi, A. (2007). Application of adaptive neuro-fuzzy inference system for epileptic seizure detection using wavelet feature extraction. *International Journal of Computers in Biology and Medicine, 37*, 227–244. doi:10.1016/j.compbiomed.2005.12.003 PMID:16480706.

Su, M., Hui, C., Zhang, Y., & Li, Z. (2009). How does the spatial structure of habitat loss affect the ecoepidemic dynamics? *Ecological Modelling, 220*, 51–59. doi:10.1016/j.ecolmodel.2008.09.009.

Sutton, R. S., & Barto, A. (1998). *Reinforcement learning: An introduction*. Boston: MIT Press.

Sutton, R. S., & Barto, A. G. (1998). *Reinforcement learning an introduction*. Boston: MIT Press.

Szathmary, L., Valtchev, P., Napoli, A., & Godin, R. (2008). Constructing iceberg lattices from frequent closures using generators. In *Proceedings of the 11th International Conference on Discovery Science (DS '08)*, (pp. 136-147). Budapest, Hungary: DS.

Szewczyk, R., Osterweil, E., Polastre, J., Hamilton, M., Mainwaring, A., & Estrin, D. (2004). Habitat monitoring with sensor networks. *Communications of the ACM, 47*(6), 34–40. doi:10.1145/990680.990704.

Szilagyi, M. (2003). An investigation of n-person prisoners' dilemmas. *Complex Systems, 14*(2).

Szilagyi, M. N. (2008). Agent-based simulation of n-person games with crossing payoff functions. *Complex Systems, 17*(4), 427.

Talukder, N., & Ahamed, S. I. (2010). Preventing multi-query attack in location-based services. In *Proceedings of the Third ACM conference on Wireless Network Security*, (pp. 25-36). ACM.

Tan, P.-N., Steinbach, M., & Kumar, V. (Eds.). (2006). *Introduction to data mining*. Reading, MA: Addison-Wesley.

Tao, Y., Faloutsos, C., Papadias, D., & Liu, B. (2004). *Prediction and Indexing of Moving Objects with Unknown Motion Patterns*. ACM SIGMOD. doi:10.1145/1007568.1007637.

Taqqu, M. S., Teverovsky, V., & Willinger, W. (1995). Estimators for long-range dependence: An empirical study. *Fractals, 3*(4), 785–798. doi:10.1142/S0218348X95000692.

Tassa, T. (2011). Generalized oblivious transfer by secret sharing. *Designs, Codes and Cryptography, 58*.

Tesauro, G., & Kephart, J. O. (2002). Pricing in agent economies using multi-agent Q-learning. *Autonomous Agents and Multi-Agent Systems, 5*(3), 289–304. doi:10.1023/A:1015504423309.

Tezel, G., & Ozbay, Y. (2009). A new approach for epileptic seizure detection using adaptive neural network. *International Journal of Expert Systems with Application, 36*, 172–180. doi:10.1016/j.eswa.2007.09.007.

Thakkar, D. (2004). *Game theoretic models of computation*. New York: Academic Press.

Thathachar, M. A. (1985). Learning systems: Stochastic automata models. *Defence Science Journal, 35*(3), 361–366.

Tian, D., & Georganas, N. D. (2002). A coverage-preserving node scheduling scheme for large wireless sensor networks. In *Proceedings of the 1st ACM Workshop on Wireless Sensor Networks and Applications*. ACM.

Tilak, S., et al. (2002). A taxonomy of wireless microsensor network models. *ACM Mobile Computing and Communications Review, 6*(2).

Tito, M., Cabrerizo, M., Ayala, M., Barreto, A., Miller, I., Jayakar, P., & Adjouadi, M. (2009). Classification of electroencephalographic seizure recordings into ictal and interictal files using correlationsum. *International Journal of Computers in Biology and Medicine*, *39*, 604–614. doi:10.1016/j.compbiomed.2009.04.005.

Toreyin, Dedeoglu, & Cetin. (2006). Contour based smoke detection in video using wavelets. In *Proceedings of the 14th European Signal Processing Conference (EUSIPCO)*. Florence, Italy: EUSIPCO.

Toreyin, B. U., Dedeoglu, Y., & Cetin, A. E. (2005). Flame detection in video using hidden markov models.[ICIP.]. *Proceedings of ICIP*, *05*, 1230–1233.

Toreyin, B. U., Dedeoglu, Y., Gudukbay, U., & Cetin, A. E. (2006). Computer vision based system for real-time fire and flame detection. *Pattern Recognition Letters*, *27*, 49–58. doi:10.1016/j.patrec.2005.06.015.

Trigoni, Yao, Demers, Gehrke, & Rajaraman. (1989). *Multi-query optimization for sensor networks* (TR2005-1989). Ithaca, NY: Cornell University.

Truong, H. L., & Dustdar, S. (2009). A survey on context-aware web service systems. *International Journal of Web Information Systems*, *5*(1), 5–31. doi:10.1108/17440080910947295.

Truong, H. L., & Dustdar, S. (2010). Context coupling techniques for context-aware web service systems: an overview. In *Enabling Context-Aware Web Services: Methods, Architectures, and Technologies* (pp. 337–364). Boca Raton, FL: Chapman and Hall/CRC. doi:10.1201/EBK1439809853-c12.

Tulone, D., & Madden, S. (2006). An energy-efficient querying framework in sensor networks for detecting node similarities. In *Proceedings of The 9th ACM International Symposium on Modeling Analysis and Simulation of Wireless and Mobile Systems*. ACM.

Tulone, D., & Madden, S. (2006). PAQ: Time series forecasting for approximate query answering in sensor networks. In *Proceedings of The 3rd European Workshop on Wireless Sensor Networks*. IEEE.

Tzallas, A., Tsipouras, M., & Fotiadis, D. (2007). Automatic seizure detection based on time–frequency analysis and artificial neural networks. *Computational Intelligence and Neuroscience*, 1–13. doi:10.1155/2007/80510 PMID:18301712.

Ulrich, T. (2008). *Wireless network monitors H2O*. Wines & Vines.

University of Melbourne. (n.d.). *Website*. Retrieved from http://www.neuroeng.unimelb.edu.au/research/epilepsy/index.html

US Government. (2001). *U.S. location privacy protection act of 2001, bill number s.1164, introduced July 11, 2001*. Retrieved from http://www.techlawjournal.com/cong107/privacy/location/s1164is.asp

Utkin, A. B., Lavrov, A. V., Costa, L., Simoes, F., & Vilar, R. (2002). Detection of small forest fires by lidar. *Applied Physics. B, Lasers and Optics*, *74*(1), 77–83. doi:10.1007/s003400100772.

van Leeuwen, J., & Wiedermann, J. (2001). *The turing machine paradigm in contemporary computing*. Mathematics Unlimited. doi:10.1007/978-3-642-56478-9_30.

Vanrompay, Y. (2011). *Efficient prediction of future context for proactive smart systems*. (PhD Dissertation). Katholieke Universiteit. Leuven, Germany

Ventos, V., & Soldano, H. (2005). Alpha galois lattices: An overview.[ICFCA.]. *Proceedings of the ICFCA*, *2005*, 299–314.

Viayan, R., & Holtman, J. (1993). *A model for analyzing handoff algorithms* (Vol. 42, p. 3). IEEE Trans. on Veh. Technol.

Want, R., Hopper, A., Falcao, V., & Gibbons, J. (1992). The active badge location system. *ACM Transactions on Information Systems*, *10*(1), 91–102. doi:10.1145/128756.128759.

Wark, T., Corke, P., Sikka, P., Klingbeil, L., Guo, Y., & Crossman, C. et al. (2007). Transforming agriculture through pervasive wireless sensor networks. *IEEE Pervasive Computing/IEEE Computer Society [and] IEEE Communications Society*, *6*(2), 50–57. doi:10.1109/MPRV.2007.47.

Waters, B. (2008). *Ciphertext-policy attribute-based encryption: An expressive, efficient, and provably secure realization*. Retrieved from http://eprint.iacr.org/

Watkins, C. J. C. H. (1989). *Learning from delayed rewards*. (PhD Thesis). King's College. Cambridge, UK.

Watkins, C. J. C. H., & Dayan, P. (1992). Q-learning. *Machine Learning*, *8*, 279–292. doi:10.1007/BF00992698.

Weiser, M. (1991). The computer of the 21st century. *Scientific American*, *265*(3), 94–104. doi:10.1038/scientificamerican0991-94.

Werbos, P. J. (2008). Foreword - ADP: The key direction for future research in intelligent control and understanding brain intelligence. *IEEE Transactions on Systems, Man, and Cybernetics. Part B, Cybernetics*, *38*(4), 898–900. doi:10.1109/TSMCB.2008.924139.

Werner-Allen, G., Johnson, J., Ruiz, M., Lees, J., & Welsh, M. (2005). Monitoring volcanic eruptions with a wireless sensor network. In *Proceedings of The 2nd European Workshop on Wireless Sensor Networks*. IEEE.

Werner-Allen, G., Lorincz, K., Welsh, M., Marcillo, O., Johnson, J., Ruiz, M., & Lees, J. (2006). Deploying a wireless sensor network on an active volcano. *IEEE Internet Computing*, *10*(2), 18–25. doi:10.1109/MIC.2006.26.

WHO. (2005). *Atlas: Epilepsy care in the world*. Geneva: World Health Organization.

Wiering, M., & van Otterlo, M. (Eds.). (2012). *Reinforcement learning: State-of-the-art*. Boston: Springer Verlag. doi:10.1007/978-3-642-27645-3.

Winkler, W. E. (1990). String comparator metrics and enhanced decision rules in the Fellegi-Sunter model of record linkage. In *Proceedings of the Section on Survey Research Methods, American Statistical Association* (pp. 354-359). ASA.

Winkler, W. E. (1999). The state of record linkage and current research problems. In *Proceedings of the Survey Methods Section*, (pp. 73-79). IEEE.

Wolf, A., Swift, J., Swinney, H., & Vastano, J. (1989). Determining lyapunov exponents from a time series. *Physica*, *16D*, 285–317.

Wolfram, S. (1994). *Cellular automata and complexity* (*Vol. 10*). Reading, MA: Addison–Wesley.

Wolfson, O., Xu, B., & Tanner, R. M. (2007). Mobile peer-to-peer data dissemination with resource constraints. In *Proceedings of the 2007 International Conference on Mobile Data Management* (pp. 16-23). MDM.

Wolsey, L. A. (1998). *Integer programming*. New York: Wiley-Interscience.

Wong, S. K., & Ho, T. K. (2010). Intelligent negotiation behaviour model for an open railway access market. *Expert Systems with Applications*, *37*(12), 8109–8118. doi:10.1016/j.eswa.2010.05.077.

Wu, S., & Xu, Y. Cho, & Lee. (2005). Swarm based sensor deployment optimization in ad hoc sensor networks. In *Proceedings of Embedded Software and Systems, Second International Conference, ICESS 2005* (LNCS), (Vol. 3820, pp. 533-541). Berlin: Springer.

Wu, Z., & Palmer, M. (1994). Verb semantics and lexical selection. In *Proceedings of the 32nd Annual Meeting of the Association for Computational Linguistics* (pp. 133–138). Las Cruces, NM: ACL.

Xia, P., Chrysanthis, P., & Labrinidis, A. (2006). Similarity-aware query processing in sensor networks. In *Proceedings of The 20th International Parallel and Distributed Processing Symposium* (pp. 178). IEEE.

Xiao, H., Zou, Y., Ng, J., & Nigul, L. (2010). An approach for context-aware service discovery and recommendation. In *Proceedings of the 17th IEEE International Conference on Web Services (ICWS)*, (pp. 163-170). IEEE.

Xiao, Y., Zhang, H., & Wang, H. (2007). Location Prediction for Tracking Moving Objects Based on Grey Theory. *IEEE FSKD 2007*.

Xiong, Z., Caballero, R., Wang, H., Finn, A. M., Lelic, M. A., & Peng, P.-Y. (2007). *Video-based smoke detection: Possibilities, techniques, and challenges*. Paper presented at SUPDET, 2007. New York.

Yang, H., Wang, Y., Wang, C. J., & Tai, H. M. (2004). Correlation dimensions of EEG changes during mental tasks. In *Proceedings of the IEEE, The 26th Annual International Conference in Engineering in Medicine and Biology Society (EMBS)*, (pp. 616-619). IEEE.

Yang, S. J. H., Zhang, J., & Chen, I. Y. L. (2008). A JESS-enabled context elicitation system for providing context-aware web services. *Expert Systems with Applications*, *34*(4), 2254–2266. doi:10.1016/j.eswa.2007.03.008.

Yasumura, Y., Kamiryo, T., Yoshikawa, S., & Uehara, K. (2009). Acquisition of a concession strategy in multi-issue negotiation. *Web Intelligence and Agent Systems*, *7*(2), 161–171.

Yavas, G., Katsaros, D., Ulusoy, O., & Manolopoulos, Y. (2005). A data mining approach for location prediction in mobile environments. *Data & Knowledge Engineering, 54*(2). doi:10.1016/j.datak.2004.09.004.

Ye, J., Li, J., Zhu, Z., Gu, X., & Shi, H. (2007). PCSM: A context sharing model in peer-to-peer ubiquitous computing environment. In *Proceedings of the International Conference on Convergence Information Technology* (pp. 1868–1873). IEEE.

Yiu, M. L., Jensen, C. S., Huang, X., & Lu, H. (2008). Spacetwist: Managing the trade-offs among location privacy, query performance, and query accuracy in mobile services.[ICDE.]. *Proceedings of, ICDE2008*, 366–375.

Yoon, S., & Shahabi, C. (2007). The clustered aggregation (CAG) technique leveraging spatial and temporal correlations in wireless sensor networks. *ACM Transactions on Sensor Networks, 3*(1), 1–38. doi:10.1145/1210669.1210672.

Yoshikawa, S. Y., Yasumura, Y., & Uehara, K. (2008). Strategy acquisition on multi-issue negotiation without estimating opponent's preference.[LNCS]. *Proceedings of Agent and Multi-Agent Systems: Technologies and Applications, 4953*, 371–380. doi:10.1007/978-3-540-78582-8_38.

Yu, E. (1995). *Modeling strategic relationships for process reengineering.* (Doctoral Thesis). University of Toronto. Toronto, Canada.

Yuan, F. N. (2008). A fast accumulative motion orientation model based on integral image for video smoke detection. *Pattern Recognition Letters, 29*, 925–932. doi:10.1016/j.patrec.2008.01.013.

Yu, C., Fang, J., Wang, J., & Zhang, Y. (2009). Video fire smoke detection using motion and color features. *Fire Technology, 46*(3), 651–663.

Zein-Sabatto, S., & Zheng, Y. (1997). Intelligent flight controllers for helicopter control. In *Proceedings of the International Conference on Neural Networks*, (pp. 617–621). IEEE.

Zein-Sabatto, S., Ma, G., & Malkani, M. J. (1998). Intelligent flight control design for helicopter yaw control. In *Proceedings of the Thirtieth Southeastern Symposium on System Theory*, (pp. 184–188). IEEE.

Zeleny, M. (1982). *Multiple criteria decision making.* New York: McGraw-Hill.

Zeng, D., & Sycara, K. (1998). Bayesian learning in negotiation. *International Journal of Human-Computer Studies, 48*, 125–141. doi:10.1006/ijhc.1997.0164.

Zerger, A., Viscarra Rossel, R. A., Swain, D., Wark, T., Handcock, R. N., & Doerr, V. A. J. et al. (2010). Environmental sensor networks for vegetation, animal and soil sciences. *International Journal of Applied Earth Observation and Geoinformation, 12*(5), 303–316. doi:10.1016/j.jag.2010.05.001.

Zhang, L., Tiwana, B., Qian, Z., Wang, Z., Dick, R. P., Mao, Z. M., & Yang, L. (2010). Accurate online power estimation and automatic battery behavior based power model generation for smartphones. In *Proceedings International Conference Hardware/Software Codesign and System Synthesis*, (pp. 105–114). IEEE.

Zhang, Z., Zhao, J., Yuan, Z., Zhang, D., Han, S., & Qu, C. (2009). Color based segmentation and shape based matching of forest fires from monocular images. In *Proceedings of the International Conference on Multimedia Information Networking and Security.* IEEE.

Zhang, Z., Zhao, J., Zhang, D., Qu, C., Ke, Y., & Cai, B. (2008). Contour based forest fire detection using FFT and Wavelet. In *Proceedings of the International Conference on Computer Science and Software Engineering.* IEEE.

Zhang, C., & Huang, Y. (2009). Cloaking locations for anonymous location based services: A hybrid approach. *Journal Geoinformatica, 13*, 159–182. doi:10.1007/s10707-008-0047-2.

Zhang, H., Zhang, F., Li, Z., Gao, M., & Li, W. (2009). Evolutionary diversity and spatiotemporal dynamics of a spatial game. *Ecological Modelling, 220*, 2353–2364. doi:10.1016/j.ecolmodel.2009.06.005.

Zhang, J. (2009). Adaptive learning via selectionism and Bayesianism: Part I: Connection between the two. *Neural Networks, 22*(3), 220–228. doi:10.1016/j.neunet.2009.03.018 PMID:19386469.

Zhao, W. Shang, & Wang. (2004). Optimizing sensor node distribution with genetic algorithm in wireless sensor network. Berlin: Springer-Verlag.

Zhao, J., Zhang, J., & Zhao, R. (2007). A practical verifiable multi-secret sharing scheme. *Computer Standards & Interfaces*, 29, 138–141. doi:10.1016/j.csi.2006.02.004.

Zhao, Q., Zhou, Z., & Perry, M. (2007). *Agent design of smart license management system using gaia methodology*. Ontario, Canada: University of Western Ontario. doi:10.1109/CONIELECOMP.2007.52.

Zhengmao, Y., & Habib, M. (2009). WSN topology control design via integration of Kalman filtering and adaptive estimation. In *Proceedings of The 6th International Conference on Electrical Engineering, Computing Science and Automatic Control* (pp. 1–5). IEEE.

Zhu, S., et al. (2003). LEAP: Efficient security mechanisms for large-scale distributed sensor networks. In *Proceedings of the 10th ACM Conference on Computer and Communication Security*. ACM.

Zhuang, Y., Pan, J., & Cai, L. (2010). Minimizing energy consumption with probabilistic distance models in wireless sensor networks. In *Proceedings of The IEEE INFOCOM* (pp. 1–9). IEEE.

Zou & Chakrabarty. (2004). Sensor deployment and target localization in distributed sensor networks. *ACM Transaction on Embedded Computing Systems*, 3, 61–91. doi:10.1145/972627.972631.

About the Contributors

Kostas Kolomvatsos received his B.Sc. in Informatics from the Department of Informatics at the Athens University of Economics and Business (AUEB) in 1995 and his M.Sc. in Computer Science from the Department of Informatics and Telecommunications at the National and Kapodistrian University of Athens (UoA) in 2005. In the beginning of 2013, he received his Ph.D. from the Department of Informatics and Telecommunications at the National and Kapodistrian University of Athens. He is currently a Postdoctoral researcher in the same Department and member of the Pervasive Computing Research Group. His research interests are in the areas of Artificial Intelligence, Computational Intelligence, Mobile and Distributed Computing. He has authored 23 publications in the above areas.

Christos Anagnostopoulos received his B.Sc., M.Sc. and Ph.D. in Informatics and Telecommunications from the Department of Informatics & Telecommunications (DIT) of the University of Athens (UoA), Athens, Greece. Since the beginning of 2011, he belongs to the faculty of the Ionian University, Department of Informatics, Corfu, Greece, where he presently is an assistant professor. His research interest focuses on mobile and distributed computing systems and context-aware computing. He is an author of over 50 publications in these research areas.

Stathes Hadjiefthymiades received his B.Sc., M.Sc. and Ph.D. in Informatics and Telecommunications from the Department of Informatics & Telecommunications (DIT) of the University of Athens (UoA), Athens, Greece. He also received a joint engineering-economics M.Sc. degree from the National Technical University of Athens. In 1992 he joined the Greek consulting firm Advanced Services Group, Ltd., as an analyst/developer of telematic applications and systems. In 1995 he became a member of the Communication Networks Laboratory of UoA. From 2001 to 2002, he served as a visiting assistant professor at the University of Aegean, Department of Information and Communication Systems Engineering. In 2002 he joined the faculty of the Hellenic Open University (Department of Informatics), Patras, Greece, as an assistant professor. Since the beginning of 2004, he has been a member of the faculty of UoA, DIT where he is presently an assistant professor. He has participated in numerous projects realized in the context of EU programmes and national initiatives. His research interests are in the areas of mobile, pervasive computing, web systems engineering, and networked multimedia applications. He is the author of over 150 publications in these areas.

* * *

Mohammad R. Akbarzadeh T. (Senior Member, IEEE) received his PhD on *Evolutionary Optimization and Fuzzy Control of Complex Systems* from the department of electrical and computer engineering at the University of New Mexico in 1998. He currently holds dual appointment as professor in the departments of electrical engineering and computer engineering at Ferdowsi University of Mashhad. In 2006-2007, he completed a one-year visiting scholar position at Berkeley Initiative on Soft Computing (BISC), UC Berkeley. From 1996-2002, he was affiliated with the NASA Center for Autonomous Control Engineering at University of New Mexico (UNM). Dr. Akbarzadeh is the founding president of the Intelligent Systems Scientific Society of Iran, the founding councilor representing the Iranian Coalition on Soft Computing in IFSA, and a council member of the Iranian Fuzzy Systems Society. He is also a life member of Eta Kappa Nu (The Electrical Engineering Honor Society), Kappa Mu Epsilon (The Mathematics Honor Society), and the Golden Key National Honor Society. He has received several awards including: the IDB Excellent Leadership Award in 2010, The IDB Excellent Performance Award in 2009, the Outstanding Faculty Award in 2008 and 2002, the IDB Merit Scholarship for High Technology in 2006, the Outstanding Faculty Award in Support of Student Scientific Activities in 2004, Outstanding Graduate Student Award in 1998, and Service Award from the Mathematics Honor Society in 1989. His research interests are in the areas of evolutionary algorithms, fuzzy logic and control, soft computing, multi-agent systems, complex systems, robotics, and biomedical engineering systems. He has published over 250 peer-reviewed articles in these and related research fields.

Sally Almanasra was born in Libya in 1983. Currently, she is a PhD student at the school of computer sciences at Universiti Sains Malaysia. She received her B.Sc and M.Sc. degrees from Alzaytoonah University and AL-Balqa Applied University in 2004 and 2007, respectively. Sally Almanasra is currently working in the field of Game theory under the supervision of Dr. Rafie. In addition, Sally has been awarded the USM Fellowship Award since 2009, and she is working as a system developer at the school of computer sciences – USM.

Theodoros Anagnostopoulos received his *first* BSc in Informatics from the Department of Informatics at the Technical Education Institution of Athens in 1997. He received his *second* BSc in Informatics from the Department of Informatics at the Athens University of Economics and Business in 2001, and his MScIS in Information Systems from the Department of Informatics at the Athens University of Economics and Business in 2002. He received his Ph.D in Informatics from the National and Kapodistrian University of Athens at the Department of Informatics and Telecommunications in 2012. His research interests are in the areas of Pervasive Computing and Machine Learning.

Daniele Apiletti is a postdoctoral researcher in Computer Engineering at the Dipartimento di Automatica e Informatica of the Politecnico di Torino. He holds a PhD (2008) and a Master (2005) degree in Computer Engineering from Politecnico di Torino. His has worked on microarray data classification, feature selection techniques in bioinformatics, network data analysis, and physiological data modeling. His current research interests are in the fields of sensor data analysis and distributed non-relational databases.

Marie-Aude Aufaure obtained a PhD in Computer Science from INRIA and the University Pierre and Marie Curie (UPMC) in 1992, and her Habilitation in 2002. She was associate professor at University Lyon 1 during 8 years. Now, she is Professor at Ecole Centrale Paris (MAS Laboratory) and head of the SAP Business Objects Chair in Business Intelligence. She is also scientific partner at INRIA in the Axis project. Her research interests deals with the analysis, retrieval and querying of unstructured data, and with bridging the gap between structured data and unstructured content using various models (graphs, ontologies, Galois lattices). The scientific topics developed in her team are related to semantic technologies, graphs, conceptual classification with user-centric point of view and are applied to semantic information retrieval, question and answering over data warehouses, social networks and recommender systems (special focus on user modeling and personalization).

Elena Baralis has been a full professor at the Dipartimento di Automatica e Informatica of the Politecnico di Torino since January 2005. She holds a Master degree in Electrical Engineering and a Ph.D. in Computer Engineering, both from Politecnico di Torino. Her current research interests are in the field of database systems and data mining, more specifically on mining algorithms for very large databases and sensor/stream data analysis. She has published over 80 papers in international journals and conference proceedings. She has served on the program committees or as area chair of several international conferences and workshops, among which VLDB, IEEE ICDM, ACM SAC, DaWak, ACM CIKM, PKDD.

Constanţa-Nicoleta Bodea is professor at the Bucharest Academy of Economic Studies, Romania. She is teaching project management and artificial intelligence. She is the president of the Project Management Romania Association. Between 2007-2012, she was the chair of Education & Training Board of the International Project Management Association - IPMA since 2007. In the last ten years, she managed more than 20 R&D and IT projects. She is author of 11 books and more than 50 papers on Project Management, Information Systems, and Artificial Intelligence, being honored by IPMA with the Outstanding Research Contributions in 2007. Her main areas of interest are knowledge management and intelligent system development, mainly for the project-oriented organizations.

Tania Cerquitelli has been an assistant professor at the Dipartimento di Automatica e Informatica of the Politecnico di Torino since October 2011. She got the master degree in Computer Engineering and the PhD degree from the Politecnico di Torino, Torino, Italy, and the master degree in Computer Science from the Universidad De Las Américas Puebla. Her research interests include the design of innovative algorithms to efficiently perform large-scale data mining, novel and efficient data mining techniques for sensor readings, innovative algorithms to extract high-level abstraction of the mined knowledge, and novel data mining algorithms for network analytics. She has been a teaching assistant in different databases and data mining courses at the Politecnico di Torino since academic year 2004-2005.

Constantinos Delakouridis, PhD Student, member of the Mobile Multimedia Laboratory, Athens University of Economics and Business (AUEB). He received his Diploma in Information and Communication Systems Engineering from University of Aegean and his Masters degree in Advanced Information Systems from University of Athens. His PhD focuses in information security and privacy aspects of pervasive computing, emphasizing in secret sharing techniques and location information dissemination. He has participated as researcher in research projects and published articles in journals and refereed conferences.

Dimitris C. Dracopoulos received the Diploma in Electrical Engineering from the National Technical University of Athens, Greece in 1990 and his PhD from the Department of Computing, Imperial College, London. He has held academic positions in various universities including Brunel University, London and Ecole Normale Superieure de Lyon, France. Between 1999 and 2004, he worked in industry as a Senior Software Engineer for various international companies. Since 2004 he is a Senior Lecturer at the School of Electronics and Computer Science at the University of Westminster, London. His research interests include neural networks and genetic algorithms for control, adaptive optimal control, learning algorithms for artificial neural networks, evolutionary computing, reinforcement learning, and control theory.

Dimitrios Effraimidis received his Diploma in Electrical and Computer Engineering from Aristoteleion University of Thessaloniki in 2005. He has been working as a Software Developer in the area of Databases and he has a Master degree at Advanced Computer Science from the University of Westminster. Currently he is completing his Ph.D degree in Artificial Intelligence at the same university. His main research interests are reinforcement learning, neural networks, evolutionary computing, and fuzzy logic.

Seyyed Abed Hosseini was born in Quchan, Iran, in 1984. He received the B.S. degree in electronics from the Sadjad Institute of higher education, Mashhad, Iran, in 2006, and the M.S. degree in biomedical engineering from the Islamic Azad University Mashhad Branch, Mashhad, Iran, in 2009. He is currently Ph.D. candidate at the Control Engineering of the Ferdowsi University of Mashhad, Iran. His research interests include recognition of emotional stress states based on the analysis of EEG and psychophysiological signals in order to improve human–computer interaction, biomedical signal processing, functional brain modeling, behavioral control, non-linear and chaotic analysis, fuzzy-neural networks, and digital design with FPGA and CPLD. He is a member of the Iranian Society for Biomedical Engineering, Tehran, Iran. He has authored over 30 journal and conference papers. He is currently a Reviewer for international journals and conferences. He participated in international conferences as a Session Chair.

George Karasmanoglou received his B.Sc. degree from the Department of Informatics and Telecommunications of the University of Athens in 2009. Currently, he is a research assistant in Pervasive Computing Research Group (p-Comp) of the same department. His research interests are in the domain of Pervasive Computing as well as in Ontological Engineering.

Leonidas Kazatzopoulos, PhD Student, member of the Mobile Multimedia Laboratory, Athens University of Economics and Business (AUEB). He received his first Diploma in Information and Communication Systems Engineering from University of Aegean (2004) and his Masters degree in Advanced Information Systems from University of Athens (2005). His PhD targets in security and privacy aspects of the distributed systems, aiming to introduce routing techniques for achieving location privacy. He has published articles in journals & refereed conferences and worked in Greek research projects PASO (PKI Applications and Security for OTE) and CORINE.

Blerina Lika received her B.Sc. degree from the Department of Informatics and Telecommunications of the University of Athens in 2010 and she is currently pursuing her M.Sc. studies in Management and Economics of Telecommunication Networks in the same department. During her postgraduate studies, she worked as a teaching assistant. She has been a research intern at INRIA. Now, she serves as a research assistant in Pervasive Computing Research Group (p-Comp) and participates in IDIRA project. Her research interests are in the domain of Pervasive Computing.

Radu-Ioan Mogos graduated from the Academy of Economic Studies, Faculty of Cybernetics, Statistics and Economic IT in 2005. He earned a PhD in Economic Cybernetics and Statistics domain in 2011. He wrote more than 20 articles, internationally published and is co-author in one book regarding artificial intelligence domain. His areas of interest are artificial intelligence, intelligent agents, neural networks, data mining, and project management. He is also part of the "Computerized Project Management" master team, performing educational activities in several disciplines. He is member of the Association of Project Management Romania and part of the organizing team of the "Knowledge Management – Project, Systems, and Technology" conference. He is also certified with IPMA level D by the Romania Project Management Association.

Nesrine Ben Mustapha obtained her Master degree in Computer Science from National School of Computer Sciences ENSI of Tunis in 2007. She obtained her PhD Diploma in june 2012 and she continues to carry out postdoctoral research at Ecole Centrale Paris (MAS Laboratory) in the context of an EU funded project FP7 Parlance. Her research interests include ontology learning from texts, machine learning applied to texts and ontology-based semantic search. In her PhD thesis, her proposal aims at improving the relevance of answers of question-based information retrieval by the integration of semantic retrieval process, case-based reasoning, and modular ontology construction. In the context of the EU funded project, she is interested in using natural language and statistical processing techniques to harness the huge amount of information on Internet, in order to incrementally build a dynamic, modular "ontological" knowledge base.

Mohammad Bagher Naghibi-Sistani received the Ph.D. degree in Electrical Engineering from the Ferdowsi University of Mashhad, Iran. He currently is Assistant Professor at the Department of Electrical Engineering, Ferdowsi University of Mashhad. His research interests include Reinforcement learning, Soft computing, Machine learning and Neural Network. He has authored or coauthored over 50 journal and conference papers.

Salma Najar is a PhD student and research assistant in the Computer Science Research Center (Centre de Recherche en Informatique) of the University of Paris 1 Panthéon-Sorbonne. She received her MSc degree in Informatics "Information Technology" in 2008. Her research interests include pervasive computing, context-aware computing, adaptation (personalization), and information systems.

Kakia Panagidi received her B.Sc. in "Informatics and Telecommunications" from the Department of Informatics and Telecommunications National at National Kapodistrian University of Athens in 2010 and her M.Sc. in "Economics and Management of Telecommunication Networks" from the same department in September 2012. Her research interests are in the fields of networked systems and network optimization, or more specifically, algorithms for decision making in distributed systems like wireless sensor networks.

Manuele Kirsch Pinheiro is Associate Professor in the Computer Science Research Center (Centre de Recherche en Informatique) of the University of Paris 1 Panthéon-Sorbonne. Previously, she occupied a post-doctoral position on the Computer Science of the Katholieke Universiteit Leuven. She received her PhD in Computer Science from the University Joseph Fourier – Grenoble I in 2006, Grenoble, France. Her research interests include ubiquitous computing, context-aware computing, adaptation (personalization), cooperative work (CSCW), group awareness, and information systems.

Muhammad Rafie was born on 1st of May 1962 in Perak, Malaysia. He received B.A in business studies degree from Macalester College, St Paul, Minnesota, USA, in 1985, and M.B.A in Management Information System from University of Dallas, Texas, USA, in 1987. Currently he is an Associate Professor at the School of Computer Sciences, Universiti Sains Malaysia, Penang. His research interest includes e-learning, multimedia systems, mobile learning, computer games, virtual reality, computer-aided instruction, and RFID.

Paolo Renna is an Assistant Professor at School of Engineering at the University of Basilicata (Italy). He took Ph.D. degree at Polytechnic of Bari in Advanced Production Systems. His academic researches principally deal with the development of innovative negotiation and production planning in distributed environments and manufacturing scheduling in dynamic environment. Several contributions have been presented on design Multi Agent Architecture and test by discrete event simulation in Business to Business environment. Among the contributions, he is co-author of two research books about e-marketplaces and production planning in production networks. Moreover, he has developed coordination approaches in multi-plant production planning environment and innovative scheduling approaches in flexible and reconfigurable manufacturing systems.

Odysseas Sekkas received his B.Sc. in Computer Science from the Department of Informatics & Telecommunications at the National and Kapodistrian University of Athens, Greece in 2003, and his M.Sc. in Communication Systems and Data Networks from the same Department in 2006. He holds a Ph.D. (2010) from the above Department in the research area of Pervasive Computing and especially in Context-Aware Data Management. He is also member of the Pervasive Computing Research Group (p-comp) and the Communication Networks Laboratory (CNL) of the National and Kapodistrian University of Athens. He has participated in several European and National founded research projects. His research interests are mainly focused in the areas of pervasive and mobile computing, wireless sensor networks and data fusion.

Carine Souveyet got her PhD Degree in Computer Sciences at the University of Paris Jussieu in 1991 and her HDR Degree at the University of Paris 1 Panthéon Sorbonne in 2006. She is Professor in Computer Sciences at the University of Paris 1 since 2008 and research member of the Centre de Recherche en Informatique (CRI) since 1991.

Luiz Angelo Steffenel is Associate Professor at the University of Reims Champagne-Ardenne, France. He obtained a Ph.D. in Computer Science in 2005 at Institut National Polytechnique de Grenoble, France. Dr Steffenel is a board member of the french Grid'5000 project. He is also its scientific coordinator for the University Reims Champagne-Ardenne. His research interests include parallel and distributed systems, grid computing, fault tolerance, and pervasive computing. Also, he works on parallel approaches for molecular docking, in collaboration with researchers from Institut de Chimie Moléculaire (ICMR/CNRS) and Matrice Extracellulaire et Dynamique Cellulaire (MEDyC/CNRS).

Khaled Suwais was born in Kuwait in 1982 but grew up in Jordan where he attended Al Albayt University at Almafraq. He received his M.Sc and Ph.D. degrees from Universiti Sains Malaysia in 2005 and 2009, respectively. Since 2009, he has been teaching at Al Imam University. Currently, he is as an Assistant Professor in Computer Science on the Riyadh campus of the Arab Open University. Suwais has published many scientific papers in Cryptography and Information Security. His research interests include information security and cryptography, parallel computing, and game theory.

Vassileios Tsetsos received his B.Sc. in Informatics from the Department of Informatics & Telecommunications at the University of Athens, Greece in 2003 and his M.Sc. in "Communication Systems and Data Networks" from the same Department in 2005. In 2010, he received his Ph.D. from the same department. He is a member of the Communication Networks Laboratory (CNL) of the University of Athens and the Pervasive Computing Research Group (p-comp). He has participated in R&D projects funded by the EU FP5 and FP7 programmes, and in several national research projects. His research interests are in the areas of pervasive and mobile computing, Semantic Web technologies and middleware for context-aware and sensor-based services.

Yves Vanrompay is a postdoctoral researcher at the MAS Laboratory of Ecole Centrale Paris. He obtained his Ms. Informatics in 2003, Ms. Artificial Intelligence in 2004, Bach. Philosophy in 2005, and PhD Engineering in 2011 from the KU Leuven, Belgium. His main research interests include context-aware systems, context reasoning, ambient intelligence, self-adaptive applications, personalization, and collaborative filtering. Within the European IST FP6 MUSIC project, he worked from 2006 to 2010 on the topics of context and adaptation. Since 2012, he is involved in the FP7 PARLANCE project, aiming at building a personalized, dynamic and context aware spoken dialogue search system for mobile users.

Professor Evagellos Zervas received his B.Sc. in Electrical Engineering from the National Technical University of Athens, Greece (1986), M.Sc. in the Northeastern University (NEU), Boston, Massachusetts (1989) and Ph.D. in Communications and Digital Processing in the NEU (1993). His is now Professor in the Dept. of Electronics in the Technological Educational Institutions, Athens, Greece. His research interests are in the area of wireless sensor networks, mobile computing, and sensor data fusion.

Index

E

Electroencephalography (EEG) 21
Electronic Market (EM) 56, 59-61, 63, 79-80, 82-84
Encapsulating Security Payload (ESP) 195
Enterprise Resource Planning (ERP) 86
entity matching 263
Epilepsy 20-22, 33-36
evolutionary computation 1, 15-16, 54, 106, 212, 216
evolutionary process 5

F

feature extraction 21-22, 34-36, 253
Finite Automata 204, 206-208, 212-214, 217
Fire Alarm System 190
Fire Detection Algorithm 190
fire detection subsystem 180-182
fire protection 179-180
Fractal Dimension (FD) 25
fuzzification 29
fuzzy logic 1-2

G

Game Theory 38, 54, 204-207, 212-216
Genetic Programming 1-2, 5-6, 9, 13, 15-16, 212, 215
Geographic Information Systems (GIS) 89
Growing Neural Gas (GNG) 266

H

Helicopter Control 15-17
Heterogeneous Environments 159
hierarchical modular ontology 166
hybrid neuroevolutionary 1

I

Inertial Navigation System (INS) 4
Information Integration 190
intelligent location service 203, 250, 295
Intensive Care Units (ICU) 21
Intentional Query Processor (IQP) 256
intention matching 261-262, 268
IPSOM (Intentional Pervasive Service Oriented Middleware 253
iterated n-player prisoners' dilemma (INPPD) 207

J

Java Development Kit (JDK) 47

K

Kernel Density Estimation (KDE) 39

L

LAN 236, 240, 247, 293
Learning Automata (LA) 209
Learning Module (LM) 256
learning process 38, 44, 263-265
linear weighted sums 186
location-based service 203, 250, 279, 295
Location Information (LocInfo) 192, 240
location prediction 218-220, 223-224, 229, 231, 234-237, 272-273
location privacy 191-192, 196, 203, 238-239, 241-242, 245-250, 276-279, 288, 292-295
location retrieval procedure 244
Location Server (LS) 245, 278
Lyapunov Exponent 20-21, 28-29, 31, 33

M

machine learning 16, 56-57, 62, 83, 218, 220, 235-237, 254, 271
market conditions 37, 39, 41, 51-53
Markov chain Monte Carlo methods (MCMC) 235
Maximal Independent Set (MIS) 119
Medium Access Control (MAC) 245, 277
Mobile Ad Hoc Network (MANET) 157-159, 165, 169, 172, 175, 178, 202, 237
Mobile IP 196, 201, 245, 247, 277, 292
Mobility Assisted Probabilistic Protocol (MAPC) 114
Multi-Criteria Decision Analysis (MCDA) 87
Multi-Layer Perceptrons (MLP) 5

N

negotiation process 37-41, 44-47, 51, 53-55, 58, 85-86, 90-92, 94, 97-98, 101-102, 107
network state 135, 142-143, 151, 170
Neural Networks (NN) 4
neuroevolutionary 1-2, 4, 7-9, 13, 15
New Product Creation 73-75
No Commitment Branch and Bound (NCCB) 88
Non-Deterministic Finite Automaton (NFA) 206
Non-Disclosure Method 195, 245, 277
nonlinear 1-2, 13, 15, 33-34, 36, 211, 216, 273
non-Reinforcement Learning (nRL) 219